The
Thousand
Recipe
Chinese
Cookbook

THE THOUSAND RECIPE

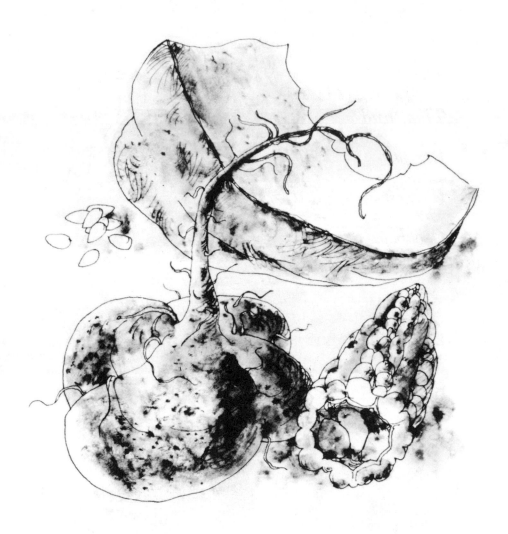

A FIRESIDE BOOK
Published by Simon & Schuster
New York London Toronto Sydney Tokyo Singapore

CHINESE COOKBOOK

Gloria Bley Miller

Drawings by Earl Thollander

Copyright © 1966 by Gloria Bley Miller
Copyright renewed © 1994 by Gloria Bley Miller

All rights reserved
including the right of reproduction
in whole or in part in any form
First Fireside Edition, 1984

Published by Simon & Schuster, Inc.
Rockefeller Center
1230 Avenue of the Americas
New York, New York 10020

Originally published by Atheneum Publishers

FIRESIDE and colophon are registered trademarks
of Simon & Schuster, Inc.

Manufactured in the United States of America

17   18   19   20

Library of Congress Cataloging in Publication Data
Miller, Gloria Bley.
   The thousand recipe Chinese cookbook.
   "A Fireside book."
   Reprint. Originally published: New York: Grosset &
Dunlap, 1970, c1966
   Includes index.
   I. Cookery, Chinese.   I. Title.   II. Title: 1000
recipe Chinese cookbook.
TX724.5.C5M5   1984   641.5951   84-18683
ISBN 0-671-50993-4

❋ FOR R.A.M. ❋

✿ INTRODUCTION ✿

I HAVE *had the pleasure of introducing many people to Chinese cooking but never imagined that a book on the subject would result from such an introduction. The fact that one has is indeed a source of additional pleasure.*

Those of us who have known this way of cooking all our lives naturally tend to take much of it for granted. To see clearly what kind of information the newcomer to Chinese cooking must have, often takes a fresh point of view. In her book, Gloria Bley Miller demonstrates this understanding beautifully. She has been able to grasp the essential points about Chinese cooking; she has been able to communicate them directly and clearly. Her recipes are models of simplicity, yet are completely authentic. The fact that they represent many regional styles of cooking makes the book richer and more diverse.

To my knowledge, there is no other single volume on the subject anywhere which encompasses the same wealth of information Mrs. Miller has brought together here. And I am equally impressed by the genuine feeling she has shown for Chinese cooking throughout.

Although Gloria Bley Miller has written this book essentially for Westerners, many of us in the Chinese-American community will, I know, find it of particular interest. We are now in our second and third generation in the United States and cannot help but note with mixed feelings the changes which have taken place in our culture. We know that many of the beautiful customs and ways handed down to us are gradually disappearing. I find it a delightful paradox, therefore, that this Chinese cookbook written by a Westerner for other Westerners might in its own special way help keep alive a culinary heritage from the Orient.

ROGER YUEN LEE

San Francisco, California

❊ FOREWORD ❊

H o w D O E S one discover the true delights of Chinese cooking? How does one learn? Where does one begin?

I began more than a dozen years ago when I visited San Francisco and was introduced by friends to architect Roger Yuen Lee and his wife, Rena. As we talked about the things a visitor might see and do in that city, the conversation naturally turned to restaurants and food. The Lees asked if we would like to join them for a Chinese meal at a nearby restaurant the following evening. The answer, of course, was "yes."

The restaurant looked to me like many others, including the on-and-off neon sign outside that read "Chop Suey." I had expected something special, but this place seemed ordinary. The dining room was full of Westerners having wonton soup, egg rolls, chow mein and the other familiars on the bill of fare.

We were led through the dining room into a quiet back room. The waiter gave Roger Lee a menu, a pad of white paper, a pencil. He wrote the order, handed the slip of paper to the waiter. The waiter read it, looked at us, shook his head doubtfully. He said something in Chinese that sounded like a protest. Roger Lee translated. The waiter, it seemed, thought we wouldn't like the authentic dishes that were ordered. He thought we would find them too "foreign."

The waiter was mistaken. When the meal came, it was memorable. After all these years I can still recall the succulence of the black mushrooms, the crispness of the duck, the green freshness of the vegetables, the delicacy of the fish. It was a whole new world and a wonderful one. That was the beginning for me. I wanted to be able to cook these marvelous dishes myself. I wanted to learn everything I could about Chinese food.

Since then I have pursued this knowledge in many ways and in many places. I have eaten in elegant and humble Chinese restaurants, haunted Chinese grocery stores, tracked down every scrap of literature on the subject, compared notes with Chinese friends and, most important, I constantly cooked and experimented.

In the process, I made a number of interesting and surprising discoveries. I found that Chinese cooking, which at first seemed complex and obscure, actually had a beautiful simplicity and logic about it. I found that, given a few fundamentals, a beginner could produce authentic Chinese dishes without difficulty; that he could do so in ordinary kitchens with ordinary utensils; and that exotic ingredients—although fascinating to use—were not always essential.

I felt these discoveries should be shared. I considered writing a magazine article on the subject. As soon as I began, I realized this art of Chinese cooking (which had been practiced with such passion and devotion for centuries) was not going to permit itself to be compressed into a few casually written pages. To do it any kind of justice, I knew, would require a book, a thoughtful and comprehensive book.

This, many years later, is the book. It is based on the premise that you, the reader (like myself when I began), know little or nothing about the preparation of Chinese food. It assumes only that you have a lively curiosity, an interest in good eating and the desire to expand your culinary horizons. In a sense, this is not one book, but two: a basic handbook to answer your many questions on the who, what, when, where and how of Chinese cooking, as well as a diversified collection of authentic Chinese recipes that are within the scope and skills of the average cook.

As you begin to use this book, you will find that Chinese cooking takes no more time than ordinary cooking. You will see it is more a matter of method than of anything else. Once you master the fundamental techniques, you'll be able to prepare delicious and distinctive meals with the ingredients you can find in any food store. You'll be able to re-create many dishes made popular by Chinese restaurants, as well as those favored by the Chinese in their home cooking but rarely served in restaurants.

Chinese cooking is a live and adventurous art, a remarkable combination of aesthetics, nutrition, surprise, mystery and delight. It has something for everyone: whether you're artistic, imaginative, health- or budget-minded, whether you live in a big, rambling house or in a small compact apartment, whether you like to dine simply or to entertain in style. On whatever level you approach Chinese cooking, it can bring you new pleasure and enjoyment. It can add a wonderful sense of harmony to your life.

The Chinese have many sayings about good cooking and good eating. One is particularly appropriate here. It notes that as those who live near water come to know the nature of fishes, as those who live near mountains become familiar with the melody of birds, so those who remain close to the kitchen acquire the knowledge of good food. This book was written for those who remain close to *their* kitchens.

GLORIA BLEY MILLER

❊ ACKNOWLEDGMENTS ❊

I wish to thank Mrs. Winifred Fu, Mrs. Rena Lee, Mrs. Laura Gong and Mrs. Beverly Hom for their kind and helpful suggestions on this book; and Mr. Honcan Bough for his invaluable guidance in the ways of Chinese food. I also want to thank Mr. Herbert Weaver of the Chinatown Museum in New York for making available to me excellent written material I might not otherwise have seen.

G. B. M.

❀ CONTENTS ❀

Part One   Background

Part Two   Recipes

Part Three   Supplementary Information

PART ONE

Background

❀ *The Chinese Diet* ❀

C H I N E S E F O O D has been called the diet of the future because it is high in nutrients, low in calories and invariably well-balanced. Meat does not predominate: vegetables (particularly the non-starchy varieties) do. The meats used are moderate in their fat content. High-protein seafood plays an important role. There are no dairy products. Animal fats are rare. Grains are plentiful, sweets negligible. Crisp, delicate foods are preferred to heavy, oily ones.

Meat does not predominate, vegetables do: The Chinese are not fascinated with great chunks of meat such as steaks, roasts, legs of lamb. They like their meat in small quantities, cut up or sliced paper-thin and combined with vegetables and other ingredients. A characteristic Chinese meat dish contains about one-fourth the meat Westerners usually expect, while a "heavy" meat dish is only three-fifths meat. (A duck, for example, that serves three or four in a Western meal will serve twice that many when prepared as a Chinese dish.) A typical Chinese family meal, however, also includes other "main" dishes made with fish, eggs, etc.

There are no dairy products: Butter, cheese and milk are practically unknown to Chinese cooking. (Cattle, few and far between in China, were more profitably put to work as beasts of burden.) Yet, with nutritional ingenuity, the Chinese created their own "cow" which produced its own "dairy" products. They took the lowly soybean, whose protein closely resembles that of meat, and transformed it in innumerable ways. They softened and ground the soybean, then mixed it with water, converting it first to milk, then to curd, and finally to cheese. (They also put it to many other uses: made it into sauce and jam; served its sprouts as vegetables; fermented, dried and roasted it; used it salty as a condiment, sweet in pastries.) Contact with the West eventually introduced milk and butter to Chinese cooking, but these dairy products were used primarily as flavoring agents and always in small quantities.

Sweets are negligible: Eating sweets is not a Chinese habit. They don't have much of a sweet tooth and are not taken with rich pastries and confections. (This is one reason Chinese women are able to keep their figures well beyond middle age.) As a rule, the Chinese prefer savories to sweets. (These savories take the form of dumplings, buns, wontons, egg rolls, etc., made with wheat- or rice-flour pastry, stuffed with various combinations of poultry, seafood, meat, vegetables, then deep-fried, steamed or boiled. Savories, or refreshments, can be taken with tea as a *tea lunch* or served with dinner as hors d'oeuvres.) The little need the Chinese have for sweets is usually satisfied by sweet-and-sour sauces served with meat and fish dishes.

Desserts as such are unknown and do not accompany family meals. On rare occasions, fresh fruit or candied ginger may be served at home after dinner. The few sweet dishes the Chinese have are reserved mainly for formal banquets and feasts. These are often hot dishes and include sweet hot fruit soups or teas, pastries filled with sweetened nuts, deep-fried sweet potatoes, and a rich steamed pudding called "Eight Precious Rice." These sometimes appear at the end of the meal, but more often as a welcome change of pace midway in a long progression of heavy or salted foods. Generally speaking, Chinese sweet dishes are not sweet at all in the Western sense. They have none of the sugary or syrupy sweetness associated with Western desserts. Even Chinese tea is taken without sugar because its natural "sweetness" is considered sufficient.

The Chinese, however, are great between-meal snack eaters and nibblers. They snack, not at regular hours (as is the case with Western coffee breaks), but whenever *not* eating becomes too monotonous. At such times they will eat various fruits (either fresh, preserved or dried), biscuits, small cakes, nuts and savories. Here again, the preference is always for light foods with subtle flavors, rather than rich sweets or heavy snacks.

(As for the meals themselves, breakfast in South China consists of a hot rice porridge called "congee," accompanied by several salty side dishes, while in the North, noodles are eaten. Lunch and dinner consist of soup, vegetables, some meat and fish, lunch being the lighter meal of the two.)

If the Western gourmet wishes to avoid the gout and related problems, he must save his rich dishes for special occasions only. On the other hand, he can indulge in Chinese food every day without suffering the consequences. Although this combination of good eating and health may seem like a paradox, the Chinese diet makes this happy arrangement possible: It simultaneously satisfies the palate while improving one's sense of well-being. Therefore it is not surprising to see that more and more health- and weight-conscious Westerners are turning to Chinese food. They have discovered its fundamental secret: This is the way to eat lightly and still eat well.

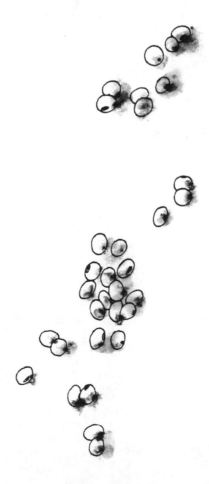

❋ *Food as Art:* *A Venerable Tradition* ❋

CHINESE CULTURE is the oldest continuous civilization in the world. It goes back some four thousand years, and the art of Chinese cooking goes back with it. The Chinese people were early farmers who planted not only staple crops, but also such spices as anise and ginger, long before anyone else knew what these were. They were among the first discoverers of fire. Most likely, they cooked their food in a civilized way while the rest of mankind was still gulping it down raw.

Many forces shaped the character of Chinese cooking. There was always a leisure class: men with the wealth, curiosity and time to cultivate their palates and delight their senses. These men dreamed about and fussed over food. One thousand years before the birth of Christ, they were already experimenting with fancy cooking, recording their recipes on silk and bamboo. As early as 1115 B.C. the Imperial Court appointed a dietitian who held the rank of medical officer. His job was not only to supervise the cooking, but to study the effects (both psychic and physical) of the various dishes served. These men of leisure brought refinement to the Chinese cuisine and discovered its rarest and most exquisite delicacies.

Yet famine as well as feast was to influence Chinese cooking. Many times in the country's history flood and drought destroyed the crops and devastated the economy. The Chinese were forced by these disasters to become great domestic economists. Fuel, for example, was chronically scarce, but the Chinese soon discovered it took less wood or charcoal to steam rice than to bake bread. And to make their limited fuel supplies go even further, they evolved several techniques for cooking food very quickly.

In order to survive, the Chinese had to put their land to the best possible use. They found, for example, that raising cattle as work animals was more economical than raising them for food. (Draft animals need no special grazing areas. They can subsist on uncultivated grass and straw.) Thus the land was used for growing grain, which in turn directly fed larger numbers of people than the beef ever could. On the other hand, pigs and poultry could be raised without agricultural displacement and so became mainstays of the diet, but not for the very poorest Chinese; the mainstays of their diet were rice and vegetables.

Adversity forced the Chinese always to seek new sources of food. They were gastronomically courageous, setting no limits as to where they would look. They explored rivers and oceans and found shrimp, crab, sea cucumber, lobster and squid. They put everything edible to use, finding wonderful ways to utilize strange plants and roots: lily buds, fungi, chrysanthemum petals. By the end of the first century A.D., the Chinese had formulated a list of 365 varieties of edible plants along with similar lists of edible seafood, fowl and animals. In addition, they evolved various salting and drying techniques to preserve many ingredients indefinitely.

In their long history, the Chinese had limitless opportunities to experiment with all kinds of foods in all kinds of ways. Their most successful experiments have become part of our culinary heritage. They represent the imaginative spirit of countless men and women, often forced by circumstance to make something of very little.

The imaginativeness of the Chinese was coupled with a strong sense of artistry. Inevitably, this artistry (beautifully demonstrated in jade, ivory, porcelain, bronze and calligraphy) was to find expression in Chinese cooking. Every aspect of food was analyzed, from palatability and texture to fragrance and color. Every dish was given proportion and balance, delicacy and harmony. In the hands of the Chinese, cooking was elevated from a menial and repetitive task to a satisfying art form.

The art was not in the cooking alone. It was in the eating as well. Sharing the pleasures of good food became part of the Chinese social tradition. Friendship and food were inseparably linked. Friends on a visit were always urged to stay for a meal. A gathering without food was considered incomplete and improper. The meal hour became the symbol of the good life, a time for relaxation and pleasantry, when the harsher realities could be forgotten—a ceremonial of friendship and sociability.

Twenty-five hundred years ago Confucius described the enjoyment of food as one of the beautiful and gentle things which contribute to the peace and harmony of society. Similar references to cooking as an art appeared in China's earliest literature, and continued to appear as a traditional theme.

For thousands of years Chinese men of letters were gourmets. As a matter of fact, China is perhaps the only country in the world where scholars wrote learned treatises on food and poets wrote cookbooks.

Yet the primary way of passing Chinese cooking from one generation to the next was not by the written word but by demonstration and word of mouth—from mother to daughter, from master chef to youthful apprentice. Each in turn was to add his own ideas, to work out his own culinary variations on what had gone before.

Thus, over the centuries, out of a relatively small range of ingredients, the Chinese created vast numbers of dishes. They invented more than two hundred ways to cook pork and so many ways to cook chicken that one might eat it every day for a week, at every meal, without tiring of it. The Chinese cuisine, unsurpassed by any other in variety, is said to include some eighty thousand different dishes.

Chinese Cooking: The Spirit and the Essence ❊

IN THE WESTERN WORLD, French cuisine is considered the highest. Yet gourmets who have sampled the best of the Chinese rank it with the French. This is not surprising. They have much in common. The Chinese and the French are skillful cooks. Both seek simplicity as their final goal—not the simplicity of short cuts—but the simplicity that comes with diligence, the simplicity of art.

The Chinese and the French also recognize that second-class ingredients (no matter how manipulated) can never produce first-class dishes; that one gets out of a dish only what one puts into it. They know that fine cooking begins not in the kitchen but at the market; that to cook well is to buy well, and to buy well is to select ingredients, not for cost as such, but for freshness and quality. These ingredients (whether commonplace or rare) must then be prepared so that they are beautiful to look at, yet with flavor never sacrificed to appearance. Flavor, as both the Chinese and French know, brings joy to eating. It is the essence of good cooking. Nothing can take its place.

Chinese cooking is an aesthetic experience: Food to the Chinese is a total experience designed to please all the senses. Certain foods are combined because their fragrances blend into memorable aromas. Others are named "ruby" or "jade" to please the ear and linger in memory. (A soup made with strips of ham and mustard cabbage becomes "golden tree branches with jade leaves," while another with alternating slices of ham and duck becomes "gold and silver broth.") The Chinese also delight in color. They love the clear gold of chicken broth, the whiteness of rice, the bright green of vegetables. They combine, blend and contrast color with the practiced eye of the painter. So color-conscious are they that hostesses have been known to include tomatoes in a dish just to match a red dress, and cooks to substitute white mushrooms for black to keep a soup lighter and more delicate in color.

The Chinese are unsurpassed in their ability to combine and contrast textures. They love to set crunchiness against smoothness: to combine crisp water chestnuts with the creaminess of bean curd; to surround crisp, tender vegetables with exquisitely smooth sauces. They also constantly stimulate the senses with contrasting tastes. Many of their greatest delicacies may seem neutral at first, almost colorless and odorless. Yet the purity of their taste, the interest of their texture are always in subtle contrast to the stronger and more decisive ingredients they are combined with.

The Chinese have a passion for creating contrast and variety in every possible way. They will play hot dishes against cold, tiny ingredients against big ones, dry dishes against those with gravies. Sweets are contrasted with salts, bland foods with those that are highly seasoned, rich dishes with light, delicate ones. Yet, despite this vast variety, the Chinese do not believe in saying too many things at once. Each dish has its own proportion, its own dominant elements. Each contributes to the coherence and essential harmony of the meal.

There is no main dish: With their passion for variety, the Chinese could never limit themselves to one main dish. Instead they prefer to dart from one dish to another, to take a few mouthfuls here, a few mouthfuls there; to change at short intervals from one taste to another, to sample at the same meal something sweet-and-sour, peppery, bitter and salty. So instead of having one main dish and several subordinate side dishes, they will serve several dishes all considered equally important. In this way, they enhance the appetite and avoid monotony and the feeling of stuffing oneself that comes from eating the same foods in comparatively large quantities.

Chinese cooking calls for maximum preparation, minimum cooking: Although the combined preparation and cooking time is roughly the same for Chinese and American dishes, the Chinese spend more time preparing and less cooking. With their quick-cooking techniques many dishes need less than 15 minutes on the stove, more often less than 10. With practice and experience, it is possible to prepare and serve a complete and excellent Chinese meal in less than an hour.

The starting point is the ingredient, not the cooking method: The Chinese housewife never begins with the idea of a stew or a roast. She begins with what she finds at the market. It may be a vegetable in season, a cut of meat, some poultry, or fish that looks particularly good. The next step is to match the cooking method to the ingredient. If it's duck, she'll want to compensate for its dry, fibrous texture by slow simmering until it's moist and tender. If it's fish, she'll steam it briefly to preserve its delicacy. In each case, her goal is to retain the ingredient's original flavor, enhance its piquancy, mask its less desirable qualities. With this individualized approach, every ingredient is made highly palatable. Meat is never tough, but exceedingly tender; poultry never dry but always savory and juicy; vegetables never overdone but crisp and crunchy; and rich dishes not too rich and never greasy.

Ingredients are usually combined, seldom cooked alone: Chinese cooking is a kind of matchmaking: ingredients are combined to bring out the best in each other (or to compensate for each other's shortcomings). They are combined to emphasize freshness, strengthen flavor or offset richness. The possible combinations of meat, poultry, seafood and vegetables are inexhaustible, the variety infinite. The blending of these ingredients produces a strength and flavor unknown in any other type of cooking. (Even commonplace ingredients such as beef and tomatoes become transformed when cooked in combination Chinese style.) The higher the level of cooking, the more superb and perfect this blending becomes. Yet within a given dish the individuality of each ingredient is never lost; its taste and texture are always retained, its individual flavor always brought out.

The cook, not the diner, seasons the food: Chinese seasoning is most effective when added *during* the cooking process. Heat sets off a chemical reaction between the condiments and other ingredients, enabling the seasoning to permeate each and every piece of meat, fish or vegetable. Seasonings so added perform a number of functions: they bring out natural flavors and aromas, suppress unwanted tastes (such as the fishiness of fish, the strong taste of liver) and form a bond between dissimilar foods. Chinese seasoning is always subtle: the condiments never betray themselves, never overwhelm or overpower the taste of other ingredients. (There is one exception: plain-cooked meats are not seasoned by the cook, but are served with various dips such as plum sauce, soy sauce and hot mustard, which the diner himself adds.)

The cook, not the diner, cuts the food: To the Chinese, knives are barbaric instruments, suitable for the kitchen but not for the table. All cutting, therefore, is done in the kitchen. (The diner needs only a pair of chopsticks and a soup spoon to manage an entire meal.) Meat and vegetables are either cut into bite-size pieces or cooked to such a tenderness that they require no cutting at all. Even when poultry and fish are served whole, chopsticks are sufficient to pick the tender meat right off the bones. As for roast meat and poultry, these too are always carved in the kitchen with the slices cut small enough to be picked up comfortably with chopsticks.

Regional Variations: The Schools of Cooking

CHINA is a vast country which varies widely from region to region in terrain, people, climate and natural resources. Chinese cooking reflects this variety: there are almost as many cooking styles as there are regions. (These differ, however, not in the cooking methods as such, but in the way various seasonings, spices and sauces are used.) Five schools predominate: The Southeastern (Canton), Western (Szechwan, sometimes called Chungking), Northeastern (Peking, or Shantung), Central (Honan) and East Coast (Fukien).

SOUTHEASTERN—THE CANTONESE SCHOOL

When Europe began trading with the Orient, the seaport of Canton became the gateway to the West. The Cantonese readily absorbed these cosmopolitan influences and, being great travelers themselves, soon emigrated to Europe and America. They were the first to establish Chinese restaurants outside their own country and to make Chinese cooking known to the West. As a result, most Chinese restaurants in the United States and Europe are Cantonese.

Cantonese cooking is original and versatile, having been encouraged by a large leisure class and abetted by the region's rich natural resources. When the Ming dynasty was overthrown in the seventeenth century, many government officials moved south from Peking to Kwangtung province (of which Canton is the capital). They also brought their chefs with them. These chefs, trained in Peking's classical style, assimilated other regional styles in their southward travels. In Canton they took advantage of the area's rich produce to expand and enlarge their cuisine into what became known as Cantonese style. As the port prospered, more emphasis was placed on fine living and dining, and the cuisine was perfected.

The Cantonese style is characterized by its ability to bring out and enhance the original taste of each ingredient and to blend natural flavors together. It uses very few seasonings (soy sauce, ginger root, wine), specializes in the quick-cooking technique known as stir-frying, and uses chicken stock as a cooking medium. The Cantonese school is also noted for roast meat and poultry, lobster, steamed pork and fish dishes, fried rice and such delicacies as Bird's Nest Soup and Shark's Fin Soup.

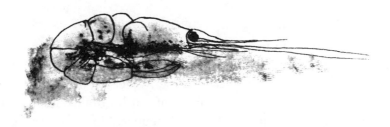

NORTHEASTERN—THE PEKING-SHANTUNG SCHOOL

Although the city of Peking and the province of Shantung are not geograph-ically close, trade between them was active, and back-and-forth migration continual. For centuries the two exchanged chefs. Eventually their cooking styles became indistinguishable. Peking, however, being the site of the Imperial Palace and China's great intellectual and cultural center, exerted the stronger influence. Its concentration of wealth attracted the country's best chefs, who brought cooking to its highest level. (Peking, the gourmet capital of China until the seventeenth century, had a great reputation for mammoth feasts and gargantuan banquets. The repasts of the Imperial Court, held in palaces of magnificent splendor, were of a grandeur unrivaled in history. Some of the meals took three days to consume.)

The Peking-Shantung school is distinguished by light, elegant, mildly seasoned rather than rich foods, and the liberal use of garlic, scallions, leeks and chives. It is known also for the delicacy of Peking Duck and Chicken Velvet, soft-fried foods, the spring roll (forerunner of the egg roll), delicious roasts and wine-cooked meats.

NOTE: Most of northern China, including the vastness of Mongolia and Manchuria, is largely barren and sparsely populated. Its people are nomadic, noted for their use of lamb and mutton and for their chafing-dish cookery.

WESTERN—THE SCHOOL OF SZECHWAN

The climate of Szechwan province is hot, almost tropical. Its people like their food highly spiced, peppery and somewhat oily. Szechwanese specialties include deep-fried chicken wrapped in paper, vegetables prepared in chicken fat, chicken and hot peppers, and a variety of mushroom dishes. Although the Szechwanese home cooking was hot and peppery, its banquet dishes were usually bland and light: northerners from Peking who had migrated to Szechwan brought such dishes with them for their formal dining. Also reflecting this northern influence is Szechwan Duck, a favorite of the region, and a variation of Peking Duck.

CENTRAL — THE SCHOOL OF HONAN

Honan province (through which the Yellow River runs) is famous for its Yellow River carp. It's noted also for its spiced concoctions, sweet-and-sour dishes and rich seasonings.

EAST COAST — THE SCHOOL OF FUKIEN

Fukien province on China's east coast is famous for seafood and for clear, light soups. These soups are noteworthy not only for their quality but also for

their quantity. At family meals, at least two such soups are served. At banquets, as many as one-fourth of all the dishes were often soups. (At one specific banquet, soup appeared for seven out of ten courses.) Fukien is noted also for its subtle use of cooking wine, its soy sauce, egg rolls and suckling pig.

NOTE: One often sees references to "Shanghai" and "Mandarin" cooking. These are not regional styles but rather restaurant designations. "Shanghai Cooking" has come to mean a menu of many regional styles, since Shanghai itself, being a great commercial center and a cosmopolitan city, reflected many influences. "Mandarin Cooking" relates to the Peking-Shantung school since it was in Peking that the mandarins or aristocrats of China lived. (The word "mandarin" means Chinese official.) The designation is a way of suggesting that the cooking is aristocratic, of the highest style, the best of its kind. It too, however, encompasses a number of styles.

Although all the regional styles are represented by the recipes in this book, no attempt has been made to indicate places of origin. In many cases this would be virtually impossible since the dishes have been adapted, varied and modified many times over the years.

❊ *The Ingredients* ❊

CHINESE COOKING calls for ingredients which are both familiar and strange. About eighty percent are familiar, the rest uniquely Chinese. The familiar ones are available in any supermarket; the others are sold mainly in Chinese food stores. Good Chinese cooking, however, does not depend on rare or unusual ingredients. It depends rather on understanding Chinese cooking methods and knowing which methods are best for cooking the ingredients on hand. Thus, authentic Chinese dishes can be prepared when the only ingredients available are meat, fish, vegetables, soy sauce and peanut oil.

MEATS

Pork is the staple and supreme Chinese meat. When cooked the Chinese way, it's more succulent than either beef or lamb. It also has a finer grain than beef, a more delicate flavor, and can be used in a greater variety of dishes. Pork, already roasted or barbecued, is sold by the pound in Chinese food stores. Ham is used more as a garnish than for its substance. The high-quality two-year-old Smithfield variety is preferred, both for color and texture, since it most closely resembles Chinese ham.

Beef originally was not eaten much in China because cattle were more valued as beasts of burden. (The buffalo was so useful in the field that both the Taoists and followers of Confucius considered it cruel and sacrilegious to eat its meat.) Contact with the West, however, made beef more popular. Lamb is used only in the North, mainly in Manchuria, where many of the people are Moslems and do not eat pork. Veal is almost never eaten.

POULTRY

Poultry is second to pork as a Chinese favorite. Duck leads, followed by chicken, squab, pheasant and occasionally turkey and goose. Poultry, like pork, can be purchased already cooked in Chinese food stores and eaten as is, or reheated.

FISH

Since China has more than three thousand miles of coast line, several mighty rivers, thousands of tributaries, streams, lakes and ponds, it's not surprising that the Chinese are great fish and seafood enthusiasts. Both fresh- and salt-water varieties are used, with the fresh-water most favored.

VEGETABLES

The Chinese use nearly every vegetable known to Americans, as well as a number of others, such as bean sprouts, bamboo shoots, water chestnuts, which are uniquely Chinese.

GRAINS

Rice grows predominantly in southern China, which has a warm climate and plenty of rain. It is usually eaten as a staple food. Among the poor, rice forms the bulk of each meal (being accompanied, at best, by soup, vegetables and a few bits of meat or fish). Among the wealthy, rice serves as a buffer to offset and neutralize rich foods.

In the North, wheat, not rice, predominates. The northerners eat wheat-flour noodles much as the southerners eat rice. (The southerners also eat noodles, but as a snack or luncheon dish rather than as a staple.) Because of their length, noodles literally symbolize longevity and are also served at birthday celebrations. Other northern grains include barley, maize and millet. These, as well as wheat, are ground into flour and made into steamed breads, buns, pastries, and pancakes similar to tortillas. In both North and South, rice, which has an almost sacred character to the Chinese, is always served on special occasions, at feasts and banquets. It is the symbol of all food and a good omen that there will always be something to eat.

FRUITS AND NUTS

Fruits are taken as between-meal snacks and sometimes at the end of a meal. They're eaten fresh, cooked and preserved. (The latter, prepared with sugar and honey, are flavored with ginger, clove, licorice, etc.) Some uniquely

Chinese fruits, such as loquats and lichees, are used also to flavor meat and poultry dishes. Canned pineapple turns up in sweet-and-pungent sauces. Nuts are eaten between meals as sweetmeats and used also as flavorings and garnishes. Walnuts and chestnuts are cooked in both sweet and salt dishes; nut-like lotus seeds are used in sweet dishes and soups. Walnuts, cashews, almonds and peanuts, when blanched and toasted, become garnishes for meat, poultry, seafood and vegetables. (Other characteristic Chinese garnishes include: mushrooms; scallion tops; dried shrimp; bamboo shoots; Chinese parsley; sesame seeds; deep-fried rice-flour noodles; and ham, lettuce or fried eggs, cut in narrow strips.)

SEASONINGS AND CONDIMENTS

The basic ingredients that give Chinese cooking its characteristically subtle taste are soy sauce, peanut oil, sherry, garlic, ginger root and scallions, salt, pepper and sugar. (Chili sauce and catsup, now used frequently, were not introduced to Chinese cooking until this century.) In addition, there are a number of special spices, sauces and seasonings available through Chinese food stores.

DRIED INGREDIENTS

Chinese dried ingredients include fish, poultry, fruit and vegetables. They are preserved either by salting or by drying in the sun and wind. These processes not only preserve the ingredients but make them more savory and flavorful. Most dried ingredients must be soaked before cooking: this reconstitutes them by restoring their moisture and also helps "develop" or bring out their flavor.

Many dried, as well as canned, Chinese ingredients may seem expensive at first. However, since they're used sparingly, they go a very long way. Because they also transform ordinary ingredients into dishes of great interest, they prove quite reasonable in the long run.

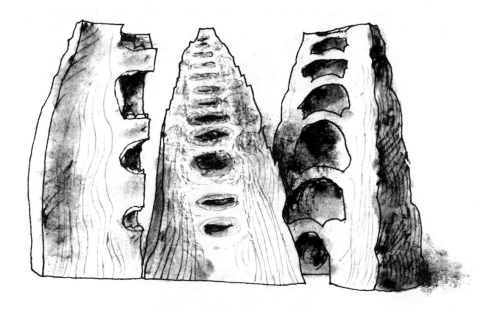

INGREDIENTS USED IN CHINESE COOKING

MEAT AND POULTRY
Bacon
Beef
Chicken
Duck
Duck Feet *
Duck Liver *
Duck, Preserved *
Duck, Roast *
Duck, Salted *
Ham *
Lamb
Pig, Roast *
Pork
Pork, Roast *
Sausage, Chinese *
Sausage, Liver *
Squab
Turkey

FISH AND SEAFOOD
Abalone *
Abalone, Dried *
Bass, Sea
Bass, Striped
Bêche de Mer *
Bluefish
Bluegill
Bream
Butterfish
Carp
Catfish

Clams
Clams, Dried *
Cod
Crab
Cuttlefish, Dried *
Dogfish
Eel
Fish, Dried *
Fish's Maw *
Flounder
Haddock
Halibut
Herring
Jellyfish, Dried *
Lobster
Mackerel
Mullet
Oysters
Oysters, Dried *
Perch
Pike
Prawn
Red Snapper
Rock Cod
Salmon
Sand Dab
Sardines
Scallops
Scallops, Dried *
Shad
Shark's Fins *
Shrimp

Shrimp Chips *
Shrimp, Dried *
Shrimp, Miniature *
Sole
Squid
Squid, Dried *
Sturgeon
Trout
Tuna
Turbot
Whitebait
Whitefish

VEGETABLES
Asparagus
Bamboo Shoots *
Bean Curd *
Bean Curd Sticks *
Beans, Black *
Beans, Red *
Bean Sprouts (Mung) *
Bean Sprouts (Soy) *
Bitter Melon *
Broccoli
Broccoli, Chinese *
Cabbage
Cabbage, Chinese *
Cabbage, Mustard *
Carrots
Cauliflower
Celery
Chives, Chinese *
Corn

* See Glossary of Chinese Ingredients for details.

Cucumbers
Eggplant
Eggplant, Chinese *
Fuzzy Melon *
Green Peas
Green Peppers
Leeks
Lettuce, Boston
Lettuce, Chinese *
Lettuce, Romaine
Lily Buds *
Lima Beans
Long Beans *
Lotus Root *
Matrimony Vine *
Mushrooms, Black
    Dried *
Mushrooms, Button *
Mushrooms, Cloud
    Ear *
Mushrooms, Grass *
Mushrooms, Snow *
Okra, Chinese *
Onions *
Parsley, Chinese *
Potatoes
Radishes
Rutabagas
Snow Peas *
Spinach
Squash, Bottle *
Squash, Chinese *
String Beans
Sweet Potatoes
Taro *
Tomatoes
Turnips
Turnips, Chinese *

Turnips, Dried *
Water Chestnuts *
Water Cress
Winter Melon *

SAUCES
Brown Bean Sauce *
Chili Sauce, Chinese *
Hoisin Sauce *
Oyster Sauce *
Plum Sauce *
Red Bean Sauce *
Shrimp Sauce *
Soy Sauce *

SPICES AND SEASONINGS
Anise, Star *
Bamboo Shoots,
    Pickled *
Bean Paste, Red *
Bean Paste, Yellow *
Beans, Black
    Fermented *
Cabbage, Dried
    Chinese *
Cabbage, Pickled *
Cabbage, Salt-Cured *
Cabbage, Salted *
Catsup
Cheese, Chinese Red *
Cheese, Chinese
    White *
Cinnamon Bark *
Curry *
Five Spices *
Garlic *
Ginger, Red *
Ginger Root *

Ginger Root,
    Preserved *
Ginger, Subgum *
Lotus Root, Dried *
Monosodium
    Glutamate *
Mustard *
Olives, Dried *
Pepper, Anise *
Pepper, Black *
Pepper, Chinese Red *
Pepper, Szechwan *
Peppers, Chili *
Red Dates *
Salt
Sesame Paste *
Soy Jam *
Sugar
Sugar, Brown
Sugar, Rock *
Tabasco
Tangerine Peel *
Tea Melon *
Turnips, Preserved *
Vinegar *
Wine *

FATS AND OILS
Chicken Fat
Lard *
Oil, Peanut *
Oil, Sesame *

RICE AND NOODLES
Rice, Glutinous *
Rice, Long-Grain *
Rice, Oval-Grain *
Noodles, Egg *

* See Glossary of Chinese Ingredients for details.

Noodles, Peastarch *
Noodles, Rice-Flour *
Noodles, Seaweed *
Noodles, Wheat-Flour *

FRUIT
Apples
Apricots
Bananas
Crab Apples
Dragon's Eyes *
Grapes
Kumquats *
Lichees *
Loquats *
Mangoes
Melons
Oranges
Peaches
Pears
Persimmons
Pineapple

Plums
Pomelo *
Strawberries
Tangerines

NUTS
Almonds *
Cashews
Chestnuts
Chestnuts, Dried *
Coconuts
Ginkgo Nuts *
Lotus Seeds *
Melon Seeds *
Peanuts *
Walnuts *

MISCELLANEOUS
Agar-Agar *
Almond Paste *
Bird's Nest *

Cornstarch *
Egg Roll Skins *
Eggs
Eggs, Preserved *
Eggs, Salted *
Flour, Glutinous-Rice *
Flour, Rice *
Flour, Water-
    Chestnut *
Flour, Wheat
Ginseng Root *
Honey
Lotus Leaves *
Mung Peas *
Pickles, Chinese *
Red Berries *
Scallions, Pickled *
Seaweed, Dried *
Seaweed, Hair *
Sweet Root *
Tea
Wonton Skins *

* See Glossary of Chinese Ingredients for details.

❋ *Techniques of Chinese Cooking* ❋

THE CHINESE sauté, steam, deep-fry and roast, but with a difference. They do their cooking with a minimum of fuel. (Originally this was a matter of necessity: in China, charcoal, wood and coal were usually in short supply.) Home cooking is always top-of-the-stove, with typical dishes being savory stews simmered for hours over small, slow fires. Baking is rarely done. Steaming, which needs only enough heat to keep water boiling, takes its place. (The fuel-conscious Chinese even use the steam that rises from cooking rice to cook bean curd, sausage, chicken and other meats.) Steaming often substitutes not only for baking, but for stewing as well. In China few families had ovens or spits. Roasting was done mainly by restaurants. Even today meat already roasted is sold in Chinese grocery stores.

In addition, the Chinese invented stir-frying, a cooking method which needs only a few minutes of intense heat. Although centuries old, it's the closest thing to "instant" cooking, and the most popular of all Chinese cooking techniques.

STIR-FRYING

This technique is used with meats, poultry, seafood and vegetables. Although similar to sautéing, it is much more rapid and fascinating. The ingredients are sliced, diced or minced, then tossed vigorously at very high temperatures in a small amount of oil. (The hot oil seals in the juices, preserves color, texture and flavor.) Next a small amount of liquid is added and the ingredients are cooked in it as quickly as possible. When done, the food not only looks good but also retains its nutritional values and is highly digestible.

The key to stir-frying is the intensity of the cooking heat. This differs, however, from stove to stove. Gas stoves are preferable to electric since their flames can be raised or lowered instantaneously.* Yet gas stoves vary considerably in the amount of heat they generate. Cooking pots also vary considerably. Generally speaking, the thinner the metal, the faster they conduct the heat. There are other heat-intensity variables, too. These include the freshness of the food (the fresher it is, the less cooking it needs) and the way it's cut (the smaller it's cut, the faster it cooks). Because of these variables, cooking times for stir-fried dishes can be standardized only up to a point and should be considered guideposts rather than absolutes. The cook must always keep her eye on the food, not the clock.

Success in stir-frying (more so than in virtually any other cooking technique) depends on knowing what you're doing and why. It's based on the simple principle that each ingredient has its own cooking time—that tender ingredients need less heat, while tougher ones need more—that each must be added to the pan separately and in sequence so all can emerge done together at the end. Stir-frying calls for split-second timing, a sense of sequence, and sensitivity to the right amount of heat, the right amount of doneness.

Stir-frying cannot be done casually. Since many ingredients are involved, the challenge becomes one of coordination: to add each to the pot separately but at the proper moment. Once the fat is literally on the fire, the tempo accelerates rapidly. Every minute counts. Ingredients must be tossed into the pan without delay, often seconds apart. Things must be stirred constantly.

* Electric stoves work best when used as follows: Set the heat where you want it in advance. Then instead of adjusting switches, lift the pan on and off the heat to regulate the temperature.

There is no time for hesitation or second thoughts. The hand must be on the stirring, the eye on the food, the mind on the next step. All the senses are involved, particularly common sense. (If, for example, a vegetable starts to scorch, the heat obviously should be lowered at once; if it begins to wilt, it should be taken out of the pan.)

Although timing is the key to stir-frying, it's not exactly a matter of do-or-die. If at any point the cook feels things are moving too fast for her, all she has to do is lift the skillet off the heat, catch her breath, get her bearings for a minute or two, then pick up where she left off.

Success in stir-frying also depends on good preparation. (This includes cutting, soaking, parboiling, measuring and mixing ingredients.) Once cooking begins, there isn't time to dash around hunting for this ingredient or that. Once the heat is turned on, everything must be on hand and ready for the pot.

Stir-frying may seem difficult at first, but practice and experience make it increasingly easy and enjoyable. Eventually it becomes a kind of freewheeling technique, done almost intuitively and with a great sense of exhilaration. To master stir-frying is to master Chinese cooking. (A step-by-step guide appears on pages 833–838.)

NOTE: When serving stir-fried dishes, it is well to remember an old Chinese proverb which says: It is better that a man wait for his meal, than the meal wait for the man. Stir-fried dishes cannot wait. They must be served as soon as they're cooked. If left on the stove even a minute or two longer, they go on cooking in their own steam. Bright green vegetables lose their color. Food that was crisp, delicious and fragrant quickly becomes overcooked, soggy and tasteless. (The dish that gets cold loses its flavor; if reheated, it gets tough.) Stir-fried dishes should *never* be put on the stove until the diners are seated at the table. Since actual cooking time averages only about five minutes, the waiting will be negligible. (Should soup be served first, the brief time gap won't even be noticed.)

DEEP-FRYING

This technique is used with meat, poultry, seafood and sometimes vegetables. Deep-frying calls for ingredients to be cut in medium-size pieces,* dredged in

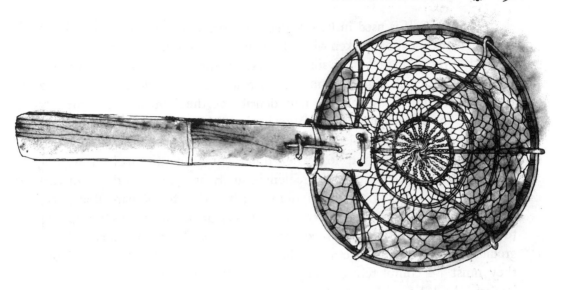

cornstarch or coated with egg-flour batter and immersed in hot oil until done. (This coating process protects the food's surfaces, keeps its juices in during cooking.) Chinese deep-frying differs from the Western variety in two ways: ingredients are often marinated first, in soy sauce and sherry, to improve flavor and aroma; and the frying is done in stages instead of all at once. In the frying process, ingredients are briefly immersed in hot oil until they are pale golden, then removed and cooled while the oil itself is reheated. The ingredients are then returned to the oil until the cooking is completed. This makes them more crisp, yet keeps the outside from cooking too quickly before the inside is done. As a result, they're done equally inside and out. If they're removed from the pot once, the technique is known as double-frying. If they're removed twice, it's called triple-frying. (If only single-frying is used, the heat should be reduced slightly once the ingredients are in the pot. Otherwise, they will char on the outside before being cooked inside.

NOTE: Many Chinese restaurants use double-frying for egg rolls, fish and pork—draining and refrigerating them after the initial frying, and then, just before serving, briefly deep-frying them again. The home cook, who likes to get as much advance preparation done as possible, can do the same.

* Fish and poultry may be left whole, but the latter needs additional cooking either before or after deep-frying. A whole chicken can be deep-fried, however, if it's basted frequently with hot oil. Some cooks pour the oil through the rear cavity and drain it out through the neck; they do this five times, then immerse the entire bird in the oil until its skin is crisp and golden.

The oil itself is used in two degrees of heat: It's ready for fish, kidneys and the white meat of chicken when it just begins to bubble. (A slice of ginger or crust of bread floated on its surface will cause the oil to foam actively along its edge.) When it begins to smoke, it's ready for beef and pork. Cooking time is determined by the size and density of the ingredients. Generally speaking, the ingredients are done when dry, crisp and golden outside but tender and still moist inside. If large amounts of oil are used, the ingredients will rise to the surface and float when done. Large quantities of oil are not necessary however. For cut-up ingredients usually one cup, or a depth of two inches, is sufficient. Ingredients should never be added to the pan all at once, but only a few at a time. This keeps the temperature of the oil from dropping too fast; allows for plenty of cooking room; and keeps batter-coated ingredients from sticking together. When ingredients are added to boiling oil, they must be completely dry or they'll spatter dangerously. Should this happen, the pot can be covered with a lid until the spattering stops.

When done, deep-fried foods are removed from the oil immediately and drained thoroughly. Some are served with salt-and-pepper dips; others with sweet-and-pungent sauces.

STEAMING

This technique is used with rice, meat, poultry, buns, dumplings, pastries and custards. It's also a favorite way of keeping fish moist and tender. Steamed foods, cooked right in their serving dishes, go directly from stove to table, with all their natural juices, flavors and nutrients preserved. Chinese steaming is known as wet or direct steaming. It calls for live steam which rises from boiling water to circulate around the food and cook it by direct contact. (The more familiar double-boiler steaming does not permit actual contact between steam and food and is known as dry or indirect steaming.)

Chinese wet steaming is done in two ways: either by rack or by bowl. Both require a covered pot containing boiling water. In rack steaming, the rack stands above 2 or 3 inches of water. The ingredients are then placed in a shallow dish (a Pyrex pie pan is fine for this) and set on the rack. The bowl method, also known as a pot-within-a-pot, calls for a bowl to sit not on a rack but on the bottom of the pan itself. The bowl is then surrounded by boiling water to about two-thirds of its height. (A greater amount will either boil over into the food or cause the bowl to float and spill its contents. A lesser amount will produce too little steam.) Both the circulating steam and the boiling water do the cooking here. The bowl method is used in steaming large cuts of meat, whole ducks and chickens.

In either case, the shallow dish or bowl should be heatproof and slightly prewarmed before steaming begins. The water should be at a vigorous rolling boil. After the food is added and the pan covered, the heat can be reduced to medium, just enough to maintain the boiling. The pan should be big enough to permit the steam to circulate; its lid snug enough to contain the steam, but not so tight that excessive pressure can build up. Depending on the ingredient, steaming can take anywhere from 15 minutes to several hours. (Steamed foods should always be cooked slightly underdone because they go on cooking in their hot serving dishes after they've been removed from the heat.) As a rule, the steamer should be opened as little as possible during cooking. With longer-cooking dishes, however, the evaporation of water must be checked from time to time. Whenever it diminishes appreciably, it should always be replenished with *boiling* water.

SLOW-COOKING

This method is used with large cuts of meat and poultry, coarse-fleshed fish and vegetables. It calls for ingredients to be simmered slowly until they become rich, mellow and extremely tender. A Dutch oven or similar heavy pan is always used. Slow-cooking includes braising and stewing. Braising requires the shorter time. It's used with vegetables such as eggplant and turnips, fish such as salmon and cod, young poultry and some cuts of meat. Braising calls for the ingredients to be browned quickly in oil first, then cooked, tightly covered, in a small amount of liquid over very low heat. (Instead of being browned or seared, meat can be scalded by a brief plunge into boiling water. This will also seal in its juices. Vegetables are sometimes deep-fried first, then simmered briefly.)

Stewing has two variations: white-stewing, which doesn't use soy sauce; and red-stewing, which does. White-stewing, sometimes called pure-stewing or clear-simmering, is used to cook fish, chicken and other delicate meats. It's usually accompanied by vegetables and produces a clear soup which retains the natural flavor of the ingredients. The soup and meat can be eaten at the same meal, but are usually served separately. (The meat, known as "plain-cooked" meat, is accompanied by a soy-sauce dip and other table condiments.)

Red-stewing gets its name from the rich, red-brown gravy produced by the soy sauce. It's used with whole poultry, large cuts of pork and beef, sometimes leg of lamb. During cooking, the meat is turned several times for even coloring as well as seasoning.

NOTE: Some cooks like to combine light and dark soy sauce for this. (See "Soy Sauce," page 868.) The light imparts a delicate flavor to the gravy; the dark gives it a rich color.

Red- and white-stewing can be combined in a technique known as pot-stewing. This calls for one hour of simmering in plain water, then another hour of simmering with soy sauce, sherry and other seasonings added.

Both red-stewed and pot-stewed meats can be served with their sauces, or the sauces can be used as gravies for noodles and rice. Some cooks set the sauce aside to be used as a cooking medium for other meats and poultry. The more frequently a given sauce is used, the more it takes on the flavors of the meats cooked in it and the more rich and subtle it becomes. Tradition tells us of such sauces, known as "Master Sauces" in China, which were kept going for two or three hundred years and, like a legacy, passed from one generation to the next.

Red-stewed dishes, prepared in advance, will keep nearly a week under refrigeration. As is the case with most stews, their flavor is improved by rewarming. They may also be extended and varied by the addition of fresh vegetables. Enough of these for a single meal should be added. If the vegetables are tender, they are stir-fried separately and added to the sauce at the last minute to preserve crispness. Longer-cooking vegetables such as carrots and turnips are added to the sauce for the last half-hour or so of cooking.

Red-stewed meats can also be served chilled. Their sauces then become jellied, like aspic. (Vegetables should be omitted here altogether because the aspic ruins their texture makes them soggy.)

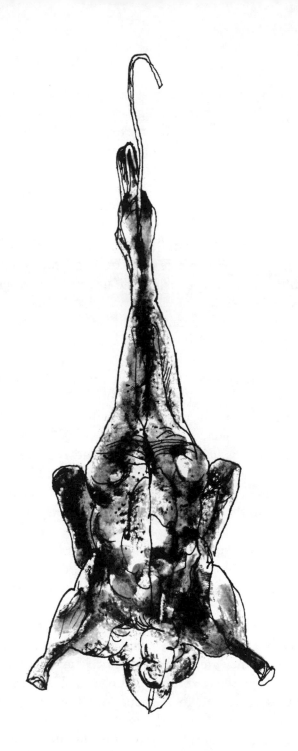

ROASTING

This method is used with whole poultry and large cuts of pork. (Roast beef and lamb are rarely used.) First the skin is rubbed with sesame oil or lard; then the meat is seared briefly in the oven or over an open flame to form a crust. The temperature is then reduced and the meat is roasted slowly until done. During this time it's basted frequently with soy sauce or a highly seasoned marinade. The meat is always elevated in some way, either on a rack or prongs, with a pan of water underneath to catch the drippings and prevent them from burning. It is always surrounded by as much air as possible and touches as little surface as possible. (Meat that sits in a flat roasting pan, stewing in its own juices, tends to become tough.) Originally in China, roasting was done in large outdoor ovens with meat either turned on a spit or hung high over the fire. These methods can be approximated today in home ovens, electric rotisseries, charcoal grills and barbecues. Chinese roasted meats are always crisp on the outside, juicy inside.

MISCELLANEOUS TECHNIQUES

Sautéing or *pan-frying* is used mainly for fish and omelets. It calls for medium heat, a longer cooking time than stir-frying and very little stirring. Dry-frying is not so much a cooking technique as a way of preserving meat. It calls for the meat to be cut up, simmered slowly until most of the stock is absorbed, then stirred constantly over low heat until it dries out completely. The result is a meat that needs no refrigeration, is rich, reddish-brown, velvety and tender.

 Boiling as such is rarely used because it destroys both flavor and nutritional value. Rice, although boiled the first few minutes, is actually steamed. Soups and stews, also brought to a boil at first, are actually simmered. Boiling liquids, however, are used in poaching, blanching and parboiling.

Poaching is related to white-stewing or clear-simmering in its absence of soy sauce, but is a quicker cooking method. It's used with delicate ingredients such as fish, chicken breast, etc. It calls for ingredients to be submerged in barely boiling liquid (with only an occasional bubble breaking through the surface) and simmered briefly until done.

Blanching and parboiling are precooking techniques.

Blanching loosens tomato skins so that they peel off easily, removes the skins of almonds and other nuts, and precooks tender young vegetables. It calls for boiling water to be poured over the ingredients, then drained off immediately, or after a minute or two.

Parboiling calls for the ingredients to be plunged into boiling water and cooked rapidly for several minutes. It is used primarily for vegetables, particularly the tougher varieties such as string beans, carrots, broccoli, cauliflower, turnips, etc. It reduces their cooking time so that the vegetables can be used in stir-fried dishes or quick-cooked soups. (If the vegetables were introduced raw, the dishes would have to cook too long.) Widely differing ingredients can be parboiled separately to bring them up to the same level of tenderness, and then added to the pot together for the final cooking. Parboiling is also useful in removing the strong or bitter tastes of certain vegetables, such as cabbage, onion, green pepper and bitter melon. Occasionally this precooking technique is used with poultry: to seal in the juices of chicken, or reduce the fattiness of duck.

NOTE: The cooking techniques described above can be—and are—used in various combinations. Thus, a chicken may be deep-fried first, cut up, then stir-fried with vegetables; or it may be steamed first, then deep-fried for a crisp, crackling surface.

Smoking is not so much a cooking technique as a way of flavoring certain foods (such as beef, chicken and fish) after they've been cooked by other methods. Smoking calls for the burning of brown sugar; such seasonings as ground anise and cinnamon and, sometimes, used black tea leaves. The burning produces a thick, strong smoke that chars the food and flavors it.

❊ *Cutting* ❊

CUTTING is extremely important to Chinese cooking, particularly for stir-frying. Ingredients cut into small pieces can be stirred easily, cooked faster with less fuel and managed comfortably with chopsticks. Cutting also improves flavor by exposing a greater amount of surface area to the seasoning agents.

In determining how to cut a given ingredient, the considerations are: the nature of the ingredient, how it's to be cooked and what it's to be combined with.

When ingredients are tough, cutting them into chunks makes them more absorbent, less tough. When they're tender, slicing them fine and cooking them quickly preserves their delicate textures. For deep-frying, they are usually cut into larger pieces; for steaming and stir-frying, into smaller ones. In stir-fried dishes the dominant vegetable determines the cutting. Peas call for diced meat, bamboo shoots for meat strips, bean sprouts for slivers. The pattern can sometimes be reversed, however, with meat that is shredded calling for shredded vegetables.

Whether sliced, diced or shredded, ingredients within a given dish should always be cut to uniform size and shape. This allows each the same amount of heat and enables them all to cook evenly. It also makes for a neater, more beautiful and harmonious dish. Eating with chopsticks becomes simpler, too: uniformly cut morsels are easier to grasp than a strip of this and a chunk of that.

This uniformity may at first seem to be in conflict with the usual Chinese emphasis on variety. But uniformity in a dish need not mean monotony in a meal. For example, if four dishes are to be served, one can be sliced, one diced, one shredded, one minced.

Chinese cutting techniques include slicing, dicing, shredding and mincing.

SLICING

This has three variations—straight, diagonal and rolling cut. Straight or vertical slicing is used with such soft, tender ingredients as mushrooms, scallops and liver. Diagonal slicing, or cutting at an angle, is used with coarse-grained meats and tough, fibrous vegetables. Rolling cut (or rolling-knife cutting), a variation of diagonal slicing, is used with coarse cylindrical vegetables such as carrots and turnips, which call for slow-cooking. In this method a diagonal cut (at about a 30-degree angle) is first made at one end of the vegetable. The vegetable is then rolled a quarter-turn and a second diagonal cut is made. (This produces an irregularly shaped slice with plenty of surface area to speed up the cooking.) The cutting and rolling continues until the vegetable is completely sliced.

DICING

This also has three variations: cube (for deep-frying and slow-cooking ingredients), dice (for stir-frying) and mince-dice (for steaming). The cubes range from ½ to 2 inches, the dice from ⅛ to ½ inch, the mince-dice from 1⁄16 to ⅛ inch. Dicing is simplest when ingredients are cut first into strips, then crosswise into cubes. When dicing irregularly shaped vegetables, begin at the narrowest section and work toward the thickest.

SHREDDING

This has two variations: the matchstick, used in steaming and stir-frying; and the threadlike strip, used in stir-frying. Matchsticks, sometimes called julienne strips, measure 2 to 3 inches in length, are about ½ inch wide, ⅛ inch thick. (When not so precise, they're known as slivers.) The threadlike strips are the same length but thinner and narrower.

MINCING

This is used mainly for steamed dishes. It is sometimes called fine chopping and consists of chopping first in one direction, then another, crosshatching continually until the ingredients look almost machine-ground. Machine-grinding, running the food through once on the coarse setting, may be substituted. This saves time but tends to mash the fibers, press out some of the juices and toughen the food. (This is why hand-minced porkballs are invariably lighter.)

OTHER CUTTING TECHNIQUES

Crushing (also called smashing) is used for garlic and ginger, to release their flavors during cooking; or for radishes and cucumbers in cold dishes, to allow the dressings to penetrate. The ingredient is either flattened with the broad side of a knife blade or else pounded with the butt of a knife handle or bottom of a glass jar. Although crushed, it remains relatively intact and does not fall apart. When crushing garlic, hold the knife blade parallel to the cutting board to prevent splattering. When crushing ginger, cut it in slices ½ inch thick and hit each firmly with the side of the knife. The fibers will hold the slice together so that each slice of ginger can be removed easily.

Scoring: This is used for whole fish and large cuts of meat. A few light incisions (either parallel or crosshatch) are made in the surface to permit hot oil and seasonings to penetrate. This speeds up cooking and improves flavor.

USING YOUR KNIFE

The best knife is either a large, heavy chef's knife or a Chinese cleaver-knife (see page 50). Another essential is a thick, solid chopping block that won't slide around.

Chef's Knife: Hold the handle in your right hand. (Reverse this procedure if you're left-handed.) With your left hand, hold the tip of the blade down on the board and don't let go. As you raise and lower the knife, the tip will act as the fulcrum of a lever, giving you greater control. To slice: move the knife up and down regularly and rapidly. To mince: use the same rocking motion, but also swing the knife back and forth, left and right in an arc, until the food is completely chopped.

Cleaver-Knife: Line up the thumb and index finger of your right hand on either side of the blade. Grasp the handle firmly but not tightly with the

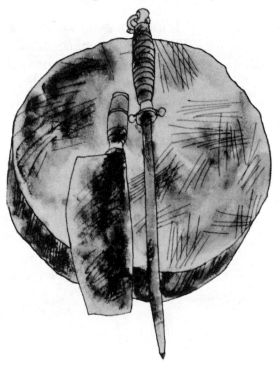

other three fingers. With your left hand make a loose fist, and rest it on the food. (This gets your fingers out of the way.) Hold the knife blade perpendicular to the chopping board, resting lightly against the middle knuckle of your left hand. Move your fist back to where you want the food cut. Raise the knife's cutting edge no higher than the level of your knuckle; then let the knife fall with a light, precise cutting stroke.* With each slice, push the food forward and move the knuckle back so the knife blade always falls in the same place. When mincing, hold the blade end down with your left hand, while lifting the blade (only near the handle) in a rapid up-and-down motion with your right. Although mincing can be done with a single knife, two knives of equal size and weight make the job much easier. These should be worked together in a lively rhythm like a drum tempo. The peppier the rhythm, the less tedious the mincing.

* Your two safeguards are: how high you raise the knife blade and how you grasp the food to be cut. The height depends on the size of your own hand and on the ingredient you're cutting. As a general rule, never raise the blade higher than 1½ to 2½ inches. When grasping the food, tuck your first two fingers under so the part between the first and middle knuckles is at right angles to the cutting board. Also keep your thumb out of the way.

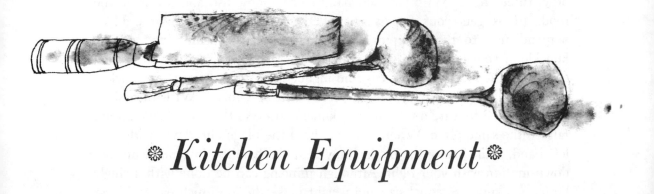

❀ Kitchen Equipment ❀

CHINESE COOKING requires no elaborate equipment. Ordinary pots, pans and utensils can do the job well. The following equipment is suggested.

POTS AND PANS

For stir-frying: a skillet or pan about 12 inches in diameter, of metal thin enough so that ingredients can heat up quickly. It should be sufficiently deep and wide so that food won't scatter over the stove during the vigors of stir-frying. (Some cooks prefer French-type iron skillets because of their rounded sides. The more seasoned by use these are, the better; their surfaces are smoother and food isn't apt to stick.) The pan must have a cover. If it doesn't, a tin or enamel saucepan lid that fits snugly will do.

For deep-frying: a pan large enough to hold several inches of oil, deep enough for the ingredients to float when done. (An inside wire basket, though not necessary, is an added convenience.)

For steaming: a covered pot large enough to hold a heatproof dish on a rack and still permit the steam to circulate freely between food and lid. The lid should be as close-fitting as possible. (See "Steamers," pages 51, 829.)

For slow-cooking: a large pot, either of heavy metal or of earthenware to hold the heat evenly and well. It must have a cover. (An asbestos pad is useful in keeping heat at a minimum.)

NOTE: Pressure cookers are not recommended. They cook foods too quickly for the seasonings to permeate and the sauces to color. Their vents also tend to become clogged by the thick gravies. When used without the pressure, however, these pots are excellent. They're made of heavy metal, have snug covers and need less water; their lids can be removed from time to time for basting or turning the ingredients.

For cooking rice: A tall and deep—rather than shallow and wide—pan which gives even heat and has a tight-fitting lid. (The high sides will keep the rice from boiling over.) Brass and copper pots conduct heat most evenly, but a heavy-bottomed aluminum one will also do. (Copper-*bottomed* pans, however, don't heat evenly and often cause rice to burn.) Since rice doubles in quantity when cooked, the pot should be large enough to permit such expansion. A two-quart pot is a good family size. (Always use the same pot in cooking rice to get consistent results from the same amount of water, the same amount of heat.)

For chafing-dish cookery: A standard chafing dish, but a very large one. A good-size soup pot set on a hot plate can substitute.

OTHER UTENSILS

For cutting: A long, heavy chef's knife with triangular blade and straight edge. (Straight blades cut faster than curved ones.) It must always be kept razor-sharp, or else it will bruise the ingredients. Also essential is a good, solid cutting board, the thicker the better. (The Chinese use a block from a tropical tree that's about 15 inches in diameter, 6 inches thick. This must be rubbed down at first with pork fat or beef fat to prevent drying and cracking. Later, constant usage will keep it moist.)

For stir-frying: A small shovel-like spatula or pancake turner to flip ingredients quickly and rapidly. The shorter the blade, the more maneuverable the spatula. A 3-inch blade is best. A metal spoon with a heatproof handle can be substituted. (Although wooden spoons are recommended for other uses, they are not suitable for stir-frying. They tend to absorb too much flavor from the liquids.)

For stirring, tasting, ladling: A variety of spoons, dippers and ladles. (The Chinese use wooden and porcelain implements rather than metal, except in stir-frying, because contact with metal changes the taste of food. Also, wooden and porcelain spoons don't burn the tongue or bruise the ingredients.)

For washing and draining vegetables, rice, noodles, etc.: The standard variety of sieves and colanders.

For draining oil from deep-fried foods: A deep-frying basket, strainer or slotted spoon. (The Chinese use shallow round brass mesh strainers with long bamboo handles, which come in a wide range of sizes. Their shallowness makes it easy to lift whole ducks and chickens out of the hot oil. They also can double as sieves.)

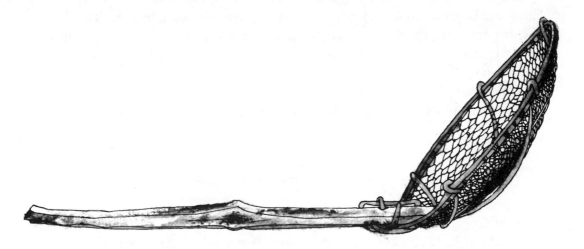

For pastries, wonton, etc.: A rolling pin. (The Chinese cut a section from a new broom or mop handle and sandpaper it to a fine smooth finish.)

SPECIAL CHINESE UTENSILS

The Chinese use three basic utensils—the wok, the cleaver-knife and chopsticks—of such versatility that with these alone just about any dish can be turned out in short order. Each is inexpensive and simple to use; all are available in Chinese hardware and food shops. Although not essential, they can add to both cooking pleasure and efficiency.

The Wok: This is an all-purpose thin-metal cooking pan which looks like an inverted coolie hat because of its flared sides and rounded bottom. (Originally these rounded bottoms fitted *into* old Chinese stoves. For modern stoves they're sold with a metal ring or collar, usually made of tin, which keeps the wok level, prevents tipping.) Woks are made of various metals: iron, copper, brass, aluminum and stainless steel. Thin tempered iron is best because it permits the most intense heat, the fastest cooking. It does need to be seasoned, however. (See "Wok," page 832.) The wok lid, usually made of aluminum, has high sloped sides, is flat on top. The wok itself has squared-off handles.

The wok's versatility seems limitless: it's shallow enough for pan-frying, deep enough for parboiling, simmering, braising, deep-frying and steaming. (It can be converted into a first-class steamer simply by setting a round wire cake rack firmly on the bottom and adding a few inches of boiling water.)

The wok's versatility extends to non-Chinese cooking as well. Small woks are fine for rolling and turning individual French omelets; larger woks, for Southern-Fried Chicken. The largest ones can be filled with charcoal and used as outdoor grills.

The wok is ideal for stir-frying. Its thin metal heats quickly. Its spherical shape and high smooth sides distribute the heat evenly, permit ingredients to be stirred vigorously without spilling. It also provides maximum cooking surface, requires less oil and, with its rounded sides, makes food easy to remove when done.

Woks come in a variety of sizes, with the 12-inch or 14-inch considered a good family size. Its spherical shape makes it adaptable for one, four and sometimes even eight people. Most Chinese kitchens have two woks: a large one for rice, a smaller one for meat, fish and vegetables.

Also available in Chinese hardware and food stores are inexpensive iron spatulas, designed to be used with the wok. Their blades have a rounded rather than a flat surface so they can slide easily around the sides of the pot and turn the food over. The blade is non-flexible and sturdy, making it excellent for stir-frying heavier ingredients. The spatula is often used in conjunction with a matching ladle. The ladle not only holds liquid seasonings, but can also be used with the spatula in a lifting, dropping, stir-frying motion that resembles tossing a salad.

The Cleaver-Knife: This all-purpose Chinese cutting tool looks like a butcher's cleaver. It has a cylindrical wooden handle and a rectangular blade made of tempered steel. (This is preferable to stainless steel, which is a harder metal and therefore more difficult to sharpen. Tempered steel will rust, however, unless thoroughly dried after each use and rubbed lightly with

vegetable oil from time to time.) The blade is about 3 by 8 inches, the handle about 4 inches long. The cleaver-knife comes in two weights. The lighter version is used for slicing softer meats and vegetables. The heavier cleaver-knife is more versatile: it performs these functions and can also chop bones and lobster and crab shells, disjoint poultry and mince meat. (The top of its blade, being blunt and thick, can even be used for mashing.) With either type of cleaver-knife, the flat side of the blade is used for transferring chopped foods from board to bowl; it is also fine for pounding and tenderizing meat, for crushing garlic, ginger and radishes.

Chopsticks: These can be used to replace spoons, forks, wire whisks, ladles and egg beaters. For cooking, bamboo and wooden chopsticks are best because of their ability to withstand high temperatures. (Metal-tipped chopsticks conduct too much heat, plastic ones can't take much heat at all.) Single chopsticks are ideal for every kind of beating, piercing, stirring or mixing. A pair of chopsticks can be used to add ingredients to the pan, lift a morsel out to see if it's done, and remove ingredients when they are ready.

In deep-frying, chopsticks are excellent for shaking off excess oil and for keeping batter-coated foods from sticking together. In stir-frying, they're fine for keeping the ingredients constantly moving, for turning the individual pieces over so they'll cook evenly; and besides, they don't bruise the softer foods. Chopsticks are easy to keep clean, never go out of commission and rarely break. At first, using chopsticks may seem awkward, but with practice they become, in effect, extensions of the fingers.

NOTE: For steaming, the Chinese use special steamer pans set in tiers, one atop the other, over boiling water. The metal pans are perforated, the bamboo have lattice-work bottoms which permit the rising steam to pass through them. (A layer of cloth is usually placed in each tray to soak up excess moisture and to keep the smaller ingredients from slipping through. The cloth is always dampened first to make it more absorbent.) A lid set on the top pan contains the steam. As many units are used as there are foods to be cooked, making this an ingenious way to steam several dishes simultaneously, using the same boiling water and the same heat.

❊ *The Basics* ❊

STOCK

Stock is essential in Chinese cooking. It's the liquid in which meat and bones have been slowly simmered until their natural sweetness and goodness have been extracted and intermingled. (The bones, with their gelatin content, also give body to the stock.) Stock has many uses: It can be a base for soups and sauces or a liquid medium for stir-fried dishes. It is the key to their flavor. When combined with other ingredients, stock enhances them in a way that water never can.

In Chinese cooking, stock never intrudes on the flavors of other ingredients. It's always neutral and delicate. Chicken stock, being the most delicate, is most preferred. Pork, often used in combination with chicken, is next. Beef stock is never used—its flavor is too hearty, too pronounced.

Stock is only as good as the ingredients which go into it. A few bones, some shreds of meat—no matter how long they're simmered—will never produce a rich, pure stock. The better the stock ingredients, the better the final dish.

There are two grades of stock: primary and secondary. Primary, made with fresh meat, is the richer, purer and more concentrated. It calls for a maximum of meat, a minimum of liquid. The meat may be a whole chicken, chicken and pork combined, or pork alone. Secondary stock uses uncooked bones from meat or poultry. Chicken bones are the first choice, pork the second. They are also good in combination. Bones left over *after* cooking can be used, but make a very weak stock.

Stock is simple to prepare. Both primary and secondary stocks are cooked in the same way: the meat or bones are placed in the pot with cold water to cover. They are then heated simultaneously. This enables the meat juices to flow out and blend with the liquid.* When the liquid comes to a boil, the heat is reduced at once to a simmer. As fat and impurities rise to the surface, they are skimmed off until they no longer accumulate. This takes about five minutes and helps keep the soup light.

NOTE: If the liquid is permitted to boil at this point, the fat and impurities will incorporate themselves with the stock and make it cloudy. (Some cooks get a clear soup by scalding the meat or poultry first, then cooking the stock according to recipe directions. The scalding is done by immersing the meat or bird in boiling water, bringing it quickly to a boil again, then pouring off all the liquid and rinsing meat or bird at once under cold running water.)

After the skimming, the soup pot is covered and the ingredients are simmered slowly for 2 to 3 hours. (The longer stock cooks, the more concentrated it becomes.) Once in the pot, stock needs little attention. It can also be turned off at any point, and the cooking resumed later. If more liquid is needed at any time, only boiling water is added. (Cold water will spoil the flavor.)

The meat and bones are then removed and the vegetables (diced or cut in chunks) are added. The vegetables, depending on their tenderness or toughness, are simmered from 15 to 30 minutes. During the last 5 minutes of cooking, the seasonings are added. (The meat from primary stock can be eaten hot or cold, accompanied by a soy or hot-mustard dip. It can also be combined with other ingredients and used in steamed, stir-fried and deep-fried recipes.)

* When cooking a whole chicken, if you're more interested in the bird than in the stock, put it in *boiling* water, which will seal in its juices and make the bird more tasty. The same is true of meat. With meat, the larger pieces can also be browned in oil first. The stock, of course, won't be as flavorful.

PRIMARY CHICKEN STOCK

1 *stewing chicken, whole*	1 *to 2 cups vegetables*
8 *to 10 cups water*	1 *teaspoon salt*
1 *tablespoon sherry*	

1. Place chicken and cold water in a saucepan; bring to a boil. Reduce heat immediately and skim the surface. Simmer covered 2 hours; then remove chicken.

2. Dice vegetables. Add to stock and simmer until done (about 15 minutes).

3. Add salt and sherry; simmer 5 minutes more. Then strain off vegetables and skim off fat.

NOTE: The chicken giblets, but not the liver, can be added with the chicken. The vegetables can include: carrots, celery, cabbage, turnips, onions, green peas, spinach, mushrooms, mustard cabbage, water chestnuts or bamboo shoots, etc., in any combination.

VARIATIONS: Quarter the chicken or cut in small cubes. (This will reduce the cooking time to about 1 to 1½ hours.)

In step 1, also add one pound lean pork, either sliced ¼ inch thick or cut in small cubes.

In step 3, also add 1 to 2 teaspoons soy sauce and/or 1 teaspoon ginger juice.

PRIMARY MEAT STOCK

1 *pound lean pork*	½ *teaspoon salt*
7 *cups water*	1 *teaspoon soy sauce*

1. Cut pork in ¼-inch slices. Place in a saucepan with cold water and bring to a boil. Reduce heat immediately and skim the surface; then simmer, covered, 30 minutes.

2. Add seasonings and simmer 5 minutes more. Then remove meat, strain the stock and skim off the fat.

VARIATIONS: For the pork, substitute 1½ pounds spareribs. Add these along with 2 celery stalks and 2 white onions to already boiling water. Simmer 90 minutes. Then remove ribs and vegetables and strain the stock.

Use ½ pound pork, ½ pound chicken giblets and simmer, covered, 30 minutes. Add ¼ cup dried black mushrooms (soaked), ¼ cup water chestnuts, both sliced; simmer 30 minutes more.

SECONDARY STOCK

1 *chicken carcass*	1 *leek*
3 *slices ginger root*	8 *cups water*
2 *pounds pork bones*	1 *cup vegetables*
½ *teaspoon salt*	

1. Chop chicken carcass in chunks. Slice ginger root. Place both in a saucepan with pork bones, leek and cold water; bring to a boil. Reduce heat immediately and skim the surface; then simmer, covered, 2 to 4 hours. Discard bones.

2. Dice vegetables. Add to stock and simmer, covered, about 15 minutes. During the last 5 minutes, add salt. Strain off vegetables and skim off fat.

VARIATIONS: For the leek, substitute 2 scallion stalks.

Use only ½ pound pork bones (preferably rib). Add 1 chicken gizzard, cut up; 2 chicken feet, cleaned and skinned; a small piece of ham; and 1 cup bamboo shoots, sliced. Place all ingredients except ham and bamboo shoots in cold water to cover. Bring to a boil. Let boil 3 to 4 minutes. Pour off the liquid and discard. Then pick up step 1, adding the ham and bamboo shoots.

TIPS ON STOCK

TO REMOVE FAT: *Fat is most easily removed after the stock is refrigerated and chilled. The fat will congeal and harden into a solid disk at the top. It can then be lifted out as one piece. (If there isn't time to chill the stock, let it stand for five minutes until fat rises to the top. Then either skim with a spoon or ladle, or draw up with a bulb-type meat baster. A lettuce leaf or paper towel floated on the surface will absorb the last few globules of fat.)*

TO COOL STOCK: *Unless cooled after cooking, stock is apt to sour. To cool, simply remove the lid and let the temperature gradually diminish. When the contents have cooled completely, cover the pot tightly.*

TO STORE STOCK: *Before storing stock, strain out all the solids and vegetables (use either a double layer of cheesecloth or a fine mesh strainer) and pour into a jar. Cover tightly and refrigerate. (If reheated to the boiling point every 3 or 4 days, stock will keep for a long period of time.)*

TO FREEZE STOCK: *Strain out all the solids and let cool. Pour the stock into plastic containers (either quart or pint), allowing about 1 inch head room in each. Seal tightly and place in the freezer.*

NOTE: Freezing makes sense because stock lends itself to preparation in quantity. Maximum storage time recommended is six months.

TO ENRICH STOCK: *Both primary and secondary stocks can be enriched by adding (during the last hour of cooking) a ham bone and one pound of peeled and diced turnips, or a slice or two of Smithfield ham, or dried scallops, squid or shrimp. Fresh seafood such as lobster, shrimp and clams may also be added. These need only about 5 minutes of cooking.*

SUBSTITUTE STOCK: *Canned chicken broth, bouillon powders or cubes can be used. Of the three, canned broths are best. Although not comparable to freshly made stock, they are concentrated, clear, economical and a time saver. Select those types seasoned with salt but not with stronger spices. Their flavor can be enriched with chicken or pork bones, chicken or duck giblets, or a few slices of fresh pork. Never add monosodium glutamate: it has already been added. For a lighter soup, use a mixture of one-half canned broth, one-half water. The next best substitute is bouillon powder. This is richer and less salty than bouillon cubes. (Should the saltier cubes be used, the amount of soy sauce and salt called for in the recipe must be reduced.*)

SCRAP STOCK: *Stock can also be made from any leftovers or odds and ends, including bits of meat, fish, vegetables, scrapings from the bottom of the skillet, water in which mushrooms have been soaked and the liquid from canned or parboiled vegetables.*

EMERGENCY STOCK: *When no stock of any kind is on hand, the following can be substituted:* 1 *teaspoon monosodium glutamate stirred into* 1 *cup water, to which* 1 *teaspoon soy sauce and a dash of pepper may also be added.*

RICE

Plain rice is to the Chinese what bread is to other peoples: the indispensable accompaniment to a meal. (As a matter of fact, when rice is cooking, its light and mellow aroma is very much like that of freshly baked bread.) The Chinese value rice for aesthetic as well as nutritional reasons: Its texture sets off the textures of other foods; its whiteness provides an ideal background for their brighter colors. Its blandness contrasts with their more definite flavors, clearing the palate between dishes. Rice also unifies and makes coherent a meal of many different courses.

Plain rice is prepared by either boiling or steaming. When properly cooked, it is dry and milky-white, with its grains standing firm and separate from each other. It is also flaky on top with natural steam holes in its dull, dry surface. Rice should always have body. It should never be lumpy, sticky, mushy, wet or shiny. It may vary in hardness or softness, according to personal preference, but must not be *too* hard or *too* soft. Even when soft, it should be quite dry, with the moisture absorbed into each grain, not lingering on the surface. (Plain rice is usually eaten as is, but a drop or two of peanut oil and soy sauce can be added for flavor. However, soy sauce in quantity should never be added: it diminishes both the color and taste of plain rice.)

Variations in hardness or softness depend in part on the type of rice used. Long-grain rice, the most commonly used variety, is absorbent and calls for a greater amount of water. It makes for a harder, firmer rice. Oval or short-grain rice is less absorbent and makes for a softer, moister rice.

Another factor affecting hardness or softness (particularly in the long-grain variety) is the quantity of water used. The less water, the harder the rice will be; the more water, the more it must absorb and the softer it will be.

NOTE: Interesting variations can be achieved by combining the two varieties in such proportions as ¾ long-grain rice to ¼ oval-grain. These work out well together because the long-grain has better texture but less flavor, while the oval-grain has better flavor but a stickier texture. The precooked varieties of rice, however, are never used.

Quantities: Since rice more than doubles in quantity when cooked, ½ cup of raw rice per person is usually sufficient. The following are rule-of-thumb ratios which can be modified according to personal preference:

> Long-grain rice (boiled): 1 cup raw rice to 1½ cups water
> (steamed): 1 cup raw rice to 3 cups water
> Oval-grain rice (boiled): 1 cup raw rice to 1 cup water
> (steamed): 1 cup raw rice to 2 cups water

Washing Rice: The secret of flaky rice is in the washing. Rice must always be washed thoroughly before it is cooked to remove the excess starch. This keeps it from becoming sticky. To wash rice:

1. Rinse under cold running water, rubbing the grains together between

the palms of the hands. Or place the rice in a fine sieve or colander (set in a saucepan or bowl) and stir with spoon or chopstick to rub the grains together.

2. Continue this rinsing and rubbing action until the rinse water runs fairly clear.

Cooking Methods: Plain rice may be either boiled or steamed. There are several ways of doing each. Steamed rice is looser in texture and takes longer to cook. It also cannot burn.

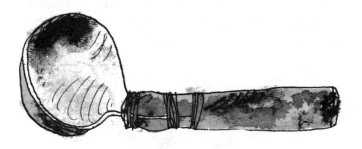

BASIC BOILED RICE I

1. Wash rice thoroughly, then spread evenly along the bottom of a saucepan.

2. Add the desired quantity of cold water for each cup of rice. (Let rice and water sit covered in pan for 30 minutes before cooking. This softens the rice, but can be omitted.)

3. Bring rice to a boil over ¾ flame. Boil covered 3 minutes. Reduce flame to ½. Boil 2 minutes more, or until most of the liquid is absorbed. (At this point, before the water is completely absorbed, some cooks stir the rice gently from the bottom up so that it will cook more evenly and have less tendency to burn on the bottom. If some rice sticks to the sides of the pot during this stirring, just scrape it down.)

4. Lower flame to a minimum. Let rice cook covered 18 to 20 minutes more. Do not lift lid or stir rice during this time. (If you lift lid, valuable steam will escape; if you stir the rice, it will stick to the bottom of the pan. When cooking is done, some cooks lift the lid and stir the rice once, loosening it gently with a lifting motion of chopsticks, then replace the lid and let the rice stand for 10 minutes.)

5. Turn off heat. Let rice sit covered in pan 10 to 15 minutes. Then, with fork or chopsticks, fluff rice to separate each grain. The rice will then be soft, flaky and ready to serve.

NOTE: Cooking time for rice varies from stove to stove and from pan to pan. Only actual experience can determine the precise cooking time.

A crust may form at the bottom of the pan, but will not burn if the heat is kept to a minimum. (Washing the pan is no problem, either, if you fill it with cold water and let it soak for a few minutes.) These crusts may be saved and refrigerated, then used in a number of ways: simmered with water to make congee or rice gruel; or broken into bite-size pieces and deep-fried, a few at a time, until golden brown, nut-like and crunchy. When used—hot from the oil—to garnish soups or stir-fried dishes, the crusts are called sizzling rice because they actually sizzle on contact with other ingredients. Deep-fried crusts can also be eaten as a cracker-like hors d'oeuvre. (Crusts from glutinous rice can be prepared in the same manner.)

BASIC BOILED RICE II

1. Wash rice thoroughly. Fill saucepan half-full of water and bring to a boil.

2. Add rice and 1 teaspoon vinegar and cook uncovered 15 to 18 minutes over medium heat, stirring occasionally.

3. Place rice in a sieve and drain. Hold sieve under hot-water tap and rinse rice thoroughly to separate grains.

Note: Never put cooked rice under the *cold*-water tap. This will wash away its flavor.

STEAMED RICE I

1. Wash rice thoroughly. Place in a pan with plenty of water.
2. Boil 5 minutes, stirring a few times. Drain.
3. Put rice in individual heatproof bowls, filling them half-full. Add the amount of water specified on page 58.
4. Place bowls on a rack in a pot containing several inches of boiling water. Cover pot and steam 1 to 1½ hours.

Note: The liquid drained in step 2 can be reserved, mixed with sugar and served separately as a thin congee.

STEAMED RICE II

1. Wash rice thoroughly. Place in a pan with plenty of water.
2. Boil 5 minutes, stirring a few times. Drain.
3. Place rice in a bamboo steamer lined with cheesecloth. Pierce rice several times with chopsticks or fork, making small holes to let the steam pass through.
4. Cover pan. Steam over medium heat for 20 minutes.

Note: See note above.

STEAMED RICE III

1. Wash rice thoroughly. Bring 4 to 5 cups of water to a boil in the bottom of a double boiler. Place rice in the top and add cold water ½ inch higher than rice.
2. Cook 1 to 1½ hours over medium heat. Do not lift lid or stir.

Note: If you're cooking just one cup of rice by this method, cook 20 minutes at medium heat; 20 minutes more at low heat.

TIPS ON RICE

Keeping Rice Warm: Steamed rice cooked in advance can be kept warm over barely boiling water. Boiled rice can be kept warm in the following ways:

1. When cooking is done, place the tightly closed pan over the lowest possible flame. (An asbestos pad is helpful here.) Do not lift the lid. The rice should keep warm for more than an hour without drying out.

2. When cooking is done, place the closed pan in a slow oven. Do not lift the lid until ready to serve.

3. Transfer rice to the top of a regular double boiler. Keep the water in the bottom heated to a slow boil.

NOTE: Never let rice get cold in its cooking pan. It will become hard and unpalatable. If you don't plan to use it within a few hours, store it as described in "Leftover Rice" (see below).

Salvaging Burned Rice: Rice will burn if the heat is too high or if there isn't enough liquid in the pot. The odor of scorching will signal trouble. When this happens, do the following:

1. Remove the lid at once. Let the odor disperse for a minute or so.

2. Place a slice of bread on top of the rice to absorb the burned, smoky flavor. Cover the pan again for a few minutes.

3. Transfer the unburned portion of the rice to another pan.

4. Add several tablespoons cold water. Cover the pan and cook over very low heat until done.

NOTE: Serving burned or improperly cooked rice to a guest is not only unattractive but considered poor etiquette as well.

Leftover Rice: Leftover rice has many uses. When reheated and eaten plain, it tastes as good as freshly cooked rice. It can also be used in soups, chowders, casseroles, congees, egg dishes or fried rice. (Recipes for these appear in the section on "Noodle and Rice Dishes," pages 628–688.) The Chinese consider leftover rice an asset rather than a liability and cook enough at once to last for several meals.

To store leftover rice:

1. While the rice is still hot, separate and loosen the grains with a fork or chopstick.

2. Let cool completely.

3. Place in covered container and refrigerate. (It should keep about a week.)

To reheat leftover rice:

1. Separate grains of rice so they will reheat evenly. (Either add 1 tablespoon cold water for every 3 cups of cooked rice and separate the grains with fork or chopstick, or dampen the hands and separate the lumps that way.)

2. Place in a saucepan. Add 1 tablespoon cold water for each cup of cooked rice.

3. Cover pan tightly. Heat 15 to 20 minutes over low flame. Do not lift lid or stir, until rice is ready to serve.

NOTE: If you have a metal or bamboo steamer, line it with a dampened layer of cheesecloth, then add the rice and steam for 5 to 10 minutes to reheat.

To combine leftover rice with fresh rice:

1. Follow steps 1, 2, and 3 under Basic Boiled Rice I.

2. Meanwhile separate the leftover rice so there are no lumps. At the end of step 3, spread it evenly over the fresh rice. Do *not* stir.

3. Follow steps 4 and 5. (The steam that cooks the fresh rice will reheat the leftover rice.)

TEA

The most fitting beverage to accompany Chinese food is Chinese tea. When taken at mealtime, the delicate fragrance and flavor of teas harmonize with the taste of food. When taken before meals, it clears the palate. When taken afterward, it refreshes it.

Tea has been the most popular beverage in China for more than a thousand years. It has been cultivated extensively in that part of the world since the fifth century A.D. There are lovely and poetic legends as to its origins. Most likely, however, tea-drinking evolved from the realization that those who drank boiled water were healthier than those who didn't. The next step was to add something to that water to make it more palatable.

Tea is taken morning, noon and night and for every occasion. It accompanies every meal and is usually served at the end of family meals. In southern China, however, tea is served *with* the meal. Since the Cantonese (from the South) were the first to open restaurants outside China, the custom of taking tea with the meal came to be thought of as typically Chinese although it is not. Tea is always served during and throughout elaborate formal dinners in all parts of China, to refresh the diner and make him more receptive to each new dish. When a visitor crosses the threshold, a characteristically hospitable gesture is to present him with a cup of tea. In shops and offices, tea is kept piping hot in basket-like tea cozies and is available all day long.

When properly brewed, Chinese tea is clear in color, naturally sweet in taste and has a fine bouquet. Since it is drunk for refreshment, not for nourishment or strength, it's always taken without cream, sugar or lemon.

Sometimes, however, when served to visitors with cake or cookies, it's given a touch of sweetness with preserved ginger or a bit of rock sugar.

Although Chinese teas vary greatly in character, flavor and aroma, they all come from the same plant—a plant belonging to the camellia family. (When it blooms, its flowers are much like the familiar camellia.) Differences in tea are created by the specific conditions under which each plant grows (its locale, climate, time of harvest, and processing.) In this sense, Chinese teas are much like wines: the conditions which create them are unique and cannot be duplicated elsewhere. All told, there are some 250 varieties of Chinese tea .(These vary in price from a few cents to hundreds of dollars per pound. The rarest are like vintage wines or fine old brandies. They are always served alone so that other tastes will not obscure their complex and delicate subtleties.) Despite this variety, there are only two basic types of tea —the green and the black—plus a subtype or combination of the two.

Green tea looks much like the leaves of the original plant because it is unfermented and receives little handling. The leaves (the smaller, younger and more tender ones from the top of the tree) are picked before they wither and are dried immediately either in the sun or with currents of warm air in special drying rooms. They are grayish-green in color and produce a pale golden brew with natural bouquet. Green tea has a refreshing and delicate taste, making it a popular drink in summer, pleasant with bland stir-fried foods and a fine foil for highly seasoned foods at any time of the year.

Black tea is fermented. Its leaves, permitted to wither on the bush, are then gathered, rolled, fermented and dried. Fermentation alters its chlorophyll content, changing the color from green to brownish-black and strengthening its flavor. Black tea produces a full-bodied rich red brew. (The Chinese name for black tea is "red" because of the color of this brew.) This warming and pungent tea is a popular winter drink and a good accompaniment for deep-fried foods.

The subtype or oolong variety is semi-fermented (or partly dried and partly fermented). The fermentation process is stopped at a certain point, making the leaves a brownish-green. Semi-fermented tea produces a rich amber brew, combining the pungent aroma of the black with the delicate fragrance of the green. These teas, often taken with the evening meal, go well with heavy foods and with such definitely flavored ones as broccoli and shrimp.

Chinese teas are often blended with fresh or dried flowers and fruit blossoms. These are the scented teas, of which jasmine is the best known. (Scented teas may be green, black or semi-fermented.) They are taken with spiced foods, with snacks, between meals and at banquets.

NOTE: The names of some specific varieties of tea appear on page 839.

Quantities: Chinese tea is usually much stronger than its color suggests. To savor tea properly, it is better to begin with fewer rather than more leaves. (This, however, does not mean the tea should be weak and watery. It should be brewed full strength, then diluted with boiling water, if desired. It's a good idea to keep an extra pot of hot water on hand for those who like their tea weaker.) If the tea is brewed too strong from the start, many of its subleties will be lost; its flavor will be overwhelming. Strength and weakness are matters of personal preference, best determined by trial and error. As a general rule, ½ to 1 teaspoon should be allowed for each measuring cup of water. Green teas, however, are generally the most potent and should be used in smaller amounts. (With some high-quality green teas, 1 heaping teaspoon can produce 6 cups of a delicately fragrant brew.)

NOTE: The number of cups of tea brewed also determines the quantity of tea leaves to use. The more boiling water there is, the greater the amount of heat on the tea leaves and consequently the stronger the infusion. Therefore, the more of the brew, the fewer the tea leaves needed.

Rules for Brewing: Whether tea is green, black, semi-fermented or scented, certain fundamental requirements must be met for the brewing of good tea. The quality of the tea must be good: no cup of tea is better than its tea leaves. The tea must always be stored properly so that its flavor is not lost. (See "Storing Information," page 879.) The tea-making utensils, teapot and cups should be used exclusively for this purpose. These are the rules for brewing tea:

1. The tea utensils must be absolutely clean. If they are not, rinse and sponge them with warm water. Never use soap. (It affects the flavor.)

2. Scald the teapot with boiling water, then drain. Keep the pot warm.

3. For the tea itself, always use freshly drawn water from the cold-water tap. (Only fresh water, freshly boiled, produces full-flavored tea. Stale water that has been allowed to stand in a kettle, or water that has been reheated, gives tea a flat taste.)

4. When the water is boiling fiercely at its highest boiling point,* pour it immediately over the tea leaves. You must be ready to brew the tea as soon as the water starts boiling. When it is added at that point, the tea leaves become active, rising first to the top quickly, then sinking slowly and gracefully to the bottom. (If the water is overboiled—and loses too much oxygen—the tea leaves sink to the bottom at once and don't steep properly. If the water is not at the boiling point, the tea leaves remain floating on top. Poorly brewed tea has a taste that's either flat or crude and bitter, and a color that's either too light or too dark.)

5. After the boiling water is added, cover the pot and let steep for 3 to 5 minutes, depending on the strength you want. Brew by the clock. Don't guess. (It takes time for the leaves to unfold and release their flavor.) Don't stir the leaves. Don't steep for a dark color. (Green tea will brew to a pale

* Brass kettles are favored for boiling the water, but any kettle or saucepan will do. Whistling tea kettles have a particular advantage: they start whistling when the water is at a rolling boil and just ready to be used.

gold, semi-fermented tea to amber, and black tea will produce a rich, red brew.) You may, however, if you wish, stir the leaves just before pouring, to make sure the tea is uniformly strong.

NOTE: To infuse means to extract flavor from the tea leaves by steeping, not boiling, them in hot water. Only the water is boiled, *not* the tea leaves. You brew the tea, you don't stew it.

Implements: Tea can be brewed in teapots, saucepans or individual cups. Teapots are best: they keep the water hot during the brewing process and then keep the tea itself hot. (Unless drunk piping hot, tea loses its flavor.) A squat, round teapot is preferable to a tall thin one: it allows for more water surface, enables the leaves to steep better. Teapots made of porcelain, crockery or glass are preferable to metal ones, which tend to impart a foreign flavor to the tea. Good-quality Chinese teapots come with their own basket-like tea cozies, which keep tea hot for hours.

To brew in a teapot:
1. Scald the pot with boiling water. Drain.
2. Add the leaves in the desired quantity.
3. Pour boiling water over tea leaves. Cover pot.
4. Let steep 3 to 5 minutes.

Saucepans are used when tea is to be drunk informally and immediately. Enamel or Pyrex ware is preferable to aluminum and other metals.

To brew tea in a saucepan:

1. For each cup of tea, measure out 1 cup of freshly drawn cold water.
2. Bring the water to a rolling boil.
3. Add tea leaves in the desired amount. Turn off the heat immediately. Cover pan.
4. Let steep 3 to 5 minutes. Strain and serve at once.

Individual cups are used for formal and ceremonial occasions. Brewing tea right in the cup is a courtesy which demonstrates that the tea is freshly made and not a reheated, dank, dark brew that's been sitting around for days in a teapot. The formal Chinese teacup is a three-piece unit consisting of a handleless cup with a concave lid and a saucer. The lid acts as a strainer by covering the tea leaves while permitting enough liquid to float over it for easy sipping. The cup is held in one hand while the forefinger of that hand pushes the lid back slightly to let the tea flow whenever the cup is tipped. (The lid is removed only when boiling water is added for a second cup or when the drinker wishes to inhale the aroma of the brewing tea.)

To brew in a teacup:

1. Scald the cup and drain.
2. Use about ½ teaspoon tea per cup.
3. Add 1 tablespoon freshly boiled water. Cover up. Let steep 1 minute.
4. Fill cup with boiling water. Let steep another 2 minutes.

NOTE: For less formal brewing, add about ½ teaspoon tea to an ordinary cup. Pour the boiling water over tea. Let steep about 4 minutes.

The Second Infusion: Most Chinese teas of good quality can be infused or brewed at least twice. The second infusion is made like the first: by pouring freshly boiled water over the original tea leaves (some like to add a few fresh tea leaves at this point) and letting the tea steep 3 to 5 minutes more. Tea connoisseurs hold that the delicate flavors and fragrances of tea don't actually manifest themselves until the second steeping and that the second infusion, therefore, is superior to the first. This, they say, is always the case with black teas, sometimes with green. Some connoisseurs consider the first infusion so immature that they quickly pour it off without tasting it and drink only the second, which they inhale with the kind of enjoyment usually reserved for fine brandies.

NOTE: With some teas, even a third infusion is possible.

Leftover Tea: Good tea, if strained (its leaves discarded) and put in a cool place, will keep about 12 hours. To use again, simply bring to a boil and serve at once.

PART TWO

Recipes

A NOTE ON QUANTITIES

A typical Chinese meal will include several "main" dishes, with the number based on the number of diners. A meal for four, for example, calls for four dishes plus rice; a meal for six, six dishes plus rice, etc.* (Each dish is placed in the center of the table and shared by all, family style. Thus, the more people, the more dishes and the greater variety within a given meal.)

This is not a hard-and-fast rule. The cook who wishes to serve fewer dishes need only increase the quantities of each dish. If she wishes to serve only one main dish, Western style, she can adjust the recipes to the amount of meat and vegetables she would normally use. (She should, however, increase the seasonings—not proportionately, but according to personal taste.)

Measurements for fresh ingredients are given *after* slicing, shelling, etc. Measurements for dried ingredients are given *before* soaking.

The amount of oil specified in stir-fry recipes may have to be adjusted according to the pan used. A wok, for example, needs less oil than a skillet.

* In Chinese restaurants, most dishes are prepared in smaller quantities. Diners, when ordering, should plan on one dish per person in addition to soup and rice.

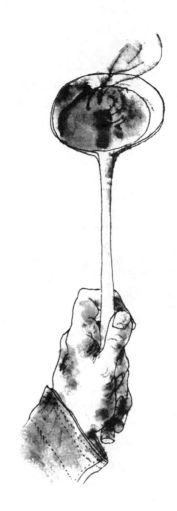

❀ *Soups* ❀

CHINESE SOUPS are extremely varied, ranging from light to heavy, from simple to complex, and from sour-pungent to sweet. Light, delicate soups, which are quickly cooked, usually accompany family dinners. Thick, hearty soups call for slow simmering and often are more solid than liquid. (These, along with rice and a vegetable dish, are sufficient for light lunches or suppers.) Sour-pungent soups—also called hot-sour soups—set off sharp flavors with bland ingredients in an unexpected way and are festive for dinner parties. Sweet soups are closer in spirit to desserts and are eaten as snacks and at formal dinners.

The simplest and lightest soup of all is the Celestial Soup or Soup for the Gods. Designed to accompany rich, heavy foods, it's simply water that has been freshly boiled, then poured over minced greens, and seasoned lightly.

The most complex and magnificent soups are the famous bird's nest and shark's fin dishes. These appear as prestige courses at formal banquets.

Chinese soups are prepared by cooking meat, poultry or seafood and vegetables in either stock or water. As a rule stock is preferred. Although stock can be served as a soup by itself, more often it becomes the base for other soups. (For details on its preparation, see the Basics: Stock.)

Thick, hearty soups are prepared like stock, with their solid and liquid ingredients added to the pot at the same time, then cooked slowly until they blend together. (Dried ingredients are invariably included in such soups for a more full-bodied flavor.)

By contrast, light soups are cooked quickly so that the color and texture of their ingredients are retained: the stock is brought to a boil, then the meat and vegetables added. Cooking time is generally determined by the type of meat and the way it's cut. Vegetables are added to light soups near the end of cooking so that they won't become overcooked or soggy. Tender green vegetables are added at the last possible moment and cooked uncovered to retain the fresh brightness of their color, while the tougher vegetables, such as carrots, string beans, turnips, etc., are either parboiled or shredded first to reduce their cooking time in the soup.

Light soups must always be clear. They should never be cooked too long or too violently: Overcooking injures flavor; boiling makes them dull and muddy. When soup comes to a boil, the heat must be reduced immediately so that the soup will simmer gently until done.

NOTE: Should the soup boil over, turn down the heat immediately, remove the pot lid, and add a small amount of cold water. Under ordinary circumstances, when more liquid is needed for soup, only *boiling* water or stock should be added. (If cold liquids in any quantity are added during cooking, they will damage the flavor of soup.)

Enriching Soup: The flavor and aroma of soup can be enhanced by any of the following: *meats*—a few thin slices of fresh lean pork or smoked ham; *seafood*—a few dried shrimp or scallops (soaked first) or several fresh shrimp, shelled, deveined and diced; *vegetables*—some slices of bamboo shoot, a few thinly sliced mushrooms, a bit of minced scallion stalk, a few sprigs of Chinese parsley; *seasonings*—a few drops of sesame oil or ginger juice, a bit of minced garlic clove, a dash of vinegar, a tablespoon of sherry or a small quantity of soy sauce.

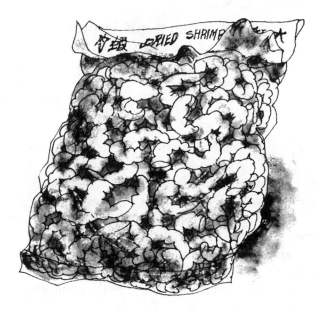

NOTE: Soy sauce should be used discreetly in light soups. If possible, it should be the light soy. (See Glossary of Chinese Ingredients.) The dark variety can destroy a soup's lightness and clarity; its strong taste can overwhelm delicate flavors. There's nothing sadder than seeing diners in Chinese restaurants dump quantities of dark soy sauce into their soup in the misguided belief that they're improving its flavor.

Thickening Soup: Thickening a soup is a matter of taste and preference, although some, like fish soups and hot-sour soups, usually are thickened. This is done by adding cornstarch paste at the end of cooking, and stirring it in over high heat until the soup becomes thick, smooth and velvety.

Garnishing Soup: Soups may be garnished with meat—strips of smoked ham or roast pork; with vegetables—Chinese parsley, chopped scallions or blanched snow peas; or with eggs. The egg garnishes may be: *egg threads or cubes,* i.e., eggs fried as thin omelets, then cut into strips or cubes; *egg flowers,* i.e., eggs that are beaten, then stirred into the soup at the last minute, the heat being turned off immediately (as in egg drop soup); or *poached eggs,* i.e., eggs poached to medium softness right in the soup or separately poached and added just before the soup is served. (The poached eggs are then pierced to let the yolk run out: this gives the soup a mild, soothing quality.)

BASIC SOUP WITH PORK (QUICK-COOKING)
4 to 5 servings

¼ pound lean pork
1 tablespoon soy sauce
1 teaspoon sugar

½ teaspoon salt
2 to 3 scallion stalks
6 cups stock

1. Slice pork thin. Combine soy sauce, sugar and salt. Add to pork and toss. Let stand half an hour, turning meat occasionally.

2. Meanwhile bring stock to a boil. Cut scallion stalks in 2-inch sections, then add. Simmer, covered, 3 to 4 minutes.

3. Add pork and simmer, covered, 5 minutes more. Skim surface to clear.

VARIATIONS: For the scallions, substitute 6 tablespoons pickled vegetables, shredded and drained. Simmer, covered, 2 minutes. Then pick up step 3, adding a few drops of sesame oil at the very end.

After step 3, add any of the following vegetables and simmer until done:

2 cucumbers, peeled or unpeeled, sliced thin

12 radishes, unpeeled and sliced thin (simmer uncovered)

1 large bamboo shoot and 8 water chestnuts, both sliced thin

1 cup fresh green peas; and ½ pound spinach, cut in 2-inch sections (simmer uncovered)

3 dried black mushrooms (soaked), cut in strips; and ¼ pound beansprouts

BASIC SOUP WITH PORK (SLOW-COOKING)
4 to 5 servings

½ pound pork shoulder
1 onion

dash of pepper

6 cups stock
¾ to 1 teaspoon salt

1. Cut pork in 1-inch cubes and onion in quarters. Place in heavy pan with cold stock and bring slowly to a boil.

2. Reduce heat, and skim surface to clear. Then simmer, covered, about 1½ hours.

3. Stir in salt and pepper. Simmer 5 minutes more.

VARIATIONS: For the onion, substitute ¼ pound fresh mushrooms, sliced, or 2 ounces dried cuttlefish (soaked).

During the last half hour of cooking, add 1 cup Chinese lettuce, cut in 1½-inch sections; and 4 water chestnuts, sliced.

PORK AND CHINESE CABBAGE SOUP

4 to 5 servings

¼ *pound lean pork*	1 *tablespoon peanut oil*
2 *slices fresh ginger root*	¾ *to 1 teaspoon salt*
½ *pound Chinese cabbage*	½ *teaspoon sugar*
6 *cups stock or water*	2 *teaspoons soy sauce*

dash of pepper

1. Mince or shred pork. Mince ginger root. Slice cabbage stems thin or shred. Bring stock to a boil.

2. In a deep pan, heat oil. Add ginger and brown lightly. Add heated stock, then salt and cabbage. Simmer, covered, 10 minutes.

3. Add pork, sugar, soy sauce and pepper. Simmer, covered, 15 minutes more.

NOTE: The tender green leaves of the cabbage may be shredded and added at the very end to simmer, uncovered, for a minute or two.

PORK AND MUSTARD CABBAGE SOUP

4 to 5 servings

¼ *pound lean pork*	¾ *to 1 teaspoon salt*
½ *pound mustard cabbage*	½ *teaspoon sugar*
6 *cups stock or water*	*dash of pepper*

1 *teaspoon soy sauce*

1. Sliver pork. Cut cabbage leaves in 1-inch sections.

2. Bring stock to a boil. Add pork and simmer, covered, about 5 minutes.

3. Add cabbage and simmer, covered, 5 minutes more. Stir in salt, sugar, pepper and soy sauce.

VARIATIONS: For the pork, substitute ¼ pound smoked ham or ¼ cup dried shrimp (soaked).

For the mustard cabbage, substitute round cabbage, shredded.

In step 3, add with cabbage, ½ cup each water chestnuts and bamboo shoots, both sliced.

Add 1 to 2 ounces peastarch noodles (soaked) at the very end, only to heat through.

Poach a Chinese salt egg and float on the soup as a garnish.

PORK AND CUCUMBER SOUP

4 to 5 servings

¼ *pound lean pork*	1 *cucumber*
1 *teaspoon cornstarch*	6 *cups stock or water*
1 *tablespoon soy sauce*	¾ *to 1 teaspoon salt*
1 *tablespoon sherry*	1 *teaspoon soy sauce*

1. Slice pork thin. Combine cornstarch, soy sauce and sherry. Add to pork and toss to coat.

2. Peel cucumber. Cut in half lengthwise; then scoop out seeds. Slice ¼ inch thick.

3. Bring stock to a boil. Add pork and simmer, covered, 8 minutes.

4. Stir in cucumber and simmer until translucent, only a minute or two. Stir in salt and remaining soy sauce.

VARIATION: For the pork, substitute ½ pound either fish fillet, sliced; or raw shrimp, shelled and deveined. Simmer, covered, 3 to 5 minutes.

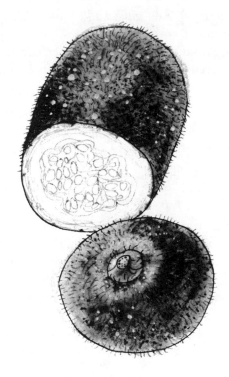

PORK AND FUZZY MELON SOUP

4 to 5 servings

¼ *pound lean pork*	6 *cups stock or water*
½ *pound fuzzy melon*	¾ *to 1 teaspoon salt*
1 *teaspoon sugar*	

1. Slice pork thin. Peel fuzzy melon; cut in half lengthwise, then in either 1-inch strips, or ¼-inch slices.

2. Bring stock to a boil. Add pork and melon and simmer, covered, 8 to 10 minutes. Add salt and sugar; simmer 2 minutes more.

VARIATIONS: For the pork, substitute 4 dried scallops (soaked) or 8 dried shrimp (soaked).

For the fuzzy melon, substitute 1 Chinese okra, trimmed and cut in ½-inch slices.

HOT-SOUR SOUP
4 to 5 servings

3 or 4 *dried black mushrooms*	5 *cups stock*
¼ *pound lean pork*	1 *cup mushroom-soaking liquid*
2 *bean curd cakes*	1 *tablespoon sherry*
1 *scallion*	2 *tablespoons white vinegar*
1 *egg*	¾ *to* 1 *teaspoon salt*
2 *tablespoons cornstarch*	1 *teaspoon soy sauce*
¼ *cup water*	¼ *teaspoon pepper*

few drops of sesame oil

1. Soak dried mushrooms. Reserve soaking liquid.
2. Sliver mushrooms, pork and bean curd. Mince scallion. Beat egg lightly. Blend cornstarch and cold water to a paste.
3. Bring stock and mushroom-soaking liquid to a boil. Add pork and mushrooms and simmer, covered, 10 minutes.
4. Add bean curd and simmer, covered, 3 minutes more.
5. Stir in sherry, vinegar, salt, soy sauce and pepper. Thicken with cornstarch paste.
6. Slowly add beaten egg, stirring gently once or twice. Remove from heat. Sprinkle with sesame oil and minced scallion.

VARIATIONS: For the pork, use half white-meat chicken and half pork.

For the white vinegar, substitute wine or cider vinegar, or lemon juice.

For the sesame oil, substitute Tabasco Sauce.

In step 3, add with pork and mushrooms, ½ cup bamboo shoots, slivered; or 4 cloud-ear mushrooms and ¼ cup lily buds (both soaked and cut in half).

Omit vinegar and pepper. (It's then called "Mandarin Soup.")

HOT-SOUR SOUP (LEFTOVERS)
4 to 5 servings

1½ *cups cooked pork*	¾ *to* 1 *teaspoon salt*
2 *eggs*	1½ *teaspoons soy sauce*
1 *cup stock*	5 *cups stock*
1 *tablespoon cornstarch*	2 *tablespoons vinegar*

dash of pepper

1. Sliver cooked meat. Beat eggs lightly. Blend cold stock, cornstarch, salt and soy sauce.

2. Bring remaining stock to a boil. Add cornstarch mixture and bring to a boil again, stirring; then reduce heat.

3. Pour eggs in slowly, stirring constantly. Add vinegar, pepper and slivered ingredients. Cook over medium heat, only to heat through.

VARIATION: For the pork, substitute cooked beef, chicken, duck or shrimp.

MATRIMONY VINE SOUP
4 to 5 servings

1 *cup lean pork*
6 *bunches matrimony vine*
¾ *to 1 teaspoon salt*

2 *eggs*
6 *cups stock*

1. Dice pork. Discard stems of matrimony vine, reserving leaves. Beat eggs lightly.

2. Bring stock to a boil. Add pork and simmer, covered, 15 to 20 minutes.

3. Add leaves and salt. Bring stock to a boil again over low heat, stirring frequently. (This should take about 5 minutes.)

4. Slowly pour in eggs; stir once gently and remove from the heat.

PORK AND SEAWEED SOUP
4 to 5 servings

3 sheets purple seaweed

¼ pound lean pork

1 scallion

6 cups stock or water

1 tablespoon soy sauce

¾ to 1 teaspoon salt

dash of pepper

1. Tear seaweed in small squares and soak. Squeeze dry.

2. Slice pork thin. Mince scallion.

3. Bring stock to a boil. Add pork and simmer, covered, 5 to 8 minutes.

4. Add seaweed and simmer, covered, 5 minutes more.

5. Stir in soy sauce, salt and pepper. Garnish with minced scallion.

VARIATIONS: For the pork, substitute either smoked ham or raw chicken.

Add with pork either 6 dried shrimp (soaked) or 4 large fresh shrimp, shelled, deveined and diced.

PORK AND WATER CRESS SOUP
4 to 5 servings

¼ pound lean pork

¼ cup celery

2 scallion stalks

1 bunch water cress

6 cups stock

¾ to 1 teaspoon salt

1. Sliver pork, celery and scallions. Cut water cress in 2-inch sections, discarding tough stems.

2. Bring stock to a boil. Add pork and celery and simmer, covered, 10 to 15 minutes.

3. Add water cress, scallions and salt. Simmer, uncovered, until water cress turns dark green (about 3 minutes).

VARIATION: For the pork, substitute ham or chicken.

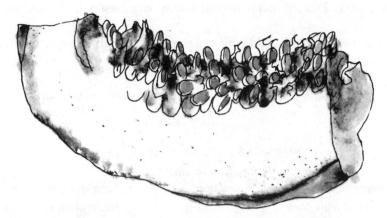

PORK AND WINTER MELON SOUP
4 to 5 servings

¼ *pound lean pork*	6 *cups stock or water*
1 *pound winter melon*	¾ *to* 1 *teaspoon salt*

1 *egg*

1. Cut pork in ½-inch cubes. Cut winter melon in 1-inch cubes, discarding rind and seeds.

2. Place pork, winter melon and stock in a saucepan. Bring slowly to a boil. Reduce heat and simmer, covered, 30 minutes.

3. Stir in salt. Beat egg, and stir in quickly. Remove from heat.

VARIATIONS: For the pork, substitute raw chicken or smoked ham, diced, or ¼ cup dried shrimp (soaked).

In step 2, add 3 dried black mushrooms (soaked), diced; or 5 water chestnuts, diced.

In step 2, bring stock to a boil first; then add pork and winter melon. Simmer, covered, 10 minutes.

PORKBALLS AND VERMICELLI SOUP
4 to 5 servings

2 *ounces vermicelli*	2 *tablespoons water*
½ *pound slightly fat pork*	4 *cups water*
1 *scallion*	6 *cups stock*
1 *teaspoon cornstarch*	1 *teaspoon soy sauce*
½ *teaspoon salt*	½ *to* ¾ *teaspoon salt*

1. Soak peastarch noodles (vermicelli). Mince or grind pork. Mince scallion.

2. Blend cornstarch, salt and cold water. Mix well with pork and form into walnut-size balls.

3. Bring remaining water to a rolling boil. Drop porkballs in one at a time. Reduce heat and simmer, covered, 5 minutes. Drain, discarding liquid.

4. Bring stock to a boil. Add porkballs and soaked vermicelli and simmer, covered, 5 minutes.

5. Add scallion, soy sauce and remaining salt. Simmer 1 to 2 minutes more.

VARIATION: For the pork, substitute beef. Simmer only 2 minutes in step 3.

BEEF AND CHINESE LETTUCE SOUP
4 to 5 servings

¼ to ½ *pound lean beef*	6 *cups stock*
1 *tablespoon soy sauce*	½ *pound Chinese lettuce*
1 *teaspoon peanut oil*	¾ to 1 *teaspoon salt*
	½ *teaspoon sugar*

1. Slice beef thin. Combine soy sauce and oil. Add to beef and toss. Let stand 30 minutes, turning meat occasionally.

2. Bring stock to a boil. Meanwhile cut lettuce in 2-inch sections.

3. Add lettuce to stock with salt and sugar and simmer, uncovered, until nearly done (about 10 minutes).

4. Add beef and simmer, uncovered, 3 to 4 minutes more.

VARIATION: For the Chinese lettuce, substitute either alone or in combination: celery, shredded; Swiss chard or spinach leaves, cut in half; or water cress, cut in 2-inch sections. Reduce cooking time in step 3 to about 2 or 3 minutes.

BEEF AND LOTUS ROOT SOUP
4 to 5 servings

1 *pound short ribs of beef*	6 *cups water*
1 *pound fresh lotus root*	1 *tablespoon soy sauce*
6 *Chinese red dates*	¾ to 1 *teaspoon salt*

1. Chop beef ribs in 1½-inch sections. Peel lotus root; cut in ¼-inch slices.

2. Place beef and lotus root in a saucepan with red dates and cold water. Bring to a boil. Reduce heat at once, skim surface to clear, then simmer, covered, 45 minutes.

3. Stir in soy sauce and salt. Simmer another minute.

VARIATION: Add with beef, etc., any or all of the following: 1 leek stalk, cut in sections; 2 slices fresh ginger root; 1 piece dried tangerine peel (soaked).

BEEF AND TURNIP SOUP

4 to 5 servings

½ *pound beef shank*   2 *white onions*
6 *cups water*   ¾ *to 1 teaspoon salt*
1 *pound Chinese white turnips*   *dash of pepper*

1. Cut beef in 1-inch cubes. Place in saucepan with cold water and bring to a boil. Then reduce heat and skim several times to clear. Simmer, covered, 1 hour.

2. Peel and dice turnips; peel and quarter onions. Add to pan and simmer, covered, 30 minutes more.

3. Season with salt and pepper. Simmer another minute.

VARIATIONS: For the beef, substitute pork or an uncooked chicken carcass.

Add with beef 1 piece dried tangerine peel (soaked).

Add with vegetables 1 tomato, peeled and diced; and either 1 carrot or 4 water chestnuts, diced.

Add with seasonings 1 tablespoon soy sauce and/or 1 teaspoon sherry.

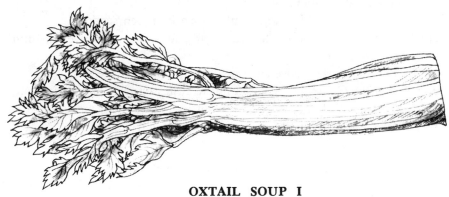

OXTAIL SOUP I

4 to 5 servings

1½ *pounds oxtails*   6 *cups water*
2 *celery stalks*   2 *tomatoes*
4 *small white onions*   ¾ *to 1 teaspoon salt*

dash of pepper

1. Chop oxtails and cut celery stalks, both in 2-inch sections; peel onions. Place in a pan with water and bring to a boil. Reduce heat and skim surface to clear. Simmer, covered, 2 hours.

2. Peel and quarter tomatoes and add with salt and pepper. Simmer, covered, 30 minutes more.

OXTAIL SOUP II
4 to 5 servings

½ cup black beans
1½ pounds oxtails
3 cups water

2 tablespoons peanut oil
6 cups water
6 Chinese red dates

¾ to 1 teaspoon salt

1. Soak black beans.
2. Chop oxtails in 2-inch sections. Bring water to a boil. Add oxtails and parboil 5 minutes. Drain, discarding liquid; then rinse meat with cold water.
3. Heat oil in a skillet; add oxtails and brown quickly.
4. Bring remaining water to a boil. Add oxtails, black beans and red dates. Bring to a boil again, and skim surface to clear. Reduce heat and simmer, covered, 2 hours. Season with salt.

Note: Don't confuse these black beans with fermented black beans, which are pungent and salty.

variation: For the black beans, substitute ½ cup raw skinless peanuts, and add with 1 piece dried tangerine peel (soaked) and 3 thin slices fresh ginger root.

CHICKEN VELVET AND CORN SOUP
4 to 5 servings

2 tablespoons smoked ham
1 chicken breast
2 teaspoons sherry
2 egg whites

1½ cups canned creamed corn
6 cups stock
¾ to 1 teaspoon salt
dash of pepper

1. Mince ham. Skin and bone chicken breast; pound meat with mallet or side of cleaver, then mince fine, removing tendons. Add sherry to chicken and mix.
2. Beat egg whites until fluffy but not stiff. Fold into chicken mixture.
3. With egg beater, beat canned corn until creamy. Bring stock to a boil. Add corn and simmer, covered, 2 minutes.
4. Add chicken mixture. Bring slowly to a boil again. Then stir in salt and pepper and remove from heat at once. Garnish with minced ham.

variations: In step 1, omit sherry and combine minced chicken with ½ cup cold stock, 1 tablespoon cornstarch and ½ teaspoon salt.

Garnish with ½ cup spinach, slivered; or ¼ cup Chinese parsley sprigs and 2 tablespoons almonds, toasted and slivered.

CHICKEN VELVET AND LETTUCE SOUP
4 to 5 servings

1 *chicken breast*	2 *tablespoons smoked ham*
½ *cup stock*	6 *cups stock*
1 *egg white*	¾ *to 1 teaspoon salt*
2 *cups lettuce*	½ *teaspoon sugar*

1. Skin and bone chicken breast; pound meat with mallet or side of cleaver, then mince fine, removing tendons. Blend in stock.

2. Beat egg white until fluffy but not stiff. Fold into chicken mixture. Cut lettuce in strips. Mince ham.

3. Bring remaining stock to a boil. Add lettuce, salt and sugar. Bring to a boil again; remove at once from heat.

4. Stir in chicken mixture. Garnish with minced ham. Serve at once.

VARIATIONS: For the chicken, substitute ¼ pound pork or ham, 4 water chestnuts and 4 dried black mushrooms (soaked), all slivered. Combine with stock, but omit egg white in step 2. Add this mixture in step 3 *before* lettuce and seasonings. Simmer, covered, 10 minutes. Add lettuce and simmer, uncovered, 2 minutes more. Season with the salt, dash of pepper and 1 teaspoon soy sauce, omitting the sugar.

For the lettuce, substitute ½ pound mustard cabbage, shredded. Then poach a Chinese salt egg and float on the soup as a garnish.

CHICKEN AND BITTER MELON SOUP
4 to 5 servings

1 *to 2 cups chicken*	6 *cups stock*
1 *bitter melon*	¾ *to 1 teaspoon salt*
2 *leaves pickled cabbage*	2 *teaspoons soy sauce*
4 *water chestnuts*	*dash of pepper*

2 or 3 eggs

1. Slice chicken thin. Cut bitter melon in half lengthwise; scoop out seeds and pulp, then slice thin. Rinse pickled cabbage; squeeze dry, then slice thin. Slice water chestnuts.

2. Bring stock to a boil. Add chicken, pickled cabbage and water chestnuts; simmer, covered, 5 minutes.

3. Add bitter melon and simmer, covered, 8 minutes more. Stir in salt, soy sauce and pepper.

4. Poach eggs in soup as a garnish.

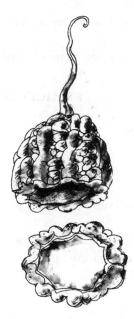

VARIATIONS: For the chicken, substitute pork, beef or ham; or ¼ cup dried shrimp (soaked) and simmer 15 minutes in step 2 before adding bitter melon.

CHICKEN AND FUZZY MELON SOUP

4 to 5 servings

1 to 2 *cups chicken*	6 *cups stock*
1 to 2 *cups fuzzy melon*	¾ to 1 *teaspoon salt*

1 *teaspoon soy sauce*

1. Skin and dice chicken. Peel and dice fuzzy melon.
2. Bring stock to a boil. Add chicken and melon and simmer, covered, 15 minutes. Stir in salt and soy sauce.

CHICKEN AND LOTUS SEED SOUP

4 to 5 servings

½ *pound dried lotus seeds*	1 *tablespoon smoked ham*
1 *cup chicken*	½ *cup green peas*
½ *cup mushrooms, fresh or canned*	6 *cups stock*

½ *teaspoon sugar*

1. Blanch dried lotus seeds (see page 826).
2. Slice chicken and mushrooms. Mince ham. Shell peas.

3. Bring stock to a boil. Add lotus seeds, chicken, mushrooms and sugar. Simmer, covered, 30 minutes.

4. Add peas and simmer, uncovered, 5 minutes more. Garnish with ham.

CHICKEN AND VERMICELLI SOUP
4 to 5 servings

2 *ounces peastarch noodles*	6 *cups stock*
1 *cup chicken*	¾ to 1 *teaspoon salt*
1 *scallion*	1 *teaspoon soy sauce*

1. Break peastarch noodles (vermicelli) in 3-inch lengths and soak. Sliver chicken. Mince scallion.

2. Bring stock to a boil. Add chicken and simmer, covered, 10 minutes.

3. Add vermicelli and simmer, covered, 10 minutes more. Stir in salt and soy sauce. Garnish with minced scallion.

THREE DELICIOUS SOUP
4 to 5 servings

1 *chicken breast*	2 *teaspoons stock*
½ *cup bamboo shoots*	6 *cups stock*
¼ *pound fresh mushrooms*	1 *tablespoon sherry*
1 *teaspoon cornstarch*	¾ to 1 *teaspoon salt*

few drops of sesame oil

1. Skin and bone chicken breast; then slice. Slice bamboo shoots and mushrooms. Blend cornstarch and cold stock to a paste.

2. Bring remaining stock to a boil. Add chicken and vegetables and simmer, covered, 5 minutes.

3. Stir in sherry and salt, then cornstarch paste. Cook, stirring over medium-high heat, until soup thickens. Sprinkle with sesame oil.

NOTE: This is also known as Three Fresh Meats Soup.

SQUAB SOUP AND GINSENG ROOT

4 to 5 servings

2 squabs	6 cups stock
1 or 2 slices fresh ginger root	⅓ cup sherry
½ cup ginseng root	1 teaspoon soy sauce

¾ to 1 teaspoon salt

1. Disjoint squabs. Cut ginger root and ginseng root in ⅛-inch slices.
2. Bring stock to a boil. Add squabs and sherry and simmer, covered, 20 minutes.
3. Add soy sauce, ginger and ginseng root. Simmer, covered, 45 minutes more. Season with salt.

NOTE: When purchasing ginseng root, be sure to specify it's for soup.

ABALONE SOUP

4 to 5 servings

4 dried black mushrooms	1 tablespoon soy sauce
½ can abalone (4 ounces)	1 tablespoon sherry
stock or water	1 tablespoon peanut oil
¼ cup smoked ham	¼ teaspoon salt
½ cup lean pork	dash of pepper
2 slices fresh ginger root	¼ teaspoon salt
1 tablespoon cornstarch	1 egg

1. Soak dried mushrooms.

Drain canned abalone, reserving liquid. Combine abalone liquid with enough cold stock or water to make six cups.

3. Cut mushrooms, abalone, ham and pork all in strips, but keep them separate. Mince ginger root.

4. Combine cornstarch, soy sauce and sherry. Add to pork and toss to coat. Let stand a few minutes.

5. Heat oil. Add salt and ginger and stir-fry a few times. Add pork and stir-fry until it loses pinkness. Remove from pan.

6. Meanwhile bring abalone-stock mixture slowly to a boil. Add mushrooms and stir-fried pork. Simmer, covered, 10 minutes.

7. Add abalone, ham strips, pepper and remaining salt. Cook only to heat through, about 2 minutes. (Don't overcook abalone; it will toughen.)

8. Garnish with a poached egg (see page 75).

VARIATION: For the pork, substitute ½ cup chicken breast, cooked. Add in step 6 after mushrooms have simmered 8 minutes, and cook only to heat through.

CLAM SOUP
4 to 5 servings

1 or 2 dried black mushrooms	½ scallion stalk
12 clams	6 cups stock
¼ cup bamboo shoots	1 tablespoon sherry
8 snow peas	dash of pepper

1. Soak dried mushrooms. Shell clams with a knife or steam about 5 minutes to open (see page 451).

2. Slice mushrooms and bamboo shoots. Stem snow peas. Mince scallion.

3. Bring stock to a boil. Add mushrooms, bamboo shoots and snow peas and simmer, uncovered, 2 minutes.

4. Stir in sherry, minced scallion and pepper. Add clams. Simmer only to heat through.

CRABMEAT SOUP I
4 to 5 servings

1 cup cooked crabmeat	¼ cup water
2 eggs	6 cups stock
½ head Boston lettuce	¾ to 1 teaspoon salt
1 tablespoon cornstarch	dash of pepper

1. Flake and pick over crabmeat. Beat eggs lightly. Chop lettuce. Blend cornstarch and cold water to a paste.

2. Bring stock to a boil. Add salt and pepper. Stir in eggs quickly; reduce heat to medium. Add cornstarch paste and cook stirring, until soup thickens and is smooth.

3. Add crabmeat and lettuce and cook, stirring, only to heat through.

CRABMEAT SOUP II
4 to 5 servings

1 cup cooked crabmeat	½ cup stock
½ pound spinach	1 tablespoon oil
1 scallion stalk	1 tablespoon sherry
2 slices fresh ginger root	5½ cups stock
1 tablespoon cornstarch	¾ to 1 teaspoon salt

1. Flake and pick over crabmeat. Remove tough stems from spinach; chop leaves. Cut scallion stalk in 1-inch sections. Mince ginger root. Blend cornstarch and cold stock.

2. In a deep pan, heat oil. Add scallion and ginger and stir-fry a few times. Add crabmeat; stir-fry 1 minute. Add sherry and stir-fry half a minute more.

3. Add remaining stock and bring to a boil. Add spinach and salt; bring to a boil again, then reduce heat to medium.

4. Add cornstarch mixture and cook, stirring, until the soup thickens and is smooth.

VARIATIONS: For the spinach, substitute 1 tomato, peeled and sliced; or 2 bean curd cakes, cubed or sliced.

In step 3, add 1 tablespoon vinegar with the salt.

Omit the spinach. In step 3, add 2 egg whites, beaten until frothy and mixed with 3 tablespoons light cream. Do not bring soup to a boil again, but add cornstarch paste immediately.

CUTTLEFISH AND LOTUS ROOT SOUP
8 to 10 servings

½ dried cuttlefish	1 quart water
1 piece tangerine peel	3 quarts water
1 pound lotus root	3 Chinese red dates
1 pound pork neck bones	¾ to 1 teaspoon salt

1. Separately soak dried cuttlefish and tangerine peel.

2. Peel lotus root. Cut in half lengthwise, then in ¼-inch slices.

3. Boil water and pour over pork bones in a soup pot. Parboil 5 minutes. Drain, discarding liquid, and rinse bones under cold running water.

4. Cover pork bones with remaining water and bring to a boil over high heat. Reduce to a simmer and skim off fat.

5. Add soaked cuttlefish, tangerine peel, lotus root, red dates and salt. Simmer, covered, 1 hour. Skim surface.

6. Add boiling water to restore to original 3 quarts. Simmer, covered, 2 hours more.

WHOLE FISH SOUP I
4 to 5 servings

1 *bass or carp* (*about 2 pounds*)	6 *cups stock*
2 *scallion stalks*	1 *tablespoon peanut oil*
2 *or 3 slices fresh ginger root*	¾ *to 1 teaspoon salt*

1. Have fish cleaned and left whole. Cut scallions in 1-inch sections. Mince ginger root.

2. Bring stock to a boil. Add fish, scallions and ginger and simmer, covered, 10 minutes.

3. Add peanut oil and salt. Simmer, covered, 10 minutes more.

NOTE: Serve the fish on a platter, the soup in a tureen.

WHOLE FISH SOUP II
4 to 5 servings

1 *bass or carp* (*about 2 pounds*)	6 *cups stock*
cornstarch	1 *tablespoon sherry*
1 *scallion stalk*	1 *tablespoon vinegar*
2 *slices fresh ginger root*	1 *teaspoon soy sauce*
1 *tablespoon oil*	*few drops of sesame oil*
2 *tablespoons oil*	2 *sprigs Chinese parsley*
	2 *whole scallions*

1. Have fish cleaned and left whole. Make three light gashes in each side. Dry thoroughly with paper toweling; dust lightly with cornstarch. Cut scallion stalk in 1-inch sections. Mince ginger root.

2. Heat oil. Add scallion and ginger and brown lightly. Remove and set aside. Heat remaining oil to smoking hot. Add fish and brown quickly on both sides.

3. Return scallion and ginger to pan with fish and add stock. Bring to a boil, then reduce heat and simmer, covered, 10 minutes.

4. Add sherry, vinegar, soy sauce and sesame oil. Simmer, covered, 10 minutes more.

5. Meanwhile, chop Chinese parsley, and mince remaining scallions. Then arrange in a long, deep serving bowl, with fish on top. Pour soup over and serve.

VARIATION: In step 2, instead of pan-frying, deep-fry fish to light golden and drain on paper toweling.

FISH FILLET SOUP I
4 to 5 servings

½ *pound fish fillets*	1 *tablespoon sherry*
2 *slices fresh ginger root*	1½ *teaspoons peanut oil*

6 cups stock

1. Sliver fish fillets against the grain. Mince ginger root and combine with sherry and oil. Add to fish and toss gently. Let stand 30 minutes, turning occasionally.

2. Distribute fish among individual soup bowls. Bring stock to a boil and pour over. (The fish will cook right in the hot stock.)

FISH FILLET SOUP II

4 to 5 servings

½ pound fish fillets	1 tablespoon soy sauce
1 small onion	1 tablespoon sherry
1 or 2 whole scallions	6 cups stock
1 tablespoon cornstarch	¾ to 1 teaspoon salt

1 tablespoon soy sauce

1. Cut fish fillets in 1-inch squares. Slice onion thin. Mince scallions.
2. Combine cornstarch, soy sauce and sherry. Add to fish and toss to coat.
3. Bring stock to a boil. Add onion, salt and remaining soy sauce; then add fish. Simmer, uncovered, 5 to 7 minutes. Garnish with scallions.

VARIATIONS: In step 3, add with fish, half a head of lettuce, cut in strips.

In step 3, add with onion ½ cup carrots and ½ cup celery, both diced, and simmer, covered, until nearly done (about 15 minutes) before adding seasoning and fish. Or add ½ cup each mushrooms, water chestnuts and bamboo shoots, all diced, and simmer, covered, 5 minutes before adding seasoning and fish.

In step 3, omit onion, salt and soy sauce; add 3 dried black mushrooms (soaked), shredded; ¼ pound peastarch noodles (soaked); 1 piece dried tangerine peel (soaked); and 1 teaspoon fresh ginger root, shredded. Bring to a boil before adding fish. Stir in salt at the end of step 3.

FISH'S MAW SOUP I

4 to 5 servings

¼ pound fish's maw	1 egg
6 water chestnuts	1 tablespoon cornstarch
2 tablespoons smoked ham	3 tablespoons water

6 cups stock

1. Soak fish's maw, then dice.
2. Dice water chestnuts. Mince ham. Beat egg lightly. Blend cornstarch and cold water to a paste.
3. Bring stock to a boil. Add fish's maw and water chestnuts, and simmer, covered, 30 minutes.
4. Add cornstarch paste and cook, stirring, until soup thickens and is smooth.
5. Remove pan from heat; stir in beaten egg. Garnish with minced ham.

FISH'S MAW SOUP II

4 to 5 servings

¼ *pound fish's maw*   1 to 2 *tablespoons smoked ham*
½ *cup chicken*   6 *cups stock*
6 *water chestnuts*   ¾ to 1 *teaspoon salt*
¼ *pound spinach*   1 *teaspoon soy sauce*

dash of pepper

1. Soak fish's maw, then dice.

2. Dice chicken and water chestnuts. Cut spinach leaves in 2-inch sections. Mince ham.

3. Bring stock to a boil. Add diced ingredients and simmer, covered, 30 minutes.

4. Add spinach and simmer, uncovered, 3 minutes. Stir in salt, soy sauce and pepper. Garnish with minced ham.

VARIATIONS: For the spinach, substitute Chinese lettuce or mustard cabbage and simmer, uncovered, 6 minutes.

For the chicken, substitute 2 slices smoked ham, cut in strips. Omit ham garnish.

For the water chestnuts and spinach, substitute 4 dried black mushrooms (soaked) and ½ cup bamboo shoots, both cut in strips. Add both in step 4, and simmer, covered, 6 minutes. (For color, garnish soup with 4 or 5 blanched snow peas.)

BASIC FISHBALL SOUP
4 to 5 servings

18 *fishballs*	6 *cups stock*
1 *scallion*	¾ *to* 1 *teaspoon salt*

1. Prepare fishballs according to recipe on page 443. Mince scallion.
2. Bring stock to a boil. Add salt. Lower fishballs in one at a time so they won't splash. Simmer, uncovered, 3 minutes. Add minced scallion. Simmer 1 minute more.

NOTE: Shrimpball soup is prepared the same way.

VARIATIONS: Before step 2, add to cold stock 4 dried black mushrooms (soaked), 1 or 2 cakes bean curd and ½ cup bamboo shoots, all slivered; bring to a boil and simmer 1 minute before adding salt and fishballs.

In step 2, add to boiling stock 1 cup Chinese cabbage stems and ½ cup celery, both slivered. Simmer, uncovered, 5 minutes before adding salt and fishballs.

Add, with fishballs, ¼ pound peastarch noodles (soaked).

Add, with scallion, ½ cup spinach or water cress, chopped.

OYSTER SOUP
4 to 5 servings

6 *dried black mushrooms*	1 *scallion*
6 *fresh oysters*	6 *cups stock*
¼ *pound lean pork*	1 *teaspoon ginger juice*
½ *cup bamboo shoots*	1 *tablespoon sherry*
6 *water chestnuts*	¾ *to* 1 *teaspoon salt*

dash of pepper

1. Soak dried mushrooms.
2. Shell and slice oysters. Slice pork thin. Slice bamboo shoots, water chestnuts and mushrooms. Mince scallion.
3. Heat stock. Extract ginger juice (see Glossary) and add. Add mushrooms, bamboo shoots and water chestnuts. Bring slowly to a boil.
4. Add pork and oysters and simmer, covered, 3 to 5 minutes. Stir in sherry, salt and pepper. Garnish with minced scallion.

TEN PRECIOUS SOUP

4 to 5 servings

½ cup bêche-de-mer	2 tablespoons peanut oil
½ cup shrimp	1 tablespoon sherry
½ cup fish fillet	5 cups stock
½ cup bamboo shoots	¾ to 1 teaspoon salt
1 scallion stalk	2 tablespoons vinegar
2 tablespoons cornstarch	few drops of sesame oil
½ cup stock	2 eggs

1. Soak bêche-de-mer.

2. Shell and devein shrimp; cut in half if large. Slice fish fillet against the grain. Shred bamboo shoots and bêche-de-mer. Mince scallion stalk. Blend cornstarch and stock to a paste.

3. Heat oil very hot and stir-fry shrimp and bamboo shoots 1 minute. Add sherry, bêche-de-mer and fish; stir-fry gently 1 minute more.

4. Add remaining stock and salt. Bring to a boil. Add cornstarch paste and cook, stirring, until soup thickens and is smooth.

5. Stir in vinegar, sesame oil and minced scallion. Beat eggs and stir in quickly, then remove from heat.

BASIC VEGETABLE SOUP

4 to 5 servings

1 to 1½ cups vegetables	6 cups stock
¾ to 1 teaspoon salt	

1. Slice any of the vegetables listed below. Bring stock to a boil.

2. Add vegetables and simmer as indicated below. (When using more than one vegetable, add each according to the time indicated by its cooking requirements.) Season with salt.

VARIATIONS: Add to stock with vegetables, 1 teaspoon ginger juice; or 1 teaspoon vinegar and a few drops of sesame oil.

CUCUMBERS: Peel. Cut in half lengthwise. Scoop out seeds and slice. Simmer, covered, 3 minutes.

LETTUCE: Chop. Simmer, uncovered, 1 to 2 minutes.

MUSHROOMS, DRIED: Soak and slice. Simmer, covered, 15 minutes.

PEAS: Shell. (You may also add ½ cup fresh mushrooms, sliced.) Simmer, uncovered, 10 minutes.

TOMATOES: Use canned tomatoes, mashed; or 6 tablespoons tomato juice. Simmer, covered, 2 to 3 minutes.

TURNIPS: Peel Chinese white turnips. Cut in chunks. Simmer, covered, 30 minutes.

WATER CRESS: Remove tough stems. Simmer, uncovered, 1 to 2 minutes.

ZUCCHINI: Use peeled or unpeeled. Cut in ¼-inch slices. Simmer, covered, 3 to 5 minutes.

EGG DROP SOUP I

4 to 5 servings

2 eggs	6 cups stock
2 teaspoons water	½ teaspoon sugar
2 scallions	¾ to 1 teaspoon salt
1 tablespoon cornstarch	1 teaspoon sherry
3 tablespoons water	1 tablespoon soy sauce

1. Beat eggs and stir in water. Mince scallions. Blend cornstarch and remaining cold water to a paste.

2. Bring stock to a boil. Reduce heat to medium and stir in sugar, salt, sherry and soy sauce.

3. Add cornstarch paste and cook, stirring, until soup thickens and is smooth.

4. Reduce heat to low. Pour eggs in slowly, stirring constantly, until they separate into shreds; then turn off heat. Garnish with minced scallions.

NOTE: This is also known as Egg Flower or Egg Petal Soup.

EGG DROP SOUP II
4 to 5 servings

2 *dried black mushrooms*	1 *scallion stalk*
¼ *pound lean pork*	½ *cup stock*
1 *tablespoon cornstarch*	2 *teaspoons cornstarch*
1 *tablespoon sherry*	6 *cups stock*
1 *egg white*	1 *tablespoon soy sauce*
few drops of sesame oil	¾ *to 1 teaspoon salt*
¼ *cup bamboo shoots*	2 *eggs*

dash of pepper

1. Soak dried mushrooms.

2. Shred pork. Combine cornstarch, sherry and egg white; add to pork and toss to coat. Sprinkle with sesame oil.

3. Shred bamboo shoots and soaked mushrooms. Mince scallion stalk. Blend cold stock and remaining cornstarch.

4. Put remaining stock in a pan with mushrooms, bamboo shoots, soy sauce and salt. Bring to a boil. Reduce heat and simmer, covered, 2 to 3 minutes.

5. Add cornstarch mixture and cook, stirring, until soup begins to thicken.

6. Add pork and cook 1 minute more. Meanwhile beat eggs.

7. Pour eggs in slowly, stirring constantly until they separate into shreds, then turn off heat. Sprinkle with minced scallions and pepper.

VARIATION: For the pork, substitute chicken.

BASIC BEAN CURD SOUP
4 to 5 servings

6 *cups stock*	2 *bean curd cakes*
¾ *to 1 teaspoon salt*	

1. Cut bean curd cakes in thin slices or 1-inch cubes.

2. Bring stock to a boil. Add bean curd and simmer, covered, only to heat through. Season with salt.

VARIATIONS: Add with bean curd any of the following vegetables:

BAMBOO SHOOTS: ½ cup, sliced thin. Simmer, covered, 3 minutes.

BEAN SPROUTS: ½ cup. Simmer, covered, 2 minutes.

CHINESE CABBAGE: 1 cup, cut in 1-inch sections. Simmer, uncovered, 3 minutes.

MUSHROOMS, FRESH: ½ cup, sliced thin. Simmer, covered, 3 minutes.

MUSHROOMS: 8 dried black (soaked), sliced. Simmer, covered, 10 to 15 minutes.

MUSTARD CABBAGE: 1 cup, cut in 1-inch sections. Simmer, uncovered, 3 to 5 minutes.

SPINACH: 1 cup, cut in 1-inch sections. Simmer, uncovered, 1 to 2 minutes.

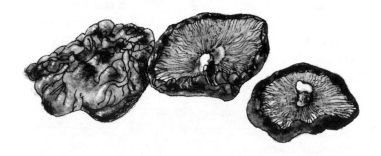

MUSHROOM SOUP
4 to 5 servings

15 *dried black mushrooms*	5 *cups stock*
mushroom-soaking liquid	¾ *to 1 teaspoon salt*

1. Soak dried mushrooms; reserve soaking liquid. Cut in half if large.
2. Place mushrooms in a deep, heatproof bowl. In a saucepan, bring mushroom-soaking liquid and stock to a boil. Pour over mushrooms.
3. Place bowl on a rack and steam over low heat for 1 hour (see page 831). Season with salt.

SPINACH SOUP
4 to 5 servings

4 *dried black mushrooms*	6 *cups stock*
½ *pound spinach*	¾ *to 1 teaspoon salt*
½ *cup bamboo shoots*	*few drops of sesame oil*

1. Soak dried mushrooms.
2. Cut spinach leaves in 1-inch sections. Slice bamboo shoots and soaked mushrooms.
3. Bring stock to a boil. Add mushrooms and bamboo shoots and simmer, covered, 10 minutes.
4. Add spinach and simmer, uncovered, 2 minutes more. Season with salt and sesame oil.

VARIATIONS: For the dried mushrooms, substitute ¼ pound fresh mushrooms, sliced.

For the bamboo shoots, substitute ½ cup celery or ½ cup carrots, diced.

For the spinach, substitute water cress.

VEGETARIAN SOUP
4 to 5 servings

½ cup cabbage
½ cup carrots
½ cup celery
1 scallion stalk
2 tablespoons peanut oil

6 cups water
1 tablespoon soy sauce
1 teaspoon sherry
1 teaspoon salt
dash of pepper

1. Cut cabbage, carrots, celery and scallion in strips.

2. Heat oil in a deep pan. Add vegetables and stir-fry until they begin to soften (2 to 3 minutes).

3. Add water, soy sauce, sherry, salt and pepper. Bring to a boil, then simmer, covered, 10 minutes.

NOTE: This soup is always made with plain water, never meat stock.

VARIATIONS: For the vegetables, substitute ½ cup fresh mushrooms, sliced; and 1 cup spinach, cut in 1-inch sections. Stir-fry the mushrooms 3 minutes, the spinach 1 to 2 minutes; then simmer, uncovered, 2 minutes.

For the vegetables, substitute ¼ cup mushrooms, ¼ cup water chestnuts, ¼ cup bamboo shoots, ⅛ cup onions, 1 tomato, ¼ cup Chinese white turnip, and ¼ cup pickled mustard cabbage, all diced. Stir-fry 5 to 6 minutes. Simmer as in step 3.

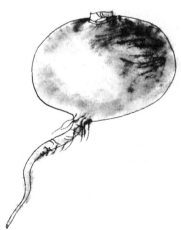

CELESTIAL SOUP
4 to 5 servings

2 whole scallions
¾ to 1 teaspoon salt

6 cups water

1 teaspoon peanut oil
2 tablespoons soy sauce

1. Mince scallions. Place in a deep bowl with salt, oil and soy sauce.

2. Bring water to a boil; pour over scallions, and let stand 1 to 2 minutes.

VARIATIONS: Add with scallions, 1 garlic clove, minced; and/or any fresh, tender greens, such as parsley, spinach or water cress, chopped.

For the peanut oil, substitute a few drops of sesame oil.

WONTON SOUP
4 to 5 servings

12 *to* 16 *wontons*	4 *cups water*
1 *to* 2 *eggs*	6 *cups stock*
1 *whole scallion*	¾ *to* 1 *teaspoon salt*

1 *teaspoon soy sauce*

1. Prepare wontons (see page 698). Make egg threads (see page 826). Mince scallion.

2. Bring water to a boil. Add wontons and simmer, uncovered, until they float (about 5 minutes). Drain. Keep wontons warm.

3. Meanwhile bring stock to a boil. Add salt and soy sauce.

4. Place wontons at the bottom of a large soup tureen or in individual soup bowls. Pour boiling stock over. Garnish with egg threads and minced scallion.

VARIATIONS: In step 3, add to the boiling stock the following and cook, covered, 5 minutes over medium heat: 5 shrimp, shelled and deveined; 2 chicken livers, cut in quarters; 1 chicken gizzard, sliced; 5 button mushrooms, sliced; 5 water chestnuts, sliced; ½ cup bamboo shoots, sliced; and 2 cups Chinese cabbage, cut in 1-inch lengths.

For the egg threads garnish, substitute ¼ cup roast pork, sliced or slivered.

❀ *Appetizers and Cold Dishes* ❀

MANY CHINESE-AMERICAN restaurants serve barbecued spareribs and egg rolls as appetizers. These dishes, when eaten at home, are not usually served as appetizers. At a family meal the appetizers are more likely to include cold chicken or duck, pork strips, ham or sausage, meatballs, fishballs, smoked fish, preserved eggs, shrimp toast, various cold vegetables, and other tidbits. At more formal meals, small dishes of melon seeds, pine nuts and salted peanuts are also set out at this time. These dishes, placed in the center of the table before the meal begins, are sampled while the cook puts the finishing touches to the dinner.

Since these various dishes are the first view of the meal, each is designed to stimulate both the eye and the appetite. Meats and vegetables are set out handsomely and decoratively—sometimes sliced thin and arranged like flower petals in layered circles. Even the plainest of ingredients are brightened with a bit of parsley or a few pink slivers of ham.

The cold vegetable dishes, while similar to salads, are never eaten raw. (Uncooked vegetables in China were not safe to eat: they had to be blanched, parboiled, salted or pickled.) Chinese vegetable dishes are characterized by light, pretty colors and crisp, crunchy textures. They are seasoned simply, with dressings that are delicious but never overpowering. They are chilled, but only briefly: they are never served so cold as to numb the taste buds.

NOTE: This section does not include the full range of dishes which can be served as appetizers. See "Appetizers" in the Index for other possibilities.

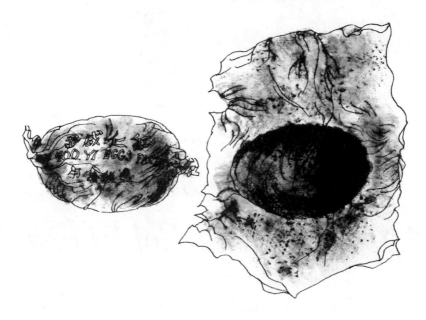

PRESERVED EGGS
Each egg is about 2 servings

1. Clean and shell preserved eggs (see page 826).
2. With a sharp knife, cut each egg crosswise in ¼-inch slices, or lengthwise in quarters.
3. Serve with any of the following sprinkled over the top:
1 teaspoon fresh ginger root, minced, combined with either 2 teaspoons vinegar or 2 teaspoons soy sauce
1 teaspoon sugar, 1 tablespoon vinegar and a few drops of sesame oil, blended together
A few drops of Tabasco, Worcestershire, soy or oyster sauce
Or serve eggs plain with sweet-and-sour pickles or subgum ginger (both cut up), or pickled scallions and red ginger (sliced).

PRESERVED EGGS WITH HAM AND VEGETABLES
6 to 8 servings

3 *preserved eggs*	1 *garlic clove*
1 *cup smoked ham*	½ *teaspoon powdered mustard*
1 *bunch water cress*	1 *tablespoon vinegar*
3 *heads endive*	1 *tablespoon soy sauce*

3 *tablespoons peanut oil*

1. Clean and shell preserved eggs (see page 826).

2. Cut eggs in ¼-inch slices. Cut ham in strips. Remove tough stems from water cress. Cut endive in 1½-inch sections.

3. Mince garlic clove, then combine with mustard, vinegar, soy sauce and oil. Pour over endive and toss.

4. Transfer to a serving platter and arrange decoratively with other ingredients.

CHINESE SAUSAGES
Each sausage is about 2 servings

1. Remove string and rinse sausage links in cold water.

2. Place sausages in a shallow heatproof dish and steam on a rack until translucent (15 to 20 minutes). See pages 33 and 831.

3. Drain and let cool. Slice diagonally in thin ovals.

SESAME HAM STICKS
About 4 servings

½ pound ham   2 teaspoons soy sauce

few drops of sesame oil

1. Slice ham, cut in strips, and arrange on a small serving dish.
2. Mix soy sauce and sesame oil, then pour over ham sticks and serve.

WHITE-CUT CHICKEN
About 8 servings

1. Prepare a white-cut chicken (see page 358).
2. With a cleaver, chop chicken, bones and all, in 2-inch sections. Arrange on a serving platter, skin side up. (You may, if you wish, bone it first, then either slice chicken thin or cut in strips.)
3. Serve in any of the following ways:
Garnish with smoked ham, slivered; and scallions and Chinese parsley, minced.
Rub a few drops of sesame oil on the chicken skin; serve a soy sauce dip on the side.
Sprinkle 1 or 2 tablespoons soy or oyster sauce over the chicken, or use in larger quantities as a dip.
Sprinkle a mixture of 3 tablespoons honey, 1½ tablespoons oyster sauce and ½ teaspoon salt over chicken; garnish with 2 slices fresh ginger root and 2 scallions, minced.
NOTE: See section on Seasonings and Sauces for other dip suggestions.

COLD CHICKEN AND CUCUMBER
About 4 servings

1 cup cooked chicken   ½ teaspoon powdered mustard
2 cucumbers   ½ teaspoon salt

2 tablespoons vinegar

1. Cut cooked chicken in strips or shred by tearing (the Chinese prefer the latter because it adds textural interest).
2. Peel cucumbers. Cut in half lengthwise and scoop out seeds; then cut in strips.
3. Arrange cucumber strips on a flat serving plate; top with chicken.

4. Combine mustard, salt and vinegar. Pour over chicken just before serving.

VARIATIONS: For the cucumbers, substitute 3 cups celery, blanched and shredded. In step 4, add to the dressing either ¼ teaspoon cayenne pepper or a few drops of Tabasco Sauce.

In step 4, substitute the following dressing: ½ teaspoon ginger root and ½ scallion stalk, both minced; ½ teaspoon sugar, 2 teaspoons vinegar, 1 tablespoon peanut oil, 1 tablespoon light soy sauce and a few drops of sesame oil.

Slice the cucumbers ¼-inch thick. Omit the dressing in step 4. Instead make a paste by gradually adding ¼ cup water to ¼ cup peanut butter, stirring until smooth. Then stir in ½ teaspoon salt and ½ teaspoon sesame oil. Add to cucumber slices and toss; then top with the chicken.

COLD CHICKEN SESAME
About 8 servings

1 *cooked chicken*	½ *head lettuce*
½ *cup water*	4 or 5 *scallion tops*
1 *teaspoon powdered mustard*	1 *tablespoon white sesame seeds*
1 *cup Chinese parsley*	½ *teaspoon salt*
pinch of sugar	

1. Strip cooked chicken from carcass and cut or tear meat in fine shreds.

2. Meanwhile boil water and let cool. Then combine just enough with mustard to make a smooth paste (about 2 teaspoons of water). Add to chicken and toss.

3. Discard tough parsley stems. Shred lettuce and green tops of scallions.

4. Heat a dry pan. Toast sesame seeds quickly and lightly. Then add to chicken and toss.

5. Sprinkle chicken with salt and sugar. Add scallions and half of parsley. Toss to mix thoroughly.

6. Line a serving platter with lettuce strips and arrange chicken on top. Garnish with remaining parsley.

NOTE: Any cooked chicken can be used, but cold deep-fried chicken has the best texture for this dish.

COLD SHERRY CHICKEN
About 8 servings

1 *cooked chicken*	1 *teaspoon ginger juice*
2 *cups sherry*	1 *tablespoon soy sauce*

½ *teaspoon sesame oil*

1. Bone cooked chicken and cut in thin slices. Add sherry and toss. Let stand 2 hours, turning once or twice. Drain, reserving sherry.

2. Meanwhile extract ginger juice, then mix well with soy sauce, sesame oil and cup of reserved sherry.

3. Arrange chicken slices on a serving platter. Pour mixture over and serve.

RED-SIMMERED CHICKEN WINGS
6 to 8 servings

8 to 10 *chicken wings*	¼ *cup sherry*
2 *scallion stalks*	½ *cup water*
¼ *cup soy sauce*	1 to 2 *tablespoons brown sugar*

1. Chop off and discard bony tips of chicken wings; then cut each wing in two. Cut scallions in 1-inch sections.

2. Place wings and scallions in a pan with soy sauce, sherry, water and sugar. Bring to a boil; then simmer, covered, 30 minutes.

3. Uncover pan and simmer 15 minutes more, stirring and basting frequently for uniform color. Refrigerate to chill.

Note: Chicken wings are considered a delicacy because of their finely textured meat and slippery skin.

variations: For the chicken wings, substitute giblets.

In step 2, substitute the following mixture: ¼ cup soy sauce, ⅓ cup water, 2 tablespoons sugar, 1 tablespoon sherry, 3 tablespoons oyster sauce, 2 slices ginger root, and 2 cloves star anise. Omit the scallions.

MARINATED ABALONE
6 to 8 servings

1 1-pound can abalone	2 tablespoons wine vinegar
3 tablespoons soy sauce	1 teaspoon sugar

few drops of sesame oil

1. Drain canned abalone (reserve liquid for soup). Slice thin or cut in strips.
2. Combine soy sauce, wine vinegar, sugar and sesame oil. Mix well, then pour over abalone and toss.
3. Refrigerate, covered, 1 hour.

variations: Cut abalone in ¾-inch cubes. Marinate 15 minutes in a mixture of ¼ cup of its own liquid, 2 teaspoons soy sauce and 1 teaspoon peanut oil. Sprinkle lightly with pepper and serve on toothpicks.

Use half a can of abalone and add 1 cup celery hearts or tender stalks, slivered. In step 2, make the dressing with 1 tablespoon soy sauce, 1 teaspoon sugar, ½ teaspoon salt and a few drops of sesame oil. Toss, then refrigerate only 30 minutes.

Use half a can of abalone and add 2 cucumbers, peeled and either sliced or cut in strips. In step 2, make the dressing with 1 tablespoon soy sauce and 1 teaspoon sesame oil. Toss, then refrigerate only 30 minutes.

CRABMEAT AND CUCUMBERS
4 to 6 servings

1 cup crabmeat	1 tablespoon soy sauce
2 cucumbers	1½ tablespoons vinegar
1 slice fresh ginger root	1 teaspoon sugar

few drops of sesame oil

1. Pick over and flake crabmeat. Peel and shred cucumbers. Place in a bowl.
2. Mince ginger, then mix well with soy sauce, vinegar, sugar and sesame oil. Pour over crabmeat-cucumber mixture and toss.

3. Refrigerate to chill (about 30 minutes).

VARIATION: For the crabmeat, substitute lobster.

SMOKED FISH
4 to 6 servings

1 *fish*	1 *slice fresh ginger root*
1 *teaspoon salt*	1 *scallion stalk*
1 *tablespoon sherry*	3 *tablespoons oil*
1 *tablespoon soy sauce*	3 *tablespoons brown sugar*

1. Have fish cleaned (but not boned) and cut in 6 pieces, each about 3 by 4 inches.

2. Sprinkle with salt, sherry and soy sauce, and let stand 15 minutes. Meanwhile mince ginger root; cut scallion stalk in ½-inch sections.

3. Heat oil. Add ginger and scallion; brown lightly and discard. Add fish and brown lightly, then remove from pan.

4. Line a heavy pan with foil for smoking fish and sprinkle with brown sugar (see page 828). Smoke fish 5 minutes.

5. Turn off heat and slowly open foil wrapping. Let smoke escape gradually. Then turn fish slices over and repeat smoking process. (If sugar is burned, remove it, and add 1 tablespoon fresh brown sugar.) Serve cold.

NOTE: This dish may be made with carp, scup, butterfish or white fish. It will keep, refrigerated, for several days.

VARIATIONS: In step 3, steam the fish 15 minutes instead of browning it.

In step 4, add with the sugar, 2 tablespoons of used black tea leaves.

PSEUDO SMOKED FISH
4 to 6 servings

1 fish

2 or 3 slices fresh ginger root

1 garlic clove

1 scallion stalk

¼ cup soy sauce

2 tablespoons sherry

½ teaspoon powdered anise

½ teaspoon sesame oil

2 teaspoons sugar

½ cup stock

2 teaspoons soy sauce

oil for deep-frying

1. Cut fish against the grain in ¼-inch slices.

2. Slice ginger root; mince garlic; cut scallion in 1-inch sections. Then combine with soy sauce, sherry, powdered anise and sesame oil. Add to fish and toss gently. Let stand 1 to 2 hours, turning occasionally.

3. Drain marinade into a saucepan; dry fish well with paper toweling.

4. Bring marinade to a boil along with sugar, stock and remaining soy sauce. Boil ½ minute (thicken with cornstarch paste); keep warm over very low heat.

5. Heat oil until smoking. Add fish, one or two pieces at a time, and deep-fry until crisp and golden.

6. Drain on paper toweling. Then dip each fish slice very briefly in warm marinade to coat. Arrange on a serving platter. Serve hot or cold.

NOTE: This dish is usually made with carp, sea bass or yellow pike.

DRIED JELLYFISH AND TURNIPS
About 6 servings

½ cup dried jellyfish

2 cups Chinese white turnips

½ teaspoon salt

1 tablespoon soy sauce

1 tablespoon vinegar

2 teaspoons sugar

few drops of sesame oil

Chinese parsley

1. Soak dried jellyfish. Drain and cut in strips about 1½ inches long and as narrow as possible.

2. Peel and shred turnips. Sprinkle with salt. Let stand 1 hour, then drain. Place in a serving bowl with jellyfish.

3. Combine soy sauce, vinegar, sugar and sesame oil. Add to bowl and toss. Serve at once, topped with a sprig or two of Chinese parsley.

VARIATION: At the end of step 2, add 2 tablespoons onion, shredded.

SHRIMP TOAST
6 to 8 servings

½ *pound shrimp*	1 *teaspoon sherry*
5 *water chestnuts*	½ *teaspoon salt*
1 *teaspoon fresh ginger root*	*dash of pepper*
1 *egg*	4 *slices white bread*
1½ *teaspoons cornstarch*	*oil for deep-frying*

1. Shell and devein shrimp; then mince with water chestnuts and ginger root. Beat egg lightly. Mix minced ingredients and egg with cornstarch, sherry, salt and pepper; blend well.

2. Trim off bread crusts. Spread shrimp mixture evenly over bread, then cut each slice in 4 squares or triangles. (To prevent shrimp mixture from sticking to knife during spreading, dip blade first in cold water.)

3. Heat oil to smoking. Place bread, shrimp side down, on a slotted spoon; then gently lower into oil. Reduce heat slightly and deep-fry a few pieces at a time, until bread is golden (about 1½ minutes). Turn each piece over and deep-fry a few seconds more. Drain on paper toweling. Serve hot.

NOTE: This dish, served originally at Chinese banquets, is excellent as an hors d'oeuvre or cocktail-party snack. (For best results, use bread that's at least 2 days old: it will absorb less oil.) Shrimp toast may be prepared in advance and kept warm by being placed, uncovered, on a cookie sheet in a slow (275-degree) oven. It may also be frozen, then reheated *without* thawing in a moderate (350-degree) oven. Leftover shrimp toast may be frozen and reheated in the same manner.

VARIATIONS: For the shrimp, substitute minced crab or lobster.

For the water chestnuts, substitute ¼ cup celery, minced.

In step 1, mince the shrimp with 1 slice ginger root and half an onion. Omit water chestnuts. Season as above, but omit cornstarch. Then fold into mixture 2 egg whites, beaten until fluffy but not stiff.

In step 1, add to shrimp mixture 1 bacon strip, minced; or ½ scallion stalk, minced.

In step 2, cut bread in 1- by 4-inch strips (these are called Shrimp Straws).

After step 2, glaze the shrimp mixture by brushing it with more beaten egg.

After step 2, press into shrimp mixture a bit of minced ham or parsley.

COLD SHRIMP AND CAULIFLOWER
4 to 6 servings

1 *small head cauliflower*	1 *tablespoon soy sauce*
¼ *pound cooked shrimp*	½ *teaspoon sesame oil*

1. Separate cauliflower in small flowerets. Parboil until tender but still crunchy (3 to 4 minutes). Place in a bowl with cooked shrimp (if large, cut shrimp in two).

2. Mix soy sauce and sesame oil. Add to bowl and toss.

3. Refrigerate, covered, only to chill (about 20 minutes).

ASPARAGUS SALAD
About 4 servings

1 *bunch asparagus*	1½ *tablespoons soy sauce*
½ *teaspoon sugar*	*few drops of sesame oil*

1. Using a rolling cut, slice asparagus in 1½-inch sections. Discard tough white ends.

2. Parboil 2 minutes. Then transfer to a bowl.

3. Mix sugar, soy sauce and sesame oil. Add to bowl and toss. Refrigerate, covered, only to chill (about 20 minutes).

VARIATIONS: In step 2, add to parboiled asparagus, ⅔ cup cooked chicken, thinly sliced. Omit sugar from dressing.

In step 3, add 4 to 5 drops hot sauce. (Do not refrigerate.) Serve at once, topped with 1 teaspoon red ginger, minced.

BRAISED BAMBOO SHOOTS
About 4 servings

2 *cups bamboo shoots*	1 *teaspoon sugar*
¼ *cup stock*	1 *teaspoon sherry*
1 *tablespoon soy sauce*	4 *tablespoons oil*

1. Cut bamboo shoots in 1½-inch strips. Combine stock, soy sauce, sugar and sherry in a cup.

2. Heat oil. Add bamboo shoots and stir-fry 2 to 3 minutes.

3. Add stock mixture. Bring to a boil, then simmer, covered, 20 minutes. Let cool.

4. Refrigerate, covered, only to chill (about 20 minutes).

BASIC COLD BEAN CURD
About 6 servings

4 *bean curd cakes*	2 *tablespoons soy sauce*
6 *cups water*	2 *tablespoons peanut oil*
dash of pepper	

1. Cut each cake of bean curd in 4 to 6 slices. Meanwhile bring water to a boil.

2. Carefully place bean curd slices, a few at a time, in a sieve. Plunge into boiling water for 30 seconds; then drain. Arrange on a serving platter and let cool.

3. Mix soy sauce and peanut oil and pour over bean curd. Serve, sprinkled with pepper.

NOTE: Bean curd is already cooked and can be eaten as is. The blanching improves its flavor and texture.

VARIATIONS: For the soy sauce, substitute oyster sauce.

For the peanut oil, substitute ½ teaspoon sesame oil.

After step 2, top bean curd with ¼ cup dried shrimp (soaked) or 2 tablespoons cooked shrimp, chopped coarsely; and 2 tablespoons scallion, minced. Season as in step 3, but omit pepper. Then refrigerate, covered, only to chill (about 20 minutes).

In step 3, use mixture as a dip instead of pouring it directly over bean curd.

In step 3, sprinkle the bean curd with the soy sauce and pepper. Garnish with ½ cup Chinese parsley, chopped, and 2 scallion stalks, shredded. Then heat the oil until smoking and pour over.

SLIVERED BEAN CURD AND SHRIMP
4 to 6 servings

4 *bean curd cakes*	1 *tablespoon vinegar*
¼ *cup dried shrimp*	2 *tablespoons peanut oil*
1 *cucumber*	*few drops of sesame oil*
½ *teaspoon salt*	

1. Press bean curd (see page 821) and sliver. Soak dried shrimp.

2. Peel cucumber and cut in half lengthwise. Scoop out and discard seeds, then sliver. Place in bowl with bean curd and shrimp.

3. Combine vinegar, peanut oil, sesame oil and salt and pour over slivered ingredients. Refrigerate, covered, 30 minutes.

BEAN SPROUT SALAD
4 to 6 servings

1 *pound bean sprouts*	1 *teaspoon sugar*
2 *tablespoons soy sauce*	*few drops of sesame oil*

1. Blanch bean sprouts. Transfer to a bowl.

2. Combine soy sauce, sugar and sesame oil. Pour over bean sprouts and toss gently. Refrigerate, covered, only to chill (about 20 minutes).

VARIATIONS: For the sesame oil, substitute 1½ tablespoons peanut oil.

Add 1 tablespoon vinegar to the dressing.

In step 1, add to the blanched bean sprouts ¼ pound water cress, cut in 1-inch lengths, with tough stems removed.

In step 1, add to the blanched bean sprouts ½ cup chicken or ham, slivered. (When using ham, substitute ½ teaspoon salt for the sugar.)

After step 2, top the bean sprouts with ½ cup chicken or ham, slivered; or ½ cup roast pork, slivered (toss the pork first in 1 tablespoon soy sauce and 1½ teaspoons peanut oil).

Garnish the bean sprouts with any of the following: egg threads, sweet red pepper, slivered; or snow peas, blanched and shredded.

PICKLED CABBAGE
8 to 10 servings

2 *pounds round white cabbage*
2 *tablespoons brown sugar*
2 *tablespoons soy sauce*

3 *tablespoons wine vinegar*
1 *teaspoon salt*
2 *tablespoons oil*

1 *tablespoon oil*

1. Discard tough outer leaves and core of cabbage. Cut in 1-inch cubes.
2. Combine brown sugar, soy sauce, vinegar and salt.
3. Heat oil. Add cabbage and stir-fry until translucent but still crisp (about 3 minutes). Transfer to a bowl.
4. Heat remaining oil. Add brown sugar-soy mixture and cook, stirring, until sugar dissolves. Then pour over cabbage and toss.
5. Transfer to a tightly covered container and refrigerate overnight.

VARIATIONS: For the white cabbage, substitute red cabbage. For the wine vinegar, substitute cider vinegar.

In step 2, add ½ teaspoon hot pepper flakes.

PICKLED CHINESE LETTUCE
About 8 servings

1 *head Chinese lettuce*
2 *tablespoons oil*
1 *garlic clove*

1 *tablespoon soy sauce*
1 *tablespoon vinegar*
few drops of sesame oil

1. Separate lettuce leaves and cut in 2-inch sections.
2. Heat oil. Add lettuce and stir-fry to soften slightly (2 to 3 minutes). Transfer to a bowl.
3. Mince garlic and combine with soy sauce, vinegar and sesame oil. Add to lettuce and toss. Serve warm or chilled.

NOTE: This will keep several days, if refrigerated and tossed once a day to moisten.

PICKLED CHINESE CABBAGE
4 to 6 servings

1 pound Chinese cabbage	2 tablespoons salt
1½ cups water	1 teaspoon Szechwan peppercorns
1 teaspoon sherry	

1. Cut cabbage stems in ½- by 2-inch strips. (Save the green leaves for soups or stir-fried dishes.) Let dry out several hours or overnight; then place in a large jar.

2. Bring water almost to a boil, then remove from heat. Stir in salt to dissolve; add Szechwan peppercorns and sherry. Let cool; then pour over cabbage.

3. Cover and refrigerate 3 days. Before serving, drain cabbage well and blot with paper toweling.

NOTE: To use marinade a second time, reheat and stir in another teaspoon of salt.

VARIATIONS: For the Chinese cabbage, substitute string beans; or celery or carrots, cut in strips about 2 inches long.

In step 1, add 1 or 2 whole dried red peppers to the jar.

PICKLED MUSTARD CABBAGE
6 to 8 servings

1½ pounds mustard cabbage	¼ cup cider vinegar
¼ to ½ cup light brown sugar	1 teaspoon salt
½ cup water	1 teaspoon sherry

1. Separate mustard cabbage leaves and cut across the grain in ½-inch sections.

2. Place sugar, water and vinegar in a deep pan. Bring to a boil over high heat, stirring until sugar dissolves.

3. Add cabbage. Bring to a boil again, stirring gently. Remove from stove and stir in salt and sherry.

4. Let cool. Then transfer to a tightly covered container and refrigerate overnight.

SWEET-AND-PUNGENT LETTUCE ROLLS
4 to 6 servings

1 pound Chinese lettuce	1 tablespoon soy sauce
2 tablespoons sugar	1 teaspoon salt
2 tablespoons vinegar	few drops of Tabasco Sauce
1 tablespoon oil	

1. Separate lettuce leaves. Parboil to soften slightly (2 to 3 minutes).

2. Roll each leaf up tightly; then cut in 1-inch sections. (If leaves are wide and unwieldy, cut in half lengthwise first.) Place in a shallow bowl.

3. Combine sugar, vinegar, soy sauce, salt and Tabasco Sauce. Heat oil. Add sugar-vinegar mixture, stirring quickly to dissolve sugar. Pour over lettuce at once.

4. Let stand 30 minutes at room temperature. Then refrigerate, covered, overnight.

VARIATION: For the Chinese lettuce, substitute round white cabbage.

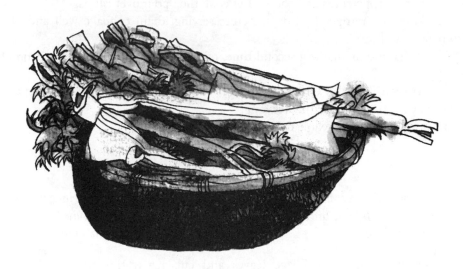

PICKLED CELERY
About 6 servings

6 *celery stalks*	½ *teaspoon salt*
1 *tablespoon soy sauce*	½ *teaspoon sugar*
1 *tablespoon vinegar*	*few drops of sesame oil*

1. Remove leaves, tough ends and stringy portions of celery stalks; then cut in 1-inch sections. (If stalks are wide, cut lengthwise in half first.) Blanch to soften slightly. Place in a bowl.

2. Combine soy sauce, vinegar, salt, sugar and sesame oil. Add to celery and toss.

3. Refrigerate, covered, only to chill (about 20 minutes).

NOTE: If the celery is young and tender, blanching isn't necessary.

VARIATIONS: Before step 2, add any of the following to the celery:

ABALONE: ½ cup canned, either slivered or cut in strips. Omit the vinegar; double the soy sauce.

CHICKEN: 1 cup cooked, either slivered or cut in strips. Omit the vinegar.

SHRIMP: ¼ cup, cooked and minced. Omit the sugar.

WALNUTS: ½ cup, shelled and blanched.

CELERY AND CARROT SALAD
About 6 servings

4 *celery stalks*	2 *teaspoons salt*
2 *carrots*	4 to 6 *cups ice water*
2 *slices fresh ginger root*	2 *tablespoons soy sauce*

½ teaspoon sesame oil

1. Shred celery stalks. Peel and shred carrots. Shred ginger root.

2. Dissolve salt in ice water and add vegetables. Let stand 30 to 40 minutes, then drain.

3. Transfer vegetables to a serving bowl. Add soy sauce and toss. Sprinkle with sesame oil and serve at once.

NOTE: This may be prepared in advance through step 2, then refrigerated. Add the dressing just before serving.

SMASHED CUCUMBERS
Allow 1 cucumber for 3 or 4 servings

1. Cut unpeeled cucumbers in ¼-inch slices. (If cucumbers are large, cut in half lengthwise, then slice.) Crush, by pounding decisively once or twice, with the side of a cleaver or the bottom of a glass. (Leave the cucumber slices intact.)

2. Add any of the dressings below and toss.

3. Refrigerate, covered, only to chill (about 20 minutes).

DRESSINGS:

1 slice ginger root, minced, placed in a saucepan with 2 tablespoons sugar and 4 tablespoons vinegar, then brought to a boil, stirring.

2 scallions, minced and marinated 10 minutes in half a cup of vinegar. (Just before serving, sprinkle cucumbers with salt and pepper to taste.)

1 garlic clove, minced, combined with 2 tablespoons vinegar and ½ teaspoon salt. (Just before serving, sprinkle cucumbers with a few drops of sesame oil.)

VARIATION: Instead of crushing the cucumbers, peel and either slice very thin or sliver.

SHREDDED CUCUMBERS
About 6 servings

2 *cucumbers*	1 *tablespoon light soy sauce*
salt	1 *tablespoon peanut oil*
½ *garlic clove*	½ *teaspoon sugar*

½ *teaspoon vinegar*

1. Peel and shred cucumbers. Sprinkle well with salt. Let stand 1 to 2 hours, then drain.

2. Mince garlic, then combine with soy sauce, peanut oil, sugar and vinegar, blending well. Add to cucumbers and toss. Serve at once.

VARIATION: For the garlic, substitute ¼ teaspoon cayenne pepper.

EGGPLANT SALAD
About 6 servings

1 *eggplant*	½ *teaspoon salt*
2 *tablespoons vinegar*	*dash of pepper*
1 *tablespoon peanut oil*	1 *garlic clove*

lettuce

1. Cut eggplant lengthwise in half if large. Leave whole if small. Place in a shallow heatproof dish (cut-side down if halved) and steam on a rack until soft (about 30 minutes). See pages 831 and 33.

2. Let cool slightly. Remove stem end and peel. Tear lengthwise in strips (this is easier than cutting); then chop fine.

3. Transfer eggplant to a bowl. Add vinegar, oil, salt and pepper, blending well.

4. Cut garlic clove in half. Rub inside of a bowl or decorative mold with cut surface of garlic; then place garlic at bottom of bowl. Pack in eggplant mixture and refrigerate overnight.

5. Arrange lettuce leaves on a serving platter. Invert eggplant onto lettuce. Remove garlic and serve.

VARIATIONS: For a coarser-textured dish, tear the eggplant as in step 2, but do not chop.

In step 3, substitute the following dressing: 1 slice ginger root, minced; 1 tablespoon sugar, 1 teaspoon salt and a few drops of sesame oil. Refrigerate, covered, only 1 to 2 hours.

SWEET-AND-PUNGENT LOTUS ROOT
About 6 servings

1 *pound lotus root*	*few drops of Tabasco Sauce*
4 *cups ice water*	1 *tablespoon sugar*
4 *cups water*	2 *tablespoons vinegar*
2 *tablespoons peanut oil*	2 *tablespoons soy sauce*

few drops of sesame oil

1. Peel lotus root. Cut lengthwise in half; then slice very thin. Soak 10 minutes in ice water and drain.

2. Meanwhile bring remaining water to a boil; then pour over lotus root and let stand 2 minutes. Drain. Cool under cold running water and drain again.

3. Heat oil. Add Tabasco Sauce and stir in quickly. Pour into a cup. Add sugar, vinegar, soy sauce and sesame oil, blending well.

4. Place lotus root in a bowl, pour dressing over and toss. Refrigerate, covered, only to chill (about 20 minutes).

BRAISED MUSHROOMS
About 8 servings

20 to 24 *dried black mushrooms*	2 *tablespoons soy sauce*
1 *slice fresh ginger root*	1 *teaspoon sugar*
3 to 4 *tablespoons oil*	½ *teaspoon salt*
1 *cup stock*	*few drops of sesame oil*

1. Soak dried mushrooms. Then squeeze dry and cut off stem ends. Mince ginger root.

2. Heat oil in a heavy pan. Stir-fry ginger a few times. Add mushrooms and stir-fry gently to coat with oil.

3. Add stock, soy sauce and sugar. Bring to a boil, stirring, then simmer, covered, until mushrooms absorb most of the liquid (about 1 hour).

4. Sprinkle with salt and sesame oil. Serve hot or cold (whole, sliced, or in bite-size pieces).

VARIATIONS: For the soy sauce, substitute sherry.

In step 2, brown a crushed garlic clove and remove before adding the ginger and mushrooms.

In step 3, add 1 clove star anise.

OYSTER SAUCE MUSHROOMS
About 8 servings

20 to 24 *dried black mushrooms*	1 *cup mushroom-soaking liquid*
1½ *tablespoons cornstarch*	¾ *cup beef stock*
¼ *cup beef stock*	2 *tablespoons oyster sauce*
	1 *teaspoon sherry*

1. Soak dried mushrooms. Squeeze dry, reserving soaking liquid; cut off stem ends.

2. Blend cornstarch and cold beef stock to a paste.

3. In a saucepan, combine mushroom-soaking liquid and mushrooms with remaining stock. Bring to a boil, then simmer, covered, 20 minutes.

4. Remove mushrooms with a slotted spoon and transfer to a deep serving dish. Arrange caps decoratively in a circular pattern; keep warm.

5. Add oyster sauce and sherry to liquids in pan and heat through, stirring. Then stir in cornstarch paste to thicken. Pour sauce over mushrooms and serve.

MARINATED MUSHROOMS I
4 to 6 servings

½ *pound fresh white mushrooms*	1 *tablespoon sherry*
3 to 4 *cups water*	⅛ *teaspoon salt*
2 *tablespoons soy sauce*	*few drops of Tabasco Sauce*
	few drops of sesame oil

1. Wipe fresh mushrooms with a damp cloth. (Cut off and discard stem ends.) Place in a colander.

2. Meanwhile bring water to a boil; pour over mushrooms to blanch. Drain well and dry gently with paper toweling. Transfer mushrooms to a bowl.

3. Combine soy sauce, sherry, salt, Tabasco Sauce and sesame oil, blending well. Add to mushrooms and toss. Refrigerate, covered, only to chill (about 20 minutes).

MARINATED MUSHROOMS II
8 to 10 servings

1 *pound fresh mushrooms*	2 *tablespoons soy sauce*
½ *cup onions*	3 *tablespoons sherry*
1 *tablespoon sugar*	4 *tablespoons vinegar*

½ teaspoon salt

1. Wipe fresh mushrooms with a damp cloth. (Cut off and discard stem ends.) Place in a bowl.

2. Mince onions. Combine in a saucepan with sugar, soy sauce, sherry, vinegar and salt. Bring to a boil, stirring. Then pour over mushrooms and toss gently.

3. Refrigerate, covered, 24 hours. Drain and serve.

STUFFED MUSHROOMS
About 10 servings

1. Soak 20 dried mushrooms. Squeeze dry. (Reserve soaking liquid for soups or sauces.) Cut off stem ends and discard.

2. Prepare any of the stuffing mixtures below.

3. Sprinkle a pinch of cornstarch into each mushroom cap. Form stuffing mixture into 20 small balls. Place one in each cap, then flatten.

4. Cook stuffed mushrooms by any of the methods indicated below. Arrange decoratively on a platter. (You may, if you wish, thicken liquids with a cornstarch paste and pour over.) Serve garnished with minced Chinese parsley.

STUFFING MIXTURES

PORK: Mince or grind together ½ pound lean pork, ½ scallion stalk and 1 slice fresh ginger root. Blend well with 1 tablespoon sherry, 1 tablespoon soy sauce, 1 teaspoon sugar, 1 teaspoon cornstarch and 1 teaspoon peanut oil. (If mixture seems too dry, add 1 tablespoon mushroom-soaking liquid.)

HAM: See Pork. Substitute ham.

SHRIMP: Mince together ½ pound shrimp, shelled and deveined; ½ cup onion; and 2 slices fresh ginger root. Combine with 1 teaspoon sugar, 1 teaspoon soy sauce and ½ teaspoon salt.

PORK AND SHRIMP: Mince or grind together ¼ pound lean pork; ¼ pound shrimp, shelled and deveined; and 1 scallion stalk. Blend well with 1 tablespoon soy sauce, 1 teaspoon cornstarch, 1 teaspoon peanut oil, and ½ teaspoon salt. (You may also, if you wish, fold in 1 egg white, beaten until fluffy but not stiff.)

PORK AND CRABMEAT: See Pork and Shrimp. Substitute crabmeat, picked over and flaked, for the shrimp.

FISH: See Pork and Shrimp. Substitute ¾ pound minced raw fish for the pork and shrimp. (Use sole, haddock, flounder or pike.)

CHICKEN AND SHRIMP: Mince or grind together ¼ pound chicken breast, skinned and boned; ¼ pound shrimp, shelled and deveined; and 2 tablespoons bamboo shoots. Blend well with 1 tablespoon sherry and ½ teaspoon salt.

WATER CHESTNUTS: Mince 6 water chestnuts and 1 to 2 cups Chinese parsley. Combine with 1 tablespoon fermented black beans (soaked), mashed.

COOKING METHODS FOR STUFFED MUSHROOMS

TO BRAISE: Heat 3 tablespoons oil. Add mushrooms, stuffing side down and brown lightly. Add 1 cup stock or mushroom-soaking liquid, ½ teaspoon salt and a dash of pepper, and simmer, covered, 10 minutes. Stir in 1½ tablespoons oyster sauce and a pinch of sugar; cook 5 minutes over high heat, basting constantly.

TO SIMMER: Heat 2 tablespoons oil. Add ½ teaspoon salt, then mushrooms, stuffing side up. Add ½ cup stock and 2 tablespoons soy sauce and simmer, covered, 8 to 10 minutes (for fish, shrimp and vegetable mixtures), or 20 to 30 minutes (for pork mixtures).

TO STEAM: Place mushrooms stuffing-side up in a shallow heatproof dish. Steam on a rack 20 minutes (for fish and vegetable mixtures); or 30 minutes (for pork mixtures). (See pages 831 and 33.) You may also glaze the stuffing with well beaten egg brushed on 5 minutes before the end of cooking.

TO STEAM AND POACH: Steam mushrooms, as above, for 15 minutes. Transfer to a pan, stuffing side up. Combine mushroom-soaking liquid with enough stock to make 2 cups; add to pan with ½ teaspoon salt. Bring to a boil; then simmer, covered, 5 minutes (for fish and vegetable mixtures), or 10 to 15 minutes (for pork mixtures).

NOTE: Serve the pork-stuffed mushrooms with hot mustard and soy sauce dips. Sprinkle the fish-stuffed mushrooms with a little heated peanut oil mixed with soy sauce.

SMASHED RADISHES
About 6 servings

20 radishes	2 tablespoons vinegar
¼ teaspoon salt	1 teaspoon sugar
1 tablespoon soy sauce	½ teaspoon salt

1 teaspoon peanut oil

1. Wash and trim radishes. Lay each on its side, then crush by pounding decisively once or twice with the side of a cleaver or the bottom of a glass. (The radishes should split open, but not break in two.)

2. Sprinkle with salt and let stand 5 to 10 minutes; then drain. Transfer to a bowl.

3. Combine soy sauce, vinegar, sugar and remaining salt. Add to radishes and toss gently. Refrigerate, covered, only to chill (about 20 minutes). Sprinkle with peanut oil just before serving.

NOTE: Instead of crushing the radishes, you may make a crisscross cut in the top of each, to let the seasonings penetrate.

VARIATIONS: For the peanut oil, substitute a few drops of sesame oil.

For the white vinegar, substitute cider vinegar.

For the white sugar, substitute light brown sugar.

At the end of step 1, add 1 small cucumber, unpeeled, cut lengthwise in thirds, then crosswise in 1-inch sections, and crushed gently, like the radishes.

At the end of step 2, add 1 green pepper, slivered.

In step 3, add 1 garlic clove, minced, to the dressing.

SPINACH SALAD WITH SHRIMP
About 6 servings

10 *dried shrimp*	½ *cup shrimp liquid*
1 *cup water*	2 *tablespoons soy sauce*
1 *pound spinach*	1 *tablespoon peanut oil*
4 *cups water*	½ *teaspoon salt*

few drops of sesame oil

1. Place dried shrimp and cold water in a small pan. Cover and bring quickly to a boil. Turn off the heat and let stand, still covered, 20 minutes.

2. Remove tough stems from spinach. Meanwhile bring remaining water to a boil. Pour over spinach, then drain at once. Cool under cold running water and drain again. Shake leaves dry, then chop coarsely. Place in a bowl.

3. Remove shrimp from pan and chop coarsely. Add to spinach.

4. Combine shrimp liquid with soy sauce, peanut oil, salt and sesame oil, blending well. Add to spinach and shrimp and toss. Serve at once.

VARIATION: For the shrimp and its dressing, substitute a hot mustard sauce, made by blending ½ tablespoon powdered mustard and 1 tablespoon cold water to a paste, then stirring in ¼ teaspoon vinegar, a pinch of salt and another 1½ tablespoons water. Add this dressing to the spinach and toss. Then sprinkle with ½ teaspoon salt and toss again. (For a milder sauce, use less mustard.)

PICKLED TURNIPS
About 6 servings

1 *Chinese white turnip*	½ *teaspoon salt*
1 *cup vinegar*	*dash of pepper*
2 *tablespoons sugar*	¼ *teaspoon paprika*

1. Peel Chinese white turnip. Cut lengthwise in half, then in ¼-inch slices. Place in a bowl.

2. Bring vinegar to a boil and stir in sugar to dissolve. Pour over turnip. Sprinkle with salt and pepper and refrigerate, covered, overnight.

3. Drain, and sprinkle with paprika before serving.

VARIATIONS: For the Chinese turnip, substitute regular turnips. Peel and slice thin. Then sprinkle with salt, let stand 1 hour and drain. Heat the vinegar and sugar, as in step 2, but add the turnips to the pan and simmer, covered, 2 minutes. Remove from heat and let cool in the pan. Then refrigerate, covered, overnight.

For the turnip, substitute the following vegetables in any combination: cauliflower (parboiled) or carrots, cucumbers, green peppers, chili peppers, round cabbage. Slice or dice the vegetables. Increase the amount of dressing as you increase the vegetables.

CHINESE PICKLES
About 10 servings

2 *cups round cabbage*	4 *cups water*
1½ *cups Chinese white turnip*	2 *slices fresh ginger root*
1 *cup carrots*	2 *or 3 dried red peppers*
1½ *cups cucumber*	8 *black peppercorns*
1 *cup celery*	1 *teaspoon sherry*
4 *tablespoons salt*	

1. Wash and core cabbage; cut in 2-inch cubes. Peel turnip and carrots; cut lengthwise in quarters, then crosswise in 2-inch sections. Peel cucumbers; cut in 2-inch slices. Cut celery stalks in 2-inch sections.

2. Wipe all vegetables with cheesecloth; then spread out to dry for four hours. Transfer vegetables to a crock or jar.

3. Bring water to a boil. Slice ginger root and add. Add dried red peppers, peppercorns, sherry and salt. Let simmer 1 minute; then remove from heat and let cool.

4. Pour over vegetables and cover tightly. Let stand (unrefrigerated) 3 to 4 days in cool weather, only 2 days in summer.

NOTE: The marinade can be used again to pickle other vegetables if ¼ cup sherry, 2 teaspoons brown sugar and ½ teaspoon salt are added.

STIR-FRIED MIXED VEGETABLES
8 to 10 servings

1 *Chinese white turnip*	4 *tablespoons oil*
2 *carrots*	1 *teaspoon salt*
4 *celery stalks*	1 *tablespoon vinegar*
1 *leek*	*few drops of sesame oil*

1. Peel Chinese white turnip and carrots and cut in thin strips. Cut celery and leek in similar strips.

2. Heat oil. Add vegetables and stir-fry 3 minutes over medium heat.

3. Add salt and vinegar and stir-fry 3 minutes more.

4. Transfer vegetables to a bowl and let cool. Refrigerate, covered, 30 minutes. Serve, sprinkled with sesame oil.

❊ *Pork* ❊

POR K, the most favored and prime meat of the Chinese, is prepared with remarkable versatility. It is stir-fried, deep fried, steamed, braised, red-simmered, white-cooked, roasted or dry-fried. It can also be cooked by a combination of these methods.

Cuts of pork used include butt, chops, fresh ham, leg, loin, shoulder, tenderloin and spareribs. Also favored is fresh bacon or belly pork, a cut with four or five layers of alternating lean and fat tissue, ending with a generous layer of lean meat. The Chinese call this Five-Flower Pork and simmer it for hours until succulent. Variety cuts include pork kidneys and liver; but just about every part of the animal is used, including the tail for soup.

COOKING TECHNIQUES AND SUITABLE CUTS OF PORK

STIR-FRYING (sliced thin, occasionally minced): butt, chops, fresh ham, shoulder and tenderloin.

DEEP-FRYING (cubed): butt, chops, fresh ham, shoulder and tenderloin.

BRAISING (whole or in chunks, with some fat): butt, chops, fresh ham, loin and shoulder.

RED-SIMMERING (whole or in chunks): butt, chops, fresh bacon, fresh ham, leg, loin and shoulder.

WHITE-COOKING (whole or in chunks): butt, chops, fresh ham, leg, loin and shoulder.

STEAMING (cubed, sliced or minced): butt, chops, fresh bacon, ham, leg, shoulder and tenderloin.

ROASTING (whole, boned): butt, fresh ham, leg, loin and shoulder.

BARBECUING: eye of butt, tenderloin (in strips); chops (¾-inch thick).

NOTE: Regardless of cut, pork should be deep pink—not too red, not too pale—with very white fat. The meat should be firm to the touch. (In larger cuts, particularly, it should be resilient and spring back when poked.) The outer skin of pork shoulder, butt and fresh ham should be smooth, clear and firm.

Tips on Selecting Pork: A good all-purpose cut of pork is shoulder or Boston butt, weighing about four pounds. The meat should be boned (with the bone reserved for stock), trimmed of all gristle and some of the fat, cut into several large pieces, each wrapped separately and then frozen. Some of the pieces will be suitable for stir-frying, others good for braising, porkballs, etc.

Porkballs should be minced with a small amount of fat, but never with skin or tendon: the fat holds the meat together, makes for a smooth texture. (If the meat is too lean, the porkballs will be dry.) The setting for machine-ground pork should be at medium grind.

Tips on Cooking Pork: Braised or red- or white-simmered pork should always be cooked in a heavy pot so that the gravy will not dry out. Salted and dried seafood, or fresh vegetables, may be added near the end of cooking. Sugar should not be added until the meat is nearly done (the gravy will become sticky and dry and the meat may burn).

Testing for Doneness: Pork is done when its color is no longer pink and when its meat is tender enough to be pierced easily by a fork or chopstick. Check for doneness by cutting into meat. Cook longer whenever necessary.

BASIC STIR-FRIED PORK I
About 4 servings

½ *pound lean pork*
1 *tablespoon cornstarch*
1 *tablespoon soy sauce*
1 *pound vegetables*
1 *or 2 scallion stalks*
1 *garlic clove*
1 *or 2 slices fresh ginger root*

¼ *cup stock*
1 *tablespoon sherry*
¼ *teaspoon salt*
2 *tablespoons soy sauce*
1½ *tablespoons oil*
¼ *teaspoon salt*
1½ *tablespoons oil*

1. Slice pork thin against the grain. Combine cornstarch and soy sauce, then add to pork and toss to coat. Let stand 15 minutes, turning occasionally.

2. Slice vegetables. Cut scallions in ½-inch sections. Crush garlic and mince ginger root. Combine stock, sherry, salt and remaining soy sauce.

3. Heat oil. Add remaining salt, then garlic and brown lightly. Add pork and stir-fry until it begins to brown (about 3 minutes). Remove from pan.

4. Heat remaining oil. Add ginger root and stir-fry a few times. Add vegetables; stir-fry to coat with oil (about 1 minute).

5. Stir in stock mixture and heat quickly. Cook, covered, over medium heat until nearly done.

6. Return pork and stir-fry to reheat and blend flavors (about 1 minute). Serve at once.

NOTE: Any vegetable can be used. (See page 583 for details on cooking time.) For suggested combinations, see page 133.

VARIATIONS: In step 1, add to the cornstarch mixture ½ teaspoon sugar and 1 tablespoon sherry.

In step 1, toss the pork instead in a mixture of 1½ teaspoons cornstarch and 1 egg, beaten; or in a mixture of 1½ tablespoons soy sauce, 1 tablespoon sherry, ½ teaspoon sugar and ¼ teaspoon salt.

In step 3, stir-fry the pork only until it loses its pinkness. Next add the vegetables and stir-fry a few times. Then add ½ cup stock and cook, covered, 2 minutes. At the end, stir in the following cornstarch mixture to thicken: 2 teaspoons cornstarch, 2 teaspoons cold water, 1 teaspoon dark soy sauce and ¼ teaspoon sugar.

BASIC STIR-FRIED PORK II
About 4 servings

½ pound lean pork	½ teaspoon salt
1 pound vegetables	1 tablespoon sherry
1 or 2 scallion stalks	½ cup stock
1 garlic clove	2 teaspoons soy sauce
1 or 2 slices fresh ginger root	2 teaspoons cornstarch
2 tablespoons oil	2 tablespoons water
2 tablespoons oil	2 teaspoons soy sauce

1. Slice pork thin against the grain. Slice vegetables. Cut scallion in ½-inch sections. Crush garlic and shred ginger root.

2. Heat oil. Add vegetables and stir-fry to soften slightly; then remove from pan.

3. Heat remaining oil. Add salt, then scallion, garlic and ginger root and brown lightly. Add pork and stir-fry until it begins to brown (about 3 minutes). Sprinkle with sherry; stir-fry ½ minute more.

4. Return vegetables. Add stock and soy sauce and simmer, covered, until done. Meanwhile blend cornstarch, cold water and remaining soy sauce to a paste. Then stir in to thicken and serve at once.

SUGGESTED VEGETABLE COMBINATIONS FOR
BASIC STIR-FRIED PORK I AND II

2 cups cabbage
3 tomatoes

1 cup peas
6 dried black mushrooms
   (soaked)

2 cups string beans
1 or 2 tomatoes
1 onion

1 head cauliflower
1 tablespoon fermented black
   beans (soaked)

1 head cauliflower
1½ tablespoons preserved sweet
   pickle
1½ tablespoons preserved sweet
   ginger

2 cups celery
1 cup carrots
½ cup peas
¼ cup almonds

½ cup water chestnuts
½ cup onions
4 to 6 dried black mushrooms
   (soaked)
1 green pepper
1 cup bean sprouts

2 cups celery
1 cup fresh mushrooms
½ cup bamboo shoots
¼ cup water chestnuts
¼ cup peas

2 green peppers
¼ pound fresh mushrooms
1 tomato
½ cup onion

2 green peppers
2 tomatoes
1 onion
1 tablespoon fermented black
   beans (soaked)

2 cups Chinese lettuce
2 cups onion
2 green peppers

½ cup lily buds (soaked)
2 tablespoons cloud ear mushrooms (soaked)

2 cups lotus root
1 cup Chinese cabbage
1 cup celery
½ cup bamboo shoots
1 onion

STIR-FRIED PORK AND BEAN CURD
About 4 servings

½ pound lean pork
4 bean curd cakes
1 large onion
1 garlic clove
1 teaspoon sugar
2 teaspoons soy sauce

1 tablespoon sherry
2 teaspoons cornstarch
2 tablespoons water
2 tablespoons oil
½ teaspoon salt
½ cup stock

1. Cut pork and bean curd cakes in ½-inch cubes. Slice onion thin; crush garlic.

2. In one cup combine sugar, soy sauce and sherry. In another, blend cornstarch and cold water to a paste.

3. Heat oil. Add salt, then garlic and brown lightly. Add pork and stir-fry until it loses its pinkness (about 2 to 3 minutes). Stir in sugar-soy mixture.

4. Add onion and stir-fry a few times. Gently stir in bean curd to heat through (or cook, tilting pan, to avoid breaking bean curd).

5. Add stock and heat quickly. Cook, covered, over medium heat until done (about 2 to 3 minutes).

6. Transfer pork and bean curd cubes to a warm serving platter. Reheat liquids in pan and stir in cornstarch paste to thicken. Pour sauce over pork and bean curd and serve at once.

VARIATIONS: Slice the pork thin against the grain. Cut each bean curd cake, first in half, then in thirds.

For the onion, substitute ¼ cup scallions, cut in ½-inch sections. Omit the sugar-soy mixture. In step 4, add with bean curd and scallions, 1 tablespoon brown bean sauce, mashed.

STIR-FRIED PORK WITH DEEP-FRIED BEAN CURD
About 4 servings

4 to 6 *dried black mushrooms*	4 *pieces deep-fried bean curd*
½ *pound lean pork*	1 *garlic clove*
1 *teaspoon cornstarch*	2 *teaspoons cornstarch*
1 *teaspoon soy sauce*	2 *teaspoons water*
2 *teaspoons sherry*	1 *tablespoon oyster sauce*
¼ *teaspoon sugar*	*pinch sugar*
¼ *teaspoon oil*	*dash pepper*
½ *cup bamboo shoots*	2 *tablespoons oil*
½ *cup celery*	½ *teaspoon salt*
¼ *cup smoked ham*	¾ *cup stock*

1. Soak dried mushrooms.

2. Shred pork. Combine cornstarch, soy sauce, sherry, sugar and oil, then add to pork and toss to coat.

3. Separately shred bamboo shoots, celery, smoked ham, deep-fried bean curd and soaked mushrooms. Crush garlic.

4. Blend remaining cornstarch and cold water to a paste, then stir in oyster sauce, remaining sugar, and pepper.

5. Heat oil. Add salt, then garlic and brown lightly. Add pork and stir-fry until it loses its pinkness (about 1 to 2 minutes).

6. Add bamboo shoots, celery and mushrooms, and stir-fry 1 minute more.

7. Stir in stock and heat quickly; then cook, covered, 2 minutes over medium heat.

8. Stir in cornstarch mixture to thicken. Then add shredded bean curd, stirring in only to heat through. Serve at once, garnished with shredded ham.

NOTE: The deep-fried bean curd is available already cooked in Chinese food stores or may be prepared at home.

STIR-FRIED PORK WITH PRESSED BEAN CURD
4 to 6 servings

3 *bean curd cakes*	2 *green peppers*
4 to 6 *dried black mushrooms*	2 *red chili peppers*
½ *pound lean pork*	1 *garlic clove*
1 *tablespoon cornstarch*	2 to 3 *tablespoons oil*
1 *tablespoon soy sauce*	½ *teaspoon salt*
1 *tablespoon sherry*	½ *cup stock*
½ *cup bamboo shoots*	¼ *teaspoon sugar*

1. Press bean curd (see page 821). Soak dried mushrooms.

2. Shred pork. Combine cornstarch, soy sauce and sherry; then add to pork and toss to coat. Let stand 15 to 20 minutes, turning occasionally.

3. Shred bamboo shoots, green peppers, red chili peppers, soaked mushrooms and pressed bean curd. Crush garlic.

4. Heat oil. Add salt, then garlic, and brown lightly. Add pork and stir-fry until it loses its pinkness (about 1 to 2 minutes).

5. Add bamboo shoots, green and chili peppers and mushrooms. Stir-fry to coat with oil (about ½ minute).

6. Stir in stock and heat quickly; then cook, covered, over medium heat until nearly done (about 2 to 3 minutes).

7. Add sugar and bean curd. Stir-fry to heat through and blend flavors (about 1 minute more). Serve at once.

STIR-FRIED PORK AND BEAN SPROUTS I
About 4 servings

½ *pound lean pork*	1 *pound bean sprouts*
1 *to* 2 *slices fresh ginger root*	1½ *tablespoons oil*
1 *tablespoon soy sauce*	1½ *tablespoons oil*
1 *tablespoon sherry*	½ *teaspoon salt*
½ *teaspoon sugar*	1 *tablespoon soy sauce*

1. Cut pork in thin strips, or shred. Mince ginger root, then combine with soy sauce, sherry and sugar. Add mixture to pork and toss.

2. Blanch bean sprouts.

3. Heat oil. Add pork and stir-fry until lightly browned (about 2 to 3 minutes). Remove from pan.

4. Heat remaining oil. Add salt, then bean sprouts and stir-fry 1 minute. Sprinkle with remaining soy sauce. Stir-fry about 1 minute more.

5. Return pork and stir-fry to reheat and blend flavors (about 1 minute). Serve at once.

STIR-FRIED PORK AND BEAN SPROUTS II
About 4 servings

½ *pound lean pork*	1 *teaspoon sugar*
1 *pound bean sprouts*	¼ *cup stock*
1 *tablespoon soy sauce*	2 *tablespoons oil*
2 *tablespoons sherry*	½ *teaspoon salt*

1. Cut pork in thin strips or shred. Blanch bean sprouts.

2. Combine soy sauce, sherry, sugar and stock.

3. Heat oil. Add salt, then pork, and stir-fry until pork loses its pinkness (1 to 2 minutes).

4. Quickly stir in and heat soy-sherry mixture. Then add bean sprouts and cook, covered, 2 minutes over medium heat. Serve at once.

VARIATION: At the end of step 3, add 3 dried black mushrooms (soaked), shredded, and ¼ cup onion, minced. Stir-fry until onion is translucent. Then pick up step 4.

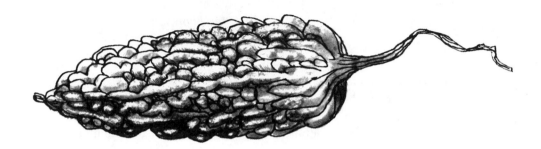

STIR-FRIED PORK AND BITTER MELON
About 4 servings

1 tablespoon fermented black beans	1 pound bitter melon
1 or 2 garlic cloves	2 teaspoons cornstarch
½ pound lean pork	1 teaspoon soy sauce
1 teaspoon cornstarch	½ teaspoon sugar
1 teaspoon soy sauce	2 teaspoons water
2 teaspoons sherry	dash of pepper
¼ teaspoon sugar	2 or 3 tablespoons oil

½ cup stock

1. Soak fermented black beans. Mince garlic, then mash with drained beans.

2. Slice pork thin against the grain. Combine cornstarch, soy sauce, sherry and sugar; then add to pork and toss to coat.

3. Cut bitter melon lengthwise in half (scoop out the seeds), then cut crosswise in $\frac{1}{16}$-inch slices. Parboil 2 to 3 minutes.

4. Blend remaining cornstarch, soy sauce and sugar to a paste with cold water and pepper.

5. Heat oil. Add garlic-black bean mixture and stir-fry ½ minute. Add pork and stir-fry until it loses its pinkness (about 2 minutes).

6. Add bitter melon and stir-fry to coat with oil (about 1 minute).

7. Stir in and heat stock quickly; then cook, covered, 2 minutes over medium heat. Stir in cornstarch mixture to thicken. Serve at once.

STIR-FRIED PORK WITH CHINESE LETTUCE AND PEPPERS
4 to 6 servings

½ *pound lean pork*
2 *cups Chinese lettuce*
2 *green peppers*
1 *cup onions*

1 to 2 *slices fresh ginger root*
1 *tablespoon soy sauce*
1 *teaspoon sugar*
½ *teaspoon salt*

2 or 3 *tablespoons oil*

1. Dice pork, lettuce, green peppers and onions.

2. Mince ginger root, then combine with soy sauce, sugar and salt.

3. Heat oil. Add pork and stir-fry until golden (about 3 to 4 minutes).

4. Add onion and stir-fry ½ minute. Add peppers; stir-fry 1 minute more. Add lettuce; stir-fry another minute.

5. Add ginger-soy mixture and stir-fry to blend flavors (1 to 2 minutes more). Serve at once.

STIR-FRIED PORK AND PRESERVED MUSTARD CABBAGE
About 4 servings

½ *pound lean pork*
1 *teaspoon cornstarch*
1 *teaspoon soy sauce*
2 *teaspoons sherry*
¼ *teaspoon sugar*
¼ *teaspoon peanut oil*
½ *pound preserved mustard cabbage*
1 *wedge fresh ginger root*

1 *teaspoon cornstarch*
1 *tablespoon water*
dash of pepper
1½ *tablespoons oil*
½ *teaspoon salt*
2½ *tablespoons oil*
1 *tablespoon sugar*
½ *teaspoon vinegar*

¼ *cup stock*

1. Slice pork thin against the grain. Combine cornstarch, soy sauce, sherry, sugar and peanut oil; then add to pork and toss to coat.

2. Rinse preserved mustard cabbage and wring dry; cut in ½-inch sections. Crush ginger root.

3. Blend remaining cornstarch, cold water and pepper to a paste.

4. Place preserved cabbage in a dry pan and stir-fry gently over medium heat until dry (3 to 4 minutes). Remove from pan.

5. Heat oil. Add salt, then ginger root and brown lightly. Add pork and stir-fry until it begins to brown (about 3 to 4 minutes). Remove from pan.

6. Heat remaining oil. Return preserved cabbage and stir-fry 2 minutes over high heat to restore crunchiness; then sprinkle with sugar and vinegar.

7. Return pork and stir-fry a few times. Stir in stock and heat quickly. Then stir in cornstarch paste to thicken. Serve at once.

NOTE: The amount of sugar and vinegar can be adjusted according to personal taste.

STIR-FRIED PORK AND CLAMS

4 to 6 servings

18 *small clams*	½ *pound lean pork*
¼ *cup clam broth*	¼ *pound fresh mushrooms*
1 *tablespoon cornstarch*	1 *cup peas*
2 *tablespoons soy sauce*	2 *tablespoons oil or lard*

1. Shell clams, reserving their broth (see page 450). Combine clam broth with cornstarch and soy sauce; then add to clams and toss to coat.

2. Slice pork thin against the grain. Slice mushrooms; parboil peas.

3. Heat oil. Add pork and stir-fry until it loses its pinkness (about 2 minutes).

4. Add mushrooms and peas. Stir-fry until mushrooms soften (about 2 minutes).

5. Add clams; stir-fry to heat through and to thicken sauce (about ½ minute). Serve at once.

STIR-FRIED PORK AND CUCUMBER
About 4 servings

½ pound lean pork	2 tablespoons oil
1 tablespoon soy sauce	¼ teaspoon salt
2 cucumbers	few drops of sesame oil

1. Slice pork thin against the grain. Add soy sauce to pork and toss. Slice cucumbers thin, but do not peel.

2. Heat oil. Add pork and stir-fry until it begins to brown (about 3 minutes).

3. Add cucumbers and salt; stir-fry 1 to 2 minutes. Then cook, covered, over medium heat until done (about 1 to 2 minutes more). Sprinkle with sesame oil and serve at once.

VARIATION: Use 1 cucumber and ½ cup bamboo shoots, sliced thin. Add as in step 3.

STIR-FRIED CURRIED PORK I
About 4 servings

½ pound lean pork	2 tablespoons water
1 onion	½ teaspoon salt
2 to 3 tablespoons curry powder	½ teaspoon sugar
½ cup stock	dash of pepper
2 teaspoons cornstarch	pinch of Five Spices

1. Slice pork thin against the grain; slice onion thin.

2. Stir curry powder and onion in a dry pan over low heat until curry smells pungent (about 2 minutes). Add pork. Stir-fry to coat with curry (2 to 3 minutes).

3. Stir in stock and heat quickly. Cook 5 minutes over medium heat, stirring occasionally.

4. Meanwhile blend cornstarch, cold water, salt, sugar, pepper and Five Spices to a paste. Then stir in to thicken and serve at once.

STIR-FRIED CURRIED PORK II
About 4 servings

½ *pound lean pork*	2 *to* 3 *tablespoons curry powder*
1 *green pepper*	½ *cup stock*
1 *onion*	½ *teaspoon lemon juice*
2 *tablespoons oil*	2 *teaspoons cornstarch*
½ *teaspoon salt*	2 *tablespoons water*

1. Cut pork and green pepper in strips. Slice onion thin.

2. Heat oil. Add salt, then pork, and stir-fry until it loses its pinkness (about 2 minutes).

3. Add pepper and onion; stir-fry to soften (about 2 minutes).

4. Add curry powder; stir-fry 2 to 3 minutes more over low heat.

5. Stir in stock and lemon juice and heat quickly; then cook 5 minutes over medium heat, stirring frequently.

6. Meanwhile blend cornstarch and cold water to a paste; then stir in to thicken. Serve at once.

STIR-FRIED PORK WITH FIVE SPICES
About 4 servings

½ *pound lean pork*	½ *teaspoon salt*
1 *tablespoon cornstarch*	1 *tablespoon sherry*
½ *teaspoon Five Spices*	2 *tablespoons oil*
	½ *cup stock*

1. Slice pork thin against the grain. Combine cornstarch, Five Spices, salt and sherry. Add to pork and toss to coat. Let stand 20 to 30 minutes, turning occasionally.

2. Heat oil. Add pork and stir-fry until it loses its pinkness (about 2 minutes).

3. Stir in stock and heat quickly, then cook, covered, over medium heat (about 2 minutes). Serve at once.

STIR-FRIED PORK AND GINGER ROOT
About 4 servings

½ *pound lean pork*	1 *scallion stalk*
1 *teaspoon cornstarch*	2 *tablespoons oil*
2 *tablespoons soy sauce*	3 *tablespoons water*
¼ *pound fresh ginger root*	1 *teaspoon sugar*

1. Slice pork thin against the grain. Dredge in cornstarch; then add soy sauce and toss.

2. Slice ginger root thin. Cut scallion in ½-inch sections.

3. Heat oil. Add pork and stir-fry until it loses its pinkness (about 2 minutes).

4. Add ginger root and scallion; stir-fry a few times. Then add water and sugar and cook, covered, until done (about 3 to 4 minutes). Serve at once.

STIR-FRIED PORK AND LEEKS
About 4 servings

½ *pound lean pork* ¼ *cup stock*
¼ *cup leeks* 1 *tablespoon soy sauce*
1 *garlic clove* 1 *tablespoon sherry*
2 *tablespoons oil* ½ *teaspoon sugar*
½ *teaspoon salt* *dash of pepper*

few drops of sesame oil

1. Mince pork and leeks. Crush garlic.

2. Heat oil. Add salt, then garlic, and brown lightly. Add pork and leeks. Stir-fry until golden (about 2 minutes).

3. Stir in stock and heat quickly, then cook, covered, 2 to 3 minutes over medium heat.

4. Meanwhile, combine soy sauce, sherry, sugar, pepper and sesame oil; then add and cook, stirring, 2 minutes more. Serve at once.

VARIATION: After step 2, add and stir-fry briefly any of the following: ½ cup water chestnuts, finely diced; 1 cup peas; 1 cup asparagus, broccoli or peppers, cut in small pieces. Pick up steps 3 and 4.

STIR-FRIED PORK WITH LETTUCE
About 8 servings

1 *pound lean pork*	1 *teaspoon soy sauce*
1 *cup water chestnuts*	*dash of pepper*
1 *head lettuce*	½ *to ¾ cup stock*
2 *tablespoons oil*	1 *tablespoon cornstarch*
½ *teaspoon salt*	3 *tablespoons water*

1. Mince pork and water chestnuts. Separate lettuce leaves and crisp in ice water.

2. Heat oil. Add pork and water chestnuts and stir-fry a few times. Then sprinkle with salt, soy sauce and pepper, and stir-fry until pork loses its pinkness.

3. Stir in and heat stock quickly, then cook, covered, 2 to 3 minutes over medium heat.

4. Meanwhile blend cornstarch and cold water to a paste, then stir in to thicken.

5. Pour mixture into a serving bowl; arrange lettuce leaves on a serving dish.

TO EAT: *The diner places about 2 tablespoons of the mixture on a lettuce leaf, folds it over, rolls it up to enclose the filling, then picks it up with his fingers.*

NOTE: This dish, usually served in summer, makes an excellent hors d'oeuvre. For the lettuce, use either Romaine or Boston.

VARIATION: For the pork and water chestnuts, substitute 2 boned squabs, 2 tablespoons pork, 6 dried black mushrooms (soaked), and ½ cup each of bamboo shoots and celery, all minced. In step 2, stir-fry 2 minutes. In step 3, cook, covered, 5 to 7 minutes. Pick up steps 4 and 5.

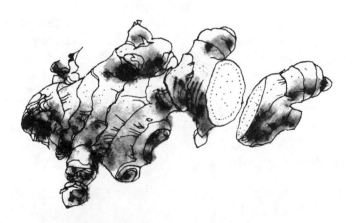

STIR-FRIED PORK AND DRIED OYSTERS WITH LETTUCE
About 8 servings

12 *dried oysters*	1 *head lettuce*
½ *pound lean pork*	2 *tablespoons oil*
½ *cup bamboo shoots*	½ *teaspoon salt*
6 *water chestnuts*	1 *tablespoon soy sauce*
2 *slices fresh ginger root*	1 *tablespoon sherry*

1. Soak dried oysters, then trim, discarding muscle.

2. Separately mince pork, bamboo shoots, water chestnuts, ginger root and soaked oysters. Separate lettuce leaves and crisp in ice water.

3. Heat oil. Add salt, then ginger root; stir-fry a few times. Add pork and stir-fry until it loses its pinkness. Sprinkle with soy sauce and sherry. Stir-fry 1 minute more.

4. Add minced oysters, water chestnuts and bamboo shoots. Stir-fry another 2 minutes. Remove from pan.

5. Serve as in step 5 above, or place lettuce on a serving dish with pork mixture arranged on top.

VARIATIONS: For the bamboo shoots, substitute celery, or string beans, parboiled, then minced.

For the ginger root, substitute ½ garlic clove, minced.

Before stir-frying, toss the pork in a mixture of 1 teaspoon cornstarch, 2 teaspoons sherry, 2 teaspoons soy sauce and ¼ teaspoon sugar. (Omit the soy sauce and sherry in step 3.)

In step 3, omit the soy sauce and sherry. In step 4, stir-fry mixture 1 minute, then stir in and quickly heat ½ cup stock and 2 tablespoons oyster sauce. Cook, covered, 3 minutes over medium heat; then stir in a cornstarch paste to thicken.

In step 5, sprinkle hoisin sauce over pork mixture.

STIR-FRIED PORK AND LILY BUDS
4 to 6 servings

½ *cup lily buds*	1 *tablespoon sherry*
4 *or 5 dried black mushrooms*	2 *teaspoons sugar*
½ *pound lean pork*	½ *teaspoon salt*
2 *tablespoons oil*	

1. Separately soak lily buds and dried mushrooms.

2. Shred pork. Slice soaked mushrooms thin. Combine sherry, sugar and salt.

3. Heat oil. Add pork and stir-fry until it loses its pinkness (about 2 minutes). Then stir in sherry-sugar mixture.

4. Add soaked mushrooms and lily buds and stir-fry 1 minute; then cook, covered, 2 minutes more over medium heat. Serve at once.

STIR-FRIED PORK WITH LILY BUDS AND EGGS
4 to 6 servings

¼ cup lily buds	1 scallion
2 tablespoons cloud ear mushrooms	1 or 2 slices fresh ginger root
½ pound lean pork	2 eggs
1 tablespoon soy sauce	1½ tablespoons oil
1 teaspoon sugar	1½ tablespoons oil

¼ teaspoon salt

1. Separately soak lily buds and cloud ear mushrooms.
2. Shred pork. Combine soy sauce and sugar; add to pork and toss.
3. Shred cloud ear mushrooms. Shred scallion stalk; cut its green leaves in 2-inch sections. Mince ginger root. Beat eggs lightly.
4. Heat oil. Add eggs and scramble quickly; remove while still moist.
5. Heat remaining oil. Add ginger root; stir-fry a few times, then add pork and stir-fry until it loses its pinkness.
6. Add salt, scallion, lily buds and cloud ear mushrooms. Stir-fry 1 minute; then cook, covered, 1 to 2 minutes more over medium heat.
7. Return scrambled eggs to pan and stir in only to reheat. Serve at once.

NOTE: This dish, known as Moo Shoo Pork or Kiangsu Egg Dish, is usually accompanied by thin pancakes called Peking Doilies (see page 783). The diner places some of the mixture on his doily, rolls it up to enclose the filling and picks it up with his fingers.

VARIATIONS: After step 5, add ½ cup bamboo shoots, shredded, and stir-fry ½ minute more.

In step 7, add with the eggs, ½ cup bean sprouts, blanched; stir-fry only to heat through.

Omit the soy sauce and sugar in step 2. In step 7, add with the eggs a mixture of ¼ teaspoon sugar, 2 teaspoons light soy sauce and a dash of pepper.

STIR-FRIED PORK AND LOTUS ROOT
4 to 6 servings

½ pound lean pork	1 tablespoon soy sauce
1 pound fresh lotus root	½ teaspoon salt
2 tablespoons sherry	2 tablespoons oil

½ cup stock

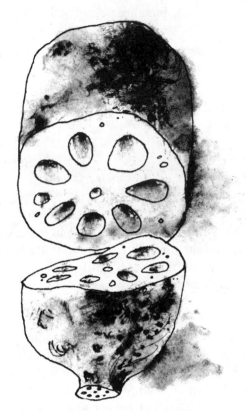

1. Slice pork thin against the grain. Peel lotus root and slice thin. Combine sherry, soy sauce and salt.

2. Heat oil. Add pork and stir-fry until it loses its pinkness (about 2 minutes).

3. Add lotus root and stir-fry 2 minutes more. Then stir in sherry-soy mixture to blend.

4. Stir in stock and heat quickly, then cook, covered, over medium heat until lotus root is done (about 5 minutes). Serve at once.

STIR-FRIED PORK WITH OYSTER SAUCE I
About 6 servings

1 *pound lean pork*	2 *teaspoons water*
1 *teaspoon cornstarch*	2 *tablespoons oyster sauce*
2 *teaspoons sherry*	¼ *teaspoon sugar*
¼ *teaspoon sugar*	*dash of pepper*
¼ *teaspoon oil*	1 *wedge fresh ginger root*
2 *teaspoons cornstarch*	2 *tablespoons oil*

¼ *cup stock*

1. Slice pork thin against the grain. Combine cornstarch, sherry, sugar and oil; then add to pork and toss to coat.

2. Blend remaining cornstarch, cold water, oyster sauce, sugar and pepper to a paste. Crush ginger root.

3. Heat oil. Add ginger root and stir-fry a few times. Add pork and stir-fry until it begins to brown (about 3 minutes).

4. Stir in stock and heat quickly; then cook, covered, 2 minutes over medium heat.

5. Stir in cornstarch-oyster sauce paste to thicken. Serve at once.

VARIATION: Before step 3, heat 2 to 3 tablespoons oil, then add 4 bean curd cakes, cut in 1-inch cubes, and stir-fry gently until lightly browned. Remove from pan. Return bean curd in step 4 after stock is heated.

STIR-FRIED PORK WITH OYSTER SAUCE II
About 6 servings

1 *pound lean pork*	1 *teaspoon soy sauce*
1 *cup scallions*	3 *tablespoons water*
1 *garlic clove*	1½ *tablespoons oil*
1 *tablespoon cornstarch*	½ *teaspoon salt*
2 *tablespoons oyster sauce*	1 *tablespoon sherry*
1 *teaspoon sugar*	1 *teaspoon soy sauce*

½ *cup stock*

1. Sliver pork. Split scallions in half, then cut crosswise in 1-inch sections. Crush garlic.

2. Blend cornstarch, oyster sauce, sugar, soy sauce and cold water to a paste.

3. Heat oil. Add salt, then garlic, and stir-fry a few times to brown lightly. Add pork and stir-fry until it begins to brown (about 2 to 3 minutes).

4. Add sherry and remaining soy sauce and stir-fry 1 minute more. Then stir in stock and heat quickly.

5. Stir in cornstarch-oyster sauce paste to thicken. Serve at once, garnished with scallion sections.

STIR-FRIED PORK WITH PEANUTS
4 to 6 servings

½ *pound lean pork*	1 *garlic clove*
1 *tablespoon cornstarch*	1½ *tablespoons oil*
1 *tablespoon soy sauce*	½ *cup raw peanuts*
1 *tablespoon sherry*	½ *teaspoon salt*
¼ *pound fresh mushrooms*	2 *tablespoons oil*
1 *or 2 celery stalks*	1 *tablespoon oyster sauce*
1 *scallion*	½ *cup stock*

1. Dice pork. Combine cornstarch, soy sauce and sherry; then add to pork and toss to coat.

2. Dice mushrooms and celery. Mince scallion; crush garlic.

3. Heat oil. Sprinkle raw peanuts lightly with salt, then add to pan and toss lightly. When peanuts begin to brown, remove and drain on paper toweling.

4. Heat remaining oil. Add garlic and brown lightly. Add pork and stir-fry until it loses its pinkness (about 2 to 3 minutes).

5. Add mushrooms and celery; stir-fry to coat with oil (about ½ minute). Add oyster sauce and stir-fry to blend in (about 1 minute).

6. Stir in and heat stock quickly. Cook, covered, over medium heat until done (about 4 minutes).

7. Stir in peanuts only to reheat. Serve at once, garnished with minced scallion.

VARIATIONS: For the mushrooms and celery, substitute 2 green peppers, diced, and 2 carrots, diced and parboiled.

Omit the oyster sauce. After step 6, stir into stock 1½ tablespoons brown sugar and dissolve. Pick up step 7, but omit the scallion garnish.

STIR-FRIED PORK AND PEPPERS I
About 4 servings

½ *pound lean pork*	2 *green peppers*
1 *teaspoon cornstarch*	1½ *tablespoons oil*
½ *teaspoon salt*	1½ *tablespoons oil*
½ *egg white*	1 *tablespoon sherry*

1. Slice pork thin against the grain, then cut in rectangles, 1 by 1½ inches. Combine cornstarch, salt and egg white; then add to pork and toss to coat. Seed and dice green peppers.

2. Heat oil. Add pork and stir-fry until it begins to brown, then remove.

3. Heat remaining oil. Add green peppers and stir-fry until they begin to soften (about 2 minutes).

4. Return pork. Sprinkle with sherry and stir-fry until done (about 2 minutes more). Serve at once.

STIR-FRIED PORK AND PEPPERS II
About 4 servings

½ *pound lean pork*	2 *tablespoons oil*
2 *green peppers*	½ *teaspoon salt*
2 *celery stalks*	½ *to ¾ cup stock*
1 *scallion stalk*	2 *teaspoons cornstarch*
1 *garlic clove*	2 *teaspoons soy sauce*
2 *tablespoons water*	

1. Dice pork in ½-inch cubes. Dice green peppers and celery. Cut scallion in ½-inch sections. Crush garlic.

2. Heat oil. Add salt, then garlic and scallion and stir-fry a few times. Add pork and stir-fry until it loses its pinkness.

3. Stir in stock and heat quickly. Cook, covered, 3 to 4 minutes over medium heat.

4. Add green peppers and celery. Cook uncovered 2 to 3 minutes more, stirring frequently.

5. Meanwhile blend cornstarch, soy sauce and cold water to a paste, then stir in to thicken. Serve at once.

STIR-FRIED PORK AND PINEAPPLE
4 to 6 servings

½ pound lean pork

1 green pepper

¼ cup water chestnuts

¼ cup sweet mixed pickles

2 or 3 canned pineapple slices

1 tablespoon cornstarch

2 teaspoons soy sauce

1 or 2 teaspoons sugar

3 tablespoons water

2 to 3 tablespoons oil

½ teaspoon salt

½ cup stock

1. Slice pork thin against the grain. Slice green pepper, water chestnuts and sweet mixed pickles. Cut each pineapple slice in 5 or 6 chunks.

2. Blend cornstarch, soy sauce, sugar and cold water to a paste.

3. Heat oil. Add salt, then pork, and stir-fry until pork begins to brown (about 3 minutes).

4. Add green pepper and stir-fry until it softens (about 2 minutes).

5. Add pineapple chunks, water chestnuts and sweet pickles; stir-fry 1 minute more.

6. Stir in stock and heat quickly. Then stir in cornstarch paste to thicken. Serve at once.

STIR-FRIED PORK AND SHRIMP
6 to 8 servings

3 dried black mushrooms

2 sticks dried bean curd

¼ pound lean pork

¼ pound smoked ham

½ cup bamboo shoots

¼ pound shrimp

2 teaspoons sugar

1 tablespoon hoisin sauce

2 tablespoons soy sauce

½ cup stock

3 tablespoons oil

½ teaspoon salt

¼ cup canned ginkgo nuts

¼ cup raw peanuts

1. Separately soak dried mushrooms and bean curd sticks.

2. Dice pork, ham, bamboo shoots, soaked mushrooms and bean curd. Shell and devein shrimp; dice if large.

3. Combine sugar, hoisin sauce, soy sauce and stock.

4. Heat oil. Add salt, then pork, and stir-fry until it loses its pinkness. Add shrimp; stir-fry ½ minute more.

5. Add ginkgo nuts, peanuts, ham, bamboo shoots, mushrooms and bean curd. Stir-fry 1 to 2 minutes more.

6. Stir in stock mixture and heat quickly. Cook, covered, 3 to 4 minutes over medium heat, stirring several times. Serve at once.

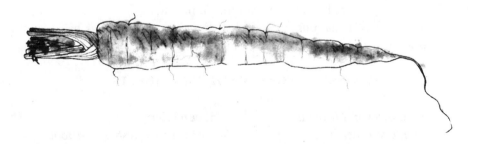

STIR-FRIED PORK WITH SPINACH AND CARROTS
About 4 servings

½ pound lean pork
2 carrots
½ pound spinach
1 scallion stalk

2 teaspoons cornstarch
2 tablespoons water
3 tablespoons oil
1 tablespoon soy sauce

½ teaspoon salt

1. Slice pork thin against the grain, then cut in strips. Peel carrots and cut in strips, then parboil. Remove tough spinach stems; cut leaves in half. Mince scallion. Blend cornstarch and cold water to a paste.

2. Heat oil. Add scallion and stir-fry until translucent. Add pork and stir-fry until it begins to brown.

3. Add carrots and soy sauce. Stir-fry 1 minute.

4. Add salt, then spinach and stir-fry until it begins to soften (about ½ minute). Then stir in cornstarch paste to thicken. Serve at once.

STIR-FRIED PORK AND STRING BEANS
About 4 servings

½ pound lean pork
1 pound string beans
2 slices fresh ginger root
1 tablespoon cornstarch
3 tablespoons water

2 tablespoons oil
½ teaspoon salt
½ cup stock
2 eggs
2 tablespoons water

1. Mince or grind pork. Dice string beans, then parboil. Mince ginger root. Blend cornstarch and cold water to a paste.

2. Heat oil. Add salt, then ginger root; stir-fry a few times. Add pork and stir-fry until lightly browned.

3. Add string beans; stir-fry ½ minute to coat with oil. Then stir in stock and heat quickly. Cook, covered, 2 minutes over medium heat.

4. Beat eggs with remaining water and stir into pan. When eggs begin to set, stir in cornstarch paste to thicken. Serve at once.

STIR-FRIED PORK WITH VERMICELLI
4 to 6 servings

4 *dried black mushrooms*	1 *cup celery*
¼ *pound vermicelli*	1 or 2 *slices fresh ginger root*
½ *pound lean pork*	2 *scallions*
1 *tablespoon cornstarch*	2 to 3 *tablespoons oil*
1 *tablespoon soy sauce*	½ *teaspoon salt*
1 *tablespoon sherry*	½ *cup stock*

1. Separately soak dried mushrooms and peastarch noodles (vermicelli).

2. Shred pork or cut in strips. Combine cornstarch, soy sauce and sherry; then add to pork and toss to coat.

3. Shred celery, ginger root and soaked mushrooms. Cut scallions in 2-inch sections; cut vermicelli in 2-inch lengths.

4. Heat oil. Add salt, then ginger root, and stir-fry a few times. Add pork and stir-fry until it loses its pinkness.

5. Add mushrooms and celery. Stir-fry 1 to 2 minutes more.

6. Stir in and heat stock quickly; then cook, covered, 2 minutes over medium heat.

7. Stir in vermicelli to heat through and blend flavors (about 2 minutes). Then stir in scallions and serve.

VARIATIONS: For the pork, substitute crabmeat; stir-fry in step 4 only to heat through.

In step 5, add 1 cup Chinese cabbage stems, shredded.

After step 5, add the vermicelli and stir-fry 1 minute. Then add the stock and simmer, covered, 3 to 4 minutes. Stir in the scallions and serve.

STIR-FRIED PORK WITH VERMICELLI AND FUZZY MELON
4 to 6 servings

3 or 4 *dried black mushrooms*	2 *tablespoons oil*
¼ *pound vermicelli*	½ to ¾ *teaspoon salt*
½ *pound lean pork*	2 *teaspoons soy sauce*
1 *medium fuzzy melon*	1 *cup stock*

1. Separately soak dried mushrooms and peastarch noodles (vermicelli).

2. Slice pork thin against the grain, then cut in strips. Peel fuzzy melon, then cut in thin strips, each about 2 inches long. Cut vermicelli in 2-inch lengths. Sliver or shred mushrooms.

3. Heat oil. Add salt, then pork, and stir-fry until it loses its pinkness (about 2 minutes).

4. Add vermicelli, mushrooms and soy sauce. Stir-fry 1 minute more.

5. Stir in and heat stock quickly; then cook, covered, 2 minutes over medium heat.

6. Add fuzzy melon and cook, uncovered, 2 minutes more, stirring frequently. Serve at once.

HAPPY FAMILY
6 to 8 servings

2 ounces bêche-de-mer	*½ cup smoked ham*
3 or 4 dried black mushrooms	*½ cup bamboo shoots*
½ cup chicken breast	*⅛ pound snow peas*
water to cover	*2 tablespoons oil*
½ pound lean pork	*1 cup stock*
1½ teaspoons soy sauce	*½ to ¾ teaspoon salt*
1½ teaspoons sherry	*½ teaspoon sugar*
½ teaspoon salt	*2 teaspoons cornstarch*
¼ teaspoon sugar	*2 tablespoons water*

1. Soak and boil bêche-de-mer; cut in ½-inch sections. Soak dried mushrooms.

2. Place chicken breast in water. Bring to a boil; then simmer, covered, 30 minutes. Let cool; then skin, bone and dice.

3. Mince or grind pork. Blend well with soy sauce, sherry, salt and sugar; form into 8 walnut-size balls.

4. Dice ham. Slice bamboo shoots. Stem snow peas and cut in half; then blanch. (See page 831.) Cut soaked mushrooms in half.

5. Heat oil. Quickly brown porkballs on all sides, then remove from pan.

6. Add stock to pan and bring to a boil. Stir in mushrooms and bamboo shoots to heat, then return porkballs. Cook, covered, 5 minutes over medium heat.

7. Add bêche-de-mer, diced chicken and ham, the remaining salt and sugar. Cook, covered, 3 to 4 minutes more.

8. Meanwhile blend cornstarch and cold water to a paste, then stir in to thicken. Stir in snow peas only to heat through and serve at once.

STIR-FRIED DEEP-FRIED PORK AND VEGETABLES

About 4 servings

½ *pound deep-fried pork cubes*　　1 *garlic clove*
1 *cup Chinese cabbage*　　　　　 1 *tablespoon cornstarch*
1 *cup celery*　　　　　　　　　　1 *tablespoon soy sauce*
½ *cup onion*　　　　　　　　　　2 *tablespoons water*
¼ *cup bamboo shoots*　　　　　　2 *or 3 tablespoons oil*
¼ *cup snow peas*　　　　　　　　½ *teaspoon salt*

½ *cup stock*

1. Dice and cook pork as in Basic Deep-fried Pork (see page 161).
2. Dice Chinese cabbage, celery, onion and bamboo shoots. Stem snow peas. Crush garlic. Blend cornstarch, soy sauce and water to a paste.
3. Heat oil. Add salt, then garlic, and stir-fry to brown lightly. Add all vegetables; stir-fry 2 minutes.
4. Stir in and heat stock quickly, then cook, covered, over medium heat until vegetables are nearly done (about 2 minutes).
5. Add deep-fried pork cubes and cook, covered, only to heat through (about 1 minute). Then stir in cornstarch paste to thicken and serve at once.

NOTE: Leftover deep-fried pork cubes can be used in this recipe. They may be combined with other stir-fried vegetables in the same way.

STIR-FRIED DEEP-FRIED PORKBALLS AND SPINACH

6 to 8 servings

1 *pound porkballs, deep-fried*　　¼ *cup water*
1 *pound spinach*　　　　　　　　1½ *tablespoons oil*
2 *garlic cloves*　　　　　　　　　½ *teaspoon salt*
1 *tablespoon cornstarch*　　　　　½ *teaspoon sugar*

1. Prepare Basic Deep-fried Porkballs (see page 166).
2. Wash spinach and remove tough stems. Crush garlic. Blend cornstarch and cold water to a paste.
3. Heat oil. Brown garlic lightly and discard. Add spinach, salt and sugar. Stir-fry until spinach softens slightly (about 1 to 2 minutes).
4. Add porkballs and stir-fry only to heat through. Then stir in cornstarch paste to thicken. Serve at once.

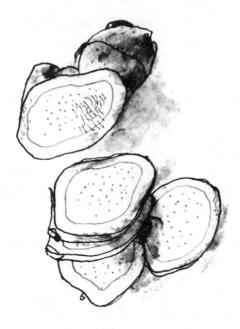

BASIC STIR-FRIED ROAST PORK

About 4 servings

½ *pound roast pork*
1 *pound vegetables (see Note)*
2 *scallion stalks*
1 *slice fresh ginger root*
1 *tablespoon cornstarch*
1 *tablespoon soy sauce*

1 *tablespoon water*
few drops of sesame oil
1½ *tablespoons oil*
1½ *tablespoons oil*
½ *cup stock*
½ *teaspoon salt*

1. Slice roast pork and vegetables. Cut scallions in 1-inch sections. Mince ginger root.

2. Blend cornstarch, soy sauce, cold water and sesame oil to a paste.

3. Heat oil. Add scallions and stir-fry until translucent. Add roast pork; stir-fry 1 minute more. Remove from pan.

4. Heat remaining oil. Add vegetables and stir-fry to coat with oil (about 1 minute). Stir in stock, salt and ginger root and heat quickly. Then cook, covered, over medium heat until nearly done.

5. Return pork and scallions, stir-frying only to reheat. Then stir in cornstarch paste to thicken. Serve at once.

NOTE: Roast pork may be purchased ready-cooked in Chinese food stores or prepared at home. For the vegetables, use in any combination bean sprouts, broccoli,

Chinese lettuce, Chinese cabbage, mustard cabbage, celery, fresh mushrooms, peppers, spinach, string beans. (See Vegetable Section for details on cooking times.)

STIR-FRIED ROAST PORK AND BEAN CURD I
About 4 servings

½ *pound roast pork*   2 *tablespoons soy sauce*
3 *or 4 bean curd cakes*   2 *tablespoons sherry*
2 *scallions*   ½ *teaspoon salt*
1 *tablespoon cornstarch*   1½ *tablespoons oil*

1½ *tablespoons oil*

1. Dice roast pork. Cut bean curd in 1-inch cubes and scallions in 1-inch sections.
2. Blend cornstarch, soy sauce, sherry and salt to a paste.
3. Heat oil. Add pork and scallions and stir-fry 1 minute. Remove from pan.
4. Heat remaining oil. Add bean curd cubes and stir-fry gently, or tilt pan to heat bean curd through (about 1 minute). Remove from pan.
5. Add cornstarch paste and simmer, stirring 1 minute.
6. Return bean curd, roast pork and scallions, stir-frying only to reheat. Serve at once.

VARIATION: Omit step 4. Deep-fry the bean curd cubes until golden instead.

STIR-FRIED ROAST PORK AND BEAN CURD II
About 4 servings

½ *pound roast pork*   *pinch of sugar*
3 *or 4 bean curd cakes*   2 *teaspoons cornstarch*
3 *tablespoons oyster sauce*   2 *tablespoons water*
½ *cup water*   1½ *tablespoons oil*

1½ *tablespoons oil*

1. Slice roast pork. Cut bean curd in half, then each half in 3 or 4 slices.
2. In one cup, combine oyster sauce, water and sugar. In another, blend cornstarch and remaining cold water to a paste.
3. Heat oil. Add roast pork, stir-fry to heat through, then remove from pan.
4. Heat remaining oil. Add bean curd and stir-fry gently, or tilt pan to heat bean curd through (about 1 minute).
5. Stir in oyster sauce mixture and heat quickly. Then cook, covered, 2 minutes over medium heat.

6. Add cornstarch paste and simmer, stirring, 1 minute.

7. Return roast pork, stir-frying only to reheat. Serve at once.

STIR-FRIED ROAST PORK WITH CHINESE LONG BEANS
About 4 servings

½ pound roast pork	2 tablespoons water
1 pound Chinese long beans	2 tablespoons oil
½ teaspoon brown bean sauce	½ teaspoon salt
½ clove garlic	1 teaspoon soy sauce
2 teaspoons cornstarch	½ cup stock

1. Dice roast pork. Cut long beans in ½-inch sections. Mash brown bean sauce. Mince garlic. Blend cornstarch and cold water to a paste.

2. Heat oil. Add salt, then garlic and brown bean sauce. Stir-fry a few times. Add roast pork; stir-fry 1 minute.

3. Add long beans and stir-fry a few times to coat with oil. Add soy sauce; stir-fry 1 minute more.

4. Stir in and heat stock quickly. Then cook, covered, over medium heat until beans are nearly done (about 3 to 4 minutes).

5. Stir in cornstarch paste to thicken. Serve at once.

VARIATION: For the pork, substitute cooked chicken, ham or beef.

STIR-FRIED ROAST PORK AND MIXED VEGETABLES
6 to 8 servings

¼ cup almond meats	4 water chestnuts
½ pound roast pork	1 scallion stalk
1 cup Chinese cabbage stems	1 tablespoon cornstarch
½ cup fresh mushrooms	3 tablespoons water
½ cup bamboo shoots	½ teaspoon sugar
½ cup onion	dash of pepper
¼ cup celery	2 tablespoons oil
12 snow peas	½ teaspoon salt

½ cup stock

1. Blanch and toast almonds. Dice roast pork, Chinese cabbage stems, fresh mushrooms, bamboo shoots, onion, celery, snow peas, and water chestnuts. Mince scallion.

2. Blend cornstarch and cold water to a paste; stir in sugar and pepper.

3. Heat oil. Add salt, then all vegetables; stir-fry to coat with oil (about 2 minutes).

4. Stir in and heat stock quickly. Then cook, covered, over medium heat until vegetables are nearly done (about 2 minutes).

5. Add roast pork, stir-frying only to heat through. Then stir in cornstarch paste to thicken. Serve at once, garnished with toasted almonds.

VARIATIONS: For the roast pork, substitute roast beef, chicken, duck or lamb.

For the vegetables, substitute the following combination: ½ cup snow peas, diced; 1 cup asparagus and 1½ cups string beans, diced and parboiled; and 2 cups broccoli, broken in flowerets and parboiled.

STIR-FRIED HAM AND SPINACH
About 4 servings

½ *pound baked ham*	½ *teaspoon sugar*
1 *pound spinach*	1 *teaspoon soy sauce*
1 *scallion stalk*	3 *tablespoons water*
½ *garlic clove*	2 *tablespoons oil*
1 *tablespoon cornstarch*	½ *teaspoon salt*

3 *tablespoons stock*

1. Cut ham in ½-inch cubes. Stem spinach, leaving leaves whole. Mince scallion and garlic. Blend cornstarch, sugar, soy sauce and cold water to a paste.

2. Heat oil. Add salt, then garlic and scallion; stir-fry to brown lightly. Add ham and stir-fry to heat through.

3. Add spinach; stir-fry a few times to coat with oil (about ½ minute). Then add stock and cook, covered, until spinach softens slightly but is not limp (1 to 2 minutes).

4. Stir in cornstarch paste to thicken. Serve at once.

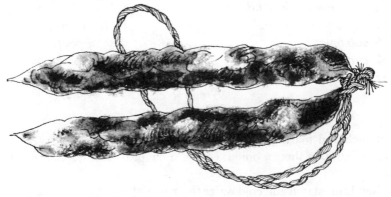

STIR-FRIED CHINESE SAUSAGE AND CABBAGE
About 4 servings

½ pound Chinese pork sausage   2 tablespoons oil
1 head round cabbage   ½ teaspoon salt
2 slices fresh ginger root   ½ to 1 cup stock

1. Steam Chinese sausage until translucent (about 15 minutes). Let cool slightly, then slice diagonally in ½-inch sections.

2. Cut cabbage in strips. Mince ginger root.

3. Heat oil. Add salt, then ginger, and stir-fry a few times. Add cabbage; stir-fry to soften (about 2 minutes).

4. Add Chinese sausage and stir-fry 1 minute more.

5. Stir in and heat stock quickly; then cook, covered, over medium heat until cabbage is done (about 10 minutes). Serve at once.

VARIATIONS: For the Chinese pork sausage, substitute Chinese liver sausage.

For the cabbage, substitute string beans, cut in 1½-inch sections; or Chinese cabbage stems, also cut in 1½-inch sections (simmer these only 2 to 3 minutes in step 5).

STIR-FRIED PORK KIDNEY AND SNOW PEAS
6 to 8 servings

4 pork kidneys   1 tablespoon sherry
2 cups snow peas   ¼ teaspoon sugar
½ cup celery   1 tablespoon cornstarch
¼ cup dried onions   3 tablespoons water
2 slices fresh ginger root   2 tablespoons oil
2 tablespoons soy sauce   ½ teaspoon salt

¼ cup stock

1. Cut pork kidneys in half and devein, then cut in ¼-inch slices. Parboil 10 minutes, then cool under cold running water. Drain well.

2. Stem snow peas. Slice celery stalks in ¼-inch sections. Dice dried onions in ½-inch cubes. Shred ginger root.

3. In one cup, combine soy sauce, sherry and sugar. In another, blend cornstarch and cold water to a paste.

4. Heat oil. Add salt, then ginger root, and stir-fry a few times. Add kidneys and stir-fry to coat with oil (about ½ minute).

5. Add celery and onions. Stir-fry 1½ minutes more.

6. Add soy-sherry mixture. Stir-fry another minute.

7. Stir in and heat stock quickly; then cook, covered, 1 minute over medium heat. Add snow peas and cook, covered, 1 minute more.

8. Stir in cornstarch paste to thicken. Serve at once.

VARIATION: For the sherry, substitute either gin or bourbon.

STIR-FRIED PORK LIVER WITH SPINACH AND MUSHROOMS
About 4 servings

4 *dried black mushrooms*	1 *tablespoon cornstarch*
½ *pound pork liver*	2 *tablespoons soy sauce*
1 *pound spinach*	2 *tablespoons sherry*
2 *scallion stalks*	2 *tablespoons water*
1 to 2 *garlic cloves*	1 to 2 *teaspoons sugar*
2 *slices fresh ginger root*	2 to 3 *tablespoons oil*

1. Soak dried mushrooms.

2. Sliver pork liver, then blanch 1 minute.

3. Stem spinach and cut leaves in half. Cut scallion stalks in 1-inch sections. Crush garlic. Mince ginger root. Sliver soaked mushrooms.

4. Blend cornstarch, soy sauce, sherry, water and sugar to a paste.

5. Heat oil. Add scallions, garlic and ginger, and stir-fry a few times. Add liver; stir-fry until it begins to brown (about 2 to 3 minutes).

6. Add mushrooms. Stir-fry 2 to 3 minutes more.

7. Add spinach. Stir-fry to soften slightly (1 to 2 minutes). Then stir in cornstarch paste to thicken and serve at once.

NOTE: The liver will sliver easily if frozen first, then thawed slightly.

VARIATION: In step 2, toss the blanched liver in a mixture of 1 tablespoon cornstarch, 1 tablespoon sherry, 2 tablespoons soy sauce, 1 teaspoon sugar and 2 slices fresh ginger root, minced. (Omit the cornstarch paste in steps 4 and 7; and the ginger root in steps 3 and 5.)

DEEP-FRIED PORK

For deep-frying, pork that is either lean or half-lean, half-fat can be used. When using the half-and-half pork, remove its coarse outer skin and score the fat in a crisscross pattern.

These are the steps in deep-frying pork: (1) cubing the meat; (2) marinating it; (3) dredging it in flour or cornstarch, or coating it with batter; (4) immersing it in hot oil and deep-frying until done; and (5) serving it sprinkled either with pepper or sesame oil, or accompanied by a sweet-and-pungent sauce.

TO CUBE: *Cut meat in ¾- to 1-inch cubes.*

TO MARINATE: (*This step is optional but greatly enhances the flavor.*) *Let pork cubes stand 15 to 30 minutes, turning meat several times, in any of the following mixtures:*

2 tablespoons soy sauce, 2 teaspoons sugar

2 tablespoons sherry, 1 teaspoon salt

2 tablespoons soy sauce, 2 tablespoons sherry (to which may be added 2 teaspoons sugar and a dash of pepper)

TO DREDGE:

marinated pork:

1. Sprinkle lightly with flour.

2. Dip in beaten egg. Roll or toss in cornstarch. Let stand until cornstarch is absorbed.

3. Dip in beaten egg. Roll or toss in flour seasoned lightly with salt.

unmarinated pork:

1. Season with salt and pepper. Roll or toss in flour or cornstarch. Dip in beaten egg.

2. Roll or toss in cornstarch. Gradually add sherry ½ teaspoon at a time, tossing cubes until coated with a thick, heavy paste.

3. Roll or toss lightly in flour. Season with salt and a dash of pepper. Sprinkle with 2 tablespoons sherry, ½ teaspoon five spices. Let stand 20 to 30 minutes, turning meat several times.

TO COAT:

marinated pork:

Instead of dredging as above, dip pork in any of the following mixtures (do not coat too thickly—the batter will absorb too much oil):

1 egg, beaten; ½ cup flour, 4 tablespoons water, ½ teaspoon salt

2 eggs, beaten; 2 tablespoons flour, 1 tablespoon water, 1 teaspoon salt

1 egg white, beaten lightly; 4 tablespoons cornstarch, ½ teaspoon salt

unmarinated pork:

Dip in the following mixture:

3 tablespoons cornstarch, 1 tablespoon soy sauce, 1 tablespoon sherry, ½ teaspoon salt, dash of pepper (to which may be added 1 egg, beaten)

TO DEEP-FRY: *Heat the oil to about 375 degrees. Add the pork cubes a few at a time. Deep-fry until golden (about 3 minutes). Lift meat out a minute to cool while reheating oil. Return pork to oil and deep-fry until done (about 3 to 4 minutes more). If a large amount of oil is used, the pork cubes will float when done. Otherwise, check for doneness by cutting a cube open to see that it is no longer pink.*

TO SERVE: *When serving pork with a sweet-and-pungent sauce, prepare the sauce first (see page 735). Then, when the pork has been deep-fried, reheat sauce, and stir the pork in briefly, only to heat through. (If pork is cooked too long in the sauce, it will lose its crispness.)*

DEEP-FRIED PORK, SIMMERED FIRST
6 servings

1 *rolled pork loin (2 pounds)*	*dash of pepper*
2 *slices fresh ginger root*	*sweet-and-pungent sauce*
2 *garlic cloves*	*oil for deep-frying*
2 *cups water*	1 *egg*
1½ *teaspoons salt*	2 *tablespoons cornstarch*

1. Wipe pork with a damp cloth. Slice ginger root and crush the garlic.

2. Boil water. Add ginger, garlic, salt and pepper. Add pork. Bring to a boil again; then simmer, covered, until tender (about 1½ hours).

3. Drain pork, reserving liquid for stock. Let pork cool, then dry thoroughly and cut in 1-inch cubes.

4. Meanwhile, prepare the sweet-and-pungent sauce (see pages 735–738). Heat oil for deep-frying.

5. Beat egg. Dip pork in egg, then sprinkle with cornstarch. Deep-fry until golden (about 2 minutes) and drain on paper toweling. Serve with the sweet-and-pungent sauce poured over.

NOTE: This method, usually used with coarser cuts, assures tenderness. Since the meat is already cooked, the deep-frying time is kept brief.

VARIATION: Slice the pork 1-inch thick, then in 1- by 2-inch strips. Cover with cold water. Bring to a boil; then simmer, covered, 30 minutes. Drain, cool and dry; then dredge lightly in cornstarch and deep-fry.

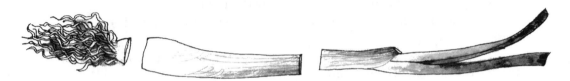

DEEP-FRIED PAPER-WRAPPED PORK

2 or 3 servings

1 *pound lean pork*	1 *tablespoon sherry*
1 *slice fresh ginger root*	1 *teaspoon sugar*
½ *garlic clove*	6 *scallion stalks*
2 *tablespoons soy sauce*	*wax paper*

oil for deep-frying

1. Cut pork in ¾-inch cubes. Mince ginger and garlic, then combine with soy sauce, sherry and sugar. Add to pork and toss. Let stand 30 minutes, turning occasionally. Drain, discarding marinade.

2. Split scallion stalks in half lengthwise, then cut crosswise in 1-inch sections. Cut wax paper or parchment in 6-inch squares.

3. Wrap one pork cube and scallion section in each square of paper.

4. Heat oil and deep-fry paper-wrapped pork until done (about 8 minutes). Drain and serve hot in wrappings.

NOTE: The diner, with chopsticks or fork, opens the paper envelopes one at a time and eats the contents.

VARIATION: Instead of wrapping pork cubes individually, put 7 or 8 together with the same number of scallion sections in a waxpaper sandwich bag. Seal tightly by folding or stapling. Deep-fry as above, one bag at a time.

GOLD COIN PORK
2 or 3 servings

8 *small dried black mushrooms*	2 *tablespoons soy sauce*
½ *pound lean pork*	1 *tablespoon sherry*
4 *bacon strips*	1 *clove star anise*
1 *slice fresh ginger root*	*oil for deep-frying*
1 *scallion stalk*	1½ *teaspoons sugar*

¼ *teaspoon sesame oil*

1. Soak dried mushrooms.

2. Slice pork in ¹⁄₁₆-inch slices, then in 1½-inch squares. Cut bacon strips in similar squares. Place both in a bowl, along with mushrooms.

3. Mince ginger and scallion, then combine with soy sauce, sherry and star anise.

4. Add to pork, bacon and mushrooms and toss gently. Let stand 1 to 2 hours, turning occasionally. Drain, transferring marinade to a saucepan.

5. Arrange mushrooms, pork and bacon squares alternately on skewers. Meanwhile, heat oil.

6. Gently lower in skewers and deep-fry ingredients until golden, turning skewers for even cooking. (Handle skewers with tongs to protect hands). Drain on paper toweling. Let cool slightly, then remove skewers.

7. Meanwhile, add sugar and sesame oil to marinade in saucepan. Heat slowly but do not boil. Briefly dip pork, bacon and mushrooms in marinade and serve.

NOTE: This dish gets its name from the squared shape of ancient Chinese coins.

DEEP-FRIED PORK AND FISH SQUARES, YANGCHOW STYLE
4 to 5 servings

sweet-and-pungent sauce	*dash of pepper*
½ *pound lean pork*	2 *tablespoons cornstarch*
½ *pound smoked ham*	¼ *cup water*
½ *pound flounder fillets*	2 *eggs*
2 *tablespoons soy sauce*	*oil for deep-frying*

flour

1. Prepare a sweet-and-pungent sauce (see pages 735–738). Keep warm.

2. Cut pork and ham in $\frac{1}{16}$-inch slices, then in 2-inch squares.

3. Cut flounder in 2-inch squares. Sprinkle with soy sauce and pepper.

4. Blend cornstarch and cold water to a paste. Separate eggs: reserve whites; beat yolks lightly, then mix with cornstarch paste to a smooth batter.

5. Dip pork, fish and ham squares alternately into batter and stack together in units of three. (The egg yolks will make them adhere.) Meanwhile, heat oil.

6. Dredge each stack lightly with flour and dip in reserved egg whites. Then add to oil, a few pieces at a time, and deep-fry until golden. Drain on paper toweling. Serve with the sweet-and-pungent sauce poured over.

DEEP-FRIED ROAST PORK SQUARES WITH CRABMEAT

2 to 3 servings

½ *cup crabmeat*	2 *teaspoons soy sauce*
¼ *cup fresh mushrooms*	½ *pound roast pork*
¼ *cup bamboo shoots*	*cornstarch*
1 *teaspoon cornstarch*	1 *egg white*
½ *teaspoon salt*	*oil for deep-frying*

¼ *cup Chinese parsley*

1. Flake crabmeat. Mince mushrooms and bamboo shoots. Then blend in cornstarch, salt and soy sauce.

2. Cut roast pork in ¼-inch slices, then in 1½-inch squares. Dust lightly with additional cornstarch.

3. Spread crabmeat mixture over half the pork squares. Top, sandwich fashion, with remaining squares. Dip each "sandwich" in egg white.

4. Meanwhile heat oil. Add pork "sandwiches" a few at a time and deep-fry until golden. Drain on paper toweling. Mince parsley and sprinkle over as a garnish.

DEEP-FRIED PORK STRIPS AND WALNUTS

4 servings

½ *cup walnut meats*	1 *tablespoon soy sauce*
1 *pound lean pork*	*oil for deep-frying*
1½ *tablespoons flour*	1 *tablespoon oil*
½ *tablespoon brown sugar*	2 *teaspoons soy sauce*

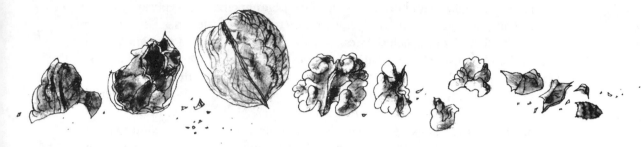

1. Blanch walnuts. Cut pork in ½-inch thick slices, then in ½- by 1½-inch strips.

2. Blend flour, brown sugar and soy sauce to a paste. Add to pork and toss to coat.

3. Heat oil until nearly smoking. Add pork strips, half a cup at a time, and deep-fry until crusty and golden. Drain on paper toweling.

4. Heat remaining oil. Add walnuts and stir-fry briefly until pale golden.

5. Return pork. Sprinkle with remaining soy sauce and stir-fry only to reheat.

BASIC DEEP-FRIED PORKBALLS
4 servings

1 *pound pork*	1 *tablespoon water*
1 *slice fresh ginger root*	½ *teaspoon salt*
1½ *tablespoons cornstarch*	2 *teaspoons soy sauce*

oil for deep-frying

1. Mince or grind pork and ginger root.

2. Blend cornstarch and cold water to a paste, then stir in salt and soy sauce. Add to pork and ginger and mix well. Form into walnut-size balls, but do not overhandle or pack too tightly. Meanwhile heat oil.

3. Add porkballs one at a time, and deep-fry several at once, turning frequently for even cooking. When porkballs float, remove from pan and let cool slightly.

4. Reheat oil. Return porkballs to fry 1 minute more. (Cut one open to make sure meat is no longer pink.) Drain on paper toweling.

5. Serve with a sweet-and-pungent sauce poured over, or with a pepper-salt mix (see page 708). Or serve as an hors d'oeuvre on a bed of lettuce strips.

NOTE: Use pork that has some fat. When using cuts such as shoulder or butt, remove skin before mincing.

VARIATIONS: For the minced ginger, substitute 1 teaspoon ginger juice.

In step 2, add to meat mixture ½ teaspoon curry powder; or add any or all of the following:

1 egg, beaten
1 scallion stalk or small onion, minced
1 garlic clove, minced
1 teaspoon sugar
1 tablespoon sherry
¼ cup dried black mushrooms (soaked), minced
¼ cup water chestnuts, minced; or celery, chopped
few drops of sesame oil

In step 3, before deep-frying, dredge porkballs lightly in cornstarch; or dredge in cornstarch and dip in beaten egg.

DEEP-FRIED HAM-AND-EGG BALLS
2 to 3 servings

½ *pound smoked ham*	3 *slices white bread*
1 *scallion stalk*	2 *teaspoons flour*
3 *eggs*	½ *teaspoon salt*

oil for deep-frying

1. Mince ham and scallion. Beat eggs. Trim off bread crusts; break bread into soft crumbs. Mix ingredients together, blending in flour and salt.
2. Form mixture into walnut-size balls. Meanwhile, heat oil.
3. Add meat balls to oil a few at a time and deep-fry until golden. Drain on paper toweling. Serve hot.

VARIATION: After step 2, roll ham-and-egg balls in rice flour noodles broken in ½-inch lengths. (When deep-fried, the noodles will curl up.)

BASIC STEAMED MINCED PORK
3 to 4 servings

1 *pound pork*	½ *teaspoon salt*
1 *teaspoon cornstarch*	2 *teaspoons soy sauce*

1. Mince or grind pork. Mix well with cornstarch, salt and soy sauce.
2. Spread mixture out flat like a pancake in a shallow heatproof dish.
3. Steam on a rack until done, about 30 minutes (see pages 831 and 33). Check with a fork to see that meat is no longer pink. Serve hot.

NOTE: This dish is best when made with slightly fat pork.

VARIATIONS: Sliver rather than grind or mince pork, and steam about 45 minutes.

In step 1, add to pork mixture any of the following:

½ teaspoon sugar

1 teaspoon peanut oil

few drops of sesame oil

1 or 2 slices fresh ginger root, minced

1 scallion stalk, minced

1 egg, beaten

¼ pound fresh mushrooms, minced; or 3 dried black mushrooms (soaked), minced

½ cup water chestnuts, minced

Or add any of the following as indicated:

BLACK BEANS: Add to pork mixture 1 tablespoon fermented black beans (soaked), mashed, and 1 garlic clove, minced.

CHINESE SAUSAGES: Place on top of pork mixture 2 Chinese sausages, either cut diagonally in ½-inch slices, or minced.

DRIED OYSTERS: Add to pork mixture 4 dried oysters (soaked), minced.

DUCK LIVERS: Add to pork mixture 2 dried duck livers (soaked), minced, and ½ cup water chestnuts, minced.

PICKLED BAMBOO SHOOTS: Place on top of pork mixture ½ cup pickled bamboo shoots, drained.

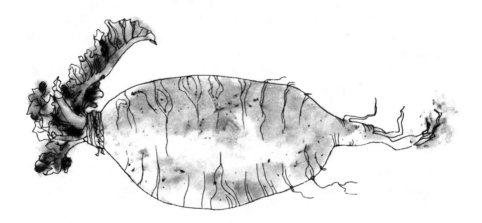

PRESERVED TURNIP: Add to pork mixture ½ bundle preserved turnip, washed and shredded, 1 tablespoon sherry and a dash of pepper.

SALT CABBAGE: Add to pork mixture ¼ to ½ cup salted or preserved cabbage, chopped. Top with 2 tablespoons water chestnuts, sliced.

SALT EGG: Separate 1 salt egg. Add the white to the pork mixture along with 1 fresh egg, beaten; 6 water chestnuts, minced, 2 teaspoons sherry and a dash of pepper. Mash or cut up salt egg yolk and sprinkle on top.

SALT FISH: Add to pork mixture ⅛ pound dried salted fish (soaked), minced, plus ¼ cup water. Or arrange on top of pork mixture 4 strips of salt fish, about ¾ inches wide by 2 inches long (soaked), and 2 slices fresh ginger root, minced. Sprinkle with 1 teaspoon sugar and 1 tablespoon oil.

TEA MELON: Add to pork mixture ½ cup tea melon, rinsed and chopped coarsely or diced. Or add 4 tablespoons tea melon and 1 cup bamboo shoots, chopped coarsely. Or add 2 tablespoons tea melon, minced; 2 tablespoons preserved turnip, minced; 1 tablespoon cloud ear mushrooms (soaked), minced, and a few drops of sesame oil.

VEGETABLES: Add to pork mixture any of the following:

1 cup cauliflower, broken into tiny flowerets or cut in 1-inch pieces and parboiled.

¼ cup carrots, diced and parboiled.

¼ cup Chinese turnips, diced and parboiled.

Instead of blending the soy sauce with the pork mixture, as in step 1, sprinkle soy over the top with a circular motion in step 2. Minced scallions can be sprinkled over the pork in the same way.

STEAMED CUBED PORK
3 to 4 servings

1 pound pork	½ cup sherry
½ cup soy sauce	1 tablespoon sugar

1. Cut pork in 1-inch cubes. Combine soy sauce, sherry and sugar. Add to pork and toss. Place in a heatproof bowl.

2. Steam on a rack until done (about 1½ hours). See pages 831 and 33.

STEAMED CUBED PORK WITH FIVE SPICES
3 to 4 servings

1 pound pork	½ teaspoon Five Spices
2 tablespoons soy sauce	½ teaspoon salt
1 teaspoon sugar	2 pounds potatoes

1. Cut pork in 1-inch cubes. Combine soy sauce, sugar, Five Spices and salt. Add to pork and toss. Refrigerate, covered, overnight.

2. Peel potatoes and cut in 1½-inch cubes. Arrange in a deep heatproof bowl with pork cubes on top. Pour the pork marinade over.

3. Steam on a rack until done (about 1½ hours). See pages 831 and 33.

STEAMED SLICED PORK WITH SHRIMP SAUCE
3 to 4 servings

1 *pound pork*	1 *clove garlic*
1 *scallion stalk*	1 *tablespoon shrimp sauce*
1 or 2 *slices fresh ginger root*	1 *tablespoon soy sauce*
	½ *teaspoon sugar*

1. Slice pork thin. Cut scallion stalk in 1-inch lengths. Mince ginger root and garlic.

2. Combine shrimp sauce, soy sauce and sugar in a heatproof bowl. Mix well with scallion, ginger and garlic. Then add pork and toss gently to coat.

3. Steam on a rack until done (about 30 minutes). See pages 831 and 33.

STEAMED SLICED PORK WITH HAM AND BEAN CURD
About 3 servings

5 *large dried black mushrooms*	*few drops of peanut oil*
½ *pound lean pork*	1 *tablespoon sherry*
¼ *pound smoked ham*	½ *teaspoon salt*
2 *bean curd cakes*	*dash of pepper*
4 *slices fresh ginger root*	2 *teaspoons cornstarch*
1 *scallion stalk*	2 *tablespoons water*

1. Soak dried mushrooms.

2. Slice pork and ham about ¼-inch thick. Slice bean curd ½-inch thick. Mince ginger root and scallion. Cut soaked mushrooms in half.

3. Rub a heatproof bowl with peanut oil. Arrange mushrooms, ham, bean curd and pork in alternating layers, with pork on top. Sprinkle with sherry, salt, pepper, minced ginger and scallion.

4. Steam on a rack until done (about 45 minutes). See pages 831 and 33.

5. Drain off gravy into a saucepan without disturbing steamed ingredients. Add water to gravy to make 1 cupful and bring slowly to a boil.

6. Meanwhile blend cornstarch and cold water to a paste. Then stir into heated gravy to thicken.

7. Invert contents of steaming bowl onto a serving platter without disturbing arrangement of layers. Pour sauce over and serve.

STEAMED SLICED PORK WITH WHITE CHEESE
3 to 4 servings

1 *pound lean pork*	1 *teaspoon soy sauce*
½ *teaspoon cornstarch*	3 *tablespoons water*

2 *cubes Chinese white cheese*

1. Cut pork in ⅟₁₆-inch slices. Place in a heatproof bowl.
2. Blend cornstarch, soy sauce and cold water. Mash white cheese cubes and blend in. Pour mixture over pork.
3. Steam on a rack until done (30 to 40 minutes). See pages 831 and 33.

STEAMED PORK STRIPS WITH GLUTINOUS RICE FLOUR
3 to 4 servings

1 *pound lean pork*	3 *tablespoons soy sauce*
1 *scallion stalk*	1 *tablespoon sherry*
1 *slice fresh ginger root*	½ *cup glutinous rice flour*

1. Cut pork in ½-inch slices, then in strips.
2. Mince scallion and ginger root; combine in a heatproof bowl with soy sauce and sherry.
3. Add pork strips and toss gently. Let stand 15 minutes, turning meat occasionally.
4. Sprinkle pork with glutinous rice flour, then toss gently again.
5. Steam on a rack 1½ hours over low heat, turning pork strips at 20-minute intervals. (See pages 831 and 33.)

NOTE: If the pork becomes dry during steaming, mix a few drops of soy sauce, sherry and water, and sprinkle over meat.

STEAMED FRESH HAM
6 to 8 servings

2 *pounds fresh ham*	1½ *tablespoons sugar*

4 *tablespoons sherry*

1. Place fresh ham in a heatproof dish and steam on a rack 1 hour. (See pages 831 and 33.)
2. Add sugar and sherry. Steam 1 hour more.
3. Let ham cool slightly, then slice and serve.

STEAMED LEG OF PORK
About 6 servings

1 *small hind pork leg* (3 *pounds*)	2 *tablespoons oil*
2 *tablespoons soy sauce*	2 *tablespoons sugar*
2 *cups water*	2 *tablespoons soy sauce*
1 *tablespoon sugar*	1 *pound spinach*
1 *tablespoon sherry*	½ *teaspoon salt*
2 *tablespoons soy sauce*	3 *to 4 cups water*
2 *or 3 garlic cloves*	2 *tablespoons cornstarch*
½ *cup water*	

1. Wipe pork with a damp cloth. Pierce skin all over with a pointed knife or skewer, then rub soy sauce into skin.

2. Place pork in a large heavy saucepan with first quantity of cold water. Bring to a boil; then simmer, covered, 40 minutes. Drain, reserving liquid for stock. Let meat cool.

3. Combine sugar, sherry and remaining soy sauce, then rub over pork. Crush garlic.

4. Heat oil and brown garlic lightly. Turn off heat; stir in remaining sugar and last of the soy sauce.

5. Transfer pork to a large heatproof bowl and pour garlic sauce over. Steam pork by the bowl-in-a-pot method until tender, about 1½ hours. (See pages 831 and 33.)

6. Wash spinach and remove tough stems. Cut leaves in 2-inch sections, then sprinkle with salt.

7. Boil second quantity of water and pour over spinach. Let stand until leaves begin to soften (1 to 2 minutes). Drain and arrange on a large serving platter.

8. When steamed pork is done, transfer to spinach bed. Pour pork gravy into a saucepan and bring to a boil.

9. Meanwhile, blend cornstarch and remaining cold water to a paste, then stir in to thicken. Pour sauce over pork and spinach and serve.

VARIATION: In step 5, add 2 cloves star anise to pork, but remove before serving.

STEAMED ROAST PIG WITH SHRIMP PASTE
3 to 4 servings

1 *pound roast pig*	1½ *tablespoons shrimp paste*
1 *slice fresh ginger root*	½ *teaspoon sugar*
few drops of sherry	

1. Cut roast pig in ¾-inch slices, then in 1½-inch squares. Arrange, skin side up, in a shallow heatproof dish.

2. Mince ginger root, then combine with shrimp paste and sugar. Dilute with a few drops of sherry and mix well. Spread mixture over each piece of roast pig.

3. Steam on a rack 20 minutes (see pages 33 and 831). Serve hot.

NOTE: Roast pig, not to be confused with roast pork, is used here. (See page 863.)

STEAMED FIVE-FLOWER PORK WITH CARROTS
3 to 4 servings

1 *pound Five-Flower pork*	½ *pound carrots*
1 *tablespoon sugar*	2 *tablespoons oil*
1 *tablespoon sherry*	2 *tablespoons stock*

1. Place pork in a heatproof bowl. Mix sugar and sherry and pour over.

2. Steam on a rack 30 minutes (see pages 33 and 831). Let meat cool, then slice thin.

3. Meanwhile scrape or peel carrots, then slice diagonally about ⅜-inch thick.

4. Heat oil. Add sliced pork and carrots and stir-fry about 3 minutes.

5. Stir in and quickly heat stock. Cook, covered, over medium heat, until carrots are done (about 3 minutes more).

VARIATION: For the carrots, substitute celery stalks.

STEAMED PORKBALLS WITH GLUTINOUS RICE
About 4 servings

1 cup glutinous rice	2 tablespoons soy sauce
1 pound pork	1 tablespoon sherry
1 or 2 scallion stalks	1 tablespoon water
2 slices fresh ginger root	2 teaspoons cornstarch
1 egg	1 teaspoon sugar

½ teaspoon salt

1. Soak glutinous rice. Drain well.

2. Mince or grind pork. Mince scallion and ginger. Beat egg and add, along with soy sauce, sherry, water, cornstarch, sugar and salt. Mix well, but do not overhandle; then form into walnut-size balls.

3. Spread soaked rice on a flat plate. Roll porkballs one at a time over rice. (The rice will adhere to and coat meat completely.)

4. Arrange porkballs on a shallow heatproof dish with ½-inch spaces between them to allow for expansion of rice.

5. Steam on a rack 1 hour (see pages 831 and 33). Serve with dips of soy sauce and hot Chinese mustard.

NOTE: Because the rice takes on a pearl-like translucence, this dish is also known as Pearl Balls. To prepare it in advance: Steam only 45 minutes in step 5; then cool and refrigerate. Before serving, steam 20 to 25 minutes more.

VARIATION: In step 2, add to meat mixture 2 or 3 dried shrimp (soaked in sherry), minced; or a few drops of sesame oil.

BASIC BRAISED PORK
6 to 8 servings

2 pounds pork	2½ cups water
2 scallion stalks	½ cup soy sauce
2 slices fresh ginger root	1 teaspoon salt
2½ tablespoons oil	1 tablespoon sugar

1. Cut pork in 1-inch cubes. Cut scallion stalks in 1-inch sections. Slice ginger root.

2. Heat oil in a heavy pan; then brown scallions and ginger lightly. Add pork and brown quickly on all sides.

3. Meanwhile boil water in another pan, then add to pork with soy sauce and salt. Simmer, covered, 1 hour, turning meat several times for even cooking and coloring.

4. Add sugar. Cook 30 minutes more, turning once again.

NOTE: This dish may be served hot or cold. If served hot, vegetables may be added (see Variations below). To serve cold, simmer pork until very tender, then chill with its sauce in a square mold. Slice and serve with the jellied sauce.

VARIATIONS: For the white sugar, substitute brown sugar.

In step 2, add with scallions and ginger 1 or 2 garlic cloves, crushed.

In step 3, add to pork 1 or 2 cloves star anise; or 2 tablespoons sherry; or ¼ pound pine nuts, shelled.

During the last 30 minutes of cooking add:

1 or 2 cups bamboo shoots, cut in 1-inch cubes

2 or 3 bean curd cakes, diced or sliced

1 pound round cabbage, cubed. (When cabbage turns a rich red after 10 minutes of cooking, add 6 dried black mushrooms (soaked) and ¼ cup dried shrimp (soaked), plus the mushroom-soaking water. Bring to a boil again, then simmer, covered, 20 minutes more.)

4 cups Chinese lettuce, cut in 1-inch sections

4 eggs, hardboiled first, then shelled. (To serve: cut eggs in half; arrange on top of pork cubes.)

¼ cup dried fish (haddock or squid), diced

1 Chinese turnip, peeled and cut in 1-inch cubes

During the last 15 minutes of cooking add:

½ pound fresh chestnuts, cut in half, parboiled and shelled

1 cup dried black mushrooms (soaked)

½ pound string beans, stemmed but left whole

BRAISED FRAGRANT PORK
6 to 8 servings

1 *piece tangerine peel*	½ *cup soy sauce*
2 *pounds pork*	½ *teaspoon anise powder*
2 *scallion stalks*	½ *cinnamon stick*
2 or 3 *slices fresh ginger root*	3 to 5 *cloves*
2½ *tablespoons oil*	1 *teaspoon salt*
1 *cup sherry*	1 *cup water*

1. Soak tangerine peel.
2. Cut pork in 1-inch cubes. Slice scallion and ginger root.
3. Heat oil to smoking in a heavy pan and brown pork quickly on all sides.
4. Add sherry, soy sauce, anise powder, cinnamon, cloves, salt and water. Bring to a boil.
5. Add tangerine peel, sliced scallion and ginger root. Then simmer, covered, until tender (about 1½ hours), turning meat occasionally.

NOTE: If water evaporates, add a small quantity of boiling water to prevent burning.

BRAISED PORK WITH RED BEAN CHEESE
6 to 8 servings

2 pounds pork	2 teaspoons sugar
3 tablespoons red bean cheese	2 teaspoons soy sauce
1 or 2 garlic cloves	2½ tablespoons oil
2 tablespoons sherry	1 teaspoon salt

3 cups stock

1. Cut pork in 1-inch cubes. Mash red bean cheese. Crush garlic cloves. Combine sherry, sugar and soy sauce.
2. Heat oil in a heavy pan. Add salt and crushed garlic. Stir-fry a few times. Add pork and brown quickly on all sides.
3. Stir in sherry-sugar mixture until it evaporates (about 1 minute). Then stir in mashed red cheese.
4. Add stock and bring to a boil. Then simmer, covered, until tender (about 1½ hours).

VARIATION: During the last 15 minutes of cooking, add 1 to 2 cups Chinese turnips, peeled and cut in 1-inch cubes.

BRAISED PORK WITH CHESTNUTS, MUSHROOMS
AND GINKGO NUTS
6 to 8 servings

1 cup dried black mushrooms	1 cup water chestnuts
1 cup chestnut meats	2 tablespoons oil
1 cup ginkgo nuts	1 teaspoon salt
2 pounds pork	1 tablespoon soy sauce

3 cups stock

1. Soak dried mushrooms. Shell and blanch chestnuts and ginkgo nuts (see page 826).

2. Cut pork in 1-inch cubes. Cut water chestnuts in half.

3. Heat oil in a heavy pan. Add salt, then pork and brown lightly on all sides.

4. Add soy sauce, turning meat constantly until soy evaporates (about 1 minute).

5. Add stock and heat; then mushrooms, ginkgo nuts, chestnuts and water chestnuts. Bring to a boil, then simmer, covered, until pork is tender (about 1½ hours).

VARIATION: In step 3, add after salt, 1 garlic clove, crushed, and brown lightly. In step 4, add (mixed with the soy sauce) 1 slice fresh ginger root, shredded; 1 tablespoon sherry and 1 teaspoon sugar. In step 5, add with mushrooms and nuts ¼ pound dried bean curd sticks, broken in 2-inch lengths (soaked); 1 cup bamboo shoots, sliced diagonally; and 10 Chinese red dates.

BRAISED CURRIED PORK WITH SWEET POTATOES
About 4 servings

2 *large sweet potatoes*	2 *tablespoons oil*
1 *pound pork*	1 *tablespoon soy sauce*
1 *onion*	½ *teaspoon salt*
1 *or* 2 *slices fresh ginger root*	*dash of pepper*
oil for deep-frying	1 *cup stock*
2 *tablespoons curry powder*	

1. Peel sweet potatoes and cut in ½-inch slices. Cut pork in ½-inch cubes. Slice onion thin. Mince ginger root.

2. Heat oil and deep-fry sweet potatoes until light golden. Drain on paper toweling.

3. Heat remaining oil. Add ginger and onion and stir-fry a few times. Add pork and brown lightly on all sides.

4. Stir in soy sauce, salt and pepper. Then add stock and curry powder and bring to a boil, stirring.

5. Add deep-fried potatoes and simmer, covered, until pork is done (30 to 40 minutes).

BRAISED PORK AND SPINACH
6 to 8 servings

3 *pounds pork loin*	1 *tablespoon brown sugar*
2 *tablespoons oil*	4 *tablespoons soy sauce*
1 *cup stock*	2 *pounds spinach*

1. Heat oil in a large heavy pan. Add pork and brown quickly on all sides. Pour off most of the fat.

2. Add stock and heat; stir in sugar and soy sauce. Then simmer, covered, until pork is done (1½ to 2 hours). Remove meat, leaving gravy in pan. Let pork cool slightly, then slice.

3. Wash spinach and remove tough stems. Add to gravy and cook, stirring gently until softened but still bright green.

4. Drain spinach and transfer to a serving platter. Arrange pork slices over the top and serve.

BRAISED PORK WITH HARDBOILED EGGS
About 8 servings

6 *eggs*	2 *tablespoons oil*
1 *onion*	½ *cup soy sauce*
2 *pounds pork*	1 *tablespoon sugar*
water to cover	4 *tablespoons sherry*

1. Hardboil eggs, then cool under running water and shell. Slice onion.

2. Place pork in a pan with water and bring to a boil. Cook, uncovered, 2 minutes, then drain, discarding liquid.

3. Heat oil in a large heavy pan. Add onion and stir-fry until translucent. Add pork and brown quickly on all sides.

4. Stir in and quickly heat soy sauce, sugar and sherry; then simmer, covered, 30 minutes, turning meat once or twice.

5. Add eggs and simmer 30 minutes more, turning meat and eggs once or twice for even cooking and coloring.

NOTE: You may score the boiled eggs lightly so the sauce can penetrate.

BRAISED PORK WITH SHRIMP SAUCE
6 to 8 servings

2 *pounds pork*	2½ *cups water*
water to cover	2 *tablespoons oil*
1 *onion*	2 *tablespoons soy sauce*
1 *scallion stalk*	1 *tablespoon shrimp paste*
2 *garlic cloves*	1 *tablespoon sugar*

1. Place pork in a pan with water. Bring to a boil, then simmer, covered, 10 minutes. Drain, discarding liquid. Cut pork in 1-inch cubes.

2. Slice onion. Cut scallion stalk in 2-inch sections. Crush garlic. Meanwhile bring remaining water to a boil.

3. Heat oil in a large heavy pan. Add onion, scallion and garlic and stir-fry to brown lightly. Add cubed pork and brown lightly.

4. Stir in soy sauce and shrimp paste to blend (about 1 minute). Then add boiling water and sugar. Simmer, covered, until meat is tender (about 40 minutes).

BRAISED PORK AND BEAN CURD
3 to 4 servings

1 *pound pork*	1½ *cups stock*
2 *cups water*	1 *tablespoon sugar*
2 or 3 *bean curd cakes*	4 *tablespoons soy sauce*
1 *onion*	½ *teaspoon salt*
1 *garlic clove*	2½ *tablespoons oil*

1. Place pork in a pan with water and bring to a boil. Cook, uncovered, 4 minutes, then drain, discarding liquid. Let pork cool.

2. Meanwhile slice or cube bean curd, slice onion, crush garlic. Combine stock, sugar, soy sauce and salt.

3. Heat oil in a large heavy pan. Add onion and garlic and brown lightly. Add pork and brown quickly on all sides.

4. Add bean curd; stir-fry gently, or tilt pan, to cover with hot oil.

5. Add stock mixture and heat; then simmer, covered, until pork is tender (about 40 minutes).

BRAISED FIVE-FLOWER PORK AND RED BEAN CHEESE
6 to 8 servings

2 *pounds Five-Flower pork*	2 *tablespoons sugar*
5 *slices fresh ginger root*	2 *tablespoons sherry*
water to cover	2 *tablespoons soy sauce*
soy sauce	1 *teaspoon salt*
¼ *cup red bean cheese*	2½ *tablespoons oil*

2 cups stock

1. Cut pork in 1-inch cubes, so there is skin on one side of each piece. Slice ginger root.

2. Bring water to a boil. Add pork and cook, uncovered, 10 minutes. Drain, discarding liquid. Let meat cool, then rub with soy sauce.

3. Mash red bean cheese. Blend to a paste with sugar, sherry, remaining soy sauce and salt.

4. Heat oil in a heavy pan. Add ginger, then meat, and brown quickly on all sides.

5. Add red bean cheese mixture, stirring to coat meat. Then turn each pork cube, skin side down, with as many touching the bottom of the pan as possible.

6. Add stock and bring to a boil. Then simmer, covered, until meat is very tender (about 2 hours). Skim off fat at intervals.

7. Drain pork cubes; arrange on a serving platter, skin side up.

BRAISED MARINATED PORK
6 to 8 servings

2 *pounds pork*	1 *tablespoon sherry*
1 *scallion stalk*	2½ *tablespoons oil*
1 *slice fresh ginger root*	1 *tablespoon sugar*
1 *garlic clove*	5 *tablespoons soy sauce*
2 *tablespoons soy sauce*	*dash of pepper*

1. Cut pork in 4 equal parts. Cut scallion in 2-inch sections.

2. Mince ginger root and garlic; then combine with soy sauce and sherry.

3. Add mixture to pork and toss gently. Let stand 30 minutes, turning meat occasionally; then drain, discarding marinade.

4. Heat oil in a heavy pan. Add pork and brown quickly on all sides.

5. Add sugar, remaining soy sauce, pepper and scallion. Simmer, covered, until pork is done (about 45 minutes). Cut in 1-inch cubes and serve.

NOTE: This dish can be made without water only if a very heavy pot is used. If pork shows signs of burning, however, add ¼ cup boiling water.

BRAISED MARINATED FIVE-FLOWER PORK WITH SPINACH
6 to 8 servings

2 *pounds Five-Flower pork*	3 *or 4 scallion stalks*
1 *tablespoon salt*	2½ *cups water*
water to cover	2 *tablespoons oil*
¼ *cup sherry*	1 *cup soy sauce*
1 *garlic clove*	1 *tablespoon sugar*
2 *or 3 slices ginger root*	2 *cloves star anise*
½ *leek stalk*	1 *pound spinach*

1. Cut pork in 1-inch cubes. Sprinkle with salt. Add water. Let stand 15 minutes; then drain.

2. Add sherry to meat and toss gently. Let stand 15 minutes more. Drain, reserving sherry.

3. Crush garlic and ginger root. Cut leek and scallion stalks in 3-inch lengths. Meanwhile bring remaining water to a boil.

4. Heat oil in a heavy pan. Add ginger, leek and scallions and brown lightly. Add pork and brown quickly on all sides.

5. Add boiling water, crushed garlic, reserved sherry, and soy sauce, sugar and star anise. Simmer, covered, 1 hour. Skim off fat.

6. Simmer 1½ hours more, skimming off fat occasionally. (The meat is done when its fatty tissue is tender and translucent.) Meanwhile wash spinach and discard tough stems.

7. When pork is done, remove and keep warm. Pour off gravy (see Note), leaving ½ cup in pan and reheat. Add spinach and cook, uncovered, until softened but still fresh and green; then drain. Arrange spinach on a serving dish with pork cubes on top.

NOTE: The reserved gravy may be strained and stored as a master sauce (see page 739). The skimmed-off fat may be kept for stir-frying vegetables.

BRAISED PORK CHOPS
6 to 8 servings

3 *tablespoons oil*	2 *cups water*
6 *thick pork chops*	1 *teaspoon sugar*
½ *cup soy sauce*	1 *pound spinach*

2 *tablespoons oil*

1. Heat oil in a heavy pan. Add pork chops 2 or 3 at a time and brown quickly. Drain on paper toweling.

2. Pour off all but 2 tablespoons of fat and return chops. Add soy sauce and water. Bring to a boil, then simmer, covered, 30 minutes.

3. Turn chops over. Simmer, covered, another 30 minutes. Add sugar and simmer, covered, 30 minutes more.

4. Wash spinach and remove tough stems. Heat remaining oil in another pan. Add spinach and stir-fry to soften slightly. Arrange on a serving platter with pork chops on top. Pour gravy over and serve.

VARIATIONS: For the spinach, substitute Chinese lettuce, cut in 2-inch sections.

In step 2, before returning chops to pan, add ½ cup onion, shredded; stir-fry until lightly browned.

BRAISED AND MARINATED PORK CHOPS
6 to 8 servings

6 *thick pork chops*	2 *scallion stalks*
3 *slices fresh ginger root*	⅓ *cup soy sauce*
1 *garlic clove*	1 *tablespoon sugar*
3 *tablespoons soy sauce*	*dash of pepper*
2 *tablespoons sherry*	3 *tablespoons oil*

1. Bone pork chops and cut meat in 1½-inch cubes. (Reserve bones for stock.)

2. Mince ginger root and garlic, then combine with soy sauce and sherry.

3. Add to pork and toss gently. Let stand 30 minutes, turning meat occasionally; then drain, discarding marinade.

4. Meanwhile cut scallion stalks in 1-inch sections. Combine remaining soy sauce with sugar and pepper.

5. Heat oil in a heavy pan. Add marinated pork and brown quickly on all sides. Add scallions and stir-fry a few times.

6. Stir in soy mixture. Bring to a boil, then simmer, covered, until tender (about 30 minutes).

BRAISED PORKBALLS AND CAULIFLOWER
4 to 5 servings

1 *pound porkballs*	1½ *tablespoons oil*
1 *medium cauliflower*	1 *cup stock*
1 *slice fresh ginger root*	2 *tablespoons cornstarch*
1½ *tablespoons oil*	2 *tablespoons soy sauce*
½ *teaspoon salt*	1 *teaspoon sugar*

¼ *cup water*

1. Prepare uncooked porkballs as in steps 1 and 2 of Basic Deep-fried Porkballs (see page 166).

2. Break cauliflower into small flowerets. Shred ginger root.

3. Heat oil in a heavy pan. Add salt and ginger, then porkballs. Brown lightly; then remove from pan.

4. Heat remaining oil. Add cauliflower and stir-fry to coat with hot oil (about 2 minutes). Return porkballs.

5. Add stock. Bring to a boil; then simmer, covered, until pork is cooked through and cauliflower is tender, but still crunchy (about 8 minutes).

6. Blend cornstarch, soy sauce, sugar and cold water to a paste, then stir in to thicken sauce.

NOTE: Uncooked porkballs may be prepared a day or two in advance, provided they are parboiled for several minutes, then drained, cooled and refrigerated until needed.

VARIATION: For the cauliflower, substitute either 1 pound string beans, stemmed and cut in thirds; or broccoli, broken in flowerets, and the stems cut diagonally in ¼-inch slices.

BRAISED PORKBALLS AND LILY BUDS
4 to 5 servings

¼ *cup dried lily buds*	1 *tablespoon soy sauce*
1 *pound porkballs*	½ *teaspoon salt*
2½ *tablespoons oil*	1 *teaspoon sugar*

2 *cups water*

1. Soak lily buds.

2. Prepare uncooked porkballs as in steps 1 and 2 of Basic Deep-fried Porkballs (see page 166). Heat oil and brown quickly on all sides.

3. Arrange soaked lily buds at the bottom of a heavy pan; top with porkballs.

4. Combine soy sauce, salt, sugar and water and add to pan. Bring to a boil, then simmer, covered, until done (about 15 minutes). Serve with porkballs arranged over lily buds.

BASIC RED-SIMMERED PORK
8 to 10 servings

3 *pounds pork*   ½ *cup soy sauce*
1 *to 2 cups water*   2 *tablespoons sherry*
4 *slices fresh ginger root*   1 *teaspoon salt*
2 *teaspoons sugar*

1. Cut pork in 1½-inch cubes. Place with water in a heavy saucepan and bring quickly to a boil.

2. Meanwhile, slice and crush ginger root. Then add to pan along with soy sauce, sherry and salt. Simmer, covered, 1 hour.

3. Add sugar. Turn meat over and simmer, covered, 30 minutes more.

VARIATIONS: For the white sugar, substitute brown sugar.

In step 2 add any of the following:

2 scallion stalks, cut in 1-inch sections
2 garlic cloves, crushed
2 cloves star anise
1 cup onion, sliced
¼ pound dried Chinese cabbage (soaked); omit the salt
¼ pound salted haddock or other dried fish (soaked), cut in 1-inch squares; omit the salt

In step 3, add ½ cup lily buds (soaked) and 2 tablespoons cloud ear mushrooms (soaked).

During the last hour of cooking, add any of the following:

1 bunch carrots, peeled and sliced rolling-cut style
2 pounds Chinese white turnips, peeled, cut in 1½-inch cubes
6 celery stalks, cut in 1½-inch sections
6 or more eggs, hardboiled and shelled
2 cups fresh squid, cut in 1-inch sections

½ pound peastarch noodles, boiled 20 minutes, then drained, and added with 1½ cups boiling water

During the last 20 minutes, add 2 or 3 bean curd cakes, cut in quarters or cubed, and/or 2 cups bamboo shoots, cut in large chunks.

During the last 3 minutes, add 1 can abalone, cut in ¼-inch slices. Also substitute 1 cup abalone liquid for the water in step 1.

RED-SIMMERED PORK WITH MUSHROOMS
3 to 4 servings

1 *pound pork*	1 *tablespoon sherry*
1 *cup water*	½ *teaspoon sugar*
1 *tablespoon soy sauce*	½ *teaspoon salt*

½ *pound fresh mushrooms*

1. Cut pork in 2-inch cubes and place with water in a heavy pan. Bring to a boil, then simmer, covered, 30 minutes. Drain, reserving liquid.

2. Add soy sauce to pork in pan. Cook over low heat, turning meat frequently until soy sauce is absorbed. Stir in sherry, sugar and salt.

3. Return reserved liquid and reheat; then simmer, covered, 20 minutes, turning meat once or twice.

4. Stem fresh mushrooms; arrange caps under pork cubes and simmer, covered, 20 minutes more.

VARIATIONS: For the fresh mushrooms, substitute 6 to 8 dried black mushrooms (soaked); or ½ pound round cabbage, cut in wedges.

RED-SIMMERED WHOLE PORK
8 to 10 servings

1 *pork shoulder (3 pounds)*
2 *slices fresh ginger root*
2 *scallion stalks*

1 *cup soy sauce*
3 *cups water*
1 *teaspoon salt*

1 *teaspoon sugar*

1. Place pork in a heavy pan. Slice ginger root; cut scallion stalks in 2-inch sections and add.
2. Add water, soy sauce and salt. Bring to a boil; then simmer, covered, 1 hour. Turn meat over; simmer, covered, 1 hour more.
3. Add sugar; simmer, covered, another 30 minutes. Let pork cool; then slice thin. Reheat gravy and pour over meat.

RED-SIMMERED LEG OF PORK
8 to 10 servings

1 *pork leg, middle cut (3 to 4 pounds)*
1 *cup soy sauce*
1½ *cups water*

4 *tablespoons sherry*
1 *teaspoon salt*
1 *tablespoon sugar*

1. Score, or make several slashes, in pork leg. Place in a heavy saucepan with soy sauce, water, sherry and salt.
2. Bring to a boil; then simmer, covered, 2½ hours, turning meat two or three times for even cooking and coloring. (If pork seems to be drying out, add just enough boiling water to keep it moist.)
3. Add sugar and cook 30 minutes more. Carve and serve.

RED-SIMMERED PORK STRIPS
6 to 8 servings

2 *pounds lean pork*
½ *cup water*

1 *cup soy sauce*

1. Cut pork in slices 2 inches thick, then in strips 6 inches long and 2 inches wide.
2. Place in a heavy pan with soy sauce and water. Bring to a boil, then simmer, covered, 1 hour. Serve hot or cold.

VARIATIONS: **In step 2,** add any or all of the following:

1 piece dried tangerine peel (soaked)	2 cloves star anise
1 scallion stalk cut in 1-inch sections	½ stick cinnamon
1 slice ginger root	1 teaspoon salt
1 or 2 garlic cloves, crushed	1 tablespoon sugar

½ cup sherry

RED-SIMMERED FRESH HAM AND CHESTNUTS
About 6 servings

1 *small fresh ham* (3 *pounds*)	2 *tablespoons sherry*
2 *scallion stalks*	¼ *cup soy sauce*
2 *garlic cloves*	2 *cups water*
3 *tablespoons brown sugar*	1 *pound chestnuts*

1. Trim off ham fat and place meat in a heavy pan. Cut scallion stalks in two; crush garlic and add along with sugar, sherry, soy sauce and water.

2. Bring slowly to a boil, then simmer, covered, 1½ hours, turning ham at half-hour intervals.

3. Meanwhile, shell and blanch chestnuts (see page 823). Add to ham and simmer, covered, 1 hour more, turning meat twice for even coloring.

WHITE-COOKED WHOLE PORK
6 to 8 servings

2 *pounds pork*	1 *teaspoon salt*
water to cover	2 *slices fresh ginger root*

1. Place pork in a heavy pan with water and bring to a boil. Add salt and ginger root; then simmer, covered, until tender (about 1½ hours). Drain, reserving liquid for stock.

2. Let pork cool, then refrigerate to chill. Slice thin and serve cold with any dip for plain-cooked pork (see page 712).

WHITE-COOKED CUBED PORK
6 to 8 servings

2 *pounds pork*	4 *cups water*
½ *cup sherry*	1 *teaspoon salt*

1 *tablespoon sugar*

1. Cut pork in 1½-inch cubes. Place in a heavy pan with sherry, water and salt. Bring to a boil; then simmer, covered, until tender (about 1 hour).

2. Add sugar and simmer 10 minutes more.

WHITE-COOKED PRESSED PORK
About 8 servings

2 to 3 pounds pork   4 tablespoons salt

water to cover

1. Have pork boned, but kept intact. Wipe clean with a damp cloth; dry with paper toweling; then rub with salt and refrigerate, covered, 2 days.

2. Wipe pork with a damp cloth to remove excess salt. Place in a heavy pan with water. Bring to a boil; then simmer, covered, until tender (about 1½ hours), turning meat several times. Drain, reserving liquid for stock.

3. Squeeze pork snugly into a deep rectangular pan (like a cake pan) and cover with a weighted tray. (Use heavy books or a kettle filled with water for the weight.) Let stand until meat is compressed and rectangular (about 2 to 3 hours).

4. Remove weights and refrigerate pork to chill. Slice ¼-inch thick, then in rectangles 1½-inches wide and 2 inches long. Serve cold with dips for plain-cooked pork. (See page 712.)

VARIATIONS: After step 1, add to the pork ½ cup sherry and 1 clove star anise. Refrigerate a third day, turning meat several times. Drain; reserve marinade and combine it with enough cold water to make 3 cups. Bring to a boil as in step 2. Continue as above.

In step 3, wrap pork in a clean cloth. Place on a plate and top with a weighted tray. Let stand overnight in a cool place, then refrigerate to chill.

DRUNKEN PORK
About 8 servings

2 to 3 pounds pork   4 to 6 cups water
2 garlic cloves   1 tablespoon salt
1 scallion stalk   dash of pepper

sherry

1. Have pork boned and rolled. Crush garlic. Cut scallion stalk in ½-inch sections.

2. Bring water to a boil. Add pork, garlic, scallions, salt and pepper. Bring to a boil again, then simmer, covered, 30 minutes.

3. Drain, reserving liquid for stock, and let meat cool; then refrigerate overnight.

4. Cut pork in large chunks. Place in a jar or crock and add enough sherry to fill. Cover tightly and refrigerate 1 week.

5. Drain pork, slice thin and serve cold.

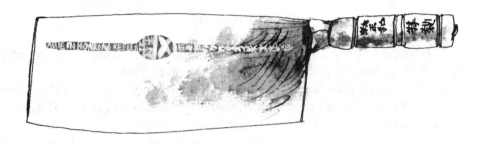

WHITE-COOKED PORK WITH LOTUS ROOT
6 to 8 servings

2 *pounds pork*	1 *teaspoon salt*
1 *pound lotus root*	*dash of pepper*
2 *tablespoons red bean cheese*	2 *teaspoons cornstarch*
water to cover	2 *tablespoons water*

1. Cut pork in 1½-inch cubes. Peel lotus root and split open slightly. Mash red bean cheese. Place in a heavy saucepan.

2. Add water, salt and pepper. Bring to a boil, then simmer, covered, 45 minutes. Remove lotus root; slice thin and set aside.

3. Blend cornstarch and remaining cold water to a paste. Add to liquids in pan and cook, stirring, to thicken. Return lotus root only to reheat.

ROAST PORK

marinade for roast pork   *pork*

1. Prepare any of the marinades for roast pork (see pages 717–720). Add to pork and let stand 2 hours, turning meat frequently. Drain, discarding marinade.

2. Preheat the oven to 425 degrees. Place pork on a rack over a drip pan. (Line pan with foil for easier cleaning.) Add several inches of water to keep drippings from burning. Roast pork 10 to 15 minutes to sear.

3. Reduce heat to 350 degrees. Roast pork until done (allow about 30 minutes per pound). Baste several times with drippings. Turn meat at half-hour intervals for even roasting.

4. Let cool slightly, then cut in 1-inch cubes, or slice thin and cut in strips 1 inch wide and 2½ inches long. Serve hot or cold.

NOTE: Roast pork can be used in stir-fried dishes, with noodles or rice, as a soup garnish, etc. For cuts of meat to use, see page 130.

BARBECUED PORK STRIPS

marinade for barbecued pork   *pork*

1. Cut pork in strips 2 inches wide, 2 inches thick and 5 inches long.

2. Prepare any of the marinades for barbecued pork strips (see page 717). Add to pork and let stand 2 hours, turning meat frequently. Drain, reserving marinade.

3. Preheat the oven to 425 degrees. Place pork strips on a rack over a shallow roasting pan containing a few inches of water; or suspend, barbecue-style, in oven. (See page 821.) Roast 10 minutes.

4. Reduce heat to 325 degrees and roast pork 30 to 40 minutes more. (Turn meat several times if not suspended.) Baste strips lightly at 5-minute intervals with peanut or sesame oil; or glaze with a thin layer of honey during the last 10 minutes of roasting.

5. Cut pork against the grain in bite-size pieces. Serve hot with reheated marinade; or cold with plum sauce, hot Chinese mustard (see page 705) or a soy sauce dip.

NOTE: Barbecued Pork Strips may be used in any dish that calls for roast pork. They can be prepared in quantity and refrigerated (they will keep about a week) or frozen in foil. (If frozen, reheat in foil without defrosting.)

VARIATIONS: Marinate a whole pork tenderloin. Roast 30 minutes at 375 degrees; 1 hour at 300 degrees. If meat is on a rack, turn at 15-minute intervals. (If suspended barbecue-style, turning isn't necessary.)

Roast the marinated pork strips 15 minutes at 350 degrees; then raise heat to 450, baste with peanut oil and roast 10 minutes more. (This will make pork very crisp.)

Cook the marinated pork strips over a hibachi, or charcoal grill, etc., allowing about 15 minutes on each side.

Broil the marinated pork strips 25 minutes, turning once. (Place about 1½ inches from flame.) Baste with the marinade at 5-minute intervals.

ROAST PORK WITH CRISP SKIN I
About 8 servings

3 *pounds pork shoulder*
1 *teaspoon salt*
1 *teaspoon Five Spices*

water
¼ *cup water*
2 *teaspoons honey*

1. Pierce meat, not skin, in several places with a skewer or sharp knife. Rub meat with salt and Five Spices and let stand 1 hour. Meanwhile preheat the oven to 350 degrees.

2. Place pork in a roasting pan, meat side up. Add enough water to submerge skin. Roast 30 minutes.

3. Remove meat from oven and turn skin side up. Pierce skin in several places with a skewer. Meanwhile, heat remaining water, then stir in honey to dissolve; rub into skin.

4. Return pork to oven and roast 1½ hours more. (The skin should be crisp, and a rich, reddish-brown.) Let meat cool slightly. Remove bones, leaving skin intact. Cut in 1-inch cubes, each with some skin, and serve.

VARIATION: Omit the Five Spices, ¼ cup water and honey. Instead, rub the meat in step 1 with a mixture containing the salt, 4 tablespoons soy sauce, 1 tablespoon peanut oil and 1 teaspoon powdered anise. In step 4, baste the skin two or three times with sesame oil.

ROAST PORK WITH CRISP SKIN II
About 8 servings

3 *pounds shoulder pork*
2 *tablespoons brown sugar*

3 *tablespoons soy sauce*
1 *tablespoon hoisin sauce*

1. Score skin of pork in a ¾-inch diamond pattern. Place skin side up under a medium broiler and let brown (about 15 minutes).

2. Preheat the oven to 350 degrees. Blend brown sugar, soy sauce and hoisin sauce; then brush over meat, not skin, of pork.

3. Place pork on a rack over a drip pan containing several inches of water and roast until done (about 1½ hours). Turn once or twice.

4. Let cool slightly. Cut in 1-inch cubes, each with some skin, or slice about 1-inch thick, then in strips ½ by 1½ inches.

ROAST PORK WITH CHINESE LETTUCE
About 8 servings

1 *garlic clove*	1½ *teaspoons salt*
1 *tablespoon sugar*	¼ *teaspoon pepper*
4 *tablespoons soy sauce*	3 *pounds pork*

1 *head Chinese lettuce*

1. Mince garlic, then combine with sugar, soy sauce, salt and pepper. Rub over pork and let stand 1 hour. Meanwhile preheat the oven to 350 degrees.

2. Place pork on a rack over a roasting pan containing several inches of water, and roast 1 hour. Meanwhile cut lettuce in 1-inch sections.

3. Remove pork and drain off fat. (Set rack aside.) Line bottom of pan with lettuce; place pork on top. Return to oven and roast 45 minutes more.

LION'S HEAD
About 4 servings

4 to 6 *dried black mushrooms*	½ *teaspoon salt*
1 *pound pork*	*dash of pepper*
10 *water chestnuts*	1 *tablespoon sherry*
2 *scallion stalks*	*oil for deep-frying*
2 *slices fresh ginger root*	1 *head mustard cabbage*
1 *egg*	2 *tablespoons oil*
1½ *teaspoons cornstarch*	1 *cup stock*
1 *teaspoon sugar*	1 *tablespoon cornstarch*

¼ *cup stock*

1. Soak dried black mushrooms.

2. Mince or coarsely grind pork (with some fat), water chestnuts, scallions, ginger root and soaked mushrooms.

3. Beat egg lightly and blend in, along with cornstarch, sugar, salt, pepper and sherry. (Use a wooden spoon and do not overhandle: if mixed too long, the meat will lose its juices.)

4. Divide mixture into 4 parts and form each into a large meatball. (This is most easily done if the hands are moistened first with water.)

5. Heat oil and, using a strainer or wire basket, deep-fry meatballs until golden

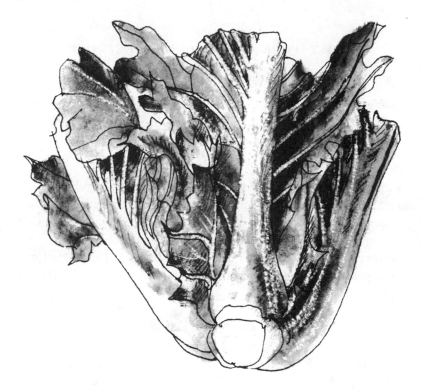

(about 5 minutes). Drain on paper toweling. Meanwhile separate leaves of mustard cabbage and cut each in 4-inch sections.

6. Heat remaining oil. Add cabbage and stir-fry until slightly softened (about 2 minutes). Transfer to a heavy pan or earthenware casserole, lining the sides and bottom.

7. Place meatballs over cabbage. Separately heat stock, then pour over. Simmer, covered, until done (about 1½ hours).

8. Arrange cabbage on a serving platter with meatballs on top. Blend cornstarch and remaining cold stock to a paste. Add to liquids in pan and cook, stirring, to thicken. Pour sauce over meatballs and serve.

NOTE: This dish gets its name because the meatball and sliced cabbage suggest the head of a lion with its mane. Lion's Head keeps well and can be made in advance and reheated.

VARIATIONS: For the pork, substitute beef.

For the dried mushrooms, substitute ¼ pound fresh mushrooms.

For the water chestnuts, substitute ½ cup bamboo shoots.

For the mustard cabbage, substitute round cabbage. (In step 7, place several slices of bread over meatballs to absorb strong odor of cabbage. Discard bread before serving.)

For the mustard cabbage, substitute Chinese cabbage (stir-fry as above and add during the last 30 minutes of cooking); or spinach (stir-fry 1 minute, then add during the last 15 minutes).

In step 2, add to pork mixture ½ pound crabmeat, picked over and flaked, 1 tablespoon soy sauce, and a few drops of sesame oil; or substitute for the crabmeat 1½ tablespoons dried shrimp (soaked) and 2 tablespoons cloud ear mushrooms (soaked).

Omit the ginger root, sugar, salt, pepper and sherry from pork mixture. Add these instead to the heated stock in step 7 along with 2 tablespoons soy sauce.

BRAISED LION'S HEAD

4 *large porkballs*   2 *tablespoons oil*
1 *head mustard cabbage*   1 *cup stock*

½ *cup soy sauce*

1. Prepare Lion's Head porkballs (see steps 1 to 4, above); cut mustard cabbage as in step 5.

2. Heat oil in a heavy pan and brown porkballs quickly. Add stock and soy sauce and bring to a boil; then simmer, covered, 30 minutes.

3. Add cabbage; simmer, covered, 30 to 40 minutes more.

VARIATION: Make smaller porkballs and sauté 15 to 20 minutes. Top with Chinese cabbage stems, cut in 3-inch sections. Simmer, covered, with no additional liquid, 10 to 15 minutes more.

SIMMERED LION'S HEAD

4 *large porkballs*   1 *head mustard cabbage*

1 *cup stock*

1. Prepare Lion's Head porkballs (see steps 1 to 4, page 193); cut mustard cabbage as in step 5.

2. Heat stock. Add porkballs and bring to a boil; then simmer, covered, 1 to 1½ hours.

3. Add cabbage; simmer, covered, 30 minutes more.

VARIATION: Stir-fry the mustard cabbage briefly to soften; then cover raw porkballs completely with cabbage. Sprinkle with ½ teaspoon salt. Add the stock and simmer, covered, about 2 hours.

STEAMED TUNG-PO PORK

2 *pounds pork shoulder or loin*　　2 *teaspoons sherry*
4 *cups water*　　4 *tablespoons soy sauce*
1 *teaspoon sugar*　　1 *to 2 pounds spinach*

3 *tablespoons oil*

1. Place pork and water in a pan, bring to a boil, then cook, covered, 15 minutes over medium heat. Drain, reserving stock.

2. Combine sugar, sherry and soy sauce, and add to pork in pan. Cook over very low heat, turning meat constantly until evenly colored. (If the pan gets dry, moisten with a few drops of reserved stock.)

3. Add remaining stock; bring to a boil, then simmer, covered, 20 minutes. Remove pork and let cool. Cut against the grain in ½-inch slices, then in strips about 1 by 2 inches.

4. Place pork slices skin side down in a deep, heatproof bowl. Steam on a rack 1 hour (see pages 831 and 33).

5. Wash spinach and remove tough stems. Heat oil, add spinach and stir-fry until softened, but still fresh and green (about 2 minutes).

6. Heap spinach over pork in the steaming bowl. Invert bowl into a deep serving dish, so that spinach is at the bottom and pork, skin side up, is on top.

NOTE: This dish, sometimes called Chinese Casserole of Pork, is attributed to Soo Tung-Po, a well-known poet of the T'ang Dynasty.

VARIATIONS: For the spinach, substitute Chinese lettuce, cut in 3-inch sections.

Simmer the pork in water to cover 1½ hours, then drain. Brown meat on all sides in oil heated to smoking. Let cool slightly and slice as above. Transfer to a shallow heatproof dish. Sprinkle with 2 tablespoons soy sauce and steam 1½ hours. Serve on a bed of stir-fried spinach leaves.

BRAISED TUNG-PO PORK I

6 to 8 servings

1 *scallion*　　1 *teaspoon salt*
2 *slices fresh ginger root*　　3 *tablespoons oil*
1 *tablespoon sugar*　　2 *pounds pork*
2 *tablespoons sherry*　　2 *cups water*
4 *tablespoons soy sauce*　　1 *head mustard cabbage*

1. Cut scallion in ½-inch sections. Slice ginger root. Combine sugar, sherry, soy sauce and salt.

2. Heat oil. Add ginger and scallion and stir-fry a few times. Stir in sugar-

sherry mixture to blend. Add pork and cook over low heat, turning constantly for even coloring.

3. Meanwhile bring water to a boil in another pan; then add to pork. Simmer, covered, until done (about 1½ hours). Separate mustard cabbage leaves.

4. Remove pork, but not liquids, from pan. Add cabbage leaves and cook, uncovered, 20 minutes, stirring occasionally. Meanwhile cut pork in slices ¼ inch thick.

5. Drain cabbage. Transfer to a serving platter. Arrange pork slices on top. Pour gravy over and serve.

VARIATION: In step 3, cook with pork, ¼ cup dried haddock, squid or turnip (soaked).

BRAISED TUNG-PO PORK II
6 to 8 servings

2 *pounds pork*	¾ *cup soy sauce*
2 *to 3 tablespoons oil*	1 *tablespoon sugar*
1½ *cups water*	4 *tablespoons sherry*
3 *slices fresh ginger root*	1 *to 2 pounds spinach*

1. Cut pork in 1½-inch cubes. Heat oil in a heavy pan and brown pork quickly.

2. Bring water to a boil in another pan. Slice and crush ginger root. Add to pork along with soy sauce. Simmer, covered, 1 hour. Skim off and reserve a ladleful of fat.

3. Add sugar and sherry to pan and simmer, covered, 30 minutes more.

4. Wash spinach and remove tough stems. Heat reserved fat. Add spinach and stir-fry until softened but still fresh and green.

5. Line a serving dish with spinach, top with pork cubes, pour gravy over, and serve.

VARIATIONS: For the spinach, substitute Chinese lettuce or Chinese cabbage, cut in 2-inch sections.

Leave the pork whole. Brown and pour off excess fat. Add to pan 1 cup water, 1½ tablespoons brown sugar and 4 tablespoons soy sauce. Heat, then simmer, covered, until pork is tender (about 1½ hours). Slice and serve over stir-fried spinach.

TWICE-COOKED PORK I
6 to 8 servings

2 *pounds pork*	2 *tablespoons oil*
3 *cups water*	½ *teaspoon salt*
1 *scallion stalk*	2 *tablespoons soy sauce*
1 *garlic clove*	1 *teaspoon sugar*
2 *to* 3 *slices fresh ginger root*	½ *teaspoon Tabasco Sauce*

1. Place pork and water in a heavy pan. Bring to a boil, then simmer, covered, 1 hour. Drain, reserving liquid for stock. Let meat cool.

2. Cut pork against the grain in ¼-inch slices, then in strips 1 by 2 inches. Cut scallion stalk in 1-inch sections. Crush garlic. Mince ginger root.

3. Heat oil. Add salt, then garlic, and brown lightly. Discard garlic. Add pork strips and stir-fry to brown (2 to 3 minutes).

4. Add scallion, ginger, soy sauce, sugar and Tabasco. Stir-fry to blend well (about 2 minutes more).

NOTE: This dish is called "Twice-Cooked" because the pork is both simmered and stir-fried. The best cuts for this are whole pork chops, boned fresh ham, or Five-Flower pork.

VARIATIONS: For the Tabasco, substitute either hot pepper oil or a dash of cayenne pepper.

In step 1, add to water 1 slice fresh ginger root and 1 teaspoon sherry.

In step 3, omit the garlic and add to heated oil: 2 green peppers, 1 red pepper, several small red hot peppers, and ½ cup bamboo shoots, all diced. Stir-fry 1 to 2 minutes; then add pork. In step 4, for the seasonings given, substitute 1½ tablespoons hoisin sauce mixed with 2 tablespoons water and 1 teaspoon sugar.

Mince the garlic instead of crushing it and add to heated oil with minced ginger. At the same time, add 1 tablespoon fermented black beans (soaked), mashed. Stir-fry 1 minute, then add pork and ½ teaspoon hot pepper flakes. In step 4, for the seasonings given, substitute 2 tablespoons soy sauce and ¼ cup reserved pork stock. Cook, covered, 2 to 3 minutes. Serve pork over stir-fried cabbage or spinach.

TWICE-COOKED PORK II
6 to 8 servings

4 to 6 cups water	2 tablespoons oil
2 pounds Five-Flower pork	½ teaspoon salt
1 green pepper	½ teaspoon sugar
1 leek stalk	2 teaspoons sherry
2 slices fresh ginger root	1 teaspoon hoisin sauce
1 to 2 garlic cloves	1 tablespoon water
1 tablespoon brown bean sauce	few drops of red pepper oil

1. Bring water to a boil and add pork. Bring to a boil again; then simmer, covered, 1 hour. Drain, reserving liquid for stock. Let meat cool.

2. Cut pork against the grain in slices $\frac{1}{16}$-inch thick. Seed and dice green pepper. Cut leek stalk in half lengthwise, then crosswise in 1-inch sections. Mince ginger root and garlic. Mash brown bean sauce.

3. Heat oil; stir in salt. Add ginger, garlic and brown bean sauce and stir-fry a few times. Add leek sections and stir-fry ½ minute more.

4. Add pork, green pepper, sugar and sherry; stir-fry 2 minutes.

5. Combine hoisin sauce and remaining water. Add and stir-fry 1 minute more. Serve sprinkled with red pepper oil.

THRICE-COOKED PORK
6 to 8 servings

2 pounds Five-Flower pork	2 tablespoons brown sugar
water to cover	3 tablespoons soy sauce
2 to 3 pieces taro	1 tablespoon honey
3 slices fresh ginger root	½ teaspoon Five Spices
1 to 2 garlic cloves	2 to 3 tablespoons oil
¼ cup red bean cheese	½ teaspoon salt
1 tablespoon sherry	

1. Cut pork in 2-inch strips with the grain. Bring water to a boil; add pork and cook, uncovered, 10 minutes. Drain, discarding liquid. Let meat cool, then cut against the grain in ¼-inch slices.

2. Peel taro; cut in ¼-inch slices, then in 1½-inch cubes. (Set aside in a bowl of cold water; drain before using.) Mince ginger root and garlic.

3. Mash red bean cheese, then blend well with sugar, soy sauce, honey and Five Spices.

4. Heat oil. Add salt, then minced garlic and ginger. Stir-fry a few times. Add pork and stir-fry to heat through (about 1 minute). Stir in sherry until it evaporates.

5. Add red bean cheese mixture and stir-fry until pork is completely coated. Remove from heat.

6. Arrange pork and taro cubes in alternating layers in a heatproof bowl. Steam on a rack 1 hour (see pages 831 and 33).

SPARERIBS

Spareribs can be cooked in many ways: stir-fried, deep-fried, steamed, braised, simmered or barbecued. With the exception of the latter, the ribs are always chopped with a cleaver into bite-size pieces (to make them maneuverable with chopsticks). For barbecuing, the rib rack is usually left intact and, after roasting, the ribs are cut apart and eaten by hand, or then chopped into bite-size pieces. Regardless of cooking method, the lean meat on the ribs can be left as is or trimmed off for later use in shredded or minced pork dishes.

An average rib rack weighs 2½ to 3 pounds. In Western-style meals (which feature one main dish), about ¾ to 1 pound is generally allowed per person. In Chinese meals, which have many "main" dishes, 1 pound of spareribs will serve 3 or 4 people. As a rule, the rib racks with shorter bones (from smaller pigs) are preferred because they're more tender.

BARBECUED SPARERIBS

TO PREPARE: *Leave the rib rack whole or cut in two. Trim off fat and gristle. With a sharp knife, cut between each rib but not clear through. (This will enable the marinade to penetrate the meat.)*

TO MARINATE: *Prepare any of the marinades for barbecued spareribs (see pages 721 to 723). Rub marinade over the ribs and into the cuts as well. Place ribs in a shallow pan and pour the marinade over them. Let stand 2 to 4 hours, basting and turning meat from time to time. (Do not marinate for a longer period: the meat will toughen.) Drain, reserving marinade.*

NOTE: Some cooks rub the ribs with salt and sugar, then let the meat stand one hour *before* adding the marinade.

TO ROAST THE RIB RACK: *Preheat oven to 375 degrees. Place the marinated ribs on a metal rack over a roasting pan nearly filled with water (this will catch the drippings and keep them from burning). Or suspend the ribs high in the oven over the drip pan, barbecue-style (see page 821). Roast about 45 minutes, basting frequently with the reserved marinade. If ribs are roasted flat on a rack, they should be turned at 15 to 20 minute intervals for even browning. (If they are suspended vertically, barbecue-style, this isn't necessary.) Halfway through cooking, the ribs may be glazed with a thin layer of either peanut oil or honey, or a mixture of 2 tablespoons honey and 1 teaspoon soy sauce.*

NOTE: Spareribs need slow, even roasting over moderate heat. High heat tends to shrivel them. The heat may be turned up to 450 degrees during the last 5 minutes of roasting, however, to crisp the ribs.

TO ROAST INDIVIDUAL RIBS: *Cut through the meat to separate ribs completely. Marinate and drain as above. Then rub each rib lightly with peanut oil. Preheat oven to 325 degrees and place ribs on a rack over a water-filled drip pan. Roast 30 minutes. Brush with reserved marinade. Roast 5 minutes more. Turn ribs over and repeat process.*

TO ROAST RIB SEGMENTS: *Cut the ribs apart; then with a cleaver chop each rib, bone and all, in 2-inch sections. Marinate and drain as above. Preheat oven to 325 degrees. Roast in a pan 35 to 45 minutes, basting frequently with marinade.*

NOTE: This method shortens roasting time and produces very crisp ribs.

TO BARBECUE OVER CHARCOAL: *To barbecue spareribs on charcoal grills, prepare as above, but increase the amount of marinade and baste more frequently to keep ribs from drying out.*

NOTE: Some cooks find it easier to barbecue spareribs partially for 50 minutes in the home oven; then to complete the cooking later, out-of-doors over charcoal. After pre-cooking, let the ribs cool, then cut in 2-rib sections, wrap in foil, and refrigerate. When ready to use the ribs, unwrap and cook them over charcoal until they're reheated and browned (about 10 minutes on each side).

TO BROIL: *Since spareribs require slow, even cooking, broiling is not recommended. It invariably results in half-cooked or charred ribs. The ribs may be cooked, however, by other methods (steaming, simmering or roasting) until nearly done, and broiled just before serving, until crisp and golden (2 to 3 minutes on each side).*

TO KEEP WARM: *Keep barbecued ribs in a slow (200 degree) oven until ready to serve.*

TO PREPARE IN ADVANCE: *Roast marinated ribs as above. Let cool. Wrap in foil and refrigerate. (These will keep several days.) Before serving, reheat the still-wrapped ribs 10 to 15 minutes in a 350-degree oven.*

TO FREEZE: *Roast marinated ribs as above. Let cool. Seal tightly in foil and freeze. When ready to use, reheat the still-wrapped ribs 30 minutes in a 400-degree oven. Do not thaw first.*

STIR-FRIED SPARERIBS WITH BLACK BEAN SAUCE
6 servings

1 to 2 tablespoons fermented black beans	1 tablespoon cornstarch
2 pounds pork spareribs	1 teaspoon sugar
2 garlic cloves	2 teaspoons soy sauce
1 scallion stalk	½ cup water
2 tablespoons sherry	2 tablespoons oil
1 tablespoon water	½ teaspoon salt
1 teaspoon soy sauce	½ cup stock

1. Soak fermented black beans.

2. Cut ribs apart, then with a cleaver, chop each, bone and all, in 1-inch sections.

3. Mince garlic and scallion stalk, then mash with soaked black beans. Combine with sherry, water and soy sauce.

4. Blend cornstarch, sugar, remaining soy sauce and cold water to a paste.

5. Heat oil to smoking; stir in salt. Add rib sections and stir-fry until golden. Drain off fat.

6. Reduce heat to medium. Stir in black bean mixture and blend with meat (about 2 minutes).

7. Add stock and heat quickly. Cook, covered, over medium heat, 3 to 4 minutes.

8. Stir in cornstarch mixture to thicken. Serve hot.

VARIATION: For the fermented black beans, substitute brown bean sauce.

STIR-FRIED SWEET-AND-PUNGENT SPARERIBS
6 servings

sweet-and-pungent sauce   *2 pounds pork spareribs*
5 tablespoons oil

1. Prepare a sweet-and-pungent sauce (see pages 735–738).

2. Cut ribs apart; then with a cleaver, chop each, bone and all, in 1-inch sections.

3. Heat oil to smoking. Add ribs and stir-fry until well browned (about 10 minutes). Drain on paper toweling.

4. Meanwhile reheat sweet-and-pungent sauce. Briefly stir in rib sections to heat through.

DEEP-FRIED SWEET-AND-PUNGENT SPARERIBS I
6 servings

sweet-and-pungent sauce	*1 egg*
1 carrot	*5 tablespoons cornstarch*
1 cucumber	*1 tablespoon soy sauce*
1 garlic clove	*¼ teaspoon Five Spices*
½ cup vinegar	*¼ teaspoon pepper*
1 tablespoon sugar	*1 teaspoon salt*
½ teaspoon salt	*1 tablespoon vinegar*
2 pounds pork spareribs	*oil for deep-frying*

1. Prepare sweet-and-pungent sauce I (see pages 735–738).

2. Peel and sliver carrot and cucumber; mince garlic. Combine with vinegar, sugar and salt. Let stand 15 minutes or more.

3. Cut ribs apart, then with a cleaver, chop each, bone and all, in 1-inch sections. Wash in cold water and drain well.

4. Beat egg. Then blend with cornstarch, soy sauce, Five Spices, pepper, and remaining salt and vinegar to make a batter.

5. Dip rib sections in batter to coat. Heat oil to smoking. Add ribs a few at a time. Reduce heat slightly and deep-fry until golden. Drain on paper toweling.

6. Reheat sweet-and-pungent sauce. Briefly stir in ribs to reheat. Drain marinated carrots and cucumber and arrange on a serving platter with ribs and sauce on top.

DEEP-FRIED SWEET-AND-PUNGENT SPARERIBS II
6 servings

sweet-and-pungent sauce	*1 teaspoon salt*
2 pounds pork spareribs	*½ teaspoon sugar*
2 tablespoons soy sauce	*oil for deep-frying*
2 tablespoons sherry	*cornstarch*

1. Prepare a sweet-and-pungent sauce (see pages 735–738).

2. Cut ribs apart; then with a cleaver, chop each, bone and all, in 1-inch sections. Wash in cold water and drain well.

3. Mix soy sauce, sherry, salt and sugar. Add to rib sections and let stand 45 minutes, turning meat occasionally. Drain, discarding marinade.

4. Heat oil to smoking. Dredge ribs lightly in cornstarch, then add to oil a few at a time. Reduce heat slightly and deep-fry until golden. Drain on paper toweling. Transfer to a serving dish.

5. Reheat sweet-and-pungent sauce. Pour over ribs and serve.

NOTE: This dish may be served cold as well as hot. Or the ribs may be deep-fried in advance, then reheated briefly with the sweet-and-pungent sauce.

VARIATION: In step 4, coat ribs instead with a batter made with 1 egg, lightly beaten, and 5 tablespoons cornstarch.

DEEP-FRIED SPARERIBS, SIMMERED FIRST
6 servings

sweet-and-pungent sauce	*2 tablespoons cornstarch*
2 pounds pork spareribs	*2 tablespoons soy sauce*
water to cover	*water*

oil for deep-frying

1. Prepare a sweet-and-pungent sauce (see pages 735–738).

2. Cut ribs apart; then with a cleaver, chop each, bone and all, in 1-inch sections.

3. Place ribs in a pan with cold water to cover. Bring to a boil, then simmer, uncovered, 20 minutes. Drain, discarding liquid. Let ribs cool.

4. Combine cornstarch and soy sauce. Gradually stir in enough water to make a smooth batter. Dip rib sections in batter to coat.

5. Heat oil to smoking. Add ribs a few at a time. Reduce heat slightly and deep-fry until golden. Drain on paper toweling.

6. Reheat sweet-and-pungent sauce. Briefly stir in ribs to reheat.

VARIATION: In step 3, instead of simmering the ribs, parboil them; plunge into boiling water and cook, uncovered, 5 minutes.

STEAMED SPARERIBS WITH BLACK BEAN SAUCE
6 servings

1 to 2 tablespoons fermented black beans   1 teaspoon cornstarch
2 pounds pork spareribs   2 teaspoons soy sauce
1 to 2 garlic cloves   1 tablespoon sugar

1. Soak fermented black beans.

2. Cut ribs apart; then with a cleaver, chop each, bone and all, in 1-inch sections. Place in a shallow heatproof dish.

3. Mince garlic and mash with soaked black beans; then combine with cornstarch, soy sauce and sugar. Pour mixture over ribs.

4. Steam 45 minutes on a rack (see pages 831 and 33). Serve hot.

VARIATION: In step 3, add to black bean mixture 1 scallion stalk, minced; 2 tablespoons stock; 2 teaspoons vinegar; 1 teaspoon sherry and 1 teaspoon peanut oil.

BRAISED SPARERIBS WITH BLACK BEAN SAUCE
6 servings

1 to 2 tablespoons fermented black beans   2 tablespoons oil
2 pounds pork spareribs   ½ cup water
1 garlic clove   1 tablespoon cornstarch
2 slices fresh ginger root   ¼ cup water

1. Soak fermented black beans.

2. Cut ribs apart; then with a cleaver, chop each, bone and all, in 1-inch sections.

3. Mince garlic and ginger root, then mash with soaked black beans.

4. Heat oil in a heavy pan. Add black bean mixture and stir-fry a few times to heat through. Add spareribs and stir-fry over high heat to brown quickly.

5. Add water, heat quickly; then simmer ribs, covered, until done (about 30 minutes). If liquid evaporates, add some boiling water to prevent burning.

6. Blend cornstarch and remaining cold water to a paste; then stir in to thicken.

BRAISED SPARERIBS WITH RED BEAN CHEESE
6 servings

2 pounds pork spareribs   ½ teaspoon sugar
½ garlic clove   ½ teaspoon salt
1 slice fresh ginger root   2 tablespoons oil
¼ cup scallion tops   ½ cup water
2 tablespoons red bean cheese   1 tablespoon cornstarch
1 teaspoon soy sauce   ¼ cup water

1. Cut ribs apart; then with a cleaver, chop each, bone and all, in 1-inch sections. Mince garlic clove and ginger root. Cut scallion tops in 1-inch lengths.

2. Mash red bean cheese and combine with soy sauce, sugar and salt.

3. Heat oil in a heavy pan. Add minced garlic and ginger and stir-fry a few times. Add spareribs and stir-fry to coat with oil. Add red bean cheese mixture and stir-fry until ribs begin to brown.

4. Add water and heat quickly; then simmer, covered, until ribs are done (about 30 minutes). If liquid evaporates, add some boiling water to prevent burning.

5. Blend cornstarch and remaining cold water to a paste; then stir in to thicken. Sprinkle with scallion tops and serve.

BRAISED SPARERIBS WITH PINEAPPLE
6 servings

2 pounds pork spareribs	2 tablespoons oil
¼ cup soy sauce	1 tablespoon flour
½ cup pineapple juice	½ teaspoon salt
¼ cup sugar	1 cup canned pineapple chunks
¼ cup vinegar	1 tablespoon cornstarch
½ cup water	3 tablespoons water

1. Cut ribs apart; then with a cleaver, chop each, bone and all, in 2-inch sections. Add soy sauce and toss. Let stand 45 minutes, turning occasionally. Drain, discarding sauce.

2. Drain canned pineapple, reserving juice. Combine juice with sugar, vinegar and water.

3. Heat oil in a heavy pan. Add ribs and stir-fry to brown (3 to 4 minutes).

4. Stir in flour, then pineapple juice mixture. Heat quickly, then simmer, covered, until ribs are tender (about 45 minutes).

5. Add salt and canned pineapple chunks, stirring in gently only to heat through.

6. Meanwhile blend cornstarch and cold water to a paste, then stir in to thicken. Serve hot.

SPARERIBS SIMMERED WITH MUSHROOMS
6 servings

9 dried black mushrooms	2 or 3 cloves star anise
2 pounds pork spareribs	3 tablespoons soy sauce
water to cover	1 teaspoon salt
water to cover	1 tablespoon cornstarch
3 tablespoons water	

1. Soak dried mushrooms.

2. Cut ribs apart; then with a cleaver, chop each, bone and all, in 2-inch sections.

3. Boil water in a heavy pot. Add spareribs and cook, uncovered, 15 minutes. Drain. Rinse ribs under cold running water. Drain again.

4. Return ribs to pot. Add fresh cold water to cover. Cut soaked mushrooms in ¼-inch slices and add, along with star anise, soy sauce and salt.

5. Bring to a boil. Then simmer, covered, until tender (about 45 minutes).

6. Blend cornstarch and remaining cold water to a paste; then stir in to thicken. Serve hot.

NOTE: This dish may be prepared in advance and reheated. The cornstarch paste, however, should be added just before serving.

SIMMERED SPARERIBS WITH SHERRY
6 servings

2 pounds pork spareribs	1 teaspoon salt
2 cups water	2 tablespoons sherry
4 tablespoons soy sauce	1 teaspoon sugar

1. Cut ribs apart; then with a cleaver, chop each, bone and all, in 1-inch sections.

2. Place in a heavy pan with cold water, soy sauce and salt. Bring to a boil, then simmer, covered, 1 hour. Drain well.

3. Heat a skillet and add ribs, sherry and sugar. Stir-fry in over high heat until liquid evaporates. Serve hot.

DEEP-FRIED SPARERIBS SIMMERED WITH CATSUP
6 servings

2 pounds pork spareribs	1 large onion
4 tablespoons soy sauce	1 cup stock
2 tablespoons sherry	¼ cup catsup
2 eggs	2 teaspoons sugar
cornstarch	1 tablespoon soy sauce
oil for deep-frying	2 tablespoons oil

1. Cut ribs apart; then with a cleaver, chop each, bone and all, in 1-inch sections. Combine soy sauce and sherry. Add to ribs and toss. Let stand 1 hour, turning occasionally. Drain, discarding marinade.

2. Beat eggs. Dip marinated rib sections in egg; then dredge in cornstarch to coat. Meanwhile, heat oil to smoking.

3. Add coated ribs a few at a time. Reduce heat slightly and deep-fry until golden. Drain on paper toweling.

4. Slice onion thin. Combine stock, catsup, sugar and remaining soy sauce.

5. Heat remaining oil. Add onion and stir-fry until translucent. Add stock-catsup mixture and simmer 1 minute.

6. Add ribs and simmer, uncovered, 10 minutes more. Serve hot.

❈ *Beef* ❈

BECAUSE OF the scarcity of cattle in China, beef cookery was never developed as fully as pork. However, contact with the West (and the greater availability of beef to the Chinese outside China) had its inevitable impact. With characteristic ingenuity, the Chinese adapted their cooking methods and seasonings to beef cookery and made it their own. Beef is cooked in many ways: stir-fried, deep-fried, steamed, braised, stewed, barbecued, dry-fried or smoked.

Many cuts are used: brisket, chuck roast, chuck steak, flank steak, pot roast, short ribs, round steak, rump roast, shank, sirloin steak, beef tenderloin; also beef liver, heart and kidneys. Particularly favored is beef plate, a coarse cut with strong fibers and muscles which, when simmered slowly for hours, becomes tender and tasty. The Chinese call this white abdomen, or hundred abdomen, of beef.

COOKING TECHNIQUES AND SUITABLE CUTS OF BEEF

STIR-FRYING (sliced thin, occasionally minced): chuck roast, chuck steak, flank steak, round steak, top rump, sirloin steak, beef tenderloin and beef liver

DEEP-FRYING (cubed or shredded): flank steak, sirloin steak, beef tenderloin, short ribs and beef kidneys

STEAMING (sliced, slivered or minced): chuck steak, flank steak, round steak, sirloin steak and top rump

BRAISING (whole or in chunks): brisket, chuck roast, chuck steak, eye round, plate, pot roast, rump roast, shank and beef heart

RED-SIMMERING (whole, in chunks or cubes): chuck steak, pot roast and shank

BARBECUING (sliced): beef tenderloin, porterhouse steak and short ribs

DRY-FRYING (sliced thin or slivered): sirloin steak

SMOKING (sliced thin): beef tenderloin

NOTE: Regardless of cut, beef should have a good red color and little fat. It should also be firm to the touch.

Tenderizing Beef: Some of the tougher cuts of meat may be tenderized before stir-frying, deep-frying, braising or red-simmering. (See page 823.)

Tips on Stir-frying: Beef should never be stir-fried by itself longer than two minutes before the vegetables, liquid seasonings, etc., are added to the pan. If cooked longer by itself, the beef will toughen.

The best general cut of beef for stir-frying is flank steak. Its flat slablike structure, with a long grain running through it in only one direction, makes it simple to handle and to cut crosswise *against* the grain. Flank steak can be bought whole (it weighs about 3 pounds), then cut lengthwise *with* the grain into 3 or 4 long thick strips, each of which can be wrapped and frozen separately until needed. When ready to use, it may be thawed slightly, and sliced easily against the grain.

Tips on Braising: Braised beef can be cooked whole or cubed, and served hot or cold. If it's to be served hot, it may be cooked with such vegetables as bamboo shoots, carrots, lily buds or turnips. Its sauce can be thickened with a cornstarch paste just before serving. If it's to be served cold, the beef should be cooked whole, cooled and refrigerated (its gravy will jell and become aspic-like), then sliced thin just before serving. Braised beef, when cooked alone, is often spiced with star anise, then chilled, sliced thin and served as an hors d'oeuvre.

Braised beef dishes will keep about a week. They can also be frozen and, when you are ready to use them, reheated without any preliminary thawing.

BASIC STIR-FRIED BEEF I
About 4 servings

½ *pound lean beef*	1 *pound vegetables*
1 *tablespoon cornstarch*	1 *or 2 slices fresh ginger root*
1 *tablespoon soy sauce*	1½ *tablespoons oil*
1 *tablespoon sherry*	1½ *tablespoons oil*
½ *teaspoon sugar*	½ *teaspoon salt*

½ *cup stock*

1. Slice beef thin against the grain. Combine cornstarch, soy sauce, sherry and sugar. Add to beef and toss to coat. Let stand 15 minutes, turning occasionally.

2. Slice vegetables. Mince ginger root.

3. Heat oil. Add beef and stir-fry until it loses its redness (about 2 minutes). Remove from pan.

4. Heat remaining oil. Add salt, then ginger root and stir-fry a few times. Add vegetables and stir-fry to heat and coat with oil.

5. Stir in stock and heat quickly. Cook, covered, over medium heat, until vegetables are nearly done.

6. Return beef and stir-fry to reheat and blend flavors (about 1 minute more). Serve at once.

NOTE: Any vegetable can be used (see page 583 for details on cooking time). For suggested combinations, see page 587.

VARIATIONS: In step 1, add to the cornstarch mixture 1 egg, beaten.

Omit the cornstarch, sherry and sugar, and double the soy sauce instead. Toss beef in the soy, then dip in beaten egg.

In step 3, before adding beef, add 1 garlic clove, crushed; and 1 scallion stalk, cut in ½-inch sections, and stir-fry a few times.

BASIC STIR-FRIED BEEF II
About 4 servings

½ pound lean beef	1 tablespoon cornstarch
1 pound vegetables	1 tablespoon sherry
1 or 2 slices fresh ginger root	2 tablespoons soy sauce
1 garlic clove	1½ tablespoons oil
1 scallion stalk	1½ tablespoons oil

½ cup stock

1. Slice beef thin against the grain. Slice vegetables. Mince ginger root. Crush or mince garlic. Cut scallion stalk in 1-inch sections.

2. Blend cornstarch, sherry and soy sauce.

3. Heat oil. Add ginger root, garlic and scallion and stir-fry a few times. Add beef and stir-fry until it loses its redness (about 2 minutes). Remove from pan.

4. Heat remaining oil. Add vegetables and stir-fry to heat and coat with oil.

5. Stir in stock and heat quickly. Cook, covered, over medium heat, until vegetables are nearly done.

6. Return beef, stir-frying to reheat and blend flavors. Then stir in cornstarch mixture to thicken. Serve at once.

NOTE: See Note above.

VARIATIONS: In step 3, add with the ginger root, etc., 1 tablespoon fermented black beans (soaked), mashed; or 1 tablespoon brown bean sauce, mashed.

Cook the vegetables first (as in steps 4 and 5) and remove from pan. Then stir-fry the beef (as in step 3). Stir in the sherry and soy sauce (omit the cornstarch). Then return vegetables, stir-frying to reheat and blend flavors.

SUGGESTED VEGETABLE COMBINATIONS FOR BASIC STIR-FRIED BEEF I OR II

½ head cabbage, 4 celery stalks, 1 small onion
½ cup mushrooms, ¼ cup bamboo shoots, ¼ cup celery, ¼ cup onion
½ cup green pepper or carrots, ½ cup celery, 1 to 2 cups bean sprouts
½ cup mushrooms, 2 cups green peas
1 small head cauliflower, 2 cups green peas (or 1 to 2 green peppers)
1 cup bamboo shoots, 12 snow peas
1½ cups potatoes, ½ cup spinach

STIR-FRIED BEEF AND BAMBOO SHOOTS
About 4 servings

½ pound lean beef	2 teaspoons soy sauce
½ cup bamboo shoots	1 tablespoon cornstarch
¼ pound fresh mushrooms	3 tablespoons water
2 slices fresh ginger root	2 to 3 tablespoons oil
3 tablespoons sherry	½ teaspoon salt
1 teaspoon sugar	dash of pepper

½ cup stock

1. Slice beef thin against the grain. Slice bamboo shoots and fresh mushrooms. Mince ginger root.

2. In one cup, combine sherry, sugar and soy sauce. In another, blend cornstarch and cold water to a paste.

3. Heat oil. Add ginger root and stir-fry a few times. Add beef and stir-fry until it loses its redness.

4. Add vegetables and stir-fry until mushrooms begin to soften (about 1 minute). Stir in sherry mixture, then salt and pepper.

5. Stir in stock and heat quickly. Cook, covered, 1 to 2 minutes, over medium heat.

6. Stir in cornstarch paste to thicken. Serve at once.

STIR-FRIED BEEF AND BEAN CURD
About 4 servings

½ *pound lean beef*	1 *tablespoon water*
1 *teaspoon cornstarch*	*dash of pepper*
1 *teaspoon soy sauce*	1 *tablespoon cornstarch*
2 *teaspoons sherry*	1 *teaspoon soy sauce*
¼ *teaspoon sugar*	¼ *teaspoon sugar*
2 *or* 3 *bean curd cakes*	2 *tablespoons oil*
1 *garlic clove*	½ *teaspoon salt*
1 *or* 2 *scallions*	½ *cup stock*

1. Mince or grind beef. Combine cornstarch, soy sauce, sherry and sugar. Add to beef and toss.

2. Cut each bean curd cake in 6 pieces. Separately mince garlic and scallion.

3. Blend cold water, pepper and remaining cornstarch, soy sauce and sugar.

4. Heat oil. Add salt, then garlic, and stir-fry a few times. Add beef and stir-fry until it loses its redness (less than a minute).

5. Stir in stock and heat quickly. Add bean curd and cook, covered, 1 to 2 minutes.

6. Stir in cornstarch mixture to thicken. Serve at once, garnished with minced scallions.

VARIATIONS: For the garlic, substitute 2 slices fresh ginger root, minced.

Omit the cornstarch mixture in step 1. Then in step 5, add with the stock a mixture of 1 tablespoon oyster sauce, 1 teaspoon soy sauce, 1 teaspoon sherry, ½ teaspoon sugar and a dash of pepper. Add bean curd and bring mixture to a boil. Pick up step 6.

STIR-FRIED BEEF AND BITTER MELON
About 4 servings

1 tablespoon fermented black beans

1 pound bitter melon

½ pound lean beef

2 teaspoons cornstarch

2 teaspoons soy sauce

¼ teaspoon salt

pinch of sugar

2 tablespoons water

1 tablespoon cornstarch

1 garlic clove

1½ tablespoons oil

¼ teaspoon salt

1½ tablespoons oil

½ cup stock

1. Soak fermented black beans.

2. Cut bitter melon lengthwise in half. Scoop out seeds; then cut in ¼-inch slices. Parboil 2 to 3 minutes.

3. Slice beef thin against the grain. Combine cornstarch, soy sauce, salt and sugar. Add to beef and toss to coat.

4. Blend water and remaining cornstarch to a paste. Drain soaked black beans. Mince garlic and mash with beans.

5. Heat oil. Add remaining salt, then beef. Stir-fry until beef loses its redness (about 2 minutes). Remove from pan.

6. Heat remaining oil. Add black bean mixture and stir-fry a few times. Add bitter melon and stir-fry to heat and coat with oil (about 1 minute).

7. Stir in stock and heat quickly. Cook, covered, 2 minutes, over medium heat.

8. Return beef and stir-fry gently to reheat and blend flavors. Then stir in cornstarch paste to thicken. Serve at once.

STIR-FRIED BEEF AND CHINESE CABBAGE
About 4 servings

½ pound lean beef

1 pound Chinese cabbage

2 tablespoons oil

½ cup stock

½ teaspoon salt

dash of pepper

2 teaspoons cornstarch

2 tablespoons water

1. Slice beef thin against the grain, then in ½- by 2-inch strips. Slice Chinese cabbage stems in similar strips.

2. Heat oil. Add beef and stir-fry until it loses its redness.

3. Add cabbage strips and stir-fry to soften slightly.

4. Stir in stock, salt and pepper and heat quickly. Cook, covered, over medium heat until done (2 to 3 minutes).

5. Meanwhile, blend cornstarch and cold water to a paste, then stir in to thicken. Serve at once.

VARIATION: In step 1, toss the beef in a mixture of 2 teaspoons cornstarch, 2 teaspoons soy sauce and 2 teaspoons sherry. Cook as in step 2; then remove from pan. In step 3, sprinkle the cabbage with ¼ teaspoon salt, ¼ teaspoon sugar and ½ teaspoon soy sauce; then stir-fry. Pick up step 4, omitting the salt and pepper. *Then* return beef to pan only to reheat and thicken with cornstarch paste.

STIR-FRIED BEEF AND PRESERVED MUSTARD CABBAGE
About 4 servings

½ pound lean beef	*2 tablespoons oil*
½ pound preserved mustard cabbage	*1 tablespoon oil*
1 tablespoon cornstarch	*1 cup stock*
2 tablespoons water	*1 to 2 tablespoons sugar*

½ teaspoon salt

1. Slice beef thin against the grain. Rinse mustard cabbage and squeeze dry; then cut in 1-inch sections.

2. Blend cornstarch and cold water to a paste.

3. Heat oil. Add beef and stir-fry until it begins to brown. Remove from pan.

4. Heat remaining oil. Add preserved cabbage and stir-fry ½ minute.

5. Add stock, sugar and salt. Cook, covered, 3 to 4 minutes over medium heat, stirring a few times.

6. Return beef, stir-frying to reheat and blend flavors (about 1 minute).

7. Stir in cornstarch paste to thicken. Serve at once.

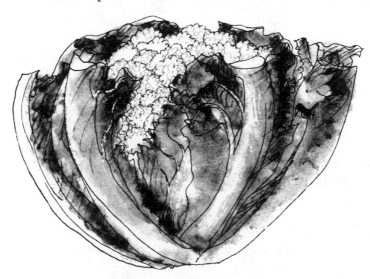

STIR-FRIED BEEF AND CAULIFLOWER
About 4 servings

½ pound lean beef
¼ teaspoon sugar
½ teaspoon salt
1 teaspoon soy sauce
1 head cauliflower
1½ tablespoons oil

1½ tablespoons oil
½ teaspoon salt
½ teaspoon sugar
1 teaspoon soy sauce
½ cup stock
1 tablespoon cornstarch

2 tablespoons water

1. Slice beef thin against the grain. Combine sugar, salt and soy sauce. Add to beef and toss to coat.
2. Break cauliflower in small flowerets; cut stalks diagonally in ½-inch slices. Then parboil.
3. Heat oil. Add beef and stir-fry until it begins to brown. Remove from pan.
4. Heat remaining oil; stir in salt. Then add cauliflower and remaining sugar and soy sauce. Stir-fry 1 minute.
5. Stir in stock and heat quickly. Cook, covered, 2 to 3 minutes over medium heat. Meanwhile blend cornstarch and water to a paste.
6. Return beef, stir-frying briefly to reheat. Then stir in cornstarch paste to thicken. Serve at once.

STIR-FRIED BEEF AND CELERY
About 4 servings

½ pound lean beef
1 teaspoon cornstarch
¼ teaspoon sugar
1 teaspoon sherry
1 teaspoon soy sauce
1 teaspoon oil
5 celery stalks

1 garlic clove
2 teaspoons cornstarch
¼ teaspoon sugar
2 tablespoons water
dash of pepper
1½ tablespoons oil
½ cup stock

1½ tablespoons oil

1. Shred beef. Combine cornstarch, sugar, sherry, soy sauce and oil. Add to beef and toss to coat.
2. Shred celery lengthwise; then cut in 1½-inch lengths. Peel but do not crush garlic.
3. Combine remaining cornstarch and sugar with water and pepper.
4. Heat oil. Rub pan with garlic clove until garlic turns brown; then discard.

(Hold garlic with chopsticks or fork.) Add celery and stir-fry a few times to coat with oil.

5. Stir in stock and heat quickly. Cook, covered, 2 minutes over medium heat. Remove celery and liquid from pan.

6. Heat remaining oil. Add beef and stir-fry until it begins to brown. Return celery and liquid, stir-frying to reheat and blend flavors.

7. Stir in cornstarch mixture to thicken. Serve at once.

STIR-FRIED CURRIED BEEF
About 4 servings

½ pound lean beef	1 tablespoon cornstarch
1 large onion	3 tablespoons water
1 to 2 slices fresh ginger root	2 tablespoons oil
½ cup stock	1 to 2 tablespoons curry
1 teaspoon sugar	1 tablespoon sherry

1. Slice beef thin against the grain. Slice onion thin. Mince ginger root.

2. In one cup, combine stock and sugar. In another, blend cornstarch and cold water to a paste.

3. Heat oil. Add onion and stir-fry until translucent (do not brown). Add curry and ginger root and stir-fry a few times more until curry smells pungent.

4. Add beef and stir-fry until it loses its redness (about 2 minutes). Stir in sherry until it evaporates (about 1 minute).

5. Then stir in stock mixture and heat quickly. Cook, covered, 1 to 2 minutes over medium heat.

6. Stir in cornstarch paste to thicken. Serve at once.

STIR-FRIED BEEF AND GINGER ROOT
About 4 servings

½ pound lean beef	2 tablespoons oil
¼ cup fresh ginger root	½ teaspoon salt
¼ cup scallion stalks	2 teaspoons soy sauce
1 tablespoon cornstarch	pinch of sugar
2 tablespoons water	¼ cup stock

1. Cut beef against the grain in ¼-inch slices, then in 1- by 2-inch strips. Peel ginger root; slice as thin as possible. Cut scallions in 1-inch sections.

2. Blend cornstarch and cold water to a paste.

3. Heat oil. Add salt, then ginger root and scallion. Stir-fry a few times. Add beef and stir-fry until it loses its redness (about 1 minute).

4. Add soy sauce and sugar and stir-fry 1 to 2 minutes more. Then add stock and stir in well.

5. Stir in cornstarch paste to thicken. Serve at once.

STIR-FRIED BEEF AND LOTUS ROOT
About 4 servings

2 tablespoons cloud ear mushrooms	1½ tablespoons oil
½ pound lean beef	1½ tablespoons oil
1 teaspoon cornstarch	½ teaspoon salt
¼ teaspoon sugar	¼ teaspoon sugar
1 teaspoon soy sauce	1 teaspoon soy sauce
1 pound fresh lotus root	½ cup stock
¾ cup celery	2 teaspoons cornstarch
½ cup dried onion	2 tablespoons water

1. Soak cloud ear mushrooms.

2. Slice beef thin against the grain. Combine cornstarch, sugar and soy sauce. Add to beef and toss to coat.

3. Peel lotus root; cut in ¼-inch slices, then each slice in 4 parts. Cut celery diagonally in ¼-inch sections. Slice dried onion thin.

4. Heat oil. Add beef and stir-fry until it begins to brown. Remove from pan.

5. Heat remaining oil. Add lotus root, celery, mushrooms and onion. Stir-fry a few times to coat with oil.

6. Add salt, remaining sugar and soy sauce and stir-fry 2 minutes more.

7. Stir in stock and heat quickly. Cook, covered, 3 minutes over medium heat. Meanwhile blend remaining cornstarch and cold water to a paste.

8. Return beef, stir-frying a few times to reheat. Stir in cornstarch paste to thicken. Serve at once.

STIR-FRIED BEEF AND MUSHROOMS
About 4 servings

½ pound lean beef	½ pound fresh mushrooms
1 tablespoon cornstarch	1 slices fresh ginger root
1 tablespoon sherry	1½ tablespoons oil
1 tablespoon soy sauce	1½ tablespoons oil
½ teaspoon sugar	½ teaspoon salt
	½ cup stock

1. Slice beef thin against the grain. Combine cornstarch, sherry, soy sauce and sugar. Add to beef and toss to coat. Let stand 15 minutes, turning occasionally.

2. Slice mushrooms thin. Mince ginger root.

3. Heat oil. Add ginger root and stir-fry a few times. Add beef and stir-fry until it loses its redness. Remove from pan.

4. Heat remaining oil. Add salt, then mushrooms. Stir-fry to soften. Return beef and stir-fry ½ minute more.

5. Stir in stock and heat quickly. Cook, covered, 1 to 2 minutes over medium heat. Serve at once.

VARIATIONS: For the fresh mushrooms, substitute canned button mushrooms.

In step 4, after the salt, add 1 cup onions, sliced thin. Stir-fry until translucent; then add mushrooms.

Use a good cut of beef steak and dice in 1-inch cubes. Also dice the mushrooms. In step 3, add to the hot oil and ginger 2 small yellow onions, diced; stir-fry until translucent. Then add beef and stir-fry as above; remove with onions from pan. In step 4, add with the mushrooms ½ celery stalk, diced. Then pick up step 5.

STIR-FRIED BEEF AND ONIONS
About 4 servings

½ pound lean beef	3 large onions
1 tablespoon cornstarch	2 tablespoons oil
1 tablespoon soy sauce	½ teaspoon salt
¼ teaspoon pepper	1½ tablespoons oil

1. Slice beef thin against the grain. Combine cornstarch, soy sauce and pepper; add to beef and toss to coat. Slice onions.

2. Heat oil. Add salt, then onions, and stir-fry until translucent but still crisp. Remove from pan.

3. Heat remaining oil. Add beef and stir-fry until it begins to brown.

4. Return onions and stir-fry to heat through and blend flavors (about 1 minute more). Serve at once.

VARIATIONS: In step 1, add to the cornstarch mixture 1 tablespoon sherry or ½ teaspoon peanut oil. Omit the pepper.

In step 3, add to the hot oil 2 teaspoons fermented black beans (soaked) and stir-fry a few times; then add beef.

After step 3, sprinkle beef with a few drops of sesame oil.

In step 4, stir in with the onions a mixture of 1 tablespoon soy sauce, 1 tablespoon sherry, ½ teaspoon salt and ½ teaspoon sugar. Omit the salt in step 2.

STIR-FRIED BEEF AND OYSTER SAUCE I

About 4 servings

½ pound beef
2 tablespoons oyster sauce
½ teaspoon salt
½ teaspoon sugar
dash of pepper

¼ cup stock
2 teaspoons cornstarch
1 teaspoon soy sauce
2 tablespoons water
2 tablespoons oil

1. Slice beef thin against the grain.

2. In one cup, combine oyster sauce, salt, sugar, pepper and stock. In another, blend cornstarch, soy sauce and water to a paste.

3. Heat oil. Add beef and stir-fry until it loses its redness (about 2 minutes).

4. Stir in oyster sauce mixture and heat quickly. Cook, covered, 1 minute over medium heat.

5. Stir in cornstarch paste to thicken. Serve at once.

VARIATIONS: In step 2, add to the oyster sauce mixture 3 scallion tops, cut in 1-inch sections.

In step 2, omit the stock from the oyster sauce mixture. Add instead: 3 tablespoons sherry, 1 tablespoon soy sauce and 1 to 2 slices fresh ginger root, minced. In step 4, stir this mixture in well. *Then* add the stock and cook, covered, 1 to 2 minutes. Pick up step 5, but omit soy sauce from the cornstarch paste.

In step 3, before adding the beef, add 1 garlic clove, crushed; and 1 small onion, sliced thin. Stir-fry until onion is translucent.

STIR-FRIED BEEF AND OYSTER SAUCE II
About 4 servings

½ *pound beef*	1 *tablespoon cornstarch*
1 *teaspoon cornstarch*	2 *tablespoons water*
1 *teaspoon soy sauce*	½ *cup scallion stalks*
¼ *teaspoon salt*	2 *tablespoons oil*
pinch of sugar	2 *tablespoons oyster sauce*
	¼ *cup stock*

1. Slice beef thin against the grain. Combine cornstarch, soy sauce, salt and sugar. Add to beef and toss to coat.

2. Blend remaining cornstarch and cold water to a paste. Cut scallions in 1-inch sections.

3. Heat oil. Add scallions and stir-fry until translucent. Add beef and stir-fry until it loses its redness.

4. Add oyster sauce and stir-fry 1 to 2 minutes more.

5. Stir in stock and heat quickly. Cook, covered, 1 to 2 minutes over medium heat.

6. Stir in cornstarch paste to thicken. Serve at once.

STIR-FRIED BEEF AND PEAS
About 4 servings

½ *pound lean beef*	½ *teaspoon salt*
1 *or 2 slices fresh ginger root*	½ *teaspoon sugar*
1 *pound peas*	1 *tablespoon cornstarch*
1 *tablespoon soy sauce*	2 *tablespoons water*
1 *tablespoon sherry*	2 *tablespoons oil*

1. Mince or grind beef. Mince ginger root. Shell and parboil peas.

2. In one cup, combine soy sauce, sherry, salt and sugar. In another, blend cornstarch and cold water to a paste.

3. Heat oil. Add ginger, then beef and stir-fry until beef begins to brown.

4. Stir in soy sauce mixture to blend.

5. Add parboiled peas and stir-fry 1 to 2 minutes more. (Taste peas to see if they're done.)

6. Stir in cornstarch paste to thicken and serve at once.

NOTE: If the mixture becomes too dry in step 5, add a few spoonfuls of liquid from the parboiled peas.

VARIATIONS: In step 1, mince or grind 4 to 6 water chestnuts with the beef.

In step 1, add to the beef and ginger root the seasonings and 2 teaspoons cornstarch. Blend well and let stand 15 minutes. Omit steps 2, 4, and 6.

In step 3, before adding the beef, add to the hot oil ¼ pound fresh mushrooms and/or 1 onion, sliced thin. Stir-fry until slightly softened; then remove from pan. Add more oil and stir-fry beef as indicated. Return mushrooms and/or onion in step 5, when adding the peas.

Do not parboil the peas. After step 4, remove the beef from pan. Add more oil and heat. Then add the peas; ¼ cup celery and ½ cup onion, both diced, and stir-fry to coat with oil. Stir in and quickly heat ½ cup stock, ¼ teaspoon sugar and 1 teaspoon soy sauce. Cook, covered, until vegetables are nearly done. Return beef and reheat; then pick up step 6.

After step 4, stir in 2 cups cooked rice. Then add the peas and a few tablespoons of their parboiling liquid to moisten the mixture. Cook, stirring, to heat through.

Prepare ⅛ pound thin rice-flour noodles as a deep-fried, crisp white garnish. (See page 827.) Arrange on a serving platter with beef and peas on top.

STIR-FRIED BEEF AND PEPPERS
About 4 servings

½ pound lean beef	2 green peppers
1 tablespoon soy sauce	1½ tablespoons oil
1 tablespoon sherry	1½ tablespoons oil
½ teaspoon sugar	½ teaspoon salt

1 tablespoon soy sauce

1. Dice beef in ½-inch cubes. Combine soy sauce, sherry and sugar. Add to beef and toss. Let stand 15 minutes, turning occasionally.

2. Seed green peppers; then dice in 1-inch squares.

3. Heat oil. Add peppers and stir-fry until slightly softened. Remove from pan.

4. Heat remaining oil. Add beef and stir-fry until it begins to brown.

5. Return peppers. Sprinkle with salt and remaining soy sauce. Stir-fry until done (about 2 minutes more). Serve at once.

NOTE: This is sometimes called Chinese Pepper Steak.

VARIATIONS: **In step 1,** substitute either of the following for the soy mixture:

1 teaspoon cornstarch, 1 teaspoon tomato sauce, 1 teaspoon sherry, 1 tablespoon soy sauce, ½ teaspoon sugar and 1 egg, beaten.

2 tablespoons soy sauce, ½ teaspoon salt, dash of pepper, and 1 small onion and 1 garlic clove, both minced. At the end of step 1, drain the beef and reserve this marinade. Then add the marinade along with the peppers in step 5, omiting the salt and soy sauce.

In step 3, add with the peppers 1 cup celery, diced.

For color contrast, use 1 green and 1 sweet red pepper.

STIR-FRIED BEEF WITH SWEET-AND-PUNGENT RADISHES
About 4 servings

½ pound lean beef	*2 tablespoons oil*
1 tablespoon cornstarch	*1½ tablespoons sugar*
2 tablespoons soy sauce	*2 tablespoons vinegar*
10 to 12 radishes	*¼ to ½ cup water*

1. Slice beef thin against the grain. Combine cornstarch and soy sauce. Add to beef and toss to coat. Slice (but do not peel) radishes.

2. Heat oil. Add beef and stir-fry until it loses its redness. Remove from pan.

3. Add to pan sugar, vinegar and water, and heat, stirring to dissolve sugar. Then return beef and stir-fry about 2 minutes more.

4. Add sliced radishes, stir-frying only to heat through. (If left in the pan too long, radishes will lose their color.) Serve at once.

STIR-FRIED BEEF AND SNOW PEAS
About 4 servings

½ pound lean beef	2 teaspoons water
1 teaspoon cornstarch	dash of pepper
¼ teaspoon sugar	½ pound snow peas
1 teaspoon soy sauce	1 wedge fresh ginger root
2 teaspoons sherry	1½ tablespoons oil
2 teaspoons cornstarch	½ teaspoon salt
½ teaspoon sugar	¼ cup stock

1½ tablespoons oil

1. Slice beef thin against the grain. Combine cornstarch, sugar, soy sauce and sherry. Add to beef and toss to coat.

2. Blend remaining cornstarch and sugar with cold water and pepper.

3. Stem and string snow peas. Crush ginger root.

4. Heat oil. Add salt, then ginger, and stir-fry a few times. Add snow peas and stir-fry to coat with oil.

5. Stir in stock and heat quickly. Cook, covered, over medium heat, ½ minute. Stir a few times and remove snow peas and liquid from pan.

6. Heat remaining oil. Add beef and stir-fry until it begins to brown. Return snow peas and stir-fry briefly to reheat and blend flavors.

7. Stir in cornstarch mixture to thicken. Serve at once.

STIR-FRIED BEEF AND STRING BEANS I
About 4 servings

½ pound lean beef	½ teaspoon salt
1 tablespoon cornstarch	1 pound string beans
1 tablespoon sherry	1½ tablespoons oil
2 tablespoons soy sauce	1½ tablespoons oil
½ teaspoon sugar	½ cup string-bean liquid

1. Slice beef thin against the grain. Combine cornstarch, sherry, soy sauce, sugar and salt. Add to beef and toss to coat.

2. Stem string beans. Cut lengthwise in strips and parboil. (Reserve parboiling liquid.)

3. Heat oil. Add beef and stir-fry until it loses its redness. Remove from pan.

4. Heat remaining oil. Add string beans and stir-fry to coat with oil.

5. Stir in reserved string-bean liquid and heat quickly. Return beef and cook, covered, over medium heat, 2 minutes. Serve at once.

VARIATION: In step 1, omit the cornstarch mixture. In step 3, stir-fry the string beans first and remove from pan. In step 4, stir-fry the beef until it loses its redness. Then stir in with the beef a mixture of ¼ teaspoon sugar, ½ teaspoon brown bean sauce and 1 teaspoon soy sauce. Return the string beans and stir-fry a few times. Then pick up step 5.

STIR-FRIED BEEF AND STRING BEANS II
About 4 servings

½ pound lean beef	½ teaspoon salt
1 small onion	1½ tablespoons oil
1 garlic clove	¼ cup stock
1 pound string beans	1 tablespoon cornstarch
1½ tablespoons oil	½ teaspoon sherry

3 tablespoons water

1. Mince or grind beef. Chop onion. Mince garlic.

2. Stem string beans, cut in 1½-inch sections; then parboil.

3. Heat oil. Add salt, then onion and garlic, and stir-fry a few times. Add beef and stir-fry until it loses its redness (about 1 minute). Remove from pan.

4. Heat remaining oil. Add parboiled beans and stir-fry to coat with oil. Stir in stock and heat quickly.

5. Return beef and cook, covered, 2 minutes over medium heat.

6. Meanwhile blend cornstarch, sherry and cold water to a paste. Then stir in to thicken. Serve at once.

VARIATION: In step 6, omit the cornstarch paste. Instead, quickly stir in 2 eggs, beaten; cook over low heat until eggs begin to set. Serve at once.

STIR-FRIED BEEF AND TEA MELON
About 4 servings

½ pound lean beef	¼ teaspoon sugar
1 teaspoon cornstarch	½ cup tea melon
2 teaspoons sherry	2 tablespoons oil
½ teaspoon soy sauce	½ teaspoon salt

1. Shred beef. Combine cornstarch, sherry, soy sauce and sugar. Add to beef and toss to coat.

2. Shred tea melon.

3. Heat oil. Add salt, then beef, and stir-fry until meat begins to brown.

4. Add tea melon and stir-fry to heat through and blend flavors (about 1½ minutes more). Serve at once.

NOTE: Use the tea melon that comes combined with preserved ginger root (shred the latter as well).

STIR-FRIED BEEF AND TOMATOES
About 4 servings

½ pound lean beef	½ teaspoon salt
3 tomatoes	¼ cup stock
1 to 2 scallion stalks	1 tablespoon cornstarch
2 tablespoons oil	3 tablespoons water

1. Cut beef against the grain in ¼-inch slices, then in 1- by 2-inch strips. Peel and quarter tomatoes. Cut scallion stalks in 1-inch sections.

2. Heat oil. Add salt, then scallions, and stir-fry until translucent. Add beef and stir-fry until it loses its redness.

3. Stir in stock and heat quickly. Cook, covered, 1 to 2 minutes over medium heat.

4. Meanwhile blend cornstarch and cold water to a paste; then stir in to thicken.

5. Stir in tomato wedges gently, only to heat through. Serve at once.

VARIATIONS: Omit the scallions. After step 2, remove beef from pan. Heat another 2 tablespoons of oil. Add 1 green pepper, diced; ½ cup celery, diced; and 2 dried onions, cut in wedges; stir-fry a minute to coat with oil. Then add the stock as in step 3, but cook, covered, 3 minutes. Next, add 1 teaspoon curry and 1 teaspoon sugar and cook, stirring, 1 minute. Then return the beef and pick up steps 4 and 5.

In step 5, stir in 2 tablespoons tomato sauce for additional color.

STIR-FRIED BEEF AND CHINESE TURNIPS
About 4 servings

½ pound lean beef
½ teaspoon cornstarch
¼ teaspoon sugar
½ teaspoon soy sauce
1 pound Chinese turnips
½ cup scallion stalks
1 to 2 garlic cloves

1½ tablespoons oil
1½ tablespoons oil
½ teaspoon salt
1 teaspoon brown bean sauce
½ teaspoon soy sauce
½ cup stock
1 tablespoon cornstarch

2 tablespoons water

1. Slice beef thin against the grain. Combine cornstarch, sugar and soy sauce. Add to beef and toss to coat.

2. Peel Chinese turnips; cut in ¼-inch slices, then in 1½-inch squares, and parboil. Cut scallion stalks in 1-inch lengths. Crush garlic.

3. Heat oil. Add beef and stir-fry until it begins to brown. Remove from pan.

4. Heat remaining oil. Add garlic and brown lightly. Add turnips and stir-fry to coat with oil. Then add salt, brown bean sauce, and remaining soy sauce. Stir-fry ½ minute more.

5. Stir in stock and heat quickly. Cook, covered, 3 minutes over medium heat. Meanwhile blend cornstarch and cold water to a paste.

6. Return beef, add scallions, and stir-fry 1 minute. Then stir in cornstarch paste to thicken. Serve at once.

STIR-FRIED BEEF AND VERMICELLI
About 4 servings

¼ pound peastarch noodles
½ pound lean beef
2 tablespoons soy sauce
1 tablespoon sherry

½ teaspoon salt
½ teaspoon sugar
1½ tablespoons oil
1½ tablespoons oil

½ cup water

1. Soak peastarch noodles (vermicelli).

2. Shred beef. Cut soaked noodles in 3-inch lengths.

3. Combine soy sauce, sherry, salt and sugar.

4. Heat oil. Add beef and stir-fry until it loses its redness. Add soy sauce mixture and stir-fry 1 to 2 minutes more. Remove beef from pan.

5. Heat remaining oil. Add soaked noodles and stir-fry a few times to coat with oil. Return beef, add water, and bring quickly to a boil. Cook, covered, over medium heat, until liquid is absorbed (about 5 minutes). Serve hot.

Note: This dish may be prepared in advance and reheated over a low flame. (Add another ¼ cup cold water if necessary.)

variations: In step 3, add the soy sauce mixture to shredded beef and toss. Pick up step 4. In step 5, substitute 1 cup stock for the water and cook, covered, 10 minutes over low heat. *Then* return the beef along with 1 scallion, minced, and stir in to reheat. (You may also add 2 eggs, beaten; stir them in at the very end, over low heat, until they begin to set.)

In step 3, add 1 cup water to the soy sauce mixture. At the end of step 4, do not remove beef from pan, but add 4 to 6 dried black mushrooms (soaked) and 1 cup Chinese cabbage stems, both shredded. Stir-fry a few times. Then add the soy-water mixture and vermicelli and simmer, covered, 5 minutes.

STIR-FRIED BEEF AND RICE-FLOUR NOODLES
About 4 servings

3 or 4 *dried black mushrooms*	2 *tablespoons oil*
½ *cup rice-flour noodles*	½ *teaspoon salt*
½ *pound lean beef*	½ *cup stock*
1 *cup bamboo shoots*	2 *teaspoons cornstarch*
1 *cup celery*	2 *tablespoons water*
⅓ *cup dried onion*	½ *teaspoon sugar*
2 *tablespoons oil*	1 *teaspoon soy sauce*

1. Soak dried mushrooms.
2. Prepare rice-flour noodles as a deep-fried, crisp, white garnish. (See page 827.)
3. Slice beef thin against the grain. Slice thin the bamboo shoots, celery, dried onion and soaked mushrooms.
4. Heat remaining oil. Add beef and stir-fry until it loses its redness. Remove from pan.
5. Heat remaining oil. Add salt, then all the vegetables, and stir-fry 2 minutes.
6. Stir in stock and heat quickly. Cook, covered, 3 minutes over medium heat. Meanwhile blend cornstarch and cold water to a paste.
7. Return beef to pan; then add sugar and soy sauce. Cook, stirring, ½ minute over high heat.
8. Stir in cornstarch paste to thicken. Top with rice-flour noodle garnish and serve at once.

variations: For the vegetables, substitute 1 cup Chinese cabbage, ¼ cup bamboo shoots, 10 snow peas and 8 water chestnuts.

In step 5, add with the vegetables 2 slices fresh ginger root, minced.

In step 8, before adding the rice-flour noodle garnish, sprinkle dish with 1 to 2 tablespoons almond meats, blanched, toasted and chopped.

STIR-FRIED ONION CRACKLE BEEF
About 4 servings

½ *pound lean beef*	2 *tablespoons sherry*
2 *scallion stalks*	2 *tablespoons oil*
1 *garlic clove*	1 *teaspoon vinegar*
2 *tablespoons soy sauce*	*few drops of sesame oil*

1. Slice beef thin against the grain. Mince scallions and crush garlic.
2. Combine scallions with soy sauce and sherry. Add to beef and let stand 30 minutes, turning occasionally. Drain, discarding marinade.
3. Heat oil. Add garlic and stir-fry a few times. Add beef and stir-fry until it loses its redness. Sprinkle with vinegar and sesame oil and stir-fry to blend in.
4. Reduce heat to low and cook, covered, 2 minutes. Serve at once.

VARIATION: For the beef, substitute tender fillet of lamb.

STIR-FRIED HOT BEEF SHREDS
About 4 servings

½ *pound lean beef*	2 *tablespoons fresh ginger root*
2 *tablespoons soy sauce*	1½ *tablespoons oil*
1 *teaspoon sherry*	1½ *tablespoons oil*
½ *cup carrots*	½ *to 1 teaspoon hot pepper flakes*
1 *cup celery*	½ *teaspoon salt*

1. Shred beef. Add soy sauce and sherry and toss.
2. Peel and shred carrots. Shred celery and ginger root.
3. Heat oil. Add beef and stir-fry until it begins to brown. Remove from pan.
4. Heat remaining oil. Add shredded ginger root and stir-fry a few times. Add hot pepper flakes and stir-fry a few times. Add carrots and stir-fry ½ minute. Add celery and stir-fry ½ minute more.
5. Add salt. Return beef and stir-fry only to reheat. Serve at once.

NOTE: The vegetables in this dish should be quite crisp.

STIR-FRIED BEEF LIVER I
About 4 servings

½ *pound beef liver*	2 *tablespoons oil*
1 *to 2 leek stalks*	1 *tablespoon sherry*
1½ *tablespoons soy sauce*	

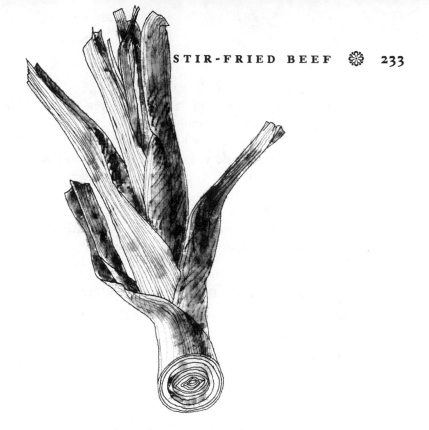

1. Cut liver in ¼-inch slices, then in strips. Cut leeks lengthwise in half, then crosswise in ½-inch sections.

2. Heat oil. Add leeks and stir-fry to brown lightly. Add liver and stir-fry until it turns pale brown (2 to 3 minutes).

3. Sprinkle sherry over and stir-fry until it evaporates. Add soy sauce and stir-fry ½ minute more. Serve at once.

NOTE: Liver is easier to cut when frozen first and then thawed slightly.

VARIATION: For the beef liver, substitute pork or calf liver.

STIR-FRIED BEEF LIVER II
About 4 servings

½ *pound beef liver*	¼ *teaspoon sugar*
1 *to 2 slices fresh ginger root*	1 *scallion stalk*
2 *teaspoons cornstarch*	1 *garlic clove*
2 *teaspoons sherry*	2 *tablespoons oil*
1 *tablespoon soy sauce*	½ *teaspoon salt*

1. Cut liver in ¼-inch slices, then in strips.

2. Mince ginger root. Combine with cornstarch, sherry, soy sauce and sugar. Add to liver and toss to coat. Let stand 15 to 20 minutes, turning occasionally.

3. Cut scallion stalk in ½-inch sections. Crush garlic.

4. Heat oil. Add salt, then garlic, and stir-fry a few times. Add liver and stir-fry until it turns pale brown (2 to 3 minutes).

5. Add scallion sections and stir-fry 1 minute more. Serve at once.

VARIATIONS: In step 4, add to heated oil 1 cup fresh mushrooms, sliced thin. Stir-fry until softened. Remove from pan. Add another 1½ tablespoons oil and heat; then add salt, garlic and liver. Cook as in steps 4 and 5. At the end of step 5, return mushrooms and stir in only to reheat.

In the above variation, for the mushrooms substitute either 2 cups shelled peas, parboiled; or 2 cups string beans, cut in 1½-inch sections and parboiled.

STIR-FRIED BEEF HEART WITH GINGER
4 to 6 servings

1 beef heart (2 pounds)	2 tablespoons sherry
2 scallion stalks	2 tablespoons water
3 or 4 slices fresh ginger root	1 teaspoon salt
1 tablespoon cornstarch	1 teaspoon sugar
2 tablespoons soy sauce	2 to 3 tablespoons oil

1. Cut beef heart lengthwise in half, then in ⅛-inch slices. (Trim off and discard fat and blood vessels.) Place meat in a bowl. Cut scallions in 1-inch sections; mince ginger root and add.

2. Combine cornstarch, soy sauce, sherry, water, salt and sugar. Add to meat and toss to coat. Let stand 15 minutes, turning occasionally. Drain, discarding marinade.

3. Heat oil. Add meat and stir-fry over medium heat until done (3 to 4 minutes). Serve at once.

DEEP-FRIED SWEET-AND-PUNGENT BEEF CUBES
3 to 4 servings

sweet-and-pungent sauce	1 garlic clove
1 pound lean beef	cornstarch
1 egg	oil for deep-frying

1. Prepare a sweet-and-pungent sauce (see pages 735–738).

2. Cut beef in ½-inch cubes. Beat egg; mince garlic and add.

3. Dip beef in egg mixture; then dredge lightly in cornstarch to coat. Meanwhile, heat oil.

4. Add beef cubes, several at a time, and deep-fry until golden. Drain on paper toweling.

5. Reheat sweet-and-pungent sauce. Stir in beef cubes only to heat through.

DEEP-FRIED PAPER-WRAPPED BEEF
3 to 4 servings

1 *pound lean beef*	½ *teaspoon salt*
1 *garlic clove*	1 *teaspoon prepared mustard*
4 *tablespoons soy sauce*	*dash of pepper*
2 *tablespoons sherry*	*few drops of sesame oil*
½ *teaspoon sugar*	*parchment or waxed paper*

oil for deep-frying

1. Cut beef against the grain in slices ½ inch thick, then in rectangles 1 by 1½ inches.

2. Mince garlic, and combine with soy sauce, sherry, sugar, salt, prepared mustard, pepper and sesame oil. Mix well, then add to beef and toss gently to coat. Let stand 1 hour, turning meat occasionally.

3. Drain well, discarding marinade. Then wrap beef in paper envelopes (see page 828). Meanwhile, heat oil.

4. Add beef a few envelopes at a time, and deep-fry until done (about 5 minutes). Drain on paper toweling and serve beef hot in wrappers.

NOTE: The wrappers help hold in flavor and retain heat. To eat, the diner breaks the envelope open with chopsticks or fork and discards the paper.

DEEP-FRIED BEEF STRIPS AND ONION
3 to 4 servings

1 *pound lean beef*	2 *tablespoons sherry*
1 *large onion*	1 *egg white*
1 *tablespoon cornstarch*	*oil for deep-frying*
2 *tablespoons soy sauce*	2 *tablespoons oil*

2 *tablespoons stock*

1. Cut beef against the grain in slices ¼ to ⅛ inch, then in strips ½ by 1½ inches. Slice onion.

2. Combine cornstarch, soy sauce and sherry, and mix well. Stir in egg white. Add beef strips and toss gently to coat. Meanwhile, heat oil.

3. Add beef strips a few at a time, stirring constantly. Deep-fry only ½ minute. Drain on paper toweling.

4. Heat remaining oil. Add sliced onion and stir-fry until translucent. Return beef only to reheat, stir-frying about 1 minute.

5. Add stock and cook, stirring, ½ minute more. Serve hot.

DEEP-FRIED CHINESE STEAK
3 to 4 servings

1 *pound lean beef*	1 *tablespoon cornstarch*
1 *scallion stalk*	1 *egg white*
1 *slice fresh ginger root*	*oil for deep-frying*
2 *tablespoons soy sauce*	4 *tablespoons soy sauce*
2 *tablespoons sherry*	½ *teaspoon sugar*

1½ *teaspoon sesame oil*

1. Cut beef against the grain in ¼-inch slices. Then pound paper-thin with flat side of a cleaver or bottom of a glass jar.

2. Mince scallion and ginger root and combine in a deep bowl with soy sauce and sherry. Add beef and toss gently. Let stand 1 to 1½ hours, turning meat occasionally.

3. Drain meat well, discarding marinade. Wipe out bowl. Blot beef dry with paper toweling and return to bowl.

4. Mix cornstarch and egg white to make a batter. Add to beef and toss gently to coat. Meanwhile, heat oil.

5. Add beef a few slices at a time, and deep-fry until golden (1 to 2 minutes). Drain on paper toweling.

6. In a saucepan, heat remaining soy sauce, sugar and sesame oil. Pour over beef and serve hot.

VARIATION: In step 6, instead of pouring heated sauce over the beef, serve it separately as a dip.

DEEP-FRIED BEEF SLIVERS WITH CELERY
3 to 4 servings

1 *pound lean beef*	*oil for deep-frying*
3 *celery stalks*	2 *tablespoons soy sauce*
1 *round onion*	1 *tablespoon sherry*
1 *scallion stalk*	½ *teaspoon sugar*
1 to 2 *slices fresh ginger root*	½ *teaspoon salt*
1 *tablespoon cornstarch*	2 *teaspoons cornstarch*
1 *egg white*	2 *tablespoons water*

2 *tablespoons oil*

1. Cut beef against the grain in thin slices, then sliver. Shred celery and onion. Cut scallion in ½-inch sections. Mince ginger root.

2. Mix cornstarch and egg white to make a batter. Add beef slivers and toss gently to coat. Meanwhile, heat oil.

3. In one cup, combine soy sauce, sherry, sugar and salt. In another, blend remaining cornstarch and cold water to a paste.

4. Place beef slivers in a wire basket. Immerse in oil until meat begins to turn golden (less than a minute). Drain on paper toweling.

5. Heat remaining oil. Add celery, onion, scallion and ginger root. Stir-fry until slightly softened (about 1 minute).

6. Stir in beef, then add soy-sherry mixture. Stir-fry only to heat through.

7. Stir in cornstarch paste to thicken. Serve at once.

VARIATION: In step 3, for the soy-sherry mixture, substitute 2 tablespoons oyster sauce.

DEEP-FRIED HOT BEEF SHREDS
3 to 4 servings

1 *pound lean beef*	1 *egg white*
2 *celery stalks*	*oil for deep-frying*
½ *chili pepper*	1 *tablespoon oil*
1 *tablespoon cornstarch*	1 *tablespoon soy sauce*
½ *teaspoon salt*	½ *teaspoon sugar*

½ to 1 teaspoon hot pepper oil

1. Cut beef against the grain, then shred. Shred celery. Crush chili pepper.

2. Blend cornstarch, salt and egg white. Add to beef and toss gently to coat. Meanwhile, heat oil.

3. Place beef in a wire basket or strainer. Immerse in oil, deep-fry 1 minute; then lift out. Reheat oil and deep-fry 1 minute more. Repeat process a third time, then drain beef on paper toweling.

4. Heat remaining oil. Add celery and chili pepper. Stir-fry a few times to soften slightly. Stir in soy sauce, sugar and hot pepper oil. Stir-fry until celery is translucent (about 2 minutes).

5. Stir in beef shreds only to reheat.

NOTE: This Szechwanese dish may be served over rice or boiled rice-flour noodles. (The triple-frying makes the meat dark and chewy.)

DEEP-FRIED BEEF LIVER CUBES
3 to 4 servings

1 *pound beef liver*	½ *teaspoon salt*
2 *celery stalks*	*flour*
1 *medium onion*	*oil for deep-frying*
1 *slice fresh ginger root*	1½ *tablespoons oil*
1 *tablespoon soy sauce*	½ *teaspoon sugar*
1 *tablespoon sherry*	2 *tablespoons soy sauce*

1. Cut beef liver in ½-inch slices, then in ½-inch cubes. Cut celery in ½-inch sections and blanch. Slice onion.

2. Mince ginger root and combine with the soy sauce, sherry and salt. Add liver cubes and toss gently. Let stand 15 to 20 minutes, turning occasionally.

3. Drain well, discarding marinade. Dredge liver in flour to coat lightly. Meanwhile, heat oil.

4. Place liver in a wire basket or strainer. Immerse in oil until liver is light brown. Drain on paper toweling.

5. Heat remaining oil. Add sliced onion and celery. Stir-fry to soften slightly. Stir in sugar and remaining soy sauce.

6. Add deep-fried liver cubes. Stir-fry only to reheat.

BASIC STEAMED BEEF
3 to 4 servings

1 *pound lean beef*	1 *tablespoon sherry*
2 *scallion stalks*	½ *teaspoon salt*
1 *slice fresh ginger root*	½ *teaspoon sugar*
1 *teaspoon cornstarch*	1 *teaspoon peanut oil*
1 *tablespoon soy sauce*	*Chinese parsley*

1. Cut beef in ¼-inch slices. Mince scallion stalks.

2. Mince ginger. Combine with cornstarch, soy sauce, sherry, salt and sugar, mixing well. Add to beef slices and toss gently to coat. Let stand 15 minutes, turning occasionally.

3. Arrange beef slices in shallow heatproof dish. With a circular motion, sprinkle oil and minced scallions over the top.

4. Steam on a rack until done (30 to 40 minutes). See pages 33 and 831.

5. Mince Chinese parsley. Serve beef in its heatproof dish, with parsley sprinkled over.

VARIATIONS: In step 1, sliver the beef or cut in julienne strips and steam 25 to 30 minutes; or mince or grind the beef and steam about 15 minutes.

In step 3, top beef with any of the following:

CLOUD EAR MUSHROOMS: 2 tablespoons cloud ear mushrooms and 1 piece tangerine peel, both soaked and slivered. (For the peanut oil, substitute a few drops of sesame oil.)

DRIED BLACK MUSHROOMS: 4 dried black mushrooms (soaked), slivered; and either 8 to 10 water chestnuts, sliced thin, or ½ cup pickles, shredded.

PICKLED BAMBOO SHOOTS: ½ cup pickled bamboo shoots. (Cut beef in julienne strips.)

PRESERVED CABBAGE: ½ to 1 cup preserved cabbage, minced.

SALTED CABBAGE: ½ cup dried salted cabbage (soaked), sliced thin.

TEA MELON: 8 tea melons, washed and sliced. (You may also add ½ bundle preserved turnips, washed and chopped coarsely.)

STEAMED BEEF CUBES
3 to 4 servings

20 small dried black mushrooms	1 tablespoon sherry
1 pound lean beef	1 cup mushroom-soaking liquid
1 scallion stalk	½ teaspoon salt
1 tablespoon soy sauce	dash of pepper

1. Soak dried mushrooms; reserve soaking liquid.

2. Cut beef in 1½-inch cubes. Place in heatproof bowl. Mince scallion and add with soy sauce and sherry to beef. Toss gently. Let stand 15 minutes, turning occasionally.

3. Steam on a rack 1½ hours, adding more boiling water as it evaporates. (See pages 33 and 831.)

4. Add soaked mushrooms and their soaking liquid. Steam 30 minutes more. Season with salt and pepper. Serve hot.

STEAMED BEEF BALLS WITH GLUTINOUS RICE
3 to 4 servings

1 cup glutinous rice	1 tablespoon soy sauce
1 pound lean beef	½ teaspoon cornstarch
2 slices fresh ginger root	½ teaspoon sugar
1 small onion	½ teaspoon salt
1 egg	1 teaspoon sherry

1. Soak glutinous rice. Drain well.

2. Mince or grind beef, removing fat and tendons. Place in a bowl. Mince ginger root and onion and add.

3. Beat egg lightly and add, along with soy sauce, cornstarch, sugar, salt and sherry. Blend well and form into walnut-size meatballs. (Do not handle meat too much; it will dry out.)

4. Spread glutinous rice on a flat plate. Roll each meatball over rice to coat completely.

5. Arrange meatballs on shallow heatproof dish with ½-inch spaces between them to allow for expansion of rice.

6. Steam on a rack 20 to 30 minutes (see pages 33 and 831). Serve hot with dips of soy sauce and Chinese mustard.

BASIC BRAISED BEEF
6 servings

2 pounds beef chuck	2 tablespoons sherry
1 scallion stalk	1 teaspoon sugar
1 garlic clove	1 teaspoon salt
2 or 3 slices fresh ginger root	dash of pepper
4 tablespoons soy sauce	2 or 3 tablespoons oil

3 cups water

1. Leave beef whole. Cut scallion stalk in 2-inch sections. Mince garlic and ginger root and combine with soy sauce, sherry, sugar, salt and pepper.

2. Heat oil in a heavy pan. Brown beef quickly on all sides. Add soy-sherry mixture and cook stirring to heat and blend (about 3 minutes). Meanwhile, boil water.

3. Add water to beef and bring to a boil again. Simmer, covered, until beef is tender (about 1½ to 2 hours).

NOTE: You may increase the soy sauce to ½ cup, the sherry to ¼ cup; then reserve the gravy as a master sauce. (See page 739.)

VARIATIONS: Cut the beef in large chunks. Cook only 1 hour in step 3.

Cut the beef in 1½-inch cubes. Sprinkle with 1 teaspoon salt; then toss in ½ tablespoon soy sauce and ½ tablespoon sherry. Let stand 20 to 30 minutes, turning occasionally. Then brown as in step 2, but omit the soy-sherry mix. Cook about 45 minutes in step 3.

Instead of browning the beef, plunge in a pan of boiling water, parboil 2 to 3 minutes, then drain.

In step 1, do not combine the soy sauce and other seasonings. Instead, after browning the beef in step 2, cook it in the soy over medium heat, until well colored (about 10 minutes). Then add the scallion, garlic and ginger root; stir in the sherry, sugar, salt, pepper and 2 cups heated stock. Cook as in step 3, but omit the boiling water.

In step 2, add any of the following:

2 cloves star anise

3 to 4 anise peppercorns and ½ teaspoon sesame oil

1-inch piece of cinnamon stick

1 piece tangerine peel (soaked)

1 tablespoon wine vinegar

During the last 30 minutes of cooking, add any of the following:

1 pound cabbage, cut in wedges
1 pound carrots, peeled and cubed
6 celery stalks, cut in 1-inch sections
½ pound chestnuts, parboiled
6 eggs, hardboiled and shelled
½ cup lily buds (soaked), cut in two
1 pound lotus root, peeled and cubed
1 cup dried black mushrooms (soaked), left whole
1 pound new potatoes, peeled and cubed
1 pound string beans, stemmed
1 pound Chinese white turnips, peeled and cubed

During the last 15 minutes of cooking, add 2 cups bamboo shoots, diced.

During the last 10 minutes of cooking, add 2 cups shelled peas or 4 tomatoes, cut in wedges.

NOTE: When adding vegetables, do *not* also add star anise, anise pepper, cinnamon stick, tangerine peel or wine vinegar. (These will overwhelm the vegetable flavors.) They are better when the beef is cooked alone.

BRAISED ANISE BEEF I
6 servings

2 *pounds beef chuck*	1 *teaspoon salt*
1 *garlic clove*	1 *teaspoon sherry*
2 *tablespoons oil*	*dash of pepper*
3 *tablespoons soy sauce*	2 *cloves star anise*
1 *tablespoon water*	1 *teaspoon sugar*

1. Leave beef whole. Crush garlic.
2. Heat oil in a heavy pan. Brown beef quickly on all sides.

3. Add garlic, soy sauce, water, salt, sherry, pepper and star anise, and heat. Simmer, covered, 1 hour. (Use an asbestos pad so meat won't burn.)

4. Turn meat. Add sugar and simmer slowly 1 hour more. Serve hot or cold.

NOTE: If the meat gets too dry during cooking, add 1 tablespoon water mixed with 1 tablespoon soy sauce.

BRAISED ANISE BEEF II
6 servings

2 pounds beef chuck
2 slices fresh ginger root
2 tablespoons oil
2 cups water

½ cup soy sauce
2 cloves star anise
1 tablespoon sugar
1 teaspoon salt

2 tablespoons sherry

1. Leave beef whole. Slice and crush ginger root.

2. Heat oil in a heavy pan. Brown beef quickly.

3. Add ginger root, water, soy sauce, star anise, sugar and salt, and heat. Simmer, covered, 1½ hours, basting occasionally.

4. Add sherry and simmer, covered, 15 minutes more.

5. Increase heat to medium and cook, uncovered, turning meat and stirring sauce, until most of the liquid is absorbed. (Be careful not to burn meat.) Serve hot or cold.

VARIATION: For the white sugar, substitute brown sugar.

In step 3, add a 1-inch piece of cinnamon stick.

BRAISED MARINATED BEEF
6 servings

2 pounds beef chuck
6 tablespoons soy sauce
4 tablespoons sherry
1 teaspoon salt

flour
2 tablespoons oil
1 tablespoon sugar
1 tablespoon vinegar

water to cover

1. Leave beef whole and pound lightly with the side of a cleaver. Pierce in several places with fork or skewer.

2. Combine soy sauce, sherry and salt. Add to meat and let stand 2 to 3 hours, turning occasionally.

3. Drain, discarding marinade. Blot meat with paper toweling. Dredge lightly with flour.

4. Heat oil in a heavy pan. Brown beef quickly. Add sugar, vinegar and water and bring to a boil.

5. Cook, covered, 15 minutes over medium heat; then simmer, covered, until tender (about 1½ hours).

NOTE: This extended marinating, being a tenderizing process, is particularly good for tough cuts of beef.

VARIATION: Cut the meat in large chunks and simmer, covered, only 1 hour in step 5.

BRAISED CURRIED BEEF
3 to 4 servings

1 pound beef chuck	1½ cups stock
4 white onions	2 tablespoons oil
2 slices fresh ginger root	½ teaspoon salt
1 tablespoon sherry	2 to 3 tablespoons curry powder
1 tablespoon water	1 tablespoon cornstarch
1 teaspoon sugar	3 tablespoons water

1. Cut beef in 1-inch cubes. Slice onions.

2. Mince ginger root and combine with sherry, water and sugar. Heat—but do not boil—stock.

3. Heat oil in a heavy pan. Add salt, then beef. Toss meat quickly in hot oil to coat.

4. Add sliced onions. Brown beef on all sides. Then add curry powder and stir to blend in with meat (2 to 3 minutes).

5. Add ginger-sherry mixture and stir in 2 minutes more.

6. Add heated stock and simmer, covered, until meat is tender (about 45 minutes).

7. Blend cornstarch and remaining cold water to a paste; then stir in to thicken sauce. Serve hot.

VARIATIONS: In step 3, add to the heated oil the salt, curry and onions, and stir-fry until onions are lightly browned; then add beef and brown. Omit the ginger-sherry mixture. Pick up steps 6 and 7.

In step 4, add with the sliced onions 1 pound raw potatoes, peeled and cut in 1½-inch cubes. Brown with the beef.

At the end of step 7, add 1 pound potatoes, peeled, cubed and deep-fried to a golden brown; or 1 large tomato, peeled and diced.

RED-SIMMERED BEEF I

6 servings

2 pounds beef chuck

½ cup soy sauce

¼ cup sherry

1 tablespoon brown sugar

2 cups water

1. Place meat, whole, in a heavy saucepan. Mix soy sauce, sherry and sugar and add to pan. Cook, covered, over low heat for 10 minutes, turning meat once.

2. Gradually add water and bring slowly to a boil. Simmer, covered, until tender (1½ to 2 hours), turning meat several times.

3. Let cool slightly and slice. Serve hot or cold.

NOTE: If meat gets too dry, add some boiling water.

VARIATIONS: In step 1, cut the meat in 1½-inch cubes and simmer only 1 hour.

In step 2, add 2 cloves star anise. Remove these before serving.

Add any of the vegetables listed in the Basic Braised Beef variations (see page 242).

RED-SIMMERED BEEF II
6 servings

2 pounds beef chuck
2 or 3 slices fresh ginger root
2 or 3 scallion stalks

½ cup soy sauce
¼ cup sherry
2 cups water

2 teaspoons sugar

1. Leave beef whole and place in a heavy saucepan. Slice and crush ginger root; cut scallion stalks in two and add.

2. Add soy sauce, sherry and water and simmer, covered, until tender (1½ to 2 hours). Turn meat several times for even color and seasoning.

3. Add sugar and simmer, covered, 30 minutes more.

VARIATIONS: See variations for Red-Simmered Beef I.

RED-SIMMERED SPICED BEEF WITH TURNIPS
6 servings

2 pounds beef chuck
2 slices fresh ginger root
1 scallion stalk
½ cup sherry
1 cup water

2 or 3 cloves star anise
1 Chinese turnip
½ cup soy sauce
2 teaspoons sugar
½ cup water

1. Leave beef whole and place in a heavy saucepan. Slice and crush ginger root; cut scallion stalk in two and add.

2. Add sherry, water and star anise and simmer, covered, 1 hour.

3. Peel Chinese turnip; cut in large cubes or slice thick by rolling-cut method. Add with soy sauce, sugar and remaining water. Simmer, covered, 1 hour more.

4. Let beef and turnip cool in stock, then slice beef. Strain stock and pour over beef and turnip. Refrigerate and serve cold.

MARINATED BEEF
3 to 4 servings

1 pound lean beef
1 or 2 garlic cloves
4 tablespoons soy sauce

2 teaspoons sugar
½ teaspoon salt
2 tablespoons oil

1. Slice beef against the grain in ¼-inch slices. Mince garlic and combine with soy sauce, sugar and salt. Add to beef slices and toss gently.

2. Let stand 1 to 2 hours, turning occasionally. Then drain, discarding marinade.

3. Heat oil very hot. Pan-fry beef until done (about 2 minutes on each side). Serve plain or over stir-fried spinach.

NOTE: When grilled as in the variations below, this is known as barbecued beef.

VARIATIONS: Broil under medium heat until done (about 3 minutes on each side).

Cook on a charcoal grill (about 2 minutes on each side).

BEEF VELVETEEN

1½ pounds lean beef	*¼ cup sherry*
½ cup soy sauce	*1 cup stock*

3 or 4 tablespoons oil

1. Trim beef of all fat and remove tendons; cube or cut in large chunks.

2. Place in a saucepan with soy sauce, sherry and stock. Cook, uncovered, over high heat, turning meat frequently until liquid evaporates.

3. Let cool; then refrigerate until chilled (about 1 to 2 hours). Shred, mince or grind beef.

4. Heat oil. Add beef and coat quickly with oil. Cook over low heat, stirring frequently, until meat dries out completely (30 to 40 minutes). Let cool, and store in a covered jar.

NOTE: This dry-fried beef needs no refrigeration. It can be used as an hors d'oeuvre, with plain congee; or as a garnish for noodles or rice.

VARIATIONS: In step 2, heat 2 tablespoons oil and brown beef lightly before adding the soy sauce, sherry and stock.

In step 2, add with the soy sauce, etc., either ½ teaspoon ground anise or ½ teaspoon cinnamon.

In step 4, add ½ teaspoon crushed red pepper to the heated oil before the beef.

SMOKED BEEF I
6 servings

1½ pounds lean beef	*1 cup water*
2 or 3 slices fresh ginger root	*1 teaspoon salt*
1 or 2 scallion stalks	*3 tablespoons brown sugar*
¼ cup soy sauce	*1 tablespoon ground anise*

1. Cut beef in ¼-inch slices. Slice ginger root; cut scallion stalks in two. Place in a heavy saucepan.

2. Add soy sauce, water and salt. Simmer, covered, until tender (1 to 1½ hours). Drain well.

3. Line a heavy pan with foil, and sprinkle with brown sugar and ground anise. Smoke beef 5 to 7 minutes (see page 828). Serve hot or cold.

SMOKED BEEF II
6 servings

1½ *pounds lean beef*	½ *cup brown sugar*
¼ *cup soy sauce*	2 *teaspoons cinnamon*
¼ *cup sherry*	2 *teaspoons ground anise*
1 *teaspoon sugar*	2 *teaspoons ground cloves*

1. Cut beef in ¼-inch slices, then in strips 1 by 2 inches. Combine soy sauce, sherry and sugar. Add to beef and toss gently. Let stand 1 hour, turning occasionally.

2. Transfer beef and its marinade to a saucepan. Cook, covered, over medium heat until tender (about 45 minutes). Drain well.

3. Line a heavy pan with foil. Sprinkle with brown sugar, cinnamon, ground anise and ground cloves. Smoke beef 5 to 7 minutes (see page 828). Serve hot or cold.

BRAISED BEEF BALLS
4 servings

1 *pound beef*	1 *teaspoon sherry*
1 *egg*	2 *tablespoons oil*
¼ *cup dry bread crumbs*	½ *cup water*
¼ *cup water*	2 *tablespoons soy sauce*
1 *tablespoon cornstarch*	1 *pound spinach*
½ *teaspoon salt*	½ *teaspoon salt*

1. Remove fat and tendons from beef; then mince or grind.

2. Beat egg lightly and add to beef, along with dry bread crumbs, cold water, cornstarch, salt and sherry. Blend well, but do not overhandle meat. Form into walnut-size balls.

3. Heat oil to smoking in a heavy pan. Brown beef balls quickly but lightly and remove. Drain fat into another pan.

4. Heat remaining water in original pan and stir in soy sauce. Return beef balls. Bring quickly to a boil; then simmer, covered, 30 minutes, turning several times.

5. Wash spinach and remove tough stems. Reheat beef fat in second pan. (If it's less than 2 tablespoons, add peanut oil to make up difference.)

6. Add remaining salt, then spinach. Stir-fry spinach until slightly softened (about 1 to 2 minutes). Top with beef balls and cook, covered, 2 minutes more over low heat. Serve hot.

VARIATION: For the spinach, substitute Chinese lettuce, cut in 2-inch sections; stir-fry until tender.

SMOKED BEEF BALLS
4 servings

1 *pound beef*	1 *tablespoon water*
1 *scallion stalk*	½ *teaspoon salt*
2 *slices fresh ginger root*	½ *teaspoon sesame oil*
1 *tablespoon cornstarch*	3 *tablespoons brown sugar*
2 *tablespoons soy sauce*	1½ *teaspoons ground anise*

1. Remove fat and tendons from beef; then mince or grind.

2. Mince scallion and ginger root and add to beef, along with cornstarch, soy sauce, cold water, salt and sesame oil. Blend well, but do not overhandle meat. Form into walnut-size balls.

3. Fill a pan three-fourths full of water. Bring to a boil. Add beef balls a few at a time (so as not to reduce water temperature); then simmer, covered, 15 to 20 minutes. Drain well, discarding liquid.

4. Line a heavy pan with foil and sprinkle with brown sugar and anise. Smoke 5 to 7 minutes (see page 828). Serve hot or cold.

SWEET-AND-PUNGENT BEEF BALLS I
4 servings

sweet-and-pungent sauce
1 pound lean beef
1 egg

2 tablespoons flour
½ teaspoon salt
dash of pepper

oil for deep-frying

1. Prepare a sweet-and-pungent sauce (see pages 735–738).

2. Remove fat and tendons from beef; then mince or grind. Form into walnut-size balls.

3. Beat egg lightly and blend with flour, salt and pepper to a smooth batter. Dip beef balls in batter to coat.

4. Meanwhile heat oil to smoking. Add beef balls a few at a time and deep-fry until golden. Drain on paper toweling.

5. Reheat the sweet-and-pungent sauce. Stir in beef balls only to heat through.

SWEET-AND-PUNGENT BEEF BALLS II
4 servings

1 *pound beef*	*dash of pepper*
2 *tablespoons onion*	1 *cup stock*
1 *egg*	2 *tablespoons brown sugar*
¼ *cup dry bread crumbs*	3 *tablespoons soy sauce*
½ *teaspoon salt*	¼ *cup vinegar*

½ *cup catsup*

1. Remove fat and tendons from beef; then mince or grind. Mince onion and add to beef.

2. Beat egg lightly and add, along with bread crumbs, salt and pepper. Blend well, but do not overhandle meat. Form into walnut-size balls.

3. Heat stock to boiling. Add beef balls a few at a time (to keep temperature of stock from dropping too rapidly) and simmer, covered, until done (about 30 minutes).

4. Meanwhile, combine brown sugar, soy sauce, vinegar and catsup.

5. Transfer meatballs to a serving platter. Leave stock in pan and add sugar-soy mixture. Cook, stirring, over medium flame, to blend and heat. Pour sauce over beef balls and serve.

BRAISED SHORT RIBS OF BEEF WITH BLACK BEANS
4 servings

1 *tablespoon fermented black beans*	1 *tablespoon soy sauce*
1½ *pounds short ribs of beef*	1 *tablespoon sherry*
½ *teaspoon salt*	1 *to 2 tablespoons oil*
1 *garlic clove*	1 *cup water*

1. Soak fermented black beans.

2. With a cleaver, chop ribs in 1- by 2-inch sections. Sprinkle with salt. Let stand 30 minutes.

3. Mince garlic and mash with soaked black beans. Stir in soy sauce and sherry.

4. Heat oil. Brown rib sections lightly. Add black bean mixture and stir-fry 2 minutes more.

5. Add water and bring quickly to a boil. Then simmer, covered, until done (about 45 minutes).

DEEP-FRIED SHORT RIBS OF BEEF
4 servings

1½ pounds short ribs of beef
1 scallion stalk
2 slices fresh ginger root
1 garlic clove
1 clove star anise
1 tablespoon soy sauce

1 teaspoon sugar
1 teaspoon salt
few drops of sesame oil
water to cover
1 egg
3 tablespoons cornstarch

oil for deep-frying

1. With a cleaver, chop ribs in 1- by 2-inch sections. Place in a saucepan.

2. Cut scallion stalk in two; slice ginger root; crush garlic. Add to pan along with star anise, soy sauce, sugar, salt and sesame oil.

3. Add cold water to cover and bring to a boil. Then simmer, covered, 45 minutes to 1 hour. Drain, reserving liquid. Let ribs cool.

4. Beat egg lightly and blend with cornstarch to a smooth batter. Thin slightly with reserved beef stock. Dip ribs in batter to coat.

5. Meanwhile, heat oil to smoking. Add ribs, several at a time, and deep-fry until golden. Drain on paper toweling and serve.

RED-SIMMERED BEEF TONGUE
8 to 10 servings

1 fresh beef tongue
water to cover
2 scallion stalks
2 to 3 slices fresh ginger root

½ cup soy sauce
4 tablespoons sherry
1 teaspoon salt
4 cups water

1 teaspoon sugar

1. Place beef tongue in heavy pan and add cold water to cover. Bring quickly to a boil and parboil, uncovered, 5 minutes. Drain, discarding liquid.

2. Let tongue cool slightly; then remove coarse outer skin. Return tongue to pot.

3. Cut scallion stalks in two; slice ginger root. Add to pot, along with soy sauce, sherry, salt and remaining water. Bring to a boil; then simmer, covered, until tender (about 2½ hours).

4. Add sugar and simmer, covered, 15 minutes more. Drain, reserving liquid.

5. Let tongue cool; then slice. Serve hot (reheat slices briefly in reserved liquid) or cold.

❀ *Duck* ❀

DUCK COOKED the Chinese way can be roasted, braised, red-simmered, white-simmered, steamed or deep-fried. It can also be preserved by salting or drying (and eaten with congee), or cured and smoked (and used as a flavoring like smoked ham).

In northern China, duck is first inflated with air, then roasted to make its skin crisp and wonderful. In the South, it is filled with liquid seasonings before roasting to make it savory. The former is Peking Duck; the latter, Cantonese duck. The Cantonese version, available ready-cooked in Chinese grocery stores, can be stir-fried briefly with vegetables or made festive with a sweet-and-pungent sauce. It can also be eaten cold at picnics. The familiar pressed duck calls for a combination of cooking techniques: the bird is steamed, boned, pressed flat and deep-fried. (Although there are special presses for this purpose, the Chinese usually press the duck by hand.)

Tips on Cooking Duck: Always be sure the oil sacs above the tail are removed. If they aren't, cut a 1½-inch slit at the back of the tail and remove them.

When a recipe calls for breast and leg meat, use the remainder of the bird (bones, neck, lower wings and lower legs) for soup or congee.

Use the same duck three ways: First roast the whole duck and serve its drumsticks and upper wings as one dish. Then stir-fry the breast meat with vegetables, or serve it cold with pineapple. Use the remainder for congee, as above. (The Chinese call this "three-in-one duck" and serve it either at the same meal or at separate meals.)

Prepare braised, steamed or simmered duck a day ahead; then refrigerate it so that the fat will congeal and can be easily lifted off. Carve or cut up the duck (see page 825) and reheat at the last moment in its own sauce.

Defrost frozen ducks completely before using them. Remove the large pieces of fat from the duck cavity and discard. Pour boiling water over the duck to cover and let stand 10 to 15 minutes (this will shrink the skin). Rinse duck in lukewarm water. If bird is to be roasted, dry well inside and out.

Test the duck to see if it's done by moving one of its legs up and down. When the leg moves easily in its joint, the duck is ready.

SIMPLE ROAST DUCK

1. Preheat oven to 350 degrees.
2. Wipe duck inside and out with a damp cloth. Place breast-side up on a rack over a drip pan containing several inches of water. Roast until tender, allowing about 30 minutes per pound. Add more water to drip pan as it evaporates.
3. Prop duck up in a bowl to permit fat to drain off. Let cool. Bone and cut bird in 1- by 2-inch sections (each with some skin).

NOTE: This can be used in recipes calling for roast or cooked duck.

LIQUID-FILLED ROAST DUCK

1. Wipe duck with a damp cloth. Dry with paper toweling. Hang bird in a cool, airy place 1 to 2 hours, or until its skin is dry.
2. Rub duck lightly, inside and out, with soy sauce or salt.
3. Tie neck of duck tightly with string to close it off. (The packaged duck in supermarkets cannot be used for this recipe: its head and neck must be intact.) Place bird tail-side up in a deep bowl and pour into its cavity any of the filling mixtures listed below.
4. Sew up the cavity securely or skewer so that the mixture cannot leak out. Meanwhile preheat oven to 400 degrees.
5. Place duck on a rack over a drip pan containing several inches of water. Roast 20 minutes; then pour off fat. Reduce heat to 350 degrees and roast until done, allowing about 25 minutes per pound. During the last 30 minutes of roasting,

reduce heat to 300 degrees. (Add water to drip pan as it evaporates.) Throughout roasting, baste duck at 20-minute intervals with any of the basting mixtures below.

6. Let duck cool slightly. Then place in a bowl and snip threads or unskewer so liquid will drain into bowl. Bone duck and cut in 1- by 2-inch sections (each with some skin). Strain liquid and reheat. Pour over duck and serve hot; or serve duck cold without sauce.

NOTE: This dish, called Cantonese Roast Duck, can also be purchased whole or in pieces at Chinese food stores. When buying, always ask for some of the liquid filling or "juice," which is delicious.

MIXTURES FOR FILLING

a. Combine 2 scallion stalks, cut in 1-inch sections; 1 teaspoon sugar, 1 teaspoon salt and 1 cup water, heated.

b. Combine in a saucepan 1 garlic clove and 2 slices fresh ginger root, both minced; 2 scallion stalks, cut in ½-inch sections; 1 teaspoon salt, 2 teaspoons sugar, 2 tablespoons sherry and 2 tablespoons soy sauce. Add 1 cup stock or water. Bring to a boil.

c. Combine in a saucepan 1 tablespoon brown bean sauce, mashed; 2 garlic cloves, crushed; 1 scallion stalk, minced; 4 tablespoons soy sauce, 2 teaspoons sugar, ½ teaspoon cinnamon and 2 cups water. Bring to a boil.

d. Combine in a saucepan 2 cloves garlic and 2 slices fresh ginger root, both crushed; 1 tablespoon salt cabbage and 1 piece tangerine peel (both soaked); 1 tablespoon brown bean sauce, mashed; 1 tablespoon sugar, 2 tablespoons soy sauce, 2 tablespoons sherry, 1 teaspoon salt, 1 teaspoon honey and 2 cups stock. Bring to a boil.

e. Combine in a saucepan 2 or 3 cloves garlic and 2 or 3 slices fresh ginger root, both crushed; 1 cup water, 1 cup sherry, 2 tablespoons soy sauce, 1 tablespoon oil and 2 teaspoons sugar. Simmer, covered, 15 minutes.

f. Heat 1 tablespoon oil. Add 1 garlic clove and 1 scallion stalk, both minced; ½ teaspoon ground star anise, and 1 teaspoon Szechwan peppercorns. Stir-fry 1 to 2 minutes. Add 2 cups water, bring to a boil, then simmer, covered, 5 minutes. Stir in 2 tablespoons soy sauce, 2 tablespoons sherry and 1 teaspoon sugar.

g. Heat 1 tablespoon oil. Add 2 garlic cloves, crushed; 4 scallion stalks and 1 or 2 slices fresh ginger root, both minced. Stir-fry 1 to 2 minutes. Add 1 cup water and bring to a boil. Stir in and heat ¾ cup soy sauce, 1 tablespoon sugar, 2 tablespoons sherry, 1 teaspoon salt, and a dash of pepper.

h. Heat 1 tablespoon oil. Add 4 tablespoons scallions and 4 tablespoons celery stalk, both minced; stir-fry 2 minutes. Add 2 cups water and bring to a boil. Stir in ½ cup soy sauce, 1 tablespoon sugar, 1 clove star anise and ½ teaspoon cinnamon.

MIXTURES FOR BASTING

a. Combine 2 cups boiling water, ¼ cup honey, 2 tablespoons vinegar, 1 tablespoon soy sauce.

b. Combine 2 cups boiling water, ½ cup honey and ¼ cup soy sauce.

NOTE: Instead of basting, combine ½ cup soy sauce and ¼ cup honey and pour over duck 6 times or more to coat before roasting.

AROMATIC ROAST DUCK
6 to 8 servings

1 *piece dried tangerine peel*	*½ cup soy sauce*
1 *duck (4 to 5 pounds)*	*2 tablespoons sherry*
1 *garlic clove*	*½ tablespoon soybean paste*
1 *scallion stalk*	*1 teaspoon sugar*
2 *or* 3 *slices fresh ginger root*	*5 tablespoons peanut oil*

1. Soak tangerine peel. Preheat oven to 350 degrees.

2. Wipe duck inside and out with a damp cloth; then dry with paper toweling. Sew up or skewer its neck opening. Place duck tail-side up in a deep bowl.

3. Mince garlic, scallion, ginger root and soaked tangerine peel. Combine with

soy sauce, sherry, soybean paste and sugar. Pour mixture into duck cavity. Sew up the cavity securely or skewer.

4. Brush duck with oil. Place on a rack over a drip pan containing several inches of water. Roast until done (about 25 minutes per pound), brushing duck with oil at 15-minute intervals. (Add more water to drip pan as it evaporates.)

5. Let duck cool; then chill. Bone and cut in bite-size pieces (each with some skin). Serve cold.

ROAST HONEY DUCK I
6 to 8 servings

1 duck (4 to 5 pounds)	2 or 3 scallions
salt	3 tablespoons soy sauce
2 garlic cloves	3 tablespoons sherry
	2 tablespoons honey

1. Wipe duck with a damp cloth. Rub lightly, inside and out, with salt. Preheat oven to 350 degrees.

2. Crush garlic and mince scallions; then combine with soy sauce and sherry. Divide mixture in half.

3. Mix honey with one half. Rub into duck skin and let stand a few minutes until dry. Then repeat. (Reserve remainder of honey mixture. Combine it with 1 cup boiling water for basting.)

4. Pour remaining half of soy mixture into duck cavity. Place bird on a rack over a drip pan containing several inches of water.

5. Roast until done (about 1¾ to 2 hours), basting with reserved honey mixture at 15-minute intervals. (Add more water to drip pan as it evaporates.)

ROAST HONEY DUCK II
6 to 8 servings

1 duck (4 to 5 pounds)	2 tablespoons soy sauce
¼ cup stock	1½ tablespoons honey
1 tablespoon sugar	1 teaspoon salt

1. Wipe duck, inside and out, with a damp cloth.

2. Combine stock, sugar, soy sauce, honey and salt in a large deep bowl. Coat duck with mixture and let stand in bowl 1 hour, turning occasionally. Drain, reserving marinade. Meanwhile preheat oven to 350 degrees.

3. Place duck on a rack over a drip pan containing several inches of water. Roast 1¾ to 2 hours, basting with marinade at ½-hour intervals.

4. Let cool slightly; then, with a cleaver, chop bones and all in bite-size pieces, or carve Western style. Serve duck plain or with a plum sauce dip.

ROAST HONEY DUCK III
6 servings

8 to 10 *cups water*	1 *tablespoon sherry*
1 *duck (4 pounds)*	1 *tablespoon sweet vegetable sauce*
2 *cups water*	1 *teaspoon sugar*
1 *cup honey*	1 *teaspoon vinegar*
1 *teaspoon salt*	½ *to 1 teaspoon Chinese hot sauce*
½ *teaspoon sesame oil*	

1. Boil water in a large pan and lower in duck to scald; then remove quickly and drain at once, discarding liquid. Hang bird to dry overnight in a cool, airy place.

2. Boil remaining water and stir in honey to dissolve. Brush over duck skin and let dry somewhat. Repeat 3 or 4 times to saturate skin with honey.

3. Rub duck cavity with salt. Hang duck overnight again to dry in a cool, airy place.

4. Combine sherry, sweet vegetable sauce, sugar, vinegar, hot sauce and sesame oil. Rub mixture into duck cavity. Meanwhile preheat oven to 450 degrees.

5. Place duck on a rack over a drip pan containing several inches of water and roast 20 minutes. Reduce heat to 250 degrees and roast 40 minutes more.

ROAST ORANGE DUCK
6 to 8 servings

1 *duck (4 to 5 pounds)*	1 *orange*
1 *garlic clove*	½ *cup sherry*
4 *tablespoons oil*	3 *or 4 slices fresh ginger root*
1 *onion*	1 *teaspoon salt*

1. Wipe duck inside and out with a damp cloth. Cut garlic clove in two and rub cut side over skin, then brush duck with oil. Meanwhile preheat oven to 325 degrees.

2. Peel onion (but not orange). With a fork pierce each in several places. Place both inside duck and sew up the cavity securely or skewer.

3. Place duck on a rack over a roasting pan containing several inches of water and roast 2 hours. (Add more water to pan as it evaporates.)

4. Remove rack. Drain off and discard fat and liquids. Place duck directly in

roasting pan and pour sherry over. Mince ginger root and sprinkle over top along with salt. Roast 30 minutes more.

5. Let bird cool slightly and unskewer. Discard orange and onion. Bone duck and cut in bite-size pieces (each with some skin).

6. Strain liquids from roasting pan and reheat; then pour over duck.

SIMMERED ROAST DUCK I
6 servings

1 duck (4 pounds)	1 teaspoon salt
2 cups sherry	2 tablespoons soy sauce

1. Wipe duck with a damp cloth and place in a pan. Add sherry and salt; bring to a boil, then simmer, covered, 15 minutes. Meanwhile preheat oven to 350 degrees.

2. Drain duck, reserving liquid, and rub with soy sauce.

3. Place bird on a rack over a drip pan containing several inches of water. Roast 1 hour, basting at 20-minute intervals with reserved liquid. (Add more water to drip pan as it evaporates.)

VARIATION: In step 2, mix the soy sauce with 1 tablespoon honey; then thin slightly with water before rubbing over duck.

SIMMERED ROAST DUCK II
6 to 8 servings

1 duck (4 to 5 pounds)	2 teaspoons sugar
4 scallions	3 tablespoons sherry
4 slices fresh ginger root	5 tablespoons soy sauce
½ teaspoon ground anise	1 cup water

hoisin sauce

1. Wipe duck inside and out with a damp cloth. Place in a large heavy pan. Cut scallions in 2-inch sections; slice ginger root and divide in two parts. Place half at bottom of pan, half in duck cavity.

2. Add to pan ground anise, sugar, sherry, soy sauce and water. Bring to a boil. Then simmer, covered, 1½ hours, turning duck 2 or 3 times. (Be careful not to puncture skin.)

3. Drain duck, reserving liquid. Let bird dry on a rack in a cool, airy place about 5 hours.

4. Preheat oven to 450 degrees. Place duck, breast-side down, on a rack over a

drip pan containing several inches of water. Roast 15 minutes. Turn bird over and roast until crisp and golden (about 10 minutes more).

5. Let cool slightly; then carve, so each slice has some crisp skin. Reheat reserved liquid and pour over. Serve duck hot with a dip dish of hoisin sauce.

NOTE: Because of its crisp skin, this dish is sometimes called "Pseudo Peking Duck."

BRAISED DUCK
6 to 8 servings

2 or 3 scallions	1 duck (4 to 5 pounds)
2 or 3 slices fresh ginger root	6 tablespoons oil
½ cup soy sauce	2 to 3 cups water
2 tablespoons sherry	1 teaspoon sugar

1. Mince scallions and ginger root. Combine with soy sauce and sherry.

2. Wipe duck with a damp cloth; then rub inside and out with mixture (reserve the remainder). Let duck stand 30 minutes.

3. Heat oil in a large heavy pan. Brown duck lightly on all sides. Drain off fat.

4. Add water and reserved mixture and bring to a boil; then simmer, covered, 1 hour.

5. Add sugar and simmer, covered, until tender (about 30 minutes more).

VARIATION: In step 2 rub duck instead with a mixture of 1 tablespoon sugar, 2 tablespoons sherry, 4 tablespoons soy sauce, 1 teaspoon cornstarch and 1 teaspoon salt. Omit step 1 and the sugar in step 5.

BRAISED DUCK WITH ONIONS
6 to 8 servings

3 to 5 dried black mushrooms	5 tablespoons soy sauce
1 duck (4 to 5 pounds)	water
1 tablespoon soy sauce	1 pound onions
1 scallion stalk	½ cup bamboo shoots
3 slices fresh ginger root	3 to 4 tablespoons oil
¼ cup oil	1 teaspoon sugar
2 tablespoons sherry	1 tablespoon cornstarch
2 tablespoons water	

1. Soak dried mushrooms.

2. Wipe duck inside and out with a damp cloth; then rub soy sauce into skin. Cut scallion stalk in 2-inch sections; crush ginger root.

3. Heat oil in a large heavy pan. Brown scallions and ginger lightly; then discard. Add duck and brown lightly on all sides. Pour off excess fat.

4. Turn duck breast-side down in pan. Add sherry, remaining soy sauce and enough water to half cover bird. Bring to a boil; then simmer, covered, 1 hour, turning occasionally for even cooking and coloring.

5. Meanwhile slice onions, bamboo shoots and soaked mushrooms. Heat remaining oil in another pan, and stir-fry onion until soft and translucent.

6. Add bamboo shoots, mushrooms, and onions to duck, and simmer, covered, until bird is tender (about 30 minutes more). Remove duck, leaving liquids in pan.

7. Let bird cool slightly. With a cleaver, chop duck, bones and all, in 2-inch sections, or carve, Western style. Arrange on a serving platter with vegetables. Keep warm.

8. Bring liquids in pan to a boil and stir in sugar. Meanwhile blend cornstarch and remaining cold water to a paste; then stir in to thicken duck liquids. Pour over duck and serve.

BONED, BRAISED DUCK
6 to 8 servings

1 duck (4 to 5 pounds)	2 teaspoons soy sauce
2 Spanish onions	½ teaspoon Five Spices
2 tablespoons oil	¼ teaspoon salt
1 garlic clove	¼ teaspoon pepper
1 to 2 slices fresh ginger root	1 teaspoon soy sauce
3 tablespoons hoisin sauce	3 to 4 tablespoons oil
1 tablespoon sherry	6 to 8 cups water
1 teaspoon sugar	1 pound spinach

salt

1. Bone duck (see page 825). Cut breast in two and spread bird out flat, skin-side down.

2. Cut onions in wedges. Heat oil and stir-fry onions to soften slightly. Transfer to a bowl.

3. Mince garlic and ginger root. Add to bowl along with hoisin sauce, sherry, sugar, soy sauce, Five Spices, salt and pepper. Blend well and spread over inside surface of duck. Sew up bird securely to seal in mixture. Rub remaining soy sauce over duck skin.

4. Heat remaining oil and brown duck on all sides. Meanwhile bring water to a boil.

5. Add 1 cup boiling water to bowl in which seasoning mixture had been blended originally; stir up leftover bits to make a sauce, then pour over duck. Add enough of remaining boiling water to barely cover duck. Simmer, covered, until duck is puffed up and tender (1 to 1½ hours). Meanwhile wash spinach and remove tough stems.

6. Transfer ½ cup duck gravy to another pan and reheat. Add spinach, stirring to soften slightly. Sprinkle spinach with salt to taste and transfer to a serving platter. Place duck on top, breast-side up.

BRAISED DUCK (IN PARTS)
4 to 5 servings

1 duck (3 to 4 pounds)	2 or 3 scallions
½ tablespoon sugar	1 garlic clove
2 tablespoons sherry	1 or 2 slices fresh ginger root
2 tablespoons hoisin sauce	3 to 4 tablespoons oil
1 teaspoon cornstarch	4 tablespoons soy sauce
1 teaspoon salt	3 cups water

1. With a cleaver, split duck down the back; then chop each half, bones and all, in 4 or 5 pieces. Combine sugar, sherry, hoisin sauce, cornstarch and salt. Rub over duck and let stand 30 minutes.

2. Cut scallions in ½-inch sections; crush garlic and ginger root.

3. Heat oil in a large heavy pan. Add scallions, garlic and ginger and stir-fry a few times. Add duck and brown lightly on all sides. Drain off excess fat.

4. Add soy sauce and water and simmer, covered, until tender (45 minutes to 1 hour).

VARIATIONS: **During the last 30 minutes of cooking**, add any of the following:

   1 to 2 cups bamboo shoots, cubed or sliced

   4 cups Chinese lettuce, cut in 1-inch sections

   1 pound chestnuts, blanched and shelled

6 eggs, hardboiled and shelled but left whole

8 to 10 dried black mushrooms (soaked)

During the last 20 minutes of cooking, add any of the following:

2 pounds potatoes, peeled and cut in 2-inch cubes

1 pound string beans, stemmed but left whole

During the last 3 minutes of cooking add:

1 green pepper, diced

BRAISED DUCK WITH MUSHROOMS
4 to 5 servings

1 duck (3 to 4 pounds)	*dash of pepper*
½ pound fresh mushrooms	*3 to 4 tablespoons oil*
1 or 2 garlic cloves	*2 tablespoons oil*
2 tablespoons sherry	*2 to 3 cups stock*
1 tablespoon soy sauce	*1 tablespoon cornstarch*
1 teaspoon sugar	*3 tablespoons water*
1 teaspoon salt	*few drops of sesame oil*

1. Wipe duck with a damp cloth. With a cleaver chop duck, bones and all, in 2-inch sections. Stem mushrooms and cut in half. Crush garlic.

2. Combine sherry, soy sauce, sugar, salt and pepper.

3. Heat oil in a large heavy pan and brown duck quickly. Add sherry-soy mixture and cook, stirring, for 2 minutes. Remove duck and seasonings from pan.

4. Heat remaining oil. Brown garlic lightly and discard. Add mushrooms and stir-fry to soften slightly. Then return duck and seasonings.

5. Add stock, bring to a boil; then simmer, covered, until done (about 45 minutes).

6. Blend cornstarch and cold water to a paste, then stir in to thicken sauce. Stir in sesame oil and serve.

VARIATION: Use only ¼ pound fresh mushrooms. Add 1 cup bamboo shoots and 1 cup celery, both diced; and ½ cup water chestnuts, sliced. In step 4, stir-fry vegetables 1 to 2 minutes; then return duck.

BRAISED DUCK WITH PEAR AND CHESTNUTS
4 servings

1 *duck (3 to 4 pounds)*	2 *tablespoons soy sauce*
½ *pound chestnuts*	2 *tablespoons sherry*
1 *or 2 slices fresh ginger root*	1 *teaspoon salt*
2 *to 3 tablespoons oil*	1 *large pear*
1 *cup stock*	1 *teaspoon sugar*

1. Wipe duck with a damp cloth. With a cleaver chop duck, bones and all, in 2-inch sections.

2. Parboil chestnuts 15 minutes; then shell. Mince ginger root.

3. Heat oil in a large heavy pan. Brown duck sections quickly; drain off excess fat. Add stock, soy sauce, sherry, salt and ginger. Bring to a boil; then simmer, covered, 30 minutes.

4. Add chestnuts and simmer, covered, 10 minutes more. Meanwhile peel pear and slice thick, then sprinkle with sugar. Add to pan and cook, covered, until heated through, but not soft (about 5 minutes).

BRAISED DUCK WITH SWEET POTATOES
4 servings

2 *large sweet potatoes*	¼ *teaspoon cinnamon*
cornstarch	¼ *teaspoon ground cloves*
oil for deep-frying	¼ *teaspoon ground star anise*
1 *duck (3 to 4 pounds)*	½ *to 1 teaspoon sugar*
1 *garlic clove*	1 *tablespoon soy sauce*
2 *or 3 slices fresh ginger root*	1 *cup stock*
3 *tablespoons oil*	1 *tablespoon cornstarch*
3 *tablespoons water*	

1. Peel sweet potatoes and cut in 1½-inch cubes; dredge lightly in cornstarch. Meanwhile heat oil. Deep-fry sweet potatoes until golden. Drain on paper toweling.

2. Bone duck and cut in 2-inch cubes. Crush garlic. Mince ginger root.

3. Heat remaining oil. Add garlic and ginger root; stir-fry a few times. Add duck cubes and brown.

4. Sprinkle with cinnamon, cloves, anise and sugar. Stir in soy sauce. Add stock and bring to a boil.

5. Add deep-fried potatoes and simmer, covered, until duck is tender (about 15 minutes).

6. Blend remaining cornstarch and cold water to a paste; then stir in to thicken sauce.

BRAISED DUCK WITH PINEAPPLE
6 to 8 servings

1 *duck (4 to 5 pounds)*	1 *or 2 slices fresh ginger root*
4 *tablespoons soy sauce*	4 *to 6 tablespoons oil*
2 *tablespoons sherry*	½ *cup pineapple juice*
½ *teaspoon sugar*	2½ *cups water*
½ *teaspoon salt*	4 *slices canned pineapple*
1 *scallion stalk*	1 *tablespoon cornstarch*
1 *garlic clove*	3 *tablespoons cold water*

1. Wipe duck inside and out with a damp cloth. Combine soy sauce, sherry, sugar and salt; rub mixture over duck inside and out.

2. Cut scallion stalk in ½-inch sections. Crush garlic. Mince ginger root.

3. Heat oil in a large heavy pan. Stir-fry scallion, garlic and ginger to soften slightly. Add duck and brown quickly on all sides.

4. Drain canned pineapple. Reserve juice and combine with water, then pour over duck. Top bird with pineapple slices. Bring to a boil, then simmer, covered, until done (about 1½ hours).

5. Transfer duck to a serving platter, leaving liquids in pan. Cut each pineapple slice in four and arrange all decoratively on duck.

6. Reheat duck liquids. Meanwhile blend cornstarch and remaining cold water to a paste, then stir in to thicken duck liquids. Pour over duck and serve.

BRAISED DUCK WITH POTATOES
8 to 10 servings

1 *duck (6 to 7 pounds)*	4 *tablespoons soy sauce*
2 *pounds potatoes*	¼ *cup sherry*
¼ *cup oil*	1 *clove star anise*
3 *garlic cloves*	1 *tablespoon oil*
2 *leek stalks*	6 *cups water*
¼ *cup red bean cheese*	1 *clove star anise*
2½ *tablespoons brown bean sauce*	½ *head lettuce*
2 *teaspoons salt*	2 *teaspoons cornstarch*
1 *tablespoon sugar*	2 *tablespoons water*

few sprigs of Chinese parsley

1. Wipe duck inside and out with a damp cloth. Peel potatoes and cut in thick slices. (Keep in cold water until ready to use.)

2. Heat oil in a large heavy pan. Brown duck quickly on all sides. Drain off excess fat. Tie or sew up duck's neck to seal. Place bird tail-side up in a deep bowl.

3. Crush garlic. Cut leeks in 2-inch sections. In one cup mash red bean cheese with brown bean sauce and salt. In another, combine sugar, soy sauce, sherry and star anise.

4. Heat remaining oil and brown garlic lightly. Add red bean cheese mixture and cook, stirring over medium heat, to blend and heat through.

5. Add water, leek sections and sugar-soy mixture. Continue stirring to blend and heat.

6. Pour 1 to 2 cups of this sauce mixture into duck cavity. Add remaining star anise. Sew up cavity securely or skewer so that liquid cannot leak out.

7. Leave remaining sauce mixture in pan and bring to a boil. Add duck and potato slices and simmer, covered, 20 minutes. Turn bird over and simmer, covered, 20 minutes more.

8. Remove duck, leaving liquids in pan. Let bird cool slightly; then chop, bones and all, in 2-inch sections. Shred lettuce and arrange on a serving platter with duck and potato slices on top.

9. Reheat liquids in pan. Meanwhile blend cornstarch and remaining cold water to a paste, then stir in to thicken liquids. Pour over duck and potatoes. Garnish with Chinese parsley.

BASIC RED-SIMMERED DUCK
8 to 10 servings

1 *duck (6 to 7 pounds)*	6 *tablespoons soy sauce*
water to cover	4 *tablespoons sherry*
2 *scallions*	2 *teaspoons salt*
2 *or 3 slices fresh ginger root*	2 *teaspoons sugar*

1. Wipe duck inside and out with a damp cloth. Place breast-side up in a heavy saucepan, tucking wings under body. Add water to cover and bring to a boil.

2. Meanwhile cut scallions in 3-inch sections and slice ginger root. Then add both, along with soy sauce, sherry and salt. Simmer, covered, 1 hour.

3. Turn bird over. Add sugar and simmer until done (about 1 hour more).

4. Cut breast meat against the grain in slices ½-inch thick. Arrange on a serving platter, reconstructing the shape of the breast. (Or chop duck, bones and all, in 2-inch sections.) Serve hot, with or without gravy. The gravy may be reserved for later use as a master sauce (see page 739). Or serve cold.

NOTE: The duck is done when the meat is so tender it nearly falls from the bones.

VARIATIONS: In step 1, use ⅓ stock, ⅔ water.

In step 2, add 5 dried black mushrooms (soaked) and ½ teaspoon sesame oil.

Use 12 to 15 whole scallions (trim root ends, but keep stalks and green leaves intact). Toss scallions in a mixture of 2 tablespoons soy sauce and ½ teaspoon sugar, then place in duck cavity with the ginger root. Bring to a boil as in step 1, then cook with seasonings as in steps 2 and 3. Serve bird whole with gravy.

For a smaller duck (3 to 4 pounds) use only 1 cup water, 2 tablespoons soy sauce, 1 tablespoon sherry and 1 teaspoon sugar. Cook 1½ hours, basting and turning for even coloring.

RED-SIMMERED DUCK WITH PINEAPPLE
4 to 5 servings

1 *duck (3 to 4 pounds)*	2 *tablespoons soy sauce*
water to cover	1 *teaspoon salt*
1 *#2 can sliced pineapple*	*dash of pepper*

1. Wipe duck inside and out with a damp cloth. Place breast-side up in a heavy pan. Add cold water to cover and bring to a boil; then simmer, covered, 1 hour.

2. Drain liquid from pineapple and add to duck, along with soy sauce, salt and pepper. Simmer, covered, 30 minutes more. Add pineapple slices during last 10 minutes of cooking.

RED-COOKED SHANGHAI DUCK
6 to 8 servings

1 *bunch scallions*

2 *slices fresh ginger root*

duck giblets

2 *or* 3 *cloves star anise*

1 *duck* (4 *to* 5 *pounds*)

⅛ *cup sugar*

¾ *cup soy sauce*

1 *cup water*

1 *tablespoon sherry*

1. Cut scallions in 3-inch sections; slice ginger root. Place in a large heavy pan, along with duck giblets and star anise. Wipe duck inside and out with a damp cloth. Place in pan breast-side down.

2. Combine sugar, soy sauce, water and sherry and pour over duck. Bring to a boil; then simmer, covered, 45 minutes.

3. Turn bird over and simmer, covered, 45 minutes more. Let duck and liquid cool, uncovered, 10 to 15 minutes. Skim off the fat that rises to the top.

4. Heat duck and liquid, uncovered, over a medium flame, basting frequently until duck skin is dark brown and the liquid reduced to a cupful (about 15 minutes).

VARIATION: For the white sugar, substitute brown sugar.

RED-COOKED DUCK WITH FIVE SPICES
4 servings

¾ *cup soy sauce*

¾ *cup sherry*

1 *duck* (3 *to* 4 *pounds*)

1 *teaspoon Five Spices*

water

1. Slowly bring soy sauce and sherry to a boil in a heavy pan. Meanwhile wipe duck inside and out with a damp cloth, then add to pan. Cook, turning to color evenly (about 2 minutes on each side).

2. Remove duck, leaving liquids in pan. Rub Five Spices into skin; then return bird to pan.

3. Add enough cold water to half cover duck. Bring to a boil; then simmer, covered, about 1 hour, turning bird at 20-minute intervals for even cooking and coloring.

4. With a cleaver, chop duck, bones and all, in 2-inch sections; or carve, Western-style. Serve hot or cold.

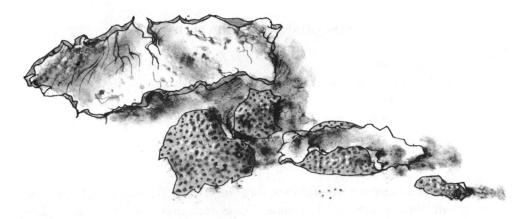

RED-COOKED DUCK WITH TANGERINE PEEL
4 to 5 servings

1 *piece dried tangerine peel*	3 *tablespoons soy sauce*
1 *duck (3 to 4 pounds)*	1 *teaspoon salt*
4 *to 6 cups water*	*dash of pepper*
½ *pound fresh mushrooms*	2 *tablespoons smoked ham*

1. Soak tangerine peel.

2. Wipe duck with a damp cloth and chop, bones and all, in 2-inch sections. Meanwhile bring water to a boil in a heavy pan.

3. Add duck and soaked tangerine peel. Bring to a boil again, then simmer, covered, 1 hour. Discard tangerine peel.

4. Meanwhile slice mushrooms; then add, along with soy sauce, salt and pepper. Simmer, covered, 20 minutes more.

5. Shred smoked ham. Serve duck hot, garnished with ham.

RED-COOKED ON-AND-OFF DUCK
4 to 5 servings

1 *duck (3 to 4 pounds)*	2 *cups sherry*
1 *scallion*	6 *tablespoons soy sauce*
2 *or 3 slices fresh ginger root*	½ *teaspoon anise pepper*

½ *teaspoon sugar*

1. Wipe duck with a damp cloth and chop, bones and all, in 2-inch sections. Place in a heavy pan. Cut scallions in 1-inch sections, slice ginger root and add, along with sherry, soy sauce, anise pepper and sugar.

2. Cook, covered, 20 minutes over medium heat. Turn off heat. (Do not remove lid.) Let stand 15 minutes.

3. Turn heat to low and simmer, covered, 15 minutes. Turn off heat. (Do not remove lid.) Let stand 10 minutes.

4. Turn on low heat again and simmer, covered, 15 minutes more. Turn off heat. (Do not remove lid.) Let stand 30 minutes, then serve.

RED-COOKED DUCK WITH PORK AND CHESTNUTS
4 to 5 servings

4 to 6 dried black mushrooms
½ pound chestnuts
1 duck (3 to 4 pounds)
½ pound lean pork

1 scallion stalk
2 or 3 slices fresh ginger root
1 cup soy sauce
4 cups water

1. Soak dried mushrooms. Blanch and shell chestnuts.

2. Wipe duck with a damp cloth and chop, bones and all, in 2-inch sections. Cut pork in 1-inch cubes. Place duck and pork in a heavy pan.

3. Cut scallion stalk in 1-inch sections; slice ginger root. Add to pan, along with soy sauce, water, soaked mushrooms and chestnuts.

4. Bring to a boil; then simmer, covered, until done (about 1½ hours).

RED-SIMMERED DUCK WITH GLUTINOUS RICE
6 to 8 servings

1 cup glutinous rice
1 duck (4 to 5 pounds)
water to cover
water to cover

½ cup soy sauce
1 tablespoon sherry
1 teaspoon salt
dash of pepper

2 scallions

1. Soak glutinous rice.

2. Wipe duck with a damp cloth. Place in a heavy pan with cold water to cover. Bring to a boil; then cook, covered, 20 minutes over medium heat. Drain, discarding liquid.

3. Stuff duck cavity with soaked rice and sew up securely or skewer. Return duck to pan.

4. Add fresh water to cover and bring to a boil; then simmer, covered, 45 minutes. Drain. (Reserve liquid for stock.)

5. Add soy sauce and sherry and simmer, covered, until tender (about 45 minutes more), turning bird frequently for even coloring.

6. Season with salt and pepper. Mince scallions and sprinkle over as a garnish.

EIGHT PRECIOUS DUCK

8 to 10 servings

½ cup glutinous rice	2 tablespoons soy sauce
4 or 5 dried black mushrooms	1 tablespoon sherry
¼ cup chestnut meats	1 duck (6 to 7 pounds)
¼ cup ginkgo nut meats	1 scallion stalk
¼ cup lotus seeds	2 or 3 slices fresh ginger root
3 to 4 cups water	3 cups stock
½ cup lean pork	1 teaspoon salt
2 tablespoons smoked ham	4 tablespoons soy sauce
¼ cup bamboo shoots	2 tablespoons sherry
6 raw shrimp	1 tablespoon sugar

1. Separately soak glutinous rice and dried mushrooms. Blanch and shell chestnuts, ginkgo nuts and lotus seeds.

2. Bring water to a boil. Add soaked rice and simmer, covered, 5 minutes, then drain. Rinse under cold running water and drain again.

3. Dice pork, ham and bamboo shoots; shell and dice shrimp; dice chestnuts and mushrooms. Combine in a bowl with cooked rice. Add soy sauce, sherry, ginkgo nuts and lotus seeds.

4. Wipe duck inside and out with a damp cloth; then stuff rice mixture into cavity, and sew up securely or skewer. Truss bird (see page 828). Place duck in a heavy pan.

5. Cut scallion stalk in 1-inch sections; slice ginger root. Add to pan along with stock, salt, remaining soy sauce and sherry.

6. Bring to a boil, then simmer, covered, 1 hour, turning duck several times for even cooking and coloring. Add sugar and simmer 1 hour more.

7. Scoop out rice stuffing and arrange on a serving dish. Chop duck, bones and all, in 1- to 2-inch sections, or carve Western-style. Arrange over stuffing and serve.

NOTE: This dish, sometimes called Eight Jewel Duck, can also be eaten cold. It will keep about a week in the refrigerator.

VARIATION: For the glutinous rice, substitute pearl barley. Bring to a boil in 2 cups cold water, then cook, covered, until soft (about 20 minutes). Drain, rinse in cold water and drain again.

WHITE-SIMMERED DUCK WITH TANGERINE PEEL
3 to 4 servings

1 *piece dried tangerine peel*	2 *scallion stalks*
1 *duck* (*4 to 5 pounds*)	2 *or 3 slices fresh ginger root*
water to cover	1 *teaspoon salt*

dash of pepper

1. Soak tangerine peel.

2. Wipe duck with a damp cloth. Place in a heavy pan with cold water to cover and bring to a boil. Meanwhile cut scallions in 2 or 3 sections, slice ginger root; then add to pan along with soaked tangerine peel.

3. Reduce heat and simmer, covered, until duck is tender (about 1½ hours). Season with salt and pepper during the last 5 minutes. Drain, reserving liquid for stock.

WHITE-SIMMERED DUCK WITH WINE
8 to 10 servings

1 *duck* (*6 to 7 pounds*)	1 *onion*
1 *teaspoon yellow bean paste*	8 *cups dry white wine*

1½ *teaspoons salt*

1. Wipe duck inside and out with a damp cloth and dry well with paper toweling. Rub duck cavity with yellow bean paste. Slice onion and place inside cavity.

2. Bring wine nearly to a boil in a large heavy pan. Add salt. Then lower bird in gently and simmer, covered, over the lowest possible heat until done (about 4 hours). Use an asbestos pad to keep heat to a minimum.

DRUNKEN DUCK I
4 to 5 servings

1 *scallion stalk*   1 *teaspoon salt*
2 *garlic cloves*   *dash of pepper*
6 to 8 *cups water*   1 *duck (3 to 4 pounds)*

2 *cups sherry*

1. Cut scallion stalk in 1-inch sections; crush garlic. Place in a large heavy pan along with water, salt and pepper, and bring to a boil.

2. Meanwhile wipe duck inside and out with a damp cloth, then add to pan. Bring to a boil again, then simmer, covered, 30 to 40 minutes.

3. Drain duck, reserving liquid for stock. Let bird cool; then dry thoroughly with paper toweling and refrigerate covered, overnight.

4. Cut duck in quarters and place in a large jar or container. Pour in sherry and cover jar tightly. Refrigerate 5 to 7 days.

5. Drain, reserving sherry (which can be re-used for cooking). Chop duck, bones and all, in bite-size pieces. Serve cold.

VARIATION: For the sherry, substitute sauterne.

DRUNKEN DUCK II
6 to 8 servings

1 *duck (4 to 5 pounds)*   2 *scallions*
salt   2 *cups sherry*
2 *slices fresh ginger root*   4 to 6 *scallions*

1. Wipe duck inside and out with a damp cloth. Rub duck cavity lightly with salt. Slice ginger root and slice off scallion roots. Put both inside cavity.

2. Place duck in a heavy pan. Add sherry and bring slowly to a boil. Then simmer, covered, until tender (about 2½ hours), turning bird several times.

3. Remove duck and let cool. Chop bird, bones and all, in bite-size pieces. Serve cold, garnished with remaining scallions, cut in 2-inch sections.

WHITE-SIMMERED DUCK IN SOUP
8 to 10 servings

6 *dried black mushrooms*   ½ *cup bamboo shoots*
1 *duck (6 to 7 pounds)*   2 *slices fresh ginger root*
8 *cups water*   ½ *pound smoked ham*

1 *teaspoon salt*

1. Soak dried mushrooms.

2. Wipe duck with a damp cloth. Place in a large heavy pan with water and bring to a boil. Skim off fat.

3. Meanwhile slice bamboo shoots and ginger root. Add to pan, along with smoked ham (in one piece) and soaked mushrooms.

4. Bring to a boil; then simmer, covered, until duck is tender (2 to 2½ hours). Add salt and simmer 5 minutes more.

5. Remove duck, ham and vegetables. Let ham cool slightly; then slice. Place duck in a deep bowl. Lay ham slices over its breast. Garnish with vegetables.

6. Reheat soup. Add to bowl and serve.

VARIATION: In step 4, during the last 30 minutes of cooking, add 2 pounds Chinese lettuce, cut in 1-inch strips. In step 5 place lettuce at the bottom of the bowl, with the duck, vegetables and ham on top. Then pick up step 6.

WHITE-SIMMERED DUCK I
8 to 10 servings

1 slice fresh ginger root	*2 slices fresh ginger root*
2 tablespoons sherry	*1 cup sherry*
½ teaspoon salt	*1 teaspoon salt*
dash of pepper	*water to cover*
1 duck (6 to 7 pounds)	*1 cup bamboo shoots*
2 scallion stalks	*¼ cup smoked ham*

1. Mince ginger root and combine it with sherry, salt and pepper. Wipe duck with a damp cloth; then rub mixture into skin. Let stand 1 hour.

2. Place bird in a heavy pan. Cut scallion stalks in 1-inch sections and slice remaining ginger root. Add to pan, along with remaining sherry and salt.

3. Add cold water to cover and bring to a boil; then simmer, covered, until tender (about 2 to 2½ hours).

4. Slice bamboo shoots and shred smoked ham; add to pan during last 10 minutes of cooking.

WHITE-SIMMERED DUCK II
8 to 10 servings

1 duck (6 to 7 pounds)	*1 scallion stalk*
2 tablespoons sherry	*2 or 3 slices fresh ginger root*
1 teaspoon salt	*4 cups sherry*
1 teaspoon ground star anise	*1 bunch scallions*

1. Wipe duck inside and out with a damp cloth. Rub sherry into its skin, then salt and ground star anise. Let stand 1 hour.

2. Cut scallion stalk in 2 or 3 sections and slice ginger root; put inside duck cavity. Place bird in a large heavy pan and add remaining sherry. Bring to a boil, then simmer, covered, 2 hours.

3. Drain and let cool; then refrigerate. Chop duck, bones and all, in bite-size pieces. Trim roots off remaining scallions and use whole as a garnish. Serve cold.

WHITE-SIMMERED ROAST DUCK
8 to 10 servings

1 duck (6 to 7 pounds)	*2½ cups water*
1 slice fresh ginger root	*1½ teaspoons salt*
1 large head Chinese cabbage	

1. Preheat oven to 400 degrees. Wipe duck with a damp cloth, then dry well with paper toweling. Truss duck (see page 828).

2. Place duck on a rack over a drip pan containing several inches of water. Roast until lightly browned (about 20 minutes).

3. Transfer duck to a heavy pan. Mince ginger root and add with water and salt. Bring to a boil; then simmer, covered, 1 hour. (If duck becomes too dry, add more boiling water.) Skim off fat.

4. Cut Chinese cabbage stems in 2-inch pieces. Place on top of duck and simmer 1 hour more.

NOTE: If the dish is prepared through step 3, then refrigerated, the fat will congeal and can be removed easily. The duck is then reheated and the cabbage added as in step 4.

WHITE-SIMMERED ROAST DUCK WITH TANGERINE PEEL
6 to 8 servings

1 *piece tangerine peel*	2 *slices fresh ginger root*
1 *duck (4 to 5 pounds)*	1 *teaspoon salt*
1 *tablespoon soy sauce*	½ *head lettuce*
1 *tablespoon peanut oil*	1 *tablespoon soy sauce*
2 *cloves star anise*	½ *teaspoon salt*
6 *to 8 cups water*	1 *tablespoon cornstarch*

3 tablespoons water

1. Soak tangerine peel.

2. Wipe duck inside and out with a damp cloth. Dry with paper toweling or hang up to dry in a cool airy place 1 to 2 hours. Meanwhile, preheat oven to 400 degrees.

3. Rub soy sauce, then peanut oil, over duck skin. Put star anise inside duck cavity. Place bird on a rack over a drip pan containing several inches of water. Roast to brown lightly (about 20 minutes), turning duck once. Meanwhile bring water to a boil.

4. Transfer duck to a large heavy pan. Mince ginger root and soaked tangerine peel and add, along with salt and boiling water to cover. Simmer, covered, 1½ hours.

5. Drain duck, reserving liquid. Let bird cool slightly; then either chop in bite-size pieces, or carve Western-style. Shred lettuce and arrange duck on top. Keep warm.

6. Strain duck liquid, then bring to a boil. Stir in remaining soy sauce and salt. Blend cornstarch and cold water to a paste, then stir in to thicken liquid. Serve as a dip with duck.

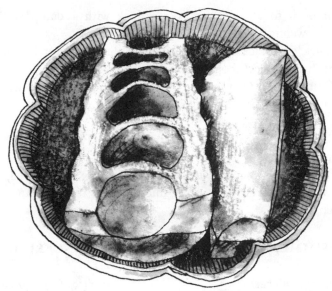

STEAMED DUCK WITH BAMBOO SHOOTS
4 to 5 servings

4 *dried black mushrooms*	½ *cup bamboo shoots*
1 *duck* (*3 to 4 pounds*)	1 *scallion stalk*
4 *cups water*	2 *slices fresh ginger root*
⅛ *pound smoked ham*	1 *teaspoon salt*

1. Soak dried mushrooms.

2. Wipe duck with a damp cloth. Place in a large heatproof bowl and add cold water.

3. Cut ham and bamboo shoots in ¼-inch slices and scallion stalk in 1-inch sections; slice ginger root; cut soaked mushrooms in half if large. Arrange over duck.

4. Steam by the bowl-in-a-pot method until duck is tender (about 2 hours). See page 831. Sprinkle with salt and serve.

VARIATION: For the ham and vegetables, substitute 4 medium parsnips, peeled and cut in half lengthwise.

STEAMED DUCK WITH TWO KINDS OF MUSHROOMS
4 to 5 servings

8 *dried black mushrooms*	2 *tablespoons sherry*
1 *duck* (*3 to 4 pounds*)	1 *teaspoon salt*
3 *cups stock*	½ *cup bamboo shoots*

¼ *cup canned button mushrooms*

1. Soak dried mushrooms.

2. Wipe duck with a damp cloth. Score bird along backbone, but do not cut through bone. Place in a large heatproof bowl and add stock, sherry and salt.

3. Steam 1½ hours by the bowl-in-a-pot method (see page 831).

4. Drain duck, straining its liquid into a saucepan. Wipe out steaming bowl. Let bird cool slightly; then bone.

5. Cut bamboo shoots in thick slices. Place at bottom of bowl, along with canned and soaked mushrooms. Place duck on top and steam 30 minutes more.

6. Reheat duck liquid, then pour over duck and vegetables and serve.

NOTE: This dish is sometimes called Angel Duck.

VARIATION: For the bamboo shoots, substitute ½ cup almond meats.

STEAMED DUCK WITH PINEAPPLE AND PRESERVED GINGER
4 to 5 servings

1 duck (3 to 4 pounds)	1 tablespoon cornstarch
½ cup pineapple juice	2 tablespoons water
3 tablespoons preserved ginger syrup	4 slices canned pineapple
1 teaspoon salt	½ cup preserved ginger

1. Wipe duck with a damp cloth. Place in a large heatproof bowl and steam by the bowl-in-a-pot method until duck is tender (about 2 hours). See page 831.

2. Remove bird and let cool slightly. With a sharp knife, make an incision along breast bone; then remove breast meat, one half at a time. Strip off skin and cut meat in ½-inch slices. Arrange on a serving platter. Keep warm.

3. Drain canned pineapple, pouring the juice into a saucepan. Add preserved ginger syrup and salt to juice and heat slowly. Meanwhile, blend cornstarch and cold water to a paste; then stir in to thicken.

4. Cut each pineapple slice in 4 pieces and slice preserved ginger; arrange over duck. Pour heated sauce over and serve.

NOTE: The remainder of the duck is generally reserved for other dishes, but the whole duck can be used if it's chopped, bones and all, in bite-size pieces.

STEAMED DUCK WITH FIVE KINDS OF SAUCE
8 to 10 servings

1 duck (6 to 7 pounds)	1 teaspoon honey
1 tablespoon soy sauce	pinch of Five Spices
1 tablespoon plum sauce	dash of pepper
1 tablespoon oyster sauce	duck giblets
2 tablespoons sweet vegetable sauce	1 cup water
2 tablespoons brown bean sauce	1 head lettuce
1 teaspoon hot sauce	1 cup Chinese parsley
1 teaspoon salt	2 teaspoons cornstarch

¼ cup water

1. Wipe duck inside and out with a damp cloth. Score bird along backbone, but do not cut through bone.

2. In a very large bowl, combine soy, plum, oyster, sweet vegetable, brown bean and hot sauces. Add salt, honey, Five Spices and pepper and blend well. Rub mixture over duck, inside and out. Then place duck in bowl with remaining mixture, and refrigerate, covered, overnight.

3. Drain duck, reserving marinade. Transfer bird to a large heatproof bowl and steam 1½ hours by the bowl-in-a-pot method (see page 831). Drain duck, let cool slightly, then bone.

4. Dice duck giblets and place in a saucepan with water. Bring to a boil, then simmer, covered, 15 minutes. Meanwhile shred lettuce and mince parsley. Arrange boned duck over lettuce.

5. Blend cornstarch and remaining cold water to a paste, then add to pan with giblets, stirring to thicken liquid. Pour giblet sauce over duck. Serve, garnished with minced parsley.

VARIATION: In step 3, place under the duck in heatproof bowl 2 pounds of either taro or potatoes, peeled and cubed; then steam as directed.

NANKING SALT DUCK
5 to 6 servings

1 tablespoon Szechwan peppercorns	1 duck (4 pounds)
6 tablespoons salt	2 tablespoons sherry

1. Put Szechwan peppercorns and salt in a dry pan and stir constantly for 5 minutes over low heat. Let cool slightly, then crush peppercorns with a rolling pin and strain through a sieve.

2. Wipe duck inside and out with a damp cloth. Rub inside and out with pepper-salt mixture. Refrigerate, covered, overnight.

3. Rinse duck briefly with cold water to remove pepper-salt coating. Transfer to a large heatproof bowl and add sherry.

4. Steam 1¼ hours by the bowl-in-a-pot method (see page 831). Turn off heat, but keep pan covered until duck has cooled to room temperature.

5. Drain duck, reserving liquid. Chop, bones and all, in 1½-inch sections; or bone and cut in 1- by 2-inch strips. Pour duck liquid over, and chill. Serve cold.

NOTE: The duck in this dish is reddish and tender. It should not be confused with preserved duck, which is heavily salted and dried.

VARIATIONS: For the Szechwan peppercorns, substitute 1 teaspoon either ground Szechwan pepper, ground black pepper, or cinnamon. In step 1, heat with the salt, stirring only 1 minute.

After step 1, add ½ teaspoon ground star anise to pepper-salt mixture.

At the end of step 2, wrap duck well in foil and refrigerate 3 to 4 days.

In step 4, instead of steaming the duck, place in a heavy saucepan with 8 cups cold water and bring to a boil. Then simmer, covered, until tender but not too soft (about 40 to 60 minutes). Pick up step 5.

STEAMED DUCK WITH HAM AND LEEKS
4 to 5 servings

1 duck (3 to 4 pounds)	2 cups duck stock
water to cover	2 slices fresh ginger root
1 pound smoked ham	2 tablespoons sherry
1 bunch leeks	3 tablespoons soy sauce

½ teaspoon salt

1. Wipe duck with a damp cloth. Place in a pan with cold water to cover and bring to a boil; then simmer, covered, 20 minutes. Drain, reserving duck stock.

2. Let bird cool. Cut meat away from bones in 1- by 2-inch rectangles. Cut smoked ham in similar-size pieces.

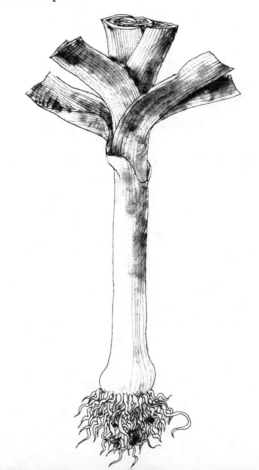

3. Cut off long, green, flexible leaves of leeks. With each leaf, tie together one piece of duck and ham, then place in a heatproof bowl.

4. Skim off fat from duck stock. Mince ginger root and combine with stock, sherry, soy sauce and salt. Mix well. Pour over duck-ham bundles.

5. Steam by the bowl-in-a-pot method until duck is tender (about 1 hour). See page 831.

NOTE: This dish is also known as Jade Belt Duck.

VARIATION: Omit the leeks. Arrange the duck and ham rectangles crosswise in alternating layers in the heatproof bowl and top with 6 canned mushrooms; or slice ham very thin and wrap each slice around one piece of duck. Steam as above.

STEAMED DUCK WITH SHERRY I
6 to 8 servings

1 duck (4 to 5 pounds)	1 cup sherry
water to cover	½ tablespoon sugar
2 scallion stalks	2 tablespoons soy sauce
2 slices fresh ginger root	1 teaspoon salt

1. Wipe duck with a damp cloth. Bring water to a boil in a large pan and lower duck in gently. Boil 5 minutes. Drain, discarding liquid. Transfer bird to a large heatproof bowl.

2. Cut scallion stalks in half and slice ginger root; add to duck. Combine sherry, sugar, soy sauce and salt. Pour over duck.

3. Steam 2 hours by the bowl-in-a-pot method (see page 831).

4. Discard scallion stalks and ginger slices. Serve duck hot in steaming bowl.

STEAMED DUCK WITH SHERRY II
6 to 8 servings

1 duck (4 to 5 pounds)	2 to 3 slices fresh ginger root
3 to 4 tablespoons oil	1 tablespoon soy sauce
salt	1 teaspoon sugar
1 large onion	1 cup sherry

1. Wipe duck inside and out with a damp cloth. Dry well with paper toweling, or hang up to dry in a cool, airy place 1 to 2 hours.

2. Heat oil in a large pan and brown duck quickly. Then rinse under cold running water (to remove oil) and drain. Sprinkle bird lightly with salt inside and out.

3. Slice onion and ginger root thin, then put inside duck cavity. Transfer duck

to a large heatproof bowl. Sprinkle with soy sauce and sugar; then pour sherry over.

    4. Steam by the bowl-in-a-pot method until duck is tender (about 2 hours). See page 831.

STEAMED TANGERINE DUCK
6 to 8 servings

1 *piece dried tangerine peel*	1 *tablespoon oil*
1 *duck (4 to 5 pounds)*	4 *cups stock*
3 *to 4 tablespoons oil*	1 *teaspoon salt*

    1. Soak tangerine peel.

    2. Wipe duck inside and out with a damp cloth. Score bird along backbone but do not cut through bone. Dry well with paper toweling, or hang up to dry in a cool, airy place 1 to 2 hours.

    3. Heat oil in a large pan and brown duck quickly. Transfer bird, breast-side down, to a deep heatproof bowl.

    4. Heat remaining oil. Add tangerine peel and stir-fry 1 to 2 minutes; then put inside duck cavity. Pour stock over duck and add salt.

    5. Steam by the bowl-in-a-pot method until duck is tender (about 2 hours). See page 831.

NOTE: This dish is sometimes called Steamed Duck Soup.

STEAMED DUCK STUFFED WITH CHINESE LETTUCE
6 to 8 servings

1 *duck (4 to 5 pounds)*	1 *head Chinese lettuce*
12 *lotus seeds*	1 *teaspoon salt*
¼ *pound smoked ham*	3 *to 4 tablespoons oil*

    1. Wipe duck inside and out with a damp cloth. Dry well with paper toweling, or hang up to dry in a cool, airy place 1 to 2 hours.

2. Blanch lotus seeds. Slice ham; cut Chinese lettuce in 1-inch sections.

3. Combine half of Chinese lettuce sections with lotus seeds and ham. Add salt and mix well. Stuff mixture into duck and sew up securely or skewer.

4. Heat oil in a large pan and brown duck quickly.

5. Place remaining lettuce sections in a large heatproof bowl; then put duck on top. Steam by the bowl-in-a-pot method until duck is tender (about 2 hours). See page 831.

STEAMED DUCK, BONED AND STUFFED
6 to 8 servings

1 duck (4 to 5 pounds)	*2 to 3 slices fresh ginger root*
6 dried black mushrooms	*½ cup stock*
12 lotus seeds	*2 tablespoons soy sauce*
½ pound lean pork	*1 tablespoon sherry*
¼ pound smoked ham	*1 tablespoon oil*
10 water chestnuts	*½ teaspoon salt*
½ cup bamboo shoots	*1 cup cooked rice*

1. Bone duck (see page 825), leaving shape and skin intact. Hang up to dry in a cool, airy place 1 to 2 hours. Meanwhile soak mushrooms; blanch lotus seeds.

2. Mince or grind pork and smoked ham. Mince water chestnuts, bamboo shoots, ginger root, soaked mushrooms and blanched lotus seeds. Mix well with stock, soy sauce, sherry, oil, salt and cooked rice. Stuff mixture into duck cavity and sew up securely or skewer.

3. Place bird in a large heatproof bowl. Steam by the bowl-in-a-pot method until duck is tender (1½ to 2 hours). See page 831. Cut in ½-inch slices and serve hot.

DEEP-FRIED STEAMED DUCK WITH MUSHROOMS AND BAMBOO SHOOTS
8 to 10 servings

5 dried black mushrooms	*¼ teaspoon sugar*
2 pieces tangerine peel	*dash of pepper*
1 duck (6 to 7 pounds)	*1 scallion*
2 teaspoons soy sauce	*2 celery stalks*
oil for deep-frying	*1 head lettuce*
1 cup bamboo shoots	*1 tablespoon cornstarch*
4 slices fresh ginger root	*1 tablespoon water*
3 to 5 cloves star anise	*1 tablespoon soy sauce*
1 teaspoon salt	*¼ teaspoon salt*

½ to 1 cup Chinese parsley

1. Separately soak dried mushrooms and tangerine peel.

2. Wipe duck inside and out with a damp cloth. Dry well with paper toweling or hang up to dry in a cool, airy place 1 to 2 hours; then rub with soy sauce.

3. Heat oil to boiling. Using a wire basket or long-handled Chinese strainer, gently lower in duck and deep-fry, basting and turning until golden. Drain on paper toweling and let cool. Then score bird along breastbone, but do not cut through bone.

4. Slice bamboo shoots and ginger root thin and combine with soaked mushrooms and tangerine peel. Mix well with star anise, salt, sugar and pepper.

5. Stuff mixture into duck cavity. Trim off scallion roots and cut celery stalks in 2 or 3 pieces; add to cavity. Sew up securely or skewer.

6. Transfer bird to a deep heatproof bowl. Steam by the bowl-in-a-pot method until done (about 2 hours). See page 831.

7. Drain duck, transferring liquids to saucepan. Let bird cool, then remove stuffing; reserve mushrooms and bamboo shoots, but discard other ingredients.

8. Carefully cut off wings and legs. Then, with the hands, carefully separate meat from bones, starting with incision on breastbone. (Keep skin and natural shape of bird as intact as possible.)

9. Spread boned duck flat on a heatproof platter, skin-side down. Bone legs and place on top. Arrange mushrooms and bamboo shoots over duck. Steam 20 minutes more.

10. Cut lettuce in strips and arrange on a serving platter. Invert duck onto lettuce, skin-side up, with mushrooms and bamboo shoots underneath.

11. Gradually reheat duck liquids in saucepan. Meanwhile blend cornstarch, water, remaining soy sauce and salt to a paste; then stir in to thicken liquids. Pour sauce over duck. Mince parsley and sprinkle over as a garnish.

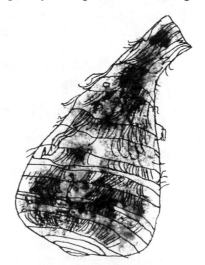

DEEP-FRIED STEAMED DUCK WITH TARO ROOT
6 to 8 servings

1 duck (4 to 5 pounds)	½ teaspoon sugar
2 teaspoons soy sauce	3 to 5 cloves star anise
oil for deep-frying	2 scallions
2 or 3 slices fresh ginger root	1 cup Chinese parsley
1 cube red bean cheese	1½ pounds taro root
1 cup stock	2 teaspoons cornstarch
1 teaspoon salt	2 tablespoons water

1. Wipe duck inside and out with a damp cloth. Dry well with paper toweling or hang up to dry in a cool, airy place 1 to 2 hours; then rub with soy sauce.

2. Heat oil to boiling. Using a wire basket or long-handled Chinese strainer, gently lower in bird and deep-fry, basting and turning, until golden. Drain on paper toweling. Let cool; then tie or securely sew up the neck opening.

3. Crush ginger root and mash red bean cheese; mix well with stock, salt, sugar and star anise.

4. Trim off scallion roots and stem parsley, then put in duck cavity. Place bird tail-side up in a deep heatproof bowl, and pour ginger-bean cheese mixture into cavity. Sew up duck securely or skewer, then turn breast-side up.

5. Peel taro root, cut in 1-inch slices and arrange around duck. Steam by the bowl-in-a-pot method until done (about 1½ hours). See page 831.

6. Carefully transfer taro slices to a serving platter. Cut threads or unskewer duck cavity and let liquids drain into a saucepan.

7. Let duck cool slightly; then chop, bones and all, in 2-inch sections; or carve Western-style. Arrange over taro and keep warm.

8. Reheat duck liquids in saucepan. Meanwhile blend cornstarch and cold water to a paste, then stir in to thicken. Pour sauce over duck and serve.

DEEP-FRIED STEAMED EIGHT PRECIOUS DUCK
6 to 8 servings

½ cup glutinous rice	½ cup crabmeat
3 dried oysters	¼ cup water chestnuts
4 dried scallops	1 tablespoon sherry
2 tablespoons dried shrimp	1 teaspoon salt
1 duck (4 to 5 pounds)	1 teaspoon sugar
2 teaspoons soy sauce	½ teaspoon garlic powder
½ cup fresh mushrooms	oil for deep-frying
¼ cup smoked ham	1 cup stock
1 Chinese sausage	½ cup green peas

1 head lettuce

1. Separately soak glutinous rice, dried oysters, dried scallops and shrimp.

2. Wipe duck inside and out with a damp cloth. Dry well with paper toweling or hang up to dry in a cool, airy place 1 to 2 hours; then rub with soy sauce.

3. Dice fresh mushrooms. Mince smoked ham, Chinese sausage, crabmeat and water chestnuts; also soaked oysters, scallops and shrimp. Mix well with soaked glutinous rice, sherry, salt, sugar and garlic powder.

4. Heat oil to boiling. Using a wire basket or long-handled Chinese strainer, gently lower in duck and deep-fry, turning and basting, until golden. Drain. Rinse in a pan of cold water and drain again.

5. Stuff duck with glutinous rice mixture. Sew up securely or skewer. Transfer bird to a large heatproof bowl and pour stock over. Steam by the bowl-in-a-pot method until tender (about 1½ hours). See page 831.

6. Parboil green peas. Cut lettuce in strips and arrange on a serving platter.

7. Let duck cool slightly; then chop, bones and all, in 2-inch sections; or carve Western-style. Arrange on lettuce bed and garnish with green peas.

VARIATIONS: For the green peas, substitute Chinese parsley.

For the sugar, substitute honey.

For the stuffing, substitute the following mixture: ½ cup glutinous rice (soaked); 2 tablespoons barley (soaked); 6 dried apricots; 12 chestnuts, blanched and shelled; 12 ginkgo nuts, shelled; ¼ cup canned lotus seeds; 1 tablespoon dried dragon's eye (soaked); ½ cup water chestnuts, diced; 1 scallion stalk, minced; 2 tablespoons sherry; 1 teaspoon sugar; and 1 teaspoon salt.

DEEP-FRIED STEAMED DUCK STUFFED WITH LOTUS SEEDS
8 to 10 servings

1 duck (6 to 7 pounds)	oil for deep-frying
2 teaspoons soy sauce	½ bunch Chinese parsley
1 cup barley	2 scallions
1 cup dried black mushrooms	3 to 5 cloves star anise
1 piece dried tangerine peel	2 cups stock
1 cup lotus seeds	dash of pepper
1 cup ginkgo nuts	¼ teaspoon salt
¼ cup ham	¼ teaspoon soy sauce
½ teaspoon salt	2 teaspoons cornstarch
½ teaspoon sugar	2 tablespoons water
½ bunch Chinese parsley	

1. Bone duck (see page 825), leaving shape and skin intact. Hang up to dry in a cool, airy place 1 to 2 hours; then rub skin lightly with soy sauce.

2. Separately soak barley, dried mushrooms and tangerine peel. Blanch lotus seeds. Shell and blanch ginkgo nuts.

3. Coarsely chop ham and soaked mushrooms. Mix well with drained barley, lotus seeds, ginkgo nuts, salt and sugar. Stuff mixture into duck cavity, then sew up securely or skewer.

4. Heat oil to boiling. Using a wire basket or long-handled Chinese strainer, gently lower in duck and deep-fry, basting and turning, until golden. Drain on paper toweling.

5. Transfer duck to a heatproof bowl. Stem parsley; trim off scallion roots; then place over duck, along with star anise and soaked tangerine peel.

6. Steam by the bowl-in-a-pot method until done (2 to 2½ hours). See page 831.

7. Discard duck topping. Let bird cool slightly, then cut in ½-inch slices.

8. Heat stock in a saucepan. Stir in pepper, remaining salt and soy sauce. Blend cornstarch and cold water to a paste, then stir into stock to thicken. Pour over duck slices and serve, garnished with remaining parsley.

DEEP-FRIED STEAMED WEST LAKE DUCK
6 to 8 servings

6 *dried black mushrooms*	1 *tablespoon soy sauce*
1 *duck (4 to 5 pounds)*	*water to cover*
2 *teaspoons soy sauce*	½ *cup duck liquid*
oil for deep-frying	½ *cup bamboo shoots*
duck giblets	½ *cup celery*
4 *slices fresh ginger root*	1½ *cups duck liquid*
1 *clove star anise*	½ *cup smoked ham*
1 *tablespoon sherry*	½ *cup Chinese parsley*
1 *teaspoon salt*	1 *tablespoon cornstarch*
1 *teaspoon honey*	¼ *cup water*

1. Soak dried mushrooms.

2. Wipe duck inside and out with a damp cloth. Dry well with paper toweling or hang up to dry in a cool, airy place 1 to 2 hours.

3. Rub duck lightly with soy sauce. Then truss (see page 828).

4. Heat oil to boiling. Using a wire basket or long-handled Chinese strainer, gently lower in duck and deep-fry, basting and turning, until golden. Drain quickly. Rinse in a pan of cold water and drain again. Untie duck.

5. Transfer bird to a large heatproof bowl. Dice giblets; slice ginger root and add, along with star anise. Combine sherry, salt, honey and remaining soy sauce and pour over. Meanwhile boil water in another pan, and also pour over duck.

6. Steam by the bowl-in-a-pot method until duck is done, but still firm (about 1¾ hours). See page 831.

7. Remove duck and let cool. Bone; then cut meat in bite-size squares, each with a piece of skin. Strain duck liquid, skimming off fat.

8. Return duck squares, skin-side up, to heatproof bowl. Add strained duck liquid and steam 15 minutes more.

9. Meanwhile shred bamboo shoots, celery and soaked mushrooms. In a saucepan, bring remaining duck liquid to a boil. Add shredded vegetables and simmer, covered, 10 minutes.

10. Cut smoked ham in strips. Chop Chinese parsley. Blend cornstarch and cold water to a paste and stir into duck liquid to thicken. Pour over duck squares and serve, garnished with ham strips and chopped parsley.

NOTE: This recipe can be made with chicken as well as duck.

VARIATIONS: In step 5, omit the seasonings given and pour over duck and giblets the following mixture: 1½ cups stock; 1 slice fresh ginger root and 1 clove garlic, both minced; and 1 cup canned button mushrooms. Also omit the water.

In step 10, arrange duck squares on a serving platter over 1 head lettuce, shredded; or over 1 pound of any of the following: asparagus, broccoli, Chinese cabbage, mushrooms, mustard greens, onions or spinach. (These must be stir-fried first.)

BASIC STEAMED DEEP-FRIED DUCK
6 to 8 servings

1 duck (4 to 5 pounds)	*oil for deep-frying*
salt and pepper	*scallions*

1. Wipe duck inside and out with a damp cloth. Rub liberally with salt and pepper. Let stand 1 hour.

2. Place bird in a deep, heatproof bowl and steam 1½ to 2 hours by the bowl-in-a-pot method (see page 831).

3. Drain duck and let cool. Wipe dry, then truss (see page 828).

4. Heat oil to boiling. Using a wire basket or long-handled Chinese strainer, gently lower in duck and deep-fry, basting and turning, until golden. Drain on paper toweling.

5. Let duck cool slightly, then chop, bones and all, in bite-size pieces. Serve with scallion brushes (see page 828), a plum or hoisin sauce dip, or any other dip for deep-fried duck (see page 711).

NOTE: The technique of double-frying can be used here. In step 4, deep-fry the duck 5 minutes, lift out; reheat the oil. Then return the bird and deep-fry again until crisp and golden.

VARIATIONS: **In step 1,** rub duck with any of the following mixtures:

2 teaspoons salt, ¼ teaspoon anise pepper and ⅛ teaspoon Five Spices

2 tablespoons sherry, 2 teaspoons salt, ½ teaspoon sugar, ¼ teaspoon red pepper

1½ tablespoons soy sauce, 1 tablespoon brown bean sauce, mashed; and ½ teaspoon Five Spices

1 to 2 scallion stalks and 3 or 4 slices fresh ginger root, both minced; 1 tablespoon Szechwan peppercorns, crushed; and 2 teaspoons salt

In step 2, before steaming, add to bowl with duck 2 scallion stalks and 2 or 3 slices fresh ginger root.

In step 3, before trussing duck, coat with a mixture of 2 tablespoons cornstarch and 1 tablespoon soy sauce; or 3 tablespoons flour and 1 egg, lightly beaten.

STEAMED DEEP-FRIED DUCK WITH TANGERINE PEEL
4 to 5 servings

1 *piece dried tangerine peel*	*water to cover*
1 *duck (3 to 4 pounds)*	½ *cup almond meats*
3 *or 4 slices fresh ginger root*	2 *tablespoons smoked ham*
1 *tablespoon sugar*	2 *tablespoons water-chestnut flour*
1 *tablespoon soy sauce*	*oil for deep-frying*
1 *tablespoon sherry*	2 *cups duck liquid*
1 *tablespoon honey*	1 *tablespoon cornstarch*
1 *teaspoon salt*	3 *tablespoons water*

1. Soak tangerine peel.

2. Wipe duck inside and out with a damp cloth. Place in a deep heatproof bowl with tangerine peel on top. Slice ginger root and add.

3. Combine sugar, soy sauce, sherry, honey and salt. Pour over duck. Bring water to a boil and also pour over.

4. Steam 1 hour by the bowl-in-a-pot method (see page 831).

5. Drain duck, reserving liquid, and let bird cool and dry. Meanwhile shell, blanch, toast and sliver almonds; mince smoked ham.

6. Rub water-chestnut flour into duck skin, then truss bird (see page 828).

7. Heat oil until boiling. Using a wire basket or long-handled Chinese strainer, gently lower in bird and deep-fry, turning and basting, until golden. Drain on paper toweling.

8. Untie duck and let cool slightly. Then chop, bones and all, in 2-inch sections; or carve Western-style.

9. Slowly heat duck liquid in a saucepan. Blend cornstarch and cold water to a paste and stir in to thicken. Pour sauce over duck and serve, garnished with ham and almonds.

VARIATION: In steps 2 and 3, omit the seasoning ingredients given and the boiling water. Pour over the duck instead a mixture of 1 cup soy sauce; ½ cup sherry; 2 tablespoons brown sugar; ½ tablespoon salt; dash of pepper; 3 scallion stalks, sliced; and 2 or 3 garlic cloves, crushed. After steaming, discard sauce and hang duck up to dry over a drip pan in a cool, airy place for several hours or overnight. Then pick up steps 6, 7 and 8, omitting step 9.

STEAMED DEEP-FRIED PRESSED DUCK
3 to 4 servings

¼ cup almond meats

1 duck (4 to 5 pounds)

½ cup soy sauce

1 teaspoon salt

1 teaspoon sugar

2 celery stalks

3 scallions

cornstarch

oil for deep-frying

½ cup sugar

½ cup vinegar

1 tablespoon catsup

few drops of hot sauce

2 teaspoons soy sauce

¼ teaspoon salt

1 tablespoon cornstarch

2 tablespoons water

½ head lettuce

1. Blanch, toast and sliver almonds.

2. Wipe duck inside and out with a damp cloth. Combine soy sauce, salt and sugar and rub over duck skin. Pour remainder into duck cavity, swishing it around to coat the interior. Drain off excess and discard.

3. Put duck in a deep heatproof bowl. Cut celery in 3 or 4 pieces; trim off scallion roots and arrange over duck. Steam 2 hours by the bowl-in-a-pot method (see page 831).

4. Drain duck, reserving liquid for stock. Let bird cool slightly; then bone, leaving skin and original shape intact (see page 825). Transfer duck to a large flat plate or cutting board.

5. With both hands, press down on duck, flattening it to a ¾-inch thickness. Then sprinkle generously on both sides with cornstarch. Return bird to heatproof bowl and steam 30 minutes more. Let cool, then cut in quarters.

6. Heat oil to boiling. Add duck, one quarter at a time, and deep-fry until golden. Drain on paper toweling. Let cool slightly; then cut bird in 1½-inch squares, each with some skin. Keep warm.

7. In a saucepan, combine sugar, vinegar, catsup, hot sauce and remaining soy sauce and salt. Bring to a boil, stirring. Meanwhile blend remaining cornstarch and cold water to a paste, then stir in to thicken.

8. Shred lettuce and arrange on a serving platter with duck squares on top. Pour sauce over and serve, garnished with toasted almonds.

NOTE: This dish is also known as Wor Shu Opp.

SIMMERED DEEP-FRIED DUCK
8 to 10 servings

1 duck (6 to 7 pounds)	1 teaspoon salt
water to cover	dash of pepper
½ cup almond meats	oil for deep-frying
1 cup canned mushrooms	2 cups duck broth
1 head Boston lettuce	¼ teaspoon salt
2 eggs	dash of pepper
4 tablespoons cornstarch	1 tablespoon cornstarch
2 tablespoons water	3 tablespoons water

1. Wipe duck inside and out with a damp cloth. Disjoint and place in a heavy pan with cold water to cover. Bring to a boil and simmer, covered, 40 minutes.

2. Meanwhile blanch, toast and sliver almonds. Drain canned mushrooms. Shred lettuce and arrange on a serving platter.

3. Drain duck, reserving liquid. Let bird cool slightly; then bone and cut meat in ½-inch squares, each with some skin. Skim fat off duck liquid.

4. Beat eggs lightly. Mix to a smooth batter with cornstarch, water, salt and pepper. Dip duck squares in batter to coat.

5. Heat oil. Add coated duck squares, a few at a time, and deep-fry until golden. Drain on paper toweling. Arrange on lettuce bed.

6. Reheat duck broth. Add canned mushrooms and remaining salt and pepper. Meanwhile blend remaining cornstarch and cold water to a paste, then stir in to thicken. Pour sauce over duck squares and serve, garnished with almonds.

VARIATION: Leave the duck whole. In step 1, add to pan ½ tablespoon salt; 3 tablespoons soy sauce; 1 scallion; 2 slices fresh ginger root; 1 garlic clove, crushed; and 2 cloves star anise. Simmer 1½ hours. Drain and cool; then chop bird, bones and all, in 2-inch sections. Dry and deep-fry without batter. Serve hot with a pepper-salt dip (see page 708).

DEEP-FRIED, SIMMERED, DEEP-FRIED DUCK
4 to 5 servings

1 duck (3 to 4 pounds)	2 teaspoons sugar
2 tablespoons soy sauce	½ cup soy sauce
oil for deep-frying	flour
4 cups water	2 cups duck liquid
1 teaspoon salt	1 tablespoon cornstarch

3 tablespoons water

1. Wipe duck inside and out with a damp cloth and cut in two. Rub each half inside and out with soy sauce.

2. Heat oil until boiling. Using a wire basket or long-handled Chinese strainer, add duck, one half at a time, and deep-fry, basting and turning, until light golden. Drain on paper toweling.

3. Transfer duck halves to a heavy pan and add water, salt, sugar and remaining soy sauce. Bring to a boil; then simmer, covered, 30 minutes.

4. Drain, reserving liquid. Let bird cool; then bone and cut in 1-inch squares, each with some skin. Dredge lightly in flour to coat.

5. Reheat deep-frying oil to boiling. Add duck squares a few at a time and deep-fry until golden brown. Drain on paper toweling. Keep warm.

6. Skim and discard fat from reserved duck liquid; then reheat. Meanwhile blend cornstarch and cold water to a paste, then stir in to thicken. Arrange duck squares on a serving platter, pour sauce over and serve.

DEEP-FRIED MARINATED DUCK STUFFED
WITH GLUTINOUS RICE
6 to 8 servings

1 *duck* (4 *to* 5 *pounds*)	2 *tablespoons sherry*
1 *scallion*	1 *tablespoon honey*
3 *or* 4 *slices fresh ginger root*	1 *teaspoon salt*
3 *tablespoons soy sauce*	1 *cup glutinous rice*

oil for deep-frying

1. Bone duck, keeping its shape and skin intact (see page 825). Place in a bowl.

2. Mince scallion and ginger root. Mix well with soy sauce, sherry, honey and salt. Add to duck and let stand 1 hour, turning occasionally.

3. Drain duck, reserving marinade. Hang up to dry over a drip pan in a cool, airy place.

4. Meanwhile cook glutinous rice. Add reserved marinade and blend in; stuff mixture into duck and sew up securely or skewer.

5. Heat oil until boiling. Using a wire basket or long-handled Chinese strainer, gently lower in duck and deep-fry, turning and basting, until crisp and golden. Drain on paper toweling.

6. Let cool slightly, then cut in ½-inch slices. Serve hot or cold with stuffing on the side.

DEEP-FRIED SWEET-AND-PUNGENT DUCK
4 to 5 servings

sweet-and-pungent sauce
1 duck (3 to 4 pounds)
2 eggs

¾ cup flour
2 tablespoons water
½ teaspoon salt

oil for deep-frying

1. Prepare a sweet-and-pungent sauce (see pages 735–738).
2. Cut duck meat in 1½-inch cubes, each with some skin.
3. Beat eggs lightly and blend to a smooth batter with flour, water and salt. Dip duck cubes in batter to coat.
4. Heat oil to boiling. Add duck cubes a few at a time and deep-fry until golden. Drain on paper toweling.
5. Meanwhile reheat sweet-and-pungent sauce. Pour over duck and serve.

VARIATION: Leave duck whole and bone it, keeping its shape and skin intact (see page 825). Brush with 1 egg, beaten; then coat with fine bread crumbs. Repeat. Deep-fry as above, then cut in bite-size pieces. Serve with the sweet-and-pungent sauce.

STIR-FRIED DUCK AND VEGETABLES
4 servings

3 dried black mushrooms
1 duck (3 to 4 pounds)
1½ teaspoons cornstarch
1 tablespoon soy sauce
½ cup bamboo shoots

½ cup water chestnuts
2 tablespoons oil
1 tablespoon oil
½ cup stock
1 tablespoon sherry

1 teaspoon salt

1. Soak dried mushrooms.
2. Remove meat from duck breast and legs and dice in 1-inch cubes. Blend cornstarch and soy sauce, then add to duck and toss gently. Let stand 30 minutes.

3. Dice bamboo shoots and soaked mushrooms. Slice water chestnuts.

4. Heat oil. Stir-fry duck until its color changes (2 to 3 minutes), then remove from pan. Drain fat from pan.

5. Heat remaining oil. Add mushrooms, bamboo shoots and water chestnuts; stir-fry 2 to 3 minutes.

6. Add stock, sherry and salt, and heat quickly; then cook, covered, 3 minutes, over medium heat. Return duck and simmer, covered, until done (about 3 minutes more). Serve at once.

VARIATIONS: Use only the duck breast and cut against the grain in ¼-inch slices. Also cut vegetables in ¼-inch slices.

For the mushrooms, substitute 1 cup Chinese cabbage stems, cut in 1-inch sections.

In step 2, omit the cornstarch and toss the duck instead in 1 tablespoon soy sauce and 1 tablespoon sherry. Then, at the very end of step 6, thicken sauce with a cornstarch paste made by blending 1 tablespoon cornstarch and 3 tablespoons cold stock.

In step 6, add with the duck, ½ cup almond meats, toasted.

STIR-FRIED DUCK AND YOUNG GINGER
4 servings

1 duck (3 to 4 pounds)	2 tablespoons soy sauce
¼ cup fresh young ginger root	2 tablespoons sherry
1 scallion stalk	½ teaspoon salt
1 tablespoon cornstarch	2 tablespoons oil

1. Remove meat from duck breast and legs and shred. Separately shred ginger root.

2. Mince scallion stalk; then combine with cornstarch, soy sauce, sherry and salt. Add to duck and toss gently. Let stand 30 minutes.

3. Heat oil. Add duck and stir-fry until its color changes (about 2 minutes).

4. Add shredded ginger. Stir-fry 3 minutes more. Serve at once.

STIR-FRIED DUCK WITH PINEAPPLE SAUCE
4 servings

1 duck (3 to 4 pounds)	1 tablespoon water
1½ tablespoons cornstarch	3 slices fresh ginger root
2 tablespoons soy sauce	2 tablespoons oil
1 8-ounce can crushed pineapple	1 tablespoon sherry
1½ teaspoons cornstarch	1 teaspoon salt

1. Dice duck meat in ½-inch cubes. Blend cornstarch and soy sauce, then add to duck and toss gently to coat. Let stand 30 minutes, turning occasionally.

2. Place crushed pineapple in a saucepan and heat slowly. Blend remaining cornstarch and cold water to a paste, then stir in to thicken pineapple. Keep warm.

3. Crush ginger root. Heat oil in a skillet. Brown ginger root and discard. Add duck and stir-fry 2 to 3 minutes. Add sherry and salt and stir-fry 1 minute more.

4. Transfer duck to a serving platter. Pour heated pineapple sauce over and serve.

PAN-FRIED DUCK
4 servings

1 duck (3 to 4 pounds)	2 eggs
1 scallion stalk	4 tablespoons cornstarch
3 slices fresh ginger root	½ teaspoon salt
2 tablespoons soy sauce	4 tablespoons water
1 tablespoon sherry	5 to 6 tablespoons oil

1. Score duck along its breast bone and remove meat in two sections. Bone legs, leaving them whole.

2. Mince scallion and ginger root, then combine with soy sauce and sherry. Add to duck and let stand 30 minutes, turning occasionally. Drain, discarding marinade.

3. Beat eggs lightly, then blend to a smooth batter with cornstarch, salt and cold water. Coat duck generously with batter.

4. Heat oil until nearly smoking and fry duck pieces 2 to 3 minutes on each side over high heat. Reduce heat to medium and cook, uncovered, turning duck occasionally until its skin is crisp and golden (15 to 20 minutes).

5. Cut in ½-inch slices. Serve hot, with a pepper-salt mix (see page 708).

STIR-FRIED COOKED DUCK WITH BAMBOO SHOOTS
About 4 servings

2 cups cooked duck meat	1 tablespoon cornstarch
2 cups fresh mushrooms	3 tablespoons water
2 cups bamboo shoots	1 teaspoon soy sauce
2 tablespoons oil	1 teaspoon salt
1½ to 2 cups stock	½ teaspoon sugar

dash of pepper

1. Bone and dice cooked duck. Dice fresh mushrooms and bamboo shoots.

2. Heat oil. Add mushrooms and bamboo shoots and stir-fry 1 to 2 minutes.

3. Add stock. Heat quickly, then simmer, covered, 5 minutes. Add duck and simmer only to heat through.

4. Meanwhile blend cornstarch, cold water, soy sauce, salt, sugar and pepper to a paste. Then stir in to thicken sauce. Serve at once.

NOTE: Any leftover duck, whether it's white-simmered, red-cooked or roasted, can be used in this recipe.

VARIATION: In step 3, add with the duck 2 tablespoons soy sauce, 1 teaspoon salt and a dash of pepper. Then, in step 4, omit all the seasonings from the cornstarch paste.

STIR-FRIED COOKED DUCK WITH BEAN SPROUTS
3 to 4 servings

2 cups cooked duck meat	1 tablespoon sherry
½ pound bean sprouts	2 tablespoons water
1 tablespoon oyster sauce	½ teaspoon salt

2 tablespoons oil

1. Bone and shred cooked duck. Blanch bean sprouts.

2. Combine oyster sauce, sherry, water and salt.

3. Heat oil. Add bean sprouts and stir-fry to heat (about ½ minute). Add duck and stir-fry to heat through.

4. Add oyster sauce mixture, stirring briefly to blend (about 1 minute). Serve at once.

NOTE: See Note above.

STIR-FRIED ROAST DUCK WITH LICHEE FRUIT I
4 to 6 servings

1 to 2 pounds roast duck	½ cup Chinese parsley
1 can lichee fruit	2 tablespoons oil
¼ pound snow peas	2 tablespoons oil
2 slices fresh ginger root	½ teaspoon salt

½ cup lichee juice

1. Bone roast duck and cut in 1- by 2-inch strips.

2. Drain canned lichees, reserving juice. Stem snow peas. Separately mince ginger root and Chinese parsley.

3. Heat oil. Stir-fry ginger root a few times. Add snow peas and stir-fry until bright green. Remove from pan.

4. Heat remaining oil. Add duck strips and stir-fry a few times; then reduce heat to medium.

5. Add salt and lichee juice and heat through. Then gently stir in lichee fruit to heat through (about 1 minute).

6. Return snow peas, stir-frying only to reheat. Serve at once, garnished with minced parsley.

NOTE: Roast ducks can be purchased ready-cooked in Chinese groceries; or the recipe for Simple Roast Duck or Simmered Roast Duck can be used.

VARIATION: For the lichee fruit, substitute pineapple chunks.

STIR-FRIED ROAST DUCK WITH LICHEE FRUIT II
4 to 6 servings

1 to 2 pounds roast duck	¼ cup pineapple juice
1 green pepper	⅓ cup duck juice
1 small can lichee fruit	¼ cup brown sugar
1 small can pineapple chunks	2 to 3 tablespoons oil
¼ cup maraschino cherries	2 teaspoons cornstarch
¼ cup lichee juice	2 tablespoons water

1. Bone roast duck and cut in 1- by 2-inch strips. Dice green pepper.

2. Drain canned lichees, pineapple chunks and maraschino cherries. Combine lichee and pineapple juices with duck juice and brown sugar.

3. Heat oil. Add diced pepper and stir-fry a few times. Add lichee fruit, pineapple chunks and cherries, stirring in gently to heat.

4. Gently stir in roast duck strips and fruit juice mixture. Cook, covered, to heat through slowly (3–5 minutes). Transfer duck and fruit to a serving dish. Keep warm.

5. Reheat liquids in pan. Meanwhile blend cornstarch and cold water to a paste, then stir in to thicken. Pour sauce over duck and fruit. Serve at once.

NOTE: When purchasing ready-cooked roast duck in Chinese groceries, ask for the duck juice in a separate container.

COLD ROAST DUCK WITH PINEAPPLE SAUCE
3 to 4 servings

1 pound roast duck	1 cup pineapple juice
2 cups lettuce	2 teaspoons cornstarch
1 small can pineapple chunks	2 tablespoons water

1. Bone and slice roast duck. Shred lettuce and arrange on a serving platter, with duck on top.

2. Drain pineapple chunks and arrange over duck. Pour pineapple juice into a saucepan and heat slowly.

3. Blend cornstarch and cold water to a paste, then stir in to thicken. Pour sauce over duck and pineapple. Refrigerate to chill before serving.

COLD ROAST DUCK WITH FRESH PINEAPPLE
4 to 6 servings

½ Spanish onion	¼ cup white sesame seeds
2 to 3 slices fresh ginger root	1 tablespoon powdered mustard
½ teaspoon salt	1 tablespoon water
1½ teaspoons sugar	1 tablespoon vinegar
3 tablespoons vinegar	½ teaspoon sugar
breast and legs of roast duck	1 tablespoon oil
½ fresh pineapple	¼ teaspoon salt

1. Shred onion and ginger root, sprinkle with salt, and let stand 10 minutes.

2. Combine sugar and vinegar, then pour over onion and ginger. Let stand 30 minutes more. Drain, discarding liquid.

3. Bone and cut roast duck in ¼-inch cubes. Put in a large bowl. Peel pineapple, cut in ¼-inch cubes and add.

4. Put sesame seeds in a dry skillet; stir over low heat, until golden. Spread out to cool, then crush with a rolling pin. Add to bowl.

5. Combine powdered mustard, water, and remaining vinegar and sugar, stirring until mustard smells pungent.

6. Add mustard mixture to bowl, along with drained onion and ginger, oil and remaining salt. Toss with duck and pineapple to blend well, and serve.

COLD ROAST DUCK WITH PICKLED VEGETABLES
4 to 6 servings

1 *cup sweet potatoes*	1 *tablespoon catsup*
1 *cup carrots*	1 *tablespoon oil*
1 *cup cucumber*	½ *teaspoon salt*
1 *cup Chinese white turnip*	½ *teaspoon hot sauce*
1 *green pepper*	*few drops of sesame oil*
1 *cup Chinese cabbage*	*pinch of cinnamon*
½ *to 1 cup sugar*	*dash of pepper*
1 *cup vinegar*	1 *head lettuce*

1 *to 2 pounds roast duck*

1. Peel and shred sweet potatoes, carrots, cucumber and Chinese white turnip. Shred green pepper and Chinese cabbage.

2. Combine sugar, vinegar, catsup, oil, salt, hot sauce, sesame oil, cinnamon and pepper. Add to shredded vegetables and toss well. Refrigerate, covered, 24 hours.

3. Toss vegetables again and refrigerate, covered, 24 hours more. Drain, discarding marinade.

4. Shred lettuce and arrange on a serving platter. Top with drained vegetables.

5. Bone and shred roast duck. Arrange over vegetables and serve.

❊ *Chicken and Other Poultry* ❊

CHICKEN COOKED CHINESE-STYLE may be stir-fried, deep-fried, steamed, poached, braised, simmered (both with and without soy sauce), roasted, jellied or smoked. Often it is cooked by a combination of methods: the chicken may be simmered and roasted; or steamed and deep-fried. This was designed originally to shorten cooking time and so conserve fuel. It has the added advantage of retaining the bird's inner tenderness while its exterior turns quickly crisp and golden.

Poultry is cooked both whole and in parts. One chicken can be used for several dishes: the legs and wings steamed or braised, the breast stir-fried, and the remainder cooked in congee or soup. Characteristically, every part of the bird is used: white meat, dark meat, liver, giblets, wings, back and bones.

Chicken wings, livers, gizzards and hearts are all considered delicacies. The wings, deep-fried, simmered or braised, are eaten both hot and cold. Their meat, being close to the bone, is particularly sweet and delectable. Chicken livers are stir-fried, deep-fried or simmered. Gizzards and hearts, if scored and parboiled first, can be used in place of chicken livers in any recipe.

(The hearts are split in two and spread open; the gizzards are cut with horizontal slashes about $\frac{1}{16}$ of an inch apart, then cut across, with a single vertical slash so that they open like flowers.) When properly cooked, they are crunchy, yet tender. Gizzards and hearts are also slow-cooked by braising and simmering.

COOKING TECHNIQUES AND SUITABLE CUTS OF CHICKEN

STIR-FRYING (sliced, cut in strips, or diced): white meat chicken, tender dark meat; also chicken livers and giblets.

DEEP-FRYING (whole, disjointed, or cubed): spring chicken, 2–3 pounds; also chicken livers and giblets.

BRAISING (whole, disjointed or chopped in 2-inch sections): spring chicken, 2–3 pounds; also chicken giblets.

WHITE-SIMMERING (whole or disjointed): young hens.

RED-SIMMERING (whole or disjointed): young hens; larger birds, 4–6 pounds.

STEAMING (whole, disjointed, chopped in 2-inch sections, slivered or minced): spring chickens, 2–3 pounds.

ROASTING (whole): larger birds, 4–6 pounds.

FOR SOUPS AND CONGEES: whole fowl, 4–6 pounds, backs and bones, also chicken giblets.

FOR CHICKEN VELVET: chicken breast, minced.

NOTE: Spring chickens, or fryers, having little fat of their own, must be cooked in someone else's fat—that is, lard or oil—and so are used in stir-fried, braised and deep-fried dishes. Older, larger birds, being more plump, can stew nicely in their own juices and so are more suitable for slow-simmered dishes and soups.

Tips on Chicken: Always wipe the chicken with a damp cloth. Better still, rinse the bird inside and out with warm water, then dry thoroughly either by blotting with paper towels to remove as much moisture as possible, or by suspending the bird in a cool, airy place for an hour or two. This will remove oil from the skin and enable the chicken to absorb more flavor during cooking.

When browning whole poultry, always truss the bird first (see page 828) to make it more manageable. If you tie an extra loop on the string, you'll have a convenient "handle" for turning the bird.

Chicken cooked in soup can also be used for stir-fried, white-cut and jellied chicken dishes, provided it has not been overcooked. The meat should be firm in texture, never soft and soggy.

Tips on Stir-frying Chicken: Although tender dark-meat chicken may be used for stir-frying, the white meat from the breast is best. The breast is simple to bone and easy to use. Remove the skin as well as the bones, but don't discard; reserve both for soup. Slice the meat thin and cut in ½-inch cubes or strips.

Pork can be substituted for chicken in any stir-fried recipe. For every 1½ cups of chicken meat, use 1 cup of diced lean pork and a set of diced chicken giblets. (Pork, however, needs longer cooking.)

To keep chicken from sticking to the pan during stir-frying, soak a few minutes in lightly salted water after slicing. Then drain well.

Stir-frying can damage the delicate texture of chicken meat. Instead of vigorous stir-frying, toss the chicken in hot oil for only half a minute. Then press against the sides of the pan a minute or two, until the chicken loses its pinkness. Sprinkle with a bit of sherry. Then turn chicken over and repeat.

When stir-frying *cooked* chicken, add it to the pan at the very end of cooking, only to heat through, so that it remains velvety, juicy and tender. If added too soon, the chicken can overcook and either crumble or become stringy.

BASIC STIR-FRIED CHICKEN I
About 4 servings

1 *chicken breast*	½ *teaspoon salt*
2 *slices fresh ginger root*	1 *pound vegetables*
1 *scallion stalk*	1½ *tablespoons oil*
1 *tablespoon cornstarch*	1½ *tablespoons oil*
1 *tablespoon sherry*	1 *tablespoon soy sauce*
2 *tablespoons water*	*pinch of sugar*

½ cup stock

1. Skin and bone chicken; then slice thin.
2. Mince ginger root and scallion, then combine with cornstarch, sherry, water and salt. Add to chicken and toss to coat. Let stand 15 minutes, turning occasionally.
3. Meanwhile slice vegetables.

4. Heat oil. Add chicken and stir-fry until it begins to brown (2–3 minutes). Remove from pan.

5. Heat remaining oil; add vegetables and stir-fry to coat with oil (1–2 minutes). Sprinkle with soy sauce and sugar.

6. Stir in stock, and heat quickly. Then simmer, covered, until vegetables are nearly done. Return chicken; stir in to reheat and blend flavors (about ½ minute). Serve at once.

NOTE: Any vegetable can be used (see page 583 for details on cooking time). For suggested combinations, see page 307.

VARIATIONS: Dice the chicken and vegetables or cut in strips.

For the ingredients in step 2, substitute either of the following mixtures:
1 tablespoon each of cornstarch, soy sauce and sherry
1 tablespoon soy sauce, 1 tablespoon oil, 1 teaspoon cornstarch, ½ teaspoon salt, dash of pepper and 1 garlic clove, minced

In step 6, add with the stock ½ teaspoon sugar, ¼ teaspoon salt and 2 teaspoons soy sauce.

BASIC STIR-FRIED CHICKEN II
About 4 servings

1 *chicken breast*	½ *teaspoon salt*
1 *pound vegetables*	½ *teaspoon sugar*
1 *garlic clove*	1½ *tablespoons oil*
2 *slices fresh ginger root*	1½ *tablespoons oil*
2 *tablespoons sherry*	½ *cup stock*
1 *tablespoon soy sauce*	2 *teaspoons cornstarch*

2 tablespoons water

1. Skin and bone chicken; then slice thin. Slice vegetables. Crush garlic. Mince ginger root.

2. Combine sherry, soy sauce, salt and sugar.

3. Heat oil. Add garlic and ginger root; stir-fry a few times. Add chicken and stir-fry until it loses its pinkness (about 2 minutes).

4. Add sherry mixture; stir in 1 minute more to blend. Remove chicken from pan.

5. Heat remaining oil. Add vegetables; stir-fry to coat with oil (1–2 minutes).

6. Stir in stock and heat quickly. Then return chicken and cook, covered, over medium heat, until done (2–3 minutes).

7. Meanwhile blend cornstarch and cold water to a paste, then stir in to thicken. Serve at once.

NOTE: See Note above.

VARIATION: Omit steps 2 and 4, and remove the chicken from the pan at the end of step 3. Then, in step 6, before returning the chicken, add to the stock a mixture of 1 tablespoon soy sauce, 1 tablespoon sherry, ½ teaspoon salt, ½ teaspoon sugar, a dash of pepper and 1 scallion stalk, minced.

SUGGESTED VEGETABLE COMBINATIONS FOR BASIC STIR-FRIED CHICKEN I AND II

1 cup onions
2 tomatoes

¼ pound fresh mushrooms
6 dried black mushrooms (soaked)

½ pound fresh mushrooms
½ pound Chinese cabbage

¼ pound fresh mushrooms
2 celery stalks
1 cup walnut meats

¼ pound fresh mushrooms
½ cup bamboo shoots

6 dried black mushrooms (soaked)
½ cup bamboo shoots
(1 cup walnut meats)

½ cup mushrooms
½ cup bamboo shoots
1 cup celery
¼ cup water chestnuts
(½ cup almond or walnut meats)
(2 tablespoons green peas)

1 cucumber
¼ pound fresh mushrooms
6 water chestnuts
1 cup celery

½ cup canned button mushrooms
1 cup celery
1 cup peas
½ cup onions
(½ cup water chestnuts)
(½ cup almond meats)

1 cucumber
½ cup bamboo shoots
1 cup peas

½ cup asparagus
½ cup bamboo shoots
1 cup bean sprouts

2 green peppers
3 celery stalks
8 scallion stalks

1 green pepper
1 red pepper
10 water chestnuts
1 onion

1 green pepper
1 Chinese turnip
4 water chestnuts
1 onion
½ cup bamboo shoots
(½ cup almond meats)

STIR-FRIED CHICKEN WITH ALMONDS AND VEGETABLES
4 to 6 servings

½ cup almond meats	2 teaspoons cornstarch
1 chicken breast	¼ teaspoon sugar
1 cup Chinese cabbage	dash of pepper
½ cup bamboo shoots	2 tablespoons water
½ cup canned mushrooms	2 tablespoons oil
¼ cup celery	½ teaspoon salt
4 water chestnuts	½ cup stock
12 snow peas	2 tablespoons oil
3 slices fresh ginger root	¼ teaspoon salt

2 teaspoons sherry

1. Blanch and toast almonds.
2. Skin and bone chicken; then dice in ½-inch cubes.
3. Dice Chinese cabbage, bamboo shoots, canned mushrooms, celery and water chestnuts. Stem and dice snow peas. Crush ginger root.
4. Blend cornstarch, sugar, pepper and cold water to a paste.
5. Heat oil. Add salt, then ginger root, and stir-fry a few times. Add diced vegetables (except for snow peas) and stir-fry 1 to 2 minutes.
6. Stir in stock and heat quickly. Then cook, covered, 2 minutes over medium heat. Remove vegetables and liquids from pan.
7. Heat remaining oil. Add remaining salt, then chicken, and stir-fry 1 minute. Sprinkle with sherry; stir-fry 1 minute more to blend in.
8. Return vegetables. Add snow peas and stir-fry another ½ minute.
9. Stir in cornstarch paste to thicken; then almonds. Serve at once.

STIR-FRIED CHICKEN WITH ALMONDS
AND WATER CHESTNUTS
8 to 10 servings

4 to 6 dried black mushrooms	1 teaspoon salt
1 chicken (2 pounds)	¼ teaspoon pepper
1 cup water chestnuts	3 to 4 tablespoons oil
½ cup almond meats	1 tablespoon soy sauce

¼ cup stock

1. Soak dried mushrooms.

2. Skin and bone chicken; then slice thin. Slice water chestnuts and soaked mushrooms.

3. Blanch and mince almonds; then combine with salt and pepper. Dip chicken slices in mixture to coat.

4. Heat oil. Quickly brown chicken slices.

5. Stir in mushrooms, water chestnuts, soy sauce and stock and heat quickly. Then cook, covered, over medium heat, until done (2 to 3 minutes).

STIR-FRIED CHICKEN AND ASPARAGUS
About 4 servings

1 tablespoon fermented black beans	2 tablespoons water
1 chicken breast	1½ tablespoons oil
1 pound asparagus	½ teaspoon salt
1 garlic clove	1½ tablespoons oil
1 tablespoon soy sauce	½ cup stock
1 tablespoon cornstarch	½ teaspoon sugar

1. Soak fermented black beans.

2. Skin and bone chicken; then dice. Cut asparagus stalks diagonally in ½-inch sections and discard tough white ends.

3. Mince garlic and mash with soaked black beans; then stir in soy sauce.

4. Blend cornstarch and cold water to a paste.

5. Heat oil. Add salt, then chicken and stir-fry until it loses its pinkness. Remove from pan.

6. Heat remaining oil. Add black bean mixture and stir-fry a few times. Then add asparagus and stir-fry 1 minute more.

7. Stir in stock and sugar and heat quickly. Return chicken and cook. covered. 2 minutes over medium heat.

8. Stir in cornstarch paste to thicken. Serve at once.

NOTE: If the asparagus is not tender, slice as above and parboil. (Do not parboil tips.)

STIR-FRIED CHICKEN AND BAMBOO SHOOTS
About 4 servings

1 chicken breast	½ teaspoon salt
½ cup bamboo shoots	½ cup stock
½ cup celery	1 tablespoon cornstarch
½ cup snow peas	3 tablespoons water
½ garlic clove	1 teaspoon soy sauce
2 tablespoons oil	¼ teaspoon sugar

1. Skin and bone chicken; then dice. Dice bamboo shoots and celery. Stem snow peas. Crush garlic.

2. Heat oil. Add salt, then garlic and stir-fry a few times. Add chicken and stir-fry until it loses its pinkness (about 2 minutes).

3. Add diced vegetables and stir-fry 1 minute. Stir in stock and heat quickly. Then cook, covered, over medium heat until vegetables are done (2 to 3 minutes). Meanwhile blend cornstarch and cold water to a paste.

4. Add snow peas, then soy sauce and sugar to pan; stir in 1 minute. Then stir in cornstarch paste to thicken. Serve at once.

VARIATIONS: For the snow peas, substitute water chestnuts, diced; add with other diced vegetables.

For the celery, substitute Chinese cabbage stems.

In step 3, add ½ cup canned button mushrooms.

At the end of step 4, garnish with 8 to 10 whole almonds, blanched and toasted.

STIR-FRIED CHICKEN AND BEAN SPROUTS
4 to 6 servings

2 dried black mushrooms	1 scallion stalk
1 chicken breast	3 tablespoons oil
2 teaspoons cornstarch	½ teaspoon salt
1 tablespoon sherry	½ teaspoon sugar
1½ pounds bean sprouts	1 tablespoon soy sauce
1 small onion	2 tablespoons oil

1. Soak dried mushrooms.

2. Skin and bone chicken; then shred. Combine cornstarch and sherry. Then add to chicken and toss to coat.

3. Blanch bean sprouts. Shred onion, scallion and soaked mushrooms.

4. Heat oil. Add bean sprouts and shredded vegetables; stir-fry 2 minutes.

5. Add salt, sugar and soy sauce and stir-fry to blend in well. Remove vegetables and liquids from pan.

6. Heat remaining oil. Add chicken and stir-fry until it loses its pinkness (about 1 minute). Return vegetables; stir-fry 1–2 minutes more. Serve at once.

NOTE: Although this dish can be served with rice, it's usually accompanied by Peking doilies (or pancake rolls). Each diner places a bit of the chicken mixture on his doily, rolls it up to enclose the filling, then picks it up with his fingers.

STIR-FRIED CHICKEN AND BITTER MELON
About 4 servings

2 teaspoons fermented black beans	1 tablespoon sherry
1 chicken breast	few drops of sesame oil
1 bitter melon	2 tablespoons oil
1 garlic clove	1 tablespoon oil
½ cup stock	1 teaspoon sugar
1 teaspoon cornstarch	1 teaspoon soy sauce

1. Soak fermented black beans.

2. Skin and bone chicken; then cut in strips. Cut bitter melon lengthwise in half and scoop out seeds; then cut in strips and parboil 3 minutes.

3. Mince garlic and mash with soaked black beans.

4. Combine stock, cornstarch, sherry and sesame oil.

5. Heat oil. Add chicken and stir-fry until it loses its pinkness (about 2 minutes). Remove from pan.

6. Heat remaining oil. Add black bean mixture and stir-fry a few times. Add bitter melon and stir-fry to heat through (about 1 minute).

7. Return chicken; then stir in stock mixture and heat quickly. Cook, covered, 2 minutes over medium heat.

8. Stir in sugar and soy sauce to blend in (about 1 minute more). Serve at once.

STIR-FRIED CHICKEN AND CHINESE CABBAGE HEARTS
About 4 servings

1 chicken breast	½ teaspoon salt
1 pound Chinese cabbage hearts	½ teaspoon soy sauce
1 garlic clove	¼ cup stock
2 tablespoons oil	2 teaspoons cornstarch
2 tablespoons water	

1. Skin and bone chicken; then slice thin and cut in ½- by 2-inch strips. Cut Chinese cabbage stems lengthwise in similar strips. Crush garlic.

2. Heat oil. Add salt, then garlic and stir-fry a few times. Add chicken and stir-fry until it loses its pinkness (1 to 2 minutes).

3. Add cabbage stems and soy sauce; stir-fry to soften slightly (about 1 minute).

4. Stir in stock and heat quickly. Then cook, covered, over medium heat until done (2 to 3 minutes). Meanwhile blend cornstarch and cold water to a paste.

5. Stir in cornstarch paste to thicken sauce. Serve at once.

NOTE: Chinese cabbage hearts are not vegetable "hearts" in the Western sense, but the very sweet and delicate inner stems of the Chinese cabbage.

VARIATION: For the chicken, substitute ½ pound shrimp, shelled and deveined.

STIR-FRIED CURRIED CHICKEN
About 6 servings

½ spring chicken	dash of pepper
1 onion	2 tablespoons water
2 teaspoons cornstarch	2 to 3 tablespoons curry powder
½ teaspoon sugar	½ cup stock
	½ teaspoon salt

1. Skin and bone chicken; then cut in thin slices. Slice onion.

2. Blend cornstarch, sugar, pepper and water to a paste.

3. Put curry powder and onion in a dry pan and stir over low heat until curry odor is pungent (about 2 minutes). Add chicken and stir-fry briefly to coat with curry.

4. Stir in stock and salt and heat quickly. Then cook, covered, over medium heat, stirring once or twice until done (2 to 3 minutes).

5. Stir in cornstarch paste to thicken sauce. Serve at once.

STIR-FRIED CHICKEN WITH EGGPLANT AND HOT PEPPERS
About 4 servings

1 chicken breast	2 or 3 chili peppers
1 tablespoon cornstarch	2 or 3 slices fresh ginger root
1 tablespoon soy sauce	1 garlic clove
1 tablespoon sherry	2 tablespoons oil
1 eggplant	2 tablespoons oil
	¼ cup stock

1. Skin and bone chicken; then slice thin and cut in strips. Combine cornstarch, soy sauce and sherry. Add to chicken and toss to coat.

2. Peel eggplant; cut in strips and parboil. Seed and shred chili peppers. Mince ginger root and garlic.

3. Heat oil. Add chili peppers; stir-fry until they change color. Remove from pan.

4. Heat remaining oil. Add chicken and stir-fry until it loses its pinkness (1–2 minutes). Add ginger root and garlic; stir-fry a few times more.

5. Add stock and eggplant; return chili peppers. Cook, stirring, 1–2 minutes to heat through and blend flavors. Serve at once.

STIR-FRIED CHICKEN AND LEEKS
About 4 servings

1 chicken breast	*1 tablespoon sherry*
½ pound young leek stalks	*¼ teaspoon salt*
2 to 3 slices fresh ginger root	*2 tablespoons oil*
2 tablespoons soy sauce	*¼ teaspoon salt*
2 tablespoons oil	

1. Skin and bone chicken; then slice thin. Cut leek stalks in 1-inch sections. Mince ginger root.

2. Combine soy sauce, sherry and salt.

3. Heat oil. Add remaining salt, then leeks and stir-fry to brown lightly. Remove from pan.

4. Heat remaining oil. Add ginger root; stir-fry a few times. Then add chicken and stir-fry until it loses its pinkness (about 2 minutes).

5. Stir in soy-sherry mixture ½ minute more to blend in.

6. Return leeks and stir-fry another minute to reheat and blend flavors. Serve at once.

STIR-FRIED CHICKEN AND BUTTON MUSHROOMS
About 4 servings

1 *chicken breast*	¼ *cup mushroom liquid*
2 *teaspoons cornstarch*	1 *tablespoon cornstarch*
½ *teaspoon salt*	1 *garlic clove*
¼ *teaspoon pepper*	2 *or 3 slices fresh ginger root*
1 *4-ounce can button mushrooms*	2 *tablespoons oil*

1. Skin and bone chicken; then dice. Combine cornstarch, salt and pepper; dredge chicken in mixture to coat.

2. Drain canned button mushrooms. Blend liquid from canned mushrooms and remaining cornstarch to a paste.

3. Mince garlic and ginger root.

4. Heat oil. Add garlic and ginger; stir-fry a few times. Add chicken and stir-fry until it begins to brown (2 to 3 minutes).

5. Add mushrooms; stir-fry only to heat through. Then stir in cornstarch paste to thicken. Serve at once.

NOTE: This is known as Moo Goo Gai Pan.

VARIATIONS: In step 1, add to the dredging mixture either 1 teaspoon sherry or 2 teaspoons soy sauce and 1 teaspoon oil. (In either case omit the pepper.) After tossing the chicken gently in the mixture to coat, let stand 10 minutes, turning occasionally.

At the end of step 4, remove the chicken from pan. Heat 2 more tablespoons oil; then add 1 green pepper, diced, and stir-fry until slightly softened (about 2 minutes). Add the mushrooms as in step 5. Return the chicken before stirring in the cornstarch paste.

At the end of step 5, garnish with either 2 tablespoons smoked ham, minced; or ¼ cup almond meats, blanched and toasted.

STIR-FRIED CHICKEN AND OYSTER SAUCE I
About 4 servings

1 *chicken breast*	2 *tablespoons water*
1 *scallion stalk*	½ *teaspoon salt*
1 *tablespoon cornstarch*	2 *tablespoons oil*
2 *tablespoons soy sauce*	2 *tablespoons oyster sauce*
1 *tablespoon sherry*	1 *teaspoon sugar*
½ *cup stock*	

1. Skin and bone chicken; then slice or dice.

2. Mince scallion, then combine with cornstarch, soy sauce, sherry, water and salt. Add to chicken and toss. Let stand 10 to 15 minutes, turning occasionally.

3. Heat oil. Add chicken and stir-fry until it loses its pinkness (about 2 minutes).

4. Add oyster sauce and sugar; stir-fry 1 to 2 minutes more.

5. Stir in stock and heat quickly. Then cook, covered, over medium heat, until done (2 to 3 minutes). Serve at once.

VARIATIONS: For the scallion, substitute 2 slices fresh ginger root, minced.

In step 4, omit the sugar; add with the oyster sauce 1 cup canned button mushrooms.

STIR-FRIED CHICKEN AND OYSTER SAUCE II
About 4 servings

1 *chicken breast*	1 *tablespoon cornstarch*
2 *scallions*	4 *tablespoons water*
1 *garlic clove*	1 *teaspoon sugar*
2 *slices fresh ginger root*	1 *teaspoon soy sauce*
2 *tablespoons oyster sauce*	2 *to 3 tablespoons oil*
1 *tablespoon soy sauce*	½ *teaspoon salt*
1 *tablespoon sherry*	¼ *cup stock*

1. Skin and bone chicken; then dice or slice. Cut scallions in 1-inch sections. Crush garlic.

2. Mince ginger root, then combine with oyster sauce, soy sauce and sherry.

3. Blend cornstarch, water, sugar and remaining soy sauce to a paste.

4. Heat oil. Add salt, then garlic, and brown lightly. Add chicken and stir-fry until it loses its pinkness (about 2 minutes).

5. Stir in oyster sauce mixture to coat chicken and blend (1 to 2 minutes).

6. Stir in stock and heat quickly. Then cook, covered, 2 to 3 minutes over medium heat. Stir in scallion sections.

7. Stir in cornstarch paste to thicken. Serve at once.

VARIATION: In step 2, add to the oyster sauce mixture 2 tablespoons catsup and 1 to 2 tablespoons curry powder; or 1 tablespoon fermented black beans (soaked), mashed.

STIR-FRIED CHICKEN AND PEANUTS I
About 4 servings

1 *chicken breast*	3 *tablespoons soy sauce*
1 *teaspoon cornstarch*	1 *tablespoon sherry*
1 *tablespoon water*	½ *teaspoon salt*
1 *egg white*	½ *teaspoon sugar*
1 *leek stalk*	2 *tablespoons oil*
1 *garlic clove*	2 *tablespoons oil*
2 *slices fresh ginger root*	½ *cup unsalted roasted peanuts*

1. Skin and bone chicken; then dice. Combine cornstarch, water and egg white. Add to chicken and toss to coat.

2. Cut leek in ½-inch sections. Mince garlic and ginger root.

3. Combine soy sauce, sherry, salt and sugar.

4. Heat oil. Add chicken and stir-fry until it loses its pinkness (about 2 minutes). Remove from pan.

5. Heat remaining oil. Add garlic, ginger root and leek; stir-fry to brown lightly (1 to 2 minutes). Return chicken and stir-fry 1 minute more.

6. Stir in soy-sherry mixture to heat through and blend flavors. Then quickly stir in roasted peanuts. Serve at once.

VARIATION: In step 5, add with the garlic, etc., 2 or 3 chili peppers, cut in half lengthwise.

STIR-FRIED CHICKEN AND PEANUTS II
About 6 servings

5 *dried black mushrooms*	2 *teaspoons cornstarch*
½ *spring chicken*	2 *tablespoons water*
2 *or 3 slices fresh ginger root*	¼ *teaspoon cayenne pepper*
1 *garlic clove*	½ *teaspoon heavy soy sauce*
2 *scallion stalks*	2 *to 3 tablespoons oil*
1 *tablespoon brown bean sauce*	1 *tablespoon sherry*
2 *tablespoons water*	½ *cup unsalted roasted peanuts*

1. Soak dried mushrooms.

2. Skin and bone chicken; then dice. Dice soaked mushrooms. Mince ginger root and garlic. Cut scallions in ½-inch sections.

3. In one cup mash brown bean sauce, then mix with water. In another, blend cornstarch and remaining cold water; then stir in cayenne pepper and soy sauce.

4. Heat oil. Add ginger root and garlic and stir-fry a few times. Add chicken and stir-fry 1 minute. Then sprinkle with sherry and stir-fry 1 minute more.

5. Add mushrooms; stir-fry another ½ minute. Add brown bean mixture, scallion sections and peanuts. Stir in to heat through and blend (about 1 minute).

6. Stir in cornstarch paste to thicken. Serve at once.

NOTE: For a spicier dish, use more cayenne pepper.

STIR-FRIED CHICKEN AND PEPPERS I

4 to 6 servings

1 *chicken breast*	1½ *tablespoons oil*
2 *green peppers*	*dash of pepper*
1½ *tablespoons oil*	2 *tablespoons oyster sauce*
½ *teaspoon salt*	¼ *cup stock*

1. Skin and bone chicken. Then dice chicken and green peppers.

2. Heat oil. Add salt, then peppers, and stir-fry until slightly softened (1 to 2 minutes). Remove from pan.

3. Heat remaining oil. Add chicken and stir-fry 1 minute. Sprinkle with ground pepper and oyster sauce; stir-fry 1 minute more.

4. Return green peppers. Stir in stock and heat quickly. Then cook, covered, 2 to 3 minutes over medium heat. Serve at once.

STIR-FRIED CHICKEN AND PEPPERS II

4 to 6 servings

1 *chicken breast*	1 *teaspoon cornstarch*
1 *tablespoon cornstarch*	1 *teaspoon soy sauce*
1 *tablespoon soy sauce*	2 *tablespoons water*
1 *tablespoon oil*	*pinch of sugar*
dash of pepper	2 *tablespoons oil*
2 *green peppers*	½ *teaspoon salt*
4 *scallion stalks*	2 *tablespoons oil*
1 *garlic clove*	½ *cup stock*

1. Skin and bone chicken; then dice. Combine cornstarch, soy sauce, oil and ground pepper; add to chicken and toss to coat. Let stand 10 minutes, turning occasionally.

2. Dice green peppers. Cut scallion stalks in ½-inch sections. Mince garlic.

3. Blend remaining cornstarch and soy sauce to a paste with water and sugar.

4. Heat oil. Add salt, then peppers, and stir-fry to soften (about 1 minute).

5. Add scallions and stir-fry until translucent (1 to 2 minutes). Remove vegetables from pan.

6. Heat remaining oil. Add garlic and stir-fry a few times. Add chicken; stir-fry until it loses its pinkness (about 2 minutes).

7. Return vegetables to pan, stir-frying briefly to reheat. Stir in stock and heat quickly. Then cook, covered, 2 minutes over medium heat.

8. Stir in cornstarch paste to thicken. Serve at once.

VARIATIONS: For one of the green peppers, substitute either 3 celery stalks or ½ cup water chestnuts, diced.

For the mixture in step 1, substitute 2 tablespoons soy sauce; 1 tablespoon sherry; and 2 or 3 slices fresh ginger root, minced.

In step 1, toss the chicken in a mixture of 1 teaspoon cornstarch, 1 tablespoon sherry and 1 egg white. Omit step 3. Then at the end of step 6, sprinkle chicken with a mixture of 1 tablespoon sherry, ½ teaspoon salt, ½ teaspoon sugar and 1 teaspoon soy sauce. Then stir-fry to blend in. Pick up step 7, but omit step 8.

STIR-FRIED CHICKEN AND HOT PEPPERS I
4 to 6 servings

1 *chicken breast*	½ *cup bamboo shoots*
1 *teaspoon cornstarch*	1 *garlic clove*
1 *tablespoon sherry*	1½ *tablespoons oil*
1 *egg white*	1½ *tablespoons oil*
1 *or 2 red chili peppers*	1 *tablespoon soy sauce*
1 *green pepper*	1 *teaspoon sugar*

½ *teaspoon salt*

1. Skin and bone chicken; then dice. Combine cornstarch, sherry and egg white. Add to chicken and toss to coat.

2. Dice chili peppers, green pepper and bamboo shoots. Crush garlic.

3. Heat oil. Brown garlic lightly and discard. Add chicken; stir-fry until it begins to brown (2 to 3 minutes). Remove from pan.

4. Heat remaining oil. Add diced peppers and bamboo shoots; stir-fry to soften peppers (about 2 minutes).

5. Return chicken. Sprinkle with soy sauce, sugar and salt. Then stir-fry to cook through and blend flavors (2 to 3 minutes). Serve at once.

VARIATIONS: Omit the chili peppers and add ½ teaspoon Tabasco Sauce with the seasonings in step 5.

In step 1, omit the egg white and add ½ teaspoon salt to the cornstarch mixture. Omit the salt in step 5.

After step 4, add 1 tablespoon hoisin sauce, and stir-fry vegetables 1 minute more. Then return chicken as in step 5, but omit the soy sauce and seasonings.

STIR-FRIED CHICKEN AND HOT PEPPERS II
About 4 servings

1 *chicken breast*	½ *teaspoon sugar*
2 *or 3 chili peppers*	3 *tablespoons oil*
1 *garlic clove*	2 *tablespoons oil*
1 *tablespoon soy sauce*	½ *cup stock*
½ *teaspoon salt*	1 *tablespoon cornstarch*

3 *tablespoons water*

1. Skin and bone chicken; cut in thin slices, then in strips. Cut chili peppers in strips.

2. Mince garlic; then combine with soy sauce, salt and sugar.

3. Heat oil. Add peppers and stir-fry until they change color (about 2 minutes). Remove from pan.

4. Heat remaining oil. Add chicken and stir-fry until it loses its pinkness (1 to 2 minutes).

5. Return peppers; stir-fry a few times. Stir in garlic-soy mixture to blend (about 1 minute).

6. Stir in stock and heat quickly. Then cook, covered, 2 to 3 minutes over medium heat.

7. Meanwhile blend cornstarch and cold water to a paste; then stir in to thicken. Serve at once.

NOTE: For color variety, use both green and red chili peppers.

STIR-FRIED CHICKEN AND PINEAPPLE I
8 to 10 servings

1 chicken (2 pounds)	10 to 12 water chestnuts
1 tablespoon cornstarch	1 celery stalk
1 tablespoon soy sauce	4 slices canned pineapple
½ teaspoon salt	2 tablespoons oil
2 teaspoons water	¼ teaspoon salt
2 small onions	2 tablespoons oil

4 tablespoons pineapple juice

1. Skin and bone chicken; then slice. Combine cornstarch, soy sauce, salt and water. Add to chicken and toss to coat. Let stand 10 minutes, turning occasionally.

2. Slice onions and water chestnuts. Cut celery diagonally in ½-inch sections. Cut each pineapple slice in 6 chunks.

3. Heat oil. Add remaining salt, then onions and stir-fry until translucent. Add celery and water chestnuts; stir-fry to soften celery (1 to 2 minutes more). Remove vegetables from pan.

4. Heat remaining oil. Add chicken and stir-fry until it begins to brown (2 to 3 minutes).

5. Return vegetables; stir-fry to reheat and blend flavors (1 to 2 minutes more).

6. Add pineapple chunks and juice, stir-frying only to heat through. Serve at once.

VARIATION: For the onions, water chestnuts and celery, substitute 6 dried black mushrooms (soaked), ¾ cup Chinese cabbage stems and ½ cup bamboo shoots—all of them sliced. Add as in step 3, but stir-fry 1 minute; then add ¼ cup stock and cook, covered, 2 minutes more. Remove vegetables and liquids from pan; pick up step 4.

STIR-FRIED CHICKEN AND PINEAPPLE II
About 4 servings

1 *chicken breast*	1 *tablespoon cornstarch*
1 *teaspoon cornstarch*	2 *tablespoons soy sauce*
1 *teaspoon soy sauce*	2 *tablespoons water*
½ *teaspoon salt*	4 *tablespoons pineapple juice*
4 *slices canned pineapple*	1 *teaspoon vinegar*
½ *garlic clove*	3 *tablespoons oil*

1. Skin and bone chicken; then dice. Combine cornstarch, soy sauce and salt. Add to chicken and toss to coat. Cut each pineapple slice in 5 or 6 chunks.

2. Mince garlic; then combine with remaining cornstarch and soy sauce the water, pineapple juice and vinegar.

3. Heat oil. Add chicken; stir-fry until it loses its pinkness. Add pineapple chunks and cook, covered, over low heat 2 to 3 minutes more; transfer to a warm serving dish.

4. Add garlic-cornstarch mixture to pan. Stir in over medium heat until thickened. Pour over chicken and pineapple chunks. Serve at once.

STIR-FRIED CHICKEN WITH PINEAPPLE AND LICHEE FRUIT
4 to 6 servings

1 *chicken breast*	1 *tablespoon soy sauce*
½ *cup pineapple juice*	2 *tablespoons sherry*
½ *cup lichee juice*	1 *tablespoon cornstarch*
2 *slices canned pineapple*	3 *tablespoons water*
1 *or 2 slices fresh ginger root*	2 *tablespoons oil*

1 *cup canned lichee fruit*

1. Skin and bone chicken; then slice as thin as possible.

2. Drain canned pineapple and lichee fruit, and combine their juices. Cut each pineapple slice in 5 or 6 chunks.

3. Mince ginger root; then combine in a cup with soy sauce and sherry. In another cup, blend cornstarch and cold water to a paste.

4. Heat oil. Add chicken and stir-fry until it loses its pinkness (about 1 minute). Sprinkle with ginger-soy mixture; stir-fry ½ minute more to blend.

5. Add pineapple chunks and lichee fruit. Cook, covered, 2 minutes over medium heat.

6. Add pineapple-lichee juice combination and heat quickly, stirring gently. Stir in cornstarch paste to thicken. Serve at once.

STIR-FRIED CHICKEN WITH PORK AND VEGETABLES
About 6 servings

1 *chicken breast*	1 *teaspoon cornstarch*
¼ *pound lean pork*	1 *egg white*
4 *tablespoons soy sauce*	2 *tablespoons oil*
½ *pound Chinese cabbage*	2 *tablespoons oil*
½ *pound fresh mushrooms*	½ *cup stock*
¼ *cup bamboo shoots*	2 *teaspoons cornstarch*
2 *or 3 slices fresh ginger root*	2 *tablespoons water*

1. Skin and bone chicken. Then cut chicken and pork in thin slices. Sprinkle both with soy sauce and toss. Let stand 30 minutes, turning occasionally.

2. Slice Chinese cabbage, mushrooms and bamboo shoots. Mince ginger root.

3. Drain chicken and pork, reserving soy sauce. Blend the soy with cornstarch and egg white; then add to chicken and pork, tossing gently to coat.

4. Heat oil. Add chicken and pork; stir-fry until they lose their pinkness (about 2 minutes). Then remove from pan.

5. Heat remaining oil. Add ginger root, then vegetables; stir-fry 2 minutes.

6. Return chicken and pork, stir-frying briefly to reheat. Then stir in stock and heat quickly. Cook, covered, over medium heat until done (about 2 minutes).

7. Meanwhile blend remaining cornstarch and cold water to a paste; then stir in to thicken. Serve at once.

STIR-FRIED CHICKEN WITH RICE-FLOUR NOODLES
About 6 servings

2 dried black mushrooms	oil for deep-frying
¼ cup almond meats	1 cup rice-flour noodles
1 chicken breast	2 tablespoons oil
2 tablespoons smoked ham	2 tablespoons sherry
½ garlic clove	2 tablespoons stock
2 slices fresh ginger root	½ teaspoon salt

½ teaspoon sugar

1. Soak dried mushrooms. Blanch almond meats.

2. Skin and bone chicken. Then dice chicken, soaked mushrooms and smoked ham. Crush garlic and ginger root.

3. Heat oil. Deep-fry almonds until lightly browned (see page 820). Drain on paper toweling.

4. Deep-fry rice-flour noodles until crisp and white (see page 827). Drain on paper toweling. Then transfer to a serving dish.

5. Heat remaining oil. Add garlic and ginger root; stir-fry to brown lightly. Add chicken and stir-fry until it begins to brown (2 to 3 minutes).

6. Add mushrooms and ham, stir-frying a few times. Sprinkle with sherry, stock, salt and sugar; then cook, stirring, about 1 minute more. Pour mixture over deep-fried noodles. Serve at once, garnished with almonds.

STIR-FRIED CHICKEN AND SNOW PEAS
About 4 servings

1 chicken breast	1 garlic clove
1 teaspoon cornstarch	2 slices fresh ginger root
1 teaspoon sherry	2 tablespoons oil
½ teaspoon sesame oil	1 tablespoon oil
1 egg white	½ cup stock
¼ pound snow peas	½ teaspoon salt

1. Skin and bone chicken; then slice. Combine cornstarch, sherry, sesame oil and egg white. Add to chicken and toss gently to coat.

2. Stem and string snow peas. Crush garlic and ginger root.

3. Heat oil. Brown garlic and ginger lightly, then discard. Add chicken and stir-fry until it begins to brown (2 to 3 minutes). Remove from pan.

4. Heat remaining oil. Add snow peas; stir-fry about 1 minute. Then stir in stock and heat quickly. Cook, covered, 1 minute over medium heat.

5. Return chicken; add salt. Cook, stirring, 1 minute more. Serve at once.

STIR-FRIED CHICKEN WITH SOY JAM
8 to 10 servings

1 chicken (2 pounds)
1 scallion stalk
2 or 3 slices fresh ginger root
1 tablespoon cornstarch

2 tablespoons sherry
2 tablespoons water
3 tablespoons oil
2 tablespoons soy jam

1 teaspoon sugar

1. Skin and bone chicken; dice in ½-inch cubes.

2. Mince scallion and ginger root; then combine with cornstarch, sherry and water. Add to chicken and toss gently to coat. Let stand 15 minutes, turning occasionally.

3. Heat oil. Add chicken and stir-fry until it begins to brown (2 to 3 minutes).

4. Add soy jam and sugar, stir-frying to heat through and blend (about 1 minute more). Serve at once.

STIR-FRIED SWEET-AND-PUNGENT CHICKEN
About 4 servings

sweet-and-pungent sauce	1 egg
1 chicken breast	cornstarch
½ teaspoon salt	2 tablespoons oil

1. Prepare a sweet-and-pungent sauce (see pages 735–738). Keep warm in its saucepan.

2. Skin and bone chicken; then shred. Sprinkle with salt; let stand a few minutes.

3. Beat egg. Dip chicken in egg; then dredge lightly in cornstarch.

4. Heat oil. Add chicken and stir-fry until it loses its pinkness (about 1 minute).

5. Transfer chicken to sweet-and-pungent sauce and stir in over medium heat to cook through and blend flavors (about 2 minutes). Serve at once.

STIR-FRIED CHICKEN AND TOMATOES I
4 to 6 servings

1 chicken breast	1 onion
1 tablespoon cornstarch	2 to 3 tablespoons oil
1 tablespoon soy sauce	¼ cup stock
1 tablespoon sherry	½ teaspoon salt
2 tomatoes	1 teaspoon sugar
1 tablespoon soy sauce	

1. Skin and bone chicken; then dice. Combine cornstarch, soy sauce and sherry. Add to chicken and toss gently to coat. Let stand 15 minutes, turning occasionally.

2. Peel and cube tomatoes. Dice onion.

3. Heat oil. Add chicken and stir-fry until it loses its pinkness (1 to 2 minutes).

4. Add onion and stir-fry until translucent (about 2 minutes more).

5. Stir in stock, salt, sugar and remaining soy sauce, and heat quickly.

6. Add tomatoes, stirring in gently only to heat through. Serve at once.

STIR-FRIED CHICKEN AND TOMATOES II
4 to 6 servings

1 *chicken breast*	1 *tablespoon sherry*
1 *scallion stalk*	2 *tomatoes*
2 *slices fresh ginger root*	2 *to 3 tablespoons oil*
2 *tablespoons soy sauce*	¼ *cup stock*

½ *teaspoon salt*

1. Skin and bone chicken; then dice.

2. Cut scallion in ½-inch sections; mince ginger root; then combine with soy sauce and sherry. Add to chicken and toss gently to coat. Let stand 15 minutes, turning occasionally. Drain, reserving marinade.

3. Meanwhile peel and cube tomatoes.

4. Heat oil. Add chicken and stir-fry until it loses its pinkness (1 to 2 minutes). Sprinkle with marinade liquid and stir-fry 1 minute more.

5. Stir in stock and salt and heat quickly. Then add tomatoes, stirring gently only to heat through. Serve at once.

STIR-FRIED CHICKEN AND TOMATOES WITH BLACK BEANS
4 to 6 servings

2 *teaspoons fermented black beans*	¼ *teaspoon salt*
1 *chicken breast*	1 *teaspoon soy sauce*
2 *tomatoes*	*dash of pepper*
1 *garlic clove*	2 *teaspoons cornstarch*
1 *tablespoon sherry*	3 *tablespoons water*
1 *teaspoon sugar*	2 *tablespoons oil*

¼ *cup stock*

1. Soak fermented black beans.

2. Skin and bone chicken; then dice. Peel and dice tomatoes. Mince garlic and mash with soaked black beans.

3. In one cup, combine sherry, sugar, salt, soy sauce and pepper. In another, blend cornstarch and cold water to a paste.

4. Heat oil. Add garlic-black bean mixture; stir-fry a few times. Add chicken and stir-fry until it loses its pinkness (about 2 minutes).

5. Sprinkle with sherry-sugar mixture; stir-fry 1 minute more.

6. Stir in stock and heat quickly. Then cook, covered, 2 to 3 minutes over medium heat. Stir in tomatoes gently to heat through.

7. Stir in cornstarch paste to thicken. Serve at once.

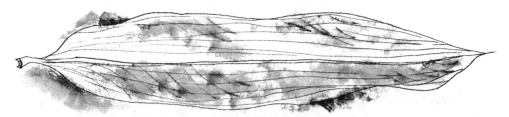

STIR-FRIED CHICKEN AND WALNUTS
4 to 6 servings

1 *chicken breast*	2 *slices fresh ginger root*
2 *teaspoons cornstarch*	1 *cup walnut meats*
½ *teaspoon salt*	*oil for deep-frying*
1 *tablespoon sherry*	2 *tablespoons oil*
½ *cup bamboo shoots*	¼ *cup stock*

1. Skin and bone chicken; dice in ¾- to 1-inch cubes. Combine cornstarch, salt and sherry. Add to chicken and toss gently to coat. Let stand 15 minutes, turning occasionally.

2. Dice bamboo shoots. Mince ginger root.

3. Blanch walnuts. Heat oil and deep-fry walnuts until golden (see page 832). Drain on paper toweling.

4. Heat remaining oil. Add ginger root and stir-fry a few times. Add chicken and stir-fry until it loses its pinkness (about 2 minutes).

5. Add bamboo shoots; stir-fry 1 minute more.

6. Stir in stock and heat quickly. Then cook, covered, 2 to 3 minutes over medium heat.

7. Stir in walnuts only to heat through. Serve at once.

VARIATIONS: For the walnuts, substitute cashew nuts.

For the bamboo shoots, substitute any of the following vegetables, diced: ½ cup mushrooms, ½ cup celery, 6 water chestnuts or 1 medium onion.

In step 1, add to the cornstarch mixture 1 teaspoon soy sauce. Or substitute the following mixture: ¼ teaspoon each of salt, pepper, sugar and oil; ½ teaspoon cornstarch; and 1 teaspoon soy sauce.

In step 1, toss the chicken in a mixture of 1 tablespoon soy sauce, 3 tablespoons sherry, ½ teaspoon sugar and ½ teaspoon salt. Let stand 30 minutes, turning occasionally. Then drain, reserving marinade. Before stir-frying, dredge chicken lightly in cornstarch; then dip in beaten egg. Add the reserved marinade with the stock in step 6.

In step 7, add 1 slice smoked ham, diced in 1-inch cubes.

STIR-FRIED DEEP-FRIED CHICKEN AND PEPPERS
4 to 6 servings

1 *chicken breast*	2 *slices fresh ginger root*
1 *tablespoon cornstarch*	*oil for deep-frying*
1 *tablespoon sherry*	2 *tablespoons cornstarch*
2 *tablespoons soy sauce*	3 *tablespoons soy sauce*
2 *green peppers*	¼ *cup stock*
1 *red chili pepper*	½ *teaspoon salt*
2 *cups onion*	1 *teaspoon sugar*
1 *garlic clove*	2 *tablespoons oil*

1. Bone chicken; then cut in 1½-inch cubes. Combine cornstarch, sherry and soy sauce. Add to chicken and toss to coat. Let stand 10 to 15 minutes.

2. Dice green peppers, red chili pepper and onion. Mince garlic and ginger root. Meanwhile heat oil.

3. Blend remaining cornstarch and soy sauce with stock, salt and sugar.

4. Add chicken to oil and deep-fry until golden. Drain on paper toweling.

5. Heat remaining oil. Add minced garlic and ginger; stir-fry a few times. Add peppers and onions and stir-fry until softened (2 to 3 minutes).

6. Stir in cornstarch-stock mixture to thicken. Slowly stir in deep-fried chicken only to reheat. Serve at once.

VARIATIONS: In step 1, for the soy sauce substitute ½ teaspoon salt.

In step 5, add with the peppers and onions 1 cucumber, peeled and diced.

STIR-FRIED DEEP-FRIED CHICKEN WITH BROWN BEAN SAUCE
About 6 servings

6 *dried black mushrooms*	1 *teaspoon cornstarch*
1 *chicken breast*	½ *teaspoon sugar*
1 *tablespoon cornstarch*	2 *teaspoons water*
1 *tablespoon sherry*	1 *to 2 tablespoons brown bean sauce*
¼ *teaspoon salt*	*oil for deep-frying*
⅓ *cup bamboo shoots*	2 *tablespoons oil*
1 *green pepper*	¼ *teaspoon salt*
1 *garlic clove*	½ *cup stock*
1 *wedge ginger root*	½ *to 1 teaspoon red pepper oil*

1. Soak dried mushrooms.

2. Bone chicken; then cut in 1½-inch cubes. Combine cornstarch, sherry and salt. Add to chicken and toss to coat. Let stand 10 to 15 minutes.

3. Dice bamboo shoots, green pepper and soaked mushrooms. Mince garlic. Crush ginger root.

4. Blend cornstarch, sugar and cold water to a paste. Mash brown bean sauce. Meanwhile heat oil.

5. Add chicken cubes to oil and deep-fry until golden. Drain on paper toweling.

6. Heat remaining oil. Add salt, then garlic and ginger root; stir-fry a few times. Add vegetables and stir-fry about 1 minute.

7. Stir in stock and heat quickly. Cook, covered, 2 minutes over medium heat.

8. Add deep-fried chicken cubes and brown bean sauce. Stir in gently only to heat through.

9. Stir in cornstarch paste to thicken. Sprinkle with red pepper oil and serve at once.

STIR-FRIED DEEP-FRIED CHICKEN WITH SOYBEAN PASTE
About 6 servings

1 *cup walnut meats*	1 *garlic clove*
1 *chicken breast*	2 *slices fresh ginger root*
1 *tablespoon cornstarch*	*oil for deep-frying*
½ *teaspoon salt*	2 *tablespoons oil*
1 *egg white*	1 *tablespoon oil*
1 *green pepper*	2 *tablespoons soybean paste*
1 *sweet red pepper*	1 *to 2 tablespoons sugar*

1 *tablespoon sherry*

1. Blanch and toast walnuts.

2. Bone chicken; then cut in 1½-inch cubes. Combine cornstarch, salt and egg white. Add to chicken and toss to coat.

3. Dice green and red peppers. Mince garlic and ginger root. Meanwhile heat oil.

4. Add chicken cubes to oil and deep-fry until golden. Drain on paper toweling.

5. Heat second quantity of oil. Add garlic and ginger; stir-fry a few times. Add peppers and stir-fry to soften (about 2 minutes). Then remove from pan.

6. Heat remaining oil. Add soybean paste and stir in 2 to 3 minutes over medium heat. Then stir in sugar until it dissolves.

7. Add deep-fried chicken cubes and sherry. Stir-fry quickly to coat chicken with soybean paste. (If sauce is too thick, thin with ¼ cup of stock).

8. Return pepper mixture; add walnuts and stir in only to heat through. Serve at once.

BASIC STIR-FRIED COOKED CHICKEN
About 6 servings

2 *cups cooked chicken*

2 *to 3 cups vegetables*

2 *to 3 tablespoons oil*

½ *teaspoon salt*

½ *cup stock*

1 *tablespoon cornstarch*

3 *tablespoons water*

1. Bone cooked chicken. Slice or dice chicken and vegetables.

2. Heat oil. Add salt, then vegetables, and stir-fry to coat with oil (about 2 minutes).

3. Stir in stock and heat quickly. Cook, covered, over medium heat, until vegetables are just about done. Then stir in cooked chicken only to heat through.

4. Meanwhile blend cornstarch and cold water to a paste; then stir in to thicken. Serve at once.

NOTE: Any vegetable can be used. (See page 583 for details on cooking time.) Also see suggested vegetable combinations below.

VARIATIONS: In step 4, add to the cornstarch paste any of the following: 1 to 2 teaspoons soy sauce, 1 teaspoon sherry, or a few drops of sesame oil.

At the end of step 4, garnish with ½ cup almond or walnut meats, blanched, toasted and slivered.

SUGGESTED VEGETABLE COMBINATIONS
FOR STIR-FRIED COOKED CHICKEN

2 cups peas
½ cup fresh mushrooms
½ cup celery
1 onion

1 cup broccoli
1 cup celery
½ cup fresh mushrooms
½ cup water chestnuts

2 dried black mushrooms (soaked)
1 cup Chinese lettuce
¼ cup bamboo shoots
¼ cup water chestnuts

1 cup Chinese cabbage
½ cup button mushrooms
12 snow peas
1 celery stalk

1 green pepper
1 tomato
½ cup Chinese cabbage
½ cup celery
¼ cup bamboo shoots
¼ cup canned button mushrooms

STIR-FRIED COOKED MARINATED CHICKEN
About 4 servings

2 cups cooked chicken
2 slices fresh ginger root
1 tablespoon cornstarch

2 tablespoons soy sauce
2 tablespoons sherry
3 to 4 tablespoons oil

1. Bone and dice cooked chicken.

2. Mince ginger root; then combine with cornstarch, soy sauce and sherry. Add to chicken and toss. Let stand 15 to 20 minutes, turning occasionally. Drain, discarding marinade.

3. Heat oil. Add chicken and stir-fry until brown and crisp. Serve at once.

STIR-FRIED COOKED CHICKEN AND PINEAPPLE
About 6 servings

2 cups cooked chicken
1 cup celery
3 slices canned pineapple
1 tablespoon cornstarch
2 teaspoons soy sauce

3 tablespoons water
2 to 3 tablespoons oil
½ teaspoon salt
dash of pepper
½ cup stock

½ teaspoon sugar

1. Bone cooked chicken; cut in ¼-inch slices. Slice celery stalks diagonally in 1-inch sections, then blanch. Cut each pineapple slice in 5 or 6 chunks.

2. Blend cornstarch, soy sauce and water to a paste.

3. Heat oil. Add salt and pepper, then chicken. Stir-fry to brown lightly.

4. Add celery, pineapple chunks, stock and sugar. Stir in gently, only to heat through.

5. Stir in cornstarch paste to thicken. Serve at once.

DEEP-FRIED CHICKEN

Chicken can be deep-fried whole, disjointed, or boned and cubed. It may be marinated beforehand in a mixture of sherry, soy sauce and other seasonings; or rubbed with such a mixture, inside and out, and hung up to dry for several hours. The chicken may then be deep-fried plain or coated with batter first.

The best birds for deep-frying are 2- to 3-pound spring chickens. (Older birds can be used if they are simmered first, then cooled and disjointed.) Some cooks pour boiling water over the young birds to clear the oil out of the skin before deep-frying.

Deep-fried chicken may be eaten plain, with various dips (see page 711), or other accompaniments such as shrimp chips or scallions. When cubed and deep-fried, the chicken may be combined with vegetables in stir-fried dishes. It is then added at the very end, only to heat through.

DEEP-FRIED WHOLE CHICKEN
About 8 servings

1 *chicken*

1 *to 2 teaspoons salt*

1 *tablespoon sherry*

1 *scallion stalk*

3 *slices fresh ginger root*

oil for deep-frying

pepper

1. Wipe chicken with a damp cloth. Rub salt and sherry into its skin.
2. Cut scallion stalk in half; slice ginger root; then place both inside cavity. Hang bird up to dry in a cool, airy place 1 to 2 hours (see page 828).
3. Heat oil. Place chicken in a wire basket or large long-handled Chinese strainer. Lower bird gently into oil and baste constantly inside and out until it turns golden.
4. Drain on paper toweling. Let cool slightly, then chop in bite-size pieces. Sprinkle with pepper and serve.

NOTE: The double or triple method of deep-frying can be used here. Lift the bird out of the oil entirely once or twice and let cool slightly. Reheat the oil each time.

DEEP-FRIED EIGHT-PIECE CHICKEN
About 8 servings

1 *chicken*

1 *egg*

2 *slices fresh ginger root*

1 *scallion stalk*

¼ *cup flour*

2 *tablespoons sherry*

oil for deep-frying

1. Wipe chicken with a damp cloth. With a cleaver, chop bird, bones and all, in 8 pieces, each approximately the same size.
2. Beat egg lightly. Mince ginger root and scallion; then add to egg, along with flour and sherry. Blend to a smooth batter.
3. Dip chicken in batter to coat. Meanwhile heat oil.
4. Add chicken, a few pieces at a time, and deep-fry until golden. Drain on paper toweling and serve.

NOTE: This dish is said to date back to 600 A.D. Some cooks prepare it by disjointing the legs and wings, then chopping breast and back each in half for a total of 8 pieces. The breast and wings need less cooking than the drumsticks and should be removed from the hot oil first.

DEEP-FRIED PEKING CHICKEN
About 8 servings

1 *chicken*	2 *slices fresh ginger root*
1 *teaspoon salt*	3 *tablespoons soy sauce*
1 *teaspoon sugar*	2 *tablespoons sherry*
¼ *teaspoon white pepper*	*cornstarch*
1 *scallion stalk*	*oil for deep-frying*

1. Wipe chicken with a damp cloth. With a cleaver, chop bird, bones and all, in 8 pieces, each approximately the same size. Place in a deep bowl. Sprinkle with salt, sugar and pepper.

2. Cut scallion stalk in 1-inch sections; mince ginger root. Add to bowl along with soy sauce and sherry. Let chicken stand 2 to 3 hours in mixture, turning occasionally.

3. Drain chicken well, discarding marinade; then dredge lightly with cornstarch. Meanwhile heat oil.

4. Add chicken a few pieces at a time and deep-fry until light golden (about 5 minutes). Lift out with a strainer or tongs and let cool slightly while reheating oil.

5. Return chicken to oil. Refry until crisp and golden (3 to 5 minutes more). Drain on paper toweling. Serve plain or with any sauce for deep-fried Peking Chicken (see pages 725–726).

NOTE: This chicken may also be chopped, bones and all, in 2-inch sections either before or after deep-frying.

VARIATIONS: For the marinade seasonings in steps 1 and 2, substitute any of the following mixtures and rub over chicken:

2 tablespoons soy sauce, 2 tablespoons oil, 1 teaspoon salt and ¼ teaspoon pepper.

2 tablespoons soy sauce and 2 tablespoons sherry.

2 tablespoons cognac, 2 tablespoons soy sauce, 1 teaspoon sugar, and 1 garlic clove, minced.

4 tablespoons soy sauce, 2 tablespoons chicken fat.

In step 3, dip chicken first in egg white, then dredge in cornstarch.

DEEP-FRIED CHICKEN HALVES
About 8 servings

1 *spring chicken*	2 *tablespoons soy sauce*
4 *slices fresh ginger root*	½ *teaspoon sugar*
3 *tablespoons sherry*	*oil for deep-frying*

1. Wipe chicken with a damp cloth. Split bird in two with a cleaver and place both halves side by side in a large, shallow platter.

2. Crush ginger root; then combine with sherry, soy sauce and sugar. Pour over chicken halves and let stand 1 to 2 hours, turning occasionally.

3. Drain chicken, discarding marinade; then blot dry with paper toweling. Meanwhile heat oil.

4. Using either a colander or long-handled Chinese strainer, suspend one chicken-half over pot. With a soup ladle, baste constantly with hot oil until evenly browned (about 7 minutes). Turn over and brown other side; then drain on paper toweling. Keep warm.

5. Deep-fry second chicken-half in the same manner.

6. With a cleaver, chop each half, bones and all, in 2-inch sections and serve.

NOTE: This kind of frying splatters, so wear a smock or other cover-up.

VARIATIONS: For the ginger root, substitute 2 scallion stalks, minced; or 1 medium onion, chopped.

For the mixture in step 2, substitute 2 tablespoons sherry, ½ teaspoon Five Spices, ½ teaspoon salt, and ¼ teaspoon pepper.

DEEP-FRIED PAPER-WRAPPED CHICKEN
4 to 6 servings

1 *large chicken breast*	1 *tablespoon sherry*
1 *tablespoon soy sauce*	*parchment or wax paper*

oil for deep-frying

1. Skin and bone chicken breast. Cut either in 1½-inch cubes; or against the grain in ¼-inch slices, then in 1- by 1½-inch strips.

2. Combine soy sauce and sherry; add to chicken and toss lightly. Let stand 30 minutes, turning occasionally. Then drain, discarding marinade.

3. Meanwhile cut parchment or wax paper in 20 to 30 4-inch squares. Wrap each piece of chicken, envelope-style, in a square of paper (see page 828).

4. Heat oil nearly to smoking. Add paper-wrapped chicken, a few pieces at a time, then reduce heat immediately. Deep-fry, flap-side down, until done (3 to 5 minutes). Drain on paper toweling.

5. Repeat process until all pieces are cooked, reheating oil each time. Serve hot in wrappers. (To eat, the diner breaks open the paper envelopes one at a time with chopsticks or fork.)

NOTE: This dish is served frequently at banquets and must be eaten hot. It may be kept warm a few minutes in a slow oven (200 degrees), but should never be reheated or it will toughen.

VARIATIONS: **In step 2,** add to the marinade any of the following:

2 slices fresh ginger root, minced; and/or 1 scallion stalk, minced

1 tablespoon peanut oil, 1 teaspoon cornstarch, ½ teaspoon salt, ½ teaspoon sugar, dash of pepper

dash of celery salt, dash of pepper

In step 2, substitute any of the following marinades:

1 tablespoon soy sauce; ½ teaspoon hoisin sauce; ½ teaspoon peanut oil; ¼ teaspoon salt; 1 teaspoon Chinese parsley, minced; and 1 teaspoon scallion stalk, minced

¼ cup scallions, minced; 1 teaspoon sugar; 2 teaspoons hoisin sauce; ½ teaspoon salt; and ¼ teaspoon sesame oil

2 tablespoons oyster sauce, ½ teaspoon sugar, ½ teaspoon soybean paste, ¼ teaspoon salt and a few drops of sesame oil

In step 3, when wrapping the chicken, include in each packet any of the following:

one or two 1-inch sections of scallion stalk

a bit of minced ginger

a sprig of Chinese parsley

a shelled pine nut

a piece of smoked ham, cut the same size as the chicken

several green peas, parboiled first

In step 4, double-fry the chicken: Heat oil first to 250 degrees and fry, a few envelopes at a time, turning constantly for 3 minutes. Drain on paper toweling. Then increase temperature of oil to 375 degrees. Return wrapped chicken and refry 2 minutes more.

DEEP-FRIED SWEET-AND-PUNGENT CHICKEN
4 to 6 servings

sweet-and-pungent sauce	*2 teaspoons soy sauce*
1 chicken breast	*½ teaspoon salt*
1 egg	*cornstarch*

oil for deep-frying

1. Prepare a sweet-and-pungent sauce (see pages 735–738).
2. Skin and bone chicken; cut in 1-inch cubes.
3. Beat egg lightly; stir in soy sauce and salt. Dip chicken cubes in mixture; then dredge in cornstarch to coat lightly.
4. Heat oil. Add chicken, a few cubes at a time, and deep-fry until golden. Drain on paper toweling.
5. Reheat sweet-and-pungent sauce. Gently stir in chicken cubes only to reheat. Serve at once.

VARIATIONS: In step 3, sprinkle chicken cubes with the soy sauce and let stand 10 to 15 minutes. Then beat the egg and blend in the salt and 3 tablespoons flour (omit cornstarch) to make a batter. Dip each cube in batter to coat and deep-fry as above.

Use half a chicken. With a cleaver chop it, bones and all, in 1-inch sections. In step 3, coat with a mixture of 5 tablespoons cornstarch, 2 tablespoons sherry and 1 teaspoon salt; then deep-fry.

DEEP-FRIED CUBED CHICKEN
4 to 6 servings

1 large chicken breast	*¼ cup water*
¼ cup flour	*½ teaspoon salt*

oil for deep-frying

1. Skin and bone chicken; cut in 1-inch cubes.
2. Blend flour, water and salt to a batter. Dip chicken in batter to coat.
3. Heat oil. Add chicken and deep-fry until golden. Drain on paper toweling.
4. Serve with a pepper-salt mix or sherry-soy dip (see pages 708 and 711).

NOTE: Although white meat is generally used for this dish, any part of the chicken, boned and cubed, can be used.

VARIATIONS: In step 2, prepare the batter with 1½ tablespoons cornstarch, 2 tablespoons sherry and ½ tablespoon vinegar. Or omit the batter. Dip chicken cubes instead first in egg white; then dredge lightly with cornstarch.

DEEP-FRIED CUBED AND MARINATED CHICKEN
About 8 servings

1 *spring chicken*

1 *or 2 slices fresh ginger root*

½ *cup soy sauce*

¼ *cup sherry*

1 *teaspoon sugar*

oil for deep-frying

cornstarch

1. Skin and bone chicken; cut in 1-inch cubes.

2. Mince ginger root; then combine with soy sauce, sherry and sugar. Add to chicken and toss gently. Let stand 1 hour, turning occasionally.

3. Drain chicken, reserving marinade; then blot dry with paper toweling. Meanwhile heat oil. Add chicken, several cubes at a time, and deep-fry until light golden. Drain on paper toweling; keep warm.

4. Transfer still-hot chicken cubes to reserved marinade. Let stand 15 minutes, turning occasionally. Drain, discarding marinade.

5. Reheat oil. Dredge chicken cubes lightly with cornstarch; then deep-fry again until crisp and golden. Drain and serve.

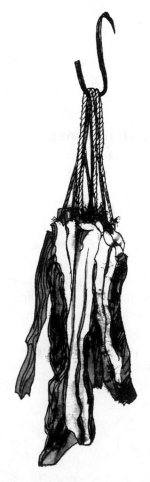

DEEP-FRIED CHICKEN CUBES WRAPPED IN BACON
10 to 12 servings

1 *spring chicken*	*few drops of sesame oil*
1 *tablespoon soy sauce*	¾ *to 1 pound bacon*
1 *tablespoon sherry*	2 *eggs*
1 *tablespoon sweet vegetable sauce*	¾ *cup flour*
½ *teaspoon salt*	*oil for deep-frying*

1 or 2 tomatoes

1. Skin and bone chicken; cut in 1-inch cubes.
2. Combine soy sauce, sherry, sweet vegetable sauce, salt and sesame oil. Mix well; then add to chicken cubes and toss. Let stand 30 minutes, turning occasionally. Drain, discarding marinade.
3. Cut bacon strips in two and wrap one piece around each chicken cube.
4. Beat eggs lightly and blend in flour to make a batter. (If batter needs thinning, add a few drops of water.) Dip bacon-wrapped chicken cubes in batter to coat.
5. Heat oil. Deep-fry cubes, a few at a time, until golden. Then drain on paper toweling. Serve hot, garnished with sliced tomatoes.

DEEP-FRIED CHICKEN CUBES WITH CURRY
About 8 servings

1 *spring chicken*	1 *teaspoon salt*
½ *head lettuce*	*dash of pepper*
2 *eggs*	*oil for deep-frying*
¼ *cup cornstarch*	2 *tablespoons oil*
½ *cup flour*	2 *tablespoons curry powder*

¼ *cup sherry*

1. Skin and bone chicken; cut in 1-inch cubes. Shred lettuce.
2. Beat eggs lightly; add cornstarch, flour, salt and pepper and blend to a batter. Dip cubes in batter to coat.
3. Heat oil. Add cubes, several at a time, and deep-fry until golden. Drain on paper toweling; keep warm.
4. Heat remaining oil. Stir in curry powder, then sherry. Cook, stirring over low heat, until mixture is smooth and thin.
5. Arrange chicken on shredded lettuce. Pour curry sauce over and serve.
NOTE: Depending on personal taste, the curry can be either increased or decreased.

VARIATION: In step 4, substitute a lemon sauce, prepared as follows: Heat 1 cup stock; stir in and heat ¼ cup sherry, 1 tablespoon soy sauce, 1 tablespoon lemon juice, and 1 teaspoon sugar. Then thicken sauce with a cornstarch paste, made with 1 tablespoon cornstarch and 3 tablespoons cold water, and pour over chicken. Garnish with lemon slices.

DEEP-FRIED SWEET-AND-PUNGENT CHICKEN WINGS
4 to 6 servings

sweet-and-pungent sauce
12 *chicken wings*
1 *or* 2 *eggs*

½ *cup cornstarch*
¼ *teaspoon salt*
dash of pepper

oil for deep-frying

1. Prepare a sweet-and-pungent sauce (see pages 735–738).
2. Leave wings intact, but with a cleaver, chop off bony tips.
3. Beat egg lightly in a bowl. Mix cornstarch, salt and pepper and spread on a flat plate or board. Dip chicken wings first in egg; then dredge in cornstarch mixture to coat.
4. Heat oil. Add wings, a few at a time, and deep-fry until golden. Drain on paper toweling.
5. Meanwhile slowly reheat sweet-and-pungent sauce. Stir in wings only to reheat.

DEEP-FRIED GOLD COIN CHICKEN I
About 6 servings

1 *large chicken breast*
1 *slice fresh ginger root*
1 *scallion stalk*
1 *tablespoon brown sugar*
1 *tablespoon sherry*

2 *tablespoons soy sauce*
2 *tablespoons cornstarch*
3 *tablespoons water*
2 *eggs*
oil for deep-frying

1. Skin and bone chicken breast; cut against the grain in slices ⅛-inch thick, then in 1-inch circles. (Reserve remainder for soup.)
2. Mince ginger root and scallion stalk; then combine with brown sugar, sherry and soy sauce. Add chicken rounds and toss gently. Let stand 20 to 30 minutes, turning occasionally. Drain, discarding marinade.
3. Blend cornstarch and water to a paste. Beat eggs lightly and blend in to

make a batter. Dip each piece of chicken in batter; then thread on metal skewers. Meanwhile heat oil.

4. With tongs, lower skewers into hot oil and deep-fry chicken until golden. (Rotate skewers during cooking.) Remove skewers, drain chicken on paper toweling, and serve.

NOTE: This dish is also called Golden Dollars.

GOLD COIN CHICKEN II
6 to 8 servings

1 *large chicken breast*	2 *tablespoons sherry*
1 *teaspoon cornstarch*	¼ *pound smoked ham*
½ *teaspoon salt*	12 *small fresh mushrooms*
	4 *tablespoons oil*

1. Skin and bone chicken breast; cut against the grain in slices ⅛-inch thick, then in 1-inch circles.

2. Combine cornstarch, salt and sherry. Add to chicken and toss gently. Let stand 10 minutes, turning occasionally.

3. Slice smoked ham ⅛-inch thick, then in 1-inch circles. Remove mushroom stems. On small skewers alternately thread chicken, ham and mushrooms.

4. Pour oil into a shallow dish and rotate skewers in dish to coat ingredients with oil.

5. Meanwhile preheat oven to 400 degrees. Place skewers on a baking tin and roast, turning once or twice until done (10 to 15 minutes). Remove ingredients from skewers and serve.

NOTE: This modernized version is best eaten immediately, but can, if necessary, be reheated in a slow (200-degree) oven. It may also be broiled 8 to 10 minutes; or cooked outdoors on a charcoal grill or hibachi.

VARIATIONS: For the smoked ham, substitute roast pork; or use ⅛ pound ham, ⅛ pound roast pork.

For the fresh mushrooms, substitute 5 water chestnuts, each cut in 3 slices.

DEEP-FRIED CHICKEN BALLS WITH LICHEE SAUCE
About 6 servings

1 large chicken breast	2 egg whites
6 water chestnuts	oil for deep-frying
1 scallion stalk	1 can lichee fruit
1 tablespoon cornstarch	½ cup lichee syrup
2 tablespoons soy sauce	¼ cup stock
2 teaspoons sherry	2 teaspoons cornstarch
½ teaspoon salt	1 tablespoon soy sauce

1 tablespoon water

1. Skin and bone chicken breast. Mince or grind coarsely with water chestnuts and scallion.

2. Then blend in cornstarch, soy sauce, sherry and salt. Beat egg whites until stiff but not dry, and fold in. Form mixture into walnut-size balls. Meanwhile heat oil.

3. Add chicken balls, a few at a time, and deep-fry until golden. Drain on paper toweling.

4. Drain canned lichee fruit. Reserve syrup and combine in a saucepan with stock. Heat slowly. Meanwhile blend remaining cornstarch and soy sauce to a paste with water. Then stir in to thicken.

5. Add chicken balls and lichee fruit to pan. Stir gently to heat through, and serve.

VARIATION: For the lichee sauce, substitute a sweet-and-pungent sauce (see pages 735–738).

SIMMERED AND DEEP-FRIED CHICKEN
10 to 12 servings

1 chicken (4 to 5 pounds)	*1 tablespoon cornstarch*
water to cover	*1 tablespoon sherry*
1 scallion stalk	*1½ tablespoons soy sauce*
2 or 3 slices fresh ginger root	*oil for deep-frying*

1. Place chicken in a pan with cold water to cover. Cut scallion in 1-inch sections and slice ginger root; add to pan. Bring to a boil; then simmer, covered, about 1 hour. Drain, reserving liquid for stock.

2. Let bird cool; then bone and (leaving skin on) cube chicken, or cut in 1- by 2-inch strips.

3. Combine cornstarch, sherry and soy sauce. Add to chicken and toss gently. Let stand 15 minutes, turning occasionally. Meanwhile heat oil.

4. Add chicken, several pieces at a time, and deep-fry until crisp and golden (about 1 minute). Drain on paper toweling.

NOTE: Depending on the size and toughness of the bird, simmering time can vary from 30 minutes to 1½ hours. The chicken should be cooked until just about done.

VARIATIONS: In step 1, add 1 tablespoon sherry and 1 tablespoon soy sauce to water.

In step 2, disjoint chicken. Drain and dry well. Brush with ½ cup soy sauce and deep-fry (omit step 3). Chop in bite-size pieces and serve.

In step 3, substitute a batter of 3 tablespoons flour; 1 egg, beaten; ½ teaspoon salt; and 1 to 2 tablespoons stock.

DEEP-FRIED CHICKEN À LA PEKING DUCK
10 to 12 servings

1 chicken (4 to 5 pounds)	*2 tablespoons sherry*
2 cups water	*1 tablespoon molasses*
¼ cup vinegar	*2 tablespoons flour*
½ cup soy sauce	*1 teaspoon salt*
½ cup honey	*oil for deep-frying*

1. Place chicken in a large pan. Boil water and pour over. Bring to a boil again; then simmer, covered, 45 minutes. Drain, reserving liquid for stock.

2. Rinse bird quickly under cold running water. Blot dry with paper toweling.

3. Combine vinegar, soy sauce, honey, sherry and molasses. Brush mixture over chicken skin. (Reserve the remainder.) Hang bird up to dry about 30 minutes in a cool, airy place.

4. Brush remainder of soy-vinegar mixture over bird. Suspend chicken again and let dry another 20 to 30 minutes. Then combine flour and salt and rub lightly into skin.

5. Heat oil until smoking. Gently lower in bird, using a wire basket or large, long-handled Chinese strainer. Deep-fry, turning and basting, until golden-brown. Drain on paper toweling.

6. Remove crisp skin, cutting it in 2-inch squares. Serve on thin slices of white bread with crusts removed, accompanied by onion brushes (see page 828) and a dip of either plum or hoisin sauce.

7. Bone remainder of chicken and cut in bite-size pieces. Serve as a separate dish with the same dip.

SIMMERED AND DEEP-FRIED CHICKEN STUFFED WITH GLUTINOUS RICE I

8 to 10 servings

¼ pound glutinous rice	dash of pepper
4 dried black mushrooms	1 medium onion
7 cups water	3 tablespoons sherry
1 chicken (3 pounds)	1 tablespoon sugar
2 chicken livers	5 tablespoons soy sauce
¼ cup smoked ham	1 egg
5 water chestnuts	5 tablespoons flour
2 tablespoons soy sauce	2 tablespoons soy sauce
1 teaspoon sugar	oil for deep-frying

1. Separately soak glutinous rice and dried mushrooms.

2. Bring water to a boil in a large pan and add chicken. Bring to a boil again; then simmer, covered, 10 minutes. Remove bird, leaving liquids in pan. Pierce chicken all over with a fork.

3. Dice chicken livers and ham; place in a bowl. Slice water chestnuts and soaked mushrooms and add, along with soy sauce, sugar, pepper and soaked rice. Blend well.

4. Stuff chicken with mixture and sew up securely or skewer. Return bird to pan. Slice onion and add, along with sherry, remaining sugar and second quantity of soy sauce.

5. Reheat chicken and simmer, covered, until liquid is nearly absorbed (about 30 minutes). Turn bird once or twice for even coloring. Drain well and blot dry with paper toweling.

6. Meanwhile beat egg lightly and blend in flour and remaining soy sauce to make a batter. Coat chicken with batter.

7. Heat oil until nearly smoking. Gently lower in bird, using a wire basket or large, long-handled Chinese strainer. Deep-fry, basting and turning, until golden. Drain on paper toweling and serve.

VARIATION: Instead of deep-frying, simmer the bird 40 to 45 minutes in step 5. (Omit steps 6 and 7.)

SIMMERED AND DEEP-FRIED CHICKEN STUFFED
WITH GLUTINOUS RICE II
8 to 10 servings

3 *dried black mushrooms*	¼ *pound smoked ham*
4 *chestnuts*	3 *canned ginkgo nuts*
10 *lotus seeds*	¼ *cup bamboo shoots*
½ *cup glutinous rice*	2 *tablespoons soy sauce*
1 *chicken* (3 *pounds*)	1 *tablespoon sherry*
¼ *pound lean pork*	*water to cover*
2 *tablespoons oil*	*cornstarch*

oil for deep-frying

1. Soak dried mushrooms. Parboil and shell chestnuts. Blanch lotus seeds. Soak glutinous rice.

2. Bone chicken, keeping its skin and natural shape intact (see page 824). Dice pork.

3. Heat oil. Add pork and stir-fry until it loses its pinkness (2 to 3 minutes). Place in a large bowl.

4. Dice ham, ginkgo nuts, bamboo shoots, mushrooms, chestnuts, and add to bowl, along with glutinous rice, lotus seeds, soy sauce and sherry. Mix well.

5. Stuff chicken with mixture and sew up securely or skewer. Wrap bird in cheesecloth (to help hold its shape) and place in a pan with water. Bring to a boil. Then simmer, covered, 30 minutes.

6. Drain chicken. Blot dry with paper toweling, then sprinkle lightly with cornstarch. Deep-fry as in step 7 above.

STEAMED AND DEEP-FRIED CHICKEN AND GLUTINOUS RICE
10 to 12 servings

2 cups glutinous rice	½ cup water
6 dried black mushrooms	1 tablespoon sherry
¼ cup chestnut meats	½ teaspoon salt
¼ cup walnut meats	1 teaspoon sugar
1 set chicken giblets	1 chicken (4 to 5 pounds)
¼ cup smoked ham	1 tablespoon soy sauce
2 Chinese sausages	½ teaspoon salt
2 scallion stalks	oil for deep-frying

Chinese parsley

1. Separately soak glutinous rice and dried mushrooms. Blanch chestnuts and walnuts.

2. Mince chicken giblets, ham, Chinese sausages, scallions, soaked mushrooms and blanched nuts. Place in a large, heatproof bowl. Add soaked rice, water, sherry, salt and sugar, blending well.

3. Steam 50 minutes (see page 831).

4. Meanwhile cut chicken through the breastbone and spread it out flat. Rub soy sauce and remaining salt into its skin. Place chicken on top of steamed ingredients. Steam 45 minutes more.

5. Remove chicken, but cover the pot again to keep rice mixture hot. Let bird cool slightly; then bone. Meanwhile heat oil until nearly smoking.

6. Add chicken and deep-fry until crisp and golden. Drain on paper toweling. Cut in bite-size pieces and arrange over rice mixture. Garnish with Chinese parsley and serve.

STEAMED AND DEEP-FRIED CHICKEN STUFFED WITH GLUTINOUS RICE
About 10 servings

2 cups glutinous rice	1 Chinese sausage
6 dried black mushrooms	1 teaspoon salt
½ cup lotus seeds	stock to cover
1 chicken (4 pounds)	cornstarch
¼ cup smoked ham	oil for deep-frying

1 lemon

1. Separately soak glutinous rice and dried mushrooms. Blanch lotus seeds.

2. Bone chicken, keeping its skin and natural shape intact (see page 824).

3. Dice smoked ham, Chinese sausage and soaked mushrooms. Mix well with salt, soaked rice and lotus seeds.

4. Stuff chicken with mixture and sew up securely or skewer. Place bird in a deep heatproof bowl. Heat enough stock to cover chicken and pour over.

5. Steam 2 hours (see page 831).

6. Drain chicken, reserving liquid for stock. Transfer bird to a platter and, with a spatula, gently flatten it, taking care that chicken does not burst. Let cool; then dust lightly with cornstarch.

7. Wash and dry original steaming bowl. Return chicken and steam 15 minutes more. Let cool briefly.

8. Heat oil. Gently lower in bird, using a wire basket or large long-handled Chinese strainer. Deep-fry, basting and turning, until golden. Drain on paper toweling, then transfer to a cutting board.

9. With a sharp knife, cut through chicken and stuffing in 2-inch slices, then in 2-inch squares. Arrange on a platter; garnish with lemon wedges and serve.

 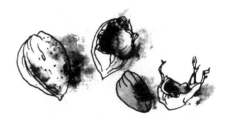

STEAMED AND DEEP-FRIED CHICKEN WITH NUTMEATS
About 6 servings

1 *spring chicken*	*oil for deep-frying*
1 *cup stock*	1 *tablespoon cornstarch*
½ *cup almond meats*	2 *tablespoons water*
1 *egg*	2 *tablespoons soy sauce*
½ *cup flour*	1 *tablespoon honey*
½ *teaspoon salt*	½ *cup water*

1. Wipe chicken with a damp cloth. With a sharp knife, make an incision along backbone, but do not cut through bone. Place bird in a heatproof bowl and add stock.

2. Steam 30 minutes. (See pages 33 and 831). Meanwhile blanch almonds and chop coarsely.

3. Let bird cool slightly; then bone. Beat egg lightly and blend in flour and salt to make a batter; then coat chicken with batter.

4. Heat oil until nearly smoking. Gently lower in chicken, using a wire basket or large long-handled Chinese strainer. Deep-fry, basting and turning until golden. Drain on paper toweling.

5. Let bird cool slightly. Carefully cut in 1½-inch strips (running from backbone to breastbone), then in 1½-inch squares. Arrange, skin-side up, on a serving platter.

6. In a cup, blend cornstarch and cold water to a paste. In a saucepan, combine soy sauce, honey and remaining water, and heat, stirring. Then add cornstarch paste and stir in to thicken. Pour over chicken. Garnish with nutmeats and serve.

VARIATION: For the almonds, substitute walnuts or pecans, or use all 3 in combination.

STEAMED AND DEEP-FRIED CHICKEN WINGS
About 4 servings

8 to 10 chicken wings	1 tablespoon cornstarch
¼ pound smoked ham	1 tablespoon oyster sauce
soy sauce	1 teaspoon sugar
oil for deep-frying	¼ teaspoon salt
2 slices fresh ginger root	3 tablespoons water
1 tablespoon water	1 teaspoon soy sauce
1 tablespoon soy sauce	1 tablespoon oil

1. Chop off bony wing tips with a cleaver; then disjoint wings and slip out bones. Mince smoked ham; stuff into wing cavities.

2. Arrange wing sections on a heatproof dish. Steam 40 minutes (see page 831). Drain wings and let cool, then rub with soy sauce.

3. Heat oil. Add wings, a few at a time, and deep-fry until golden. Drain on paper toweling; keep warm.

4. Mince ginger root; then combine in a cup with water and the second quantity of soy sauce. In another cup, blend cornstarch, oyster sauce, sugar, salt, the remaining water and soy sauce to a paste.

5. Heat remaining oil. Stir in ginger-soy combination 1 minute over medium heat. Then stir in cornstarch paste to thicken. Add deep-fried wings only to reheat. Serve at once.

STEAMED CHICKEN

Chicken can be steamed whole, disjointed or chopped in 2-inch sections. It can also be boned first, then cubed or slivered. (Boned chicken needs the shortest cooking time.) Both spring and boiling chickens can be used. A spring chicken, steamed whole, calls for only 1 cup of stock or water. A boiling fowl requires much more, and is usually served in a large bowl with its own soup. Cooking time depends on the tenderness of the chicken. The bird is done when the meat comes off the bones easily.

BASIC STEAMED SPRING CHICKEN
4 to 6 servings

1 *spring chicken*	2 *or 3 slices fresh ginger root*
2 *tablespoons sherry*	1 *scallion*
1 *teaspoon salt*	1 *cup stock or water*

1. Rub chicken inside and out with sherry and salt. Place bird in a heatproof bowl.

2. Slice ginger root and trim scallion stalk; place inside bird's cavity. Then pour stock over.

3. Steam until done (35 to 40 minutes). See page 831.

NOTE: This chicken can be served hot or cold. When using it for cold dishes, remove skin, slice meat thin and serve either in salads or with dips for white-cut chicken. (See pages 709–711.)

VARIATIONS: In step 1, rub the chicken first with 2 tablespoons soy sauce, then with 1 tablespoon peanut oil and a few drops of sesame oil.

Add the sherry, salt, scallion and ginger root to the stock instead of the chicken.

After step 3, transfer 1 cup of chicken liquid to a large saucepan. Add 4 tablespoons soy sauce, 1 tablespoon sugar and ½ teaspoon sesame oil. Heat slowly, stirring. Then add chicken and cook over medium heat, turning frequently until bird is evenly colored. Let cool slightly. With a cleaver chop, bones and all, in 1½-inch sections; or carve Western-style. Serve hot or cold, garnished with Chinese parsley.

BASIC STEAMED FOWL
8 to 10 servings

1 chicken (4 to 5 pounds)   5 cups water
¼ cup fresh mushrooms   salt

1. Place chicken in a large heatproof bowl. Add mushrooms, whole, along with water.

2. Steam 2 hours. (See page 831.) Add salt to taste. Serve as above.

NOTE: A larger bird, steamed slowly 3 to 4 hours in 8 cups of water, makes a dish that's nutritious and easily digestible for expectant mothers, convalescents and small children.

STEAMED CHICKEN WITH ANISE
4 to 6 servings

1 spring chicken   1 cup water
1 cup soy sauce   2 teaspoons sugar

4 or 5 cloves star anise

1. Wipe chicken with a damp cloth. Place in a colander over a large bowl.

2. Combine soy sauce, water, sugar and star anise in a saucepan. Bring to a boil slowly, stirring; then baste chicken, inside and out, with mixture to color evenly.

3. Return leftover mixture to saucepan and slowly reheat, stirring. Then repeat basting process. Discard mixture.

4. Transfer chicken to a heatproof bowl. Steam until done (about 30 minutes). See page 831.

STEAMED CHICKEN, BANQUET STYLE
About 8 servings

8 dried black mushrooms   1 garlic clove
18 lily buds   3 tablespoons soy sauce
1 chicken (3 to 4 pounds)   4 tablespoons sherry
3 scallion stalks   1 teaspoon sugar
2 slices fresh ginger root   ½ teaspoon salt

dash of pepper

1. Separately soak dried mushrooms and lily buds.

2. Wipe chicken with a damp cloth. Place in a heatproof bowl.

3. Cut scallions in 1-inch sections; slice ginger root; crush garlic. Cut soaked lily buds in half; also soaked mushrooms, if large. Arrange all over top of chicken.

4. Combine soy sauce, sherry, sugar, salt and pepper. Pour over chicken.

5. Steam until done (about 2 hours). See page 831.

STEAMED CHICKEN STUFFED WITH LOBSTER

8 to 10 servings

1 chicken (3 to 4 pounds)	1 tablespoon smoked ham
1 lobster	¾ teaspoon salt
½ pound pike	dash of pepper

1. Bone chicken, leaving its skin and natural shape intact (see page 824).

2. Shell and mince lobster. Bone and mince pike. Mince smoked ham. Then combine with salt and pepper.

3. Stuff chicken with mixture; then sew up securely or skewer. Place in a large heatproof bowl. Steam until done (about 2 hours). See page 831.

STEAMED CHICKEN AND ASPARAGUS

6 to 8 servings

1 piece dried tangerine peel	½ teaspoon sugar
1 chicken (4 pounds)	4 cloves star anise
2 slices fresh ginger root	1 16-ounce can asparagus tips
1 garlic clove	½ cup cream (half-and-half)
1 bunch Chinese parsley	¼ teaspoon salt
½ teaspoon salt	2 tablespoons cornstarch
2 tablespoons water	

1. Soak tangerine peel.

2. With a sharp knife, make an incision along the chicken's backbone, but do not cut through bone.

3. Mince ginger root, garlic and soaked tangerine peel; stem parsley. Combine with salt and sugar.

4. Spread mixture evenly inside bird's cavity. Add star anise. Then sew up cavity securely or skewer.

5. Place chicken in a large heatproof bowl. Steam 40 minutes (see pages 33 and 831). Then transfer bird to a cutting board and let cool.

6. Meanwhile, transfer chicken liquids to a saucepan. Drain canned asparagus tips; mash ½ cup of these and add to saucepan. Arrange remainder in a shallow heatproof dish.

7. When chicken has cooled, carefully cut in 1½-inch strips, running from backbone to breastbone; then in 1½-inch squares. Arrange, skin-side down, over asparagus, in heatproof dish. (Reserve chicken legs and wings for other dishes.)

8. Steam on a rack 20 minutes more.

9. Add cream and remaining salt to saucepan with chicken liquids and mashed asparagus. Heat slowly, stirring, but do not boil. Meanwhile blend cornstarch and water to a paste; then stir in to thicken.

10. Remove heatproof dish from steamer. Place a serving platter on top and invert quickly so that chicken squares are skin-side up, topped by asparagus tips. Pour thickened sauce over and serve.

STEAMED CHICKEN AND CHINESE SAUSAGE
About 6 servings

1 *spring chicken*	2 *tablespoons sherry*
2 *Chinese sausages*	½ *teaspoon salt*
2 *teaspoons water-chestnut flour*	½ *teaspoon sesame oil*

1. With a cleaver, chop chicken, bones and all, in 1½- to 2-inch sections. Cut Chinese sausages diagonally in ½-inch slices.

2. Combine water-chestnut flour, sherry, salt and sesame oil, mixing well. Add to chicken sections and toss gently to coat.

3. Arrange chicken in a shallow heatproof dish. Top with Chinese sausage. Steam on a rack until done (about 40 minutes). See page 831.

VARIATION: Omit step 2. Instead, dredge chicken sections in 2 tablespoons cornstarch. In step 3, add 6 dried black mushrooms (soaked), sliced. Reserve 1 cup mushroom soaking liquid and add to it the salt, sherry and sesame oil. Pour this over the chicken, mushrooms and sausages; then steam as in step 3.

STEAMED CHICKEN AND MUSHROOMS
4 to 6 servings

4 to 6 dried black mushrooms	*2 scallion stalks*
1 chicken (2½ pounds)	*2 or 3 slices fresh ginger root*
4 teaspoons cornstarch	*½ teaspoon salt*
2 tablespoons soy sauce	*dash of pepper*

1. Soak dried mushrooms.

2. With a cleaver, chop chicken, bones and all, in 1½- to 2-inch sections. Blend cornstarch and soy sauce to a paste and rub over chicken to coat. Place in a heatproof dish.

3. Mince scallion stalks and ginger root; slice soaked mushrooms. Arrange over chicken. Sprinkle with salt and pepper.

4. Steam until done (about 30 minutes). See page 831.

VARIATIONS: Bone and cube the chicken; then steam only 10 to 15 minutes in step 4.

In step 2, add to cornstarch paste 1 teaspoon sugar, 1 teaspoon peanut oil and 2 teaspoons sherry.

In step 3, add ½ cup bamboo shoots and 8 water chestnuts, both sliced.

STEAMED CHICKEN AND GRASS MUSHROOMS
About 6 servings

10 *Chinese dried grass mushrooms*	½ *cup bamboo shoots*
4 *Chinese red dates*	2 *or 3 slices fresh ginger root*
1 *piece dried tangerine peel*	1 *tablespoon cornstarch*
1 *spring chicken*	½ *teaspoon salt*
1 *set chicken giblets*	½ *teaspoon sugar*

2 teaspoons soy sauce

1. Separately soak dried grass mushrooms, Chinese red dates and tangerine peel.
2. With a cleaver, chop chicken, bones and all, in 1½- to 2-inch sections; cut giblets in ½-inch slices. Arrange on a shallow heatproof platter.
3. Slice bamboo shoots thin. Shred ginger root, soaked mushrooms and tangerine peel. Pit soaked red dates, then shred. Combine in a bowl.
4. Blend cornstarch, salt, sugar and soy sauce to a paste. Add to bowl, mixing well.
5. Spread mixture evenly over chicken sections. Steam until done (30 to 40 minutes). See page 831.

VARIATION: For the grass mushrooms, substitute ½ cup lily buds (soaked), cut in two.

STEAMED CHICKEN AND HAM
6 to 8 servings

1 *spring chicken*	½ *teaspoon salt*
1 *cup smoked ham*	2 *scallion stalks*
1 *tablespoon oil*	*Chinese parsley*

1. With a cleaver, chop chicken, bones and all, in 1½- to 2-inch sections. Slice smoked ham ½-inch thick, then in 1½-inch squares.
2. In a heatproof bowl, arrange alternating layers of chicken sections, skin-side up, and squares of ham.
3. Sprinkle with oil, using a circular motion. Season with salt. Mince scallion stalks and sprinkle over the top.
4. Steam until done (about 45 minutes). See page 831. Garnish with Chinese parsley and serve.

VARIATION: After step 1, toss the chicken sections gently to coat in a mixture of 1 tablespoon cornstarch; 2 tablespoons soy sauce; 2 tablespoons sherry, 2 tablespoons ginger root, minced; 1 tablespoon oil or chicken fat; ½ teaspon salt; and a dash of pepper. In step 2, top with the ham squares and 1 cup canned button mushrooms. Omit step 3; pick up step 4.

STEAMED MINCED CHICKEN AND HAM
About 4 servings

1 *chicken breast*	¼ *cup smoked ham*
2 *teaspoons cornstarch*	½ *cup stock*
½ *teaspoon salt*	1 *tablespoon cornstarch*
1 *teaspoon peanut oil*	1 *tablespoon soy sauce*
1 *tablespoon soy sauce*	3 *tablespoons water*

1. Skin and bone chicken; then mince coarsely or grind. Combine with cornstarch, salt, oil and soy sauce.

2. Spread chicken mixture out flat like a pancake in a shallow heatproof dish. Mince or grind ham and sprinkle over the top.

3. Steam until done (about 15 minutes). See page 831.

4. Heat stock. Meanwhile blend remaining cornstarch and soy sauce to a paste with cold water. Then stir in to thicken. Pour over steamed chicken and serve.

STEAMED SLIVERED CHICKEN AND VEGETABLES
About 6 servings

¼ *cup lily buds*	2 or 3 *slices fresh ginger root*
4 *Chinese red dates*	2 *tablespoons soy sauce*
4 *dried black mushrooms*	1 *tablespoon sherry*
2 *tablespoons cloud ear mushrooms*	½ *teaspoon salt*
1 *large chicken breast*	½ *teaspoon sugar*
¼ *cup bamboo shoots*	*dash of pepper*
6 *water chestnuts*	*few drops of sesame oil*

1. Separately soak dried lily buds, red dates, and black and cloud ear mushrooms.

2. Skin, bone and sliver chicken breast. Place in a shallow heatproof dish.

3. Sliver bamboo shoots. Mince water chestnuts, ginger root, soaked black mushrooms and red dates. Coarsely chop soaked lily buds and cloud ear mushrooms. Combine in a bowl.

4. In a cup, combine soy sauce, sherry, salt, sugar, pepper and sesame oil. Add to bowl and blend well.

5. Spread mixture over slivered chicken. Steam until done (10 to 15 minutes). See page 831.

VARIATION: For the chicken, substitute pork. Steam until cooked through (30 to 40 minutes).

DEEP-FRIED AND STEAMED CHICKEN WITH PINEAPPLE

1 *spring chicken*	½ *teaspoon salt*
oil for deep-frying	1 *teaspoon sugar*
3 *slices fresh ginger root*	½ *cup chicken liquids*
1 *leek stalk*	½ *cup pineapple juice*
3 *tablespoons soy sauce*	1 *cup canned pineapple chunks*
1 *tablespoon sherry*	1 *tablespoon cornstarch*

3 *tablespoons water*

1. Wipe chicken with a damp cloth; dry well with paper toweling or hang in a cool, airy place 1 to 2 hours.

2. Heat oil. Gently lower in bird, using a wire basket or large colander. Deep-fry, turning and basting, until golden. Drain on paper toweling.

3. Transfer chicken to a deep heatproof bowl. Slice ginger root; cut leek in 1-inch sections, and add. Combine soy sauce, sherry, salt and sugar and pour over chicken.

4. Steam until done (about 30 minutes). See page 831.

5. Transfer chicken to a cutting board and let cool slightly. Then bone, but do not skin; cut in 2-inch squares. Arrange skin-side up on a warm serving platter.

6. Pour chicken liquids into a saucepan. Drain canned pineapple, adding its juice to the pan. Heat slowly. Add pineapple chunks and heat.

7. Meanwhile blend cornstarch and cold water to a paste; then stir in to thicken. Pour sauce over chicken and serve.

WHITE CUT CHICKEN

White cut chicken is poached chicken which is white-cooked, or cooked *without* soy sauce. Either a spring or boiling chicken can be used. (The Chinese prefer 4- to 5-pound pullets or young hens.) In any case, the best birds are the plump ones with a thin layer of fat beneath the skin. (The skin, after cooking, becomes fine and satiny.) White cut chicken, because of its delicate texture and flavor, is never served with heavy, overwhelming sauces; it's usually eaten cold with various dips. It can also be used in any recipe that calls for cooked chicken.

WHITE CUT CHICKEN (YOUNG BIRD)

4 to 6 servings

8 to 10 *cups water*	1 *spring chicken*
3 *slices fresh ginger root*	1 *tablespoon sherry*
1 or 2 *scallion stalks*	1 *teaspoon salt*

1. Bring water to a boil in a heavy saucepan. Slice ginger root; cut scallion stalk in 1-inch sections, and add to pan.

2. Add chicken, sherry and salt. Cover pan and bring to a boil again over medium heat.

3. Turn off heat and let stand, covered, 1 hour. (Do not remove lid.) Drain, reserving liquid for stock.

4. Let chicken cool; then refrigerate to chill. Chop in 2-inch sections, or carve

Western-style. Serve with dips for white cut chicken (see pages 709–711).

NOTE: To test for doneness, pierce chicken leg with a fork at the end of step 3; if no blood is drawn, the bird is done. Otherwise, bring liquid to a boil again. Turn off heat and let stand, covered, 30 minutes more.

WHITE CUT CHICKEN (PULLET)
About 8 servings

8 to 10 cups water

1 pullet (4 to 5 pounds)

4 scallion stalks

1. Bring water to a boil in a heavy saucepan and add chicken. Cut scallion stalks in 1-inch sections and add. Bring to a boil again; then simmer, covered, 15 minutes.
2. Turn bird over and simmer, covered, 15 minutes more.
3. Turn off heat and let stand, covered, 30 minutes. (Do not remove lid.)
4. Drain, reserving liquid for stock. Let bird cool; then refrigerate and cut up as above.

NOTE: Some cooks, after step 3, rinse the bird under cold running water to make the skin smooth and firm.

VARIATION: In step 1, omit scallions, and add 3 slices fresh ginger root; 2 onions, sliced; and 6 celery stalks, cut diagonally in ½-inch sections.

WHITE CUT CHICKEN (STEWING FOWL)
8 to 10 servings

1 fowl (4 to 6 pounds)

2 or 3 slices fresh ginger root

2 scallion stalks

water to cover

1 teaspoon salt

1. Place chicken in a heavy saucepan. Slice scallion stalks and ginger root and add, along with cold water and salt. Bring to a boil; then cook, covered, over medium heat 30 minutes.
2. Turn off heat and let stand, covered, 30 minutes more. (Do not remove lid.)
3. Drain, reserving liquid for stock. Let cool; then refrigerate and cut up, as above.

WHITE CUT CHICKEN AND VEGETABLES
10 to 12 servings

1 chicken (4 to 5 pounds)

2 pounds broccoli

½ pound smoked ham

sauce for white cut chicken

1. Cook chicken by the white cut method. Cool, bone and cut in 1- by 2-inch strips.

2. Cut smoked ham in ⅛-inch slices, then in 1- and 2-inch strips. Arrange ham and chicken on a serving platter, in an alternating striped pattern.

3. Break broccoli in flowerets and plunge into boiling salted water. Parboil until tender but still crunchy. Drain; chill immediately under cold running water, then drain again. Arrange decoratively on the serving platter.

4. Prepare any sauce for white cut chicken and vegetables (see page 727). Pour over both meat and vegetable and serve.

NOTE: This dish, sometimes called Gold and Jade, appears frequently at formal dinners and wedding banquets. It's sometimes garnished with real flowers, such as yellow or white crysanthemums, white roses or lilies.

VARIATIONS: For the broccoli, substitute cauliflower (broken in flowerets and parboiled), and freshly cooked green peas, or asparagus tips. Or substitute raw carrots, cucumbers and tomatoes, cut in flower-like shapes.

Cut cooked chicken and ham in thin slices. In step 2, arrange sandwich-style on the platter, with a slice of ham between 2 slices of chicken.

WHITE CUT CHICKEN BREAST
4 to 6 servings

1 *large chicken breast*	1 *tablespoon sherry*
3 *cups water*	1 *teaspoon sugar*
1 *scallion*	1 *teaspoon vinegar*
1 *or 2 slices fresh ginger root*	½ *teaspoon salt*
3 *tablespoons soy sauce*	*few drops of sesame oil*

few drops of Tabasco Sauce

1. Place chicken breast in a saucepan. Boil water and pour over chicken. Simmer, covered, 10 minutes.

2. Drain, reserving liquid for stock. Let chicken cool; then bone. With a sharp knife, cut in ¾-inch strips. Arrange, skin-side up, on a serving dish.

3. Mince scallion and ginger root and sprinkle over chicken. Combine soy sauce, sherry, sugar, vinegar, salt and sesame oil. Pour over chicken. Then sprinkle with Tabasco Sauce and serve.

WHITE-COOKED CHICKEN IN SOUP I

About 8 servings

1 *chicken (4 to 5 pounds)*	2 *slices fresh ginger root*
8 *cups water*	1 *tablespoon sherry*
1 *scallion stalk*	1 *teaspoon salt*

dash of pepper

1. Place chicken and cold water in a pan. Bring to a boil; then reduce heat to low. Skim surface to clear.

2. Meanwhile mince scallion and ginger root; then add, along with sherry, salt and pepper. Simmer, covered, 2 hours.

3. Remove bird and let cool slightly; then cut up (see page 824) and arrange on a serving platter. Serve with any dip for white cut chicken (see pages 709–711).

4. Reheat soup and serve in individual bowls.

VARIATIONS: In step 2, add with other ingredients ½ cup bamboo shoots and 3 dried black mushrooms (soaked), both sliced.

During the last 30 minutes of cooking, add 1 or more slices smoked ham and 2 cups Chinese lettuce, cut in 1-inch sections.

In step 3, thinly slice only the white meat (reserving rest of chicken for other dishes). Return white meat to soup along with several thin slices of smoked ham and 1 teaspoon soy sauce. Simmer 10 to 15 minutes more and serve.

WHITE-COOKED CHICKEN IN SOUP II

6 to 8 servings

4 *to 6 dried black mushrooms*	2 *slices fresh ginger root*
2 *tablespoons cloud ear mushrooms*	4 *to 6 red dates*
1 *chicken (4 pounds)*	8 *cups water*

sherry

1. Separately soak dried black and cloud ear mushrooms.

2. With a cleaver, chop chicken, bones and all, in 3-inch sections. Place in a saucepan. Slice ginger root and add, along with red dates, cold water and soaked mushrooms.

3. Bring quickly to a boil; then reduce heat, and skim surface to clear. Simmer, covered, 1 hour.

4. Ladle soup and ingredients into individual bowls. Add 1 tablespoon sherry to each and serve.

VARIATION: For the sherry, substitute 1 to 2 teaspoons gin for each bowl.

WHITE-COOKED CHICKEN WITH MUSHROOMS AND PEAS
About 6 servings

1 spring chicken	*1 pound peas*
4 tablespoons cornstarch	*1½ cups water*
¼ cup water	*½ teaspoon salt*
2 egg whites	*dash of pepper*
8 cups water	*2 tablespoons cornstarch*
½ pound fresh mushrooms	*¼ cup water*

1 tablespoon soy sauce

1. Skin and bone chicken; cut in 2-inch squares.

2. Blend cornstarch and cold water to a paste. Add egg whites and beat until smooth. Coat chicken with mixture and let stand 10 minutes.

3. Bring water to a boil. Add coated chicken, one piece at a time (to maintain the boiling). Cook, uncovered, 2 to 3 minutes. Then drain, discarding liquid. Rinse chicken under cold running water and drain again.

4. Stem mushrooms and cut in two; shell peas. Bring the second quantity of water to a boil. Add mushrooms and peas and cook, uncovered, 3 minutes.

5. Add chicken squares, salt and pepper. Simmer, covered, until chicken is done (about 10 minutes).

6. Blend remaining cornstarch and cold water to a paste, then stir in to thicken. Stir in soy sauce and serve.

WHITE-COOKED CHICKEN AND TOMATOES
4 to 6 servings

1 spring chicken	*1 tablespoon sherry*
2 cups water	*1 tablespoon oil*
2 tomatoes	*½ teaspoon salt*

1. Disjoint chicken. Place in a saucepan with water and bring to a boil. Then simmer, covered, 20 minutes.

2. Peel tomatoes; cut in quarters if large, or in halves if small. Add to pan, along with sherry, oil and salt. Simmer, covered, 10 minutes more.

3. Remove chicken and let cool slightly. With a cleaver, chop in bite-size pieces. Reheat sauce and pour over.

NOTE: When using a stewing chicken, simmer, covered, about an hour in step 1.

WHITE-COOKED CHICKEN AND CURRY I
About 6 servings

1 spring chicken	1 teaspoon cornstarch
1 cup Chinese white turnip	3 tablespoons water
1 cup round cabbage	1 to 2 tablespoons curry powder
2 cups water	2 scallions

1. With a cleaver, chop chicken, bones and all, in 2-inch sections. Place in a saucepan.

2. Peel Chinese turnip. Cut turnip and cabbage in 2-inch cubes and add to pan, along with cold water. Bring to a boil; then simmer, covered, 30 minutes.

3. Remove chicken and vegetables to a warm serving platter, leaving liquids in pan.

4. Blend cornstarch and remaining cold water to a paste; then stir in curry powder. Add to liquids in pan and cook, stirring, to thicken.

5. Pour sauce over vegetables. Mince scallions; then sprinkle over and serve.

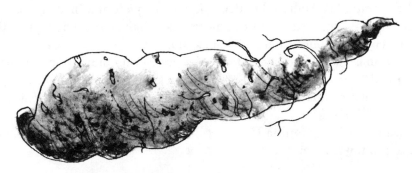

WHITE-COOKED CHICKEN AND CURRY II
6 to 8 servings

1 spring chicken	3 tablespoons oil
2 onions	1 to 2 tablespoons curry powder
4 potatoes	1½ cups water
1 teaspoon salt	

1. With a cleaver, chop chicken, bones and all, in 2-inch sections.

2. Cut onions in 2-inch cubes. Peel and cube potatoes, but leave in cold water until ready to use.

3. Heat oil. Add onions and curry powder and stir-fry until onions are translucent and softened.

4. Add chicken sections and water. Bring to a boil; then simmer, covered, 10 minutes.

5. Add salt and cubed potatoes. Simmer, covered, until done (about 20 minutes more).

WHITE- AND RED-COOKED CHICKEN
About 8 servings

1 chicken (4 to 5 pounds)	4 tablespoons soy sauce
4 cups water	1 tablespoon sherry
1/4 pound fresh mushrooms	1 teaspoon salt

1. Wipe chicken with a damp cloth and place in a heavy pan with cold water. Bring to a boil over medium heat; then simmer, covered, 30 minutes. Pour off liquid, reserving it for stock.

2. Stem fresh mushrooms. Add to chicken, along with soy sauce, sherry and salt.

3. Simmer, covered, 1 hour, turning bird once or twice for even coloring.

WHITE- AND RED-COOKED STUFFED CHICKEN WINGS
About 4 servings

8 to 10 chicken wings	1 tablespoon soy sauce
water to cover	1/2 teaspoon salt
1/4 pound smoked ham	1 tablespoon cornstarch
2 slices fresh ginger root	3 tablespoons water
1 cup stock	2 tablespoons sherry

1. Chop off bony wing tips with a cleaver; then chop chicken wings in two. Place in a pan with cold water. Bring to a boil; then simmer, covered, 30 minutes. Drain, reserving liquid for stock.

2. Let wings cool; then carefully slip out bones without breaking skin. Sliver smoked ham and stuff into wing-bone cavities.

3. Mince ginger root and add to saucepan along with reserved stock, soy sauce and salt. Simmer 2 minutes. Meanwhile blend cornstarch and remaining cold water to a paste. Then stir in to thicken.

4. Stir in sherry. Return stuffed chicken wings and cook only to heat through.

VARIATION: In step 2, stuff wing cavities with a half-and-half mixture of slivered ham and bamboo shoots.

RED-COOKED OR SOY CHICKEN I
4 to 6 servings

1 *spring chicken*   1 *cup soy sauce*

water to cover

1. Wipe chicken with a damp cloth. Place in a heavy pan with soy sauce and cold water. Bring to a boil over medium heat; then simmer, covered, until done (30 to 40 minutes). Turn once or twice for even coloring.

2. Let chicken cool slightly. With a cleaver, chop, bones and all, in 2-inch sections; or carve Western-style. Serve hot with its sauce; or serve cold, reserving sauce for later use as a master sauce. (See page 739.)

NOTE: Simmer a 4- to 5-pound bird about an hour.

RED-COOKED OR SOY CHICKEN II
4 to 6 servings

4 *scallion stalks*	1 *cup sherry*
¼ *cup brown sugar*	1 *cup water*
1 *cup soy sauce*	1 *spring chicken*

1. Cut scallion stalks in ½-inch sections. Place in a large heavy pan, along with brown sugar, soy sauce, sherry and water. Bring to a boil over medium heat.

2. Wipe chicken with a damp cloth and add to pan. Bring to a boil again; then simmer, covered, 40 minutes, turning bird once or twice for even coloring.

3. Let chicken cool slightly. With a cleaver, chop, bones and all, in 2-inch sections; or carve Western-style. Serve hot with its sauce; or serve cold, reserving sauce for later use as a master sauce. (See page 739.)

NOTE: For a 4- to 5-pound bird, cook 30 minutes on each side, basting frequently.

VARIATION: In step 1, for the scallions, substitute 3 slices fresh ginger root; 1 garlic clove, crushed; and 1 clove star anise.

RED-COOKED OR SOY CHICKEN III
4 to 6 servings

1 *spring chicken*	1 *scallion stalk*
1 *slice fresh ginger root*	2 *slices fresh ginger root*
2 *tablespoons soy sauce*	2 *tablespoons oil*
1 *tablespoon sherry*	1 *cup soy sauce*
½ *teaspoon salt*	1 *cup water*
dash of pepper	1 *teaspoon sugar*

1. Wipe chicken with a damp cloth. Mince ginger root; then combine with soy sauce, sherry, salt and pepper. Rub mixture over chicken inside and out. Let stand 1 hour.

2. Cut scallion stalk in ½-inch sections. Slice and crush remaining ginger root.

3. Heat oil. Add scallion and ginger root; stir-fry a few times. Add remaining soy sauce and bring to a boil. Cook 2 minutes over medium heat.

4. Hold chicken upside down over a bowl. Pour heated soy mixture into its cavity, letting it drain out through the neck into the bowl. Repeat 5 times, reheating sauce after the second and fourth time.

5. Transfer sauce to a large pan and slowly bring to a boil. Add chicken and cook, turning, until evenly colored (about 10 minutes).

6. Boil water and add to chicken and sauce. Simmer, covered, 10 to 15 minutes. Add sugar and simmer, covered, 2 minutes more.

RED-STEWED CHICKEN I
About 8 servings

1 chicken (4 pounds)
4 cups water
1 cup fresh mushrooms
1 cup bamboo shoots

6 water chestnuts
2 tablespoons soy sauce
½ teaspoon salt
dash of pepper

1. Wipe chicken with a damp cloth; then, with a cleaver, chop, bones and all, in 2-inch sections. Place in a heavy saucepan.

2. Boil water and pour over chicken. Bring to a boil again; then simmer, covered, 30 minutes.

3. Meanwhile slice mushrooms, bamboo shoots and water chestnuts. Add to chicken, along with soy sauce, salt and pepper; and simmer, covered, 30 minutes more.

RED-STEWED CHICKEN II
8 to 10 servings

1 chicken (5 to 6 pounds)
3 or 4 slices fresh ginger root
3 scallion stalks

3 cups water
½ cup soy sauce
¼ cup sherry

1 tablespoon sugar

1. Disjoint chicken and cut breast in two. Slice ginger root; trim scallion stalks.

2. Place chicken and cold water in a heavy pan. Bring to a boil over medium heat; then add ginger, scallions, soy sauce and sherry. Reduce heat and simmer, covered, 1 hour, turning chicken sections once or twice for even coloring.

3. Add sugar and simmer, covered, 30 minutes more.

NOTE: Simmer 2- to 3-pound chickens only 30 minutes in step 2, and 15 minutes in step 3.

RED-COOKED SPICED CHICKEN
4 to 6 servings

1 spring chicken
2 slices fresh ginger root
1 scallion stalk
2 cloves star anise
½ cinnamon stick

1 tablespoon Szechwan peppercorns
¼ cup soy sauce
¼ cup sherry
¼ cup sesame oil
1 tablespoon sugar

2 scallions

1. Wipe chicken with a damp cloth. Slice ginger root and cut scallion stalk in two; place in chicken cavity.

2. Put star anise, cinnamon stick and Szechwan peppercorns on a square of cheesecloth. Gather up the corners and tie with thread.

3. In a large heavy pan, heat soy sauce, sherry and sesame oil. Add chicken and spice bag and simmer, covered, until nearly done, about 40 minutes. (Turn bird once or twice for even coloring.) Add sugar and simmer, covered, 5 minutes more.

4. Let bird cool slightly. With a cleaver, chop, bones and all, in 2-inch sections; or carve Western-style. Sliver remaining scallions; sprinkle over and serve.

VARIATION: At the beginning of step 3, add 1 piece dried tangerine peel (soaked).

BASIC BRAISED CHICKEN
4 to 6 servings

1 *spring chicken*	½ *cup soy sauce*
2 *scallion stalks*	2 *cups water*
2 or 3 *slices fresh ginger root*	½ *teaspoon salt*
3 to 4 *tablespoons oil*	1 *tablespoon sugar*
3 *tablespoons sherry*	*Chinese parsley*

1. With a cleaver, chop chicken in 1½- to 2-inch sections. Trim scallion stalk and slice ginger root.

2. Heat oil in a large heavy pan and brown chicken sections quickly.

3. Add sherry, soy sauce, water, salt, scallions and ginger root. Bring to a boil; then simmer, covered, 20 to 30 minutes.

4. Add sugar and simmer, covered, 10 to 15 minutes more.

5. Transfer chicken sections to a serving bowl. Strain sauce and pour over. Garnish with Chinese parsley and serve.

VARIATIONS: For the scallions, substitute 2 garlic cloves, crushed. For the water, substitute 2 cups sherry.

In step 1, rub chicken sections with 1 tablespoon soy sauce, ¼ teaspoon salt.

In step 1, toss chicken sections in a mixture of 2 tablespoons soy sauce, 2 tablespoons sherry, ½ teaspoon salt, ½ teaspoon sugar and a dash of pepper. Let stand 15 minutes, turning occasionally. Brown as in step 2, but omit steps 3 and 4. Instead add to chicken 2 cups stock, plus the scallions and ginger root. Bring to a boil; then simmer, covered, 30 to 45 minutes.

In step 2, after browning, remove chicken from pan. Heat 1 more tablespoon

oil. Then add the scallion stalks, cut in ½-inch sections; the ginger slices, and 1 garlic clove, both crushed. Stir-fry 1 or 2 minutes; then stir in the soy sauce, sherry and water and bring to a boil. Return chicken, add the salt and sugar, and simmer as in steps 3 and 4 above.

During the last 20 minutes of cooking, add any of the following:

6 eggs, hardboiled and shelled; increase the soy sauce (added in step 3) to ¾ cup.

4 bamboo shoots, cut in 1-inch sections; and 1 teaspoon sugar.

15 to 20 dried black mushrooms (soaked); increase the soy sauce (added in step 3) to ¾ cup.

6 dried black mushrooms (soaked); and 6 Chinese red dates.

1½ pounds string beans, stemmed and cut in 1½-inch sections; increase the soy sauce (added in step 3) to ¾ cup.

1 cup celery stalks, cut diagonally in 1½-inch sections; 1 cup cabbage, shredded; and ½ cup fresh mushrooms, sliced.

1 cup dried black mushrooms (soaked); 1 cup bamboo shoots and ½ cup water chestnuts, all sliced. Garnish in step 5 with shredded smoked ham.

During the last 10 minutes of cooking, add 4 cups Chinese lettuce, cut in 1-inch sections.

During the last 5 minutes of cooking, add 1 small head cauliflower, broken in flowerets and parboiled.

BRAISED WHOLE CHICKEN
About 8 servings

1 *chicken (4 to 5 pounds)*	1 *cup water*
2 *scallion stalks*	½ *cup soy sauce*
2 *or 3 slices fresh ginger root*	3 *tablespoons sherry*
4 *to 5 tablespoons oil*	1 *teaspoon sugar*

1. Wipe chicken with a damp cloth. Cut scallion stalks in 2-inch sections; slice ginger root.

2. Heat oil in a large heavy pan. Truss chicken and brown quickly on all sides.

3. Boil water and add to chicken, along with soy sauce, scallions and ginger. Bring quickly to a boil again; then simmer, covered, 30 minutes, turning bird once.

4. Add sherry and sugar and simmer, covered, 30 minutes more, turning bird once or twice for even coloring.

VARIATION: Omit the scallions. In step 2, add to the heated oil 2 cups onion, chopped; stir-fry until translucent and remove. Heat more oil, if needed; add chicken and brown. Return onions when adding other ingredients in step 3.

BRAISED CHESTNUT CHICKEN
About 8 servings

6 *dried black mushrooms*	2 *to 3 tablespoons oil*
30 *chestnuts*	2 *cups water*
2 *pounds chicken legs*	3 *tablespoons soy sauce*
2 *or 3 sets chicken giblets*	2 *tablespoons sherry*
2 *slices fresh ginger root*	½ *teaspoon salt*

1. Soak dried mushrooms. Shell chestnuts (see page 823); then cut in half.

2. With a cleaver, chop chicken legs, bones and all, in 2-inch sections. Chop giblets in 2-inch sections. Slice ginger root and soaked mushrooms.

3. Heat oil in a heavy pan. Quickly brown chicken and giblet sections. Add ginger root and mushrooms; stir-fry about 1 minute.

4. Meanwhile heat, but do not boil, water; then stir in soy sauce, sherry and salt. Pour over chicken and bring to a boil. Then simmer, covered, 30 to 35 minutes.

5. Add chestnuts and simmer, covered, 15 minutes more.

NOTE: This dish is often served at holiday feasts and elaborate dinners.

VARIATION: Brown chicken as in step 3; then sprinkle with 1½ tablespoons soy sauce, 2 tablespoons sherry and 3 tablespoons cold water. Stir in to heat. Add the salt and ginger root and simmer, covered, 30 minutes without additional water. Then pick up step 5.

BRAISED CHICKEN WITH DRIED CHESTNUTS
About 6 servings

½ to 1 cup dried chestnuts

1 spring chicken

2 to 3 tablespoons oil

2 cups water

2 slices fresh ginger root

2 tablespoons soy sauce

2 tablespoons sherry

½ teaspoon salt

½ teaspoon sugar

1. Parboil dried chestnuts (see page 850).

2. With a cleaver, chop chicken, bones and all, in 2-inch sections.

3. Heat oil in a heavy pan. Brown chicken sections quickly. Meanwhile bring water to a boil.

4. Mince ginger root; then combine with soy sauce, sherry, salt and sugar. Stir into pan with chicken. Add chestnuts and water; then simmer, covered, until done (about 45 minutes).

BRAISED GINGER CHICKEN I
4 to 6 servings

1 spring chicken

¼ cup fresh ginger root

½ cup oil

½ teaspoon salt

¼ teaspoon pepper

1. Wipe chicken with a damp cloth. Dry thoroughly with paper toweling; or hang up to dry in a cool, airy place 1 to 2 hours.

2. With a cleaver, chop chicken, bones and all, in 2-inch sections. Slice ginger root thin.

3. Heat oil to smoking in a heavy pan. Add chicken and ginger and brown quickly. Sprinkle with salt and pepper.

4. Reduce heat to medium and cook chicken, covered, until done (about 30 minutes). Pour off oil; discard ginger, and serve.

BRAISED GINGER CHICKEN II
4 to 6 servings

⅛ pound fresh ginger root

1½ cups water

4 to 6 dried black mushrooms

1 spring chicken

1 garlic clove

1 scallion stalk

½ cup sherry

3 tablespoons oil

2½ tablespoons soy sauce

1 teaspoon sugar

2 cups water

1. Peel ginger root and place in a pan with water. Bring to a boil; then simmer, covered, 45 minutes. Cut 1 slice from ginger root, discarding the remainder. Reserve ginger liquid.

2. Meanwhile soak dried mushrooms. With a cleaver, chop chicken, bones and all, in 2-inch sections. Crush garlic. Cut scallion in 1-inch sections.

3. Combine sherry with reserved ginger liquid and add to chicken. Let stand 15 minutes, turning occasionally; then drain well.

4. Heat oil. Add garlic, scallion and ginger slice; stir-fry a few times. Add chicken and brown lightly.

5. Add soy sauce, sugar, remaining water and soaked mushrooms. Bring to a boil; then simmer, covered, 30 minutes.

BRAISED HONEY CHICKEN
About 6 servings

1 chicken (3 pounds)	½ cup sherry
1 scallion stalk	2 tablespoons honey
2 slices fresh ginger root	2 tablespoons soy sauce
3 to 4 tablespoons oil	1 teaspoon salt

1. With a cleaver, chop chicken, bones and all, in 2-inch sections. Cut scallion stalk in ½-inch sections. Mince ginger root.

2. Heat oil in a heavy pan. Add scallion and ginger; stir-fry a few times. Brown chicken sections quickly, then drain off excess oil.

3. Combine sherry, honey, soy sauce and salt. Slowly pour over chicken and heat. Simmer, covered, until done (about 40 minutes).

BRAISED LILY BUD CHICKEN I
About 6 servings

6 dried black mushrooms	2 tablespoons sherry
12 to 15 lily buds	1 to 2 teaspoons sugar
1 chicken (3 pounds)	½ teaspoon salt
1 slice fresh ginger root	½ cup oil
3 tablespoons soy sauce	3 cups water

1. Separately soak dried mushrooms and lily buds.

2. Wipe chicken with a damp cloth. Mince ginger root; then combine with soy sauce, sherry, sugar and salt. Rub mixture over chicken skin and let stand 30 minutes.

3. Heat oil in a large heavy pan. Truss chicken and brown quickly on all sides, then drain off excess oil.

4. Boil water and add to chicken along with soaked mushrooms and lily buds. Bring to a boil; then simmer, covered, until done (about 1 hour).

5. Let chicken cool slightly; then, with a cleaver, chop chicken, bones and all, in 2-inch sections; or carve Western-style. Serve with lily buds, mushrooms and sauce poured over.

VARIATIONS: Omit step 2. Brown chicken as in step 3. Then add the sherry, sugar, salt and water, and bring to a boil. Add the soy sauce, ginger root, soaked mushrooms and lily buds. Simmer as in step 4.

In step 2, omit the ginger-soy mixture and rub chicken instead with 2 tablespoons soy sauce. Let stand 10 minutes. Then add ¼ cup sherry, 2 cups boiling water, the salt, sugar, mushrooms and lily buds. Simmer as in step 4.

In step 4, add, with the black mushrooms and lily buds, 2 tablespoons cloud ear mushrooms (soaked) and 6 Chinese red dates.

BRAISED LILY BUD CHICKEN II
4 to 6 servings

4 dried black mushrooms	3 tablespoons oil
12 lily buds	1 tablespoon soy sauce
1 spring chicken	2 tablespoons sherry
2 slices fresh ginger root	1 cup stock

1. Separately soak dried mushrooms and lily buds.

2. Disjoint chicken; or chop, bones and all, in 2-inch sections. Crush ginger root. Cut mushrooms in strips. (If lily buds are long, cut in half.)

3. Heat oil in a large heavy pan and brown chicken sections quickly.

4. Add soy sauce, sherry and ginger root, stirring them in to heat and blend.

5. Meanwhile heat stock separately. Add to chicken, along with mushrooms and lily buds. Bring to a boil; then simmer, covered, until done (30 to 40 minutes).

BRAISED CHICKEN WITH FRESH MUSHROOMS I
6 to 8 servings

1 chicken (3 pounds)	5 tablespoons oil
½ pound fresh mushrooms	1½ tablespoons sherry
2 garlic cloves	2 tablespoons soy sauce

1. With a cleaver, chop chicken, bones and all, in 2-inch sections. Remove mushroom stems, leaving caps intact. Crush garlic.

2. Heat oil in a heavy pan. Brown garlic lightly and discard. Add chicken sections and brown quickly.

3. Reduce heat to medium. Add mushroom caps and stir in gently to coat with oil. Cook, covered, 5 minutes.

4. Stir in sherry, then soy sauce. Cook, covered, over low heat until chicken is done (25 to 30 minutes).

BRAISED CHICKEN WITH FRESH MUSHROOMS II
6 to 8 servings

1 *chicken (3 pounds)*	2 *tablespoons oil*
1 *garlic clove*	5 *tablespoons oil*
1 *or 2 slices fresh ginger root*	½ *teaspoon sugar*
2 *tablespoons soy sauce*	½ *teaspoon salt*
1 *tablespoon sherry*	*dash of pepper*
chicken liver and gizzard	¾ *cup water*
½ *pound fresh mushrooms*	2 *teaspoons cornstarch*
3 *scallion stalks*	3 *tablespoons water*

1. Cut chicken in half; wipe with a damp cloth. Mince garlic and ginger root; then combine with soy sauce and sherry. Rub mixture over chicken, inside and out. Let stand 30 minutes.

2. Meanwhile dice chicken liver and gizzard. Stem and dice mushrooms. Cut scallion stalks in ½-inch sections.

3. Heat oil in a large heavy pan. Add diced ingredients and scallion and stir-fry until cooked through (about 3 minutes). Remove from pan.

4. Heat remaining oil. Brown each chicken-half separately. Then place side by side in pan.

5. Add sugar, salt, pepper and water. Bring to a boil; then simmer, covered, until done (30 to 40 minutes).

6. Remove chicken, leaving liquids in pan. With a cleaver, chop in bite-size pieces. Arrange on a serving platter and keep warm.

7. Reheat liquids. Return stir-fried ingredients and reheat.

8. Meanwhile blend cornstarch and remaining cold water to a paste; then stir in to thicken. Pour sauce over chicken and serve.

BRAISED BLACK MUSHROOM CHICKEN
6 to 8 servings

10 *to 15 dried black mushrooms*	1 *teaspoon sugar*
1 *chicken (3 pounds)*	2 *to 3 tablespoons oil*
4 *tablespoons soy sauce*	2 *cups water*
2 *tablespoons sherry*	½ *teaspoon salt*
	dash of pepper

1. Soak dried mushrooms.

2. Wipe chicken with a damp cloth and disjoint. Combine soy sauce, sherry and sugar.

3. Heat oil in a large heavy pan. Brown chicken quickly. Then stir in soy-sherry mixture. Reduce heat and cook, covered, 5 minutes, turning pieces once.

4. Boil water separately. Add to chicken, along with mushrooms, salt and pepper. Bring to a boil again; then simmer, covered, until done (35 to 40 minutes).

VARIATIONS: For the water, substitute stock.

Omit the water. Increase the soy sauce and sherry to ½ cup each and the sugar to 1 tablespoon. Add with the other ingredients after chicken is browned; and simmer, covered, about 40 minutes.

In step 3, add to heated oil 2 slices ginger root, crushed; and 1 scallion stalk, cut in 2-inch sections. Stir-fry a minute; then add chicken and brown.

In step 3, after browning chicken, add the soaked mushrooms and ½ cup bamboo shoots, sliced. Stir-fry to coat with oil; then continue with steps 3 and 4.

In step 4, add with the mushrooms, 10 Chinese red dates.

During the last 10 minutes of cooking, add ¼ cup fresh green peas.

BLACK MUSHROOM CHICKEN, DEEP-FRIED AND BRAISED
6 to 8 servings

10 to 15 dried black mushrooms	oil for deep-frying
1 chicken (3 pounds)	2 tablespoons oil
soy sauce	½ teaspoon salt
4 or 5 slices fresh ginger root	2½ cups water
1 bamboo shoot	½ teaspoon sugar
4 water chestnuts	dash of pepper
2 scallion stalks	2 teaspoons cornstarch

3 tablespoons water

1. Soak dried mushrooms.

2. Cut chicken in half and wipe with a damp cloth. Rub, inside and out, with soy sauce. Let stand 10 minutes.

3. Meanwhile slice ginger root. Shred bamboo shoot, water chestnuts and soaked mushrooms. Cut scallion stalks in 1-inch sections.

4. Heat oil to bubbling. Gently lower in chicken, one half at a time, and brown lightly. Drain on paper toweling.

5. Heat remaining oil. Add salt and ginger root; stir-fry a few times. Add shredded vegetables and scallions; stir-fry 1 to 2 minutes.

6. Stir in and heat water; add sugar and pepper. Return chicken halves and bring to a boil; then simmer, covered, until tender (about 20 minutes).

7. Remove chicken, leaving liquids in pan. Let bird cool slightly; then chop, bones and all, in bite-size pieces. Arrange on a serving platter.

8. Gently reheat liquids in pan. Meanwhile blend cornstarch and remaining cold water to a paste; then stir in to thicken. Pour sauce over chicken and serve.

VARIATION: In step 7, instead of chopping the chicken, disjoint and bone the legs and wings. Cut the breast meat in slices and arrange decoratively on a platter with legs and wings.

BRAISED CHICKEN AND POTATOES I
About 8 servings

1 *chicken (3 pounds)*	2 *cups water*
1 *small onion*	2 *to 3 tablespoons oil*
1 *garlic clove*	1 *tablespoon sugar*
2 *slices fresh ginger root*	3 *tablespoons soy sauce*

2 *potatoes*

1. Wipe chicken with a damp cloth. With a cleaver chop, bones and all, in 2-inch sections.

2. Slice onion. Mince garlic and ginger root. Heat water.

3. Heat oil in a heavy pan. Add onion, garlic and ginger; stir-fry to brown lightly. Add chicken and brown quickly.

4. Add heated water, sugar and soy sauce. Bring to a boil; then simmer, covered, 20 minutes.

5. Meanwhile peel potatoes and cut in 1-inch cubes. Add to pan and simmer, covered, until done (about 10 minutes more).

BRAISED CHICKEN AND POTATOES II
About 8 servings

1 *chicken (3 pounds)*	1 *teaspoon sugar*
2 *potatoes*	½ *teaspoon Five Spices*
2 *tablespoons red bean cheese*	¼ *teaspoon salt*
2 *cups water*	2 *to 3 tablespoons oil*
3 *tablespoons soy sauce*	¼ *teaspoon salt*

1. Wipe chicken with a damp cloth. With a cleaver, chop, bones and all, in 2-inch sections.

2. Peel potatoes and cut in 2-inch cubes, but leave in cold water until ready to use.

3. Mash red bean cheese; then blend with water, soy sauce, sugar, Five Spices and salt.

4. Heat oil in a heavy pan. Add remaining salt; then add chicken sections and brown.

5. Pour red bean cheese mixture over. Bring to a boil, stirring constantly. Add potatoes and simmer, covered, until done (about 30 minutes).

BRAISED CHICKEN WITH RED DATES AND BACON
About 8 servings

1 chicken (3 pounds)	1 tablespoon soy sauce
1 leek stalk	2 tablespoons sherry
½ pound bacon	¾ cup Chinese red dates

1. Wipe chicken with a damp cloth; and chop, bones and all, in 2-inch sections. Cut leek in ½-inch sections.

2. Slice bacon thick; then cut in 1-inch strips. Place in a cold pan and brown lightly over medium heat. Drain on paper toweling.

3. Reheat bacon fat. Add leek; stir-fry a few times. Add chicken and brown quickly.

4. Return bacon. Add soy sauce, sherry and red dates. Reduce heat and simmer, covered, stirring occasionally until tender (about 30 minutes).

VARIATION: Disjoint chicken, instead of chopping it in sections. Simmer about 45 minutes in step 4.

BRAISED CURRIED CHICKEN I
6 to 8 servings

1 chicken (3 pounds)	3 tablespoons oil
1 or 2 scallions	2 cups stock
3 tablespoons oil	1 tablespoon cornstarch
1 to 2 tablespoons curry	3 tablespoons water

1. With a cleaver, chop chicken, bones and all, in 2-inch sections. Mince scallions.

2. Heat oil in a heavy pan. Brown chicken sections quickly; remove from pan. Add stock to pan and heat until nearly boiling.

3. Meanwhile in a dry skillet, heat curry over a low flame, stirring constantly. When pungent, blend in remaining oil.

4. Return chicken to pan with stock; stir in curry mixture and simmer, covered, 45 minutes.

5. Transfer chicken to a heated serving platter, leaving liquids in pan. Blend cornstarch and cold water to a paste; then stir in to thicken liquids. Pour sauce over chicken and serve, garnished with minced scallions.

VARIATIONS: Before browning chicken, add 3 onions, sliced, to heated oil; stir-fry to brown lightly. Then turn off heat and let cool a few minutes. Add 2 tablespoons curry powder, ½ teaspoon chili powder, ½ teaspoon crushed red pepper and ½ teaspoon salt. Cook, stirring, 5 minutes over medium heat. Then add chicken and brown. Stir in the heated stock; then simmer and thicken as above.

During the last 30 minutes of cooking, add 1 pound potatoes, peeled and cubed.

BRAISED CURRIED CHICKEN II
6 to 8 servings

1 chicken (3 pounds)	3 tablespoons oil
½ cup green pepper	½ teaspoon salt
2 onions	1 to 2 tablespoons curry powder
1 clove garlic	2 teaspoons soy sauce

2 cups stock

1. With a cleaver, chop chicken, bones and all, in 2-inch sections.
2. Cut green peppers in 1-inch squares. Slice onions; crush garlic.
3. Heat oil in a heavy pan. Stir in salt; add chicken and brown quickly.
4. Add green pepper, onions, garlic, curry, soy sauce and stock. Bring to a boil, stirring; then simmer, covered, 40 to 45 minutes.

BRAISED CURRIED CHICKEN WITH ANISE
8 to 10 servings

1 chicken (3 pounds)	1 to 2 tablespoons curry powder
2 onions	1 tablespoon sugar
1 garlic clove	2 tablespoons soy sauce
2 slices fresh ginger root	2 cups stock
2 tablespoons oil	½ teaspoon salt
3 tablespoons oil	2 cloves star anise
1 tablespoon flour	1 pound potatoes

1. Bone chicken and cut in 2-inch cubes. Separately mince onions, garlic and ginger root.
2. Heat oil. Add onions; stir-fry to brown lightly; then remove from pan. Heat remaining oil; add garlic and stir-fry a few times. Then stir in ginger, flour and curry to blend.
3. Return onions and stir in 1 minute over low heat. Add chicken. Raise heat to medium and gently stir in 3 minutes to coat.

4. Add sugar, soy sauce, stock, salt and star anise. Bring to a boil; then simmer, covered, 20 minutes.

5. Meanwhile peel potatoes and cut in 1½-inch cubes. Then add to pan and simmer, covered, until done (about 20 minutes).

BRAISED CHICKEN BREAST
4 to 6 servings

3 *dried black mushrooms*	2 *to 3 tablespoons oil*
1 *large chicken breast*	2 *tablespoons oil*
1 *tablespoon cornstarch*	1 *cup water*
1 *tablespoon soy sauce*	1 *tablespoon sherry*
½ *teaspoon salt*	2 *tablespoons soy sauce*
½ *pound leeks*	1 *tablespoon cornstarch*
½ *cup bamboo shoots*	2 *tablespoons water*
2 *tablespoons smoked ham*	1 *teaspoon sugar*

Worcestershire Sauce

1. Soak dried mushrooms.

2. Skin and bone chicken breast and cut in 2-inch squares. Combine cornstarch, soy sauce and salt. Add to chicken and toss gently to coat.

3. Cut leeks in 1-inch sections; slice bamboo shoots and soaked mushrooms. Mince ham.

4. Heat oil. Add leeks and stir-fry to brown lightly; then remove. Heat remaining oil. Add chicken; stir-fry until it loses its pinkness. Return leeks to pan.

5. Add water and bring to a boil. Stir in sherry and remaining soy sauce; then reduce heat and simmer, covered, 10 minutes.

6. Add sliced bamboo shoots and mushrooms; simmer, covered, 20 minutes more. Remove chicken and vegetables, leaving liquids in pan. Arrange on a serving platter and keep warm.

7. Blend remaining cornstarch and cold water to a paste; stir in sugar. Then add to liquids in pan, stirring to thicken. Pour sauce over chicken. Garnish with ham, sprinkle with Worcestershire Sauce and serve.

NOTE: This Shanghai-style dish is sometimes called Princess Chicken.

BRAISED CHICKEN WINGS WITH BLACK BEAN SAUCE
About 8 servings

1 *to 2 tablespoons fermented black beans*	½ *teaspoon salt*
2 *pounds chicken wings*	1 *cup stock*
½ *cup green pepper*	1 *teaspoon soy sauce*
½ *cup onion*	*dash of pepper*
1 *garlic clove*	1 *tablespoon cornstarch*
3 *tablespoons oil*	2 *tablespoons water*

1. Soak fermented black beans.

2. With a cleaver, chop off bony wing tips and discard; then chop each wing in 5 sections.

3. Dice green pepper and onions. Mince garlic and mash with soaked black beans.

4. Heat oil. Add salt, then black bean-garlic mixture. Stir-fry a few times to heat through. Add chicken sections and brown lightly.

5. Stir in stock and heat quickly. Then simmer, covered, 10 minutes.

6. Add green pepper and onion and simmer, covered, 10 minutes more. Then stir in soy sauce and pepper.

7. Meanwhile blend cornstarch and cold water to a paste; then stir in to thicken sauce.

BRAISED CHICKEN BALLS AND OYSTER SAUCE
4 to 6 servings

1 large chicken breast	2 to 3 slices fresh ginger root
1 tablespoon cornstarch	2 tablespoons oyster sauce
1 tablespoon sherry	¼ cup water
½ teaspoon salt	1 teaspoon sugar
1 egg	2 to 3 tablespoons oil
1 to 2 scallion stalks	dash of pepper

1. Skin, bone and mince chicken breast. Place in a bowl with cornstarch, sherry and salt. Beat egg lightly and add. Blend mixture, then form into walnut-size balls.

2. Mince scallion and ginger root; then combine with oyster sauce, water and sugar.

3. Heat oil. Brown chicken balls quickly but lightly.

4. Stir in oyster sauce mixture and heat quickly. Then simmer, covered, 15 to 20 minutes, stirring occasionally. Sprinkle with pepper and serve.

BASIC ROAST CHICKEN
About 8 servings

1 chicken (4 to 5 pounds)	marinade for roast chicken

1. Wipe chicken with a damp cloth. Dry well with paper toweling; or hang up to dry in a cool, airy place for 1 to 2 hours. Transfer to a deep bowl.

2. Prepare any marinade for roast chicken (see page 724). Then pour over chicken and rub into skin. Let stand 1 to 2 hours, turning occasionally. Drain, reserving marinade.

3. Preheat the oven to 350 degrees. Place chicken on a rack over a drip pan containing several inches of water (this will keep the drippings from burning). Roast until bird is tender and browned, basting with marinade at 15-minute intervals and turning bird occasionally. (Allow about 30 minutes roasting time per pound.)

4. With a cleaver, chop chicken, bones and all, in 2-inch sections; or carve Western-style, and serve.

VARIATION: After step 2, brush bird with melted chicken fat.

SIMMERED AND ROASTED CHICKEN
About 8 servings

2 *scallion stalks*	3 *to 4 cups water*
3 *or 4 slices fresh ginger root*	1 *teaspoon sugar*
1 *cup soy sauce*	1 *teaspoon salt*
½ *cup sherry*	1 *chicken (4 to 5 pounds)*

1. Cut scallion stalks in 2-inch sections. Slice ginger root. Place in a large heavy saucepan along with soy sauce, sherry, water, sugar and salt. Bring to a boil.

2. Wipe chicken with a damp cloth and add. Bring to a boil again; then cook, covered, 15 minutes over medium heat. Turn off heat, but do not remove lid. Let stand 20 minutes. Meanwhile preheat oven to 450 degrees.

3. Drain chicken, reserving liquid for master sauce (see page 739). Place bird on a rack over a drip pan containing several inches of water. Roast until well browned (about 15 minutes).

4. With a cleaver, chop bird, bones and all, in 2-inch sections. Arrange, skin-side up, on a serving platter. Serve with a pepper-salt dip (see page 708).

BONELESS ROAST CHICKEN STUFFED WITH PORK
8 to 10 servings

1 *chicken (4 to 5 pounds)*	1 *tablespoon soy sauce*
water to cover	1 *tablespoon sherry*
¾ *pound lean pork*	½ *teaspoon salt*
3 *scallion stalks*	½ *teaspoon sugar*
2 *slices fresh ginger root*	2 *to 3 tablespoons water*
1 *tablespoon cornstarch*	¼ *cup oil*
1 *tablespoon soy sauce*	

1. Wipe chicken with a damp cloth. Place in a heavy saucepan with cold water. Bring to a boil; then simmer, covered, 30 minutes.

2. Drain, reserving liquid for stock. Let bird cool slightly; then bone.

3. Mince or grind pork; mince scallions and ginger root, then combine with

cornstarch, soy sauce, sherry, salt, sugar and remaining water. Meanwhile preheat the oven to 400 degrees.

4. Stuff chicken with pork mixture; then sew up securely or skewer. Place in a roasting pan with oil and remaining soy sauce.

5. Roast chicken, basting frequently until cooked through and tender (about 30 minutes). Cut through stuffing in ½-inch slices and serve.

ROAST CHICKEN, LIQUID-FILLED
About 8 servings

1 *piece dried tangerine peel*	2 *teaspoons soy sauce*
1 *chicken (4 to 5 pounds)*	1 *teaspoon brown bean sauce*
2 *cups stock*	1 *to 2 tablespoons soy sauce*

1. Soak dried tangerine peel.

2. Wipe chicken with a damp cloth. Then dry thoroughly with paper toweling; or hang up to dry in a cool, airy place 1 to 2 hours.

3. Preheat the oven to 450 degrees. Mince soaked tangerine peel; then combine with stock, soy sauce and brown bean sauce.

4. Tie chicken's neck tightly with string to make it leakproof. Then hold bird upside-down over a bowl and pour stock mixture into body cavity. Sew up cavity securely or skewer to seal in liquid.

5. Rub bird with remaining soy sauce. Place on a rack over a drip pan containing several inches of water. Roast 10 minutes. Then reduce heat to 300 degrees and continue roasting until done (about 30 minutes more).

6. Let bird cool slightly. Place in a bowl and snip threads or unskewer, letting liquids drain into bowl. Cut bird in bite-size pieces. Strain liquids and reheat; then pour over chicken and serve. Or serve cold without sauce.

NOTE: The packaged chicken sold in supermarkets cannot be used for this dish: the head and neck must be intact.

VARIATIONS: For the brown bean sauce, substitute hoisin sauce.

In step 6, thicken the reheated sauce with a cornstarch paste.

ROAST CHICKEN STUFFED WITH CHESTNUTS
AND DRIED MUSHROOMS
About 8 servings

12 *dried black mushrooms*	½ *teaspoon salt*
½ *pound chestnuts*	*dash of pepper*
1 *chicken (4 to 5 pounds)*	1 *tablespoon sherry*
1 *onion*	1 *tablespoon soy sauce*
2 *tablespoons soy sauce*	1 *tablespoon peanut oil*
salt and pepper	

1. Soak dried mushrooms. Shell chestnuts.

2. Wipe chicken with a damp cloth. Then dry thoroughly with paper toweling; or hang up to dry in a cool, airy place 1 to 2 hours.

3. Preheat oven to 375 degrees. Mince onion, mushrooms and chestnuts; then mix well with soy sauce, salt and pepper. Stuff chicken with mixture; then sew up securely or skewer.

4. Combine sherry with remaining soy sauce and rub over bird. Rub in oil. Sprinkle lightly with remaining salt and pepper; then truss.

5. Place on a rack over a drip pan containing several inches of water. Roast 20 minutes, basting frequently with drippings.

6. Reduce heat to 325 degrees and roast 40 minutes more, basting frequently. (Replenish water in drip pan as it evaporates.)

VARIATION: For the chicken, substitute turkey.

ROAST CHICKEN STUFFED WITH FRESH MUSHROOMS
About 8 servings

1 chicken (4 to 5 pounds)	1 tablespoon sugar
salt	2 tablespoons soy sauce
¼ to ½ pound fresh mushrooms	¼ cup sherry
3 or 4 slices fresh ginger root	1 cup stock
1 bunch scallions	1 tablespoon cornstarch
2 tablespoons oil	3 tablespoons water

1. Wipe chicken with a damp cloth. Dry well. Then rub lightly with salt, inside and out. Preheat the oven to 350 degrees.

2. Slice mushrooms and ginger root. Cut scallions, stalk and leaf, in 2-inch sections.

3. Heat oil. Add ginger root; stir-fry a few times. Add scallions and mushrooms; stir-fry until softened, but not browned. Remove from pan and let cool.

4. Stuff bird with scallion-mushroom mixture. Sew up securely or skewer: then truss. Place bird in a roasting pan.

5. Combine sugar, soy sauce, sherry and stock and pour over bird. Roast, basting frequently, until done (about 1½ hours).

6. Carve chicken and arrange with stuffing on a serving platter. Keep warm.

7. In a saucepan, slowly reheat ½ cup of chicken drippings. Meanwhile blend cornstarch and cold water to a paste; then stir in to thicken. Pour sauce over chicken and serve.

CHICKEN VELVET

Chicken Velvet, known also as Chicken Essence, is an elegant and festive dish. It calls for chicken breast (skinned, boned and minced to a pulp) to be combined with egg whites and then either sauteed in oil or poached briefly in a rich concentrated stock.

The basic preparation includes the following steps:

    1. Skin and bone the chicken breast; then pound flat with a mallet or the side of a cleaver.

    2. Cut the meat in 1-inch cubes; then mince or grind in any of the following ways:

    a. Mince on a hardwood cutting board, removing tendons.

    b. Grind in a mortar and pestle. Remove tendons.

    c. Blend at low speed in a blender, turning the motor on and off. Remove and discard gristle that attaches to blades.

    d. Run twice through a hand grinder (set at the finest setting). Remove gristle.

    3. During the mincing or grinding above, add about 1 tablespoon of water, a

drop at a time, to give the mixture a paste-like consistency. (Sherry may be used in place of water.)

4. Beat the egg whites until fluffy, but not stiff and dry; then fold into chicken mixture.

CHICKEN VELVET SAUTÉED
4 to 6 servings

1 *large chicken breast*	4 *egg whites*
1 *tablespoon water*	1 *cup rich stock*
2 *tablespoons smoked ham*	1 *teaspoon sherry*
1 *teaspoon cornstarch*	¼ *teaspoon salt*
½ *teaspoon salt*	1 *tablespoon cornstarch*
1 *egg white*	3 *tablespoons stock*
¼ *cup water*	3 *tablespoons oil*

1. Skin, bone and mince (or grind) chicken breast, as in steps 1 to 3 above, gradually adding water. Mince smoked ham.

2. Place chicken mixture in a bowl. Add cornstarch, salt and unbeaten egg white. With a fork or wire whisk, gradually and very slowly add and blend in remaining water. (If it's added too quickly, the mixture won't hold together.)

3. Beat remaining egg whites until stiff, but not dry; then fold into chicken mixture.

4. Slowly heat stock, sherry and remaining salt. Meanwhile, in a cup, blend remaining cornstarch and cold stock to a paste. Then stir in to thicken. Keep warm over very low heat.

5. Heat oil in a skillet. When warm, but not hot, add chicken mixture. Heat 1 minute; then remove pan from stove and stir mixture rapidly to absorb oil.

6. Increase heat to medium; return pan to stove. Cook until mixture sets slightly—is firm, but not browned (about 20 seconds). Transfer to a serving dish.

7. Pour heated sauce over; garnish with minced ham and serve.

VARIATIONS: For the oil, substitute chicken fat.

Increase oil to ½ cup. Cook as in steps 5 and 6; then place mixture in a sieve to let excess oil drain off.

Increase oil to 1 to 2 cups and heat to 365 degrees. Drop chicken mixture in by the teaspoonful. Brown very lightly; then remove to a sieve and drain.

CHICKEN VELVET AND CORN
4 to 6 servings

1 *large chicken breast*	1 *teaspoon salt*
1 *tablespoon water*	1 *#2 can cream-style corn*
2 *tablespoons smoked ham*	2 *cups stock*
2 *egg whites*	1 *tablespoon cornstarch*
1 *tablespoon sherry*	3 *tablespoons water*

1. Skin, bone and mince (or grind) chicken breast, as in steps 1 to 3 of basic preparation (page 387), gradually adding water. Mince smoked ham.

2. Beat egg whites until stiff, but not dry; then fold into chicken mixture, along with sherry and salt.

3. With an egg beater, beat canned corn until creamy.

4. Bring stock to a boil. Add chicken mixture and corn. Slowly bring to a boil again. Meanwhile blend cornstarch and remaining cold water to a paste; then stir in to thicken.

5. Pour chicken-corn mixture into a deep serving bowl. Garnish with minced ham and serve.

DRUNKEN CHICKEN I
4 to 6 servings

1 *spring chicken*	2 *teaspoons salt*
12 *cups water*	*sherry*

1. Wipe chicken with a damp cloth and truss (see page 828).

2. Bring water to a rolling boil in a large heavy saucepan. Add salt and carefully lower in chicken. Cover pan tightly and turn off heat at once. Let stand to cool for an hour or so without removing lid.

3. Drain chicken, reserving liquid for stock. Place bird in large bowl or glass container and add sherry to cover. Seal container tightly. Place in coolest part of refrigerator; let stand 7 days.

4. Drain chicken, reserving sherry (which can be reused in cooking). Remove string. Then, with a cleaver, chop chicken, bones and all, in 2-inch sections. Serve cold.

VARIATIONS: For the sherry, substitute sauterne.

In step 2, add to boiling water 1 scallion stalk, cut in 1-inch sections; and 2 garlic cloves, crushed.

For a 3- to 4-pound chicken, simmer 30 minutes in step 2, instead of turning off the heat and letting the chicken stand. Then drain bird, let cool and dry; and refrigerate overnight. Cut chicken in half and pick up steps 3 and 4.

DRUNKEN CHICKEN II
4 to 6 servings

1 *spring chicken*	1 *scallion stalk*
1 *tablespoon sherry*	4 *teaspoons salt*
2 *slices fresh ginger root*	¾ *cup stock*

¾ *cup sherry*

1. Wipe chicken with a damp cloth. Rub sherry into chicken cavity. Slice ginger root, cut scallion stalk in two; then place inside cavity.

2. Put bird in a heatproof bowl and steam 1 hour (see page 831).

3. Drain chicken, reserving liquid for stock. Let cool; then quarter bird and sprinkle with salt. Place in a covered dish; let stand overnight at room temperature.

4. Combine stock and remaining sherry and pour over chicken. Refrigerate, covered, overnight. Then with a cleaver, chop in 1½- to 2-inch sections and serve.

DRUNKEN CHICKEN III
4 to 6 servings

2 slices fresh ginger root	1 large chicken breast
1 scallion stalk	½ teaspoon salt
2½ cups water	½ cup sherry

1. Slice ginger root. Cut scallion stalk in 2-inch sections.

2. Bring water to a boil. Add chicken breast, ginger root and scallion. Simmer, covered, 10 minutes.

3. Turn off heat but do not remove lid. Let stand 10 minutes more. Drain chicken, reserving liquid for stock.

4. Skin and bone chicken breast. Then sprinkle with salt. Place in a container and pour sherry over. Cover tightly and refrigerate overnight. Drain, cut in 1-inch cubes and serve.

JELLIED CHICKEN
About 4 servings

1 spring chicken	1 teaspoon salt
2 or 3 scallion stalks	15 to 20 peppercorns
2 or 3 slices fresh ginger root	2 cloves star anise
6 to 8 cups water	radishes, cucumbers, celery, etc.
1 tablespoon sherry	½ head lettuce
water-cress, parsley or scallions	

1. Wipe chicken with a damp cloth. Trim scallion stalks; slice ginger root.

2. Bring water to a boil in a large heavy saucepan. Add chicken, scallions, ginger root, sherry and salt. Bring to a boil again; then reduce heat and simmer, covered, 30 minutes.

3. Drain chicken and let cool, leaving liquids in pan. Disjoint legs and wings; cut breast in two. Remove skin and bones (but do not discard); then cut meat in either ½-inch cubes or ½- by 2-inch strips.

4. Return skin and bones to liquids in pan. Add peppercorns and star anise. Bring to a boil; then simmer, covered, 1 hour. Strain, discarding solids.

5. Meanwhile arrange chicken pieces in a deep bowl or mold. Surround decoratively with sliced radishes, diced cucumbers, chopped celery, or parboiled green peas. Pour strained stock over to half cover ingredients. Let set partially.

6. Add more stock to cover completely. Let cool; then refrigerate overnight.

7. Shred lettuce and arrange on a serving platter.

8. Unmold chicken by dipping bowl quickly in hot water and inverting it onto the serving platter. (Or dip a cloth in hot water, wring out, and wrap around bowl; then invert.) Garnish with water cress, parsley or minced scallions, and serve.

NOTE: This dish, usually made with spring chicken, or chicken breasts, can also be made with a bigger bird if, at the end of step 2, the bird is left in the pan to cool for 3 hours without removing the lid.

VARIATION: After step 3, heat 2½ cups of the stock. Add 1 teaspoon soy sauce, ¼ teaspoon salt and a dash of pepper. Meanwhile dissolve 1 package unflavored gelatin in ¼ cup cold water. Add to heated stock, mixing well. Pour over chicken (and vegetables, if desired) and let cool. Then refrigerate until set. (Omit steps 4, 5 and 6.)

SALT ROASTED CHICKEN I

4 to 6 servings

1 spring chicken   *3 to 5 pounds salt*

1. Wipe chicken with a damp cloth. Dry well with paper toweling; or hang up to dry in a cool, airy place 1 to 2 hours.

2. Place salt in a heavy iron pot slightly larger than the chicken. (If the pot is too much larger, the salt will shift too much.) Then heat over a medium flame, stirring frequently, until salt is very hot (about 30 minutes or more).

3. Scoop out some of the hot salt, leaving a layer of at least 2 inches in the bottom of the pan. (Transfer the scooped-out salt to another pan temporarily.) Place chicken, breast-side down, on the layer of salt; then return remaining hot salt, packing it around the bird with a spoon so that only the rump end is visible.

4. Cover pot tightly and reduce heat to very low. Let cook undisturbed 1 hour. Remove bird and brush off any salt that adheres.

5. Let cool slightly. Then with a cleaver, chop chicken, bones and all, in 2-inch sections; or carve Western-style. Serve hot or cold.

NOTE: This chicken turns out to be not salty at all but surprisingly sweet, tender and juicy. The salt itself can be reused later.

SALT ROASTED CHICKEN II
4 to 6 servings

1 *spring chicken*	1 *teaspoon Chinese parsley*
3 *to 5 pounds salt*	1 *cup water*
1 *scallion*	1 *tablespoon sherry*
2 *slices fresh ginger root*	*dash of pepper*
½ *teaspoon salt*	

1. Follow steps 1 and 2 above.

2. Mince scallion, ginger root and Chinese parsley; then combine with water, sherry, pepper and remaining salt.

3. Tie chicken's neck tightly with string to make it leakproof. Then invert bird in a bowl and pour liquid mixture into its cavity. Sew up securely or skewer.

4. Follow steps 3 and 4 above, but cook chicken only 30 to 40 minutes in hot salt.

5. Cut through strings to unskewer cavity and let liquid drain into a saucepan. Chop chicken as in recipe above. Reheat liquid and serve as a sauce with chicken.

NOTE: The packaged chicken sold in supermarkets cannot be used for this dish: the head and neck must be intact.

VARIATION: For the salt, use coarse crystal salt.

SMOKED CHICKEN
4 to 6 servings

1 *chicken* (3 *pounds*)	4 *tablespoons brown sugar*
2 *teaspoons salt*	1 *to 2 teaspoons sesame oil*

1. Wipe chicken with a damp cloth. Dry well with paper toweling; or hang up to dry in a cool, airy place 1 to 2 hours.

2. Rub bird, inside and out, with salt. Refrigerate, covered, overnight.

3. Place chicken in a heatproof bowl. Steam 45 minutes (see page 831). Drain, reserving liquid for stock.

4. Smoke chicken, breast-side up, 5 to 10 minutes, with brown sugar (see page 828).

5. Turn off heat. Let chicken stand, still sealed in, 10 minutes more; then rub skin with sesame oil. With a cleaver, chop, bones and all, in 2-inch sections. Serve hot or cold.

VARIATIONS: Cook the chicken by the white cut method. Drain and dry well with paper toweling. Rub inside and out with the salt. Then pick up step 4.

Rub the chicken inside and out with soy sauce. Place in a pan with the salt and add boiling water to cover. Simmer, covered, 40 minutes. Drain and dry well. Then pick up steps 4 and 5.

Disjoint the chicken and cut in 10 to 12 pieces. Place in a pan with 3 cups water; 3 onions, sliced; and 1 teaspoon salt. Bring to a boil; then simmer, covered, 30 minutes. Add ½ cup soy sauce, 3 tablespoons sherry and simmer, covered, 30 minutes more. Drain and dry thoroughly. Then pick up step 4, but let stand only 5 minutes in step 5.

STIR-FRIED CHICKEN LIVERS WITH BAMBOO SHOOTS
About 4 servings

½ pound chicken livers	2 to 3 tablespoons oil
2 tablespoons sherry	1 tablespoon soy sauce
¼ cup bamboo shoots	1 tablespoon sherry
¼ cup water chestnuts	¼ cup stock
1 scallion stalk	½ teaspoon salt

½ teaspoon sugar

1. Cut chicken livers in ½-inch slices. Add sherry, toss gently, and let stand 5 minutes.

2. Meanwhile slice bamboo shoots thin, then in ½-inch strips. Slice water chestnuts. Mince scallion.

3. Heat oil. Add livers and stir-fry until they change color (about 1 minute).

4. Add soy sauce and remaining sherry, stirring to blend in (about ½ minute).

5. Add bamboo shoots and water chestnuts; stir-fry a few times. Then add stock and salt and stir-fry to heat through.

6. Add sugar and scallion; stir-fry ½ minute more. Serve at once.

VARIATION: For the bamboo shoots and water chestnuts, substitute any of the following: blanched bean sprouts; celery, cut in ½-inch sections; broccoli or cauliflower (broken into flowerets), parboiled.

STIR-FRIED CHICKEN LIVERS WITH SNOW PEAS
About 4 servings

½ pound chicken livers	*1 to 2 slices fresh ginger root*
1 teaspoon cornstarch	*2 teaspoons cornstarch*
1 teaspoon sherry	*¼ cup water*
1 tablespoon soy sauce	*2 tablespoons oil*
¼ pound snow peas	*½ teaspoon salt*
2 tablespoons oil	

1. Cut chicken livers in ½-inch slices. Combine cornstarch, sherry and soy sauce. Add to livers and toss gently. Let stand 15 minutes, turning occasionally.

2. Stem and string snow peas. Mince ginger root. Blend remaining cornstarch and cold water to a paste.

3. Heat oil. Add salt, then ginger; stir-fry a few times. Add snow peas and stir-

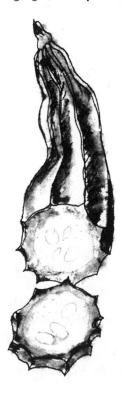

fry over medium heat to soften slightly (high heat will scorch them). Remove snow peas from pan.

4. Heat remaining oil. Add chicken livers and stir-fry over high heat until nearly cooked through (2 to 3 minutes).

5. Stir in cornstarch paste to thicken. Return snow peas only to heat through. Serve at once.

VARIATION: In step 4, add to the hot oil, 1 garlic clove, crushed; stir-fry a few times. Add chicken livers and stir-fry 1 minute. Add ½ cup water chestnuts, sliced; and 2 tablespoons cloud ear mushrooms (soaked), sliced. Continue with steps 4 and 5.

STIR-FRIED CHICKEN LIVERS WITH OYSTER SAUCE
About 4 servings

½ pound chicken livers	½ cup stock
¼ pound fresh mushrooms	½ teaspoon sugar
1 onion	1 tablespoon cornstarch
2 tablespoons oyster sauce	3 tablespoons water
1 tablespoon soy sauce	2 tablespoons oil
1 tablespoon sherry	2 tablespoons oil

1. Cut chicken livers in two. Slice fresh mushrooms and onion thin.

2. In a small bowl, combine oyster sauce, soy sauce, sherry, stock and sugar. In a cup, blend cornstarch and cold water to a paste.

3. Heat oil until smoking. Add chicken livers and stir-fry until their color begins to change (2 to 3 minutes). Remove livers from pan.

4. Heat remaining oil. Add sliced mushrooms and onion; stir-fry until softened but not browned.

5. Return chicken livers and stir-fry a few times to reheat. Stir in oyster sauce mixture and cook, covered, 2 to 3 minutes over medium heat.

6. Stir in cornstarch paste to thicken. Serve at once.

STIR-FRIED CHICKEN LIVERS AND GIZZARDS WITH MUSHROOMS
About 4 servings

¼ pound chicken livers	½ pound fresh mushrooms
¼ pound chicken gizzards	½ cup bamboo shoots
2 teaspoons cornstarch	1 onion
1 tablespoon soy sauce	2 tablespoons oil
1 tablespoon sherry	½ teaspoon salt
2 tablespoons oil	

1. Cut chicken livers in quarters. Remove fat and outer membrane of gizzards. Then score with a number of parallel slashes (to speed up cooking), and also cut in quarters.

2. Combine cornstarch, soy sauce and sherry. Add to livers and gizzards and toss gently. Let stand 15 minutes, turning occasionally.

3. Sliver fresh mushrooms, bamboo shoots and onion.

4. Heat oil. Add salt, then onion; stir-fry a few times. Add mushrooms and bamboo shoots and stir-fry until nearly cooked through (2 to 3 minutes). Remove vegetables from pan.

5. Heat remaining oil. Add livers and gizzards and stir-fry until just about done (2 to 3 minutes). Return vegetables, stir-frying only to reheat. Serve at once.

STIR-FRIED SWEET-AND-PUNGENT CHICKEN LIVERS I
About 4 servings

sweet-and-pungent sauce	*½ garlic clove*
½ pound chicken livers	*1 or 2 slices fresh ginger root*
4 cups water	*2 tablespoons oil*
	½ teaspoon salt

1. Prepare a sweet-and-pungent sauce (see pages 735–738). Keep warm.

2. Cut chicken livers in two. Boil water and pour over livers to blanch. Stir once or twice, then drain. Rinse quickly in cold water and drain again. Mince garlic and ginger root.

3. Heat oil. Add salt, then garlic and ginger; stir-fry a few times. Add chicken livers and stir-fry 2 minutes.

4. Pour sweet-and-pungent sauce over chicken livers and stir in well. Cook slowly, 2 to 3 minutes more. Serve at once.

STIR-FRIED SWEET-AND-PUNGENT CHICKEN LIVERS II
About 4 servings

½ pound chicken livers	*3 tablespoons sugar*
1 cucumber	*1 tablespoon soy sauce*
1 carrot	*½ cup vinegar*
2 celery stalks	*¼ cup water*
1 garlic clove	*2 to 3 tablespoons oil*
2 slices fresh ginger root	*½ teaspoon salt*
1 tablespoon cornstarch	*dash of pepper*

1. Cut and blanch chicken livers as above.

2. Peel cucumber and cut in half lengthwise; then seed and slice crosswise in

½-inch sections. Slice carrot and celery in similar ½-inch sections. Crush garlic; slice ginger root.

3. Combine cornstarch, sugar, soy sauce, vinegar and water.

4. Heat oil. Brown garlic and ginger root lightly. Add chicken livers and stir-fry gently to coat with oil.

5. Stir in vegetables, salt, pepper and cornstarch mixture. Simmer, covered, until done (3 to 5 minutes).

VARIATION: In step 2, sprinkle the cucumber, carrot and celery with ½ teaspoon salt and let stand 10 minutes. Or marinate these vegetables in a mixture of 2 tablespoons sugar, 2 tablespoons water and ½ cup vinegar. Drain, reserving this marinade, and add 1 tablespoon cornstarch, 1 tablespoon sugar and 1 teaspoon soy sauce. Substitute this for the mixture in step 3.

STIR-FRIED CHICKEN LIVERS WITH PINEAPPLE
About 4 servings

½ pound chicken livers	2 to 3 tablespoons oil
1 tablespoon cornstarch	½ teaspoon salt
1 tablespoon sugar	dash of pepper
1 tablespoon vinegar	1 cup pineapple chunks
2 tablespoons soy sauce	¼ cup stock

1. Cut and blanch chicken livers as in Stir-Fried Sweet-and-Pungent Chicken Livers I.

2. Blend cornstarch, sugar, vinegar and soy sauce to a paste.

3. Heat oil. Add chicken livers and stir-fry gently to coat with oil. Sprinkle with salt and pepper.

4. Add pineapple chunks and stock and heat quickly. Then simmer, covered, 3 minutes.

5. Stir in cornstarch paste to thicken. Serve at once.

DEEP-FRIED CHICKEN LIVERS
6 to 8 servings

1 pound chicken livers	oil for deep-frying
cornstarch	salt and pepper

1. Cut each chicken liver in 2 or 3 pieces. Dredge lightly in cornstarch.

2. Heat oil. Add livers, about half a cup at a time, and deep-fry until golden. Drain on paper toweling.

3. Serve hot, sprinkled with salt and pepper (or with a pepper-salt mix—see page 708), and with a side dip of hot mustard or lemon juice.

NOTE: Chicken livers can be cut in smaller pieces, deep-fried as above, and then served, speared on toothpicks, as hors d'oeuvres.

VARIATION: Instead of dredging livers in cornstarch, toss gently in a mixture of 1 egg white, 1 tablespoon cornstarch, 1 teaspoon sherry and ½ teaspoon soy sauce.

MARINATED AND DEEP-FRIED CHICKEN LIVERS
6 to 8 servings

1 *pound chicken livers*	½ *teaspoon sugar*
2 *tablespoons soy sauce*	½ *cup flour*
1 *tablespoon sherry*	¼ *cup water*
½ *teaspoon salt*	*oil for deep-frying*

1. Cut each chicken liver in 2 or 3 pieces.

2. Combine soy sauce, sherry, salt and sugar. Add to livers and toss gently. Let stand 15 minutes, turning occasionally. Drain, discarding marinade.

3. In a bowl, blend flour and water to a paste. Add livers and toss gently to coat.

4. Deep-fry as in step 2, above, and serve as in step 3.

VARIATION: In step 2, add to the marinade 1 or 2 slices fresh ginger root, minced; and 1 clove garlic minced. For the white sugar, substitute 2 teaspoons brown sugar.

SIMMERED AND DEEP-FRIED CHICKEN LIVERS
6 to 8 servings

1 *pound chicken livers*	½ *teaspoon cinnamon*
2 *cups water*	2 *tablespoons almond meats*
½ *cup soy sauce*	2 *whole scallions*
1 *tablespoon brown sugar*	*oil for deep-frying*

flour

1. Place chicken livers in a saucepan, along with water, soy sauce, sugar and cinnamon. Bring to a boil; then simmer, covered, 15 minutes. Drain, discarding liquid, and let cool.

2. Meanwhile mince almond meats and scallions.

3. Heat oil. Dredge livers with flour; then add, half a cup at a time, and deep-fry until golden. Drain on paper toweling.

4. Serve hot, sprinkled with minced almonds and scallions.

VARIATIONS: For the sugar and cinnamon, substitute ½ teaspoon salt and 2 or 3 cloves star anise.

In step 3, omit the flour. Cut each chicken liver in 5 pieces and wrap each, along with a whole water chestnut, in half a strip of bacon. Deep-fry until bacon is crisp. (Omit almond and scallion garnish.)

DEEP-FRIED CHICKEN GIZZARDS
6 to 8 servings

1 *pound chicken gizzards*	½ *teaspoon salt*
1 *tablespoon cornstarch*	*oil for deep-frying*
2 *tablespoons soy sauce*	*pepper*

1. Remove fat and outer membrane of gizzards. Make a few parallel slashes in each; then cut in thirds.

2. Combine cornstarch, soy sauce and salt. Add to gizzard sections and toss gently to coat.

3. Heat oil. Add gizzards, about half a cup at a time, and deep-fry until golden. Drain on paper toweling. Serve hot, sprinkled with pepper.

VARIATION: After step 1, marinate the gizzards 20 to 30 minutes in a mixture of 1 tablespoon sherry, ½ teaspoon sugar, plus the soy sauce and salt. Then drain, discarding marinade. Omit step 2. Before deep-frying, dredge gizzards lightly in cornstarch.

BRAISED CHICKEN GIZZARDS
About 4 servings

½ *pound chicken gizzards*	2 *tablespoons oil*
6 *water chestnuts*	4 *tablespoons soy sauce*
½ *cup bamboo shoots*	1 *tablespoon sherry*
1 *onion*	½ *teaspoon salt*
2 *or* 3 *slices fresh ginger root*	1½ *cups water*

1. Remove fat and outer membrane of gizzards; cut each in 6 slices. Slice water chestnuts, bamboo shoots and onion. Mince ginger root.

2. Heat oil. Add onions and ginger; stir-fry a few times. Add gizzards and stir-fry 1 to 2 minutes. Stir in soy sauce, sherry and salt.

3. Add water chestnuts, bamboo shoots and water. Heat quickly; then simmer, covered, until tender (20 to 30 minutes).

SIMMERED CHICKEN LIVERS
4 to 6 servings

4 *cups water*	½ *cup water*
1 *pound chicken livers*	1 *scallion stalk*
½ *cup soy sauce*	2 *or* 3 *slices fresh ginger root*
¼ *cup sherry*	2 *cloves star anise*
1 *tablespoon sugar*	¼ *teaspoon peppercorns*

1. Boil water and pour over chicken livers. Stir a few times, then drain. Rinse quickly with cold water and drain again.

2. In a saucepan, combine soy sauce, sherry, sugar and remaining water; bring slowly to a boil.

3. Meanwhile cut scallion in ½-inch sections; shred ginger root. Then **add to** pan along with livers, star anise and peppercorns. Heat quickly; then simmer, covered, 10 minutes.

4. Turn off heat. Let stand 5 minutes more, without removing lid. Drain, discarding sauce.

5. Refrigerate livers to chill. Cut in bite-size pieces and serve.

NOTE: When preparing this dish a day or two ahead, refrigerate the livers in sauce until ready to serve.

VARIATIONS: For the peppercorns, substitute ¼ teaspoon crushed red peppers.

Omit step 1. Combine steps 2 and 3, adding all the ingredients to saucepan, except the water. Bring to a boil, gently stirring. Then add the water and bring to a boil again. Pick up steps 4 and 5.

CHICKEN LIVERS SIMMERED IN OYSTER SAUCE
4 to 6 servings

1 *pound chicken livers*	2 *tablespoons oyster sauce*
4 *cups water*	2 *tablespoons soy sauce*
1 *or* 2 *scallion stalks*	1 *teaspoon sugar*
2 *tablespoons smoked ham*	½ *teaspoon salt*
1 *cup stock*	2 *teaspoons cornstarch*

2 *tablespoons water*

1. Blanch chicken livers as in step 1 above; then cut in ½-inch slices. Separately mince scallion stalks and smoked ham.

2. Heat stock. Add oyster sauce, soy sauce, sugar, salt and scallions. Bring to a boil.

3. Add chicken livers. Reduce heat to medium and cook, covered, until done (about 3 minutes).

4. Meanwhile blend cornstarch and cold water to a paste; then stir in to thicken. Garnish with minced ham and serve.

SIMMERED CHICKEN GIBLETS AND BEAN CURD
About 4 servings

1 cup chicken giblets	½ teaspoon salt
water to cover	dash of pepper
4 cakes bean curd	2 teaspoons cornstarch
2 cups stock	3 tablespoons water

1. Place chicken giblets in a saucepan with cold water. Bring to a boil; then simmer, covered, 30 minutes. Drain, discarding liquid. Dice giblets and bean curd.

2. Rinse out saucepan. Add stock and bring slowly to a boil. Add giblets and bean curd along with salt and pepper. Cook only to heat through.

3. Blend cornstarch and cold water to a paste. Then stir in to thicken and serve.

DEEP-FRIED SQUAB
4 to 6 servings

3 squabs	oil for deep-frying
¼ cup soy sauce	½ head lettuce
2 tablespoons sherry	lemon wedges

salt

1. With a cleaver, chop each squab in quarters. Place in a bowl.

2. Combine soy sauce and sherry, then rub into skin. Let stand 30 minutes, turning occasionally. Drain, discarding marinade.

3. Heat oil. Add squabs, a few pieces at a time, and deep-fry 1 minute. Drain on paper toweling. Let cool slightly.

4. Reheat oil and return squab sections. Deep-fry, turning frequently, until crisp and golden. Drain again on paper toweling.

5. Cut lettuce in strips and arrange on a serving platter. Arrange squab over lettuce. Serve with lemon wedges and salt.

NOTE: The diner squeezes lemon juice over the squab, then dips each section in salt before eating.

VARIATIONS: In step 2, add to the soy-sherry mixture 2 slices fresh ginger root, minced.

In step 2, rub the squabs with soy sauce only; then deep-fry. After step 4, heat in a saucepan 1 tablespoon sugar, 2 tablespoons sherry, 2 teaspoons soy sauce, the juice of ½ lemon, and a few drops of sesame oil. When this mixture comes to a boil, add deep-fried squab sections and simmer, uncovered, 2 to 3 minutes. Garnish with lemon slices and serve.

Omit steps 1 and 2. With a cleaver, chop the squabs, bones and all, in 1½-inch squares. Then coat with a batter of ½ cup water-chestnut flour; 1 egg, beaten; ½ garlic clove and ½ scallion stalk, both minced; ½ teaspoon salt, 2 teaspoons soy sauce and a dash of pepper. Deep-fry as in steps 3 and 4.

STEAMED DEEP-FRIED SQUAB
About 4 servings

1 *piece dried tangerine peel*	¼ *teaspoon powdered star anise*
1 *garlic clove*	2 *squabs*
2 *slices fresh ginger root*	*soy sauce*
2 *scallion stalks*	*oil for deep-frying*
½ *teaspoon salt*	*cornstarch*
½ *teaspoon cinnamon*	*lemon wedges*

1. Soak dried tangerine peel.

2. Mince garlic, ginger root, scallions and soaked tangerine peel; then combine with salt, cinnamon and star anise, mixing well.

3. Wipe squabs with a damp cloth. Coat with mixture. Then place in a heatproof bowl.

4. Steam 45 minutes (see page 831). Remove squabs. Rinse off seasonings under cold running water. Dry well with paper toweling.

5. Rub skin lightly with soy sauce; return to heatproof bowl and steam 10 minutes more. Remove and let cool. Refrigerate, covered, overnight.

6. Heat oil. Dredge squabs lightly in cornstarch; then add, one at a time, and deep-fry, turning and basting, until golden. Drain on paper toweling.

7. With a cleaver, chop each in quarters; garnish with lemon wedges and serve.

NOTE: Use about 6 inches of oil to cover the squabs completely when deep-frying.

RED-COOKED DEEP-FRIED SQUAB

About 4 servings

1 *piece dried tangerine peel*   *4 to 5 cups water*
2 *slices fresh ginger root*   *1-inch piece cinnamon stick*
¼ *cup sugar*   *2 or 3 cloves star anise*
1 *cup soy sauce*   *2 squabs*

oil for deep-frying

1. Soak dried tangerine peel.

2. Slice ginger root. Then place in a heavy pan, along with sugar, soy sauce, water, cinnamon, star anise and soaked tangerine peel. Bring to a boil.

3. Wipe squabs with a damp cloth. Add to pan and bring to a boil again. Then simmer, covered, 30 minutes, turning frequently for even coloring. Drain well and let cool. Dry with paper toweling.

4. Heat oil. Add squabs one at a time and deep-fry until crisp and golden. Drain on paper toweling.

5. With a cleaver, chop birds, bones and all, in bite-size pieces. Serve with a pepper-salt mix (see page 708).

NOTE: See Note above on deep-frying squabs.

DEEP-FRIED STEAMED AROMATIC SQUAB
4 to 6 servings

1 *stick dried bean curd*	2 *cloves star anise*
2 *or 3 squabs*	1-*inch piece cinnamon stick*
oil for deep-frying	¼ *cup bamboo shoots*
2 *slices fresh ginger root*	2 *scallion stalks*
1 *scallion stalk*	1 *tablespoon cornstarch*
2 *tablespoons soy sauce*	¼ *cup stock*
2 *tablespoons sherry*	2 *tablespoons oil*

½ teaspoon salt

1. Soak dried bean curd.
2. Wipe squabs with a damp cloth and dry well with paper toweling.
3. Heat oil. Add squabs, one at a time, and deep-fry, turning and basting, until light golden. Drain on paper toweling.
4. With a cleaver, chop squabs, bones and all, in 1- by 2-inch pieces. Transfer to a heatproof bowl. Slice ginger root, mince scallion; and add, along with soy sauce, sherry, star anise and cinnamon stick.
5. Steam 30 minutes (see page 831).
6. Meanwhile slice bamboo shoots and soaked bean curd. Cut remaining scallion stalks in 1-inch sections. Blend cornstarch and cold stock to a paste.
7. Heat oil. Add bamboo shoots, bean curd and scallions. Stir-fry to cook through (3 to 4 minutes).
8. Stir in salt. Then stir in cornstarch paste to thicken. Pour over squabs in their steaming bowl and serve.

STEAMED SQUABS STUFFED WITH BIRD'S NEST
About 4 servings

1 *ounce bird's nest*	½ *to 1 teaspoon salt*
2 *squabs*	3 *cups stock*

2 *tablespoons smoked ham*

1. Soak bird's nest.
2. Bone squabs, leaving their shape and skin intact (see page 824). Rub birds, inside and out, with salt.
3. Stuff squabs with soaked bird's nest and sew up securely or skewer. Place in a heatproof bowl; pour stock over.
4. Steam over low heat until squabs are tender (about 2 hours). See page 831.
5. Mince smoked ham; sprinkle over the top. Serve squabs in their steaming bowl with stock.

VARIATIONS: For the whole bird's nest, substitute ½ cup dried bird's-nest chips. Instead of boning squabs, score them along the backbone, but do not cut through bone. Steam birds cut-side up. Serve cut-side down.

ROAST TURKEY
About 20 servings

6 *slices fresh ginger root*	2 *tablespoons sugar*
4 *scallion stalks*	1½ *teaspoons salt*
3 *cups soy sauce*	½ *teaspoon pepper*
1 *cup sherry*	1 *turkey* (10 *pounds*)
10 *cups water*	1 *tablespoon sesame oil*

1 *head lettuce*

1. Slice ginger root and trim scallion stalks; combine in a large, heavy saucepan with soy sauce, sherry, water, sugar, salt and pepper. Bring to a boil.

2. Wipe turkey with a damp cloth and lower into pan. Bring to a boil again; then simmer, covered, 45 minutes, turning once or twice for even coloring. Meanwhile heat the oven to 350 degrees.

3. Transfer bird and some of its stock to a roasting pan. Roast 1 hour, basting with stock at 10-minute intervals.

4. Sprinkle bird with sesame oil. Turn oven up to 450 degrees. Let bird brown thoroughly (10 to 15 minutes more); then remove and let cool slightly.

5. Shred lettuce and arrange on a serving platter. With a cleaver, chop turkey, bones and all, in bite-size pieces. Arrange over lettuce and serve.

NOTE: The breast may be eaten hot at one meal, and the remainder of the bird, cold, at another. To serve the breast, remove it whole, then slice against the grain in 1- by 2-inch strips.

❋ *Fish* ❋

THE CHINESE like their fish as fresh as possible. They prefer the fresh-water varieties, which can be kept alive in tubs until the last moment, to the salt-water varieties, which cannot. The latter are also second choice because they're considered "salted" from birth and therefore less "fresh."

The Chinese custom is to serve the fish whole. A fish without head or tail is considered incomplete and unaesthetic. The reasons for serving fish whole, however, are not aesthetic only: the meat in the fish's cheek is tender and much prized; and the juices of the fish are better retained when the body is kept intact. (Even when head and tail must be removed, as with fillets, fish steaks and fishballs, these parts are not discarded but simmered separately to make stock.) Although the head, fins and tail are retained, the fish itself is always thoroughly cleaned and scaled (except for shad, whose scales are left on to protect it from drying out).

The Chinese cook fish in a wide variety of ways: steaming, clear-simmering (or poaching), deep-frying, pan-frying and stir-frying. Whatever the cooking method, fish cooked and seasoned the Chinese way is never oily, but fresh and light in taste, flaky in texture and invariably moist and tender.

The most typical cooking techniques are steaming and clear-simmering. Steaming, generally used with smaller fish (1½ to 2 pounds), permits the fish to cook in its own juices, keeps its skin and flesh moist, and produces a quantity of gravy. Steamed fish is cooked either whole or in steaks or slices. It is placed in the steamer when the boiling water is at its maximum heat and removed when about 90 percent cooked. (Since the fish is served in its hot steaming platter, it cooks until done right at the table.) As a rule, the Chinese undercook fish because overcooking coarsens its texture and makes the fish dry and tasteless. Clear-simmering is generally used with larger fish (which won't fit into a steamer), and calls for the fish to be poached or cooked directly in boiling water. Just before a steamed or clear-simmered fish is served, several tablespoons of peanut oil can be heated to smoking and poured over it. This technique, known as "flavor-smoothing," forces the seasonings into the fish and completes the cooking process.

Deep-frying is another frequently used method. Fish can be deep-fried either whole or in steaks, strips or rolls. The fish used whole for deep-frying are usually no larger than 2 to 3 pounds, since bigger ones are too hard to handle in boiling oil. (Small fish such as sprats, however, can be deep-fried 5 or 6 at a time. Flat fish, which would dry out too quickly, are never deep-fried whole.) In deep-frying, the fish is coated with flour or a batter, then cooked in a large quantity of hot oil. Fish may be partially deep-fried in advance, then refried just before it is served. This double-frying not only permits preparation long before the meal, but makes for a crisper fish as well.

Braising and pan-frying are used for the whole fish or fish steaks. Since both methods call for small quantities of oil, there's always the possibility that the fish will stick to the pan and lose some of its skin. To prevent this, the fish is dried completely with paper toweling, rubbed lightly with cornstarch or flour, and then browned quickly in smoking hot oil. Another solution to the "sticking" problem is to hold the fish by the head over the pan, baste it with boiling oil until its skin is well browned, and then lower it gently into the pan to complete the cooking.

COOKING METHODS AND SUITABLE FISH

STEAMING: black bass, bluefish, butterfish, carp, catfish, flounder, halibut, mackerel, mullet, perch, pike, porgy, salmon, sand dab, sea bass, shad, red snapper, sole trout and whitefish.

CLEAR-SIMMERING: black bass, bluefish, mullet, pike, sea bass, shad and whitefish

DEEP-FRYING: *Whole fish*—black bass, bluefish, bream, buffalo carp, bullhead,

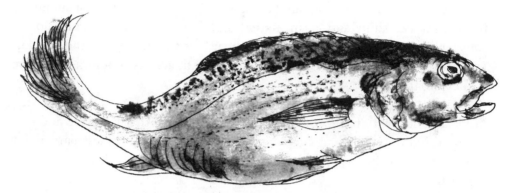

butterfish, carp, cod, halibut, haddock, mackerel, mullet, perch, porgy, red snapper, rock salmon, sea bass, small herring, smelts, sprats, sturgeon, trout, whitefish and yellow pike

  Fish steaks—black bass, carp, halibut, rock cod and yellow pike

  Strips—flounder, haddock and sole

 BRAISING: black bass, carp, perch, porgy, rock cod, salmon, scup, sea bass, swordfish, trout and tuna

  PAN-FRYING: black bass, bluefish, flounder, porgy, rock cod and sole

  STIR-FRYING: *Fish steaks or slices*—black bass, pike, rock cod and sea bass

  Strips—flounder, haddock and sole

  MINCING OR GRINDING: *Fishballs and fishcakes*—black bass, carp, cod, flounder, haddock, halibut, pike, sole, whiting and whitefish

  NOTE: This is a list of possibilities; it does not pretend to be complete.

Seasonings for Fish: Characteristic Chinese fish seasonings include ginger root, garlic, scallions, soy sauce, oil and wine. These are sometimes referred to as "defishers" since they enhance those fish flavors which are agreeable, while subtly counteracting those which are not. Other frequently used seasonings are the pungent fermented black beans and the delicate dried lily buds. A wide variety of vegetables are also fine complements for fish. Among these are: asparagus, bamboo shoots, bean curd, bean sprouts, bitter melon, broccoli, carrots, Chinese cabbage, Chinese lettuce, Chinese white turnip, eggplant, mushrooms and preserved mustard cabbage.

Leftover Fish: Fish toughens when reheated and therefore is better eaten cold. Leftover fish cakes and fishballs, however, can be used in hot vegetable dishes, provided the vegetables are stir-fried first and the fish added at the very end only to be heated through.

How to Buy Fish: Select a fish with bright, clear (never dull) eyes, bright red (never brownish) gill flaps and an open, gaping mouth. Its odor should be fresh, its scales shiny and clean, its tail and fins firm, and its skin smooth, translucent and moist. When you poke the fish, it should be firm and resilient (not soft) to the touch. The impression of your fingertips should not remain. If they do, the fish is not fresh.

How to Store Fish: Rinse the fish under the cold-water tap. Pat dry, inside and out, with paper toweling. Sprinkle lightly with salt, inside and out. Wrap in foil or transparent wrap and place the fish in the coldest part of the refrigerator (but not the freezer). Use the same day, if possible, or the next day at the latest.

How to Score Fish: (Scoring or slashing the fish permits a better penetration of heat and seasonings and enables the fish to cook evenly.) Make 3 or 4 parallel diagonal slashes, slanting from backbone to tail, on each side of the fish. These should be about 1 to 1½ inches apart and about 1 inch deep. They should cut down to the bone, but not through it, so that the flesh will still adhere to the bone. The slashes should not be made too close to the tail since this could weaken the tail and make it fall off.

How to Bone Fish: Make a horizontal gash just below the gill on one side of the fish, being careful not to cut through bone. Then grasp the fish by the tail and, holding a sharp knife parallel to its backbone, cut the flesh away from the backbone, working from the tail toward the head. Remove the meat in one piece as a single fillet. Repeat this process with the other half. (Discard head and bones or use them for stock.) To remove the skin, place fillet skin-side down and cut the meat away in one slice.

How to Mince Fish: Cut each fillet lengthwise in half. Coarsely chop, then mince fine. (Sprinkle fish with a pinch or two of cornstarch to prevent it from adhering to the knife blade.)

How to Test Fish for Doneness: Test smaller fish with a fork. The flesh should flake off easily; the eyes should pop and look chalky white. To test larger fish, make a cut to the bone in the thickest part, close to the head, with a small sharp knife. If meat is white and opaque, the fish is done; if it's still pink and translucent, cook a few minutes longer.

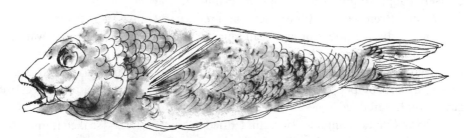

BASIC STEAMED FISH

Allow about ½ pound for each serving

1. Have fish cleaned and scaled, but left whole. Rinse in cold water. Dry well with paper toweling; then rub lightly with salt, inside and out. Place in a shallow heatproof dish. (If fish is too large, cut it in two.)

2. Prepare any of the topping mixtures below and spread over fish.

3. Steam until done (see pages 33 and 831). (Allow about 30 minutes for a 2½-pound fish; 20 minutes for a 1½-pound fish; 15 minutes for a ¾-inch thick fish steak; and 7 to 10 minutes for a thinly sliced or flat fish.)

4. Garnish fish with shredded scallions and Chinese parsley. Serve immediately.

VARIATIONS: In step 3, during the last 10 minutes of steaming, top whole fish with several clams in their shells (scrub them clean first). The shells will open when steamed.

In step 3, steam 2 cakes of bean curd, sliced or cubed, with the fish.

Steam the fish, topped only with ½ teaspoon salt, 2 slices fresh ginger root and 1 scallion, both shredded. Then heat ¼ cup peanut oil to smoking and pour over fish. Sprinkle immediately with 3 tablespoons soy sauce and serve at once, garnished with shredded scallion.

Steam the fish, topped with a mixture of 2 tablespoons sherry, ½ teaspoon salt and 1 teaspoon ginger juice. Then serve with a Five Willow or sweet-and-pungent sauce poured over (see pages 733–738).

TOPPING MIXTURES FOR STEAMED FISH

Basic: Combine 1 tablespoon sherry; 2 tablespoons soy sauce; ½ teaspoon sugar; ½ teaspoon salt; 1 teaspoon peanut oil; 2 slices fresh ginger root, shredded; and 1 to 2 scallions, cut in ½-inch sections.

Black Bean Sauce I: Omit sherry in basic mixture and add 1 tablespoon fermented black beans (soaked), mashed with 1 garlic clove, minced.

Black Bean Sauce II: Omit sherry and salt in basic mixture, and add 1 tablespoon fermented black beans (soaked); ½ bundle preserved turnip, washed and coarsely chopped; and a few drops of sesame oil.

Brown Bean Sauce I: Omit sherry and reduce soy sauce to 2 teaspoons in basic mixture. Add 2 teaspoons brown bean sauce, mashed; and 4 tablespoons water.

Brown Bean Sauce II: Combine 2 teaspoons brown bean sauce, mashed to a paste, with ¼ cup stock; ½ teaspoon sugar; 1 teaspoon soy sauce (dark); 2 teaspoons sherry; a dash of pepper; 1 tablespoon oil; 1 scallion, minced; and 2 slices fresh ginger root, shredded.

Dried Olives: combine ⅛ pound dried Chinese olives (soaked), minced; 1 garlic clove, minced; and 1 slice fresh ginger root, minced; 2 tablespoons oil; ½ teaspoon salt.

Ham: Omit sherry in basic mixture and add ⅛ pound smoked ham, shredded; and 1 teaspoon vinegar.

Lily Buds I: Omit scallions in basic mixture and add 12 lily buds (soaked), cut in two; and 2 teaspoons vinegar. Blend to a paste 1 teaspoon cornstarch, ½ teaspoon salt, 1 teaspoon soy sauce and 2 tablespoons cold water; spread over fish. Top with 10 lily buds (soaked), cut in two; 4 dried black mushrooms (soaked), sliced; and 2 tablespoons preserved parsnips (soaked), slivered.

Lily Buds II: Combine 1 teaspoon cornstarch, ¼ teaspoon salt, ½ teaspoon sugar, dash of pepper, 1 tablespoon soy sauce, and 1 tablespoon oil; rub over fish. Repeat these ingredients. Combine in a bowl, adding 12 lily buds (soaked), cut in two; 2 dried black mushrooms (soaked), slivered; 2 Chinese red dates (soaked), pitted and slivered; 2 slices fresh ginger root, shredded; and 1 thin slice smoked ham, slivered. Mix well and spread over fish.

Mushrooms I: Omit scallion in basic mixture and add ⅛ pound fresh mushrooms, and 1 small onion, both sliced.

Mushrooms II: Add to basic mixture 2 or 3 dried black mushrooms (soaked), sliced; and 2 teaspoons vinegar.

Mushrooms III: Omit sherry and salt in basic mixture and add 5 dried black mushrooms (soaked), shredded; and ½ bundle preserved turnip, washed and shredded.

Shrimp Sauce: Omit sherry, soy sauce and sugar in basic mixture and add 1 tablespoon shrimp sauce.

Tea Melon: Add to basic mixture 2 tablespoons tea melon, slivered (½ cup bamboo shoots, sliced, may also be added).

NOTE: The various mixtures above may be added in two ways—the liquid seasonings sprinkled over first, then the minced or shredded ingredients arranged on top; or all the ingredients combined and spread over the fish. Before these mixtures are added, the fish may be scored with parallel diagonal slashes, then rubbed, inside and out, with oil to coat.

STEAMED FISH WITH SUBGUM GINGER
3 to 4 servings

1 *fish* (1½ *pounds*)	1 *tablespoon smoked ham*
½ *teaspoon salt*	2 *scallion stalks*
2 *tablespoons soy sauce*	1 *garlic clove*
4 *tablespoons subgum ginger*	2 *or* 3 *tablespoons peanut oil*

1. Have fish cleaned and scaled but left whole. Wash and dry. Steam as in Basic Steamed Fish (but without any topping). Drain well and sprinkle with salt and soy sauce.

2. Meanwhile mince subgum ginger and smoked ham; split scallion stalks lengthwise in 4 or 5 long strips and then cut crosswise in 2-inch sections. Sprinkle ingredients over fish.

3. Crush garlic and place in a pan with oil. Heat until oil begins to smoke.

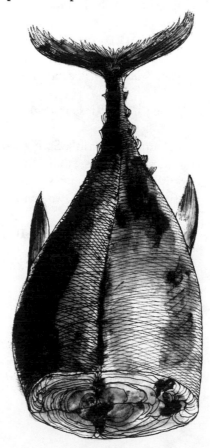

Remove from heat and let stand 1 minute. Discard garlic and pour oil over fish. Serve at once.

VARIATION: In step 3, add a few drops of sesame oil to the peanut oil before heating.

STEAMED WHITEFISH STEAK
3 to 4 servings

1 white fish steak (1½ pounds)	1 teaspoon preserved lemon peel
½ cup fresh mushrooms	2 tablespoons soy sauce
½ cup smoked ham	2 tablespoons oil
2 to 3 slices fresh ginger root	½ teaspoon salt

1. Score skin of fish crosswise with several slashes. Place fish in a heatproof dish.

2. Slice mushrooms, ham, ginger root and preserved lemon peel, then combine with soy sauce, oil and salt. Pour mixture over fish. Refrigerate, covered, 30 minutes.

3. Steam until done, about 20 minutes (see pages 33 and 831). Serve at once.

VARIATION: For the oil, substitute chicken fat.

STEAMED DRIED FISH

dried fish	2 slices fresh ginger root
2 tablespoons peanut oil	

1. Cut dried fish in ¾-inch strips. Rinse in cold water; then place in a shallow heatproof dish.

2. Shred ginger root and arrange over fish. Sprinkle with oil.

3. Steam 15 to 20 minutes (see pages 33 and 831).

NOTE: This pungent dish is essentially a flavoring for rice and should be eaten accordingly, in small quantities. Allow about two ¾-inch strips per person.

CLEAR-SIMMERED FISH I
4 to 5 servings

1 fish (2 to 2½ pounds)	1 tablespoon salt
2 quarts water	1 tablespoon sherry
2 or 3 slices fresh ginger root	2 tablespoons oil

1. Have fish cleaned and scaled, but left whole. Rinse in cold water and score on both sides.

2. Bring water to a vigorous boil in a large pan. Crush ginger root and add to

water along with salt, sherry and oil.

3. Gently lower fish into pan. Cover tightly at once and turn off heat. Let stand 30 minutes without removing lid. (The steam will cook the fish.)

CLEAR-SIMMERED FISH II
4 to 5 servings

1 *fish (2 to 2½ pounds)*	1 *teaspoon salt*
3 *to 4 cups water*	2 *scallions*
3 *tablespoons soy sauce*	3 *slices fresh ginger root*
1 *tablespoon sherry*	3 *tablespoons oil*

1. Have fish cleaned and scaled, but left whole. Rinse in cold water and score on both sides.

2. Bring water to a vigorous boil in a large pan. Gently lower fish into pan. Bring to a boil again; then cook, covered, 3 minutes over medium heat. Turn off heat and let stand 10 minutes more without removing lid.

3. Meanwhile combine soy sauce, sherry and salt. Mince scallions and ginger root.

4. Transfer fish to a warm serving platter. Sprinkle with soy mixture; then top with minced ingredients.

5. Heat oil to smoking and pour over fish. Serve at once.

VARIATIONS: In step 2, add 2 slices fresh ginger root, crushed, to the boiling water before the fish. Then in step 5, when heating the oil, add 2 more slices ginger root, shredded. Stir-fry to brown and pour over fish with the oil.

Omit step 3. In step 4, sprinkle the fish with 1 teaspoon salt; then top with a mixture of 4 tablespoons soy sauce; ¼ teaspoon cinnamon; ¼ teaspoon preserved lemon peel, shredded; 2 slices fresh ginger root, minced; and 3 scallion stalks, split lengthwise in half, then cut crosswise in 2-inch sections. Pick up step 5.

Omit step 3. In step 4, sprinkle the fish with 1 tablespoon soy sauce, 1 teaspoon salt and a dash of pepper. Top with 4 pieces of tea melon, 1 scallion stalk, 1 tablespoon smoked ham and 1 tablespoon Chinese parsley, all shredded. Pick up step 5.

CLEAR-SIMMERED FISH III
6 to 7 servings

1 *fish (2½ to 3 pounds)*	1 *scallion stalk*
2 *tablespoons soy sauce*	½ *cup smoked ham*
2 *tablespoons sherry*	5 *slices fresh ginger root*
1 *teaspoon salt*	2 *cups water*

1. Have fish cleaned and scaled, but left whole. Rinse in cold water and score on both sides.

2. Combine soy sauce, sherry and salt, and sprinkle over fish.

3. Mince scallion stalk; slice ham and ginger root thin and arrange on top.

4. Add water, pouring it down the sides of pan so as not to disturb topping. Bring to a boil over moderate heat; then simmer, covered, until fish is done (30 to 40 minutes).

5. Serve hot, with dips of soy sauce, ginger and vinegar.

VARIATION: Omit steps 2 and 3; sprinkle the fish with 1 tablespoon sherry, 1 teaspoon salt and 1 teaspoon ginger juice. Simmer as in step 4. Then drain and transfer to a serving dish. Serve with a Five Willow Sauce poured over (see page 733).

RED-SIMMERED FISH
About 6 servings

2½ pounds smelts	2 cups vinegar
6 scallion stalks	1½ cups soy sauce
8 slices fresh ginger root	3 to 5 tablespoons sugar

½ teaspoon sesame oil

1. Have smelts cleaned; slice scallions and ginger root. Place in a pan.

2. Add vinegar, soy sauce, sugar and sesame oil. Bring to a boil; then simmer, covered, 2 hours.

3. Drain fish, discarding liquid. Refrigerate to chill. Serve cold.

NOTE: These fish are simmered so long that their bones are soft enough to eat. This dish may be prepared in advance for several meals. It will keep about a week.

VARIATION: For the smelts, substitute any small fish, about 3 to 5 inches long.

BASIC DEEP-FRIED FISH (WHOLE)
Allow about ½ pound for each serving

1. Have fish cleaned and scaled, but left whole. Wash; then dry well with paper toweling. Score on each side with 3 diagonal slashes. Rub lightly with salt.

2. Cover fish with any of the coatings indicated below.

3. Heat oil. (Use enough to cover fish completely.) Add fish and deep-fry until done, 8 to 15 minutes, depending on size. (Allow about 1 minute on each side over high heat, about 4 minutes on each side over medium heat, and about 1 minute on each side over high heat again.) Drain on paper toweling.

4. Serve hot with a sweet-and-pungent or Five Willow Sauce, a soy sauce dip or pepper-salt mix (see Seasonings and Sauces).

COATINGS FOR DEEP-FRIED FISH (WHOLE)

a. Dredge fish in cornstarch to coat.

b. Dip fish in beaten egg. Dredge in flour to coat.

c. Coat fish with a paste made of 3 tablespoons each of cornstarch and flour, and sherry to thin.

d. Coat fish with a batter made of 1 egg, lightly beaten, and 5 tablespoons flour.

e. Omit salt. Coat fish with a batter made as follows: combine 4 tablespoons flour, 2 tablespoons cornstarch, 1 teaspoon baking powder and 1 teaspoon salt; then add 1 egg, lightly beaten, and 1 tablespoon oil or lard.

DEEP-FRIED FISH WITH VEGETABLES
About 6 servings

4 to 6 dried black mushrooms	1 teaspoon sugar
½ cup bamboo shoots	1 teaspoon soy sauce
¼ cup water chestnuts	¼ cup water
1 cup Chinese cabbage	½ head lettuce
2 slices fresh ginger root	1 fish (2 pounds)
2 tablespoons sherry	oil for deep-frying
1 tablespoon water	2 tablespoons oil
1 teaspoon soy sauce	½ teaspoon salt
¼ teaspoon pepper	½ cup stock
1 tablespoon cornstarch	Chinese parsley

1. Soak dried mushrooms.

2. Shred bamboo shoots, water chestnuts, Chinese cabbage and soaked mushrooms.

3. Mince ginger root; then combine with sherry, water, soy sauce and pepper.

4. Blend cornstarch, sugar, remaining soy sauce and water to a paste.

5. Shred lettuce and arrange on a serving platter.

6. Deep-fry whole fish as in Basic Deep-fried Fish (whole), above. Drain on paper toweling. Keep warm.

7. Heat remaining oil. Add salt, then shredded vegetables. Stir-fry 2 minutes.

8. Add ginger-sherry mixture and stir-fry 1 minute more.

9. Add stock and bring to a boil. Cook, covered, 2 to 3 minutes over medium heat.

10. Stir in cornstarch paste to thicken. Place fish on lettuce bed. Pour thickened sauce over and serve, garnished with parsley.

VARIATIONS: For the water chestnuts, substitute 12 lily buds (soaked). In step 4, use dark or heavy soy sauce and add 2 teaspoons sherry. In step 7, add to reheated oil, after the salt, ⅛ pound lean pork, shredded. Stir-fry 1 minute until meat changes color; then add vegetables and stir-fry. Continue with step 8.

In step 7, add with the vegetables ½ cup roast pork, shredded.

DEEP-FRIED SWEET-AND-PUNGENT FISH, SHANGHAI STYLE

5 to 6 servings

2 *dried black mushrooms*	⅛ *cup bamboo shoots*
1 *fish (2 pounds)*	½ *scallion stalk*
1 *teaspoon salt*	*oil for deep-frying*
1 *scallion stalk*	*flour*
1 *or 2 slices fresh ginger root*	2 *tablespoons oil*
2 *tablespoons sherry*	½ *cup stock*
2 *tablespoons smoked ham*	4 *tablespoons sugar*
⅛ *cup green pepper*	4 *tablespoons vinegar*
1 *tablespoon fresh red chili pepper*	1 *tablespoon soy sauce*
2 *slices fresh ginger root*	2 *tablespoons cornstarch*

2 tablespoons water

1. Soak dried mushrooms.

2. Have fish cleaned and scaled, but left whole. Wash; then dry well with paper toweling. Score on both sides. Sprinkle inside and out with salt.

3. Mince scallion and ginger root; arrange over fish. Sprinkle fish with sherry. Let stand 10 to 20 minutes.

4. Meanwhile mince ham, green pepper, fresh red chili pepper, remaining ginger root and soaked mushrooms. Slice bamboo shoots. Cut remaining scallion stalk in ½-inch sections.

5. Heat oil. Sprinkle fish with flour to coat. Using a wire basket or long-handled Chinese strainer, lower in fish and deep-fry 3 minutes. Lift out and drain.

6. Repeat twice more (reheat oil each time) until fish is crisp and golden. Drain on paper toweling. Keep warm.

7. Heat remaining oil. Add ham and vegetables and stir-fry 1 to 2 minutes. Remove from pan.

8. Add stock, sugar, vinegar and soy sauce to the same pan and bring to a boil. Meanwhile blend cornstarch and cold water to a paste; then stir in to thicken.

9. Return ham and vegetables to sauce only to heat through. Pour mixture over fish and serve.

BASIC DEEP-FRIED FISH (IN PIECES)
Allow about ½ pound for each serving

1. Bone fish, discarding the head, and cut crosswise in 1½- to 2-inch sections, or in ¾-inch cubes.

2. Wash fish; then dry well with paper toweling. (When using thick fillets or fish steaks, score the skin of each with crisscross gashes.) Season lightly with salt and a dash of pepper.

3. Cover with any of the coatings indicated below.

4. Heat oil for deep-frying. Add fish sections and deep-fry until golden. Drain on paper toweling.

5. Serve with a sweet-and-pungent sauce or with any dip or sauce for deep-fried fish (see pages 713, 732–734).

COATINGS FOR DEEP-FRIED FISH (IN PIECES)

a. Dredge fish in cornstarch or flour.

b. Coat fish with a paste made by blending 1 tablespoon cornstarch and 3 tablespoons cold water.

c. Dip fish in a mixture made of 1 egg, beaten; 1 tablespoon soy sauce; and ¼ teaspoon salt. Then dredge lightly in cornstarch.

d. Dip fish in any of the following batter mixtures:

1 cup flour, 2 teaspoons baking powder, and water to thin

1 cup flour, ½ cup water, ½ teaspoon salt and ¼ teaspoon pepper, mixed to a paste; then 1 tablespoon baking powder blended in

1 egg, lightly beaten; and ½ cup flour

1 egg white, 1 tablespoon cornstarch, 2 teaspoons sherry and 1 teaspoon soy sauce

1 egg yolk, 1½ tablespoons cornstarch, 1½ teaspoons sherry and ½ teaspoon salt

DEEP-FRIED FISH SECTIONS WITH VEGETABLES
4 to 5 servings

3 or 4 dried black mushrooms	2 tablespoons oil
½ cup bamboo shoots	½ teaspoon salt
1 scallion stalk	½ cup stock
2 slices fresh ginger root	1 tablespoon soy sauce
1 fish (2 pounds)	1 tablespoon cornstarch
oil for deep-frying	3 tablespoons water

1. Soak dried mushrooms.

2. Slice bamboo shoots and soaked mushrooms. Cut scallion stalk in ½-inch sections. Crush ginger root.

3. Prepare fish as in steps 1 through 4 of Basic Deep-fried Fish (in Pieces), above. Keep warm.

4. Heat remaining oil. Add salt, then scallion sections and ginger root; stir-fry a few times.

5. Add mushrooms and bamboo shoots; stir-fry 2 minutes more.

6. Add stock and soy sauce and bring to a boil. Then cook, covered, 2 to 3 minutes over medium heat.

7. Meanwhile blend cornstarch and cold water to a paste. Then stir in to thicken. Pour sauce over fish and serve.

NOTE: If the fish needs rewarming, return it to pan in step 7, just as the sauce begins to thicken.

VARIATIONS: In place of (or in addition to) the bamboo shoots, use any of the following: bean sprouts; cauliflower, broken into flowerets and parboiled; celery, cut in 1-inch sections and blanched; lily buds, soaked; mushrooms, fresh or canned, sliced; or onion, sliced.

In step 5, add ⅓ cup roast pork and ⅓ cup water chestnuts, both sliced.

In step 6, for the stock substitute ½ cup water. Add, with the soy sauce and 1 tablespoon sherry, 1 teaspoon sugar and ½ teaspoon salt.

In step 7, prepare the cornstarch paste with 1 teaspoon cornstarch, 1 teaspoon soy sauce, 1 tablespoon cold stock and 1 tablespoon sherry.

DEEP-FRIED FILLETS WITH EGG WHITES
2 or 3 servings

½ *pound fish fillets*	*cornstarch*
2 *tablespoons sherry*	1 *egg white*
½ *teaspoon salt*	1 *tablespoon cornstarch*
dash of pepper	*oil for deep-frying*

1. Cut fish fillets crosswise in 1- by 1½-inch strips. Sprinkle first with sherry, then with salt and pepper. Dredge lightly in cornstarch.

2. Beat egg white and remaining cornstarch until stiff but not dry. Dip fish strips in mixture.

3. Heat oil. Add fish, a few pieces at a time, and deep-fry until pale golden. Drain on paper toweling.

4. Serve hot, with a pepper-salt mix (see page 708).

NOTE: Use the fillets of thick fish such as bass, halibut or pike.

DEEP-FRIED FISH SQUARES, SZECHWAN STYLE
About 6 servings

2 dried black mushrooms
2 tablespoons bamboo shoots
½ fresh red chili pepper
1 scallion stalk
2 or 3 slices fresh ginger root
¼ cup lean pork
1 pound fish fillets
½ teaspoon salt
dash of pepper
flour
1 egg
3 tablespoons sherry
5 tablespoons flour

oil for deep-frying
2 tablespoons oil
1 teaspoon vinegar
3 tablespoons soy sauce
2 tablespoons oil
½ teaspoon ground chili pepper
1 tablespoon sherry
1 teaspoon soy sauce
1 cup stock
½ teaspoon hot pepper oil
2 tablespoons sherry
1 tablespoon cornstarch
2 tablespoons water

1½ teaspoons sugar

1. Soak dried mushrooms.

2. Mince bamboo shoots, fresh chili pepper, scallion, ginger root and soaked mushrooms. Mince or grind the pork.

3. Cut fish fillets in 2-inch squares. Season with salt and pepper. Dredge lightly in flour.

4. Beat egg; then blend in sherry and remaining flour to make a batter. Dip fish squares in batter to coat.

5. Meanwhile heat oil. Add fish, a few pieces at a time, and deep-fry until light golden (about 2 minutes). Drain on paper toweling.

6. Heat the second quantity of oil. Add minced vegetables and stir-fry 2 minutes. Stir in vinegar and soy sauce to heat; then remove vegetables from pan.

7. Heat remaining oil. Add minced pork and stir-fry until it loses its pinkness (1 to 2 minutes). Add ground chili pepper and the second quantity of sherry; stir-fry another 2 minutes. Stir in remaining soy sauce.

8. Return vegetables. Add stock, hot pepper oil and remaining sherry. Stir to heat through. Add fish and simmer, uncovered, 3 to 5 minutes.

9. Blend cornstarch and cold water to a paste; then stir in to thicken. Stir in sugar and serve.

NOTE: Use the fillets of thick fish, such as bass, halibut or pike.

DEEP-FRIED FISH FILLETS WITH VINEGAR SAUCE

4 to 5 servings

1 *pound fish fillets*	½ *teaspoon salt*
1 *slice fresh ginger root*	*oil for deep-frying*
½ *scallion stalk*	1 *cup stock*
1 *egg white*	1 *tablespoon sugar*
2 *tablespoons cornstarch*	1 *tablespoon vinegar*
1 *tablespoon sherry*	1 *tablespoon cornstarch*

2 tablespoons stock

1. Cut fish fillets in ½- by 1½-inch strips. Mince ginger root and scallion.

2. Combine egg white, cornstarch, sherry and salt. Add to fish strips and toss gently to coat.

3. Meanwhile heat oil. Add fish, several strips at a time, and deep-fry, stirring constantly, until pale golden (about 1 minute). Drain on paper toweling.

4. Bring stock to a boil in another pan; then add sugar, vinegar, minced ginger and scallion.

5. Meanwhile blend cornstarch and remaining cold stock to a paste. Then stir in to thicken sauce. Add fish strips, stirring in briefly to reheat.

NOTE: Use sole or flounder.

DEEP-FRIED MARINATED SWEET-AND-PUNGENT FISH (WHOLE)

4 to 5 servings

1 *fish (2 pounds)*	1 *teaspoon soy sauce*
1 *small onion*	1 *teaspoon sherry*
2 *slices fresh ginger root*	*cornstarch*
½ *teaspoon salt*	*sweet-and-pungent sauce*
dash of pepper	*oil for deep-frying*

1. Have fish cleaned and scaled, then split.

2. Mince onion and ginger root; then combine with salt, pepper, soy sauce and sherry. Rub mixture over fish, inside and out. Let stand 30 minutes.

3. Dredge fish lightly in cornstarch. Let stand 5 minutes more.

4. Meanwhile prepare a sweet-and-pungent sauce (see pages 735–738). Keep warm.

5. Heat oil. Add fish and deep-fry, turning and basting, until golden. Drain on paper toweling. Then transfer to a serving platter.

6. Pour sweet-and-pungent sauce over and serve.

VARIATION: In step 2, coat fish with a mixture of 4 tablespoons cornstarch, 2 tablespoons sherry, 2 tablespoons soy sauce and 1 teaspoon ginger juice. Omit step 3.

DEEP-FRIED SMALL MARINATED FISH
About 4 servings

6 *small fish*	1 *tablespoon sherry*
4 *slices fresh ginger root*	1 *clove star anise*
½ *cup soy sauce*	*oil for deep-frying*

few drops of sesame oil

1. Have fish cleaned, but left whole.

2. Slice ginger root; then combine with soy sauce, sherry and star anise. Add to fish and let stand 30 minutes, turning occasionally.

3. Drain fish, discarding marinade; then blot dry with paper toweling. Meanwhile heat oil.

4. Add fish, several at a time, and deep-fry until crisp and golden. Drain on paper toweling.

5. Let cool; then refrigerate to chill. Sprinkle with sesame oil and serve.

NOTE: Any fish 3 to 5 inches long can be used.

DEEP-FRIED MARINATED FISH (IN PIECES)
6 to 8 servings

1 fish (2 to 3 pounds)	¼ teaspoon salt
2 scallion stalks	dash of pepper
2 or 3 slices fresh ginger root	few drops of sesame oil
1 garlic clove	oil for deep-frying
4 tablespoons soy sauce	2 tablespoons soy sauce
2 tablespoons sherry	¼ teaspoon salt
2 teaspoons sugar	1 teaspoon sugar

½ cup stock

1. Bone fish and cut crosswise in 1½-inch sections.

2. Mince scallion, ginger root and garlic; then combine with soy sauce, sherry, sugar, salt, pepper, and sesame oil. Add to fish sections and let stand 1 hour, turning occasionally.

3. Drain fish, discarding marinade; then blot dry with paper toweling. Meanwhile heat oil.

4. Add fish, a few pieces at a time, and deep-fry until golden. Drain on paper toweling.

5. In a saucepan, combine remaining soy sauce, salt and sugar with stock. Bring to a boil.

6. Add fish sections and cook over moderate heat, stirring gently until sauce has nearly evaporated. Serve hot or cold.

VARIATION: In step 4, reserve the marinade, and substitute it for the ingredients in step 5. Heat the marinade; dip each fish section in it for about 5 seconds, then drain on paper toweling. Arrange fish on a serving platter. Sprinkle with ½ teaspoon Five Spices, and serve.

DEEP-FRIED MARINATED FISH FILLETS WITH SESAME SEEDS
4 to 5 servings

1 pound fish fillets	½ teaspoon salt
1 small onion	1 egg
1 to 2 slices fresh ginger root	1½ tablespoons cornstarch
½ cup sherry	3 tablespoons flour
1½ teaspoons sugar	white sesame seeds

oil for deep-frying

1. Cut fish fillets in narrow strips.

2. Mince onion and ginger root; then combine with sherry, sugar and salt.

3. Add to fish strips and let stand 15 minutes, turning occasionally. Drain, discarding marinade.

4. Beat egg lightly; then blend in cornstarch and flour to make a batter. Dip fish strips in batter; then roll in sesame seeds to coat. Meanwhile heat oil.

5. Add fish strips, several at a time, and deep-fry until golden (less than a minute). Drain on paper toweling and serve at once.

DEEP-FRIED FISH ROLLS WITH ALMONDS
6 to 8 servings

¾ cup almond meats	*1 teaspoon sugar*
3 fish fillets	*½ teaspoon salt*
3 slices smoked ham	*2 teaspoons soy sauce*
1 scallion stalk	*1 teaspoon sherry*
½ teaspoon ginger juice	*1 egg*
1 teaspoon cornstarch	*oil for deep-frying*

1. Blanch and mince almonds.

2. Cut fish fillets in 2- by 3-inch pieces, smoked ham in 1- by 2-inch pieces.

3. Mince scallion stalk; extract ginger juice; then combine with cornstarch, sugar, salt, soy sauce and sherry. Beat egg lightly and blend in.

4. Dip fish pieces in mixture; then coat on one side only with minced

almonds. Wrap each piece of fish (almond side in) around one strip of ham and roll up. (Fasten with a toothpick or tie with white thread.) Meanwhile heat oil.

5. Add fish rolls, a few at a time, and deep-fry until golden. Drain briefly on paper toweling and serve.

DEEP-FRIED FISH ROLLS WITH HAM AND SPINACH
6 to 8 servings

3 fish fillets	*1 egg*
2 teaspoons ginger juice	*1 cup flour*
½ teaspoon salt	*⅔ cup water*
¼ cup smoked ham	*1 tablespoon white sesame seeds*
½ cup fresh spinach	*oil for deep-frying*

1. Cut fish fillets in 2- by 3-inch pieces. Extract ginger juice and sprinkle over fish, along with salt.

2. Shred ham and spinach; then top fish with mixture. Roll up each piece of fish to enclose stuffing. (Fasten with a toothpick or tie with white thread.)

3. Beat egg lightly; then blend to a batter with flour and water. Stir in sesame seeds. Dip each fish roll in batter. Meanwhile heat oil.

4. Add fish rolls, a few at a time, and deep-fry until golden. Drain briefly on paper toweling and serve.

DEEP-FRIED FISH ROLLS WITH PORK
6 to 8 servings

3 fish fillets	*1 teaspoon soy sauce*
1 cup cooked pork	*2 tablespoons sherry*
3 tablespoons sherry	*½ teaspoon sugar*
1 teaspoon sugar	*1 tablespoon cornstarch*
¼ cup onion	*3 tablespoons water*
1 or 2 slices fresh ginger root	*oil for deep-frying*
½ cup stock	

1. Cut fish fillets in 2- by 3-inch pieces.

2. Mince or grind cooked pork, then combine with sherry and sugar. Top fish strips with mixture, then roll up each piece to enclose stuffing. (Fasten with a toothpick or tie with white thread.)

3. Mince onion and ginger root; then combine in a cup with soy sauce, remaining sherry and sugar. In another cup, blend cornstarch and cold water to a paste. Meanwhile heat oil.

4. Add fish rolls, a few at a time, and deep-fry until golden. Drain on paper toweling.

5. Heat stock in a pan. Add onion-ginger mixture and cook, stirring, 2 minutes. Stir in cornstarch paste to thicken. Pour sauce over fish rolls and serve.

VARIATIONS: Serve the fish rolls with deep-fried eggs, sliced lengthwise (see page 571).

For the mixture in step 2, substitute ⅓ cup cooked pork, ⅓ cup cooked shrimp and ⅓ cup onion, blended with ½ teaspoon salt.

Instead of deep-frying the stuffed fish rolls, poach them: Omit steps 3, 4 and 5. Place fish instead in a shallow pan with ½ cup sherry, ½ cup water and 1 tablespoon soy sauce and let stand 30 minutes, turning occasionally. Then bring nearly to a boil over very low heat. Transfer to a serving dish. Sprinkle lightly with salt and pepper; spoon some of the liquid over and serve.

BASIC BRAISED SOY FISH
About 4 servings

1 fish (2 pounds)	1 cup water
½ teaspoon salt	4 tablespoons soy sauce
flour	2 tablespoons sherry
3 slices fresh ginger root	½ teaspoon sugar
1 or 2 scallions	½ teaspoon salt

4 to 6 tablespoons oil

1. Have fish cleaned and scaled, but left whole. Rinse in cold water. Dry well, inside and out, with paper toweling and score on both sides.

2. Sprinkle fish with the salt and let stand 10 minutes. Then coat lightly with flour.

3. Mince ginger root and scallions; then combine with water, soy sauce, sherry, sugar and remaining salt.

4. Heat oil in a heavy pan until nearly smoking. Gently lower in fish; fry over high heat 1 minute on each side, then over medium heat 2½ minutes on each side. Baste continually with hot oil. (To turn fish over, loosen it with the back of a spatula and turn gently. The pan may be removed temporarily from the burner while the fish is being turned.)

5. Pour ginger-scallion mixture over fish and bring quickly to a boil. Then cook, covered, over medium heat until done (15 to 20 minutes), turning fish halfway through cooking.

NOTE: Braised soy fish is good served hot or cold. It may be prepared in quantity and served cold as a side dish or with drinks. (Its sauce is delicious when jellied.) Braised fish may also be browned in advance, then cooked in sauce, as in step 5, just before serving. Once it's completely cooked, however, it should never be reheated.

VARIATIONS: For the water, substitute stock.

For the white sugar, substitute brown sugar.

In step 2, omit the salt and rub fish lightly with soy sauce before coating with flour.

In step 3, add to the sauce mixture any or all of the following: 2 tablespoons smoked ham, minced; 1 celery stalk, minced; few drops of sesame oil or vinegar.

During the last few minutes of cooking, add 1½ cups fresh tomatoes, peeled and diced; or 2 cups bean curd, sliced or cubed. Cook only to heat through.

BRAISED SOY FISH WITH MUSHROOMS AND BAMBOO SHOOTS I

5 to 6 servings

4 or 5 dried black mushrooms	1 fish (2 pounds)
⅓ cup bamboo shoots	¾ cup water
1 bunch scallions	1 tablespoon brown sugar
2 tablespoons oil	5 tablespoons soy sauce

1 tablespoon sherry

1. Soak dried mushrooms.

2. Slice bamboo shoots and soaked mushrooms. Cut scallions in 2-inch sections.

3. Heat oil. Add scallions, bamboo shoots and mushrooms. Stir-fry 1 to 2 minutes; then remove from pan.

4. Pick up steps 1, 2 and 4 of Basic Braised Soy Fish, above.

5. Return vegetables. Add water, sugar, soy sauce and sherry. Bring to a boil; then simmer, covered, 5 minutes.

6. Turn heat up to medium and baste fish until all but ½ cup of the sauce has evaporated. Serve at once with remaining sauce.

BRAISED SOY FISH WITH MUSHROOMS AND BAMBOO SHOOTS II
5 to 6 servings

6 *dried black mushrooms*	1 *cup stock*
½ *cup bamboo shoots*	3 *tablespoons soy sauce*
3 *scallion stalks*	1 *tablespoon sherry*
2 *slices fresh ginger root*	½ *teaspoon salt*
2 *garlic cloves*	1 *clove star anise*
1 *fish* (2 *pounds*)	½ *teaspoon sugar*

1. Soak dried mushrooms.

2. Slice bamboo shoots and soaked mushrooms. Cut scallions in ½-inch sections. Mince ginger root; crush garlic.

3. Pick up steps 1, 2 and 4 of Basic Braised Soy Fish.

4. Add to fish all the vegetables, along with stock, soy sauce, sherry and salt. Bring to a boil; then simmer, covered, 5 minutes.

5. Add star anise and sugar. Simmer, covered, 15 minutes more, turning fish once. Serve hot.

VARIATION: In step 4, add ¼ pound pork with some fat, slivered.

BRAISED SOY FISH WITH OYSTER SAUCE
4 to 5 servings

1 *fish* (2 *pounds*)	1 *tablespoon oil*
4 *scallion stalks*	2 *tablespoons oyster sauce*
1 *or* 2 *slices fresh ginger root*	2 *tablespoons soy sauce*
1 *garlic clove*	1 *teaspoon sugar*
1 *cup stock*	*few drops of Tabasco Sauce*

1. Prepare fish as in steps 1, 2 and 4 of Basic Braised Soy Fish. Turn off heat and leave fish in pan.

2. Cut scallions in ½-inch sections. Mince ginger root and garlic. Meanwhile heat stock separately.

3. In a skillet, heat remaining oil. Add scallion, ginger root and garlic, and stir-fry a few times. Add oyster sauce, soy sauce, sugar and Tabasco Sauce. Cook, stirring, 1 minute. Then pour over fish.

4. Add heated stock to fish and simmer, covered, until done (about 15 minutes), turning fish once.

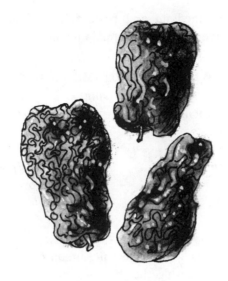

BRAISED SOY FISH WITH RED DATES
About 8 servings

6 *Chinese red dates*	1 *teaspoon salt*
10 *dried black mushrooms*	1½ *cups water*
½ *cup bacon*	1 *tablespoon soy sauce*
½ *cup bamboo shoots*	2 *tablespoons sherry*
¼ *cup water chestnuts*	1 *teaspoon sugar*
2 *slices fresh ginger root*	⅛ *teaspoon pepper*
1 *scallion stalk*	*few drops of sesame oil*
1 *garlic clove*	1 *head lettuce*
1 *fish (2 to 3 pounds)*	*Chinese parsley*

1. Separately soak Chinese red dates and dried mushrooms.

2. Shred bacon, bamboo shoots, water chestnuts, ginger root, soaked dates and mushrooms. Mince scallion stalk; crush garlic.

3. Pick up steps 1, 2 and 4 of Basic Braised Soy Fish, but add salt and crushed garlic to heated oil before fish.

4. Arrange shredded ingredients and scallion on top of fish in pan. Add water, soy sauce, sherry, sugar, pepper and sesame oil. Bring to a boil; then simmer, covered, 20 minutes.

5. Shred lettuce and arrange on a serving platter. Place fish, with topping intact, on lettuce bed. Garnish with Chinese parsley and serve.

VARIATIONS: In step 4, add with shredded ingredients ½ teaspoon tangerine peel (soaked), shredded. Omit the sesame oil.

When fish is done, transfer to a serving platter, as in step 5; then thicken liquids in saucepan with a cornstarch paste and pour sauce over.

BRAISED CARP IN CHICKEN FAT I
About 6 servings

1 carp (2½ to 3 pounds)
2 scallion stalks
¼ cup chicken fat

2 tablespoons soy sauce
2 tablespoons sherry
¾ cup water

1. Prepare fish as in steps 1 and 2 of Basic Braised Soy Fish.
2. Cut scallions in ½-inch sections. Heat chicken fat in a large, deep pan. Add scallions and stir-fry to brown lightly. Add carp and brown quickly (about 3 minutes on each side).
3. Pour soy sauce and sherry over. Cook 1 to 2 minutes over moderate heat.
4. Add water and bring to a boil; then simmer, covered, 7 minutes more. Gently turn fish over. Cook, covered, another 7 minutes and serve.

NOTE: Carp is noted for the delicacy and soft texture of its flesh. The chicken fat enhances these qualities.

VARIATION: For the scallions, substitute 2 garlic cloves, crushed.

BRAISED CARP IN CHICKEN FAT II
6 to 7 servings

1 carp (2½ to 3 pounds)
1 garlic clove
3 slices fresh ginger root
4 scallion stalks
¼ cup chicken fat

few drops of Tabasco Sauce
2 tablespoons oyster sauce
1 teaspoon sugar
stock to cover
2 cakes bean curd

1. Prepare fish as in steps 1 and 2 of Basic Braised Soy Fish.
2. Mince garlic and ginger root. Cut scallions in 2-inch sections.

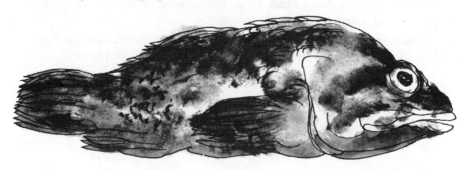

3. Heat chicken fat in a large, deep pan. Stir in Tabasco and oyster sauce. Add garlic, ginger root, scallions and sugar, and stir-fry a few times.

4. Add carp and brown quickly on both sides. (The pan should now be very hot.)

5. Add enough stock to cover fish. Bring to a boil; then simmer, covered, about 15 minutes. Meanwhile, dice bean curd.

6. Transfer fish to a warm serving platter, leaving liquids in pan. Add bean curd to pan and simmer, covered, to heat through (3 to 5 minutes).

7. Arrange bean curd cubes around fish. Pour sauce over and serve.

BRAISED FISH WITH DEEP-FRIED BEAN CURD
4 to 6 servings

1 fish (2 pounds)	¼ teaspoon salt
1 or 2 slices fresh ginger root	1 cup water
1 scallion stalk	1½ teaspoons cornstarch
2 cakes bean curd	1 teaspoon sugar
oil for deep-frying	1 teaspoon soy sauce
4 tablespoons oil	1 teaspoon sherry
¼ teaspoon salt	dash of pepper
1 tablespoon oil	3 tablespoons water

1. Prepare fish as in steps 1 and 2 of Basic Braised Soy Fish.

2. Shred ginger root. Cut scallion in ½-inch sections.

3. Cut each bean curd cake in 9 cubes. Heat oil to bubbling and deep-fry bean curd until light golden. Drain on paper toweling.

4. Heat the second quantity of oil until nearly smoking. Add salt, then fish; brown well on each side (about 3 minutes). Remove from pan.

5. Heat remaining oil. Add remaining salt, along with shredded ginger root, and stir-fry a few times. Add water and bring to a boil.

6. Add fish and bean curd. Top with scallion sections and simmer, covered, about 10 to 15 minutes. Meanwhile, in a cup, blend cornstarch, sugar, soy sauce, sherry, pepper and remaining water to a paste.

7. Transfer fish and bean curd to a warm serving platter, leaving liquids in pan. Stir in cornstarch paste, to thicken. Pour sauce over fish and serve.

BRAISED FISH STUFFED WITH PORK
4 to 6 servings

1 fish (2 pounds)	1 teaspoon ginger juice
¼ pound lean pork	4 to 5 tablespoons oil
1 scallion stalk	1 garlic clove
1 tablespoon cornstarch	5 slices fresh ginger root
1 tablespoon soy sauce	1 leek stalk
1 tablespoon sherry	2 cups water
1 teaspoon sugar	1 tablespoon sugar

3 tablespoons soy sauce

1. Prepare fish as in steps 1 and 2 of Basic Braised Soy Fish.

2. Mince or grind pork and mince scallion; then combine with cornstarch, soy sauce, sherry and sugar. Extract ginger juice and blend in. Stuff mixture into fish cavity.

3. In a large, deep pan, heat oil until nearly smoking. Add fish and brown on both sides. Remove fish; drain oil from pan.

4. Crush garlic; mince ginger root; cut leek in ½-inch sections. Then add to pan with water and remaining sugar and soy sauce; bring to a boil.

5. Return fish and simmer, covered, 20 minutes. Carefully turn fish over and simmer, covered, 10 minutes more.

BRAISED FISH STEAKS WITH BEAN CURD
4 to 6 servings

1 fish (2 pounds)	4 or 5 tablespoons oil
2 cakes bean curd	1 tablespoon soy sauce
1 scallion stalk	2 tablespoons sherry
2 or 3 slices fresh ginger root	½ cup water

½ teaspoon salt

1. Cut fish crosswise into 2 to 3 inch steaks. Wipe dry.

2. Cut each bean curd cake in 9 cubes; cut scallion in 1-inch sections. Mince ginger root.

3. Heat oil until nearly smoking. Brown fish steaks quickly on both sides.

4. Add soy sauce, sherry, water, salt, minced ginger root and scallion. Bring to a boil; then simmer, covered, 10 minutes.

5. Add bean curd cubes. Simmer, covered, until fish is done (5 to 10 minutes more).

BRAISED FISH STEAKS AND VEGETABLES
4 to 6 servings

4 dried black mushrooms	*½ cup stock*
1 fish (2 pounds)	*2 tablespoons soy sauce*
cornstarch	*1 tablespoon sherry*
½ cup bamboo shoots	*1½ teaspoons brown sugar*
1 garlic clove	*½ teaspoon salt*
2 slices fresh ginger root	*4 to 5 tablespoons oil*
1 scallion stalk	*1 tablespoon oil*

1. Soak dried mushrooms.

2. Cut fish crosswise into 2 to 3 inch steaks. Wipe dry; then dredge lightly in cornstarch.

3. Slice bamboo shoots and soaked mushrooms. Mince garlic, ginger root and scallion.

4. Combine stock, soy sauce, sherry, brown sugar and salt.

5. Heat oil until nearly smoking. Brown fish steaks quickly on both sides. Remove from pan.

6. Heat remaining oil. Add minced garlic, ginger and scallion and stir-fry a few times. Add mushrooms and bamboo shoots and stir-fry 1 minute more.

7. Add stock-soy mixture and bring to a boil. Return fish and simmer, covered, until done (about 15 minutes).

SIMPLE PAN-FRIED FISH
4 to 6 servings

1 fish (2 pounds)	*4 to 6 tablespoons oil*
soy sauce	

1. Prepare fish as in steps 1 and 2 of Basic Braised Soy Fish.

2. Heat oil. Brown fish quickly on both sides over high heat.

3. Reduce heat to medium and fry fish until done (about 5 minutes on each side). Remove from pan. Sprinkle generously with soy sauce and serve.

PAN-FRIED SWEET-AND-PUNGENT FISH
4 to 6 servings

sweet-and-pungent sauce	*3 tablespoons cornstarch*
1 fish (2 pounds)	*2 tablespoons water*

4 to 6 tablespoons oil

1. Prepare a sweet-and-pungent sauce (see pages 735–738).

2. Clean and score fish as in step 1 of Basic Braised Soy Fish.

3. Blend cornstarch and cold water to a paste; then coat fish well with it.

4. Heat oil very hot. Hold fish by the head over pan and baste with hot oil until the flesh exposed by scoring is well browned.

5. Gently lower fish into pan and fry on both sides, over medium heat, until crisp. Remove from pan and drain on paper toweling. Then transfer to a warm serving platter.

6. Reheat sweet-and-pungent sauce. Pour over fish and serve.

PAN-FRIED MARINATED FISH STEAKS
4 to 6 servings

1 fish (2 pounds)	*1 or 2 slices fresh ginger root*
2 tablespoons sherry	*4 scallion stalks*
¾ teaspoon salt	*1 tablespoon vinegar*
2 garlic cloves	*3 to 4 tablespoons oil or lard*

1. Have fish cleaned and scaled, but left whole. Rinse in cold water; then dry well with paper toweling. Sprinkle fish with sherry and salt, wrap in foil or transparent wrap, and refrigerate overnight.

2. Cut fish crosswise into 2 to 3 inch steaks.

3. Mince garlic, ginger root and scallions; then blend well with vinegar.

4. Heat oil to smoking. Brown fish steaks quickly. Remove from pan when done. Top at once with vinegar mixture and serve.

NOTE: Use haddock or whiting.

PAN-FRIED STUFFED FISH SKIN
About 8 servings

4 dried shrimp
4 dried black mushrooms
1 fish, (3 pounds)
⅛ pound smoked ham
6 water chestnuts
3 scallion stalks
2 sprigs Chinese parsley

2 tablespoons ice water
1 tablespoon soy sauce
1 tablespoon oil
2 teaspoons cornstarch
½ teaspoon sugar
¼ teaspoon salt
dash of pepper

4 tablespoons oil

1. Separately soak dried shrimp and dried mushrooms.

2. Hold fish by the tail. With a sharp knife, cut the flesh away from the bone, working along the spine from tail to head. (Discard head and bones.) Then, using a spoon or knife, scrape the flesh away from the skin, taking care not to tear the skin. Keep both halves of the fish skin intact and lay them out flat.

3. Mince fish flesh with ham, water chestnuts, scallions, parsley, soaked shrimp and mushrooms. Then blend with ice water, soy sauce, oil, cornstarch, sugar, salt and pepper.

4. Pile mixture onto one fish skin and shape it to the form of the skin, leaving about a ½-inch margin. Top with the second skin. Press edges of the skins together or fasten with toothpicks.

5. Heat remaining oil. Cook stuffed fish skin 1 to 2 minutes, on each side, over high heat. Then cook, on each side, over medium heat until golden.

NOTE: Use carp, bass or red snapper.

VARIATION: Instead of pan-frying as in step 5, simmer the fish. Dredge lightly in cornstarch at the end of step 4. Then simmer, covered, 20 minutes in a mixture of ½ cup water, 1 tablespoon sugar, 1 tablespoon soy sauce, 2 tablespoons sherry, and 1 to 2 slices fresh ginger root, minced.

PAN-FRIED SWEET-AND-PUNGENT FISH STEAKS
4 to 6 servings

sweet-and-pungent sauce
1 fish (2 pounds)

1 egg
cornstarch

4 to 5 tablespoons oil

1. Prepare a sweet-and-pungent sauce (see pages 735–738).
2. Cut fish crosswise into 2 to 3 inch steaks.
3. Beat egg. Dip fish in egg; then dredge in cornstarch.
4. Heat oil until smoking. Brown fish on both sides. Then reduce heat to medium and cook until done. Transfer to a serving platter.
5. Reheat sweet-and-pungent sauce. Pour over fish and serve.

VARIATION: Substitute either of the following for step 3: Dip the fish in egg white; then dredge in flour. Repeat process. Or dip the fish in a batter made by blending 2 eggs, beaten, with 2 tablespoons cornstarch.

PAN-FRIED FISH FILLETS WITH EGGS
About 6 servings

1½ pounds fish fillets	2 or 3 slices fresh ginger root
3 eggs	1 tablespoon sherry
½ teaspoon salt	2 tablespoons water
2 tablespoons cornstarch	½ teaspoon salt
1 or 2 scallion stalks	4 tablespoons oil

1. Cut fish fillets across the grain in 1½-inch sections.
2. Beat eggs lightly with salt. Gradually fold in cornstarch, blending until smooth.
3. Dip fish strips in mixture to coat. (Reserve excess egg mixture.)
4. Mince scallion and ginger root. Add to remaining egg mixture, along with sherry, water and remaining salt. Mix well.
5. Heat oil almost to smoking. Add fish strips and brown lightly (about 2 minutes on each side).
6. Add scallion-egg mixture (restir it first). Cook, stirring, over moderate heat until sauce thickens and is smooth. (Turn fish gently several times.) Serve at once.

PAN-FRIED FISH FILLETS WITH PINEAPPLE
About 4 servings

1 pound fish fillets	2 eggs
1 scallion stalk	1 tablespoon cornstarch
2 tablespoons soy sauce	1 8-ounce can sliced pineapple
1 tablespoon sherry	¼ cup pineapple juice
½ teaspoon salt	3 tablespoons oil

1. Cut fish fillets against the grain in 1-inch strips.

2. Mince scallion; then combine with soy sauce, sherry and salt. Add fish strips and let stand 10 to 15 minutes, turning occasionally. Drain fish, discarding marinade.

3. Beat eggs lightly and blend with cornstarch to a batter. Dip fish strips in batter to coat. (Reserve excess batter.)

4. Drain canned pineapple. Combine juice in a saucepan with excess batter. Cut pineapple slices in quarters and add.

5. Heat oil in a skillet. Brown fish strips lightly on both sides. Transfer to a serving platter.

6. Meanwhile cook pineapple-batter mixture over medium heat, stirring until it thickens. Pour over fish strips and serve.

STIR-FRIED FISH AND BEAN SPROUTS
4 to 6 servings

1 fish (2 pounds)	*½ teaspoon salt*
1 pound bean sprouts	*2 tablespoons oil*
½ cup scallions	*1 tablespoon soy sauce*
1 or 2 slices fresh ginger root	*¼ cup stock*
3 tablespoons oil	*1 tablespoon cornstarch*

3 tablespoons water

1. Bone fish and cut against the grain in ¼-inch slices.

2. Blanch bean sprouts. Cut scallions in 1-inch sections. Mince ginger root.

3. Heat oil. Add salt, then ginger root, and stir-fry a few times. When oil is nearly smoking, add fish and stir-fry gently until half done (about 1 minute on each side). Remove fish.

4. Heat remaining oil. Add bean sprouts and stir-fry 1 minute. Add scallion sections and soy sauce; stir-fry a few times.

5. Add stock and bring to a boil. Return fish and cook, covered, over medium heat, until done (about 2 minutes).

6. Meanwhile blend cornstarch and cold water to a paste; then stir in to thicken sauce. Serve at once.

VARIATION: In step 4, add with the bean sprouts and scallions 2 tablespoons Chinese preserved sweet pickle and 1 tablespoon preserved ginger, both shredded. Omit the soy sauce.

STIR-FRIED FISH WITH VEGETABLES
4 to 6 servings

1 *fish* (2 *pounds*)	1 *garlic clove*
1 *tablespoon cornstarch*	2 *tablespoons oil*
¼ *teaspoon salt*	¼ *teaspoon salt*
2 *teaspoons sherry*	½ *cup stock*
¼ *cup bamboo shoots*	½ *teaspoon sugar*
1 *cup Chinese lettuce*	*dash of pepper*
3 *water chestnuts*	3 *slices fresh ginger root*
12 *snow peas*	2 *tablespoons oil*

¼ teaspoon salt

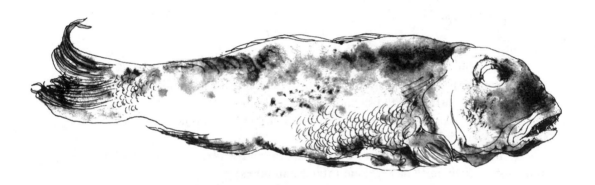

1. Bone fish and cut against the grain in ¼-inch slices. Combine cornstarch, salt and sherry. Add to fish and toss gently to coat.

2. Slice bamboo shoots, Chinese lettuce and water chestnuts thin. Stem and string snow peas. Crush garlic.

3. Heat oil. Add the second quantity of salt, then crushed garlic; stir-fry a few times. Add vegetables and stir-fry to coat with oil (about 1 minute).

4. Add stock, sugar and pepper and bring to a boil. Cook, covered, 2 minutes over medium heat; then remove vegetables and liquid from pan. Meanwhile mince ginger root.

5. Heat remaining oil. Add remaining salt, then minced ginger; stir-fry a few times. Add fish slices and stir-fry gently until done (about 3 minutes).

6. Return vegetables and their liquid. Stir-fry gently only to heat through. Serve at once.

VARIATIONS: For the Chinese lettuce, substitute Chinese cabbage.

For the vegetables, substitute ½ head cauliflower, broken into flowerets and parboiled; and 1 cup fresh mushrooms, sliced thin.

In step 3, add with the vegetables 2 tablespoons cloud ear mushrooms (soaked).

STIR-FRIED FISH WITH LILY BUDS
4 to 6 servings

12 *lily buds*	3 *tablespoons stock*
1 *fish (2 pounds)*	2 *tablespoons soy sauce*
1 *tablespoon cornstarch*	1 *tablespoon sherry*
2 *tablespoons water*	2 *teaspoons cornstarch*
1 *scallion stalk*	2 to 3 *tablespoons oil*

½ teaspoon salt

1. Soak lily buds.

2. Bone fish and cut against the grain in ½-inch slices. Blend cornstarch and cold water to a paste. Add to fish and toss gently to coat.

3. Mince scallion. Cut soaked lily buds in two. Combine stock, soy sauce, sherry and remaining cornstarch.

4. Heat oil. Add salt, then minced scallion, and stir-fry a few times. Add fish and stir-fry gently until nearly done (about 4 minutes).

5. Add lily buds and stir-fry 2 minutes more. Transfer fish and lily buds to a warm serving platter, leaving liquids in pan.

6. Stir in stock-cornstarch mixture to thicken. Pour sauce over fish and lily buds. Serve at once.

STIR-FRIED MINCED FISH AND CHINESE TURNIP
About 6 servings

1 *pound Chinese white turnip*	1 *slice fresh ginger root*
1 *pound fish fillet*	½ *cup raw peanuts*
1 *egg white*	2 *tablespoons oil*
1 *teaspoon cornstarch*	1 *teaspoon soy sauce*
1 *tablespoon sherry*	½ *teaspoon sugar*
½ *teaspoon salt*	½ *teaspoon salt*
dash of pepper	2 *tablespoons oil*
1 *scallion stalk*	1 *teaspoon sherry*

1. Peel Chinese turnip and parboil until cooked through but still crunchy (about 3 minutes); then shred.

2. Mince fish; then blend well with egg white, cornstarch, sherry, salt and pepper.

3. Mince scallion stalk and ginger root. Mince or grind peanuts.

4. Heat oil. Add parboiled turnip and stir-fry 2 to 3 minutes. Add soy sauce, sugar and remaining salt; stir-fry a few times. Transfer mixture to a serving dish and keep warm.

5. Heat remaining oil. Add minced scallion and ginger root; stir-fry a few times. Add minced fish mixture and stir-fry only to heat through (about 1 minute). Add remaining sherry; stir-fry 1 minute more.

6. Arrange fish over turnips. Garnish with peanuts and serve.

BASIC FISHBALLS

Fishballs can be used in a variety of ways: they can be deep-fried and served with a sweet-and-pungent sauce, combined with stir-fried vegetables, or added to soups and red-cooked dishes.

Preparing the fish: Use either fish fillets or whole fish. With the latter,

have the fish split in half and the head and big bones removed. Then, with a spoon or blunt knife, scrape the flesh from the skin. Always work from tail to head. (If you work the other way, the fine bones will come loose and be difficult to separate out.)

Making the fish mixture: Follow any of the four recipes below.

Forming the fishballs: If the fish mixture is moist, take a fistful and squeeze it through a hole made by joining thumb and index finger, to form walnut-size balls. Or, if the mixture is of a drier consistency, shape the fishballs between the palms of the hands. (Moisten the hands first.)

Cooking the fishballs: Bring 4 to 5 cups of water almost to a boil. Add fishballs and cook over medium heat until done (3 to 5 minutes). The fish liquid may be enriched with 4 beaten egg yolks and 1 teaspoon salt, stirred in at the end of cooking, and then served with the fish. Or a fish stock may be substituted and the fishballs cooked in it. To prepare stock, simmer the fish head and bones in 4 to 5 cups of water for an hour. Then stir in 1 tablespoon vinegar, a few drops of sherry, and either 1 tablespoon lard or a few drops of sesame oil.

Storing fishballs: Fishballs cannot be stored raw, but must be parboiled first. Plunge fishballs, a few at a time, into boiling water and cook until they float. Drain and let cool. Place in a large bowl of cold water, cover, and refrigerate. The fishballs will keep several days.

NOTE: Two pounds of fish fillets make about 20 fishballs.

FISHBALL MIXTURE A
About 8 servings

2 pounds fish fillets	½ teaspoon salt
2 eggs	dash of pepper
1 teaspoon ginger juice	1 teaspoon cornstarch

1 tablespoon sherry

1. Mince or grind fish.

2. Beat eggs; extract ginger juice. Add to fish along with salt, pepper and cornstarch, and sherry. Blend well.

VARIATIONS: In step 1, mince the fish with 1 or 2 slices fresh ginger root. Omit the ginger juice in step 2.

In step 1, while mincing the fish, gradually add ½ cup water. For the whole eggs, substitute 2 egg whites, beaten until stiff. Fold in with the other ingredients.

For the ingredients in step 2, substitute ¼ cup water, 3 tablespoons flour, ½ teaspoon sugar, 1 teaspoon salt, and a dash of pepper.

FISHBALL MIXTURE B
About 8 servings

1 scallion stalk

2 slices fresh ginger root

¼ cup water

2 pounds fish fillets

2 egg whites

1 tablespoon sherry

1 teaspoon cornstarch

½ teaspoon salt

½ cup water

1. Crush scallion and ginger root. Combine with water and mash to a pulp.
2. Add pulp to fish fillets and mince or grind together.
3. Add egg whites, sherry, cornstarch and salt. Beat with an egg beater, gradually adding remaining water, until ingredients are well blended.

FISHBALL MIXTURE C
About 8 servings

2 scallion stalks

2 slices fresh ginger root

1 cup water

½ teaspoon salt

2 pounds fish fillets

1 egg white

2 tablespoons cornstarch

1. Mince scallion stalks and ginger root. Add to water and let stand 20 minutes. Then strain water, discarding minced ingredients. Add salt.
2. Cut fish fillets in ½- to 1-inch cubes. Place in a blender, with salted water. Blend about 1 minute at low speed. Transfer to a bowl.
3. Beat egg white until stiff. Fold into fish, along with cornstarch.

VARIATION: Omit scallions and ginger root, adding water and salt directly to blender in step 2.

FISHBALL MIXTURE D
About 8 servings

2 pounds fish fillets

½ cup water

½ teaspoon salt

1 teaspoon cornstarch

½ teaspoon sugar

1. Mince or grind fish. Place in a large bowl. Add water, salt, cornstarch and sugar. Knead mass by hand to blend.

2. Stir mixture firmly, in one direction only, until it takes on a fluffy, marshmallow-like consistency.

3. Lift mass and toss it back hard against the bottom of the bowl. Repeat 15 to 20 times, or until mixture stops spattering and has an adhering quality.

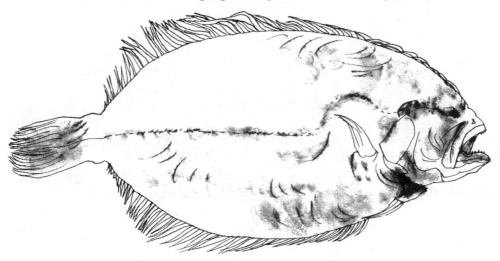

DEEP-FRIED FISHBALLS AND CHINESE CABBAGE
About 4 servings

1 head Chinese cabbage	¼ cup sherry
2 slices fresh ginger root	1 teaspoon soy sauce
10 fishballs	¼ teaspoon sugar
oil for deep-frying	dash of pepper
2 tablespoons oil	½ teaspoon salt
salt	1 tablespoon cornstarch
⅓ cup stock	3 tablespoons water

1. Cut Chinese cabbage in 2-inch sections. Crush ginger root.

2. Prepare fishballs from any of the mixtures above.

3. Heat oil to bubbling. Add fishballs, a few at a time, and deep-fry until golden. Drain on paper toweling.

4. Heat remaining oil. Add ginger root and stir-fry a few times. Add Chinese cabbage and stir-fry until tender but still crisp. Transfer to a warm serving platter and sprinkle lightly with salt. Place fishballs on top.

5. Meanwhile, in a saucepan, heat stock. Stir in sherry and soy sauce and heat; then add sugar, pepper, and remaining salt.

6. Blend cornstarch and cold water to a paste; then stir in to thicken. Pour sauce over fishballs and cabbage and serve.

STEAMED FISHBALLS
4 to 6 servings

2 or 3 *dried black mushrooms*	1 *tablespoon sherry*
1 *pound fish fillets*	½ *teaspoon salt*
¼ *cup smoked ham*	*dash of pepper*
¼ *cup bamboo shoots*	1 *egg white*
½ *cup Chinese cabbage*	1 *cup stock*
1 or 2 *slices fresh ginger root*	¼ *teaspoon salt*
1 *tablespoon cornstarch*	½ *tablespoon cornstarch*

1 *tablespoon water*

1. Soak dried mushrooms.

2. Cut fish in strips 1-inch long. Cut ham, bamboo shoots, Chinese cabbage and soaked mushrooms in similar strips.

3. Mince ginger root; then combine in a deep bowl with cornstarch, sherry, salt, pepper and egg white. Add fish strips and toss gently to coat; then add ham and vegetable strips, tossing to coat. Form into walnut-size balls and place in a shallow heatproof dish.

4. Steam until done (about 7 minutes). See page 831.

5. Heat stock in a saucepan and add remaining salt. Meanwhile blend cornstarch and cold water to a paste; then stir in to thicken. Pour sauce over fishballs and serve.

Note: Unlike the minced fishballs, these, which are made with fish strips, have a ridged surface. This dish is also known as Rainbow Fish or Yangchow Fishballs.

variations: For the Chinese cabbage, substitute fresh spinach.

In step 3, add 2 teaspoons oil to the cornstarch-sherry mixture.

PAN-FRIED FISH CAKES
About 4 servings

¼ *cup dried shrimp*	1 *tablespoon soy sauce*
4 or 5 *dried black mushrooms*	1 *tablespoon sherry*
½ *pound fish fillets*	½ *teaspoon sugar*
1 *teaspoon cornstarch*	¼ *teaspoon salt*
¼ *teaspoon salt*	2 *teaspoons cornstarch*
¼ *teaspoon stock*	3 *tablespoons water*
¼ *cup smoked ham*	2 to 3 *tablespoons oil or lard*
½ *cup bamboo shoots*	*few drops of sesame oil*

1. Separately soak dried shrimp and mushrooms.

2. Mince fish together with soaked shrimp. Blend in cornstarch, salt and stock. Shape in small cakes.

3. Dice smoked ham, bamboo shoots and soaked mushrooms.

4. In one cup, combine soy sauce, sherry, sugar and remaining salt. In another, blend remaining cornstarch and cold water to a paste.

5. Heat oil. Brown fish cakes lightly on each side over medium heat. Remove to a warm serving platter.

6. Reheat oil, adding more if necessary. Add diced ham and vegetables and stir-fry 2 minutes. Add soy-sherry mixture; stir-fry 1 minute more.

7. Stir in cornstarch paste to thicken. Then stir in sesame oil. Pour sauce over fish cakes and serve.

DEEP-FRIED BEAN CURD STUFFED WITH MINCED FISH
About 8 servings

½ pound shrimp	*½ teaspoon salt*
½ pound fish fillets	*6 bean curd cakes*
1 egg white	*oil for deep-frying*

1. Shell and devein shrimp. Mince or grind together with fish.

2. Add egg white and salt and knead well to blend thoroughly. Divide in 16

parts, forming each into a ball. Then toss each ball hard against a cutting board, or other solid surface, 15 to 20 times. (This will remove the air.)

3. Cut each bean curd cake diagonally in 4 separate triangles. On one cut surface of each triangle, cut a pocket by starting near the apex and making a slit running ¾ of the way down. (Do not cut clear through bean curd triangle.)

4. Stuff a fishball into each slit or pocket, flattening and shaping fish to fit. Meanwhile heat oil.

5. Add bean curd triangles, a few at a time, and deep-fry until golden (3 to 5 minutes). Drain on paper toweling and serve.

BRAISED BITTER MELON STUFFED WITH MINCED FISH
8 to 10 servings

2 teaspoons fermented black beans	½ garlic clove
1 pound shrimp	3 tablespoons oil
1 pound fish fillets	1½ cups stock
1 egg white	½ teaspoon salt
½ teaspoon salt	½ teaspoon sugar
2 pounds bitter melon	1 tablespoon cornstarch

2 tablespoons water

1. Soak fermented black beans.

2. Shell and devein shrimp. Mince or grind together with fish. Add egg white and salt and knead well to blend thoroughly.

3. Slice each bitter melon crosswise in 4 thick sections. Scoop out pulp and discard. Stuff fish mixture into pulp cavity, making a mound at the top.

4. Mince garlic and mash together with soaked black beans.

5. Heat oil. Add bitter melon sections, mound-side down, and brown fish lightly. Remove from pan.

6. Add garlic-black bean mixture and stir-fry about 1 minute. Then stir in stock, salt and sugar. Return bitter melon sections and bring to a boil. Then simmer, covered, 20 minutes.

7. Remove bitter melon to a warm serving platter, leaving liquids in pan. Blend cornstarch and cold water to a paste; then stir in to thicken. Pour sauce over bitter melon and serve.

❊ *Other Seafood* ❊

THE CHINESE use a wide variety of seafood: abalone, bêche-de-mer, clams, crabs, lobsters, oysters, scallops, shrimp, snails and squid. These are stir-fried, steamed or deep-fried. Regardless of method, cooking time for seafood is always kept brief since prolonged exposure to heat toughens it. Seafood can be bought fresh, dried, canned or frozen. The frozen varieties should be thawed completely in their original wrappings, then drained well or dried with paper toweling.

CLAMS are extremely versatile. In addition to being steamed, stuffed or stir-fried, they can be used as a substitute for pork in curried pork, for shrimp in lobster sauce and for lobster in deep-fried sweet-and-pungent lobster.

TO BUY: *Select only tightly closed clams, avoiding those with open or cracked shells.*

TO SHELL: *Wash in cold water; scrub thoroughly with a brush to remove sand. Insert a blunt knife blade between the two shells and press downward toward the hinges. This will slash the clam's strong tensile muscle, making it easy to pry the shells apart. With the knife, scrape each shell to loosen the meat; carefully remove any shell fragments. Reserve the clam broth for soups. Note: Clams can also be opened by steaming or boiling (see page 460).*

CRABS come in two varieties, salt-water and fresh-water. These can be used interchangeably, although the latter is generally preferred. Crabs are purchased live, washed in cold water, then boiled or steamed, and shelled for use in various recipes. Frozen or canned crabmeat can substitute for fresh.

TO BOIL: *Plunge the crabs, head down, in enough boiling water to cover. Add a crushed garlic clove; then cook, covered, until done (about 15 minutes for a small crab, 30 minutes for a large one).*

TO STEAM: *Place the crabs in a heatproof dish and cover with 5 to 6 slices fresh ginger root and 4 tablespoons sherry. Steam until done (15 to 30 minutes.) See page 831.*

TO SHELL: *Remove and discard the tail or apron and force upper and lower shells apart. Discard soft, spongy parts. With nutcracker or hammer, lightly crush large claws or pincers. Then remove meat from shells and pincers, discarding the white cartilage.*

LOBSTER, although familiar to Chinese restaurants, is little known in China itself, outside of Canton and the nearby coastal areas. Like crab, lobster is best purchased live. Generally it is cut up and cooked immediately: this way its resiliency, its smooth, shiny texture and its succulent, juicy taste are all retained.

TO BUY: *Allow about ½ pound of lobster per person. Select those with the hardest shells and with claws intact.*

TO CUT UP: *Place live lobster on its back on a wooden board. With a sharp knife or cleaver, quickly chop lobster through at the point where the body and tail are joined. (This will sever the spinal cord.) Chop off and discard head (along grooved semicircle). Chop off claws at joints. Chop body in half lengthwise. Discard gills, lungs and intestinal tract. The coral (of females) and the dark liver are considered delicacies, however, and retained. Remove and dice meat from both body and claws. Or else chop each half of the body crosswise, shell and all, in 2-inch sections; and chop each claw, shell and all, in 2 to 3 pieces.*

Live lobster may also be prepared by parboiling—plunging it briefly, head first, into boiling water, then cutting it up as above for use in various recipes. It can also be boiled or steamed until thoroughly cooked: the shells will turn bright red. The lobster is then cleaned and shelled, cut into neat shapes and served hot or cold with a ginger-vinegar dip (see page 713). NOTE: When buying *cooked* lobster, select one whose tail, when straightened out, will spring back to the same position. (This indicates that the lobster was alive when originally boiled.)

S C A L L O P S , bought fresh, should be cut in thin, round slices for stir-frying and in halves and quarters—depending on their size—for deep-frying. The latter can be prepared as in Basic Deep-fried Shrimp (see page 514). Dried scallops must be soaked, either in water or in sherry; the latter enhances their delicate flavor. Sometimes the dried ones are boiled and shredded instead, and used as a substitute for shrimp in various stir-fried recipes.

S H R I M P figure importantly in Chinese cooking. They are deep-fried, steamed, stir-fried or, occasionally, poached (but rarely boiled since boiling tends to toughen shrimp and make them dry). Deep-fried shrimp are especially succulent: the hot oil seals in their moisture and flavor, and insures juicy tenderness. Stir-frying calls for considerable care, to prevent the shrimp's delicate meat from being cooked either too much or too unevenly. The size of the shrimp will determine cooking time: smaller ones need 2 to 3 minutes of stir-frying; larger ones, 4 to 5 minutes. If very large, the shrimp should be cut in several pieces first.

Shrimp, whether stir-fried, deep-fried or pan-fried, are often cooked and served right in their shells. The shells help retain maximum flavor and also serve as insulation against the heat, so there is less chance of overcooking. Shrimp in their shells are best eaten with chopsticks: The diner pops the shrimp directly into his mouth and neatly removes the shell as he eats the shrimp in several bites. With his chopsticks he delicately and unobtrusively returns the shell to his plate. At no time do his fingers touch either the shrimp or its shell.

TO BUY: *Choose those shrimp which are a translucent gray, tinged with blue (an opaque whitish color, tinged with pink, indicates that the shrimp aren't as fresh). Size in itself is no indication of superiority: while large or jumbo shrimp are generally required for "butterflying," the small and medium varieties are appropriate for most dishes and often have a finer texture and flavor.*

TO STORE: *Place fresh unshelled shrimp, covered, in the meat section of the refrigerator. They will keep several days.*

TO SHELL AND DEVEIN: *With shears or a sharp knife, cut shrimp along the back, cutting to—but not through—the last tail segment. Hold cut portion under cold running water to wash gritty vein away. (Or lift up vein with a toothpick and discard.) Strip off shell and legs, leaving the tail intact.*

TO DEVEIN SHRIMP IN ITS SHELL: *Rinse shrimp first in lightly salted water; then strip off and discard legs. Using a toothpick or tweezers, draw out the vein (the dark, gritty strip along the back) in one piece if possible. If this is too difficult, slit the shell along the back with a sharp knife or shears, and, using the knife point or a toothpick, remove the vein without loosening the shell. Rinse and dry shrimp.*

FANTAIL (OR PHOENIX-TAIL) SHRIMP is the term used for shrimp cooked with the tail intact. The tail acts as a decorative indicator of "doneness" because it turns a brilliant red, like the tail of the phoenix, when the shrimp is cooked. For deep-frying, the tail becomes a convenient handle, permitting the cook to dip the shrimp neatly in batter and afterward being useful to the diner if he's eating the shrimp by hand. The tail itself should never be coated with batter, which would conceal its lovely red color. For stir-frying, however, the tail shell is always removed (see below), but the delicate fin-like meat is retained for color as well as taste.

TO REMOVE THE TAIL-SHELL SEGMENT: *Hold shrimp in one hand; pinch its tail between thumb and forefinger of the other hand. Press hard, then gently pull tail shell. It should slip right off, leaving the meat of the tail intact.*

"BUTTERFLY" SHRIMP is not a variety or a cooking method, but a way of spreading the shrimp out to make them seem larger and fuller. It also enables the shrimp to cook quickly and evenly.

TO BUTTERFLY: *Use large or jumbo shrimp. Shell and devein, leaving the tail shell intact. With a sharp knife, score each shrimp along its inner curve (do not cut all the way through), scoring each about three-quarters down its length. Tap shrimp lightly with the side of a knife to separate the halves; then spread them open to form wings.*

SQUID, bought fresh, is used primarily in stir-fried dishes. The dried variety is generally cooked in soup.

TO CLEAN: *Remove skin with scissors or a knife (if squid is young, the skin will slip off easily). Remove, but do not puncture, ink sac. Cut off tentacles, gelatinous portions and transparent cartilage. Rinse in cold running water and drain or dry well.*

ABALONE

STIR-FRIED ABALONE WITH OYSTER SAUCE
About 4 servings

1 15-ounce can abalone

2 tablespoons smoked ham

1 tablespoon cornstarch

⅓ cup abalone liquid

1 tablespoon soy sauce

3 tablespoons oyster sauce

2 tablespoons oil

1. Drain canned abalone and cut in 1-inch cubes. Reserve liquid. Mince smoked ham.

2. Blend cornstarch and abalone liquid to a paste; then stir in soy and oyster sauces.

3. Heat oil. Add abalone; stir-fry to heat through (about 1 minute).

4. Then stir in cornstarch mixture to thicken. (Do not cook more than 1½ minutes or the abalone will toughen.) Garnish with minced ham and serve.

NOTE: Save the remainder of the abalone liquid for soup.

VARIATIONS: Omit the oyster sauce. Double the quantity of soy sauce.

In step 2, instead of adding the soy and oyster sauces to the cornstarch paste, add them in step 3, after abalone has been stir-fried ½ minute. Then pick up step 4.

STIR-FRIED ABALONE WITH MUSHROOMS AND BAMBOO SHOOTS
4 to 6 servings

4 dried black mushrooms

1 15-ounce can abalone

1 cup bamboo shoots

2 scallion stalks

2 to 3 tablespoons oil

½ teaspoon salt

½ cup abalone liquid

1 tablespoon sherry

1. Soak dried mushrooms.

2. Drain canned abalone and cut in ⅛-inch slices. Reserve liquid. Cut bamboo shoots and soaked mushrooms in ⅛-inch slices. Cut scallion stalks in 1-inch sections.

3. Heat oil. Stir in salt, then bamboo shoots and mushrooms; stir-fry to heat through.

4. Add abalone liquid and sherry. Bring to a boil; then cook, covered, 3 minutes over medium heat.

5. Gently stir in abalone slices and scallions and bring to a boil again. Serve at once.

VARIATIONS: For the dried mushrooms, substitute 1 cup canned button mushrooms.

At the end of step 5, thicken with a cornstarch paste made of 1 tablespoon cornstarch, 3 tablespoons cold water and a few drops of sesame oil.

STIR-FRIED ABALONE WITH MIXED VEGETABLES
About 6 servings

3 or 4 dried black mushrooms	2 tablespoons oil
1 15-ounce can abalone	½ teaspoon salt
1 cup Chinese cabbage stems	1 tablespoon soy sauce
½ cup bamboo shoots	2 tablespoons sherry
2 stalks celery	½ teaspoon sugar
1 onion	½ teaspoon pepper
2 slices smoked ham	1 garlic clove
½ cup snow peas	2 slices fresh ginger root

2 tablespoons oil

1. Soak dried mushrooms.

2. Drain canned abalone; cut in thin strips. (Reserve liquid for soup.) Also cut in strips Chinese cabbage stems, bamboo shoots, celery, onion, soaked mushrooms, smoked ham and snow peas.

3. Heat oil. Stir in salt, then Chinese cabbage, bamboo shoots, celery, onion and mushrooms. Stir-fry to heat through (about 1 minute).

4. Cover pan and let vegetables steam in their own liquids, over low heat, until cooked through (about 3 minutes). Then remove from pan.

5. Meanwhile combine soy sauce, sherry, sugar and pepper. Mince garlic and ginger root.

6. Heat remaining oil. Add minced garlic and ginger root; stir-fry a few times. Add abalone and stir-fry ½ minute.

7. Stir in soy-sherry mixture and heat. Then add snow peas. Return vegetables and gently stir-fry to reheat (about 1½ minutes more). Garnish with ham strips and serve.

VARIATIONS: In step 5, add to the soy-sherry mixture 1 tablespoon oyster sauce.

Shred the abalone; sliver the vegetables. In step 6, add with abalone ½ cup roast pork, ½ cup cooked chicken and ¼ cup ham, all shredded. In step 7, add ½ cup abalone liquid after the soy-sherry mixture and cook, covered, 1½ minutes over low heat. Omit the snow peas and the ham garnish.

STIR-FRIED ABALONE WITH CHICKEN AND ASPARAGUS
6 to 8 servings

1 15-ounce can abalone	1 tablespoon sherry
1 small chicken breast	½ teaspoon sugar
½ cup bamboo shoots	½ teaspoon salt
2 cups asparagus	1 tablespoon cornstarch
1 cup abalone liquid	3 tablespoons water
1 cup stock	2 tablespoons oil

1. Drain canned abalone and cut in 1-inch cubes. Reserve liquid. Bone and skin chicken breast, then dice. Slice bamboo shoots.

2. Cut fresh asparagus in 1-inch sections. Parboil until tender but still crisp.

3. In a bowl, combine abalone liquid, stock, sherry, sugar and salt. In a cup, blend cornstarch and cold water to a paste.

4. Heat oil. Add chicken cubes and stir-fry until they lose their pinkness. Add abalone and bamboo shoots; stir-fry only to heat through (about 1 minute).

5. Add asparagus sections, then stock-sherry mixture. Bring to a boil, stirring gently.

6. Stir in cornstarch paste to thicken and serve at once.

STIR-FRIED ABALONE WITH MINCED PORK

About 6 servings

4 dried black mushrooms	½ cup water
1 15-ounce can abalone	½ teaspoon sesame oil
1 cup lean pork	1 tablespoon cornstarch
¼ cup water chestnuts	1 teaspoon sugar
½ cup bamboo shoots	1 teaspoon soy sauce
1 garlic clove	1 tablespoon water
1 or 2 slices fresh ginger root	2 tablespoons oil
2 tablespoons sherry	½ teaspoon salt
2 tablespoons oyster sauce	½ cup abalone liquid

1. Soak dried mushrooms.

2. Drain canned abalone and cut in 1-inch cubes. Reserve liquid.

3. Mince or grind pork. Mince water chestnuts, bamboo shoots and soaked mushrooms. Crush garlic.

4. Mince ginger root; then combine in a cup with sherry, oyster sauce, water and sesame oil. In another cup, blend cornstarch, sugar, soy sauce and cold water to a paste.

5. Heat oil. Stir in salt. Add garlic; stir-fry to brown lightly. Add minced pork and stir-fry until it loses its pinkness (about 1 minute).

6. Add abalone; stir-fry another ½ minute. Add minced vegetables and stir-fry ½ minute more.

7. Stir in sherry-oyster sauce mixture and heat through. Then add abalone liquid and cook, covered, 1 minute over medium heat.

8. Stir in cornstarch paste to thicken and serve at once.

STIR-FRIED DRIED ABALONE WITH OYSTER SAUCE
4 to 6 servings

½ pound dried abalone	*2 tablespoons oil*
1 tablespoon cornstarch	*½ teaspoon salt*
2 tablespoons water	*½ cup stock*

2 tablespoons oyster sauce

1. Soak dried abalone and cut in ⅛-inch slices.
2. Blend cornstarch and cold water to a paste.
3. Heat oil. Stir in salt; then add abalone slices; stir-fry to coat with oil.
4. Add stock and oyster sauce and cook, stirring, 1 minute. Then cover and cook 2 minutes more over medium heat.
5. Stir in cornstarch paste to thicken and serve.

BÊCHE-DE-MER

STIR-FRIED BÊCHE-DE-MER WITH PORK AND BAMBOO SHOOTS
About 6 servings

8 bêche-de-mer	*½ cup sherry*
½ pound lean pork	*4 tablespoons soy sauce*
1 cup bamboo shoots	*1 cup water*
1 slice fresh ginger root	*2 to 3 tablespoons oil*
1 scallion stalk	*¼ teaspoon sugar*

1. Soak bêche-de-mer; then boil until soft (see page 881).
2. Separately shred pork, bamboo shoots and bêche-de-mer. Mince ginger root. Cut scallion stalk in ½-inch sections.
3. Combine sherry, soy sauce and water.
4. Heat oil. Add pork and stir-fry until it loses its pinkness. Add shredded bêche-de-mer; stir-fry 2 to 3 minutes more.
5. Add bamboo shoots and stir-fry ½ minute. Stir in sherry-soy mixture and heat quickly. Cook, covered, 3 minutes over medium heat.
6. Stir in sugar, minced ginger and scallion. Stir-fry ½ minute more. Serve at once.

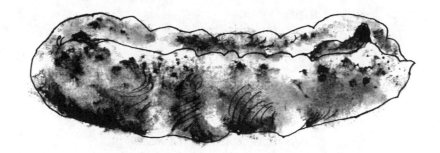

SWEET-AND-PUNGENT BÊCHE-DE-MER
About 4 servings

8 *bêche-de-mer*   3 *tablespoons sherry*
1 *cup bamboo shoots*   3 *tablespoons vinegar*
3 *leeks*   ½ *cup stock*
4 *tablespoons sugar*   2 *to 3 tablespoons oil*
4 *tablespoons soy sauce* 2 *teaspoons cornstarch*

¼ *cup water*

1. Soak bêche-de-mer. Split in half.
2. Slice bamboo shoots. Cut leeks in 3-inch sections.
3. Combine sugar, soy sauce, sherry, vinegar and stock.
4. Heat oil. Add leek and bamboo shoots; stir-fry 2 to 3 minutes. Add soaked bêche-de-mer and stir-fry 1 minute more.
5. Stir in sugar-soy mixture and heat quickly. Then simmer, covered, 15 minutes.
6. Blend cornstarch and cold water to a paste; then stir in to thicken.

VARIATIONS: For the leeks, substitute 1 scallion stalk, 1 garlic clove and 1 slice fresh ginger root, all minced.

For the sugar-soy mixture in step 3, substitute ½ cup stock, 1 tablespoon sherry, 1 teaspoon soy sauce and ½ teaspoon salt.

CLAMS

BASIC STEAMED CLAMS
Allow 4 to 6 clams per person

1. Prepare a dip for clams (see page 713).
2. Wash clams, in their shells, under cold running water to remove sand. Scrub with a brush if necessary.
3. Place clams on a shallow heatproof platter. Steam until clam shells open (5 to 10 minutes). See page 831.
4. Serve clams in their shells, with the dip on the side.

Note: Clams may also be opened by boiling. Pour over boiling water to cover and boil until shells open.

variations: In step 3, place in a deep heatproof bowl 1 pound fresh spinach, with tough stems removed. Sprinkle with 2 tablespoons soy sauce and top with unopened clams. Steam as directed.

After step 3, shell clams and toss them in the clam dip; then refrigerate to chill.

After step 3, shell clams; arrange them on a heatproof platter. Pour over a mixture of 2 tablespoons soy sauce; 1 tablespoon sherry; 1 leek stalk and 2 slices fresh ginger root, both minced. Steam 5 minutes more.

In the variation above, substitute for the seasoning mixture 1 tablespoon shrimp sauce and 1 leek stalk, minced.

STEAMED CLAMS STUFFED WITH PORK
About 6 servings

24 clams	1 tablespoon soy sauce
½ pound lean pork	1 tablespoon sherry
2 slices fresh ginger root	½ teaspoon salt
1 scallion stalk	½ teaspoon sugar

1. Steam clams as above. Shell clams, reserving the shells.
2. Mince pork together with ginger root, scallion and clam meat. Blend in soy sauce, sherry, salt and sugar.

3. Stuff mixture into half-shells. Arrange, stuffing-side up, on a heatproof platter.

4. Steam until pork is cooked through (about 15 minutes). See page 831.

PORK-STUFFED CLAMS, DEEP-FRIED AND SIMMERED
About 6 servings

24 *clams*	1 *tablespoon sherry*
2 *slices fresh ginger root*	1 *teaspoon cornstarch*
1 *scallion stalk*	2 *teaspoons water*
1 *tablespoon sherry*	*oil for deep-frying*
½ *pound lean pork*	1 *cup stock*
1 *tablespoon cornstarch*	1 *teaspoon sugar*
3 *tablespoons soy sauce*	1 *teaspoon soy sauce*
½ *teaspoon salt*	2 *tablespoons cornstarch*

¼ *cup water*

1. Wash clams as in step 2 of Basic Steamed Clams. Place in a deep heatproof bowl.

2. Slice ginger root; cut scallion stalk in 2-inch sections. Add to bowl along with sherry and steam as in step 3 of Basic Steamed Clams.

3. Shell clams, reserving the shells. (Reserve the clam broth for soup.)

4. Mince or grind pork together with clam meat. Blend in cornstarch, soy sauce, salt and remaining sherry.

5. Stuff mixture into half-shells. Blend the second quantity of cornstarch to a paste with water; then, with fingertips, rub paste over the stuffing to coat. (This will seal in the mixture.)

6. Heat oil. Carefully lower in clams, stuffing-side up, a few at a time. Deep-fry, basting with hot oil, until golden. Drain on paper toweling.

7. Combine stock, sugar and remaining soy sauce; then bring to a boil, stirring. Add stuffed clams and simmer, covered, 20 minutes.

8. Blend remaining cornstarch and cold water to a paste. Transfer clams to a warm serving platter, leaving liquids in pan. Stir in cornstarch paste to thicken; then pour sauce over clams and serve.

NOTE: This Shanghai-style dish is served during the Chinese New Year.

STIR-FRIED CLAMS IN SHELLS
4 to 6 servings

24 *clams*	1 *onion*
2 *or 3 garlic cloves*	4 *tablespoons oil*

½ *teaspoon salt*

1. Wash clams as in step 2 of Basic Steamed Clams. Mince garlic and onion.

2. Heat oil. Add salt, then garlic and onion; stir-fry a few times. Add clams in their shells and stir-fry gently to heat.

3. Reduce heat to medium and cook clams, covered, until their shells open (about 7 minutes).

4. Stir-fry clams (still in their shells) gently 1 minute more, basting with hot oil and clam liquids. Serve at once.

CRABS

BASIC STIR-FRIED CRABMEAT
About 4 servings

1 *pound lump crabmeat*	2 *tablespoons sherry*
3 *or 4 scallion stalks*	½ *teaspoon salt*
2 *slices fresh ginger root*	2 *tablespoons oil or lard*
2 *tablespoons soy sauce*	1 *tablespoon cornstarch*

¼ cup water

1. Pick over and shred crabmeat. Cut scallion stalks in ½-inch sections. Mince ginger root.

2. Combine soy sauce, sherry and salt.

3. Heat oil. Add crabmeat and minced ginger root; stir-fry about 1 minute over medium heat. Add scallion sections; stir-fry a few times more.

4. Stir in soy-sherry mixture and heat quickly. Simmer, covered, 2 to 3 minutes.

5. Meanwhile blend cornstarch and cold water to a paste; then stir in to thicken. Serve at once, either plain or with a vinegar dip (see page 713).

VARIATIONS: For the lump crabmeat, substitute canned crabmeat or 2 crabs, shelled.

For the minced ginger, substitute 1 teaspoon ginger juice and blend into crabmeat.

In step 4, instead of simmering, stir-fry the ingredients over low heat until the liquids are nearly absorbed. Omit the cornstarch paste.

With Black Bean Sauce—Mash together 1 tablespoon fermented black beans (soaked) and 1 garlic clove, minced. Add to heated oil in step 3, stir-frying a few times. Then add the crabmeat. Omit the ginger root and soy sauce; increase the sherry to ½ cup.

With Chinese Cabbage I—Shred and blanch 1 pound Chinese cabbage stems. Add with the scallion in step 3.

With Chinese Cabbage II—Cut 1 pound Chinese cabbage stems in 3-inch sections. Cook until tender in stock or water; then drain and keep warm. After step 5, arrange crabmeat mixture over cooked cabbage stems and serve.

With Mushrooms—Drain ½ cup canned button mushrooms and add with scallions in step 3. Pick up steps 4 and 5.

STIR-FRIED CRABMEAT WITH PORK
About 6 servings

1 *pound lump crabmeat*	2 *tablespoons soy sauce*
¼ *pound lean pork*	2 *tablespoons sherry*
2 *slices fresh ginger root*	2 *tablespoons water*
2 *eggs*	½ *teaspoon salt*
2 *scallions*	½ *teaspoon sugar*

2 to 3 tablespoons oil

1. Pick over and shred crabmeat. Mince or grind pork; mince ginger root. Beat eggs lightly. Shred scallions.

2. Combine soy sauce, sherry, water, salt and sugar.

3. Heat oil. Add pork and stir-fry until it loses its pinkness (1 to 2 minutes). Add crabmeat and ginger; stir-fry a few times. Then gently stir in eggs.

4. Add soy-sherry mixture and cook, stirring, over low heat 3 to 4 minutes. Garnish with shredded scallions and serve.

SIMMERED CRABS WITH PORK
4 to 6 servings

2 *crabs*	1 *teaspoon sugar*
¼ *pound lean pork*	¼ *teaspoon salt*
1 *garlic clove,*	½ *teaspoon pepper*
2 *scallions*	4 *tablespoons oil*
1 *egg*	¼ *teaspoon salt*
1 *cup stock*	1 *tablespoon cornstarch*
2 *tablespoons soy sauce*	¼ *cup water*

1. Clean crabs. With a cleaver, chop each, shell and all, in 6 to 8 pieces.
2. Mince or grind pork. Crush garlic; mince scallions. Beat egg lightly.
3. Heat stock and stir in soy sauce, sugar, salt and pepper. Keep warm.

4. Heat oil. Add remaining salt, then garlic, and stir-fry a few times. Add pork and stir-fry until it loses its pinkness (1 to 2 minutes).

5. Stir in stock mixture. Then add crab sections and heat quickly. Cook, covered, 8 to 10 minutes over medium heat.

6. Blend cornstarch and cold water to a paste; then stir in to thicken.

7. Turn off heat. Gently stir in beaten egg until it sets. Garnish with minced scallions and serve.

STEAMED MARINATED CRABS WITH GLUTINOUS RICE
8 to 12 servings

4 large crabs	*2 cups glutinous rice*
2 slices fresh ginger root	*4 cups water*
2 scallion stalks	*1 tablespoon oil*
¼ cup sherry	*½ teaspoon salt*
2 tablespoons soy sauce	*½ teaspoon sugar*

1 tablespoon soy sauce

1. Clean crabs. Mince ginger root and scallions; then combine with sherry and soy sauce. Add to crabs and let stand 30 to 40 minutes, turning occasionally. Drain, reserving marinade.

2. Meanwhile wash and cook glutinous rice (see page 826).

3. Transfer rice to a deep heatproof bowl. Blend in oil, salt, sugar and remaining soy sauce. Top with crabs. Pour the reserved marinade over.

4. Steam until done (about 1 hour). See page 831.

DEEP-FRIED CRABS
8 to 10 servings

6 crabs	½ cup flour
2 eggs	½ teaspoon salt

oil for deep-frying

1. Place crabs on a heatproof platter and steam 10 minutes. See page 831.

2. Clean and shell crabs; remove claws but not legs. Cut each crab in 4 to 6 sections, leaving a leg on each as a "handle."

3. Beat eggs lightly and blend to a smooth batter with flour and salt. Dip crab sections in batter to coat.

4. Heat oil. Add crab sections a few at a time and deep-fry until golden. Drain on paper toweling. Serve hot with any seafood dip (see pages 713–714).

DEEP-FRIED MARINATED CRABS
About 8 servings

6 dried black mushrooms	½ head lettuce
6 soft-shelled crabs	2 eggs
½ garlic clove	½ cup flour
2 slices fresh ginger root	pinch of salt
2 tablespoons soy sauce	dash of pepper
2 tablespoons sherry	oil for deep-frying
1 tablespoon water	2 tablespoons oil
few drops of sesame oil	½ teaspoon salt
1 cup bamboo shoots	½ cup stock
¼ cup water chestnuts	1 tablespoon cornstarch
¼ cup snow peas	1 teaspoon sugar
1 cup Chinese cabbage stems	1 teaspoon soy sauce
1 garlic clove	½ cup water

1. Soak dried mushrooms.

2. Clean crabs and, with a cleaver, chop each in 4 pieces.

3. Mince garlic and ginger root; then combine with soy sauce, sherry, water and sesame oil. Add to crab sections and let stand 30 minutes, turning occasionally. Drain, reserving marinade.

4. Meanwhile shred bamboo shoots, water chestnuts, snow peas, Chinese cabbage stems and soaked mushrooms. Crush remaining garlic. Cut lettuce in strips.

5. Beat eggs lightly; then combine with flour and beat to a smooth batter. Add salt and pepper; beat 1 minute more. Dip crab sections in batter to coat.

6. Heat oil. Add crab sections, a few at a time, and deep-fry until golden. Drain on paper toweling. Keep warm.

7. Heat remaining oil. Add remaining salt, then crushed garlic; stir-fry a few times. Add shredded vegetables (but not lettuce) and stir-fry 2 minutes.

8. Add crab marinade and stir-fry 2 minutes more. Stir in stock and heat quickly. Then simmer, covered, over medium heat, another 2 minutes.

9. Meanwhile blend cornstarch and sugar to a paste with remaining soy sauce and water. Then stir in to thicken.

10. Arrange crabs on shredded lettuce. Pour sauce over and serve, either with lemon slices or a vinegar dip (see page 713).

DEEP-FRIED SWEET-AND-PUNGENT CRABMEAT BALLS
4 to 6 servings

sweet-and-pungent sauce	*1 tablespoon sherry*
1 pound lump crabmeat	*½ teaspoon salt*
2 to 3 scallion stalks	*dash of pepper*
¼ pound fresh mushrooms	*1 egg*
1½ tablespoons oyster sauce	*cornstarch*

oil for deep-frying

1. Prepare a sweet-and-pungent sauce (see pages 735–738).

2. Pick over crabmeat; then mince, together with scallions. Chop mushrooms coarsely and add. Blend in oyster sauce, sherry, salt and pepper. Shape mixture into walnut-size balls.

3. Beat egg. Dip crabmeat balls in egg; then dredge lightly in cornstarch.

4. Heat oil. Add crabmeat balls, a few at a time, and deep-fry until golden. Drain on paper toweling.

5. Reheat sweet-and-pungent sauce. Stir in crabmeat balls only to reheat.

DEEP-FRIED CRABMEAT FRITTERS WITH VEGETABLES
6 to 8 servings

4 dried black mushrooms	1 pound lump crabmeat
1 cup bamboo shoots	¼ teaspoon garlic salt
1 cup celery	dash of pepper
¼ cup water chestnuts	oil for deep-frying
¼ cup snow peas	2 tablespoons oil
1 garlic clove	½ teaspoon salt
2 slices fresh ginger root	½ cup stock
1 teaspoon soy sauce	1 tablespoon cornstarch
1 teaspoon sherry	1 teaspoon sugar
few drops of sesame oil	¼ cup water
3 eggs	1 teaspoon soy sauce
½ cup flour	Chinese parsley

1. Soak dried mushrooms.

2. Shred bamboo shoots, celery, water chestnuts, snow peas and soaked mushrooms. Crush garlic.

3. Mince ginger root; then combine with soy sauce, sherry and sesame oil.

4. Beat eggs. Blend in flour and beat vigorously to a smooth batter. Pick over and mince crabmeat; then add to batter along with garlic salt and pepper. Blend in well.

5. Heat oil. Drop in crabmeat mixture, 1 tablespoon at a time, and deep-fry until golden. Drain on paper toweling. Keep warm.

6. Heat remaining oil. Add salt, then crushed garlic; stir-fry to brown lightly. Add shredded vegetables and stir-fry 2 to 3 minutes.

7. Add ginger-soy mixture; stir-fry 1 minute more. Then add stock and heat quickly. Cook, covered, 2 to 3 minutes over medium heat.

8. Meanwhile blend cornstarch, sugar, water and remaining soy sauce to a paste. Then stir in to thicken. Pour vegetable mixture over crabmeat. Garnish with sprigs of Chinese parsley and serve.

VARIATION: For the parsley garnish, substitute ¼ cup mixed nuts, crushed.

PAN-FRIED CRABMEAT CAKES
About 4 servings

½ pound bean sprouts	5 eggs
½ cup bamboo shoots	1 tablespoon cornstarch
1 onion	2 tablespoons soy sauce
2 tablespoons oil	¼ teaspoon salt
½ pound lump crabmeat	dash of pepper

1½ tablespoons oil

1. Blanch bean sprouts. Sliver bamboo shoots and onion.

2. Heat oil. Add vegetables and stir-fry about 1 minute. Transfer to a deep bowl.

3. Pick over and mince crabmeat; add to vegetables. Beat eggs and add along with cornstarch, soy sauce, salt and pepper. Mix well to blend.

4. Heat remaining oil. Add crabmeat mixture about 2 tablespoons at a time, dropping it like pancake batter to form thin cakes.

5. Brown cakes lightly on one side; turn with a spatula and brown on the other. Repeat (adding more oil as needed) until crabmeat mixture is used up. Keep cakes warm until ready to serve.

VARIATIONS: For the bean sprouts, substitute shredded celery.

Mince the vegetables and, add directly to the crabmeat. (Omit step 2.)

BRAISED CRABMEAT IN CLAM SHELLS
About 6 servings

2 or 3 dried black mushrooms	2 tablespoons sherry
2 dozen clam shells	½ teaspoon salt
1 pound lump crabmeat	3 tablespoons flour
¼ pound lean pork	oil for deep-frying
1 tablespoon smoked ham	1 onion
1 slice fresh ginger root	2 tablespoons oil
½ scallion stalk	¼ cup stock
1 egg	2 tablespoons sherry

1. Soak dried mushrooms. Wash clam shells.

2. Pick over crabmeat; then mince together with pork, ham, ginger root, scallion and soaked mushrooms.

3. Beat egg lightly; add to minced ingredients, along with sherry and salt. Mix well to blend. Stuff mixture into clam shells and dust lightly with flour to seal in.

4. Heat oil. Lower in clam shells, a few at a time, stuffing-side up; and deep-

fry, basting with hot oil, until golden (about 3 minutes). Drain on paper toweling.

5. Shred onion. Heat remaining oil. Add onion and stir-fry to soften slightly (about 1 minute). Then add stock and heat quickly.

6. Add stuffed clam shells and simmer, covered, 10 minutes. Add remaining sherry; simmer, covered, 10 minutes more, and serve.

LOBSTER

STIR-FRIED LOBSTER AND MUSHROOMS
About 4 servings

1 *pound lobster meat*	1 *garlic clove*
1 *tablespoon cornstarch*	2 *tablespoons soy sauce*
¼ *cup water*	1 *tablespoon sherry*
¼ *pound fresh mushrooms*	2 *tablespoons oil*
2 *scallion stalks*	3 to 4 *tablespoons oil*

½ *teaspoon salt*

1. Cut lobster meat in 1-inch cubes. Blend cornstarch and cold water to a paste; add to lobster cubes and toss gently to coat.

2. Slice mushrooms. Cut scallion stalks in 1-inch sections.

3. Mince garlic; then combine with soy sauce and sherry.

4. Heat oil. Add scallions; stir-fry a few times. Add mushrooms and stir-fry until nearly done (2 to 3 minutes). Remove vegetables from pan.

5. Heat remaining oil. Add salt and lobster cubes. Stir-fry until cubes begin to curl at the edges (about 3 to 4 minutes).

6. Quickly stir in garlic-soy mixture. Then return mushrooms and scallions. Stir-fry to reheat and blend flavors (about 2 minutes more). Serve at once.

VARIATIONS: For the mushrooms, substitute any of the following: 1 cup bamboo shoots, carrots, celery, green pepper or snow peas, cut in strips.

In step 1, coat the lobster cubes with a batter made of 1 egg, beaten; ¼ cup flour; and 1½ tablespoons water.

In step 3, add to the garlic-soy mixture 3 slices fresh ginger root, minced.

STIR-FRIED LOBSTER AND MIXED VEGETABLES
4 to 6 servings

¼ cup almond meats	2 tablespoons sherry
1 lobster (1½ to 2 pounds)	½ teaspoon sugar
½ cup celery	2 to 3 tablespoons oil
½ cup bamboo shoots	½ teaspoon salt
1 small can button mushrooms	1 tablespoon cornstarch
1 garlic clove	2 teaspoons soy sauce
2 slices fresh ginger root	3 tablespoons water
½ cup stock	few drops of sesame oil

1. Blanch and toast almonds.

2. With a cleaver, chop lobster lengthwise in half; then clean. Chop, shell and all, in ½-inch cubes.

3. Slice celery diagonally in ¼-inch sections. Slice bamboo shoots ¼-inch thick, then in ¾-inch squares. Drain canned mushrooms. Crush garlic.

4. Mince ginger root; then combine with stock, sherry and sugar.

5. Heat oil. Add salt, then garlic, and stir-fry a few times. Add lobster; stir-fry 1 minute. Add vegetables and stir-fry 2 minutes more.

6. Stir in ginger-stock mixture and heat quickly. Then cook, covered, 3 minutes over medium heat.

7. Meanwhile blend cornstarch, soy sauce and cold water to a paste; then stir in to thicken. Sprinkle with sesame oil; garnish with toasted almonds and serve.

NOTE: This dish is also called Subgum Lobster.

VARIATIONS: For the whole lobster, substitute 2 lobster tails. Discard shell and cut meat in ½-inch slices.

For the vegetables, substitute any of the following: asparagus, bean sprouts, Chinese cabbage stems, cucumbers, green peppers, fresh or dried mushrooms, or onions. Or any of the following, parboiled: broccoli, carrots, cauliflower, Chinese turnips, green peas or string beans. (All, with the exception of the bean sprouts and green peas, should be diced.)

LOBSTER CANTONESE I

4 to 6 servings

1 lobster (1½ to 2 pounds)	2 teaspoons soy sauce
¼ pound lean pork	½ cup stock
1 to 2 garlic cloves	2 eggs
3 to 4 tablespoons oil	¼ cup water
½ teaspoon salt	1 tablespoon cornstarch

3 tablespoons water

1. With a cleaver, chop lobster lengthwise in half; then clean. Chop each half, shell and all, in 1½-inch sections. Chop claws in two.

2. Mince or grind pork. Crush garlic.

3. Heat oil. Add salt, then garlic, and brown lightly. Add pork and stir-fry until it loses its pinkness (1 to 2 minutes). Sprinkle with soy sauce; stir-fry ½ minute more.

4. Add lobster sections; stir-fry 1 minute. Stir in stock and heat quickly. Then cook, covered, over medium heat, until done (about 3 minutes): the meat should be chalky white; the shell bright red.

5. Meanwhile, in one cup, beat eggs lightly with water and set aside. In another cup, blend cornstarch and remaining water to a paste.

6. Stir in cornstarch paste to thicken; then turn off heat and stir in beaten eggs until creamy. (Turning off the heat helps retain the egg's rich yellow color and makes for a smooth-flowing sauce; it prevents the egg from overcooking, coagulating and turning white.) Serve at once.

NOTE: For best results, start with a live lobster.

VARIATIONS: For the lobster, substitute 6 crabs. Shell, crack claws, discard feet. Chop each crab in 4 pieces.

In step 3, omit the salt and garlic clove. Mash 1 tablespoon fermented black beans (soaked) with 1 garlic clove, minced, and add to the hot oil. (You may also at this point add 1 slice fresh ginger root, minced; and/or a few drops of sesame oil.) Stir-fry a few times to heat; then add minced pork.

In step 4, before adding the stock, sprinkle lobster with ¼ teaspoon salt, ¼ teaspoon sugar, a dash of pepper and 1 teaspoon sherry. Stir-fry a few times to blend in.

In step 4, substitute for the stock a mixture of 1 tablespoon soy sauce, 1 tablespoon sherry, ¼ cup water, ½ teaspoon sugar and 1 slice fresh ginger root, minced.

In step 5, add to the cornstarch paste ¼ teaspoon sugar and 2 teaspoons soy sauce.

In step 6, add with the beaten eggs 1 scallion stalk, minced.

LOBSTER CANTONESE II
4 to 6 servings

1 *lobster* (1½ *to* 2 *pounds*)	2 *tablespoons cornstarch*
¼ *pound lean pork*	2 *tablespoons sherry*
1 *scallion*	2 *tablespoons soy sauce*
2 *slices fresh ginger root*	½ *teaspoon salt*
2 *eggs*	½ *cup water*

3 to 4 tablespoons oil

1. Clean and chop lobster as in recipe above.

2. Mince or grind pork; mince scallion and ginger root. Beat eggs lightly. Then combine with cornstarch, sherry, soy sauce, salt and water, blending well.

3. Heat oil. Add lobster sections and stir-fry over medium heat until the shell turns bright red (about 3 minutes).

4. Add pork mixture and cook, stirring, over low heat until meat is cooked through (3 to 5 minutes). Serve at once.

BASIC DEEP-FRIED LOBSTER
About 4 servings

1 *lobster* (1½ *to* 2 *pounds*)	½ *teaspoon salt*
2 *eggs*	*oil for deep-frying*
4 *tablespoons cornstarch*	*lettuce*
2 *tablespoons water*	*pepper*

1. Clean and shell lobster. Cut meat in ½-inch cubes.

2. Beat egg lightly and blend to a batter with cornstarch, water and salt. Dip lobster cubes in batter to coat.

3. Heat oil. Add lobster cubes, a few at a time, and deep-fry about ½ minute. Then reduce heat to medium and deep-fry until golden. Drain on paper toweling.

4. Arrange lobster on a bed of shredded lettuce, sprinkle with pepper and serve.

VARIATIONS: **After step 1,** marinate lobster cubes in a mixture of 2 tablespoons sherry, 1 tablespoon oyster or soy sauce, and 2 slices fresh ginger root, minced. Let stand 30 minutes, tossing cubes occasionally; then drain, discarding marinade. Pick up step 2.

After step 1, wrap each lobster cube in half a strip of bacon. Pick up step 2.

In step 2, for the cornstarch batter, substitute either of the following:

2 eggs, lightly beaten, and ¾ cup flour. (If necessary, add a few drops of water to thin.)

2 eggs, lightly beaten; ¼ cup flour; ¼ cup water-chestnut flour; ½ teaspoon salt; and ¼ teaspoon garlic powder.

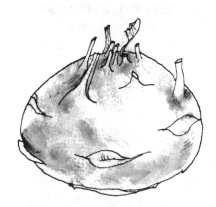

DEEP-FRIED LOBSTER AND VEGETABLES
6 to 8 servings

deep-fried lobster cubes
1 cup canned button mushrooms
1 cup snow peas
½ cup bamboo shoots
½ cup onion
¼ cup water chestnuts
1 cup Chinese cabbage stems
½ cup celery
1 garlic clove
1 or 2 slices fresh ginger root

1 tablespoon oyster sauce
2 tablespoons sherry
2 tablespoons oil
few drops of sesame oil
½ teaspoon salt
½ cup stock
1 tablespoon cornstarch
1 teaspoon sugar
1 teaspoon soy sauce
¼ cup water

1. Deep-fry lobster as in recipe above (marinating it as in the first variation). Drain and set aside.

2. Slice canned button mushrooms, snow peas, bamboo shoots, onion and water chestnuts. Slice Chinese cabbage stems and celery, both diagonally. Crush garlic.

3. Mince ginger root; then combine with oyster sauce and sherry.

4. Heat oil and sesame oil. Add salt, then garlic; stir-fry a few times. Add vegetables and stir-fry 2 or 3 minutes.

5. Add ginger-oyster sauce mixture; stir-fry 1 minute more.

6. Add stock and heat quickly. Then cook, covered, 3 minutes over medium heat.

7. Meanwhile blend cornstarch, sugar, soy sauce and cold water to a paste. Then stir in to thicken. Add lobster cubes only to reheat. Serve at once.

VARIATION: In step 4, add after the salt and garlic, ¾ cup chicken or lean pork, shredded; stir-fry until pork or chicken loses its pinkness. Then, in place of the vegetables listed above, stir in the following, all shredded: ¾ cup each bamboo shoots, Chinese cabbage and celery; ½ cup fresh mushrooms and ¼ cup water chestnuts.

DEEP-FRIED SWEET-AND-PUNGENT LOBSTER
About 4 servings

sweet-and-pungent sauce	1½ tablespoons soy sauce
1 pound lobster meat	1 egg
½ teaspoon salt	flour
1 teaspoon sugar	oil for deep-frying

1. Prepare a sweet-and-pungent sauce (see pages 735–738).

2. Clean and shell lobster. Cut meat in ½-inch cubes and sprinkle lightly with salt.

3. Combine sugar and soy sauce; then add to lobster cubes and toss gently. Let stand 15 minutes, turning occasionally. Drain, discarding marinade.

4. Beat egg lightly. Dip lobster cubes in egg; then dredge in flour.

5. Deep-fry as in Basic Deep-fried Lobster and drain on paper toweling.

6. Reheat sweet-and-pungent sauce. Pour over lobster and serve.

VARIATIONS: For the marinade in step 3, substitute 1 tablespoon lemon juice, 1 teaspoon soy sauce.

Omit step 4 and coat the cubes instead with the batter (or its variations) given in Basic Deep-fried Lobster.

STEAMED LOBSTER
About 4 servings

1 lobster (1½ to 2 pounds)	½ teaspoon salt
1 scallion stalk	1 tablespoon sherry
2 tablespoons oil	

1. With a cleaver, chop lobster lengthwise in half, shell and all; then clean. Split claws. Place lobster, meat-side up, on a heatproof platter.

2. Mince scallion stalk and sprinkle over lobster, along with salt, sherry and oil.

3. Steam until lobster shell is bright red (15 to 20 minutes). See page 831. Serve at once.

VARIATIONS: In step 2, add, with other ingredients, 3 slices fresh ginger root, minced; and 1 teaspoon soy sauce.

Omit the oil in step 2. Then, at the end of step 3, heat the oil plus a few drops of sesame oil until nearly smoking. Pour over lobster and serve.

STEAMED LOBSTER WITH PORK
About 6 servings

1 *lobster* (1½ *to 2 pounds*)	2 *tablespoons soy sauce*
¼ *pound lean pork*	1 *tablespoon sherry*
2 *scallion stalks*	½ *teaspoon salt*
2 *slices fresh ginger root*	1 *teaspoon sugar*
2 *eggs*	*dash of pepper*
2 *tablespoons oil*	*lettuce*

1. With a cleaver, chop lobster lengthwise in half; then clean. Chop each half, shell and all, in 1½-inch sections. Chop claws in two. Arrange lobster, meat-side up, on a heatproof platter.

2. Mince or grind pork, scallions and ginger root; beat eggs lightly. Then combine, together with oil, soy sauce, sherry, salt, sugar and pepper. Blend well.

3. Spread mixture over lobster and stream until done (about 30 minutes). See page 831. Garnish with shredded lettuce and serve.

VARIATIONS: For the lobster, substitute 6 crabs.

For the pork mixture, substitute either of the following combinations:

¼ pound pork, minced; 1 teaspoon fermented black beans (soaked), mashed together with 2 garlic cloves, minced; 2 eggs, lightly beaten; 1 tablespoon smoked ham and 1 scallion stalk, both minced; and ½ teaspoon salt.

¼ pound pork, minced; 4 dried black mushrooms (soaked), minced; 4 water chestnuts, minced; 1 tablespoon oil, 1 teaspoon sherry, ½ teaspoon salt, ½ teaspoon sugar and the white of a Chinese salt egg. (After spreading mixture over lobster, mash the yolk of the salt egg and sprinkle on top.)

STEAMED LOBSTER TAILS STUFFED WITH PORK
8 to 10 servings

4 *dried black mushrooms*	1 *teaspoon salt*
2 *tablespoons fermented black beans*	1 *garlic clove*
4 *large lobster tails*	2 *teaspoons cornstarch*
¼ *cup water chestnuts*	½ *cup water*
½ *pound lean pork*	2 *tablespoons soy sauce*
2 *tablespoons oil*	2 *tablespoons oil*

1. Separately soak dried mushrooms and fermented black beans.

2. Remove lobster meat from tails, reserving the shells. Mince lobster, together with water chestnuts and soaked mushrooms. Separately mince or grind pork.

3. Heat oil. Add pork and stir-fry to brown lightly (2 to 3 minutes).

4. Let pork cool; then add to lobster mixture, along with salt, mixing well to blend. Divide mixture in 4 parts, forming each into a ball. Toss each ball hard against a chopping board 10 to 15 times to drive out the air. Then stuff mixture into lobster shells. Arrange, stuffing-side up, on a shallow heatproof dish.

5. Steam until done (about 20 minutes). See page 831.

6. Meanwhile mince garlic; then mash with soaked black beans. Blend cornstarch, cold water and soy sauce to a paste.

7. Heat remaining oil. Add garlic-black bean mash; stir-fry a few times. Then stir in cornstarch paste to thicken. Pour sauce over lobster tails and serve.

SIMMERED LOBSTER AND VERMICELLI

About 4 servings

6 *dried black mushrooms*	½ *teaspoon salt*
¼ *pound vermicelli*	*dash of pepper*
1 *cup cooked lobster meat*	¼ *teaspoon garlic powder*
2 *slices fresh ginger root*	½ *cup celery*
1 *tablespoon soy sauce*	2 *cups stock*
2 *tablespoons sherry*	2 *scallions*

1. Separately soak dried mushrooms and vermicelli (peastarch noodles).

2. Shred lobster meat. Mince ginger root; then combine with soy sauce, sherry, salt, pepper and garlic powder. Add to lobster and toss gently.

3. Shred celery and soaked mushrooms. Cut vermicelli in 5- to 6-inch lengths.

4. Bring stock to a boil. Add soaked vermicelli; simmer, covered, 4 minutes. Add celery and mushrooms and simmer, covered, another 3 minutes.

5. Add lobster shreds and simmer 3 minutes more. Shred scallions; sprinkle over as a garnish and serve.

NOTE: This recipe calls for *cooked* lobster meat. When using live lobster, parboil it 2 minutes, rinse in cold water; then shell.

OYSTERS

DEEP-FRIED OYSTERS
About 6 servings

24 to 30 oysters   1 or 2 scallions
salt and pepper   batter

oil for deep-frying

1. Shell oysters; then season lightly with salt and pepper. Mince scallions.

2. Coat oysters with any of the batter combinations listed below.

3. Heat oil. Add oysters, a few at a time, and deep-fry until golden. Drain on paper toweling. Garnish with scallions and serve.

VARIATIONS: Instead of seasoning the oysters with salt and pepper, toss them in a mixture of 1 tablespoon sherry and 1 teaspoon salt. Then coat with batter.

In step 2, add the minced scallions to the batter mixture.

BATTERS FOR DEEP-FRIED OYSTERS

a. 1 egg, beaten; ½ cup flour; 1 cup water.

b. 1 cup flour, 2 teaspoons baking powder, ¾ cup water.

c. 1 cup flour, 1 teaspoon baking powder, 4 tablespoons cornstarch, 1 tablespoon lard, ¾ cup water.

DEEP-FRIED BACON WRAPPED OYSTERS
About 4 servings

12 oysters

1 slice fresh ginger root

2 tablespoons soy sauce

2 tablespoons sherry

1 cup mixed nutmeats

3 bacon strips

3 tablespoons smoked ham

2 scallion stalks

1 egg

½ cup flour

pinch of salt

dash of pepper

oil for deep-frying

½ head lettuce

lemon wedges

Chinese parsley

1. Shell oysters. Mince ginger root; then combine with soy sauce and sherry. Add to oysters and let stand 15 minutes, turning occasionally. Drain, discarding marinade.

2. Meanwhile crush nutmeats almost to a powder. Cut each bacon strip crosswise in 4 sections. Sliver smoked ham. Cut scallion stalks in ½-inch sections.

3. Dip each oyster in crushed nutmeats; then top with a few ham slivers and a piece of scallion. Wrap oysters in bacon sections.

4. Beat egg lightly and blend to a batter with flour, salt and pepper. Dip wrapped oysters in batter to coat.

5. Meanwhile heat oil. Add oysters, a few at a time, and deep-fry until crisp and golden. Drain on paper toweling.

6. Arrange on a bed of shredded lettuce. Garnish with lemon wedges and Chinese parsley.

VARIATION: For the smoked ham, substitute Chinese sausage.

PAN-FRIED OYSTERS AND BACON
About 4 servings

12 oysters

3 bacon strips

1 egg

1 tablespoon water

⅔ cup onions

1 tablespoon cornstarch

1 teaspoon soy sauce

½ cup stock

1 tablespoon oil

2 tablespoons oil

1. Shell oysters. Cut each bacon strip crosswise in 4 sections. Wrap bacon around each oyster.

2. Beat egg lightly with water; then dip wrapped oysters in mixture to coat.

3. Chop onions. In a cup, blend cornstarch, soy sauce and cold stock to a paste.

4. Heat oil. Gently add oysters and brown well on both sides. Drain on paper toweling. Keep warm. Pour off and discard bacon fat.

5. Heat remaining oil. Add onions and stir-fry until translucent. Then stir in cornstarch paste to thicken. Pour sauce over oysters and serve.

STIR-FRIED DRIED OYSTERS AND VEGETABLES
About 6 servings

12 *dried oysters*	½ *teaspoon salt*
4 *dried black mushrooms*	1 *teaspoon soy sauce*
½ *cup bamboo shoots*	*dash of pepper*
½ *cup water chestnuts*	1 *tablespoon cornstarch*
1 *head lettuce*	3 *tablespoons water*
1 *tablespoon sherry*	2 *to 3 tablespoons oil*
	½ *cup stock*

1. Separately soak dried oysters and dried mushrooms.

2. Dice bamboo shoots, water chestnuts and soaked mushrooms. Mince soaked oysters. Cut lettuce in strips; arrange on a serving platter.

3. In one cup, combine sherry, salt, soy sauce and pepper. In another, blend cornstarch and cold water to a paste.

4. Heat oil. Add minced oysters and stir-fry a few times. Add diced vegetables; stir-fry 1 minute.

5. Add sherry mixture; stir-fry 1 minute more. Add stock and heat quickly. Then cook, covered, 2 to 3 minutes over medium heat.

6. Stir in cornstarch paste to thicken. Spoon mixture over lettuce and serve.

VARIATIONS: For the diced vegetables, substitute 1 cup celery, 1 cup Chinese cabbage and ½ cup snow peas, all minced.

In step 3, add to the sherry mixture 1 slice fresh ginger root, minced, and a few drops of sesame oil.

In step 3, add to the cornstarch paste 1 tablespoon oyster sauce, 1 teaspoon soy sauce and a few drops of hot sauce.

In step 4, add, with the oysters, 1 cup lean pork, minced or ground. Stir-fry until the pork loses its pinkness; then add the vegetables.

BRAISED DRIED OYSTERS AND PORK I
About 8 servings

12 *dried oysters*	1 *tablespoon sugar*
½ *pound pork*	3 *tablespoons soy sauce*
water to cover	2 *tablespoons sherry*
1 *or 2 garlic cloves*	½ *cup oyster soaking liquid*
1 *scallion stalk*	2 *tablespoons oil*

2 cups water

1. Soak dried oysters (reserve soaking liquid).
2. Place pork in water and boil 15 minutes; discard liquid.
3. Cut meat in 1-inch cubes. Mince soaked oysters. Crush garlic. Cut scallion stalk in 1-inch sections.
4. Combine sugar, soy sauce, sherry and oyster-soaking liquid.
5. Heat oil. Stir-fry garlic and scallions to brown lightly. Add pork cubes; stir-fry to brown lightly.
6. Add sugar-soy mixture and minced oysters. Cook, stirring, 1 minute.
7. Add remaining water. Bring to a boil; then simmer, covered, until pork and oysters are tender (about 30 minutes).

VARIATION: In step 7, after the water boils, add 6 water chestnuts, sliced.

BRAISED DRIED OYSTERS AND PORK II
6 to 8 servings

12 *dried oysters*	2 *tablespoons oil*
4 *dried black mushrooms*	2 *cups stock*
¼ *pound lean pork*	2 *teaspoons cornstarch*
1 *cup bamboo shoots*	3 *tablespoons water*
1 *garlic clove*	1 *teaspoon soy sauce*

salt and pepper

1. Separately soak dried oysters and dried mushrooms.
2. Cut pork in ¼-inch slices. Slice bamboo shoots, soaked oysters and mushrooms. Crush garlic.
3. Heat oil. Add garlic. Stir-fry to brown; then discard. Add pork; stir-fry until it loses its pinkness.
4. Add sliced vegetables and oysters. Stir-fry 2 minutes more.
5. Add stock and bring to a boil; then simmer, covered, about 1 hour.
6. Blend cornstarch and cold water to a paste; then stir in to thicken. Transfer to a serving dish. Sprinkle with soy sauce; season lightly with salt and pepper, and serve.

BRAISED DRIED OYSTERS WITH BEAN CURD STICKS
About 8 servings

12 *dried oysters*
6 *dried black mushrooms*
4 *to 6 bean curd sticks*
2 *teaspoons red bean cheese*
2 *tablespoons oil*

½ *teaspoon salt*
2 *cups stock*
¼ *teaspoon sugar*
1 *tablespoon oil*
2 *teaspoons cornstarch*

2 *tablespoons water*

1. Separately soak dried oysters, dried mushrooms and bean curd sticks.
2. Dice soaked oysters and mushrooms. Cut bean curd sticks in 2-inch lengths. Mash red bean cheese.
3. Heat oil. Add salt, then red bean cheese, and stir-fry 1 minute. Stir in oysters, mushrooms and bean curd.
4. Add stock, sugar and remaining oil. Bring quickly to a boil, stirring gently. Then simmer, covered, 45 minutes, stirring occasionally.
5. Blend cornstarch and cold water to a paste; then stir in to thicken, and serve.

STUFFED AND DEEP-FRIED DRIED OYSTERS
8 to 10 servings

¼ *pound dried oysters*
¼ *pound shrimp*
¼ *pound lean pork*
1 *slice fresh ginger root*
½ *teaspoon salt*

1 *teaspoon sugar*
2 *teaspoons soy sauce*
1 *tablespoon sherry*
1 *egg*
cracker meal

oil for deep-frying

1. Soak dried oysters.
2. Shell and devein shrimp. Mince or grind pork, shrimp and ginger root; then combine with salt, sugar, soy sauce and sherry. Mix well.
3. Cut each oyster lengthwise in half. Spread 1 tablespoon shrimp-pork mixture on one oyster half. Top, sandwich-style, with the second half.
4. Beat egg lightly. Dip stuffed oyster in egg; then dredge in cracker meal (or fine bread crumbs).
5. Meanwhile heat oil. Add stuffed oysters a few at a time and deep-fry until golden. Drain on paper toweling and serve.

STEAMED AND DEEP-FRIED DRIED OYSTER BALLS

About 12 servings

24 *dried oysters*	3 *tablespoons cornstarch*
¼ *pound shrimp*	2 *teaspoons sugar*
½ *pound lean pork*	¾ *teaspoon salt*
½ *pound fish fillets*	*dash of pepper*
4 *scallion stalks*	2 *eggs*
2 *garlic cloves*	*cracker meal*
3 *slices fresh ginger root*	*oil for deep-frying*

1. Soak dried oysters.

2. Shell and devein shrimp; then mince or grind along with pork, fish, scallions, garlic and ginger root.

3. Blend in cornstarch, sugar, salt and pepper, mixing well. Roll soaked oysters in mixture to coat, shaping each into a ball.

4. Place oyster balls on a shallow heatproof dish and steam 20 minutes (see page 831). Let cool, then refrigerate either several hours or overnight.

5. Beat eggs lightly. Dip oyster balls in egg; then dredge in cracker meal (or fine bread crumbs).

6. Meanwhile heat oil. Add oyster balls a few at a time and deep-fry until golden. Drain on paper toweling and serve, with a seafood dip (see pages 713–714).

NOTE: These oyster balls, prepared in advance and deep-fried at the last minute, are usually eaten as snacks.

SCALLOPS

STIR-FRIED SCALLOPS AND ONION
4 to 6 servings

1 *pound scallops*	½ *teaspoon salt*
1 *yellow onion*	*dash of pepper*
2 *to 3 tablespoons oil*	1 *tablespoon sherry*

1. Quarter scallops or cut in ¼-inch slices if large; cut in half if small. Slice onion thin.

2. Heat oil. Add onion and stir-fry to soften. Add scallops and stir-fry quickly to brown.

3. Sprinkle with salt and pepper, then with sherry. Stir-fry over medium heat until scallops are done (2 to 3 minutes). Serve at once.

STIR-FRIED SCALLOPS WITH GINGER ROOT
4 to 6 servings

1 *pound scallops*	1 *tablespoon cornstarch*
2 *or 3 slices fresh ginger root*	4 *tablespoons water*
1 *scallion stalk*	2 *tablespoons oil*

½ *teaspoon salt*

1. Cut scallops as in recipe above. Mince ginger root. Cut scallions in 1-inch sections. Blend cornstarch and cold water to a paste.

2. Heat oil. Add salt, then ginger root and scallions; stir-fry a few times. Add scallops and stir-fry to cook through (2 to 3 minutes).

3. Stir in cornstarch paste to thicken, and serve at once.

VARIATIONS: In step 2, add with the scallops either 1 or 2 green peppers, diced; or ½ pound fresh mushrooms, sliced.

For the cornstarch paste, substitute 2 tablespoons soy sauce and 1 teaspoon sugar. Add in step 3, stirring in to blend.

STIR-FRIED SCALLOPS WITH MIXED VEGETABLES
About 6 servings

1 *pound scallops*	2 *teaspoons soy sauce*
½ *cup bamboo shoots*	¼ *cup water*
½ *cup celery*	3 *tablespoons oil*
½ *cup dried onions*	½ *teaspoon salt*
6 *snow peas*	½ *cup stock*
1 *tablespoon cornstarch*	½ *teaspoon sugar*

1. Cut scallops as in Stir-fried Scallops and Onion.

2. Cut bamboo shoots first in ¼-inch slices, then in ½-inch sections. Slice celery in ¼-inch sections. Slice dried onions. Stem snow peas.

3. Blend cornstarch, soy sauce and cold water to a paste.

4. Heat oil. Add salt, then scallops, and stir-fry to coat with oil (about ½ minute). Add vegetables and stir-fry about 2 minutes more.

5. Add stock and sugar and heat quickly. Then cook, stirring, over medium heat, until vegetables are done (2 to 3 minutes).

6. Stir in cornstarch paste to thicken. Serve at once.

VARIATIONS: For the vegetables, substitute 1 pound string beans, cut in ½-inch lengths and parboiled; and 2 tomatoes, peeled and cubed. Add the beans in step 4, the tomatoes after step 5.

Or substitute ½ cup water chestnuts, ½ cup white onions and ½ cup celery, all sliced. Add in step 4. Then, after step 5, add ½ cup canned pineapple chunks.

In step 1, dredge the scallops lightly with flour.

In step 3, add a few drops of sesame oil to the cornstarch paste.

In step 4, add to the hot oil 2 slices fresh ginger root and 1 garlic clove, both minced, and stir-fry to brown lightly. Then stir-fry scallops. Sprinkle with the salt and a dash of pepper *before* adding the vegetables.

STIR-FRIED SCALLOPS WITH EGG
About 4 servings

¾ *pound scallops*	½ *teaspoon salt*
2 *tablespoons smoked ham*	*dash of pepper*
2 *tablespoons sherry*	2 *eggs*
1 *teaspoon sugar*	3 *tablespoons oil*

1. Cut scallops as in Stir-fried Scallops and Onion. Mince smoked ham.

2. Combine sherry, sugar, salt and pepper.

3. Separate eggs. Combine 2 yolks with 1 white and beat until smooth. (Reserve remaining white for another recipe.)

4. Heat oil. Add scallops and stir-fry to brown lightly (2 to 3 minutes). Add sherry-sugar mixture; stir-fry 1 minute more.

5. Add beaten eggs; then cook, stirring, over high heat until scallops are coated with egg. Garnish with minced ham and serve.

STEAMED MARINATED SCALLOPS AND HAM
About 6 servings

1 pound scallops	1 or 2 slices fresh ginger root
sherry to cover	½ teaspoon salt
¼ cup onion	½ cup smoked ham
1 teaspoon sugar	

1. Cut each scallop in half. Add sherry and let stand 15 minutes, turning occasionally. Drain, discarding marinade. Arrange scallop sections on a heatproof dish.

2. Mince onion and ginger root and sprinkle over scallops. Then season with salt. Shred ham and arrange on top; sprinkle with sugar.

3. Steam until done (about 3 to 5 minutes). See page 831.

NOTE: Use sea scallops, not bay scallops, for this dish.

STIR-FRIED DRIED SCALLOPS WITH STRING BEANS
4 to 6 servings

10 *dried scallops*
½ *cup sherry*
1 *pound string beans*
1 *cup water*

4 *tablespoons soy sauce*
4 *tablespoons oil*
2 *tablespoons oil*
½ *cup stock*

1. Soak dried scallops in sherry 2 hours, turning occasionally. Drain and discard sherry.

2. Cut string beans diagonally in 3 sections; then parboil.

3. Place scallops in a pan with water. Bring to a boil; then simmer, covered, until soft (15 to 20 minutes).

4. Add soy sauce and cook, stirring, over high heat until the liquid has nearly evaporated.

5. Heat oil. Add scallops and stir-fry over low heat until they come apart in shreds and are dry. Remove from pan.

6. Heat remaining oil. Add parboiled string beans and stir-fry 2 minutes.

7. Add stock and heat quickly. Then cook, covered, over medium heat, until beans are nearly done (about 2 minutes). Return scallop shreds only to reheat, and serve at once.

VARIATION: For the string beans, substitute either 1 cup peas, parboiled; or 2 to 3 cups Chinese cabbage, cut in 2-inch sections.

STEAMED DRIED SCALLOPS WITH HAM
4 to 6 servings

10 *dried scallops*
1 *cup sherry*
½ *cup smoked ham*

2 *tablespoons onion*
1 *or 2 slices fresh ginger root*
½ *teaspoon sugar*

1. Soak dried scallops in sherry 12 hours, turning occasionally. Drain and discard sherry.

2. Cut scallops in half. Arrange on a heatproof dish. Chop ham coarsely; mince onion and ginger root and sprinkle over scallops. Then season with sugar.

3. Steam until done (about 1 hour). See page 831.

BRAISED DRIED SCALLOPS AND RADISHES
4 to 6 servings

10 *dried scallops*   ½ *teaspoon salt*
1½ *cups soaking liquid*   30 *radishes*
1 *cup stock*   2 to 3 *tablespoons oil*
2 *tablespoons sherry*   1 *teaspoon cornstarch*

1 *tablespoon water*

1. Soak dried scallops. (Reserve soaking liquid.)

2. Strain soaking liquid; then combine with stock, sherry and salt. Trim and peel radishes.

3. Heat oil. Add scallops and radishes; stir-fry 2 minutes.

4. Add soaking liquid-stock mixture and heat quickly. Then simmer, covered, until scallops are tender (about 15 minutes).

5. Meanwhile blend cornstarch and remaining cold water to a paste. Then stir in to thicken, and serve.

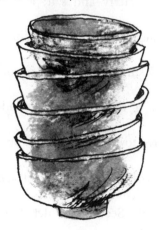

SHRIMP

BASIC STIR-FRIED SHRIMP I
4 to 6 servings

½ pound shrimp	*2 slices fresh ginger root*
2 teaspoons cornstarch	*1 tablespoon cornstarch*
1 tablespoon sherry	*2 tablespoons water*
½ teaspoon salt	*1½ tablespoons oil*
1 pound vegetables	*2 tablespoons oil*
1 garlic clove	*½ cup stock*

1. Shell and devein shrimp. Combine cornstarch, sherry and salt; add to shrimp and toss to coat.

2. Slice or dice vegetables. Crush garlic. Mince ginger root. Blend remaining cornstarch and cold water to a paste.

3. Heat oil. Brown garlic lightly. Add shrimp and stir-fry until pink (2 to 3 minutes). Remove from pan.

4. Heat remaining oil. Add ginger root; stir-fry a few times. Then add vegetables; and stir-fry briefly to coat with oil.

5. Stir in and heat stock quickly. Then cook, covered, over medium heat, until nearly done.

6. Return shrimp, stir-frying to reheat. Then stir in cornstarch paste to thicken. Serve at once.

NOTE: Any vegetable can be used. (See Vegetable Section for details on cooking time.) For suggested combinations, see page 492.

VARIATIONS: **In step 1,** add to the cornstarch mixture any or all of the following:

1 teaspoon sugar
2 teaspoons soy sauce
1 scallion stalk, minced
2 slices fresh ginger root, minced (omit it in step 4)

In step 1, toss the shrimp instead in any of the following combinations:
1 tablespoon cornstarch, 1 tablespoon sherry and ½ teaspoon salt. Then in step

3, after shrimp turn pink, quickly stir in to blend 2 tablespoons soy sauce and 1 teaspoon sugar. Pick up steps 4 to 6.

1 tablespoon cornstarch, 2 teaspoons sherry and 1 egg white. After shrimp turn pink in step 3, quickly stir in to blend 1 more tablespoon sherry, 1 teaspoon sugar and ½ teaspoon salt. Pick up steps 4 to 6.

1 tablespoon sherry, 1 tablespoon soy sauce, ½ teaspoon salt and a dash of pepper. At the end of step 4, sprinkle the vegetables with 2 more teaspoons sherry. Pick up steps 4 to 6.

1 tablespoon sherry, ½ teaspoon cornstarch and ½ teaspoon salt. When returning shrimp in step 6, add ½ teaspoon sugar and a pinch of salt. Then stir in cornstarch paste to thicken.

BASIC STIR-FRIED SHRIMP II
4 to 6 servings

½ pound shrimp	*1 tablespoon soy sauce*
1 pound vegetables	*1 tablespoon sherry*
1 scallion stalk	*1½ tablespoons oil*
2 slices fresh ginger root	*¼ teaspoon salt*
1 garlic clove	*2 tablespoons oil*
1 teaspoon cornstarch	*¼ teaspoon salt*

½ cup stock

1. Shell and devein shrimp. Slice or dice vegetables. Cut scallion in ½-inch sections. Mince ginger root. Crush garlic.
2. Blend cornstarch, soy sauce and sherry to a paste.
3. Heat oil. Add salt, then scallion and ginger root; stir-fry a few times. Add shrimp and stir-fry until pink (about 3 minutes). Remove ingredients from pan.
4. Heat remaining oil. Add remaining salt, then garlic, and stir-fry a few times. Add vegetables; stir-fry to coat with oil.
5. Stir in stock and heat quickly. Then cook, covered, over medium heat, until nearly done.
6. Return shrimp, stir-frying to reheat and blend flavors (about 1 minute more).
7. Stir in cornstarch paste to thicken. Serve at once.
NOTE: See Note above.
VARIATIONS: In step 1, sprinkle the shrimp with 1½ tablespoons sherry and let stand 5 minutes, turning several times.

For the cornstarch paste in step 2, substitute any of the following and add in step 7:

1 tablespoon cornstarch, 3 tablespoons cold water, 2 teaspoons soy sauce

2 teaspoons cornstarch, 1 teaspoon sugar, ½ teaspoon salt, 1 teaspoon soy sauce and 3 tablespoons cold stock

1 teaspoon cornstarch, 1 tablespoon oyster sauce, 2 tablespoons soy sauce, 3 table-spoons cold water and 2 slices fresh ginger root, minced

½ teaspoon salt, 2 teaspoons soy sauce, 2 teaspoons sherry, 3 tablespoons stock and 1 or 2 slices fresh ginger root, minced.

After adding the shrimp in step 3, stir-fry only ½ minute, then sprinkle with 1 more tablespoon sherry and stir-fry until pink.

SUGGESTED VEGETABLE COMBINATIONS FOR BASIC STIR-FRIED SHRIMP I AND II

2 green peppers	½ cup string beans
2 tomatoes	½ cup bean sprouts
	½ cup celery
½ cup peas	½ cup tomatoes
4 dried black mushrooms (soaked)	1 onion
6 water chestnuts	
2 slices smoked ham	2 cups celery
	½ cup almond meats
1 cup peas	
1 cup fresh mushrooms	1 cup celery
½ cup bamboo shoots	4 to 6 dried black mushrooms (soaked)
2 cups bean sprouts	
1 cup celery	1 scallion
½ cup onion	2 cups broccoli
6 water chestnuts or	1 cup celery
1 green pepper	½ cup onion
2 cups string beans	1 cup Chinese cabbage
10 dried black mushrooms (soaked)	¼ cup bamboo shoots
	¼ cup peas
2 cups string beans	¼ cup button mushrooms
1 cup onion	6 snow peas
	6 water chestnuts

STIR-FRIED SHRIMP WITH ALMONDS
4 to 6 servings

½ cup almond meats
½ pound shrimp
2 slices fresh ginger root
1 tablespoon cornstarch
½ teaspoon salt
1 or 2 celery stalks

1 garlic clove
1 teaspoon soy sauce
1 teaspoon sherry
2 tablespoons water
2 tablespoons oil
dash of pepper

1. Blanch and toast almonds.

2. Shell, devein, and butterfly shrimp. (Leave tail segments intact.)

3. Mince ginger root; then add to shrimp, along with cornstarch and salt. Toss to coat.

4. Mince celery; crush garlic. Combine soy sauce, sherry and water.

5. Heat oil. Brown garlic and discard. Add shrimp; stir-fry until pinkish (about 2 minutes).

6. Add minced celery and pepper; stir-fry 2 minutes more. Quickly stir in soy-sherry mixture and stir-fry another minute. Garnish with almonds and serve at once.

VARIATION: For the almonds, substitute walnuts.

STIR-FRIED SHRIMP WITH ANISE
6 to 8 servings

1 *pound shrimp*
1½ *tablespoons sherry*
1 *tablespoon soy sauce*

½ *teaspoon sugar*
½ *cup stock*
3 *tablespoons oil*

⅛ *teaspoon powdered anise*

1. Shell and devein shrimp; cut lengthwise in half if large.
2. Combine sherry, soy sauce, sugar and stock.
3. Heat oil. Add shrimp and stir-fry until pinkish.
4. Stir in sherry-soy mixture and heat quickly. Then cook, covered, 2 minutes over medium heat.
5. Sprinkle shrimp with powdered anise and serve at once.

STIR-FRIED SHRIMP AND ASPARAGUS
About 4 servings

½ *pound shrimp*
1 *pound asparagus*
2 *slices fresh ginger root*
2 *tablespoons soy sauce*

1 *tablespoon sherry*
1 *teaspoon sugar*
½ *teaspoon salt*
2 to 3 *tablespoons oil*

1. Shell and devein shrimp; cut in 3 or 4 pieces if large.
2. Cut asparagus diagonally in 1-inch sections, discarding tough white ends; then parboil. Mince ginger root.
3. Combine soy sauce, sherry, sugar and salt.
4. Heat oil. Stir-fry shrimp until pinkish. Add asparagus sections and ginger root and stir-fry a few times.
5. Add soy-sherry mixture and heat quickly. Then cook, covered, 2 minutes over medium heat. Serve at once.

STIR-FRIED SHRIMP AND BAMBOO SHOOTS I
4 to 6 servings

½ *pound shrimp*
salt
1 *cup bamboo shoots*
2 *tablespoons smoked ham*
2 *tablespoons sherry*
½ *teaspoon sugar*

2 *teaspoons soy sauce*
1½ *tablespoons oil*
1½ *tablespoons oil*
2 to 3 *tablespoons stock*
few drops of vinegar
few drops of sesame oil

1. Shell and devein shrimp; cut in 3 or 4 pieces if large. Sprinkle lightly with salt.

2. Slice bamboo shoots. Mince smoked ham. Combine sherry, sugar and soy sauce.

3. Heat oil. Add shrimp and stir-fry until pinkish. Then remove from pan.

4. Heat remaining oil. Add bamboo shoots; stir-fry to heat through (about 1 minute). Then quickly stir in sherry-sugar mixture to blend.

5. Return shrimp; stir in stock. Cook, covered, 2 to 3 minutes over medium heat. Transfer to a serving dish.

6. Sprinkle first with minced ham, then with vinegar and sesame oil. Serve at once.

STIR-FRIED SHRIMP AND BAMBOO SHOOTS II
4 to 6 servings

½ pound shrimp	*2½ tablespoons soy sauce*
1 cup bamboo shoots	*1 teaspoon sugar*
1 cup onions	*1 tablespoon cornstarch*
2 slices fresh ginger root	*3 tablespoons water*
1½ tablespoons sherry	*3 to 4 tablespoons oil*

1. Shell and devein shrimp; cut in 1-inch sections.

2. Slice bamboo shoots and onion thin. Mince ginger root.

3. In one cup, combine sherry, soy sauce and sugar. In another, blend cornstarch and cold water to a paste.

4. Heat oil. Add shrimp and stir-fry until pinkish. Quickly stir in sherry-soy mixture to blend.

5. Add ginger root; stir-fry a few times more. Then add bamboo shoots and onions. Stir-fry until onions are translucent (about 2 minutes).

6. Stir in cornstarch paste to thicken and serve at once.

STIR-FRIED SHRIMP AND BEAN CURD I
4 to 6 servings

½ *pound shrimp*	¼ *cup stock*
2 *slices fresh ginger root*	3 *tablespoons oil*
1 *scallion stalk*	1½ *tablespoons oil*
1 *tablespoon sherry*	1 *tablespoon soy sauce*
2 *or 3 bean curd cakes*	1 *teaspoon sugar*
1 *tablespoon cornstarch*	½ *teaspoon salt*

1. Shell and devein shrimp. Mince ginger root and scallion; then add to shrimp, along with sherry. Let stand 10 minutes, turning occasionally.

2. Meanwhile cut each bean curd cake first in half, then in 4 slices. Blend cornstarch and cold stock to a paste.

3. Heat oil. Add bean curd; stir-fry gently until lightly browned. Remove from pan.

4. Heat remaining oil. Add shrimp and stir-fry until pinkish. Sprinkle with soy sauce, sugar and salt; stir-fry ½ minute more to blend.

5. Stir in cornstarch paste to thicken. Then return bean curd and stir in gently to reheat. Serve at once.

VARIATIONS: In step 1, toss the shrimp in a mixture of 1 teaspoon cornstarch, 1 teaspoon ginger juice and ½ teaspoon salt. In step 3, add to the hot oil ½ leek stalk, minced; *then* add the bean curd. In step 4, for the soy sauce, substitute sherry.

In step 5, add with the bean curd 1 cucumber, peeled and cut in thin strips.

STIR-FRIED SHRIMP AND BEAN CURD II
4 to 6 servings

½ *pound shrimp*	1 *tablespoon soy sauce*
3 *or 4 bean curd cakes*	½ *teaspoon salt*
¼ *pound fresh mushrooms*	*dash of pepper*
½ *pound peas*	1½ *tablespoons oil*
2 *tablespoons sherry*	1½ *tablespoons oil*

1. Shell, devein and dice shrimp. Dice bean curd. Slice fresh mushrooms. Shell and parboil peas.

2. Combine sherry, soy sauce, salt and pepper.

3. Heat oil. Add shrimp and stir-fry until pink. Remove from pan.

4. Heat remaining oil. Add mushrooms; stir-fry to soften slightly. Then add parboiled peas and stir-fry 1 minute more.

5. Add diced bean curd and sherry-soy mixture. Stir-fry gently until bean curd is heated through.

6. Return shrimp and cook, gently stirring, to reheat and blend flavors (about 1 minute). Serve at once.

VARIATIONS: In step 1, toss the shrimp in 1 tablespoon sherry. Let stand 10 to 15 minutes, turning occasionally.

In step 3, stir-fry shrimp ½ minute; then add sherry-soy mixture and stir-fry until shrimp turns pink. In step 5, add ½ cup stock with bean curd and simmer, covered, to heat through.

STIR-FRIED SHRIMP WITH DEEP-FRIED BEAN CURD
4 to 6 servings

½ pound shrimp	oil for deep-frying
1 tablespoon sherry	2 tablespoons oil
3 or 4 bean curd cakes	½ teaspoon salt
1 scallion stalk	2 tablespoons soy sauce
1 garlic clove	½ teaspoon sugar

1. Shell and devein shrimp. Sprinkle with sherry and let stand 10 to 15 minutes, turning occasionally.

2. Cut bean curd in 1-inch cubes. Cut scallion in ½-inch sections. Crush garlic. Meanwhile heat oil.

3. Add bean curd cubes to oil, several at a time, and deep-fry until golden. Drain on paper toweling.

4. Heat remaining oil. Add salt, then garlic and scallions; stir-fry a few times. Add shrimp and stir-fry until pinkish.

5. Quickly stir in soy sauce and sugar to blend; then cook, covered, 1 to 2 minutes over medium heat.

6. Return bean curd, stirring gently, only to heat through. Serve at once.

VARIATIONS: For the bean curd, substitute 4 slices slightly stale white bread. (Remove crusts, cut in cubes, then deep-fry until golden.)

In step 5, omit the soy sauce. Add 3 tablespoons catsup and a pinch of salt with the sugar. Stir-fry with the shrimp 2 minutes; then pick up step 6.

STIR-FRIED SHRIMP AND BEAN SPROUTS I
4 to 6 servings

½ pound shrimp	¼ teaspoon salt
1 tablespoon sherry	1 tablespoon soy sauce
1 pound bean sprouts	½ teaspoon sugar
2 tablespoons oil	¼ teaspoon salt

dash of pepper

1. Shell and devein shrimp. Add sherry and toss. Let stand 10 to 15 minutes, turning occasionally.

2. Blanch bean sprouts.

3. Heat oil. Add salt, then shrimp, and stir-fry until pinkish. Add bean sprouts; stir-fry 1 minute more.

4. Add soy sauce, sugar and remaining salt. Stir-fry 1 minute more.

5. Sprinkle with pepper. Serve at once.

STIR-FRIED SHRIMP AND BEAN SPROUTS II
4 to 6 servings

½ pound shrimp	1 teaspoon soy sauce
1 pound bean sprouts	1 tablespoon cornstarch
1 tablespoon preserved sweet pickles	3 tablespoons water
1 garlic clove	dash of pepper
1 or 2 slices fresh ginger root	1 teaspoon soy sauce
2 tablespoons sherry	2 tablespoons oil
1 teaspoon sugar	½ teaspoon salt

½ cup stock

1. Shell, devein and butterfly shrimp. (Leave tail segments intact.)

2. Blanch bean sprouts. Shred sweet pickles. Crush garlic.

3. Mince ginger root; then combine in a cup with sherry, sugar and soy sauce. In a second cup, blend cornstarch, cold water, pepper and remaining soy sauce to a paste.

4. Heat oil. Add salt, then garlic, and stir-fry to brown lightly. Add shrimp; stir-fry until pinkish.

5. Add ginger-sherry mixture; stir-fry 1½ minutes more.

6. Add bean sprouts and pickles and stir-fry another minute.

7. Stir in stock and heat quickly. Then cook, covered, 1 to 2 minutes over medium heat.

8. Stir in cornstarch paste to thicken and serve at once.

VARIATION: For the bean sprouts, substitute any of the following: 1 pound broccoli, broken in flowerets and parboiled; 1 pound string beans, cut in 2-inch lengths and parboiled; or ½ pound snow peas.

STIR-FRIED SHRIMP WITH BEAN SPROUTS AND SNOW PEAS

6 to 8 servings

2 tablespoons cloud ear mushrooms	2 teaspoons cornstarch
½ pound shrimp	1 teaspoon sugar
1 pound bean sprouts	1 tablespoon soy sauce
½ cup snow peas	1 tablespoon sherry
2 celery stalks	dash of pepper
1 or 2 scallion stalks	2 to 3 tablespoons oil
1 garlic clove	½ teaspoon salt
2 slices fresh ginger root	1½ tablespoons oil

1. Soak cloud ear mushrooms.

2. Shell and devein shrimp; cut each in 2 or 3 pieces. Blanch bean sprouts. Stem snow peas.

3. Slice celery thin; also scallions and soaked mushrooms. Mince garlic and ginger root.

4. Blend cornstarch, sugar, soy sauce, sherry and pepper to a paste.

5. Heat oil. Add salt, then sliced vegetables; stir-fry about 1 minute. Add bean sprouts and stir-fry 1 minute more. Remove from pan. (The vegetables should be tender but still crisp.)

6. Heat remaining oil. Add minced garlic and ginger root; stir-fry a few times. Add shrimp and stir-fry until pinkish.

7. Add snow peas and stir-fry ½ minute more. Return other vegetables; stir-fry briefly to reheat.

8. Stir in cornstarch paste to thicken and serve at once.

STIR-FRIED SHRIMP WITH BLACK BEAN SAUCE I

4 to 6 servings

1 tablespoon fermented black beans	3 tablespoons water
½ pound shrimp	2 tablespoons oil
2 green peppers	½ teaspoon salt
½ cup dried onion	½ cup stock
1 garlic clove	½ teaspoon sugar
1 tablespoon cornstarch	1 teaspoon soy sauce

1. Soak fermented black beans.

2. Shell and devein shrimp. Slice green peppers and dried onion.

3. Mince garlic; then mash with soaked black beans in one cup. In another, blend cornstarch and cold water to a paste.

4. Heat oil. Add salt, then black bean mixture, and stir-fry a few times. Add shrimp; stir-fry 1 minute.

5. Add green pepper and onion; stir-fry to soften slightly (1 to 2 minutes).

6. Stir in stock and heat quickly. Then cook, covered, over medium heat, until done (2 to 3 minutes).

7. Stir in sugar and soy sauce to blend. Then stir in cornstarch paste to thicken. Serve at once.

VARIATION: At the end of step 7, stir in 1 egg, beaten. (Remove from heat as soon as egg begins to set.)

STIR-FRIED SHRIMP WITH BLACK BEAN SAUCE II

6 to 8 servings

1 tablespoon fermented black beans	dash of pepper
1 pound shrimp	1 tablespoon cornstarch
1 garlic clove	3 tablespoons water
2 slices fresh ginger root	1 teaspoon soy sauce
1 tablespoon soy sauce	2 tablespoons oil
2 tablespoons sherry	½ teaspoon salt
1 teaspoon sugar	½ cup stock

1. Soak fermented black beans.

2. Shell and devein shrimp. Crush garlic.

3. Mince ginger root; then combine in a cup with soy sauce, sherry, sugar and pepper. In another cup, blend cornstarch, cold water and remaining soy sauce to a paste.

4. Heat oil. Add salt, then garlic, and stir-fry to brown lightly. Add shrimp; stir-fry until pinkish (about 2 minutes).

5. Add ginger-soy mixture and stir-fry ½ minute more. Add soaked black beans; stir-fry another ½ minute.

6. Stir in stock and heat quickly. Then cook, covered, 1 to 2 minutes over medium heat.

7. Stir in cornstarch paste to thicken and serve at once.

STIR-FRIED SHRIMP WITH CATSUP I
6 to 8 servings

1 *pound shrimp*	1 *tablespoon cornstarch*
1 *garlic clove*	3 *tablespoons water*
2 *slices fresh ginger root*	1 *teaspoon soy sauce*
1 *tablespoon soy sauce*	2 *tablespoons oil*
2 *tablespoons sherry*	½ *teaspoon salt*
1 *teaspoon sugar*	2 to 3 *tablespoons catsup*
⅛ *teaspoon pepper*	½ *cup stock*

1. Shell and devein shrimp. Mince or crush garlic.

2. Mince ginger root; then combine in a cup with soy sauce, sherry, sugar and pepper. In another cup, blend cornstarch, cold water and remaining soy sauce to a paste.

3. Heat oil. Add salt, then garlic, and stir-fry a few times. Add shrimp; stir-fry until pinkish (about 2 minutes).

4. Add ginger-soy mixture and stir-fry 1 minute. Then add catsup; stir-fry ½ minute more.

5. Stir in stock and heat quickly. Then cook, covered, 2 minutes over medium heat.

6. Stir in cornstarch paste to thicken and serve at once.

VARIATIONS: For the catsup, substitute 1 to 2 tablespoons oyster sauce.

Omit the ginger-soy mixture in step 2, but add the minced ginger root in step 3 with the garlic. In step 4, add to the shrimp 2 teaspoons sherry and ¼ cup stock; cook, covered, 2 minutes over medium heat. Then stir in ¼ cup catsup to coat the shrimp evenly. Omit step 5. Pick up step 6.

STIR-FRIED SHRIMP WITH CATSUP II
6 to 8 servings

1 pound shrimp
½ teaspoon salt
⅛ teaspoon pepper
6 scallion stalks
1 garlic clove
2 slices fresh ginger root

2 tablespoons catsup
2 tablespoons soy sauce
2 tablespoons vinegar
2 teaspoons sugar
1 tablespoon cornstarch
3 tablespoons cold water

2 tablespoons oil

1. Shell and devein shrimp. Sprinkle with salt and pepper.
2. Slice scallion stalks; mince garlic and ginger. Then combine with catsup, soy sauce, vinegar and sugar. Blend cornstarch and cold water to a paste.
3. Heat oil. Add shrimp and stir-fry until pinkish (about 2 minutes).
4. Add scallion-catsup mixture and cook 2 minutes over low heat, stirring frequently. Then stir in cornstarch paste to thicken and serve at once.

STIR-FRIED SHRIMP WITH CELERY AND ALMONDS
About 4 servings

½ cup almond meats
½ pound shrimp
3 or 4 celery stalks
2 slices fresh ginger root

1½ tablespoons oil
¼ teaspoon salt
2 teaspoons sherry
1½ tablespoons oil

¼ teaspoon salt

1. Blanch and toast almonds; then chop coarsely.
2. Shell, devein and dice shrimp. Dice celery. Mince ginger root.
3. Heat oil. Add ginger root; stir-fry a few times. Add shrimp and stir-fry until

pinkish (about 2 minutes). Then sprinkle with salt and sherry; stir-fry 1 minute more and remove from pan.

4. Heat remaining oil. Add celery and almonds; stir-fry 1 minute. Then stir in remaining salt.

5. Return shrimp, stir-frying only to reheat. Serve at once.

NOTE: The celery should be quite crisp.

STIR-FRIED SHRIMP WITH CHICKEN AND VEGETABLES
6 to 8 servings

½ pound shrimp	*1 tablespoon cornstarch*
½ cup cooked chicken	*½ teaspoon sugar*
½ cup bamboo shoots	*¼ cup stock*
½ pound fresh mushrooms	*2 tablespoons oil*
¼ pound snow peas	*½ teaspoon salt*
1 garlic clove	*½ cup stock*

1. Shell and devein shrimp. Slice cooked chicken thin, also bamboo shoots and fresh mushrooms. Stem and string snow peas. Crush garlic.

2. Blend cornstarch, sugar and cold stock to a paste.

3. Heat oil; add garlic and stir-fry to brown lightly. Add shrimp and stir-fry 1 minute.

4. Add bamboo shoots and mushrooms; stir-fry until mushrooms begin to soften (2 to 3 minutes).

5. Stir in chicken, salt and remaining stock. Heat quickly; then cook, covered, 2 minutes over medium heat.

6. Add snow peas; cook, stirring, 1 minute more.

7. Stir in cornstarch paste to thicken, and serve at once.

VARIATION: For the snow peas, substitute 1 cup bean sprouts, blanched.

STIR-FRIED SHRIMP WITH CUCUMBERS AND ONIONS
4 to 6 servings

½ pound shrimp	*1 garlic clove*
¼ teaspoon salt	*1 or 2 slices fresh ginger root*
dash of pepper	*2 tablespoons oil*
1 tablespoon cornstarch	*2 teaspoons sherry*
1 or 2 cucumbers	*1 tablespoon oil*
1 white onion	*¼ teaspoon salt*

1. Shell and devein shrimp. Sprinkle with salt and pepper; then add cornstarch and toss to coat.

2. Peel cucumbers. Cut lengthwise in half and seed; then cut crosswise in ¼-inch slices. Slice onion thin. Crush garlic. Mince ginger root.

3. Heat oil. Add garlic; stir-fry a few times. Add onion and stir-fry until translucent (1 to 2 minutes).

4. Add shrimp and stir-fry until pink (2 to 3 minutes). Add sherry; stir-fry until it evaporates. Remove ingredients from pan.

5. Heat remaining oil. Add remaining salt, then minced ginger root; stir-fry a few times. Add cucumber slices and stir-fry over medium heat until translucent (1 to 2 minutes).

6. Return shrimp, stir-frying only to reheat. Serve at once.

VARIATION: For the cucumbers and onion, substitute 2 or 3 green peppers, diced.

STIR-FRIED CURRIED SHRIMP
6 to 8 servings

1 *pound shrimp*	*dash of pepper*
1 *onion*	2 *to 3 tablespoons oil*
2 *teaspoons cornstarch*	½ *teaspoon salt*
2 *tablespoons water*	2 *teaspoons sherry*
½ *teaspoon sugar*	2 *to 3 tablespoons curry powder*

½ *cup stock*

1. Shell and devein shrimp. Cut onion in half; then slice thin.

2. Blend cornstarch, water, sugar and pepper to a paste.

3. Heat oil. Add salt, then shrimp, and stir-fry 1 minute. Sprinkle shrimp with sherry; stir-fry until pinkish (about 1 minute more), then remove. Clean and dry the pan.

4. Add curry powder; stir in ½ minute over low heat. Add onion and stir-fry until curry smells pungent (about 1 minute more).

5. Return shrimp. Stir in stock and heat quickly. Then cook, stirring, until onion softens.

6. Stir in cornstarch paste to thicken and serve at once.

STIR-FRIED SHRIMP AND LETTUCE
4 to 6 servings

½ *pound shrimp*	1 *garlic clove*
1 *tablespoon cornstarch*	2 *tablespoons oil*
2 *or 3 slices fresh ginger root*	½ *teaspoon salt*
1 *head lettuce*	¼ *cup stock*

1. Shell and devein shrimp. Add cornstarch and toss to coat. Mince ginger root and sprinkle over shrimp.

2. Shred lettuce coarsely. Crush garlic.

3. Heat oil. Add salt, then garlic; stir-fry to brown lightly. Add shrimp and stir-fry until pinkish (about 2 minutes).

4. Add lettuce; stir-fry to soften slightly (about 1 minute more).

5. Stir in stock and heat quickly. Serve at once.

STIR-FRIED SHRIMP WITH LOBSTER SAUCE
4 to 6 servings

lobster sauce
½ pound shrimp
1 tablespoon cornstarch

2 teaspoons sherry
2 tablespoons oil
½ teaspoon salt

1. Prepare lobster sauce (see page 735). Keep warm in pan.

2. Shell, devein and butterfly shrimp. Combine cornstarch and sherry; then add to shrimp and toss to coat.

3. Heat oil. Add salt, then shrimp; stir-fry until pinkish (about 2 minutes).

4. Transfer shrimp to lobster sauce and cook, stirring gently, over low heat to blend flavors (1 to 2 minutes). Serve at once.

VARIATION: In step 3, add with the salt 1 garlic clove, crushed; and/or 2 slices fresh ginger root, minced. Stir-fry a few times; then add the shrimp.

STIR-FRIED SHRIMP AND CHINESE MUSHROOMS
6 to 8 servings

10 dried black mushrooms
½ pound shrimp
2 or 3 slices fresh ginger root
1½ tablespoons oil

1 tablespoon soy sauce
½ teaspoon salt
2 tablespoons oil
¼ cup stock

1. Soak dried mushrooms.

2. Shell and devein shrimp. Crush ginger root. Slice soaked mushrooms.

3. Heat oil. Add ginger; stir-fry a few times. Add shrimp and stir-fry until pinkish (about 2 minutes).

4. Add soy sauce and salt; stir-fry 2 minutes more. Remove shrimp from pan.

5. Heat remaining oil. Add mushrooms; stir-fry to coat with oil. Stir in stock and heat quickly. Then cook, covered, 2 to 3 minutes over medium heat.

6. Return shrimp and stir in only to reheat and blend flavors (about 1 minute). Serve at once.

STIR-FRIED SHRIMP WITH PEPPERS AND TOMATOES
6 to 8 servings

½ *pound shrimp*	1 *tablespoon cornstarch*
2 *green peppers*	1 *tablespoon soy sauce*
1 *or 2 tomatoes*	3 *tablespoons water*
1 *garlic clove*	2 *to 3 tablespoons oil*
2 *slices fresh ginger root*	½ *teaspoon salt*
3 *scallions*	½ *cup stock*

1. Shell, devein and butterfly shrimp. Dice peppers. Cut each tomato in 6 wedges. Crush garlic, mince ginger root and chop scallions.

2. Blend cornstarch, soy sauce and cold water to a paste.

3. Heat oil. Add salt, then garlic and ginger root; stir-fry a few times. Add shrimp and stir-fry until pinkish (about 2 minutes).

4. Add green peppers; stir-fry 1 minute more.

5. Stir in stock and heat quickly. Then cook, covered, 2 to 3 minutes over medium heat.

6. Gently stir in tomato wedges to heat through. Then stir in cornstarch paste to thicken. Sprinkle with chopped scallions and serve at once.

STIR-FRIED SHRIMP WITH PICKLES
6 to 8 servings

1 *pound shrimp*	2 *teaspoons cornstarch*
2 *tablespoons sweet pickles*	3 *tablespoons water*
2 *scallion stalks*	2 *tablespoons oil*
2 *slices fresh ginger root*	2 *tablespoons sherry*
1 *garlic clove*	3 *tablespoons soy sauce*

½ *teaspoon sugar*

1. Shell and devein shrimp. Chop sweet pickles. Cut scallion stalks in 1-inch sections. Mince ginger root. Crush garlic.

2. Blend cornstarch and cold water to a paste.

3. Heat oil. Add scallions, ginger root and garlic; stir-fry a few times. Add shrimp and stir-fry until pinkish (about 2 minutes).

4. Add sweet pickles and sherry; stir-fry 1 minute more over high heat. Remove shrimp, leaving pickles and liquids in pan.

5. Stir in soy sauce and sugar to heat and blend. Then stir in cornstarch paste to thicken.

6. Return shrimp, stirring, to reheat and blend flavors (about 1 minute). Serve at once.

STIR-FRIED SHRIMP AND VEGETABLES I
6 to 8 servings

3 or 4 dried black mushrooms
½ pound shrimp
1 teaspoon cornstarch
¼ teaspoon salt
1 tablespoon sherry
1 cucumber

½ cup bamboo shoots
1 cup carrots
2 slices fresh ginger root
1½ tablespoons oil
2 tablespoons oil
½ teaspoon sugar

¼ teaspoon salt

1. Soak dried mushrooms.

2. Shell and devein shrimp. Combine cornstarch, salt and sherry; then add to shrimp and toss to coat.

3. Peel and sliver cucumber. Sliver bamboo shoots and soaked mushrooms. Sliver and parboil carrots. Mince ginger root.

4. Heat oil. Add ginger root; stir-fry a few times. Add shrimp and stir-fry until pink (about 3 minutes). Remove from pan.

5. Heat remaining oil. Add slivered vegetables and stir-fry until nearly done (2 to 3 minutes).

6. Return shrimp, along with sugar and remaining salt. Stir-fry only to heat through and blend flavors (about 1 minute). Serve at once.

STIR-FRIED SHRIMP AND VEGETABLES II
6 to 8 servings

½ pound shrimp
2 slices fresh ginger root
2 tablespoons sherry
1 tablespoon soy sauce
1 or 2 green peppers
1 onion

4 celery stalks
1 tablespoon cornstarch
2 tablespoons water
1½ tablespoons oil
2 tablespoons oil
½ teaspoon salt

½ cup stock

1. Shell and devein shrimp. Mince ginger root; then combine with sherry and soy sauce. Add to shrimp and toss. Let stand 15 minutes, turning occasionally.

2. Dice green pepper, onion and celery. Blend cornstarch and cold water to a paste.

3. Heat oil. Add shrimp and stir-fry until pinkish (2 to 3 minutes). Remove from pan.

4. Heat remaining oil. Add salt, then diced vegetables; stir-fry to soften slightly (1 to 2 minutes).

5. Stir in stock and heat quickly. Then cook, covered, 2 to 3 minutes over medium heat.

6. Return shrimp; stir in only to reheat and blend flavors (about 1 minute). Then stir in cornstarch paste to thicken, and serve at once.

STIR-FRIED SHRIMP IN SHELLS I
6 to 8 servings

1 *pound shrimp*	2 *tablespoons sherry*
1 *scallion stalk*	½ *teaspoon salt*
2 *slices fresh ginger root*	3 *tablespoons oil*
2 *tablespoons soy sauce*	1 *teaspoon sugar*

1. Wash shrimp. Remove legs, leaving shells intact; then devein (see page 453).

2. Mince scallion stalk and ginger root; then combine with soy sauce, sherry and salt.

3. Heat oil. Add shrimp and stir-fry until pinkish (1 to 2 minutes). Add sugar; stir-fry ½ minute more.

4. Add scallion-soy mixture and stir-fry another 2 minutes. Serve hot or cold.

NOTE: These shrimp, served cold, are excellent as appetizers, buffet dishes or picnic snacks.

VARIATIONS: For the scallion-soy mixture prepared in step 2 and added in step 4, substitute any of the following:

2 tablespoons soy sauce, 2 tablespoons sherry, 1 teaspoon sugar, 1 teaspoon vinegar and ½ teaspoon salt. Then at the end of step 3 add 2 scallion stalks and 1 garlic clove, both minced; stir-fry a few times. Add the substitute mixture as in step 4.

2 tablespoons brown sugar, 2 tablespoons soy sauce, 2 tablespoons sherry, 2 slices fresh ginger root, minced, and ½ tablespoon vinegar. Add as in step 4 and heat quickly, stirring. Then cook, covered, over medium heat until shrimp are done (2 to 3 minutes).

2 teaspoons sugar, 2 tablespoons soy sauce and 1 scallion stalk. In step 3, add to the hot oil 1 garlic clove and 1 slice fresh ginger root, both crushed. (Stir-fry a few times before adding shrimp.) For the sugar in step 3, substitute 1 tablespoon sherry. Pick up step 4.

1 teaspoon soy sauce, 2 tablespoons stock and ¼ cup scallions, cut in ½-inch sections. In step 3, add to the hot oil ½ teaspoon salt, before adding shrimp. Pick up step 4.

2 tablespoons hoisin sauce, 1 tablespoon vinegar, ½ teaspoon salt and 1 teaspoon sugar. At the end of step 3, add 6 scallion stalks, cut in 1-inch sections and 1 slice fresh ginger root, minced. Stir-fry a few times; then pick up step 4.

STIR-FRIED SHRIMP IN SHELLS II
6 to 8 servings

1 *pound shrimp*	1 *tablespoon cornstarch*
1 *scallion stalk*	1 *teaspoon sugar*
1 *garlic clove*	*dash of pepper*
2 *slices fresh ginger root*	3 *tablespoons water*
2 *tablespoons catsup*	2 *tablespoons oil*
2 *tablespoons sherry*	½ *teaspoon salt*
2 *tablespoons water*	1 *tablespoon oil*

1. Wash shrimp. Remove legs, leaving shells intact; then devein (see page 453). (If large, cut each shrimp, shell and all, in 2 or 3 pieces.) Cut scallion in ½-inch sections. Crush garlic; mince ginger root.

2. In one cup, combine catsup, sherry and water. In a second cup, blend cornstarch, sugar, pepper and remaining cold water to a paste.

3. Heat oil. Add salt, then garlic; stir-fry to brown lightly. Add shrimp and stir-fry until pink (2 to 3 minutes). Remove from pan.

4. Heat remaining oil. Add ginger root and scallion; stir-fry a few times. Stir in catsup-sherry mixture and heat quickly.

5. Return shrimp and stir in only to reheat. Then stir in cornstarch paste to thicken and serve at once.

STIR-FRIED MARINATED SHRIMP IN SHELLS
6 to 8 servings

1 *pound shrimp*	2 *tablespoons sherry*
1 *scallion stalk*	½ *teaspoon salt*
1 *teaspoon ginger juice*	½ *teaspoon sugar*
3 *tablespoons soy sauce*	*few drops of sesame oil*

4 to 6 tablespoons oil

1. Wash shrimp. Remove legs, leaving shells intact, then devein (see page 453).

2. Mince scallion and extract ginger juice; then combine with soy sauce, sherry, salt, sugar and sesame oil. Add to shrimp and toss. Let stand 20 to 30 minutes, turning occasionally. Drain, discarding marinade.

3. Heat oil. Add shrimp and stir-fry until pink, with tails that are bright red (about 3 minutes). Serve hot or cold.

NOTE: These shrimp, called Golden Hooks, may also be baked in their own marinade. Preheat the oven to 325 degrees and bake about 15 minutes.

VARIATION: For the mixture in step 2, substitute 1 tablespoon brown sugar, 1 tablespoon soy sauce, 1 tablespoon sherry, and 1 teaspoon Worcestershire Sauce.

STIR-FRIED MINIATURE SHRIMP
8 to 10 servings

1 *pound frozen miniature shrimp*	*water to cover*
½ *teaspoon salt*	1 *or 2 scallion stalks*

2 *tablespoons oil*

1. Thaw shrimp. Add salt and water and let stand a few minutes. Meanwhile mince scallion.

2. Drain shrimp, then rinse several times with fresh water. Drain again and blot dry with paper toweling.

3. Heat oil. Add shrimp and scallion and stir-fry until done (2 to 3 minutes). Serve at once.

STIR-FRIED MINIATURE SHRIMP AND PEAS
8 to 10 servings

1 *pound frozen miniature shrimp*	½ *egg white*
1 *or 2 slices fresh ginger root*	1 *cup shelled peas*
½ *teaspoon salt*	1 *teaspoon cornstarch*
water to cover	2 *tablespoons stock*
1 *teaspoon cornstarch*	2 *tablespoons oil*
½ *teaspoon salt*	1 *tablespoon sherry*

1. Thaw and prepare shrimp as in steps 1 and 2 above.

2. Mince ginger root; then combine with cornstarch, salt and egg white. Add to shrimp and toss to coat.

3. Parboil peas.

4. Blend remaining cornstarch and cold stock to a paste.

5. Heat oil. Add shrimp and stir-fry until they turn white (1 to 2 minutes).

6. Add sherry and peas; stir-fry ½ minute more. Then stir in cornstarch paste to thicken, and serve at once.

STIR-FRIED MINIATURE SHRIMP AND VEGETABLES
About 6 servings

4 *dried black mushrooms*	¼ *cup canned button mushrooms*
½ *pound frozen miniature shrimp*	10 *water chestnuts*
½ *teaspoon salt*	12 *snow peas*
water to cover	1 *garlic clove*
1 *slice fresh ginger root*	2 *teaspoons cornstarch*
½ *teaspoon cornstarch*	2 *teaspoons water*
½ *teaspoon salt*	¼ *teaspoon sugar*
½ *egg white*	*dash of pepper*
1 *cup Chinese cabbage*	2 *tablespoons oil*
¼ *cup bamboo shoots*	3 *tablespoons oil*

½ *cup stock*

1. Soak dried mushrooms.

2. Prepare shrimp as in steps 1 and 2 of Stir-fried Miniature Shrimp.

3. Dice Chinese cabbage, bamboo shoots, canned and soaked mushrooms and water chestnuts. Stem and dice snow peas. Crush garlic.

4. Blend cornstarch, water, sugar and pepper to a paste.

5. Heat oil. Add shrimp, stir-fry 2 minutes; then remove from pan.

6. Heat remaining oil. Add garlic; stir-fry to brown lightly. Then add all vegetables, except snow peas, and stir-fry to coat with oil (about 1 minute).

7. Stir in stock and heat quickly. Then cook, covered, over medium heat, until nearly done (about 2 minutes).

8. Add snow peas and stir in ½ minute. Return shrimp; stir in only to reheat (about ½ minute more).

9. Stir in cornstarch paste to thicken and serve at once.

STIR-FRIED COOKED SHRIMP
6 to 8 servings

1 garlic clove	½ teaspoon salt
4 tablespoons catsup	1 tablespoon cornstarch
¼ cup water	3 tablespoons water
1 teaspoon sugar	2 tablespoons oil

1 pound cooked shrimp

1. Crush garlic. In one cup, combine catsup, water, sugar and salt. In another, blend cornstarch and remaining water to a paste.

2. Heat oil. Brown garlic lightly. Add catsup mixture and bring to a boil, stirring. Then stir in cooked shrimp only to heat through.

3. Stir in cornstarch paste to thicken and serve at once.

DEEP-FRIED SHRIMP WITHOUT BATTER
6 to 8 servings

1 pound shrimp	oil for deep-frying
2 tablespoons sherry	4 tablespoons soy sauce
½ teaspoon salt	¼ teaspoon salt

1. Shell and devein shrimp. Sprinkle with sherry and salt and toss. Let stand 10 to 15 minutes, tossing occasionally. Then drain.

2. Meanwhile heat oil. Add shrimp, then reduce heat to medium. Deep-fry until bright pink, and drain on paper toweling.

3. Combine soy sauce and remaining salt with 2 tablespoons of the hot oil.

Blend well; pour over shrimp and serve at once.

NOTE: If the heat of the oil is not reduced right after the shrimp are added, they will burn on the outside and be raw inside.

DEEP-FRIED SHRIMP IN SHELLS WITHOUT BATTER
6 to 8 servings

1 *pound shrimp*
oil *for deep-frying*
1 *slice fresh ginger root*

1 *scallion stalk*
4 *tablespoons soy sauce*
2 *tablespoons sherry*

1 *teaspoon sugar*

1. Wash shrimp. Remove legs, leaving shells intact, then devein (see page 453). Dry well with paper toweling.

2. Heat oil. Add shrimp, then reduce heat to medium. Deep-fry until bright pink and drain on paper toweling. Transfer shrimp to a shallow bowl.

3. Mince ginger root and scallion; then combine with soy sauce, sherry and sugar. Pour mixture over shrimp, tossing well to coat.

4. Refrigerate, covered, 30 minutes to 1 hour and serve. (If refrigerated for a longer period, the shrimp will discolor and darken.)

NOTE: See Note above.

BASIC DEEP-FRIED SHRIMP
6 to 8 servings

1 *pound shrimp*

batter

oil *for deep-frying*

1. Shell and devein shrimp, leaving tail segments intact.

2. Prepare any of the batters given on pages 515–516. Then holding each shrimp by the tail, dip in batter to coat.

3. Meanwhile heat oil. Add shrimp one by one (if dropped in all at once, they'll form a solid mass), or place in a wire basket and lower into oil.

4. Reduce heat to medium and deep-fry until shrimp float and are golden on both sides. (Depending on size, this will take 3 to 5 minutes.) Drain on paper toweling.

5. Serve hot, garnished with lettuce strips and Chinese parsley, and accompanied by plum sauce, hot mustard, catsup or a pepper-salt mix. (For additional dips, see pages 713-714.) Or serve with a sweet-and-pungent sauce (see pages 735-738).

NOTE: See Note under Deep-fried Shrimp without Batter.

VARIATIONS: In step 1, strip off legs and devein, but leave the shells intact; or else butterfly the shrimp. (See page 453.)

After step 1, marinate the shrimp in a mixture of 2 tablespoons soy sauce, 3 tablespoons sherry, 1 teaspoon ginger root, minced; and ¼ teaspoon salt. Let stand 10 to 15 minutes, turning occasionally. Drain, discarding marinade. Then coat with batter as in step 2, or dredge lightly in flour.

In the above variation, add to the marinade any or all of the following: 1 scallion, minced; ½ teaspoon garlic powder; a few drops of sesame oil.

EGG BATTER FOR DEEP-FRIED SHRIMP

4 tablespoons flour	1 egg
½ teaspoon salt	2 to 4 tablespoons water

1. Combine flour and salt.
2. Beat egg lightly and add. Then stir in water to thin.

VARIATIONS: In step 1, use 3 tablespoons flour and 1 tablespoon cornstarch; or 2½ tablespoons flour and 1½ tablespoons water-chestnut flour.

In step 1, add any of the following:

½ teaspoon baking powder

1 teaspoon sherry

1 teaspoon sugar

4 or 5 drops ginger juice

½ teaspoon garlic powder

dash of white pepper

In step 2, for the water, substitute either beer or sour milk.

EGGLESS BATTER FOR DEEP-FRIED SHRIMP

½ cup flour
¼ cup water
½ teaspoon salt
dash of pepper
1½ teaspoons baking powder

1. Combine flour, water, salt and pepper. Beat with a fork until smooth.
2. Then blend in baking powder.

VARIATION: In step 1, add 2 tablespoons cornstarch and 1 tablespoon each of soy sauce and sherry.

EGG-WHITE BATTER FOR DEEP-FRIED SHRIMP

3 egg whites
2 tablespoons cornstarch
¼ teaspoon salt
¼ teaspoon salt
2 tablespoons cornstarch

1. Beat egg whites until stiff; fold in cornstarch and salt.
2. Combine remaining cornstarch and salt in another dish. Dredge shrimp in this; then dip in egg-white mixture to coat.

SEPARATED EGG BATTER FOR DEEP-FRIED SHRIMP

1 egg
⅔ cup flour
½ teaspoon salt
few drops of water
2 tablespoons oil

1. Separate egg. Combine yolk with flour and salt. Add water to thin and mix until smooth.
2. Blend in oil. Beat egg white until stiff, then fold in gently.

DEEP-FRIED SHRIMP WITH SHERRY
6 to 8 servings

1 pound deep-fried shrimp
⅓ cup sherry

½ head lettuce

1. Deep-fry shrimp as in Basic Deep-fried Shrimp.
2. Shred the lettuce and arrange on a serving platter.
3. In a large skillet, heat sherry to boiling. Add deep-fried shrimp and simmer, uncovered, until sherry is absorbed, turning shrimp once. Arrange over lettuce and serve.

DEEP-FRIED SHRIMP WITH SHERRY SAUCE
6 to 8 servings

1 pound deep-fried shrimp
1 onion
1 tablespoon cornstarch

2 tablespoons sherry
2 teaspoons soy sauce
½ cup stock

2 tablespoons oil

1. Deep-fry shrimp as in Basic Deep-fried Shrimp and keep warm. Mince onion.
2. Blend together cornstarch, sherry, soy sauce and stock.
3. Heat remaining oil. Add minced onion and stir-fry until translucent (1 to 2 minutes).
4. Add cornstarch-sherry mixture and cook, stirring, until sauce thickens. Pour over shrimp and serve.

DEEP-FRIED SHRIMP WITH CATSUP SAUCE
6 to 8 servings

1 pound deep-fried shrimp
5 tablespoons onion
2 slices fresh ginger root
4 tablespoons catsup

½ teaspoon salt
2 teaspoons sugar
1 tablespoon cornstarch
½ cup water

2 tablespoons oil

1. Deep-fry shrimp as in Basic Deep-fried Shrimp (but only for 1 to 2 minutes). Then drain. Mince onion and ginger root.
2. In a cup, combine catsup, salt and sugar. In another cup, blend cornstarch and cold water.

3. Heat remaining oil. Add onion and ginger root; stir-fry a few times. Add deep-fried shrimp and stir-fry briefly to reheat.

4. Stir in catsup mixture only to heat through. Then stir in cornstarch paste to thicken, and serve at once.

DEEP-FRIED SHRIMP WITH HOT SAUCE
6 to 8 servings

1 *pound deep-fried shrimp*	1 *tablespoon sugar*
2 *chili peppers*	1 *tablespoon soy sauce*
1 *garlic clove*	1 *tablespoon sherry*
2 *slices fresh ginger root*	½ *teaspoon salt*

2 tablespoons oil

1. Deep-fry shrimp as in Basic Deep-fried Shrimp.

2. Mince chili peppers, garlic and ginger root. In a cup, combine sugar, soy sauce, sherry and salt.

3. Heat remaining oil. Add chili peppers, garlic and ginger root; stir-fry to brown lightly (1 to 2 minutes).

4. Stir in sugar-soy mixture and heat quickly.

5. Stir in deep-fried shrimp only to reheat; then serve at once.

VARIATIONS: For the chili peppers, substitute a few drops of Tabasco Sauce and add in step 5.

Omit the chili peppers. Reduce the sugar to 1 teaspoon. In step 1, deep-fry the shrimp only 2 minutes. Return as in step 5 to reheat. Then stir in ¼ teaspoon crushed red pepper, 1 tablespoon catsup and 1 tablespoon Chinese chili. Serve at once.

DEEP-FRIED SHRIMP WITH CROUTONS
8 to 10 servings

1 *pound deep-fried shrimp*	½ *teaspoon salt*
3 *slices white bread*	½ *teaspoon sugar*
12 *water chestnuts*	1 *tablespoon cornstarch*
3 *tablespoons soy sauce*	2 *tablespoons water*
2 *tablespoons sherry*	2 *tablespoons oil*

1. Deep-fry shrimp as in Basic Deep-fried Shrimp but only for 1 to 2 minutes.

2. Remove bread crusts and cut bread in 2-inch cubes (or approximately the size of the shrimp). Slice water chestnuts.

3. In one cup, combine soy sauce, sherry, salt and sugar. In another cup, blend cornstarch and cold water to a paste.

4. Reheat deep-frying oil. Add bread cubes and deep-fry until golden. Drain on paper toweling; arrange on a serving platter.

5. Heat remaining oil. Add water chestnuts; stir-fry a few times. Add deep-fried shrimp; stir-fry ½ minute to reheat.

6. Add soy-sherry mixture and bring quickly to a boil. Then simmer, covered, 2 minutes.

7. Stir in cornstarch paste to thicken. Spoon mixture over bread cubes and serve at once.

NOTE: Slightly stale bread is best for the croutons.

DEEP-FRIED SHRIMP AND PEAS
8 to 10 servings

1 *pound deep-fried shrimp*	½ *teaspoon salt*
½ *pound peas*	*dash of pepper*
1 *tablespoon sherry*	2 *teaspoons cornstarch*
2 *teaspoons soy sauce*	3 *tablespoons water*

2 tablespoons oil

1. Deep-fry shrimp as in Basic Deep-fried Shrimp.

2. Shell and parboil peas.

3. In one cup, combine sherry, soy sauce, salt and pepper. In another cup, blend cornstarch and cold water to a paste.

4. Heat remaining oil. Add deep-fried shrimp and parboiled peas; stir-fry briefly to heat through. Add sherry-soy mixture and bring to a boil over high heat, stirring constantly.

5. Stir in cornstarch paste to thicken, and serve at once.

VARIATIONS: For the peas, substitute the following (diced, and in any combination): smoked ham, water chestnuts, bamboo shoots, or snow peas.

Instead of coating shrimp with batter, as in Basic Deep-fried Shrimp, dredge in a mixture of 1 tablespoon cornstarch and 1 teaspoon salt. Deep-fry until pinkish and drain on paper toweling. Omit steps 3 and 5. In step 4, add with the shrimp and peas 2 teaspoons sherry and stir-fry 2 minutes. Then serve at once.

DEEP-FRIED SHRIMP WITH LICHEES
8 to 10 servings

1 *pound deep-fried shrimp*	⅓ *cup sugar*
½ *to 1 cup canned lichee fruit*	½ *teaspoon salt*
2 *slices fresh ginger root*	½ *teaspoon heavy soy sauce*
⅓ *cup vinegar*	1 *tablespoon oil*

1. Deep-fry shrimp as in Basic Deep-fried Shrimp and keep warm. Drain lichee fruit (reserve liquid for other uses).

2. Mince ginger root, then combine with vinegar, sugar, salt and soy sauce.

3. Heat remaining oil. Stir in ginger-vinegar mixture and bring to a boil; then simmer, stirring, 2 minutes.

4. Stir in lichee fruit only to heat through. Spoon sauce over shrimp and serve at once.

VARIATION: For the lichee fruit, substitute pineapple chunks.

DEEP-FRIED SHRIMP WITH VEGETABLES I
8 to 10 servings

1 *pound deep-fried shrimp*	1 *tablespoon sherry*
½ *cup carrots*	1 *teaspoon soy sauce*
½ *cup bamboo shoots*	1 *teaspoon vinegar*
2 *slices fresh ginger root*	1 *tablespoon cornstarch*
½ *cup leek stalk*	3 *tablespoons water*
1 *tablespoon sugar*	2 *tablespoons oil*
2 *tablespoons catsup*	½ *teaspoon salt*

1. Deep-fry shrimp as in Basic Deep-fried Shrimp.
2. Dice carrots and parboil. Dice bamboo shoots. Slice ginger root and leek.

3. In one cup, combine sugar, catsup, sherry, soy sauce and vinegar. In another cup, blend cornstarch and cold water to a paste.

4. Heat remaining oil. Add salt, then ginger root and leek; stir-fry a few times.

5. Add carrots and bamboo shoots and stir-fry briefly to heat through.

6. Add sugar-catsup mixture; stir-fry 2 minutes more to heat and blend.

7. Stir in deep-fried shrimp only to reheat. Then stir in cornstarch paste to thicken and serve at once.

DEEP-FRIED SHRIMP WITH VEGETABLES II
10 to 12 servings

1 *pound deep-fried shrimp*	1 *garlic clove*
1 *cup bamboo shoots*	1 *tablespoon cornstarch*
1 *cup Chinese cabbage stems*	1 *tablespoon soy sauce*
1 *cup celery*	1 *teaspoon sugar*
½ *cup water chestnuts*	*dash of pepper*
½ *cup onion*	3 *tablespoons oil*
½ *cup fresh mushrooms*	*few drops of sesame oil*
½ *cup snow peas*	1 *teaspoon salt*
2 *scallion stalks*	1 *cup stock*

1. Shell, devein and butterfly shrimp. Marinate as in the second or third variation of Basic Deep-fried Shrimp, then deep-fry. (Reserve the marinade.)

2. Slice bamboo shoots thin; also Chinese cabbage stems, celery, water chestnuts, onion and mushrooms.

3. Cut snow peas in 2 or 3 pieces. Split scallions in half lengthwise; then cut crosswise in 1-inch sections. Crush garlic.

4. Blend cornstarch, soy sauce, sugar and pepper to a paste.

5. Heat remaining oil along with sesame oil. Add salt and garlic; stir-fry to brown lightly. Add all vegetables except scallions and stir-fry 2 to 3 minutes to heat through.

6. Add reserved shrimp marinade and stir-fry 2 minutes more.

7. Add scallions; stir-fry a few times. Then add stock and heat quickly. Cook, covered, over medium heat, until vegetables are nearly done (about 3 minutes).

8. Stir in deep-fried shrimp to reheat. Then stir in cornstarch paste to thicken and serve at once.

DEEP-FRIED SHRIMP WITH BACON I
8 to 10 servings

1 *pound large shrimp*	*pepper*
6 *bacon strips*	*oil for deep-frying*

lemon wedges

1. Shell, devein and butterfly shrimp, leaving the tail segments intact.

2. Cut bacon strips in two and wrap each half around a shrimp. Sprinkle lightly with pepper.

3. Meanwhile heat oil. Add shrimp and deep-fry until golden. Drain on paper toweling. Serve hot, accompanied by lemon wedges.

VARIATION: Omit the pepper in step 2, and before deep-frying, coat the bacon-wrapped shrimp in the following batter: Blend 2 eggs, beaten, with ¼ cup flour and ¼ cup water-chestnut flour. Then blend in ¼ cup mixed nutmeats, toasted and crushed to a powder, and ½ teaspoon salt.

DEEP-FRIED SHRIMP WITH BACON II
8 to 10 servings

1 pound large shrimp	½ teaspoon salt
6 bacon strips	2 teaspoons soy sauce
1 egg	¾ cup cornstarch

oil for deep-frying

1. Shell, devein and butterfly shrimp, leaving the tail segments intact.

2. Cut bacon strips in 1-inch sections. Place one section on each shrimp; then re-close shrimp, pressing its edges to seal in bacon.

3. Beat egg; then stir in salt and soy sauce. Holding each shrimp by the tail, dip first in egg mixture, then in cornstarch to dredge lightly.

4. Transfer shrimp to a covered dish and refrigerate 30 minutes to 1 hour.

5. Meanwhile heat oil. Then add shrimp, and deep-fry until golden. Drain on paper toweling and serve at once.

DEEP-FRIED SHRIMP STUFFED WITH BACON AND ALMONDS
6 to 8 servings

1 pound large shrimp	salt
¼ cup almond meats	1 egg
2 strips lean bacon	1 cup flour

oil for deep-frying

1. Shell, devein and butterfly shrimp, leaving the tail segments intact.

2. Blanch and toast almonds; chop coarsely. Shred bacon, then mix with almonds. Place about ½ teaspoon of mixture on each shrimp. Re-close shrimp, pressing its edges to seal in filling. Sprinkle lightly with salt.

3. Beat egg. Holding shrimp by the tail, dip first in egg, then in flour to dredge lightly. Meanwhile heat oil.

4. Add shrimp and deep-fry until golden. Drain on paper toweling and serve at once.

VARIATION: For the almonds and bacon, substitute walnuts and smoked ham.

DEEP-FRIED SHRIMP STUFFED WITH HAM
8 to 10 servings

1 *pound large shrimp*	2 *tablespoons soy sauce*
¼ *pound smoked ham*	1 *tablespoon sherry*
oil for deep-frying	¼ *cup flour*
1 *egg*	⅛ *cup cornstarch*
3 *tablespoons onion*	½ *teaspoon salt*
½ *garlic clove*	*dash of pepper*

1. Shell and devein shrimp, leaving the tail segments intact. Butterfly shrimp, making 2 slits in the back of each.

2. Slice ham thin; then cut in 1- by 3-inch strips. Thread 1 strip through each shrimp, working from back to front so that ham is mostly inside. Meanwhile heat oil.

3. Beat egg. Mince onion and garlic and add, along with soy sauce and sherry. Then sift in flour, cornstarch, salt and pepper; beat to a smooth batter.

4. Holding shrimp by the tail, dip in batter to coat. Add to oil, 1 at a time, and deep-fry until golden. Drain on paper toweling; serve at once.

DEEP-FRIED COATED BUTTERFLY SHRIMP
10 to 12 servings

2 *dried oysters*	1 *egg*
1 *pound large shrimp*	⅓ *cup cornstarch*
1 *pound fish fillets*	½ *teaspoon salt*
1½ *bacon strips*	⅛ *teaspoon pepper*
2 *tablespoons smoked ham*	*oil for deep-frying*
1 *tablespoon Chinese sausage*	1 *egg*
1 *scallion stalk*	1 *cup cornmeal*
1 *garlic clove*	½ *head lettuce*
½ *teaspoon fresh ginger root*	*few sprigs of Chinese parsley*

1 *lemon*

1. Soak dried oysters.
2. Shell, devein and butterfly shrimp, leaving the tail segments intact.
3. Mince fish fillets, bacon, smoked ham, Chinese sausage, scallion, garlic, ginger root and soaked oysters.
4. Beat egg and add to minced ingredients, along with cornstarch, salt and pepper. Blend mixture to a smooth paste.
5. Roll each shrimp in about 3 tablespoons of this paste to coat. (First oil the palms of the hands lightly with peanut oil to prevent sticking.) Meanwhile heat deep-frying oil.
6. Beat remaining egg. Holding shrimp by the tail, dip first in egg, then in cornmeal to dredge lightly. Add shrimp to oil, 1 at a time, and deep-fry until they float. Drain on paper toweling.
7. Shred lettuce and arrange on a serving platter with shrimp on top. Chop Chinese parsley; sprinkle over as a garnish. Serve hot, accompanied by lemon wedges.

NOTE: For the fish fillets, use sea bass, pike or haddock.

VARIATION: For the Chinese sausage, substitute 1 tablespoon dried duck (soaked).

PAN-FRIED BACON-WRAPPED BUTTERFLY SHRIMP I
8 to 10 servings

1 *pound large shrimp*	*dash of pepper*
6 *bacon strips*	1½ *tablespoons oil*

½ *cup catsup*

1. Shell, devein and butterfly shrimp, leaving the tail segments intact.
2. Cut each bacon strip in two and wrap one half around each shrimp.

Sprinkle lightly with pepper.

3. Heat oil. Pan-fry shrimp on both sides until pinkish.

4. Add catsup and cook, stirring occasionally, until shrimp are done (about 2 minutes more). Serve hot.

VARIATIONS: In step 2, dip the bacon-wrapped shrimp in beaten egg. Then sprinkle with the pepper.

In step 4, substitute for the catsup a mixture of ¾ cup stock, 1 tablespoon cornstarch and 1 teaspoon soy sauce. Cook, stirring, over medium heat until mixture thickens.

PAN-FRIED BACON-WRAPPED BUTTERFLY SHRIMP II
8 to 10 servings

1 *pound large shrimp*	2 *or 3 teaspoons sugar*
3 *or 4 bacon strips*	*dash of pepper*
1 *large onion*	½ *cup water*
1 *garlic clove*	2 *teaspoons cornstarch*
1 *or 2 eggs*	2 *tablespoons water*
4 *tablespoons flour*	3 *tablespoons oil*
¼ *cup catsup*	1 *tablespoon oil*
2 *tablespoons Worcestershire Sauce*	½ *teaspoon salt*

1. Shell, devein and butterfly shrimp, leaving the tail segments intact. Cut bacon strips in ½-inch sections. Slice onion thin. Crush garlic.

2. Beat eggs. Then add flour and beat with a wire whisk until batter thickens. (It should not be runny: if it is, add more flour.) Dip bacon in batter, 1 section at a time, and place on the flattened surface of each shrimp.

3. In one cup, combine catsup, Worcestershire Sauce, sugar, pepper and water. In another cup, blend cornstarch and remaining cold water to a paste.

4. Heat oil. Add shrimp, bacon-side down, and pan-fry 2 minutes over medium heat. Cover and cook another ½ minute. Turn shrimp over and pan-fry 2 minutes more. Remove and drain shrimp on paper toweling.

5. Add onion slices and stir-fry until softened and translucent; then drain. Arrange on a serving dish with shrimp on top. Keep warm.

6. Heat remaining oil. Add salt and crushed garlic; stir-fry to brown lightly. Add catsup mixture and bring to a boil, stirring.

7. Then stir in cornstarch paste to thicken. Spoon sauce over shrimp and serve at once.

VARIATIONS: In step 2, substitute for the batter, a mixture of 2 egg whites, 4 tablespoons flour and ½ teaspoon salt.

In step 2, top each shrimp with a strip of smoked ham. (Slice ham thin, cut in 1- by 2-inch strips, and dip in batter to make it adhere.) Then top with a bacon section as above.

In step 4, for the catsup mixture, substitute ½ cup catsup and 1 cup stock.

In step 4, add to the cornstarch paste 1 teaspoon soy sauce and a dash of pepper.

STEAMED SHRIMP
6 to 8 servings

1 *pound shrimp*	1 *tablespoon soy sauce*
3 *or 4 slices fresh ginger root*	1 *tablespoon sherry*

1. Shell and devein shrimp.

2. Mince ginger root; then combine with soy sauce and sherry. Add to shrimp and toss. Let stand 10 to 15 minutes, turning occasionally.

3. Transfer shrimp and its marinade to a shallow heatproof dish. Steam over low heat until shrimp turn pink (15 to 20 minutes). See page 831.

VARIATIONS: In step 2, add to the marinade ½ teaspoon salt, ½ teaspoon sugar and a dash of pepper.

Omit step 2. Sprinkle the shrimp instead with 2 tablespoons sherry before steaming. Then season with salt to taste and serve cold.

In step 3, add with the shrimp 2 cakes bean curd, sliced or cubed; or ½ cup fresh mushrooms and ¼ cup water chestnuts, both sliced.

POACHED SHRIMP
6 to 8 servings

1 *pound shrimp*	2 *cups water*
½ *teaspoon salt*	

1. Wash shrimp. Remove legs, leaving shells intact, then devein.

2. Bring water to a boil. Add salt, then shrimp, and simmer, uncovered, until shrimp turn bright pink (about 4 minutes). Drain, discarding liquid.

3. Let shrimp cool; then shell and devein. Serve cold, with a dip (see page 713).

NOTE: Do not overcook, or the shrimp will toughen and dry out.

POACHED SHRIMP WITH HAM AND BEAN CURD
6 to 8 servings

½ pound shrimp	4 cakes bean curd
½ cup smoked ham	3 cups stock

few sprigs of Chinese parsley

1. Shell and devein shrimp; dice in ½-inch sections. Dice ham and bean curd in ½-inch cubes. Place in a saucepan.
2. Pour stock over. Bring to a boil; then simmer, uncovered, until shrimp turn bright pink.
3. Serve hot, in a deep bowl, garnished with Chinese parsley.

POACHED SHRIMP WITH EGG SAUCE
6 to 8 servings

1 pound shrimp	3 egg yolks
½ head lettuce	¼ cup white vinegar
4 cups water	1 teaspoon dry mustard
1 teaspoon salt	pinch of salt
1 tablespoon sherry	¼ cup oil

1 Shell and devein shrimp. Shred lettuce.
2. Bring water to a boil. Add salt, sherry and shrimp; then simmer, uncovered, until shrimp turn bright pink (about 4 minutes). Drain, discarding liquid. Cut shrimp in bite-size pieces and keep warm.
3. Beat egg yolks and blend with vinegar, dry mustard and remaining salt.
4. Heat oil. Add egg mixture and cook, stirring, over low heat until eggs begin to thicken. Then remove from heat. (Do not let them set.)
5. Arrange lettuce on a serving platter with shrimp on top. Spoon egg sauce over and serve at once.

DRUNKEN SHRIMP
6 to 8 servings

1 pound shrimp	4 to 6 tablespoons sherry
4 cups water	½ teaspoon salt
2 tablespoons soy sauce	2 slices fresh ginger root

1 teaspoon vinegar

1. Wash shrimp. Remove legs, leaving shells intact; then devein.

2. Boil water and poach shrimp until pinkish (about 2 minutes); then drain.

3. Combine soy sauce, sherry and salt; pour over shrimp and toss. Let stand 1 hour, turning occasionally. Drain, discarding marinade.

4. Mince ginger root and sprinkle over shrimp. Also sprinkle vinegar over. Let stand 30 minutes more, turning occasionally; then serve.

NOTE: These shrimp, served in their shells, should be as fresh as possible. In China, live shrimp were used.

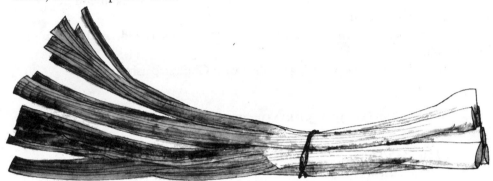

MARINATED SHRIMP WITH EGGS
6 to 8 servings

1 pound shrimp
½ teaspoon ginger root
½ teaspoon scallion
½ teaspoon salt
2 teaspoons sherry
2 teaspoons soy sauce
½ teaspoon ginger root

½ teaspoon scallion
1 teaspoon vinegar
2 tablespoons stock
2 teaspoons soy sauce
flour
3 or 4 eggs
2 tablespoons oil

½ head lettuce

1. Shell and devein shrimp.

2. Mince ginger root and scallion; then combine with salt, sherry and soy sauce. Add to shrimp and toss. Let stand 15 minutes, turning occasionally.

3. Mince remaining ginger root and scallion. Then combine with vinegar, stock and remaining soy sauce.

4. Drain shrimp, discarding marinade; sprinkle lightly with flour. Beat eggs; then add shrimp and toss gently to coat.

5. Heat oil. Add coated shrimp and stir in. Add soy-vinegar mixture and cook over low heat, stirring occasionally, until shrimp turn pink (about 5 minutes).

6. Shred lettuce and arrange on a serving platter. Top with shrimp mixture and serve at once.

BARBECUED SHRIMP
10 to 12 servings

1 *pound large shrimp*
5 *bacon strips*
½ *pound chicken livers*
½ *garlic clove*
2 *slices fresh ginger root*

1½ *tablespoons sugar*
½ *cup soy sauce*
½ *teaspoon salt*
dash of pepper
white bread

1. Shell, devein and butterfly shrimp, leaving the tail segments intact. Cut each bacon strip crosswise in 4 sections. Slice chicken livers thin and cut in similar-size sections.

2. Place a piece of chicken liver, then bacon, on the flattened surface of each shrimp. Arrange in a shallow dish.

3. Mince garlic and ginger root; then blend with sugar, soy sauce, salt and pepper. Pour over shrimp and let stand 15 to 20 minutes.

4. Thread shrimp (with liver and bacon sections) on skewers. Either broil in the oven or barbecue over charcoal, turning once or twice until shrimp turn pink (about 5 minutes).

5. Serve hot, accompanied by thin slices of white bread, trimmed of their crusts.

CURRIED SHRIMP I
6 to 8 servings

1 *pound shrimp*
3 *or 4 scallions*
1 *to 2 tablespoons curry*

½ *teaspoon salt*
5 *tablespoons oil*
½ *cup stock*

1. Wash shrimp. Remove legs, leaving shells intact; then devein (see page 453). Mince scallions.

2. Heat a dry pan. Add curry and salt and stir a few times. Gradually add oil, blending in until smooth and heated through.

3. Add shrimp; stir-fry gently until well coated and browned.

4. Add stock and heat quickly. Then simmer, covered, until shrimp are done (3 to 4 minutes).

5. Stir in minced scallions only to heat through; serve at once.

CURRIED SHRIMP II
6 to 8 servings

1 *pound shrimp*	1 *to 2 tablespoons curry*
2 *small white onions*	½ *cup milk*
3 *tablespoons oil*	2 *teaspoons cornstarch*

2 tablespoons water

1. Shell and devein shrimp; cut in two, if large. Cut onions in wedges.

2. Heat oil. Add curry; stir in until it begins to smell pungent.

3. Add onion wedges and stir-fry until translucent (3 to 4 minutes).

4. Add shrimp; stir in quickly to coat. Then add milk. Cook, covered, over medium-low heat, stirring occasionally, until shrimp turn pink (5 to 7 minutes).

5. Blend cornstarch and cold water to a paste. Then stir in to thicken and serve at once.

BASIC DEEP-FRIED SHRIMP BALLS
6 to 8 servings

1 *pound shrimp*	2 *slices fresh ginger root*
6 *to 10 water chestnuts*	2 *teaspoons cornstarch*
1 *egg*	1 *tablespoon sherry*
½ *scallion stalk*	½ *teaspoon salt*

oil for deep-frying

1. Shell and devein shrimp. Then mince or grind with water chestnuts.

2. Beat egg lightly; mince scallion and ginger root; then add to shrimp mixture along with cornstarch, sherry and salt. Blend to a smooth paste.

3. Shape mixture into walnut-size balls. (To prevent sticking, wet 2

teaspoons in a bowl of cold water; then spoon up a teaspoon of the mixture and toss it between the 2 spoons to form a round, smooth ball.)

4. Meanwhile heat enough oil to float shrimp balls. Add them a few at a time. (Don't crowd: allow room for stirring and for even browning.) Reduce heat to medium and deep-fry, turning shrimp balls occasionally, until golden. Remove with a slotted spoon and drain on paper toweling.

5. Repeat process until mixture is used up, reheating oil each time.

6. Serve shrimp balls hot, sprinkled with nutmeg and lemon juice and garnished with Chinese parsley; or accompanied by a sweet-and-pungent sauce.

VARIATIONS: For the shrimp, substitute fresh crabmeat.

For the water chestnuts, substitute either ½ cup bamboo shoots or ¼ cup celery, minced.

Omit the whole egg. Substitute 1 egg white in step 2; or else dip shrimp balls in the egg white to coat after step 3.

Omit the cornstarch in step 2. After step 3, dredge shrimp balls lightly in flour; then dip in whole egg, beaten.

In step 2, add 2 bacon strips, minced; or 1 or 2 tablespoons unrendered leaf lard, minced; or ¼ pound pork, with some fat, minced.

In step 2, add any or all of the following: ½ garlic clove, minced; a few sprigs of Chinese parsley, chopped; 1 tablespoon soy sauce; ½ teaspoon sugar; a few drops of sesame oil.

At the end of step 3, roll each shrimp ball in minced smoked ham (about 2 ounces for 1 pound of shrimp) to coat.

Omit step 3. Instead of shaping into balls, drop shrimp mixture directly into the hot oil from a teaspoon. (Dip teaspoon in cold water each time to prevent sticking.)

FLUFFY DEEP-FRIED SHRIMP BALLS
6 to 8 servings

1 *pound shrimp*	1 *teaspoon water*
1½ *tablespoons leaf lard*	1 *egg white*
½ *teaspoon salt*	1 *tablespoon flour*

oil for deep-frying

1. Shell and devein shrimp; then mince with unrendered leaf lard. Knead together in a mixing bowl.

2. Dissolve salt in water and add, along with egg white and flour. Stir mixture by hand in one direction 15 to 20 minutes.

3. Pick up mixture and toss vigorously back into bowl. Repeat several times. (The mixture will now be whitish.)

4. Continue stirring and tossing until mixture is quite stiff and pinkish. (Squeeze a small amount of the mixture into a bowl of cold water. If it holds its shape well and is not sticky, it's ready.)

5. Meanwhile heat oil. Place some shrimp mixture in the palm of the hand; then make a fist and squeeze mixture through the hollow between thumb and index finger, shaping it into as round a ball as possible. Drop shrimp balls carefully into hot oil.

6. Deep-fry a few at a time, as in Basic Deep-fried Shrimp Balls. Then drain on paper toweling and serve.

DEEP-FRIED SHRIMP BALLS IN BATTER
8 to 10 servings

1 *pound shrimp*	*few drops of sesame oil*
½ *cup bamboo shoots*	1 *egg white*
½ *cup canned button mushrooms*	1 *egg*
1 *scallion*	1 *cup flour*
½ *teaspoon salt*	1 *teaspoon baking powder*
dash of pepper	3 *teaspoons oil*

oil for deep-frying

1. Shell and devein shrimp. Then mince, along with bamboo shoots, canned button mushrooms and scallion. Place in a mixing bowl.

2. Blend in salt, pepper and sesame oil. Then fold in egg white. Stir in one direction until mixture is fluffy. Then form into walnut-size balls.

3. Beat whole egg lightly. Add flour, baking powder and oil and blend to a smooth batter. (If necessary, add water to thin slightly.) Meanwhile heat deep-frying oil.

4. Dip shrimp balls, one at a time, in batter to coat; then carefully drop into hot oil. Deep-fry a few at a time, as in Basic Deep-fried Shrimp Balls. Then drain on paper toweling and serve.

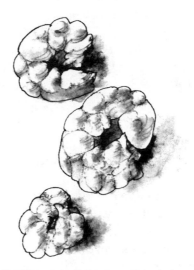

SHRIMP BALLS FOR SOUP
About 4 servings

½ pound shrimp	*½ teaspoon sugar*
¼ cup smoked ham	*2 teaspoons cornstarch*
1 egg white	*1 teaspoon soy sauce*
¼ teaspoon salt	*4 to 6 cups water*

soup stock

1. Shell and devein shrimp. Then mince with smoked ham.

2. Blend egg white into shrimp mixture, along with salt, sugar, cornstarch and soy sauce. Form into walnut-size balls.

3. Bring water to a boil and carefully drop in shrimp balls, a few at a time. Cover and cook gently until they float (3 to 4 minutes). Drain, discarding liquid.

4. Place shrimp balls in a large tureen. Bring stock to a boil and pour over. (The richer the soup stock, the better the dish).

NOTE: These shrimp balls may be prepared a day or two in advance and refrigerated.

VARIATIONS: In step 1, omit the ham and add 1 slice fresh ginger root, minced.

In step 2, omit the sugar, cornstarch and soy sauce; add 1 tablespoon sherry.

In step 3, instead of cooking the shrimp balls in water, bring the stock (in which they're to be served) to a boil; then simmer shrimp balls, covered, 5 minutes.

BASIC BRAISED SHRIMP BALLS
8 to 10 servings

1 *pound shrimp*	½ *teaspoon salt*
¼ *pound pork*	1 *tablespoon cornstarch*
1 *tablespoon sherry*	2 *tablespoons water*
1 *tablespoon soy sauce*	3 *tablespoons oil*
1 *teaspoon sugar*	3 *tablespoons water*

1. Shell and devein shrimp; mince or grind with pork. Then blend in sherry, soy sauce, sugar and salt.

2. Blend cornstarch and cold water to a paste. Add to shrimp mixture, mixing well. Form into walnut-size balls; then flatten each slightly.

3. Heat oil. Brown shrimp balls lightly on all sides.

4. Add remaining water and cook, covered, over medium heat, turning several times, until done (6 to 8 minutes).

NOTE: The pork used should have some fat.

VARIATIONS: For the oil, substitute lard.

With Chinese cabbage: In step 4, place 1 pound Chinese cabbage stems, cut in 1-inch sections, at the bottom of the pan with the shrimp balls on top. Add ½ cup water and ½ teaspoon salt; then simmer, covered, 15 to 20 minutes.

With cucumbers: In step 4, place 2 medium cucumbers, peeled and cut in 1-inch slices, at the bottom of the pan with the shrmip balls on top. Add ½ cup water and 1 tablespoon soy sauce; then simmer, covered, 10 minutes.

With lily buds: In step 4, place ½ cup lily buds (soaked) at the bottom of the pan with the shrimp balls on top. Add 1 cup water and 2 teaspoons soy sauce; then simmer, covered, 20 minutes.

With mushrooms: In step 4, add to the shrimp balls ½ cup water and simmer, covered, 10 minutes. Then add ½ pound fresh mushrooms, sliced; and simmer, covered, 3 to 4 minutes more.

With spinach: In step 4, add to the shrimp balls ½ cup water and simmer, covered, 10 minutes. Then add 1 pound whole leaf spinach and ½ teaspoon salt; and simmer, covered, 3 minutes more.

STIR-FRIED SHRIMP BALLS AND TOMATOES
8 to 10 servings

2 dried black mushrooms	1 green pepper
1 pound shrimp	2 celery stalks
½ garlic clove	4 scallion stalks
2 teaspoons cornstarch	1 garlic clove
½ teaspoon sugar	1 tablespoon cornstarch
1 tablespoon soy sauce	1 teaspoon soy sauce
½ teaspoon salt	½ teaspoon sugar
1 egg	¼ cup mushroom liquid
4 to 6 cups water	3 tablespoons oil
2 large tomatoes	½ teaspoon salt

1. Soak dried mushrooms; reserve soaking liquid.

2. Shell and devein shrimp. Mince shrimp and garlic; then combine with cornstarch, sugar, soy sauce and salt. Beat egg; then blend in well. Form into walnut-size balls.

3. Bring water to a boil. Carefully drop in shrimp balls, a few at a time, and cook gently until they float (3 to 4 minutes). Drain, discarding liquid.

4. Meanwhile peel tomatoes and chop to a pulp. Dice pepper in 1-inch squares. Cut celery stalks and scallions in 1-inch sections. Crush remaining garlic. Slice soaked mushrooms.

5. Blend remaining cornstarch, soy sauce and sugar to a paste with the mushroom-soaking liquid.

6. Heat oil. Add remaining salt and garlic; stir-fry to brown lightly. Add green pepper, celery and mushrooms, and stir-fry a few times. Then cook, covered, 2 minutes over medium heat.

7. Add scallions and stir-fry until translucent (1 to 2 minutes more).

8. Add shrimp balls and tomato pulp; stir in to heat through.

9. Then stir in cornstarch mixture to thicken and serve at once.

PAN-FRIED SHRIMP CAKES WITH PORK
6 to 8 servings

½ pound shrimp	½ teaspoon salt
½ pound lean pork	¼ teaspoon pepper
½ cup scallions	3 to 4 tablespoons oil

soy sauce

1. Shell and devein shrimp; cut pork in chunks and scallions in thirds. Mince together, or machine-grind twice at a medium setting.

2. Blend in salt and pepper and form mixture into small cakes, about 1½ inches in diameter and ½ inch thick.

3. Heat oil. Pan-fry shrimp cakes over medium heat until cooked through and golden on both sides. Then sprinkle with soy sauce and serve.

VARIATION: For the pork and scallions, substitute ½ pound fish fillets, ½ cup blanched almond meats and 2 bacon strips. In step 2, omit the pepper and add 1 tablespoon cornstarch, 1 tablespoon soy sauce and 1 teaspoon oil. Cook as in step 3, but do not sprinkle with soy sauce when serving.

PAN-FRIED SHRIMP CAKES WITH CHINESE CABBAGE
8 to 10 servings

1 *pound shrimp*	½ *teaspoon salt*
10 *water chestnuts*	*dash of pepper*
1 *scallion stalk*	1 *to 2 tablespoons stock*
1 *slice fresh ginger root*	3 *to 4 tablespoons oil*
1 *egg*	1 *pound Chinese cabbage*
1 *teaspoon cornstarch*	2 *tablespoons oil*
½ *teaspoon salt*	

1. Shell and devein shrimp; then mince or grind with water chestnuts, scallion stalk and ginger root.

2. Beat egg and blend into mixture, along with cornstarch, salt, pepper and stock. Form into cakes, as in step 2 above.

3. Heat oil. Pan-fry shrimp cakes over medium heat until cooked through and golden on each side. Remove from pan.

4. Meanwhile cut Chinese cabbage stems in 1-inch sections and blanch.

5. Heat remaining oil. Add remaining salt, then Chinese cabbage. Stir-fry to cook through (about 2 minutes). Return shrimp cakes; cook, covered, only to reheat. Serve at once.

NOTE: The shrimp mixture can be pan-fried as 1 large pancake, then cut in ¾-inch cubes and reheated.

SQUID

STIR-FRIED FRESH SQUID
About 4 servings

1 *pound fresh squid*	2 *tablespoons water*
1 *scallion stalk*	2 *tablespoons oil*
1 *slice fresh ginger root*	1 *tablespoon soy sauce*
1 *tablespoon cornstarch*	1 *tablespoon sherry*

1. Clean squid and cut in 1-inch squares. Cut scallion stalk in 1-inch sections. Crush ginger root.

2. Blend cornstarch and cold water to a paste.

3. Heat oil. Add scallion and ginger root; stir-fry a few times. Add squid and stir-fry to coat with oil (about 1 minute).

4. Sprinkle with soy sauce and sherry; stir-fry 2 minutes more.

5. Stir in cornstarch paste to thicken and serve at once.

STIR-FRIED FRESH SQUID WITH MUSHROOMS
About 6 servings

3 or 4 dried black mushrooms	1 tablespoon cornstarch
1 pound fresh squid	3 tablespoons water
1 cup Spanish onion	2 to 3 tablespoons oil
2 slices fresh ginger root	1½ tablespoons oil
1 tablespoon soy sauce	½ cup stock
2 tablespoons sherry	½ teaspoon salt

1. Soak dried mushrooms.

2. Clean squid and cut in 2-inch pieces. Slice onion and soaked mushrooms.

3. Mince ginger root; then combine in a cup with soy sauce and sherry. In another cup, blend cornstarch and cold water to a paste.

4. Heat oil. Add squid and stir-fry to coat with oil (about 1 minute).

5. Add ginger-soy mixture; stir-fry 1 to 2 minutes more. Remove squid from pan.

6. Heat remaining oil. Add sliced onion and mushrooms; stir-fry until onion is translucent. Then return squid.

7. Add stock and salt and heat quickly. Then cook, covered, 2 minutes over medium heat. Stir in cornstarch paste to thicken and serve at once.

STIR-FRIED FRESH SQUID AND VEGETABLES
6 to 8 servings

1 pound fresh squid	½ teaspoon sugar
½ cup bamboo shoots	1 teaspoon soy sauce
½ cup celery	1 teaspoon cornstarch
½ cup dried onion	1 teaspoon water
¼ pound snow peas	3 tablespoons oil
⅓ cup stock	½ teaspoon salt

1. Clean squid and cut in 1-inch squares.

2. Slice bamboo shoots, celery and dried onion. Stem and blanch snow peas.

3. In one cup, combine stock, sugar and soy sauce; in another, blend cornstarch and cold water to a paste.

4. Heat oil. Add salt, then squid; stir-fry to coat with oil (about 1 minute).

5. Add sliced vegetables and stir-fry ½ minute more.

6. Add stock-sugar mixture and heat quickly. Then cook, covered, over medium heat until vegetables are nearly done (2 to 3 minutes).

7. Stir in blanched snow peas to heat through. Then stir in cornstarch paste to thicken. Serve at once.

DEEP-FRIED SQUID
About 4 servings

1 *pound fresh squid*	½ *teaspoon salt*
½ *cup flour*	1 *egg*
¼ *cup cornstarch*	⅓ *cup water*
½ *teaspoon baking powder*	1½ *tablespoons oil*

oil for deep-frying

1. Clean squid and cut each in 4 parts.

2. Blend together flour, cornstarch, baking powder and salt. Then beat egg and add, along with cold water and oil. Beat with an egg beater until batter is smooth. Dip squid in this batter to coat.

3. Meanwhile heat deep-frying oil. Add squid, a few pieces at a time, and deep-fry until golden. (Do not overcook.) Drain on paper toweling and serve.

❀ *Egg Dishes* ❀

SO VERSATILE are the Chinese with eggs that whole cookbooks have been written on the subject. Eggs are cooked in all possible ways: steamed, stirred or scrambled, pan-fried, deep-fried, boiled, poached, simmered (in soy sauce, gravies and tea); or used in omelets, soufflés and egg puddings.

Eggs are not usually cooked alone but combined with other ingredients. These may be meat or seafood and vegetables. (If already cooked, the ingredients are cut up fine and combined directly with the eggs. If raw, they're usually stir-fried first.)

Fried eggs, stirred eggs and omelets are all cooked quickly over high heat. In the case of fried eggs, the oil or lard must be nearly smoking. This makes for egg whites that are crisp and crusty; for yolks that retain their moistness. Stirred or scrambled eggs are cooked over medium-high heat. They are pushed about quickly with a spatula while the pan is tilted so that most of the liquid egg comes directly in contact with the hot oil. This puffs up the eggs, makes them light and airy. Stirred eggs are removed from the stove while still quite moist: they cook to the right consistency in their own heat by the time they reach the table. Chinese omelets cooked over high heat are characteristically browned on the outside, soft on the inside, with their ingredients or fillings quickly heated through.

The original or classic egg foo yung is a light, airy soufflé made with egg whites and minced chicken breast. (Its name derives from both a white hibiscus flower and a Chinese bird whose colors resemble pure white jade.) The foo yung more familiar to Westerners is a hearty combination of whole eggs, shredded meat or seafood, and vegetables, cooked together as a thick, solid pancake. There are two versions of the more familiar variety: home-style and restaurant-style. Home-style egg foo yung is pan-fried either as one large omelet or as several small ones. The restaurant version is deep-fried, with the mixture dropped from a ladle into the hot oil to make a number of small omelets.

Boiled eggs (invariably hard-boiled) are eaten with a soy sauce dip or else pot-stewed afterward—that is, shelled and then simmered in the sauce of red-cooked meat or poultry until permeated with the savory flavors of these sauces. Poached eggs are used as garnishes for steamed rice and soups. Steamed custard-like eggs have their smooth blandness set off by ingredients that are highly flavored or salty.

NOTE: Leftover egg whites can be used in soufflés, chicken velvet, bird's nest soup and various batters for deep-fried foods. Leftover yolks can be used in omelets, egg puddings, as egg threads; or poached directly in hot soup as a garnish.

BASIC STEAMED EGGS
About 4 servings

2 scallions
1 cup stock
3 or 4 eggs
2 teaspoons sherry

1 teaspoon oil
½ teaspoon salt
¼ teaspoon sugar
soy sauce

1. Mince scallions. Heat (but do not boil) stock.
2. Beat eggs very lightly; then combine with sherry, oil, salt, sugar and scallions.

Slowly stir in heated stock. Transfer mixture to a shallow heatproof dish.

3. Steam over low heat until eggs are custard-like (20 to 30 minutes). See page 831. (Check with a toothpick or knife to see if eggs are done: they should be semi-solid. If they're still runny, steam a few minutes more.)

4. Sprinkle lightly with soy sauce and serve right in the steaming dish.

NOTE: Steamed eggs are delicately flavored and nourishing. Their texture will be smooth and custard-like *only* if the air content is kept to a minimum. For this reason the eggs should not be overbeaten. Also stock, rather than water, is generally used (it has already been brought to a boil and the air is driven out). Heating the stock first also contributes to the smoothness by enabling it to blend better with the eggs. Steaming should always be done over low heat: too much heat causes the eggs to separate and form holes in the surface of the custard.

VARIATIONS: For the stock, substitute milk. Scald before adding, but do not boil. (Water is not recommended as a substitute, but if it is to be used, it should be brought to a boil first to drive out the air, then cooled slightly before adding.)

In step 2, add 1 teaspoon ginger juice to the egg mixture.

After step 2, add any of the following, either alone or in the combinations indicated below:

Meat—½ cup lean pork, minced
  ½ cup roast pork, diced
  ¼ cup smoked ham, minced
  2 or 3 bacon strips, minced
  1 Chinese sausage, diced
  ½ cup beef, minced
  ½ cup chicken, minced
  ½ cup any leftover cooked meat, minced with 1 slice fresh ginger root
Seafood—½ cup cod fish, minced
  ½ cup clams, fresh or canned, minced (for the stock, substitute clam broth)
  ½ cup crabmeat, flaked
  ½ cup lobster, flaked
  ½ cup oysters, minced
  ½ cup shrimp (raw or cooked), minced
  2 or 3 dried scallops (soaked), shredded
  4 to 6 dried shrimp (soaked), minced
Vegetables—½ cup celery, chopped
  ½ cup fresh mushrooms, chopped
  ½ cup Chinese parsley, chopped
  ½ cup scallion stalks, chopped
  1 cup spinach, chopped
  ½ cup water chestnuts, chopped

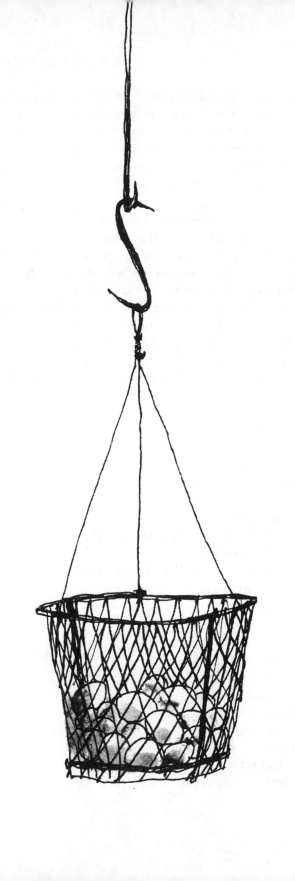

Combinations—½ cup lean pork and 8 water chestnuts, both minced
    ¼ cup lean pork and ½ cup raw shrimp, both minced
    ½ cup lean ham and ¼ cup bamboo shoots, both diced
    ½ cup crabmeat, flaked; and 3 dried scallops (soaked), shredded
    10 raw oysters, ¼ cup fat pork and 2 Spanish onions, minced. (Omit the oil and reduce stock to ¾ cup.)

In step 4, omit the soy sauce and sprinkle over eggs any of the following garnishes:
    1 tablespoon oyster sauce
    a few drops of sesame oil
    1 scallion stalk, minced
    a few sprigs of Chinese parsley, chopped

In step 4, top eggs with a garnish, stir-fried as follows: Heat 2 tablespoons oil. Add 2 onions, minced; ½ cup bamboo shoots, slivered; ¼ cup smoked ham, slivered; and 4 fresh mushrooms, sliced. Stir-fry 1 to 2 minutes. Then add 2 leaves of Chinese cabbage, shredded, and stir-fry 1 minute more. Sprinkle with the soy sauce and ½ teaspoon salt and stir in. Arrange over the steamed eggs and serve.

With clams in their shells: Use about 12 clams. Scrub their shells; then immerse 15 minutes in salted water (this will make the clams eject any grit or sand). Rinse and arrange on a shallow heatproof dish. Prepare the egg mixture as in steps 1 and 2 of Basic Steamed Eggs and pour over clams. Steam 30 minutes. Sprinkle with the soy sauce and a few drops of sesame oil.

With whole lobster: Chop a live lobster lengthwise in half and clean. Remove shell, leaving meat from each half intact. Pick up steps 1 to 3 of Basic Steamed Eggs, cooking eggs until they begin to set (about 10 minutes). Then top with the lobster meat and steam 10 minutes more. Sprinkle with the soy sauce.

STEAMED EGGS AND STIR-FRIED PORK
About 6 servings

¼ to ½ pound lean pork	2 tablespoons soy sauce
10 water chestnuts	½ teaspoon salt
1 scallion stalk	½ cup stock
2 tablespoons oil	4 eggs

1. Mince pork, water chestnuts and scallion.

2. Heat oil. Add minced ingredients; stir-fry until pork loses its pinkness (about 2 minutes).

3. Stir in soy sauce and salt to blend. Then drain mixture and transfer to a shallow heatproof dish.

4. Heat (but do not boil) stock. Beat eggs very lightly; then slowly stir in stock and pour over pork mixture.

5. Steam over low heat until eggs set (20 to 30 minutes). See page 831. Serve right in the steaming dish.

STEAMED EGGS AND FISH FILLETS
About 6 servings

½ *pound fillet of sole*	1 *tablespoon oil*
cornstarch	½ *cup stock*
1 *tablespoon green pepper*	3 *eggs*
1 *scallion stalk*	½ *teaspoon salt*

1. Sliver fish fillets (or cut against the grain in ¾-inch strips). Dredge them lightly in cornstarch; then arrange in a shallow heatproof dish.

2. Mince green pepper and scallion; sprinkle over fish. Also sprinkle oil over.

3. Heat (but do not boil) stock. Beat eggs very lightly. Slowly stir in stock, add salt; then pour over fish.

4. Steam over low heat until done (30 to 40 minutes). See page 831. Serve right in the steaming dish.

VARIATIONS: For the oil, substitute chicken fat.

For the sole, substitute pike, skinned and diced. In step 2, add 1 tablespoon smoked ham, minced. (This dish is called Fish Swimming in a Golden Pond.)

In step 3, add to the egg mixture either 1 teaspoon ginger juice or a pinch of cinnamon.

STEAMED GOLD-AND-SILVER EGGS
6 to 8 servings

6 *eggs*	1 *tablespoon smoked ham*
1½ *cups water*	½ *teaspoon salt*
½ *pound fish fillets*	1 *tablespoon peanut oil*
½ *teaspoon salt*	*few sprigs of Chinese parsley*

1. Separate eggs. Boil water, then let cool slightly.

2. Mince fish and add, with half the water and salt, to egg whites. Beat lightly.

3. Mince smoked ham and add, with remaining water and salt, to egg yolks. Beat lightly.

4. Pour egg white mixture into a shallow heatproof dish. Slowly pour egg yolk mixture over as a separate layer on top.

5. Steam over low heat until eggs set (about 20 minutes). See page 831.

6. In another pan, heat oil to smoking; then pour over eggs immediately. Garnish with Chinese parsley and serve right in the steaming dish.

STEAMED PRESERVED EGGS
About 4 servings

1 *preserved egg*   3 *fresh eggs*

½ teaspoon salt

1. Clean and shell preserved egg (see page 826). Then rinse, dry and dice.

2. Beat fresh eggs very lightly. Then stir in salt and preserved egg. Transfer mixture to a shallow heatproof dish.

3. Steam over low heat until eggs are set and custard-like (about 15 minutes). See page 831.

4. Let cool; then cut in bite-size cubes. Serve cold.

STEAMED THREE-KINDS-OF-EGGS
About 4 servings

1 *preserved egg*	2 *cups stock*
2 *fresh eggs*	1 *teaspoon peanut oil*
1 *salt egg*	*½ teaspoon salt*

1 scallion

1. Clean and shell preserved egg (see page 826); then rinse and dry. Dice egg and arrange on a shallow heatproof dish.

2. Beat fresh eggs very lightly in a bowl. Separate salt egg. Add its white to bowl; then dice its yolk and add.

3. Heat (but do not boil) stock. Slowly stir stock into fresh-and-salt-egg mixture, along with peanut oil and salt. Pour over diced preserved egg.

4. Steam over low heat until eggs are set and custard-like (15 to 20 minutes). See page 831.

5. Mince scallion; sprinkle over the top. Serve eggs right in the steaming dish.

VARIATION: In step 3, add to the egg mixture ¼ teaspoon sugar and 1 teaspoon sherry.

BASIC STIRRED EGGS
About 4 servings

4 to 6 eggs	2 tablespoons oil
2 scallion stalks	½ teaspoon salt

1. Beat eggs well. Shred or sliver scallion stalks.
2. Heat oil. Add salt, then scallions, and stir-fry a few times.
3. Pour in beaten eggs and cook over medium-high heat. As eggs begin to set, draw them with a fork or spatula away from the edges of the pan and toward the center. (Do not overcook: eggs are best when semi-solid or partly set.) Serve at once.

NOTE: Stirred eggs are seldom cooked alone; they're combined with various meats, seafood and vegetables as in the variations below.

VARIATIONS: In step 1, add to the beaten eggs ¼ teaspoon sugar and 2 teaspoons sherry.

In step 2, add with the scallions 1 slice fresh ginger root, minced.

With bacon and string beans—In step 2, omit the oil. Add 2 bacon strips, cut in ½-inch sections and pan-fry until nearly done; pour off half the fat. Add to the pan 2 cups string beans, cut diagonally in 1-inch sections and parboiled. Stir-fry string beans until softened but still bright green. Then add the eggs and cook as in step 3.

With bean sprouts—In step 2, add ½ pound bean sprouts, blanched. Stir-fry 2 to 3 minutes, then add eggs. (You may also add with the bean sprouts ½ cup bamboo shoots, shredded.)

With crabmeat I—In step 2, add 1 cup crabmeat, picked over and flaked, and stir-fry 2 minutes. Then add ¼ cup bamboo shoots, cut in strips and 3 fresh mushrooms, sliced; stir-fry 2 minutes more. Add eggs and cook as in step 3. (For the oil, you may substitute chicken fat.)

With crabmeat II—In step 2, add the crabmeat as above and stir-fry 2 minutes. Next add 1 cup bean sprouts, blanched; sprinkle lightly with salt and pepper and stir-fry 1 to 2 minutes more. Then add eggs and cook as in step 3.

With fish—In step 1, add to beaten eggs ½ pound fish fillets, coarsely chopped. Then pick up steps 2 and 3.

With ham—In step 1, add to beaten eggs ¼ pound smoked ham, coarsely chopped. Then pick up steps 2 and 3.

With mushrooms I—In step 1, add to the beaten eggs ½ cup fresh mushrooms, shredded. Then pick up steps 2 and 3.

With mushrooms II—In step 2, add 2 tablespoons cloud ear mushrooms (soaked), sliced, and stir-fry 1 to 2 minutes. Then add eggs and cook as in step 3.

Before serving, sprinkle eggs with 1 teaspoon each soy sauce and oyster sauce.

With oyster sauce—In step 1, add to eggs 1 tablespoon oil and a dash of pepper; then cook as in steps 2 and 3. When eggs are nearly done, turn off heat; sprinkle with 1 tablespoon oyster sauce and scramble once more (they will go on cooking in their own heat). Garnish with ¼ cup smoked ham, shredded, and a few sprigs of Chinese parsley.

With peas—In step 2, add after the scallions 1 cup peas, shelled and parboiled; stir-fry 2 minutes. Then add eggs and cook as in step 3. Sprinkle with 1 tablespoon soy sauce and serve. (Before adding the peas, you may add either 1 slice smoked ham, diced, and/or 1 bacon strip, diced. When bacon is used, reduce oil to 1 tablespoon.)

With preserved eggs—In step 1, add to beaten eggs 2 preserved eggs, cleaned, shelled, cut in half lengthwise, then crosswise in 8 slices. For the scallion, substitute 1 small bunch Chinese chives, cut in 2-inch lengths. In step 2, stir-fry the chives 2 minutes over medium heat. Then add the egg mixture and cook as in step 3.

With scallions—In step 1, add to beaten eggs 6 whole scallions, minced, and 1 teaspoon soy sauce. Pick up steps 2 and 3.

With scallops (dried) I—In step 1, add to beaten eggs 10 dried scallops (soaked overnight in 1 cup water, first heated to boiling), 1 tablespoon sherry, ½ teaspoon salt, and ½ teaspoon sugar. (You may also add in step 1 the scallop-soaking liquid, which will enhance the flavor of the eggs.)

With scallops (dried) II—In step 2, add 10 dried scallops (soaked overnight in sherry), shredded, and stir-fry 2 minutes. Then add eggs and cook as in step 3.

With shrimp—In step 2, add ½ pound shrimp, shelled, deveined and chopped coarsely, and 3 fresh mushrooms, sliced. Stir-fry until shrimp turns pink (about 2 minutes). Then add eggs and cook as in step 3.

With shrimp (dried)—In step 1 add to beaten eggs ¼ cup dried shrimp, which first have been brought to a boil with 1 cup water, left to stand 20 minutes in the covered pan with the heat turned off, then coarsely chopped. (You may also add in step 1 the shrimp water, which will enhance the flavor of the eggs.) Pick up steps 2 and 3.

With spinach—In step 2, add ½ pound whole leaf spinach to pan. Stir-fry in 1 to 2 tablespoons heated oil until spinach turns bright green but does not wilt. Remove and chop fine. Stir into the beaten eggs along with the salt. Then add another tablespoon of oil or lard to pan and cook eggs as in step 3.

With tomatoes—In step 3, cook eggs, stirring vigorously for 1 minute; then add 2 tomatoes, peeled and cubed. Cook, stirring gently, until eggs begin to set.

With vegetables—In step 1, beat the eggs with 1 cup water. Then add 1 teaspoon soy sauce, a dash of pepper and a pinch of garlic powder. In step 2 add a few drops of sesame oil to the peanut oil. Then add 1 cup of any of the following

vegetables, sliced or diced—Chinese cabbage, green peppers, onions, snow peas, asparagus, broccoli or string beans (the last 3 need parboiling first). Stir-fry until nearly done. Then add eggs and cook as in step 3.

With leftovers—In step 2, add ½ to 1 cup cooked poultry, meat, fish or vegetables, shredded or diced. Stir-fry only to heat through. Then add eggs and cook as in step 3.

STIRRED EGGS AND PORK I
About 6 servings

¼ to ½ pound lean pork *4 to 6 eggs*
1 to 2 tablespoons soy sauce *½ teaspoon salt*
2 tablespoons oil or lard

1. Slice pork paper-thin, or shred; then add soy sauce and toss.
2. Beat eggs lightly with salt.
3. Heat oil almost to smoking. Add pork and stir-fry to brown lightly (about 2 minutes).
4. Add eggs and cook over medium-high heat, as in Basic Stirred Eggs, above, until they begin to set. Serve at once.

VARIATION: In step 1, toss the pork in a mixture of 1 tablespoon soy sauce, 1 tablespoon sherry, 1 teaspoon cornstarch and the salt.

STIRRED EGGS AND PORK II
About 6 servings

¼ to ½ *pound lean pork*   3 *tablespoons water*
¼ *pound fresh mushrooms*   2 *tablespoons oil*
1 to 2 *scallion stalks*   2 *tablespoons oil*
4 to 6 *eggs*   ½ *teaspoon salt*

1. Slice pork paper-thin or shred. Slice fresh mushrooms. Mince scallion stalks.
2. Beat eggs together with water.
3. Heat oil. Add eggs and cook over medium-high heat as in Basic Stirred Eggs until half done. (They should be quite moist.) Remove from pan.
4. Heat remaining oil. Add scallions and stir-fry a few times until translucent. Add pork; stir-fry until it loses its pinkness (about 2 minutes).
5. Add mushrooms and salt; stir-fry until mushrooms begin to soften.
6. Return eggs and cook, stirring, until they just begin to set. Serve at once.
VARIATIONS: For the fresh mushrooms, substitute 4 or 5 dried mushrooms (soaked), sliced.

For the water, substitute ¼ to ½ cup milk.

In step 5, add with the mushrooms ¼ cup bamboo shoots, sliced.

In step 6, when returning the eggs, stir in a mixture of 1 tablespoon sherry, 1 tablespoon soy sauce and ½ teaspoon sugar.

STIRRED EGGS AND PORK III
About 6 servings

3 *dried black mushrooms*   4 to 6 *eggs*
¼ *pound lean pork*   1 to 2 *teaspoons soy sauce*
½ *cup bamboo shoots*   ½ *teaspoon sesame oil*

2 *tablespoons oil*

1. Soak dried mushrooms.
2. Mince or grind pork. Dice bamboo shoots and soaked mushrooms.
3. Beat eggs, together with soy sauce and sesame oil. Then stir in pork and vegetables.
4. Heat oil. Add egg mixture and cook as in Basic Stirred Eggs, until mixture begins to set. Serve at once.

STIRRED EGGS WITH PORK AND SHRIMP
About 8 servings

¼ *pound lean pork*	2 *tablespoons sherry*
½ *pound shrimp*	1 *tablespoon soy sauce*
1 *scallion stalk*	½ *teaspoon salt*
1 *or 2 slices fresh ginger root*	2 *tablespoons oil*
1 *teaspoon cornstarch*	4 *eggs*
1 *tablespoon water*	2 *tablespoons oil*

1. Mince pork. Shell and devein shrimp; if large, cut in two.
2. Mince scallion and ginger root; then combine with cornstarch, cold water, sherry, soy sauce and salt. Add to pork and shrimp, and toss to coat.
3. Heat oil. Add pork and shrimp and stir-fry until pork begins to brown and shrimp turn pinkish (2 to 3 minutes). Remove from pan.
4. Beat eggs in a bowl; then stir in pork and shrimp.
5. Heat remaining oil. Add egg mixture and cook until done as in Basic Stirred Eggs. Serve at once.

STIRRED EGGS WITH PORK AND VERMICELLI
6 to 8 servings

½ *to 1 cup vermicelli*	*dash of pepper*
¼ *pound lean pork*	1 *slice smoked ham*
1 *tablespoon oil*	1 *celery stalk*
1 *teaspoon cornstarch*	3 *scallion stalks*
2 *teaspoons soy sauce*	¼ *cup Chinese parsley*
½ *teaspoon salt*	2 *to 3 tablespoons oil*
½ *teaspoon sugar*	4 *to 6 eggs*

1. Soak vermicelli (peastarch noodles).
2. Mince or grind pork. Combine oil, cornstarch, soy sauce, salt, sugar and pepper; then add to pork and toss to coat.
3. Sliver smoked ham. Coarsely chop celery and scallions, then parsley.
4. Heat remaining oil. Add celery and scallions and stir-fry until translucent.
5. Add pork and ham; stir-fry until pork loses its pinkness.
6. Stir in soaked noodles and cook, covered, 2 minutes over medium heat.
7. Meanwhile beat eggs. Then add to pan with chopped parsley. Cook, as in Basic Stirred Eggs, until mixture just begins to set (about 1 minute). Remove from heat and continue stirring until eggs are firmer but still moist (about 1 minute more). Serve at once.

STIRRED EGGS AND FISH
About 6 servings

1 *fish (1 to 1½ pounds)*   2 *tablespoons oil*
1 *slice fresh ginger root*   1 *tablespoon soy sauce*
1 *scallion stalk*   ½ *teaspoon salt*
3 *eggs*   2 *tablespoons water*

1. Have whole fish cleaned and scaled. Steam 20 minutes (see Basic Steamed Fish, page 411). Let cool slightly; remove bones and flake meat coarsely.

2. Mince ginger root and scallion. Beat eggs.

3. Heat oil until smoking. Add fish flakes and stir-fry to coat with oil. Then quickly stir in ginger, scallion, soy sauce and salt.

4. Add eggs and cook over medium-high heat as in Basic Stirred Eggs. When eggs just begin to set, add water and continue stirring until eggs are cooked through, but still moist. Serve at once.

BASIC OMELET
About 6 servings

6 *eggs*   *dash of pepper*
½ *teaspoon salt*   2 *to 3 tablespoons oil*

1. Beat eggs; then season with salt and pepper.

2. Heat oil very hot. Add eggs; stir in quickly a few times, but do not scramble.

3. Cook until eggs begin to set, shaking or tilting the pan gently to distribute eggs over its surface and insure even cooking. (The uncooked part will roll around and under the cooked part.) Cook 1 minute more and serve.

NOTE: When the bottom is lightly browned, the omelet may be loosened with a spatula, inverted onto a platter, then slid carefully back into the pan and cooked ½ minute more on the other side.

VARIATIONS: Add any of the following ingredients and cook as directed:

With bean curd I—Add to the heated oil 2 cakes bean curd (dried well first with paper toweling), mashed. Stir-fry only to heat through. Then add eggs and cook as in steps 2 and 3.

With bean curd II—Add to the heated oil 2 cakes bean curd, cut in 1-inch cubes. Gently shake pan to heat them through. Then add ¼ cup water, heat quickly and cook, covered, 2 to 3 minutes over medium heat. Remove bean curd and drain. Heat 2 more tablespoons oil. Add eggs and cook as in step 2 until bottom browns lightly; then invert omelet. Top with bean curd, cook 1 minute more and garnish with Chinese parsley or minced smoked ham.

With bean sprouts I—In step 1, add to the beaten eggs 1 cup bean sprouts, blanched, and 1 tablespoon soy sauce. In step 2, pour only half the egg mixture into the pan and sprinkle with ½ cup smoked ham, minced. Then carefully pour remaining egg mixture over the top as a separate layer. Finish cooking as in steps 2 and 3, inverting the omelet to brown lightly on both sides.

With bean sprouts II—Add to the heated oil 2 cups bean sprouts, blanched; ¼ cup onion, minced; ¼ cup green pepper, minced, the salt and pepper. Stir-fry 1 to 2 minutes; then add eggs and cook as in steps 2 and 3. Garnish with minced scallions.

With ham—In step 1, add ½ teaspoon oil to beaten eggs. Cook as in steps 2 and 3, inverting omelet to brown lightly on both sides. Top with ¼ cup smoked ham, slivered; and a few sprigs of Chinese parsley, minced.

With lobster—Add to the heated oil 2 scallion stalks, minced, and stir-fry until translucent. Add 1 cup lobster meat, diced; stir-fry only to heat through. Then add eggs and cook as in steps 2 and 3.

With pork I—Add to the heated oil 1 small onion, minced, and stir-fry until translucent. Then add ¼ to ½ pound lean pork (either minced or ground); stir-fry until it loses its pinkness and begins to brown. Add eggs and cook as in steps 2 and 3. During the last minute of cooking you may also add 1 tomato, peeled and cubed.

With pork II—Add to the heated oil ¼ to ½ pound lean pork, shredded, and stir-fry until it loses its pinkness. Then add 1 cup Chinese chives, cut in 3-inch lengths; stir-fry 1 minute more and remove. Stir pork and chives into beaten eggs. Heat 1 more tablespoon oil; then add egg-pork mixture and cook as in steps 2 and 3.

With roast pork—Add to the heated oil ¼ cup roast pork, ½ cup bamboo shoots, ½ cup dried onion, ¼ cup snow peas and 2 dried black mushrooms (soaked), all sliced thin; stir-fry 2 to 3 minutes. Then add eggs and cook as in steps 2 and 3. (This dish is called Precious Flower Egg.)

With scallops—In step 1, add to the beaten eggs 1 teaspoon soy sauce and 2 scallion stalks, minced. In step 2 add to the heated oil ¾ cup onions, chopped, and stir-fry until translucent. Add ½ pound scallops (cut in quarters if large; left whole if small) and stir-fry over medium heat to brown lightly. Then add eggs and cook as in steps 2 and 3.

With shrimp I—Add to the heated oil 2 slices fresh ginger root, minced, and stir-fry a few times. Add ½ pound shrimp, shelled and deveined; stir-fry until pink. Then sprinkle with 1 tablespoon sherry. Add eggs and cook as in steps 2 and 3.

With shrimp II—Add to the heated oil ½ pound shrimp, shelled and deveined, then dredged in a mixture of 1 teaspoon cornstarch, 1 teaspoon soy sauce, 1 teaspoon sherry and 2 slices fresh ginger root, minced. Stir-fry shrimp until they turn pink; then add eggs and cook as in steps 2 and 3.

With vegetables—Add to the heated oil 1 onion, minced, and stir-fry until translucent. Then add 1 green pepper and 3 celery stalks, both diced, and 4 fresh mushrooms, sliced; stir-fry until vegetables begin to soften (2 to 3 minutes). Then drain and add to beaten eggs. Heat 1 more tablespoon oil and cook egg-vegetable mixture as in steps 2 and 3. Cut omelet in 2-inch cubes and serve.

OYSTER OMELET
6 to 8 servings

16 oysters	*1 cup milk*
¼ cup lean pork	*½ teaspoon salt*
¼ cup fresh mushrooms	*2 to 3 tablespoons oil*
⅛ cup bamboo shoots	*1 tablespoon cornstarch*
2 scallion stalks	*½ cup cold water*
4 eggs	*1 teaspoon soy sauce*

1 teaspoon oyster sauce

1. Shell oysters. Shred pork. Slice mushrooms and bamboo shoots. Mince scallion stalks.

2. Beat eggs. Stir in milk, salt, oysters and minced scallion.

3. Heat oil. Add shredded pork and stir-fry until it loses its pinkness (about 2 minutes). Add mushrooms and bamboo shoots; stir-fry 2 minute more.

4. Add egg mixture and cook as in Basic Omelet, above. When the bottom sets, fold omelet in half with a spatula. Turn it over and lightly brown the other side.

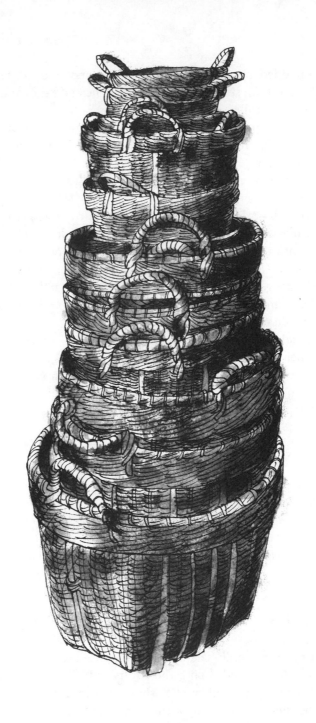

5. Meanwhile in a saucepan, blend cornstarch and cold water to a paste. Then add soy and oyster sauce and heat, stirring, until mixture thickens. Pour over omelet and serve at once.

OYSTER PANCAKES
About 6 servings

1½ *cups oysters*	*4 tablespoons flour*
4 scallion stalks	*½ teaspoon baking powder*
4 eggs	*¼ cup oyster liquid*
½ teaspoon salt	*oil*
dash of pepper	*6 tablespoons vinegar*

1 or 2 teaspoons hot sauce

1. Shell oysters reserving their liquid, and chop coarsely. Cut scallion stalks in ½-inch sections.

2. Beat eggs. Then stir in salt, pepper, oysters and scallions.

3. Sift flour, together with baking powder. Blend to a paste with oyster liquid; then stir into egg mixture.

4. Heat a skillet and grease lightly with a drop of oil. Spoon oyster batter onto skillet (with a large spoon) to make pancakes 2 inches in diameter. Brown lightly on each side. Remove and keep warm.

5. Repeat, re-oiling skillet each time batter is added. Serve pancakes with a dip made by mixing vinegar and hot sauce.

SHRIMP PANCAKES
About 4 servings

1 *tablespoon dried shrimp*	*½ cup stock*
1 *egg*	*2 whole scallions*
⅔ *cup flour*	*2 teaspoons oil*
½ teaspoon salt	*2 teaspoons oil*

1. Soak dried shrimp.

2. Blend egg, flour, salt and stock to a batter. Mince scallions and soaked shrimp; then stir in.

3. Heat oil in an 8- or 10-inch skillet over medium heat. Add half the batter, tilting pan to distribute it evenly, and cook until edge of pancake browns lightly. Then flip with a spatula and lightly brown the other side. Remove and keep warm.

4. Heat remaining oil and repeat the process.

VARIATION: For the dried shrimp, substitute 1 bacon strip, minced.

SHARK'S FIN OMELET I
About 8 servings

½ cup dried shark's fin
6 eggs
¼ cup smoked ham

½ cup bamboo shoots
2 tablespoons oil
¼ teaspoon salt

1. Soak and process shark's fin (see page 884).
2. Beat eggs. Sliver smoked ham and bamboo shoots.
3. Heat oil. Add salt, then bamboo shoots; stir-fry 1 minute.
4 Add shark's fin; stir-fry gently to heat through. Then add ham and stir-fry to heat.
5. Add eggs and cook as in Basic Omelet.

VARIATION: Omit the ham and bamboo shoots. Add soaked shark's fin to the beaten eggs, along with 1 tablespoon sherry, 1 teaspoon ginger juice, ½ teaspoon salt and ½ teaspoon sugar. Cook as in Basic Omelet or scramble until nearly set.

SHARK'S FIN OMELET II
About 8 servings

½ cup dried shark's fin
2 scallion stalks
2 slices ginger root
1 cup stock
2 tablespoons sherry

½ teaspoon salt
dash of pepper
2 tablespoons oil
6 eggs
½ teaspoon salt

3 to 4 tablespoons oil

1. Soak shark's fin. Cut scallions in 1-inch sections. Slice ginger root.

2. Combine stock, sherry, salt and pepper.

3. Heat oil. Add scallions and ginger root; stir-fry a few times. Add shark's fin and stock-sherry mixture. Heat quickly; then simmer, covered, 5 minutes over medium-low heat. Drain, discarding liquid, scallions and ginger root.

4. Beat eggs, then season with remaining salt. Stir in shark's fin.

Heat remaining oil. Add egg mixture and cook as in Basic Omelet. When the bottom begins to set, slowly fold omelet over with a spatula. Let it brown lightly while keeping the inside still soft and semi-liquid. Serve at once.

VARIATION: Omit steps 2 and 3. Place the shark's fin in a saucepan with water to cover. Add 1 scallion stalk, sliced; 1 slice fresh ginger root, crushed; and 2 tablespoons sherry. Bring to a boil; then simmer 15 minutes. Rinse and drain; then add fins to the beaten eggs, along with the salt, 1 tablespoon sherry, a dash of pepper, and 1 slice fresh ginger root and 1 scallion, both minced. Cook egg mixture as in step 5.

BASIC PAN-FRIED EGG FOO YUNG
About 8 servings

6 eggs	1 cup cooked meat or seafood
¾ teaspoon salt	1½ cups vegetables
	2 tablespoons oil

1. Beat eggs; then season with salt.

2. Shred or dice meat and vegetables (see combinations on page 558). Mix well with eggs.

3. Heat oil. Spoon 2 to 3 tablespoons of egg mixture into pan to make one small omelet. (Fry each omelet separately.) Turn it over when bottom is done and brown lightly on the other side. Remove omelet and keep warm.

4. Repeat process, adding more oil as needed. Serve omelets either plain, or with Egg Foo Yung sauce (see page 728).

VARIATIONS: In step 1, add to the beaten eggs any or all of the following:

1 or 2 scallion stalks, minced

2 teaspoons soy sauce

1 teaspoon sherry

¼ teaspoon garlic powder

dash of pepper

BASIC DEEP-FRIED EGG FOO YUNG
About 8 servings

6 eggs	1 cup cooked meat or seafood
1 teaspoon salt	1½ cups vegetables
	oil for deep-frying

1. Follow steps 1 and 2 above. (You may, if you wish, *not* beat the eggs first but stir them in with the meat and vegetables until well mixed.)

2. Heat oil until it foams (it should be about 2½ inches deep). Carefully drop egg mixture into oil with a ladle, tipping the ladle to release the omelets. (For a 3-inch omelet, allow ½ cup of egg mixture; for a smaller one, ¼ cup.)

3. Let omelet rise to the top (this will take about 2 minutes). Baste with hot oil to brown. Then flip omelet over, using a spoon and spatula, or 2 spoons, and baste to brown the other side. Lift out with a slotted spoon and drain on paper toweling. Keep warm.

4. Repeat process until egg mixture is used up. Serve omelets either plain, sprinkled lightly with soy sauce, or with Egg Foo Yung sauce (see page 728).

VARIATIONS: See the variations for Basic Pan-fried Egg Foo Yung above.

COMBINATIONS FOR BASIC PAN-FRIED OR DEEP-FRIED EGG FOO YUNG

With chicken I—Add to the beaten eggs 1 cup cooked white meat chicken, ½ cup onions; ½ cup celery, blanched; and ½ cup canned mushrooms.

With chicken II—Add to the beaten eggs ½ cup cooked white meat chicken, ½ cup ham, ½ cup green peppers, ½ cup bamboo shoots and ½ cup water chestnuts.

NOTE: For either of the vegetable combinations above, you may substitute 1 cup bean sprouts, blanched (or 1 cup string beans, shredded and parboiled), and ½ cup tomatoes, peeled.

With clams—See chicken. Substitute 1 cup raw clams.

With crabs—Add to the beaten eggs 1 cup crabmeat, 1 cup bean sprouts, blanched, ¼ cup scallions and 1 teaspoon fresh ginger root, minced. (For the vegetables, you may substitute bamboo shoots, or canned mushrooms, and green peas.)

With ham—Add to the beaten eggs ¼ cup smoked ham, ½ cup canned mushrooms and 2 teaspoons soy sauce.

With oysters—See chicken. Substitute 1 cup raw oysters.

With pork—Add to the beaten eggs ½ to 1 cup cooked pork, ½ cup onions, ½ cup green pepper and ½ cup canned mushrooms. (For the vegetables, you may substitute 1 cup bean sprouts, blanched; and 2 scallions, or else 1 cup onions.)

With shrimp—Add to the beaten eggs 1 cup cooked shrimp, ½ cup canned mushrooms and ¼ cup water chestnuts. (For the vegetables, you may substitute 1 cup bean sprouts, blanched; or 1 cup onions.)

With turkey—See chicken. Substitute 1 cup cooked turkey.

With vegetables—Add to the beaten eggs 1 cup bean sprouts, blanched; ½ cup onion; ½ cup celery, blanched; and ½ cup canned mushrooms. (For the vegetables, you may substitute any of the following in any combination: asparagus, broccoli and peas, parboiled; celery, blanched; tomatoes, peeled; and canned mushrooms. Fresh mushrooms may be used, but only if shredded. You may also add ½ cup almond meats, blanched, toasted and minced.)

PORK AND SHRIMP EGG FOO YUNG
8 to 10 servings

1 *cup lean pork*	2 *tablespoons oil*
½ *pound shrimp*	6 *eggs*
1 *cup Chinese cabbage stems*	¾ *teaspoon salt*
½ *cup onion*	*oil*

1. Shred pork. Shell, devein and sliver shrimp. Shred Chinese cabbage stems and onion.
2. Heat oil. Add pork and stir-fry until it loses its pinkness (about 2 minutes).
3. Add shrimp, Chinese cabbage and onion; stir-fry about 1 minute more. Then cook, covered, 3 minutes over medium heat. Drain and let cool.
4. Beat eggs. Stir in salt and stir-fried ingredients.
5. Either pan-fry or deep-fry as in the Basic Egg Foo Yungs above.

VARIATIONS: For the pork, substitute crabmeat. For the Chinese cabbage, substitute celery. In step 2, stir-fry the celery and onions to soften. Then add crabmeat with the shrimp in step 3.

In step 3, before cooking the shrimp and vegetables, covered, sprinkle them with 1 tablespoon soy sauce, ½ teaspoon sugar.

ROAST PORK EGG FOO YUNG
8 to 10 servings

6 *dried black mushrooms*	2 *tablespoons oil*
¼ *pound roast pork*	6 *eggs*
1 *cup Chinese cabbage stems*	½ *teaspoon salt*
½ *cup bamboo shoots*	½ *teaspoon sugar*
¼ *cup water chestnuts*	1 *to 2 tablespoons oil*

1. Soak dried mushrooms.
2. Shred roast pork, Chinese cabbage stems, bamboo shoots and soaked mushrooms. Slice water chestnuts thin.
3. Heat oil. Add vegetables and pork and stir-fry 1 minute. Then cook, covered, 1 to 2 minutes over medium heat. Drain and let cool.
4. Beat eggs. Stir in salt, sugar and stir-fried ingredients.

5. Heat remaining oil. Fry mixture as small omelets (as in Basic Pan-fried Egg Foo Yung), or divide mixture in half and pan-fry as 2 separate large omelets. Turn over to brown each side.

NOTE: This omelet is sometimes called Subgum Egg Foo Yung because of its many and varied ingredients.

VARIATIONS: For the bamboo shoots, substitute 1 cup bean sprouts, blanched. For the Chinese cabbage, substitute celery, blanched.

In step 3, add with vegetables and pork 1 slice fresh ginger root, minced; 6 scallion stalks, slivered; and ¼ cup smoked ham, shredded.

HAM EGG FOO YUNG
About 10 servings

½ cup bamboo shoots	½ teaspoon salt
½ cup celery	2 teaspoons soy sauce
½ cup water chestnuts	dash of pepper
½ cup onion	1 tablespoon flour
2 to 3 tablespoons oil	½ pound ham
½ teaspoon sugar	6 eggs

1 to 2 tablespoons oil

1. Dice bamboo shoots, celery and water chestnuts. Mince onion.

2. Heat oil. Add vegetables and stir-fry 1 minute. Sprinkle with sugar, salt, soy sauce and pepper; stir-fry 1 minute more.

3. Remove vegetables from pan; drain, and let cool. Then sprinkle with flour.

4. Mince or shred ham. Beat eggs. First fold stir-fried vegetables, then ham, into eggs.

5. Reheat remaining oil. Spoon egg mixture into pan, 2 tablespoons at a time, and cook as in Basic Pan-fried Egg Foo Yung.

6. Repeat process until egg mixture is used up, adding more oil as needed.

NOTE: This is sometimes called Mandarin-style ham and eggs.

BASIC STUFFED OMELETS
8 to 10 servings

omelet filling	½ teaspoon salt
6 eggs	2 to 3 tablespoons oil

1. Prepare and stir-fry either of the fillings below. Drain and keep warm.

2. Beat eggs and season with salt.

3. Heat oil very hot. Pour eggs in slowly (do not stir). Then reduce heat to medium. When bottom begins to set (check this by lifting the edge with a spatula), top omelet with the filling, placed over to one side. Cook ½ minute.

4. With the spatula, fold omelet in half to cover filling. Cook 1 minute more. Then gently turn folded omelet over and lightly brown the other side.

VARIATION: In step 2, beat the eggs with ½ cup water.

PORK FILLING FOR OMELETS

¼ to ½ pound lean pork
2 celery stalks
2 scallion stalks

¼ pound bean sprouts
2 tablespoons oil
2 tablespoons soy sauce

1 teaspoon sugar

1. Shred pork, celery and scallions. Blanch bean sprouts.

2. Heat oil. Add pork and stir-fry until it loses its pinkness (1 to 2 minutes).

3. Add celery, scallions and bean sprouts; stir-fry 1 minute. Add soy sauce and sugar; stir-fry 1 minute more.

4. Remove from pan and drain well. Use as a filling for Basic Stuffed Omelets.

VARIATION: For the pork, substitute chicken, fish or crabmeat. In step 3, when adding the soy sauce and sugar, also stir in 1 tablespoon sherry.

SHRIMP FILLING FOR OMELETS

½ pound shrimp
¼ cup celery

¼ cup onion
1 tablespoon oil

1 tablespoon soy sauce

1. Shell, devein and cut shrimp in ½-inch pieces. Shred celery and onion.

2. Heat oil. Add shrimp and stir-fry until they turn pinkish (about 1 minute). Sprinkle with soy sauce and stir in to blend.

3. Add celery and onion; stir-fry 1 minute more.

4. Remove from pan and drain well. Use as a filling for Basic Stuffed Omelets.

STEAMED OMELET ROLLS
About 6 servings

6 eggs
½ teaspoon salt
½ tablespoon oil
1 cup cooked chicken
1 slice fresh ginger root

1 small onion
½ teaspoon salt
½ cup stock
2 tablespoons sherry
½ teaspoon salt

1. Beat eggs and season with salt.

2. Lightly oil an 8-inch skillet; then heat over a low flame until very hot. Remove skillet from heat and add ⅓ eggs, tilting pan so they spread evenly over the bottom.

3. Return skillet to stove and cook eggs over low heat until they have set but are still moist. Gently invert omelet onto a platter. Repeat process to make 2 more omelets; let them cool slightly.

4. Meanwhile mince or grind cooked chicken, together with ginger root and onion. Season with remaining salt. Divide the mixture into 3 parts.

5. Top each omelet with mixture and roll it tightly around the topping. Then secure with toothpicks. Arrange omelet rolls on a heatproof dish and steam on a rack 10 to 15 minutes (see pages 33 and 831).

6. Transfer omelet rolls to a warm serving dish and cut each in 1-inch sections. Meanwhile heat stock in a saucepan. Stir in sherry and last of the salt. Then pour over omelet rolls and serve.

VARIATION: For the cooked chicken, substitute cooked pork.

EGG POUCH OMELETS
About 6 servings

filling mixture	½ *teaspoon salt*
6 *eggs*	*dash of pepper*

oil

1. Prepare egg pouch filling as in recipe below. Place conveniently near the stove.

2. Beat eggs. Season with salt and pepper.

3. Lightly grease a 4-inch skillet (or a wok) with a drop of oil, and heat to the crackling point. Then pour in 1 tablespoon of beaten egg.

4. Rotate pan so egg forms a thin layer at the bottom. Cook quickly until bottom sets but upper surface is still moist. Then reduce heat to medium.

5: Scoop up 1 teaspoon of filling and place over egg. Fold egg in half to make a semi-circular pouch; then press lightly along the edges with a spatula to seal in filling.

6. Let cook ½ minute to brown lightly. Turn over and lightly brown the other side (about ½ minute more).

7. Repeat process until eggs and filling mixture are used up, re-oiling the skillet as necessary. Keep omelets warm in the top of a double boiler until all are cooked. Serve on a bed of lettuce strips or surrounded by stir-fried spinach.

NOTE: These tiny stuffed omelets are also called egg dumplings or egg pockets. They may be prepared in advance and frozen, then reheated, without thawing, by being steamed for 10 minutes. They're excellent as party snacks.

VARIATIONS: Instead of using a skillet, grease a Chinese ladle (with a wooden handle) and hold it directly over the flame to heat. Cook the egg right in it, add the stuffing and fold egg in two. Then flip egg over with chopsticks to cook the other side.

Make the omelets larger by using 2 tablespoons of beaten egg and 1 tablespoon of filling. For easier handling, the filling can be shaped in 1-inch balls before adding it to eggs.

Cook omelets stuffed with *pork* as follows:

For smaller omelets—When all the omelets are browned, add 3 tablespoons water and cook over medium heat until liquid is absorbed.

For larger omelets—When all the omelets are browned, simmer 5 to 10 minutes in ½ cup stock, 1 tablespoon soy sauce and ½ teaspoon sugar.

FILLING FOR EGG POUCH OMELETS

¼ to ½ pound pork	¼ teaspoon salt
1 scallion stalk	¼ teaspoon sugar
2 tablespoons oil	2 teaspoons soy sauce

1. Mince or grind pork. Cut scallion stalk in ½-inch sections.

2. Heat oil. Add scallion and stir-fry until translucent. Add pork; stir-fry until it loses its pinkness (about 1 minute).

3. Sprinkle with salt, sugar and soy sauce and stir-fry 1 minute more. Remove from pan; then drain, and let cool.

VARIATIONS: For the pork, substitute beef, ham, shrimp, or fish fillet.

In step 1, mix the meat with 1 teaspoon cornstarch, 2 teaspoons sherry and the salt. (Omit salt in step 3.)

In step 2, add with the scallions 1 or 2 slices fresh ginger root, minced.

After step 2, add either ¼ cup celery, minced; or ¼ pound fresh mushrooms, shredded. Then stir-fry 1 minute more.

CHICKEN SOUFFLÉ
About 6 servings

1 cup chicken breast	½ teaspoon salt
2 tablespoons stock	6 egg whites

4 to 6 tablespoons oil

1. Skin and bone chicken; then mince or grind as fine as possible. Blend to a smooth paste with stock and salt.

2. Beat egg whites until frothy and stiff, but not dry; then fold in chicken mixture.

3. Heat oil to smoking. Add chicken-egg mixture, then remove pan from heat

at once and stir briskly a few times. Return pan to stove and cook, stirring, over medium-high heat until mixture is firm, but not browned. Serve at once, either by itself, or on a bed of spinach (which has been separately stir-fried).

NOTE: This dish is the original egg foo yung—more soufflé than omelet. It must be eaten immediately because its fine, firm texture will not keep.

VARIATIONS: In step 1, mince 1 tablespoon ham fat with the chicken. Increase the stock to ½ cup.

In step 1, while mincing the chicken, add 3 tablespoons water, a few drops at a time. Then blend in the salt, 1 tablespoon cornstarch and 1 teaspoon sherry. (Omit the stock.)

In step 1, instead of mincing the chicken, cut it in ½-inch wide strips. In step 2, add the salt to the egg whites along with 1 tablespoon sherry and 1 tablespoon water; then beat. (Omit the stock.) Fold chicken strips into mixture and pick up step 3.

In step 3, add to the heating oil 1 scallion stalk, cut in 1-inch sections and 3 slices fresh ginger root, shredded; stir-fry a few times, then add chicken-egg mixture.

In step 3, after removing the pan from the heat, stir the chicken-egg mixture slowly until it begins to form lumps. Then transfer to a colander and drain off the oil. Meanwhile blend to a paste 1 teaspoon cornstarch, ¼ teaspoon salt, 2 teaspoons sherry and 2 tablespoons cold water. In a pan, heat 5 tablespoons stock; then stir in the cornstarch paste to thicken. Add the drained chicken-egg mixture and cook gently, stirring, 2 minutes more.

CRABMEAT SOUFFLÉ I
About 6 servings

1 cup crabmeat	1½ tablespoons cornstarch
5 or 6 egg whites	¾ cup milk
½ teaspoon salt	¼ cup oil

1. Pick over and flake crabmeat.
2. Beat egg whites, with salt, until frothy and stiff, but not dry.
3. Blend cornstarch and milk and fold into egg whites. Then fold in crabmeat.
4. Heat oil to smoking. Add egg mixture and cook quickly, stirring, over medium-high heat until thick and fluffy. Serve at once.

NOTE: The Cantonese call this dish Fried Milk.

VARIATIONS: In step 1, combine the crabmeat with 1 tablespoon sherry and 1 teaspoon ginger juice.

In step 3, fold in with the crabmeat 1 tablespoon smoked ham, minced.

At the end of step 4, serve the soufflé in a nest of deep-fried rice-flour noodles.

CRABMEAT SOUFFLÉ II
6 to 8 servings

1 cup crabmeat	2 tablespoons cornstarch
1 slice fresh ginger root	¼ cup water
1 scallion stalk	½ teaspoon salt
2 tablespoons oil	5 or 6 egg whites
¼ teaspoon salt	¼ cup oil
1 tablespoon sherry	½ cup stock
½ cup milk	salt and pepper
½ cup stock	few drops of sesame oil

1. Pick over and flake crabmeat. Mince ginger root and scallion.

2. Heat oil. Add ginger root and scallion; stir-fry a few times. Add crabmeat and stir-fry to heat through. Stir in salt and sherry. Then remove mixture from pan and let cool.

3. In a bowl, combine milk and stock. In a cup, blend cornstarch and cold water to a paste; then blend into milk-stock mixture along with remaining salt.

4. Beat egg whites until frothy and stiff, but not dry. Fold in milk-stock mixture. Then fold in stir-fried crabmeat.

5. Heat remaining oil to smoking. Add crabmeat-egg mixture and cook over medium-high heat, stirring constantly, while gradually adding remaining stock.

6. When mixture thickens, season with salt and pepper to taste. Sprinkle with sesame oil and serve at once.

SHRIMP SOUFFLÉ
6 to 8 servings

½ pound cooked shrimp	5 or 6 egg whites,
3 slices fresh ginger root	½ teaspoon salt
1 tablespoon sherry	4 tablespoons oil
1 teaspoon soy sauce	dash of pepper

1. Dice cooked shrimp and mince ginger root; then combine with sherry and soy sauce.

2. Beat egg whites, with salt, until frothy and stiff, but not dry. Fold in shrimp mixture.

3. Heat oil to smoking. Add shrimp-egg mixture and cook over medium-high heat, stirring constantly, until eggs begin to set (3 to 4 minutes).

SHRIMP AND BEAN SPROUT SOUFFLÉ
About 6 servings

¼ to ½ pound shrimp	4 tablespoons oil
1 small onion	½ teaspoon salt
¼ pound bean sprouts	½ cup stock
6 egg whites	1 teaspoon cornstarch
1 teaspoon cornstarch	2 tablespoons water
2 tablespoons sherry	dash of pepper

1. Shell, devein and cut each shrimp in 2 or 3 pieces. Mince onion.

2. Parboil bean sprouts 2 minutes in boiling salted water. Then drain and keep warm.

3. Beat egg whites until frothy and stiff, but not dry. Blend cornstarch and sherry to a paste; then fold in.

4. Heat oil. Add salt, then minced onion; stir-fry until translucent. Add shrimp and stir-fry until pink (about 2 minutes).

5. Slowly pour in egg mixture and stir only once. Then reduce heat to low and cook until egg barely sets.

6. Meanwhile heat stock in another pan. Blend remaining cornstarch and water to a paste; then stir in to thicken.

7. Gently transfer soufflé to a serving dish and surround with parboiled bean sprouts. Pour thickened stock over. Sprinkle with pepper and serve at once.

VEGETABLE SOUFFLÉ
8 to 10 servings

1 pound spinach	4 tablespoons oil
½ cup bamboo shoots	2 tablespoons oil
1 slice smoked ham	½ cup stock
10 egg whites	¼ teaspoon salt
½ teaspoon salt	2 teaspoons cornstarch

3 tablespoons cold water

1. Stem and wash spinach; cut leaves in 2-inch sections. Shred bamboo shoots. Mince smoked ham.

2. Beat egg whites, with salt, until frothy and stiff, but not dry.

3. Heat oil to smoking. Add eggs and cook, gently stirring, over medium-high heat until they just begin to set. Transfer to a colander and drain off oil.

4. Heat remaining oil. Add bamboo shoots and spinach; stir-fry until spinach turns a brighter green and just begins to soften (about 1 minute). Remove to a serving platter.

5. Heat stock; add remaining salt. Meanwhile blend cornstarch and cold water to a paste; then stir into stock to thicken.

6. Add egg whites to stock, stirring for a moment to reheat. Then pour mixture over stir-fried vegetables. Garnish with ham and serve at once.

FISH SOUFFLÉ
About 6 servings

3 eggs	*1 teaspoon soy sauce*
½ teaspoon salt	*1 pound fish fillets*
¼ teaspoon pepper	*2 to 3 tablespoons oil*
¼ teaspoon sugar	*catsup*

1. Separate eggs. Beat 2 yolks lightly; then combine with salt, pepper, sugar and soy sauce. (Reserve the third yolk for another dish.)

2. Cut each fish fillet crosswise in 3 or 4 pieces; then coat with egg yolk mixture.

3. Heat oil. Carefully add fish pieces and brown lightly, on one side only, over medium heat. Remove pan from heat and turn fish pieces over with a spatula.

4. Meanwhile beat the 3 egg whites until frothy and stiff, but not dry. Spread evenly over browned surface of fish. Return pan to heat and lightly brown underside of fish.

5. Carefully turn fish over so that the egg-white surface is now at the bottom. Turn heat up to medium-high and cook until egg white sets and is golden (about 1 minute).

6. Invert onto a serving platter, egg-white side up. Garnish with catsup, sprinkled over generously and decoratively.

FRIED EGGS WITH SOY SAUCE
4 to 6 servings

3 tablespoons oil   soy sauce
6 eggs   pepper

lettuce

1. Heat oil almost to smoking.
2. Break 1 egg gently onto a flat plate, then slide into the center of the pan. Cook over medium-high heat so that the bottom browns quickly while the yolk remains soft and semi-liquid. (Cook the eggs only 1 at a time.)
3. Sprinkle each egg with 1 teaspoon soy sauce and a dash of pepper. Then carefully turn it over with a spatula and cook ½ minute more. Remove and keep warm. Repeat until all eggs are done, adding more oil as needed. Serve on a bed of lettuce strips.

VARIATIONS: For the soy sauce, substitute oyster sauce.

Omit the soy sauce in step 3. Then, when all the eggs are cooked, heat 1 tablespoon peanut oil to smoking and mix with 1 tablespoon soy sauce. Sprinkle mixture over eggs.

Instead of turning the eggs over in step 3, fry them sunny-side up ½ minute more. Serve topped with a sweet-and-pungent sauce (see page 738).

COIN PURSE EGGS
4 to 6 servings

3 tablespoons oil   salt and pepper
6 eggs   soy sauce

Chinese parsley

1. Follow steps 1 and 2 above. Then sprinkle the egg lightly with salt and pepper.
2. As soon as its edge begins to brown slightly and while the whites are still moist, flip one half of the egg over with a spatula and fold it to form a half-moon shape. Immediately press the edges lightly together with the spatula to seal, so it can hold this shape. (The still-soft egg white will act as an adhesive.)
3. Cook over medium heat until the bottom surface is a rich golden. Turn over and brown the other side.
4. Remove and keep warm until all the eggs are done. Sprinkle lightly with soy sauce. Garnish with Chinese parsley and serve on a platter or over rice.

NOTE: This fried egg gets its name because the folded-over white looks like a purse, while the yolk inside is like a large golden coin. These eggs are most easily cooked in a concave pot like a wok, but can be managed in flat-bottomed pans as well.

VARIATION: Omit the salt, pepper and soy sauce. In step 4, sprinkle each egg with 1 teaspoon oyster sauce.

DEEP-FRIED EGGS AND VEGETABLES
6 to 8 servings

4 dried black mushrooms	2 tablespoons oil
1 cup Chinese cabbage stems	½ teaspoon salt
½ cup bamboo shoots	½ cup stock
¼ cup water chestnuts	1 tablespoon cornstarch
oil for deep-frying	¼ cup water
6 eggs	½ teaspoon sugar
½ head lettuce	dash of pepper

1. Soak dried mushrooms.

2. Shred Chinese cabbage, bamboo shoots, water chestnuts and soaked mushrooms.

3. Heat oil in a small pan. Break one egg gently onto a flat plate, then slide into hot oil. Deep-fry until its edges begin to brown (2 to 3 minutes). Remove with a slotted spoon and drain on paper toweling. (Fry only one egg at a time.)

4. Cut lettuce into strips. Arrange on a serving platter with eggs on top.

5. Heat remaining oil. Add salt, then shredded vegetables, and stir-fry 2 minutes.

6. Add stock and heat quickly; then simmer, covered, 2 to 3 minutes.

7. Meanwhile blend cornstarch and cold water to a paste. Then add, along with sugar and pepper, and cook, stirring, to thicken. Pour over deep-fried eggs and serve at once.

VARIATIONS: For the Chinese cabbage, substitute asparagus, broccoli, celery or snow peas.

After step 5, sprinkle the vegetables with a mixture of 1 tablespoon sherry, ½ teaspoon sugar and 1 teaspoon soy sauce. Stir-fry 1 minute more.

STUFFED EGGS: HARD-BOILED, STEAMED AND DEEP-FRIED
8 to 10 servings

water to cover	1 teaspoon ginger juice
6 eggs	oil for deep-frying
¾ pound lean pork	1 cup steaming liquids
1 tablespoon cornstarch	2 tablespoons soy sauce
3 tablespoons water	½ teaspoon salt
1 tablespoon sherry	1 teaspoon sugar
1 tablespoon cornstarch	

1. Place eggs in cold water to cover. Bring to a boil, then simmer gently 12 to 15 minutes.

2. Meanwhile mince or grind pork. Blend cornstarch and cold water to a paste; then add to pork along with sherry and ginger juice, mixing well. Divide mixture into 12 parts. Form each into a ball, then flatten into a thick patty.

3. Cool eggs thoroughly under cold running water; then shell. Cut each egg in half lengthwise. Then cut a small slice from the back of each half so that it will lie flat when turned yolk side up.

4. Arrange eggs yolk-side up on a shallow heatproof dish; top each with a meat patty. Steam for 10 minutes (see page 831). Drain eggs, reserving the liquids.

5. Heat oil. Carefully lower in stuffed eggs, meat-side up. Deep-fry, basting with hot oil, until golden. Drain on paper toweling.

6. Meanwhile in a saucepan blend steaming liquids, soy sauce, salt, sugar, and remaining cornstarch. Bring to a boil, stirring to thicken. Then pour sauce over eggs and serve at once.

VARIATION: For the pork, substitute beef.

DEEP-FRIED COATED EGGS
About 6 servings

4 eggs	1 tablespoon sherry
1 cup lean pork	2 tablespoons soy sauce
2 scallion stalks	½ teaspoon salt
1½ tablespoons cornstarch	oil for deep-frying

lettuce

1. Hardboil eggs as above, and shell, but leave eggs whole.

2. Meanwhile mince pork and scallion stalks; then combine with cornstarch, sherry, soy sauce and salt, blending well.

3. Coat each egg with about 3 tablespoons of the pork mixture, using a knife to spread mixture as evenly as possible.

4. Heat oil. Gently lower in coated eggs and deep-fry, basting with hot oil, until golden. Drain on paper toweling.

5. Cut eggs in half lengthwise. Serve on a bed of lettuce strips.

BASIC EGG PUDDING
4 to 6 servings

6 egg yolks	½ teaspoon salt
1 tablespoon cornstarch	4 to 4 tablespoons oil
2 tablespoons water	2 tablespoons smoked ham

1. Beat egg yolks until thick and lemon-colored. Blend cornstarch and cold water to a paste; then add to eggs, along with salt. Stir in well.

2. Heat oil to smoking. Add eggs; then reduce heat to medium-low. Cook, stirring in one direction, until mixture is smooth, thick and pudding-like.

3. Pour into a serving bowl. Mince smoked ham and sprinkle over as a garnish.

NOTE: Other names for this dish are Imperial Eggs and Flowing Yellow.

VARIATIONS: For the egg yolks, substitute whole eggs.

In step 1, add to the egg mixture any or all of the following:

1 cup stock

1 to 2 tablespoons sherry

¼ cup bamboo shoots, minced

¼ cup water chestnuts, minced

¼ cup smoked ham, minced (omit ham garnish)

2 dried black mushrooms (soaked), minced

2 tablespoons dried shrimp (soaked), minced

In step 2, when the egg mixture begins to thicken, stir in ½ cup cooked shrimp, minced.

EGG PUDDING WITH DRIED SCALLOPS
About 8 servings

12 *dried scallops*	1 *scallion stalk*
4 *cups water*	3 *eggs*
½ *pound lean pork*	½ *teaspoon salt*

1. Place dried scallops and water in a saucepan. Bring to a boil; then simmer, covered, 2 hours.

2. Slice pork thin; mince scallion. Beat eggs. Add to pan and stir in well.

3. Simmer, covered, until done (about 30 minutes more). Season with salt and serve.

NOTE: The mixture should have a mush-like consistency. If it seems to be getting too dry in step 3, add more water.

IRON POT EGGS
About 6 servings

5 *eggs*	½ *cup water*
¼ *pound lean pork*	½ *teaspoon soy sauce*
½ *tablespoon lard*	½ *teaspoon salt*

1. Beat eggs. Mince or grind pork. Melt lard. Combine with water, soy sauce and salt, and mix well.

2. Transfer egg mixture to an iron pot or Pyrex pan large enough for it to expand to about three times its original size. Cover and cook over a very low flame

until eggs puff up and push against the lid (about 30 minutes). Serve at once.

NOTE: Unless eaten immediately, these eggs will shrink. Because of the way they puff up, they're also called Grown Eggs.

HARD-BOILED SALT EGGS
Allow about 1 egg for each serving

salt eggs   water to cover
1 to 2 tablespoons peanut oil

1. Wash salt eggs to remove the brine. Then place in a saucepan with cold water and cook slowly 25 to 30 minutes.

2. Shell eggs and cut each in half or quarters.

3. Heat peanut oil to smoking; then pour over eggs. Serve with rice.

SWEET-AND-PUNGENT PRESERVED EGGS
About 6 servings

sweet-and-pungent sauce   *4 tablespoons oil*
4 preserved eggs   salt

1. Prepare a sweet-and-pungent sauce (see pages 735–738). Keep warm in its saucepan.

2. Clean and shell preserved eggs (see page 826). Cut each in 4 slices.

3. Heat oil. Gently pan-fry egg sections 1 minute to heat. Then sprinkle lightly with the salt.

4. Add eggs to sweet-and-pungent sauce. Cook, stirring gently, to blend flavors (1 to 2 minutes); then serve.

SOY EGGS
4 to 6 servings

5 to 6 eggs	½ cup soy sauce
water to cover	½ cup water
¼ cup sugar	lettuce

1. Place eggs in cold water to cover and bring to a boil over medium heat. Then cook gently 10 to 12 minutes.

2. Cool eggs thoroughly under cold running water (about 5 minutes); then shell.

3. Combine sugar, soy sauce and water in a saucepan. Then heat, stirring, to dissolve sugar.

4. Add eggs and baste to brown evenly. Simmer, covered, 1 hour, turning several times for even coloring.

5. Turn off heat and let stand, covered, 30 minutes more, turning eggs once or twice.

6. Cut each egg in 4 wedges with a sharp knife. Serve yolk-side up on a bed of lettuce strips. Either garnish with tomatoes and Chinese parsley, or serve with dip dishes of plum sauce, catsup or hot sauce.

NOTE: These eggs, also known as pot-stewed or red-stewed eggs, are eaten for breakfast or as a late supper dish. They can also be served cold as an hors d'oeuvre.

VARIATIONS: For the white sugar, substitute brown sugar.

For the sugar-soy mixture, substitute ¼ cup soy sauce; 2 cups stock; 2 tablespoons sherry; 1 medium onion, cut in wedges; and 2 slices fresh ginger root.

After step 2, add eggs to any red-cooked chicken, duck or pork dish for the last 30 to 40 minutes of cooking, making sure each egg is covered with sauce. Serve either with the meat or poultry or as a separate dish.

In step 3, also add 2 scallion stalks, minced; and 1 tablespoon lard or peanut oil; or ½ teaspoon sesame oil.

SOY DUCK EGGS
6 to 8 servings

1 piece dried tangerine peel	2 garlic cloves
6 duck eggs	½ cup soy sauce
water to cover	8 cups water
1 leek stalk	1 tablespoon honey
1 teaspoon salt	

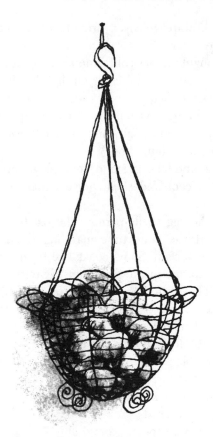

1. Soak dried tangerine peel.

2. Place duck eggs in water to cover and bring to a boil over medium heat; then cook gently 8 to 10 minutes more.

3. Cool eggs thoroughly under cold running water (about 5 minutes); then shell.

4. Meanwhile cut leek in 1½-inch sections and crush garlic. Combine in a saucepan with soy sauce, water, honey, salt and soaked tangerine peel. Bring to a boil, stirring.

5. Add eggs and simmer, covered, 2 hours. (Add more boiling water if necessary.)

6. Serve as in step 6 of Soy Eggs above.

TEA EGGS
8 to 10 servings

8 *to* 10 *eggs*	3 *tablespoons black tea*
water to cover	1 *tablespoon salt*

1. Place eggs in cold water to cover. Bring to a boil, then simmer gently 12 to 15 minutes. Reserve the water.

2. Cool eggs thoroughly under cold running water for 5 minutes. Then either roll each egg gently on a board or table, or tap lightly with a spoon to crackle the entire shell. (Do not remove shell.)

3. Bring the reserved water to a boil again. (There should be 3 to 4 cups. If not, add more water.) Add tea leaves, salt, and crackled eggs; then simmer, covered, until egg shells turn brown (about 1 hour).

4. Turn off the heat and let eggs stand, covered, 30 minutes more.

5. Drain eggs, then cool and shell. Serve either cut in half lengthwise or quartered.

NOTE: Crackling the egg shells permits the tea liquid to seep through and flavor the eggs, while at the same time marbling them and creating an effect somewhat like antique porcelain. Some cooks like to let the unshelled eggs stand overnight at room temperature in the tea liquid. (If refrigerated in the liquid, they will keep several days. They taste best, however, on the first and second days.) Tea eggs are sometimes eaten at lunch and dinner, but more often at breakfast or as a snack. They're also excellent for picnics and should be left in their shells (which keep the eggs moist) until actually ready to eat.

VARIATIONS: For the black tea, substitute either jasmine or lichee tea. For the salt, substitute ½ cup rock sugar.

In step 3, also add any of the following:

1 piece tangerine peel (soaked)

4 cloves star anise or 1 teaspoon ground anise

¼ cup soy sauce and 1 cinnamon stick

❋ *Vegetable Dishes* ❋

THE EXCELLENCE and unparalleled repertory of Chinese vegetable cookery grows directly out of the Buddhist tradition, which prohibits the eating of meat. This tradition, however, places great stress on culinary skills, with these skills being devoted exclusively to the preparation of vegetables. At Buddhist banquets in China, where ten or more vegetarian dishes were served, a fantastic ingenuity would be demonstrated. Not only were these dishes tremendously varied, but they also included artful and convincing reconstructions that looked for all the world like chicken, fish, ham and duck. Their actual ingredients, however, were bean curd, vegetables and flour.

The Chinese consider vegetables as savories in their own right, to be prepared with as much care as fish or fowl. Chinese vegetable dishes are characterized by crispness, excellent flavor and bright color. The vegetable, in fact, looks as fresh as it did before cooking. The secret: it has not been cooked to death but only partially cooked until half tender and half crunchy. Chinese vegetables are never soft, with the color and flavor boiled out of them, but neither are they raw.

In Chinese vegetable cookery, the technique is primary and the vegetable secondary: once the method is understood, one vegetable can readily substitute for another. Any vegetable, whether it be a familiar domestic variety or a uniquely Chinese one,* can be cooked the Chinese way.

Depending on the nature of the vegetable and how it's cut, it may be stir-fried, braised, steamed or deep-fried. Stir-frying, the most typical technique, calls for the vegetable to be tossed quickly first in a small amount of peanut oil or lard, then to finish cooking in the juices it generates itself, or in liquid which is added later. The pan must be well heated before the oil is added. When the oil begins to sizzle, salt (which makes green vegetables turn a brighter green) is added, and then the vegetable itself. The vegetable is quickly stir-fried or tossed until it becomes coated with the oil. (If the oil is not hot enough at this point, the vegetable will become soft, limp and watery. However, once the vegetable is in the pot, the heat of the oil must be reduced slightly to prevent scorching.)

Soft vegetables such as spinach, lettuce, water cress, tomatoes and bean sprouts generally need no additional liquid. When subjected to heat, they quickly render up their own juices and continue cooking in them. (In the case of leafy vegetables, enough liquid will cling to the vegetable after washing to keep it from sticking to the pan until it does render up its own juices.) Still other soft vegetables, like mushrooms and zucchini, can be stir-fried in oil for a minute, then cooked, covered, for another minute or two without additional liquids.

With hard and semi-hard vegetables, additional liquid must be added. (Hard vegetables include asparagus, broccoli, cauliflower, carrots, string beans and turnips. The semi-hard are bamboo shoots, bitter melon, celery, lotus root, mustard cabbage and snow peas.) Except of course in soup, the Chinese-style vegetable is never cooked in any more liquid than is absolutely necessary. Just enough is added to enable the vegetable to render up and steam in its own juices. The liquid used may be stock or water. (Stock is preferred because it enhances and enriches the vegetable's flavor.) It is added after the vegetable has been well coated with oil, and is poured not directly over the vegetable but down the sides of the pan to heat. The pan is then covered tightly and the vegetable steamed until done.

* Some of these, sold fresh in Chinese food stores, are grown on Chinese farms in California, New Jersey and Florida; others are imported canned and dried from the Orient.

This stir-frying or quick-cooking method has many advantages: it retains the vegetable's individual characteristics, its color, texture and taste. The hot oil seals in the vegetable's juices, while at the same time extracting its flavor. Since there are no excess liquids to pour down the drain, the vegetable's valuable vitamin and mineral content is not lost.

When several vegetables are cooked together, those needing longer cooking time (onions, celery, green peppers) go into the pan first, while the more tender ones (spinach, bean sprouts, tomatoes) go in last. In the case of vegetables with stalks and leaves (such as Chinese cabbage), the stalks, being tougher, go into the pan first; the soft, tender leaves are added at the last minute only to be heated through.

Hard and semi-hard green vegetables should be cooked, covered, as briefly as possible, to retain their fresh color. The cover should never be lifted more than once during cooking. If it is, the vegetable will turn yellowish. A good method of color retention is to blanch or parboil the vegetable first. This will reduce the time the vegetable needs to be cooked covered. Blanching and parboiling are described on page 831.

The color in vegetable cookery is important, but not only for aesthetic reasons. With green vegetables, it indicates when the vegetable is done. As a green vegetable cooks, it turns successively from bright green to dark green to olive drab. When it's somewhere between bright and dark green, it should be removed from the heat.

Cutting vegetables: Vegetables, depending on their own nature and the nature of the ingredients they're to be cooked with, may be sliced, diced, minced or shredded. As often as possible, they should be cut in shapes to match the other ingredients. Soft vegetables are sliced straight or vertically; hard and semi-hard vegetables are cut diagonally. As a rule, vegetables should not be cut until actually ready to use (they will dry out or wilt). If they must be cut up in advance, they should be wrapped well, in transparent wrap or foil, and refrigerated.

Seasoning vegetables: Vegetables, after being stir-fried in oil, are frequently seasoned with soy sauce, then stir-fried a minute or so longer. (When additional liquid is needed, it's added afterward.) Another common seasoning for vegetables is sugar, added in small quantities at the very end. When the sugar is mixed with vinegar (in the ratio of 1 teaspoon sugar to 1 tablespoon vinegar) it makes a sweet-and-pungent sauce that combines well with such vegetables as carrots and cabbage.

Cooking vegetables in advance: Hard and semi-hard vegetables such as broccoli, Brussels sprouts, carrots, cauliflower and string beans may be cooked in advance and reheated; they are stir-fried briefly in oil, then cooked, covered, in ¼ cup of liquid over medium heat until nearly done. They are then stirred a few times and cooked, covered, another minute or two until all the liquid is absorbed. The vegetable is then left to cool, uncovered, to retain its natural color and texture. When ready to use, it is stir-fried again in a small amount of oil, just long enough to be reheated.

Salads: The Chinese rarely eat raw vegetables, and so have no tradition of eating salads. Originally the reasons were hygienic: it wasn't safe to eat vegetables raw. If they weren't actually cooked, vegetables were always quickly scalded or blanched first. This scalding not only destroyed harmful bacteria, but enhanced the vegetable's taste and brightened its color without

in any way damaging its fresh texture. After blanching, however, the vegetables were treated like salads: that is, tossed lightly in dressings made with various combinations of soy sauce, salt and oil, and then chilled for about 20 minutes—long enough for the dressings to flavor the vegetables, but not long enough to discolor or wilt them.

Frozen vegetables: Because frozen vegetables are less crisp and flavorful than fresh ones, they are not generally recommended. If necessary, however, frozen peas and string beans can be used. These should always be thawed first, then drained on paper toweling to remove as much moisture as possible. Since their water content is higher than that of fresh vegetables, the frozen varieties need only brief stir-frying in hot oil. (Additional liquid should never be added, nor should the vegetables be parboiled first.) Minced garlic or ginger root, added to the hot oil, will improve the vegetable's flavor.

To store vegetables: Do not buy fresh vegetables too far in advance. Do not leave them at room temperature for any length of time, but refrigerate them as quickly as possible in a vegetable crisper or perforated plastic bag. Do not wash the vegetables until actually ready to cook. (Vegetables, particularly the leafy varieties, will wilt and rot. Others will lose many of their water-soluble vitamins if exposed to moisture for any length of time.) If, for any reason, the vegetables must be washed in advance, then drain and dry completely before refrigerating.

BASIC STIR-FRIED VEGETABLES
About 4 servings

1 *pound vegetables*	1 *tablespoon soy sauce*
3 *slices fresh ginger root*	½ *teaspoon sugar*
¼ to ½ *cup stock*	2 *tablespoons oil*
½ *teaspoon salt*	

1. Prepare vegetables as indicated in the instructions below. (They may be prepared individually, or as in the suggested combinations on page 587.) Mince or crush ginger root.

2. Combine stock, soy sauce and sugar.

3. Heat oil. Add salt, then ginger root, and stir-fry a few times. Add vegetable (adjust heat to prevent scorching). Stir-fry to coat with oil and heat through.

4. Add stock-soy mixture and heat quickly. Then simmer, covered, over medium heat until vegetable is done. (See Cooking Instructions for Specific Vegetables below.)

NOTE: All cooking times indicated below are approximate. They depend on the vegetable's tenderness, the way it's cut, the amount of heat and the type of pan used. Taste the vegetable to check for doneness: it should be tender but still crunchy.

VARIATIONS: For the ginger root, substitute 1 garlic clove, minced; or 1 scallion stalk, cut in ½-inch sections. (With stronger-tasting vegetables such as cabbage, ginger root is better than garlic.)

For the oil, substitute chicken fat, bacon fat or lard. (Chicken fat is particularly good with Chinese cabbage and Chinese lettuce; bacon fat with other varieties of lettuce.)

For the mixture in step 2, substitute 1 teaspoon cornstarch, 1 teaspoon sugar, 1 teaspoon soy sauce, 2 tablespoons sherry, ½ cup water and 1 to 2 slices fresh ginger root, minced. (Omit the ginger root in step 3.)

Omit the soy sauce in step 2. Then, after step 3, sprinkle the soy sauce over the vegetables and stir in. Add the stock and sugar as in step 4.

After step 3, stir into the vegetables ¼ to ½ teaspoon shrimp sauce.

In step 4, add ¼ cup dried shrimp or scallops (soaked), shredded. (The soaking water may be substituted for the stock.)

After step 4, thicken the sauce with a cornstarch paste made of 1 teaspoon cornstarch and 2 tablespoons cold stock or water.

Serve the vegetables garnished with blanched, toasted and coarsely chopped almonds or walnuts.

COOKING INSTRUCTIONS FOR SPECIFIC VEGETABLES

Asparagus—Discard tough fibrous ends. Cut stalks diagonally in 1- to 1½-inch sections. Blanch the stalks if young and tender. If not, parboil them. (Do not blanch or parboil the delicate tips.) In step 4, cook 2 to 3 minutes.

Bamboo Shoots (canned)—Drain. Slice thin lengthwise; then dice or sliver. In step 4, cook 2 to 3 minutes.

Bamboo Shoots (fresh)—Remove outer leaves. Parboil 10 to 15 minutes; then drain. Slice, and cook as above.

Bean Sprouts—Blanch (this shortens cooking time, keeps them crunchy). Stir-fry with the salt and soy sauce until done. (Omit the stock and sugar.) Do not overcook: the bean sprouts will become discolored and dry. For the soy sauce you may substitute 1 teaspoon vinegar or a few drops of sesame oil.

Bitter Melon—Cut in half lengthwise. Scoop out spongy pulp and seeds, then cut crosswise in ½- to 1-inch slices. Parboil 3 minutes. In step 4, cook 3 to 4 minutes.

Broccoli—Break into small flowerets. Trim off tough ends, then cut stems diagonally in ½-inch slices (split heavy stems in half). Parboil. In step 4, cook 3 minutes. Then cook, uncovered, 1 minute more, stirring gently. (If broccoli is cooked, covered, too long, it discolors and turns yellow.) **NOTE:** Chinese broccoli is more tender and needs less cooking.

Brussels Sprouts—Leave whole if tender; cut in half if tough. Parboil. In step 4, cook 2 to 3 minutes.

Cabbage, Chinese—Discard tough outer leaves. Separate the stalks and leaves. Split lower stalks lengthwise in half; then cut either diagonally in 1-inch sections, or lengthwise in ½- by 2-inch strips. Cut the leaves in 2-inch sections. Stir-fry stalks as in step 3. Then, in step 4, cook about 3 minutes. Stir in leaves at the very end, only to soften.

Cabbage, Mustard—Separate the leaves. Cut in 2-inch sections and blanch. In step 4, cook 3 to 4 minutes. (The stalk and leafy portions may be added separately: In step 3, stir-fry the stalks 2 minutes; then add the leaves and stir-fry 1 minute more. Pick up step 4.)

Cabbage, Preserved—Wash and squeeze dry. Slice leaves lengthwise in 3 sections, then crosswise in ¼-inch sections. In step 4, cook 3 to 4 minutes. For the soy sauce, you may substitute 1 to 2 teaspoons vinegar.

Cabbage, Round (new)—Cut young cabbage leaves in 1-inch lengths, or shred coarsely as for coleslaw. In step 4, cook 3 minutes.

Cabbage, Round (old)—Cut cabbage in 1½-inch cubes or 2-inch wedges. In step 4, cook 15 to 20 minutes. (Or slice thin and parboil; then cook as for new cabbage.)

Carrots—Peel or scrape. Cut diagonally in ¼-inch slices. (If large, cut lengthwise in halves or quarters first.) Parboil. In step 4, cook 2 to 3 minutes. For the soy sauce, you may substitute 1 to 2 teaspoons vinegar.

Cauliflower—Break into small flowerets. Cut stems diagonally in ½-inch slices. Parboil. In step 4, cook 3 minutes.

Celery—Trim off leaves and tough stem ends. Cut stalks diagonally in 1-inch sections. Parboil if tough; blanch if tender. In step 4, cook 2 minutes. (If celery is young, omit stock mixture and continue stir-frying as in step 3 until done.)

Cucumber—Peel. If small, cut in ¼-inch slices. If large, cut in half lengthwise and scoop out seeds; then cut crosswise in ¼-inch slices. Reduce soy sauce to 1 teaspoon. In step 4, cook 2 to 3 minutes.

Eggplant—Peel. Cut in 1-inch cubes or strips. In step 4, cook 3 to 4 minutes. (Or omit the stock and sugar and, in step 3, stir-fry gently until eggplant begins to give off its own moisture, about 2 to 3 minutes. Then sprinkle with the soy sauce and cook, covered, over low heat until done, about 13 minutes, stirring gently from time to time.)

Lettuce—Separate the leaves. Tear each in half or in 2-inch squares. Omit step 2. Stir-fry as in step 3 over medium heat until leaves begin to soften but are not limp. (Or stir-fry briefly in step 3, then cook, covered, without additional liquid another minute or two.)

Lettuce, Chinese—Separate the leaves and cut diagonally against the grain in ½- to 1-inch sections. Omit the soy sauce. Reduce the stock to 3 tablespoons because this vegetable gives off considerable liquid of its own. In step 4, cook 2 minutes.

Lotus Root—Peel and slice thin. Parboil. In step 4, cook 2 to 3 minutes.

Mushrooms, Dried—Soak, then squeeze dry. Slice, discarding tough stems. In step 4, cook 3 to 5 minutes, or longer. You may substitute the soaking liquid for stock.

Mushrooms, Fresh—Wipe with a damp cloth. Trim tough stem ends. Leave whole if small or cut vertically in ⅛-inch slices. Omit steps 2 and 4. At the end of step 3, sprinkle with the soy sauce and continue stir-frying until soft but not limp. For the soy sauce, you may substitute oyster sauce.

Onions—Trim off tops and bottoms. Cut in half lengthwise, then peel. Place halves flat-side down and slice crosswise. In step 4, cook 2 minutes.

Peas—Shell and blanch. Omit the soy sauce. In step 4, cook 3 to 4 minutes.

Peppers—Cut in half and remove seeds. Dice or cut in strips. In step 4, cook 2 to 3 minutes. (Stop cooking while peppers are still bright green. If overcooked, they become drab and bitter.)

Pumpkin—Peel. Remove spongy pulp and seeds. Cut in 2-inch cubes and score back of each cube with crisscross slashes. Omit the soy sauce. In step 4, cook 10 to 15 minutes.

Potatoes—Peel and dice. Parboil. Omit the soy sauce. In step 4, cook 3 to 5 minutes.

Snow Peas—Stem and string. Leave whole if tender; if not, cut in two diagonally. Blanch. In step 4, cook 1 to 2 minutes.

Spinach—Wash, then shake off excess water. Trim tough stem ends. (If tender, leave stems on with about ½ inch of the pink root for color contrast.) Leave leaves whole or tear in 2-inch squares. Omit steps 2 and 4. At the end of step 3, sprinkle with the soy sauce and continue stir-frying until leaves turn a brighter green and are slightly softened, but not limp. (Or cover pan after step 3 and cook 1 minute without additional liquid. Then uncover, sprinkle with the soy sauce and stir-fry ½ minute more.) In either case, add the sugar at the very end.

Squash—(Chinese squash, summer squash or zucchini) Peel. Cut in ⅛- to ¼-inch slices. In step 4, cook 3 to 4 minutes.

String Beans—Stem, then cut or break in 1- to 2-inch sections. Parboil. In step 4, cook 4 to 5 minutes. (In step 3, you may also add 1 tablespoon soy jam to the hot oil, along with 1 garlic clove, crushed, before adding the beans.)

Swiss Chard—Separate root end from the leafy part. Cut diagonally in 1-inch sections. (Add leafy part at the end of step 3.) In step 4, cook 4 minutes.

Tomatoes—Peel. Quarter if small; cube if large. Omit steps 2 and 4. Stir-fry only to heat through. Sprinkle with the soy sauce and sugar; then stir-fry once or twice more.

Turnips, Chinese White—Peel, then shred or grate. Omit steps 2 and 4. Continue stir-frying as in step 3 until done. (Or peel, and dice or slice ½-inch thick; then parboil. In step 4, cook 3 minutes.)

Water Chestnuts (fresh)—Peel. Slice thin. In step 4, cook 2 minutes.

Water Chestnuts (canned)—Drain. Slice and cook as above.

Water Cress—Wash. Wrap in a clean towel and shake out excess moisture. Trim off tough stems. Cut in 1- to 2-inch lengths. Omit steps 2 and 4. Continue stir-frying in step 3 until bright green and softened, but not limp. Sprinkle with the soy sauce and sugar; then stir-fry once or twice more.

Winter Melon—Peel. Cut in 1-inch cubes. In step 4, cook about 4 minutes. Serve sprinkled with a few drops of peanut or sesame oil.

SUGGESTED COMBINATIONS FOR BASIC STIR-FRIED VEGETABLES

1 cup fresh mushrooms, sliced; ½ cup bamboo shoots, sliced; and 1 pound spinach leaves, left whole.

12 to 16 dried black mushrooms (soaked); and either 6 water chestnuts or 1 cup bamboo shoots, sliced.

½ pound bean sprouts, blanched; ½ pound asparagus, cut in 1-inch sections; and 1 celery stalk, cut in strips.

½ pound bean sprouts, blanched, with any of the following: 2 tomatoes, peeled and cubed; 2 green peppers, seeded and cut in strips; or 1 cup preserved cabbage, cut in 2-inch sections.

½ pound Chinese cabbage stems, cut in 2-inch sections, with any of the following: 6 strips of bacon, cut in 1-inch sections; 1½ cups fresh mushrooms, sliced; ½ cup bamboo shoots, sliced; or 6 to 8 lily buds (soaked).

¼ pound each Chinese white turnips and carrots, cut in strips and parboiled; ¼ pound each, celery and leeks, cut in strips.

NOTE: The individual vegetables are added to the pot, according to their specific cooking times. (See details above.) Remember: the toughest vegetables are added first; the most tender ones last.

BASIC SWEET-AND-PUNGENT VEGETABLES
About 4 servings

1 pound vegetables	½ teaspoon salt
2 to 3 tablespoons sugar	1 tablespoon cornstarch
3 tablespoons vinegar	2 tablespoons water
1 tablespoon soy sauce	2 tablespoons oil

1. Prepare vegetables as in Basic Stir-fried Vegetables above.

2. In one cup, combine sugar, vinegar, soy sauce and salt. In another, blend cornstarch and cold water to a paste.

3. Heat oil. Add vegetable and stir-fry until half done.

4. Add sugar-vinegar mixture; stir-fry 2 minutes more.

5. Then stir in cornstarch paste to thicken and serve at once.

NOTE: Any of the following vegetables are suitable for this recipe: asparagus, cabbage, carrots, celery or zucchini.

VARIATION: In step 2, add a drop or two of Tabasco Sauce to the sugar-vinegar mixture.

MIXED VEGETABLES I
About 4 servings

5 dried black mushrooms	¼ cup snow peas
½ cup round cabbage	½ cup stock
1 carrot	½ teaspoon salt
½ cup bamboo shoots	1 teaspoon sugar
1 cucumber	2 teaspoons soy sauce

3 to 4 tablespoons oil

1. Soak dried mushrooms.

2. Cut cabbage in 2-inch cubes and parboil. Cut carrot in 1½-inch strips and parboil. Cut bamboo shoots in similar strips. Peel and slice cucumber. Stem snow peas.

3. Combine stock, salt, sugar and soy sauce.

4. Heat oil. Add cabbage and stir-fry 2 to 3 minutes. Add remaining vegetables; stir-fry 2 to 3 minutes more.

5. Add stock mixture and heat quickly. Cook, covered, 3 to 4 minutes over medium heat. Serve at once.

VARIATION: Shred all the vegetables. Then, in step 4, stir-fry only 1 to 2 minutes. In step 5, add to heated stock ¼ pound vermicelli (soaked), cut in 3-inch lengths.

MIXED VEGETABLES II
About 4 servings

¼ pound broccoli
¼ pound string beans
¼ pound cabbage
¼ pound fresh mushrooms
1 large onion

1 garlic clove
3 tablespoons oil
½ teaspoon salt
½ cup stock
1 tablespoon soy sauce

1. Break broccoli into flowerets and parboil. Cut string beans in 1-inch sections and parboil separately.

2. Dice cabbage, mushrooms and onion. Crush garlic.

3. Heat oil. Add salt, then garlic, and stir-fry a few times. Add onion, cabbage and string beans; stir-fry 2 minutes.

4. Add broccoli and mushrooms; stir-fry 2 minutes more. Add stock and soy sauce, and heat quickly. Then cook, covered, 2 to 3 minutes over medium heat. Serve at once.

MIXED VEGETABLES III
About 4 servings

½ cup cauliflower
½ cup asparagus
½ cup peas
½ cup celery
½ cup Chinese cabbage stems
½ cup bamboo shoots

½ cup fresh mushrooms
2 slices fresh ginger root
2 to 3 tablespoons oil
½ teaspoon salt
1 tablespoon soy sauce
½ cup stock

1. Break cauliflower into small flowerets and parboil. Cut asparagus in 1-inch sections. Shell peas.

2. Dice celery, Chinese cabbage stems, bamboo shoots and fresh mushrooms. Mince ginger root.

3. Heat oil. Add ginger root and stir-fry a few times. Add cauliflower, asparagus, peas and celery; stir-fry 2 minutes.

4. Add Chinese cabbage, bamboo shoots, and mushrooms; stir-fry 2 minutes more. Sprinkle with salt and soy sauce and stir-fry briefly to blend in.

5. Add stock and heat quickly. Cook, covered, 2 minutes over medium heat. Serve at once.

MIXED VEGETABLES IV

About 4 servings

2 green peppers

1 small head lettuce

1 cucumber

1 zucchini

2 tomatoes

1 garlic clove

2 to 3 tablespoons oil

½ teaspoon salt

1. Seed and dice green peppers. Separate lettuce leaves. Peel and dice cucumber, zucchini and tomatoes. Crush garlic.

2. Heat oil. Add salt, then garlic, and stir-fry a few times. Add green pepper; stir-fry 1 minute.

3. Add cucumber and zucchini and stir-fry 1 minute more. Add tomatoes and lettuce; gently stir-fry another ½ minute.

4. Cover and cook 2 minutes more over medium heat. Serve at once.

NOTE: These vegetables need no stock; they will cook in their own liquids.

MIXED VEGETABLES V

About 4 servings

½ pound bean sprouts

¼ pound Chinese cabbage stems

6 water chestnuts

12 snow peas

2 to 3 tablespoons oil

½ teaspoon salt

½ cup stock

½ teaspoon sugar

1. Blanch bean sprouts. Cut Chinese cabbage stems diagonally in 2-inch sections. Slice water chestnuts. Stem snow peas.

2. Heat oil. Add salt, then vegetables, and stir-fry 2 minutes.

3. Add stock and sugar and heat quickly. Cook, covered, 2 minutes more over medium heat. Serve at once.

STIR-FRIED ASPARAGUS WITH EGG SAUCE
About 4 servings

1 *pound asparagus*	1 *cup stock*
1 *egg*	2 *tablespoons oil*
1 *tablespoon cornstarch*	1 *tablespoon sherry*
¼ *teaspoon salt*	¼ *teaspoon salt*

1. Trim off tough asparagus ends; set tips aside. Cut stalks in 1-inch lengths and parboil. Beat egg lightly.

2. Combine cornstarch, salt and stock in a saucepan and bring to a boil, stirring.

3. Slowly stir in some heated stock with beaten egg. Then add egg mixture to pan and cook, stirring, over medium heat until stock thickens. Keep warm.

4. Heat oil in another pan. Add asparagus stalks and tips; stir-fry until tender but still crisp (about 3 minutes). Stir in sherry and remaining salt.

5. Transfer asparagus to a serving platter. Pour the warm egg sauce over and serve at once.

VARIATION: For the whole egg, substitute 2 egg whites.

STIR-FRIED BAMBOO SHOOTS AND MUSHROOMS
About 4 servings

10 *to* 12 *dried black mushrooms*	1 *tablespoon soy sauce*
2 *cups bamboo shoots*	1 *teaspoon sugar*
3 *tablespoons oil*	1 *tablespoon cornstarch*

½ *cup mushroom-soaking liquid*

1. Soak dried mushrooms; reserve the soaking liquid.

2. Cut bamboo shoots lengthwise in thin slices, then in 1- by 1½-inch strips. Leave mushrooms whole if small; quarter if large.

3. Heat oil. Add mushrooms and stir-fry 2 to 3 minutes.

4. Add bamboo shoots; stir-fry 2 minutes more. Then blend in soy sauce and sugar.

5. Transfer vegetables to a serving platter, leaving liquids in pan. Arrange bamboo shoots underneath, mushrooms on top.

6. Blend cornstarch and mushroom-soaking liquid to a paste. Add to pan and cook, stirring, to thicken liquids. Pour sauce over vegetables and serve at once.

DEEP-FRIED BAMBOO SHOOTS
About 4 servings

2 *cups bamboo shoots*	1 *teaspoon sugar*
oil for deep-frying	½ *cup water*
1 *tablespoon cornstarch*	1 *to* 2 *tablespoons oil*
1 *tablespoon soy sauce*	

1. Cut bamboo shoots in strips as for french-fried potatoes.

2. Heat oil and deep-fry bamboo shoots until pale golden. Drain on paper toweling.

3. Blend cornstarch, sugar and cold water.

4. Heat remaining oil. Add bamboo shoots; stir-fry to heat through. Sprinkle with soy sauce and blend in.

5. Then stir in cornstarch paste to thicken and serve at once.

VARIATION: Omit the cornstarch paste. In step 4, add 2 teaspoons chili sauce to the oil and heat before adding the bamboo shoots. At the end of step 4, stir in the sugar with the soy sauce.

DEEP-FRIED BAMBOO SHOOTS AND SALTED CABBAGE
About 4 servings

½ *cup dried salted cabbage*	¼ *teaspoon salt*
1½ *cups bamboo shoots*	1 *teaspoon sugar*
oil for deep-frying	1 *teaspoon sesame oil*
¼ *teaspoon sugar*	

1. Soak dried salted cabbage.

2. Cut bamboo shoots in strips, as for French-fried potatoes. Cut soaked cabbage in 1-inch sections.

3. Heat oil and deep-fry bamboo shoots until pale golden. Drain on paper toweling. Sprinkle with salt and sugar; keep warm.

4. In another pan, heat sesame oil. Add cabbage and stir-fry to heat through. Sprinkle with remaining sugar.

5. Arrange cabbage strips on a platter with bamboo shoots on top, and serve at once.

VARIATION: For the dried cabbage, substitute fresh mustard cabbage. (See Basic Stir-fried Vegetables for details.)

STEAMED BAMBOO SHOOTS WITH CHICKEN AND HAM

4 to 6 servings

2 cups bamboo shoots
½ cup chicken breast
½ cup smoked ham

¼ cup water chestnuts
2 egg whites
1 tablespoon cornstarch

Chinese parsley

1. Cut bamboo shoots lengthwise in 2-inch strips.
2. Mince chicken together with smoked ham and water chestnuts.
3. Blend egg whites with cornstarch; then add to minced ingredients and mix to a smooth paste.
4. Roll bamboo strips one at a time in the paste to coat well and arrange on a heatproof dish.
5. Steam for 10 minutes (see page 831). Serve hot, garnished with Chinese parsley.

BASIC STIR-FRIED BEAN CURD

About 4 servings

4 cakes bean curd
1 scallion stalk
3 to 4 tablespoons oil

¼ teaspoon salt
2 tablespoons soy sauce
¼ teaspoon salt

1. Cut each bean curd cake in 6 to 8 pieces or in 1-inch cubes. Cut scallion stalk in 1-inch sections.
2. Heat oil. Add salt; then scallion, and stir-fry a few times until translucent.

Add bean curd; stir-fry gently until heated through (2 to 3 minutes).

3. Sprinkle with soy sauce and remaining salt and stir in gently.

NOTE: Since bean curd is fragile, vigorous stir-frying will demolish it. Therefore shake or tilt the pan from time to time to baste the bean curd with hot oil; or else separately turn the pieces so they can heat through evenly.

VARIATIONS: For the soy sauce, substitute oyster sauce.

Use 4 or 5 whole scallions, cut in 1-inch lengths.

Before serving, sprinkle bean curd with a few drops of sesame oil; or garnish with minced raw scallion.

With Chinese sausage: Steam 4 Chinese sausages 15 minutes; then slice thin. Add to heated oil in step 2 and brown lightly; then stir-fry scallion and bean curd.

With mushrooms (fresh): In step 2, add after the scallion, ¼ pound fresh mushrooms, sliced, and stir-fry until slightly softened. Then add the bean curd and continue as in steps 2 and 3.

With mushrooms (dried): After step 2, add 10 dried black mushrooms (soaked), sliced, the soy sauce and ½ teaspoon sugar. Then gently stir in ½ cup of the mushroom-soaking liquid or stock. Bring to a boil and simmer, covered, 5 minutes over medium heat.

With roast pork: In step 2, add after the scallion, ¼ cup roast pork, sliced or diced, and stir-fry a few times. Then add the bean curd and continue as in steps 2 and 3.

With shrimp: In step 2, add after the scallion ¼ cup raw shrimp, shelled, deveined and cut in 1-inch pieces; stir-fry until pinkish. Then add bean curd and continue as in steps 2 and 3.

BASIC DEEP-FRIED BEAN CURD
About 4 servings

4 cakes bean curd	*oil for deep-frying*

salt

1. Cut bean curd cakes in 1-inch cubes. Blot gently with paper toweling to remove as much moisture as possible.

2. Heat oil and deep-fry bean curd cubes, several at a time, until puffed up and golden. Drain on paper toweling. Sprinkle with salt and serve hot.

NOTE: Deep-fried bean curd cubes can be added to any stir-fried dish. They should be added at the very end, only to heat through (so as not to lose their interesting texture and crispness). Speared on toothpicks, these are also excellent as an hors d'oeuvre to serve with cocktails.

VARIATION: At the end of step 2, also sprinkle lightly with hot sauce.

DEEP-FRIED BEAN CURD WITH DRIED SHRIMP SAUCE
4 to 6 servings

2 tablespoons dried shrimp	½ teaspoon salt
4 cakes deep-fried bean curd	2 teaspoons soy sauce
1 scallion stalk	2 tablespoons oil
1 cup stock	1 teaspoon cornstarch
2 tablespoons sherry	1 tablespoon water

1. Soak dried shrimp.

2. Deep-fry bean curd as above. Mince scallion. Combine stock, sherry, salt and soy sauce.

3. Heat oil. Add scallion and soaked shrimp; stir-fry a few times. Add stock mixture and heat quickly. Then simmer, covered, 5 minutes.

4. Add deep-fried bean curd cubes; stir in only to heat through. Meanwhile, blend cornstarch and cold water to a paste; then stir in to thicken.

VARIATION: For the dried shrimp and scallion, substitute 1 tablespoon brown bean sauce, mashed, and 1 garlic clove, minced; stir-fry as in step 3. Then add plain stock (omit the sherry, salt and soy sauce). In step 4, add 2 tablespoons oyster sauce with the bean curd cubes.

STEAMED STUFFED BEAN CURD
6 to 8 servings

¼ to ½ pound lean pork	1 teaspoon sesame oil
1 scallion stalk	4 bean curd cakes
1 teaspoon soy sauce	1 teaspoon soy sauce
1 teaspoon sherry	½ teaspoon sherry

1. Mince pork and scallion stalk. Blend together with soy sauce, sherry and sesame oil. Divide mixture in 8 parts.

2. Cut each bean curd cake diagonally in 2 triangles. Carefully scoop out a hole or pocket on 1 cut surface of each triangle. Stuff pork mixture into the pockets.

3. Arrange stuffed bean curd on a shallow heatproof dish and sprinkle with remaining soy sauce and sherry. Steam until done (about 30 minutes). See page 831.

MISCELLANEOUS BEAN CURD

Dice bean curd cakes, or cut in 1- by 2-inch pieces. Pan-fry in a little oil to brown lightly on each side. Serve hot.

Dice or slice bean curd cakes. Immerse briefly in boiling water, only to heat through. Serve with a dip (see page 714) or with a sweet-and-pungent sauce (see pages 735–738).

STIR-FRIED BEAN SPROUTS AND CELERY
4 to 6 servings

1 *pound bean sprouts*	½ *teaspoon salt*
2 *to 4 celery stalks*	1 *tablespoon soy sauce*
2 *tablespoons oil*	¼ *cup stock*

1. Blanch bean sprouts. Shred celery.

2. Heat oil. Add celery and stir-fry 1 minute. Add bean sprouts; stir-fry 1 minute more.

3. Add salt, soy sauce and stock. Heat quickly; then cook, covered, 2 to 3 minutes over medium heat. Serve at once.

VARIATIONS: In step 2, add, with the celery, 4 to 6 dried black mushrooms (soaked), shredded.

In step 3, add, with the seasonings and stock, 1 slice fresh ginger root and 1 scallion stalk, both shredded.

After step 3, thicken the sauce with a paste made of 1 teaspoon cornstarch and 2 tablespoons cold water.

STIR-FRIED BEAN SPROUTS WITH TWO KINDS OF PEPPERS
About 4 servings

½ pound bean sprouts
2 green peppers
2 red chili peppers
1 slice fresh ginger root

2 tablespoons oil
½ teaspoon salt
¼ cup stock
¼ teaspoon sugar

1 teaspoon sherry

1. Blanch bean sprouts. Seed green and chili peppers; then cut in thin strips. Crush ginger root.

2. Heat oil. Add salt, then ginger, and stir-fry a few times. Add green and chili peppers; stir-fry 1 to 2 minutes. Add bean sprouts; stir-fry ½ minute more.

3. Add stock and heat quickly. Then cook, covered, 2 to 3 minutes over medium heat.

4. Stir in sugar and sherry. Serve at once.

STIR-FRIED BEAN SPROUTS AND PORK
About 6 servings

1 pound bean sprouts
½ cup lean pork
2 teaspoons cornstarch
2 teaspoons sherry
½ teaspoon sugar

¼ teaspoon salt
1 tablespoon soy sauce
1 tablespoon oil
2 tablespoons oil
¼ cup stock

¼ teaspoon salt

1. Blanch bean sprouts. Cut pork in matchstick-like strips.

2. Combine cornstarch, sherry, sugar, salt and soy sauce. Add to pork and toss to coat. Let stand 15 minutes, turning meat occasionally.

3. Heat oil. Add bean sprouts; stir-fry 1 to 2 minutes, then remove from pan.

4. Heat remaining oil. Add pork and stir-fry until it loses its pinkness (about 2 minutes).

5. Add stock and heat quickly. Then cook, covered, 2 to 3 minutes over medium heat.

6. Return bean sprouts, stir in only to reheat. Sprinkle with remaining salt and serve at once.

VARIATIONS: For the pork, substitute lean beef, chicken, duck or shrimp.

In step 3, add with the bean sprouts any of the following, slivered: bamboo shoots, celery, cucumbers or mushrooms.

BRAISED STUFFED BITTER MELON
About 8 servings

1 *tablespoon fermented black beans*	2 *teaspoons cornstarch*
½ *pound lean pork*	½ *teaspoon sugar*
¼ *cup Chinese parsley*	½ *teaspoon salt*
2 *scallion stalks*	*dash of pepper*
1 *garlic clove*	4 *medium bitter melons*
1 *tablespoon soy sauce*	4 *tablespoons oil*
1 *tablespoon oil*	½ *garlic clove*

½ *cup water*

1. Soak fermented black beans.
2. Mince pork, together with parsley, scallions and garlic. Then blend well with soy sauce, oil, cornstarch, sugar, salt and pepper.
3. Cut each bitter melon in 1½-inch slices. With a sharp knife, scoop out the spongy white pulp and seeds at the center of each slice.
4. Stuff pork mixture into centers, letting meat bulge out slightly (it will shrink during cooking).
5. Heat remaining oil. Brown bitter melon slices lightly on both sides; then remove from pan.
6. Mash soaked black beans; crush remaining garlic. Add to pan; add water, and bring to a boil, stirring.
7. Return stuffed bitter melon and bring to a boil again. Then simmer, covered, over medium heat, until done (about 20 minutes).

STEAMED STUFFED BITTER MELON
About 8 servings

1 *tablespoon fermented black beans*	1 *tablespoon soy sauce*
½ *pound lean pork*	1 *tablespoon sherry*
1 *garlic clove*	½ *teaspoon salt*

4 *medium bitter melons*

1. Soak fermented black beans.
2. Mince pork and garlic. Mash soaked beans and add to meat along with soy sauce, sherry and salt. Blend in well.
3. Cut bitter melons lengthwise in half. With a spoon, scoop out the seeds and spongy white pulp at the center. Stuff with meat mixture.
4. Arrange bitter melon, stuffing-side up, on a heatproof dish. Steam until done (about 30 minutes). See page 831.

VARIATION: For the pork stuffing, substitute ½ pound fish fillets, ½ teaspoon cornstarch, ½ teaspoon salt, ¼ teaspoon sugar and ⅛ cup water blended together.

CREAMED CHINESE CABBAGE
About 6 servings

1 to 1½ pounds Chinese cabbage	½ teaspoon salt
2 tablespoons cornstarch	1 cup stock
1 cup milk	4 tablespoons smoked ham
3 tablespoons chicken fat	dash of pepper

1. Cut Chinese cabbage stems diagonally in 2-inch sections. Stir cornstarch into milk to dissolve.

2. Heat chicken fat. Add Chinese cabbage and stir-fry 2 minutes.

3. Add salt and stock and bring to a boil. Then cook, covered, over medium heat until cabbage is softened (4 to 5 minutes).

4. Gradually stir in cornstarch mixture over low heat (the milk should not boil). Then simmer, covered, 3 to 5 minutes more, stirring once or twice.

5. Mince smoked ham. Sprinkle cabbage with pepper and ham. Serve hot.

NOTE: Unlike other Chinese vegetables, this one is better overcooked than undercooked. Although milk is not often used, its presence here enhances the vegetable's sweetness, freshness and delicacy.

VARIATIONS: For the Chinese cabbage, substitute Chinese lettuce, cut in 2-inch cubes or in strips ¼ inch wide and 2 inches long.

For the fresh milk, substitute ½ cup evaporated milk.

For the chicken fat, substitute oil or lard.

In step 3, add to the chicken fat 6 dried shrimp (soaked). Stir-fry 1 to 2 minutes; then add cabbage.

Omit the smoked ham. Garnish the cabbage instead with 4 fresh mushrooms, diced and stir-fried separately until cooked through.

STIR-FRIED CHINESE CABBAGE AND WHITE CHEESE
About 4 servings

1 pound Chinese cabbage	3 tablespoons oil
¾ cup water	1 to 2 tablespoons Chinese white cheese

1. Cut Chinese cabbage stems diagonally in 1½-inch sections. Bring water to a boil.

2. Heat oil. Add Chinese cheese to pan and mash. Add cabbage stems and stir-fry until cheese melts.

3. Stir in hot water and bring to a boil again. Then simmer, covered, 2 minutes more.

4. Stir cabbage and simmer, covered, again until done (1 to 2 minutes more). Serve at once.

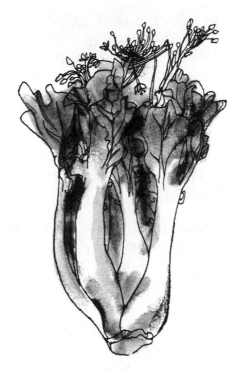

STIR-FRIED CHINESE CABBAGE AND DRIED SHRIMP

6 to 8 servings

8 *dried shrimp*	2 *tablespoons oil*
4 *dried black mushrooms*	½ *cup mushroom-soaking liquid*
1 *pound Chinese cabbage*	½ *teaspoon salt*
½ *cup bamboo shoots*	1 *teaspoon cornstarch*

2 tablespoons water

1. Separately soak dried shrimp and dried mushrooms. Reserve mushroom-soaking liquid.

2. Cut cabbage stems in 2-inch sections. Slice bamboo shoots and soaked mushrooms.

3. Heat oil. Add cabbage and stir-fry 1 minute. Add bamboo shoots; stir-fry 1 minute more.

4. Add soaked shrimp, mushrooms and mushroom liquid. Bring to a boil; then simmer, covered, 3 minutes.

5. Add salt. Stir mixture once again and simmer, covered, again until done (about 2 minutes more).

6. Meanwhile blend cornstarch and cold water to a paste. Then stir in to thicken, and serve at once.

BRAISED CHINESE LETTUCE AND CHESTNUTS
6 to 8 servings

2 or 3 *dried scallops*	1 *cup stock*
15 *chestnuts*	½ *teaspoon salt*
1 *pound Chinese lettuce*	1 *teaspoon cornstarch*
1 or 2 *tablespoons oil*	2 *tablespoons water*

1. Soak dried scallops.

2. Shell chestnuts. Cut Chinese lettuce in 2-inch cubes and blanch. Shred scallops.

3. Heat oil. Add lettuce and stir-fry to coat with oil.

4. Add stock, salt, scallops and chestnuts. Bring to a boil; then simmer, covered, until chestnuts are soft (about 20 minutes).

5. Blend cornstarch and cold water to a paste; then stir in to thicken. Serve hot in a deep bowl.

VARIATION: In step 3, add with the lettuce 5 dried mushrooms (soaked), sliced.

BRAISED CHINESE LETTUCE AND DRIED SHRIMP
6 to 8 servings

8 to 10 *dried shrimp*	2 *tablespoons oil*
4 *dried black mushrooms*	½ *teaspoon salt*
1 *pound Chinese lettuce*	1 *cup mushroom-soaking liquid*
6 *cups water*	2 *tablespoons soy sauce*

1 *teaspoon sugar*

1. Separately soak dried shrimp and dried mushrooms. Reserve mushroom-soaking liquid.

2. Cut lettuce in 2-inch cubes. Bring water to a boil. Blanch lettuce 1 to 2 minutes, then drain.

3. Heat oil. Add shrimp and stir-fry 2 minutes. Add lettuce; stir-fry to coat with oil. Then sprinkle with salt.

4. Add mushroom liquid. Bring to boil; then simmer, covered, 10 minutes.

5. Add soaked mushrooms, soy sauce and sugar. Simmer, covered, 10 minutes more.

VARIATIONS: In step 3, after stir-frying the lettuce, add ½ cup bamboo shoots, sliced; stir-fry 1 minute more. Then sprinkle with salt.

In step 5, also add 1 sweet red pepper, sliced or diced.

After step 5, thicken sauce with a cornstarch paste made of ½ tablespoon cornstarch and 2 tablespoons cold water.

STEAMED CHINESE LETTUCE I
4 to 6 servings

1 to 1½ pounds Chinese lettuce

1 tablespoon cornstarch

½ teaspoon salt

1½ cups stock

1. Separate lettuce leaves, and cut each in 4 sections. Place in a deep heatproof bowl.

2. Steam 15 minutes (see page 831).

3. In a saucepan, blend together cornstarch, salt and cold stock. Then cook, stirring, until mixture thickens. Pour over steamed lettuce and serve.

STEAMED CHINESE LETTUCE II
About 6 servings

4 to 6 dried shrimp

4 to 6 dried black mushrooms

1 pound Chinese lettuce

1 tablespoon smoked ham

½ teaspoon salt

½ cup mushroom-soaking liquid

1. Separately soak dried shrimp and dried mushrooms. Reserve mushroom-soaking liquid.

2. Cut Chinese lettuce in 2-inch cubes. Chop ham. Dice soaked mushrooms.

3. Arrange lettuce cubes on a shallow heatproof dish. Sprinkle with salt. Top with mushrooms, shrimp and ham. Then pour mushroom liquid over.

4. Steam until done (about 30 minutes). See page 831.

VARIATION: For the dried shrimp and mushrooms, substitute fresh shrimp and mushrooms. For the mushroom-soaking liquid, substitute stock.

SWEET-AND-PUNGENT MUSTARD CABBAGE
4 to 6 servings

1 pound mustard cabbage

3 sweet red peppers

1 garlic clove

2 tablespoons sugar

2 tablespoons vinegar

1 tablespoon soy sauce

½ teaspoon salt

1 teaspoon cornstarch

2 teaspoons water

2 tablespoons oil

1. Separate mustard cabbage leaves and cut each in 2-inch sections. Dice sweet red peppers. Crush garlic.

2. In one cup, combine sugar, vinegar, soy sauce and salt. In another, blend cornstarch and cold water to a paste.

3. Heat oil. Add garlic and peppers; stir-fry 2 minutes. Add cabbage and stir-fry 2 minutes more.

4. Add sugar-vinegar mixture; stir-fry another 2 minutes. Then stir in the cornstarch paste to thicken and serve at once.

NOTE: If the mustard cabbage is not tender, blanch it first.

MUSTARD CABBAGE AND MEAT SAUCE
4 to 6 servings

meat sauce	*1 teaspoon salt*
6 cups water	*1 pound mustard cabbage*

1. Prepare a meat sauce (see pages 729–730) and keep warm.

2. Bring water to a boil and add salt. Meanwhile, separate cabbage leaves and cut each in 2-inch sections.

3. Parboil cabbage until bright green and tender (about 3 minutes). Drain at once; then arrange on a serving platter.

4. Pour the meat sauce over and serve.

STIR-FRIED PRESERVED CABBAGE AND PEAS
6 to 8 servings

1 pound preserved cabbage	*2 tablespoons oil*
1 pound peas	*2 tablespoons soy sauce*

1. Separate preserved cabbage leaves. Rinse and squeeze dry; cut in 1½-inch sections. Shell and parboil peas.

2. Heat oil. Add peas and stir-fry to coat with oil. Add cabbage and soy sauce; stir-fry 2 to 3 minutes more. Serve at once.

STIR-FRIED SWEET-AND-PUNGENT PRESERVED CABBAGE
About 4 servings

1 pound preserved cabbage	*1 tablespoon cornstarch*
1 teaspoon cornstarch	*¼ cup water*
1 tablespoon sugar	*2 tablespoons oil*
1 tablespoon vinegar	*¼ cup water*

1. Rinse and cut cabbage as above.

2. In one cup, combine cornstarch, sugar and vinegar. In another cup, blend remaining cornstarch and cold water to a paste.

3. Heat oil. Add preserved cabbage and stir-fry to coat with oil.

4. Add remaining water and heat quickly. Then cook, covered, 2 to 3 minutes more over medium heat.

5. Stir in cornstarch-sugar mix to blend (1 to 2 minutes). Then stir in cornstarch paste to thicken. Serve at once.

DEEP-FRIED CARROT BALLS
About 4 servings

1 *pound carrots*	*water to cover*
2 *slices fresh ginger root*	½ *teaspoon salt*
1 *scallion stalk*	*oil for deep-frying*

1. Scrape carrots. Mince ginger root and scallion stalk.

2. Bring water to a boil. Add carrots and boil, uncovered, until soft but not mushy. Then drain and mash.

3. Blend in salt, ginger root and scallion. Form carrot mixture into walnut-size balls.

4. Heat oil. Deep-fry carrot balls, a few at a time, until golden. Drain on paper toweling.

5. Return carrot balls to oil; deep-fry ½ minute more. Drain quickly and serve.

STIR-FRIED CAULIFLOWER WITH MUSHROOMS AND WATER CHESTNUTS

About 4 servings

5 *dried black mushrooms*
1 *medium cauliflower*
6 *water chestnuts*
¼ *cup stock*
2 *tablespoons soy sauce*

1 *tablespoon sherry*
½ *cup mushroom-soaking liquid*
2 *tablespoons oil*
1 *teaspoon cornstarch*
2 *tablespoons water*

1. Soak dried mushrooms; reserve their soaking liquid.
2. Break cauliflower in flowerets; cut the stems in ½-inch slices; then parboil. Slice water chestnuts and soaked mushrooms.
3. Combine stock, soy sauce, sherry and mushroom liquid.
4. Heat oil. Add mushrooms and stir-fry to coat with oil. Add water chestnuts; stir-fry to coat with oil.

5. Stir in stock-soy mixture and heat quickly.

6. Add cauliflower and bring to a boil; then cook, covered, 2 minutes over medium heat.

7. Meanwhile blend cornstarch and cold water to a paste; then stir in to thicken. Serve at once.

STIR-FRIED CELERY AND MUSHROOMS
About 4 servings

2 cups celery

½ pound fresh mushrooms

1 tablespoon sherry

3 tablespoons oil or lard

¼ teaspoon salt

1. Trim off leaves and tough ends of celery. Cut stalks diagonally in 1½-inch sections. Slice fresh mushrooms.

2. Heat oil. Add celery and stir-fry 2 to 3 minutes.

3. Add mushrooms; stir-fry until they soften (about 2 minutes more).

4. Sprinkle with salt and sherry and stir in quickly. Serve at once.

NOTE: If the celery is not tender, blanch it first.

STIR-FRIED SESAME CUCUMBERS
About 4 servings

2 cucumbers

salt

1½ tablespoons sesame oil

¼ teaspoon sugar

1. Peel cucumbers and cut in half lengthwise. Scoop out seeds with a spoon; then cut crosswise in ½-inch slices.

2. Arrange slices on a flat plate and sprinkle well with salt. Let stand 1 hour; then squeeze each slice gently to press out as much moisture as possible.

3. Heat sesame oil. Add cucumbers and stir-fry until softened and translucent (1 to 2 minutes).

4. Then stir in sugar and serve at once.

NOTE: Because of their semicircular shape, these are sometimes called Cucumber Moon Slices.

SIMMERED CUCUMBERS AND SHRIMP
6 to 8 servings

3 large cucumbers

10 to 12 dried shrimp

2 cups water

½ teaspoon salt

1. Peel cucumbers. Cut in half lengthwise, then crosswise in 1½-inch slices.

2. Place in a saucepan with dried shrimp and water. Bring to a boil quickly.

Then simmer, covered, until done (about 30 minutes). Season with salt and serve.

VARIATION: After step 2, remove cucumber slices, leaving liquids in pan. Then blend 1 tablespoon cornstarch and 2 tablespoons cold water to a paste and stir in to thicken. Pour the sauce over the cucumbers and serve.

STUFFED CUCUMBERS I
About 8 servings

filling mixture
3 large cucumbers
flour
3 tablespoons oil

¾ cup stock
1 teaspoon soy sauce
3 tablespoons sherry
1 tablespoon cornstarch

3 tablespoons water

1. Prepare either of the filling mixtures on pages 608 and 609.

2. Peel cucumbers; then cut crosswise in 2-inch sections. Scoop out seeds from one side only of each section, not clear through.

3. Stuff the center of each section with filling, packing it in tightly and rounding out the edges. Dredge stuffed sections lightly with flour.

4. Heat oil. Add cucumber sections, stuffing-side down, and brown lightly. Turn over and cook 1 to 2 minutes more.

5. Add stock, soy sauce and sherry and bring to a boil. Then simmer, covered, until tender (about 20 minutes), turning once or twice for even cooking. Remove cucumbers to a serving platter, leaving liquids in pan.

6. Blend cornstarch and cold water to a paste; then stir in to thicken liquids. Pour sauce over stuffed cucumbers and serve.

STUFFED CUCUMBERS II
About 8 servings

filling mixture
3 large cucumbers
3 tablespoons cornstarch
1 tablespoon tomato sauce

¼ cup water
oil for deep-frying
½ cup water

1. Prepare either of the filling mixtures below.

2. Leave cucumbers unpeeled; or peel them lengthwise in alternating strips. (The latter are not only decorative, but help the cucumbers hold their shape after cooking.) Cut crosswise in 2-inch sections.

3. Scoop out seeds and stuff cucumbers with filling mixture as above, but do not dredge with flour.

4. Blend cornstarch and cold water to a paste and brush over stuffed cucumber sections to coat. Reserve remaining paste.

5. Heat oil to smoking. Add cucumber sections a few at a time; then reduce heat and deep-fry until pale golden. Drain on paper toweling.

6. Bring remaining water to a boil. Gently lower in cucumbers; then simmer, covered, 10 minutes over very low heat.

7. Remove cucumbers to a serving platter, leaving liquids in pan. Add reserved cornstarch paste and tomato sauce, and stir in to thicken. Pour sauce over cucumbers and serve.

VARIATIONS: For the tomato sauce, substitute soy sauce.

In step 6, top each stuffed cucumber section with either a mushroom cap or a 1-inch square of smoked ham.

TO SIMMER: *Omit steps 4 and 5. Place cucumber sections, stuffing-side up, in a pan with 1 cup water and ½ teaspoon salt. Bring to a boil; then simmer, covered, until done (30 to 40 minutes). Pick up step 7.*

TO STEAM: *Omit steps 4, 5 and 7. Arrange cucumber sections, stuffing-side up, on a heatproof platter. Steam on a rack 20 minutes (see pages 33 and 831). Season with salt and serve.*

CUCUMBER FILLING I

½ pound lean pork
1 egg
1 tablespoon cornstarch

1 tablespoon sherry
1 teaspoon soy sauce
½ teaspoon salt

1. Mince or grind pork. Beat egg and add.

2. Then add cornstarch, sherry, soy sauce and salt; blend well.

VARIATION: For the pork, substitute beef, chicken or shrimp.

CUCUMBER FILLING II

3 dried black mushrooms

½ pound lean pork

2 slices fresh ginger root

1 scallion stalk

1 tablespoon soy sauce

1 tablespoon sherry

1 teaspoon sugar

½ teaspoon salt

1 teaspoon oil

1. Soak dried mushrooms.

2. Mince or grind pork, together with ginger root, scallion and soaked mushrooms.

3. Then add remaining ingredients and blend in.

STIR-FRIED FRAGRANT EGGPLANT

About 6 servings

4 dried black mushrooms

1 tablespoon dried shrimp

½ cup cooked chicken

2 tablespoons smoked ham

1 cup bamboo shoots

2 walnuts

6 almonds

6 peanuts

1 eggplant

cornstarch

oil for deep-frying

2 tablespoons soy sauce

2 tablespoons sherry

½ teaspoon salt

¼ teaspoon sugar

2 tablespoons oil

1. Separately soak dried mushrooms and dried shrimp.

2. Dice cooked chicken, smoked ham, bamboo shoots, soaked mushrooms and shrimp.

3. Shell, blanch and coarsely chop walnuts and almonds. Halve the peanuts.

4. Peel eggplant and cut in ½-inch cubes. Then dredge lightly in cornstarch.

5. Heat oil and deep-fry eggplant cubes until golden. Drain on paper toweling.

6. Meanwhile combine soy sauce, sherry, salt and sugar in a cup.

7. Heat remaining oil. Add all diced ingredients. Stir-fry to heat through (about 2 minutes).

8. Return eggplant cubes. Add soy-sherry mixture and stir-fry 2 minutes more. Garnish with nutmeats and serve.

BRAISED EGGPLANT
About 4 servings

1 eggplant	1 cup stock
1 or 2 cloves garlic	2 tablespoons soy sauce
3 tablespoons oil or lard	½ teaspoon salt

1. Peel eggplant; cut lengthwise in quarters, then crosswise in 1-inch sections. Crush garlic.

2. Heat oil. Add garlic; stir-fry a few times. Add eggplant and stir-fry gently to coat with oil (1 to 2 minutes).

3. Add stock, soy sauce and salt and bring to a boil. Then simmer, covered, until done (10 to 15 minutes).

NOTE: Overcooking makes eggplant mushy. It's at its best when soft on the outside, but still firm inside.

VARIATIONS: After step 2, add 1 tablespoon shrimp sauce and stir-fry 1 minute more. Then pick up step 3, omit the soy sauce and salt.

In step 3, add 2 tablespoons of dried shrimp (which have been simmered 10 minutes in 1 cup of water). Then, during the last 5 minutes of cooking, add the soy sauce and salt. (The shrimp water may be substituted for the stock.)

BRAISED EGGPLANT WITH BACON AND TOMATOES
6 to 8 servings

6 bacon strips	1 to 2 garlic cloves
4 tomatoes	¼ teaspoon salt
1 eggplant	dash of pepper

1. Cut bacon strips in 2-inch sections. Peel and quarter tomatoes. Peel eggplant and cut in 1-inch cubes. Crush garlic.

2. Place bacon in a cold pan; then heat and brown lightly. (Do not pour off fat.) Add garlic and stir-fry a few times.

3. Add eggplant cubes; stir-fry gently to coat with bacon fat. Then reduce heat to medium and cook, covered, until eggplant begins to soften (about 5 minutes), stirring once or twice.

4. Gently stir in tomatoes. Reduce heat to low and cook, covered, until eggplant is done (about 5 minutes more). Season with salt and pepper and serve.

VARIATION: Increase the garlic cloves to 6.

STEAMED EGGPLANT
About 4 servings

1 eggplant	½ teaspoon salt
1 tablespoon soy sauce	few drops of peanut oil

1. Wash eggplant. Score its skin with a few lengthwise slashes about ½-inch deep. Place on a heatproof dish.

2. Steam until done (15 to 20 minutes). See page 831.

3. Let cool slightly; then strip off skin and tear eggplant lengthwise in shreds.

4. Add soy sauce, salt and peanut oil and blend in. Serve hot or cold.

NOTE: Tearing the cooked eggplant gives it a more interesting texture than chopping or mincing does.

VARIATIONS: For the peanut oil, substitute sesame oil.

In step 4, also add 1 or 2 slices fresh ginger root and ½ clove garlic, both minced.

After step 4, arrange eggplant shreds on a serving dish radiating out like flower petals. Leave a space in the center about 3 inches in diameter and fill this with stirred or scrambled eggs, cooked and then broken in small pieces. (For the egg mixture, use 2 eggs, beaten; 2 scallion stalks, minced; 2 teaspoons soy sauce and ½ teaspoon sugar.)

STEAMED STUFFED EGGPLANT
6 to 8 servings

filling for eggplant	1 eggplant

1. Prepare either of the fillings below.

2. Wash eggplant. Cut in half lengthwise and scoop out seeds. Stuff filling into bottom half of eggplant and cover with top half.

3. Place on a heatproof dish. Then steam until done (about 30 minutes). See page 831.

4. Cut eggplant crosswise, through stuffing, in ½- to 1-inch slices, and serve.

VARIATIONS: *To cut*—Cut a 1½-inch slice from each end of the eggplant, reserving the slices. With a sharp knife or apple corer, hollow out the eggplant's center about 1 inch in diameter. Then stuff with filling and replace the end slices, fastening them with toothpicks. After steaming, cut crosswise as in step 4.

To simmer—After step 2, boil 1½ cups water. Add eggplant and simmer, covered, 45 minutes, turning several times for even cooking. Remove eggplant; slice and keep warm. Then add to liquids in pan 1 egg yolk, beaten; ½ teaspoon salt and a dash of pepper. Cook, stirring, until sauce thickens. Pour sauce over eggplant and serve.

EGGPLANT FILLING I

½ pound lean pork	*½ teaspoon salt*
dash of pepper	

1. Mince or grind pork.
2. Combine with salt and pepper.

EGGPLANT FILLING II

8 dried black mushrooms	*2 tablespoons soy sauce*
½ pound lean pork	*1 tablespoon sherry*
1 scallion stalk	*½ teaspoon salt*
1 slice fresh ginger root	*½ teaspoon sugar*

1. Soak dried mushrooms.
2. Mince or grind pork. Mince scallion, ginger and soaked mushrooms; combine with pork.
3. Blend in remaining ingredients.

VARIATION: For the dried black mushrooms, substitute 10 water chestnuts.

DEEP-FRIED STUFFED LOTUS ROOT
About 8 servings

filling for lotus root	*½ cup water*
2 pounds lotus root	*½ cup flour*
1 egg	*¼ teaspoon salt*
oil for deep frying	

1. Prepare the filling below and let it cool slightly.
2. Peel lotus root and cut in ⅛-inch slices.

3. Spread filling evenly over one slice; then cover, sandwich-style, with a second slice. Repeat until done.

4. Beat egg together with water; then blend in flour and salt to make a batter. Dip lotus root "sandwiches" in batter to coat. Let dry a few minutes; then dip in batter again.

5. Heat oil; add "sandwiches" a few at a time, and deep-fry until golden. Drain on paper toweling and serve.

VARIATIONS: In step 2, cut the lotus root in ¼-inch slices; then cut each slice in half, but not clear through. Stuff the filling between the still-joined halves; then press the edges together.

In step 4, make the batter with 2 eggs, beaten; 2 tablespoons cornstarch and 2 tablespoons flour.

FILLING FOR LOTUS ROOT

1 cup lean pork
1 cup onion
1 slice fresh ginger root

1 to 2 tablespoons oil
2 tablespoons soy sauce
¼ teaspoon salt

1. Mince or grind pork. Chop onion. Mince ginger root.

2. Heat oil. Add onion and stir-fry a few times until translucent. Add pork; stir-fry until it loses its pinkness (about 2 minutes).

3. Remove pan from heat. Stir in soy sauce, salt and minced ginger root to blend.

VARIATION: Reduce pork to ½ cup. In step 3, add, along with the other ingredients, 1 cup tightly packed spinach, parboiled and chopped fine.

STIR-FRIED DRIED MUSHROOMS WITH SNOW PEAS AND BAMBOO SHOOTS
About 4 servings

1 cup dried black mushrooms	½ teaspoon salt
1 cup bamboo shoots	2 tablespoons oil
¼ pound snow peas	2 tablespoons soy sauce
2 tablespoons oil	½ teaspoon sugar

¼ cup stock

1. Soak dried mushrooms.
2. Slice bamboo shoots and soaked mushrooms. Stem snow peas.
3. Heat oil. Add salt, then snow peas, and stir-fry until bright green (less than 1 minute). Remove from pan.
4. Heat remaining oil. Add mushrooms and bamboo shoots; stir-fry to coat with oil (about 1 minute).
5. Add soy sauce, sugar and stock and heat quickly. Then simmer, covered, 3 minutes.
6. Return snow peas and stir-fry only to reheat. Serve at once.

VARIATIONS: In step 4, first stir-fry briefly 1 garlic clove and 1 slice fresh ginger root, both minced. Then add the mushrooms and bamboo shoots.

In step 4, also add 1 cup celery, ½ cup water chestnuts and 2 tablespoons cloud ear mushroom (soaked), all sliced. Stir-fry 2 to 3 minutes with the mushrooms and bamboo shoots. In step 5, increase the stock to ½ cup.

STEAMED DRIED MUSHROOMS
6 to 8 servings

20 to 24 dried black mushrooms	1 cup mushroom-soaking liquid
3 cups stock	2 tablespoons chicken fat

1 teaspoon sugar

1. Soak dried mushrooms; reserve their soaking liquid.
2. Stem mushrooms and arrange caps in a heatproof bowl. Pour stock and mushroom liquid over. Add chicken fat and sugar.
3. Steam 1½ hours (see page 831). Serve hot right in the steaming bowl.

SIMMERED STUFFED GREEN PEPPERS

4 to 6 servings

stuffing for peppers
4 green peppers
½ cup stock
½ teaspoon salt

dash of pepper
1 tablespoon cornstarch
1 tablespoon soy sauce
¼ cup water

1. Prepare any of the stuffing mixtures below.

2. With a sharp knife, cut the tops off peppers; then scoop out the seeds. Stuff peppers with filling mixture; replace the tops as lids.

3. Stand stuffed peppers upright in a pan. Add stock, salt and pepper. Bring to a boil, then simmer, covered, 1 hour.

4. Remove peppers, leaving liquids in pan. Then blend cornstarch, soy sauce and cold water to a paste and stir in to thicken liquids. Pour sauce over peppers and serve.

VARIATION: After step 2, place peppers upright in a heatproof bowl and steam 45 minutes. (See page 831.) Omit steps 3, 4 and 5.

PORK STUFFING FOR GREEN PEPPERS

¾ pound lean pork ½ teaspoon salt
2 scallion stalks ¼ teaspoon pepper
1 tablespoon soy sauce 1 teaspoon oil

1. Mince pork and scallion stalks.
2. Blend in the remaining ingredients.

VARIATIONS: Reduce the pork to ½ pound. Add 1 slice smoked ham and 4 water chestnuts, both minced, 1 teaspoon sugar and 1 teaspoon cornstarch. Or add to the pork instead, the following, all minced: ½ cup fillet of sole, ¼ cup crabmeat, 4 dried black mushrooms (soaked), and 1 scallion stalk, all minced. (In either case, omit the pepper and oil.)

FISH STUFFING FOR GREEN PEPPERS

¾ pound fish fillets 1 tablespoon oil
1 scallion stalk 2 tablespoons water
2 teaspoons cornstarch ½ teaspoon salt
dash of pepper

1. Flake fish. Mince scallion stalk.
2. Blend in the remaining ingredients.

NOTE: Use haddock or halibut.

VARIATION: Reduce fish fillets to ½ pound. Add ¼ pound shrimp, shelled, deveined, and minced.

VEGETABLE STUFFING FOR GREEN PEPPERS

1 cup carrots 3 tablespoons catsup
1 cup onions 1 teaspoon sugar
2 tablespoons oil ½ teaspoon salt
dash of pepper

1. Shred carrots and onions.
2. Heat oil. Add carrots and onions and stir-fry to soften slightly (about 2 minutes). Then combine with the remaining ingredients.

DEEP-FRIED POTATOES AND CARROTS
4 to 6 servings

3 *dried black mushrooms*	½ *teaspoon salt*
1 *carrot*	1 *tablespoon sherry*
1 *pound potatoes*	½ *cup stock*
cornstarch	1 *teaspoon cornstarch*
oil for deep-frying	½ *teaspoon sugar*
2 *tablespoons oil*	1 *teaspoon soy sauce*

1 tablespoon water

1. Soak dried mushrooms.
2. Dice carrots and parboil. Dice soaked mushrooms. Peel and slice potatoes as for french-fries; then parboil and drain well. Dredge potatoes lightly in cornstarch.
3. Heat oil and deep-fry potato strips until golden. Drain on paper toweling.
4. Heat remaining oil. Add salt, then carrots and mushrooms; stir-fry to coat with oil.
5. Add sherry and stock and heat quickly. Then cook, covered, 2 to 3 minutes over medium heat.
6. Meanwhile, blend remaining cornstarch to a paste with sugar, soy sauce and water. Then stir in to thicken. Add deep-fried potatoes; stir in only to reheat. Serve at once.

VARIATION: After step 5, for color, add 1 tablespoon green peas, parboiled.

STIR-FRIED SNOW PEAS WITH MUSHROOMS
6 to 8 servings

15 to 20 *dried black mushrooms*	2 *tablespoons oil*
½ *pound snow peas*	1½ *cups stock*
4 *scallion stalks*	½ *cup mushroom-soaking liquid*
1 or 2 *slices fresh ginger root*	1 *teaspoon cornstarch*
1 *teaspoon cornstarch*	2 *tablespoons water*
1 *teaspoon sugar*	2 to 3 *tablespoons oyster sauce*
½ *teaspoon salt*	1½ *tablespoons oil*
½ *teaspoon soy sauce*	¼ *teaspoon salt*

1. Soak dried mushrooms; reserve their soaking liquid.
2. Stem, string and blanch snow peas. Cut scallion stalks in 1-inch lengths. Shred ginger root.

3. Combine cornstarch, sugar, salt and soy sauce. Add to mushrooms and toss to coat.

4. Heat oil. Add mushrooms and stir-fry 2 minutes. Add scallions and ginger root; stir-fry 2 minutes more.

5. Add stock and mushroom liquid and bring to a boil; then simmer, covered, 10 minutes.

6. Meanwhile blend remaining cornstarch and cold water to a paste. Then stir in to thicken. Stir in oyster sauce to blend and remove pan from heat.

7. Heat remaining oil in another pan. Add remaining salt, then snow peas, and stir-fry 1 minute. Transfer to a serving platter. Pour mushroom mixture over and serve at once.

STIR-FRIED SNOW PEAS WITH PORK, MUSHROOMS AND BAMBOO SHOOTS
About 4 servings

3 dried black mushrooms
½ pound snow peas
¼ cup lean pork
½ cup bamboo shoots
2 tablespoons oil

¼ cup stock
1 tablespoon cornstarch
pinch of sugar
¼ cup water
1 teaspoon soy sauce

1. Soak dried mushrooms.

2. Stem and string snow peas. Slice pork thin. Slice bamboo shoots and soaked mushrooms.

3. Heat oil. Add pork and stir-fry until it loses its pinkness (2 to 3 minutes).

4. Add mushrooms and stir-fry to coat with oil. Then add bamboo shoots; then snow peas, stir-frying each briefly.

5. Add stock and heat quickly. Then cook, covered, 3 minutes over medium heat.

6. Meanwhile blend cornstarch, sugar and cold water to a paste. First sprinkle vegetables with soy sauce; then stir in cornstarch paste to thicken. Serve at once.

VARIATION: For the pork, substitute white meat chicken.

STIR-FRIED SPINACH AND WHITE CHEESE
About 4 servings

1 pound spinach
1 garlic clove
1 tablespoon Chinese white cheese
½ teaspoon salt

2 tablespoons water
½ teaspoon sugar
3 tablespoons peanut oil

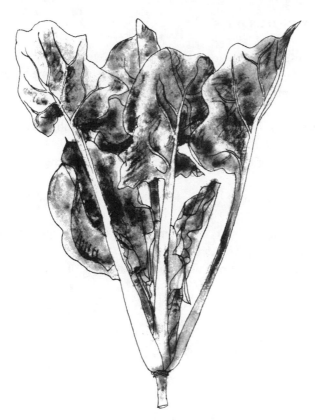

1. Wash and stem spinach; cut leaves in half. Crush garlic.

2. Mash Chinese white cheese; then blend to a paste with water and sugar.

3. Heat oil. Add salt, then garlic, and stir-fry to brown lightly. Add spinach; stir-fry 1 minute.

4. Stir in white cheese mixture and cook, covered, over medium heat, until spinach begins to soften (1 to 2 minutes more).

5. Uncover pan and stir-fry spinach another ½ minute over high heat. Serve at once.

VARIATION: For the spinach, substitute either lettuce or water cress. Omit the garlic.

STIR-FRIED SPINACH AND MUSHROOMS
About 6 servings

12 to 14 dried black mushrooms	*2 or 3 tablespoons oil*
1 pound spinach	*½ cup mushroom-soaking liquid*
4 tablespoons soy sauce	*1 tablespoon cornstarch*
1 tablespoon sherry	*1 tablespoon water*
1 teaspoon sugar	*1½ tablespoons oil*
¼ teaspoon salt	*½ teaspoon salt*

1. Soak dried mushrooms; reserve their soaking liquid.

2. Stem and wash spinach; shake off excess moisture. Leave soaked mushrooms whole if small; cut in half if large.

3. Combine soy sauce, sherry, sugar and salt.

4. Heat oil. Add mushrooms and stir-fry 2 minutes. Stir in soy-sherry mixture to blend.

5. Add mushroom liquid and heat quickly. Then cook, covered, about 10 minutes over medium heat.

6. Blend cornstarch and cold water to a paste. Then stir in to thicken. Keep warm.

7. Heat remaining oil in another pan. Add remaining salt, then spinach; stir-fry until bright green and softened (about 2 minutes).

8. Transfer spinach to a serving dish. Pour mushrooms and their sauce over. Serve at once.

SPINACH AND PEANUTS
4 to 6 servings

2 tablespoons raw peanuts
oil
¼ cup smoked ham

6 cups water
1 pound spinach
½ teaspoon salt

1 tablespoon oil

1. Toast peanuts quickly in a small amount of oil; then chop coarsely. Mince smoked ham. Meanwhile boil water.

2. Wash and stem spinach. Pour boiling water over and let stand 2 to 3 minutes. Then drain. Chop spinach and drain again.

3. Add peanuts, half the ham, salt and remaining oil; toss well to blend.

4. Transfer spinach mixture to a serving dish. Garnish with remaining smoked ham and serve.

VARIATION: In step 3, also add a few drops of sesame oil and either 2 tablespoons vinegar or ½ teaspoon powdered mustard.

STIR-FRIED STRING BEANS AND WHITE CHEESE
About 4 servings

1 pound string beans
1 garlic clove
1 tablespoon Chinese white cheese
½ teaspoon salt

½ cup stock
¼ teaspoon sugar
2 tablespoons oil

1. Stem string beans; cut or break in 1½-inch sections, and parboil. Crush garlic.

2. Blend Chinese white cheese with cold stock and sugar.

3. Heat oil. Add salt, then garlic and brown lightly. Add string beans and stir-fry to coat with oil.

4. Stir in and heat white cheese mixture; then cook, covered, 2 to 3 minutes over medium heat. Serve at once.

VARIATIONS: For the string beans, substitute broccoli or cauliflower, parboiled; or else celery or mustard cabbage, blanched.

In step 2, add to the white cheese mixture 1 teaspoon soy sauce, 2 teaspoons sherry, 2 teaspoons white cheese liquid from jar, and 1 slice fresh ginger root, minced.

BRAISED SQUASH WITH FISH
8 to 10 servings

fish mixture
2 to 3 pounds Chinese squash
3 to 4 tablespoons oil
2 tablespoons soy sauce

1 tablespoon sherry
¾ cup water
½ teaspoon salt
Chinese parsley

1. Prepare the fish mixture below.

2. Cut squash in ¾-inch slices and spread each evenly with the fish mixture.

3. Heat oil. Add squash, fish-side down, and brown lightly over medium heat.

4. Meanwhile combine soy sauce, sherry, water and salt. Add to pan and bring to a boil. Then simmer, covered, until squash is tender (20 to 30 minutes). Garnish with Chinese parsley and serve.

VARIATION: In step 3, instead of pan-frying squash, deep-fry, fish-side up, basting with hot oil until golden. Then pick up step 4.

FISH MIXTURE FOR SQUASH

¾ to 1 pound fish fillets
1 teaspoon cornstarch

1 teaspoon salt
½ teaspoon sugar

2 tablespoons water

1. Mince fish.

2. Blend in the remaining ingredients.

VARIATION: Add to minced fish 6 almonds, blanched and chopped; 2 tablespoons smoked ham, and 1 scallion stalk, both minced.

BRAISED TURNIPS WITH MEAT SAUCE

About 4 servings

1 *pound Chinese white turnips*	1 *teaspoon sugar*
1 *scallion stalk*	2 *tablespoons oil*
2 *tablespoons pork gravy*	½ *cup stock*
2 *tablespoons soy sauce*	*dash of pepper*

1. Peel turnips; cut in ½-inch cubes.
2. Mince scallion; then combine with pork gravy, soy sauce and sugar.
3. Heat oil. Add turnips and stir-fry 2 minutes.
4. Add stock and heat quickly. Then cook, covered, 5 minutes over medium heat.
5. Add scallion-gravy mixture and simmer 5 minutes more. Sprinkle with pepper and serve.

NOTE: The sauce from any red-cooked pork or beef dish can be used for the gravy.

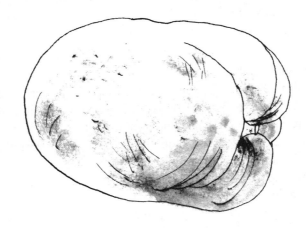

DEEP-FRIED SIMMERED WINTER MELON

4 to 6 servings

5 *dried black mushrooms*	2 *tablespoons oyster sauce*
1 *pound wedge of winter melon*	2 *teaspoons cornstarch*
2 *tablespoons smoked ham*	2 *teaspoons water*
oil for deep-frying	½ *teaspoon salt*
½ *cup stock*	½ *teaspoon sugar*

dash of pepper

1. Soak dried mushrooms.

2. Peel and seed winter melon wedge; then cut crosswise in half. Cut soaked mushrooms in half. Shred ham.

3. Heat oil and separately deep-fry each winter melon section until golden. Drain on paper toweling. Let cool; then cut in ¾-inch sections.

4. Bring stock to a boil. Add winter melon and soaked mushrooms; simmer, covered, 10 minutes. Then stir in oyster sauce to blend.

5. Transfer melon and mushrooms to a serving platter, leaving liquids in pan. Blend cornstarch, cold water, salt, sugar and pepper to a paste; then stir in to thicken liquids. Pour sauce over melon and mushrooms. Garnish with shredded ham and serve.

BASIC BUDDHIST VEGETABLE DISH
8 to 10 servings

9 *to 12 vegetables, nuts, etc.*	1 *tablespoon cornstarch*
1 *to 2 cups water*	*pinch of sugar*
3 *tablespoons soy sauce*	3 *tablespoons water*
1 *teaspoon sherry*	1 *teaspoon soy sauce*
½ *teaspoon salt*	½ *teaspoon salt*
4 *tablespoons oil*	*few drops of sesame oil*

1. Select 9 to 12 of the ingredients listed below, choosing some from each category: dried, fresh and miscellaneous. (Although less typical, as few as 4 or 5 ingredients may be used.) Prepare each ingredient, as indicated below.

2. Combine water, soy sauce, sherry and salt.

3. Heat oil. Add selected ingredients, and stir-fry 3 to 5 minutes. (This will take a large pan. If one is not available, cook 3 or 4 ingredients at a time, then assemble them in step 5 and reheat before adding cornstarch paste.)

4. Add water-soy mixture and heat quickly; then simmer, covered, until vegetables are tender (about 15 minutes).

5. Blend cornstarch and sugar to a paste with remaining cold water, soy sauce and salt; then stir in to thicken. Sprinkle vegetable mixture with sesame oil; stir in and serve.

NOTE: This vegetarian dish is known as the Feast of Arahats or Food for the Saints; the Chinese name is Lo (or Loo) Hon Ji, or Lohan Tsai. It will keep about a week and can be reheated several times without loss of flavor.

VARIATION: In step 4, stir 2 tablespoons Chinese red cheese, mashed, into the water-soy mixture; then heat quickly.

DRIED INGREDIENTS FOR BUDDHIST VEGETABLE DISH

⅛ *pound rice or peastarch noodles (soaked), cut in 3-inch lengths*

½ *cup lily buds (soaked)*

½ *cup dried black mushrooms (soaked), cut in half*

2 *tablespoons cloud ear mushrooms (soaked)*

½ *cup hair seaweed (soaked)*

½ *cup dried bamboo shoots (soaked), cut in 2-inch lengths*

¼ *cup dried chestnuts (parboiled)*

3 *sticks dried bean curd, broken in 2-inch lengths and soaked; or 1 or 2 sheets dried bean curd (soaked), cut in squares or rectangles*

2 *pieces dried lotus root (soaked)*

FRESH INGREDIENTS FOR BUDDHIST VEGETABLE DISH

½ *cup celery, shredded*

½ *cup green pepper, shredded*

½ *cup mushrooms, shredded*

½ *cup mustard cabbage, shredded*

½ *cup onion, shredded*

½ *cup bean sprouts, blanched*

½ *cup cauliflower, broken in small flowerets*

½ *cup Chinese cabbage, cut in 2-inch sections*

½ cup snow peas, stemmed
1 cup winter melon, diced
1 cup zucchini, cut in 2-inch slices

MISCELLANEOUS INGREDIENTS FOR BUDDHIST VEGETABLE DISH
1 cup canned bamboo shoots, shredded
½ cup ginkgo nuts or lotus seeds, shelled and blanched
½ cup raw peanuts
5 cakes bean curd, deep-fried
½ cup vegetable steak

FOOD OF THE FOREST
6 to 8 servings

1 cup dried black mushrooms	3 tablespoons oil
2 tablespoons cloud ear mushrooms	3 tablespoons stock
½ cup lily buds	1 tablespoon soy sauce
¾ cup chestnuts	3 tablespoons oil
½ pound asparagus	½ teaspoon salt
2 cups bamboo shoots	1 teaspoon oil
2 slices fresh ginger root	1 teaspoon soy sauce

1 teaspoon sugar

1. Separately soak dried black mushrooms, cloud ear mushrooms and lily buds.

2. Blanch and shell chestnuts. Cut soaked mushrooms in half if large.

3. Discard tough ends of asparagus; cut stalks in 1½-inch sections. Cut bamboo shoots in matchstick-like strips; sliver ginger root.

4. Heat oil. Add ginger root and stir-fry a few times. Add black mushrooms and chestnuts; stir-fry 2 minutes. Add cloud ear mushrooms; stir-fry a few times to coat with oil.

5. Add stock and soy sauce; then cook, uncovered, 10 minutes over medium heat, stirring frequently. Remove ingredients from pan.

6. Heat the second quantity of oil. Add asparagus and bamboo shoots and stir-fry 2 to 3 minutes. Stir in salt; then remove vegetables from pan.

7. Heat remaining oil. Add lily buds; stir-fry 2 minutes. Then stir in remaining soy sauce.

8. Return mushrooms and chestnuts to pan and cook, covered, 5 minutes over medium heat, stirring occasionally.

9. Return asparagus and bamboo shoots. Sprinkle with sugar and stir-fry only to reheat. Serve at once.

NOTE: To keep the ingredients from drying out in step 5, add more stock as needed, 1 tablespoon at a time.

SOFT IMMORTAL FOOD
About 8 servings

¼ cup peastarch noodles	2 tablespoons Chinese red bean cheese
2 cups dried black mushrooms	water to cover
4 bean curd sticks	2 tablespoons cornstarch
12 cakes bean curd	2 teaspoons soy sauce
	¼ cup water

1. Separately soak peastarch noodles and dried mushrooms. Break bean curd sticks in 3-inch lengths and also soak.

2. Cut each bean curd cake in 4 parts. Cut soaked peastarch noodles in 3-inch lengths. Cut mushrooms in half, if large.

3. Place noodles, mushrooms and the dried and fresh bean curd in a saucepan. Mash red bean cheese and add, along with water. Bring to a boil; then simmer, covered, 1 hour.

4. Blend cornstarch, soy sauce and remaining cold water to a paste. Then stir in to thicken and serve.

HARD IMMORTAL FOOD
About 8 servings

2 cups ginkgo nuts	4 tablespoons oil
2 cups winter melon	2 tablespoons Chinese red cheese
12 cakes bean curd	2 cups water

1. Shell and blanch ginkgo nuts. Peel and cube winter melon. Cut each bean curd cake in 4 parts.

2. Heat oil. Add ginkgo nuts, melon and bean curd and stir-fry gently 3 minutes (or else shake or tilt the pan to avoid breaking the bean curd).

3. Mash red cheese and add, along with water. Bring to a boil; then simmer, covered, 1 hour, and serve.

THREE WINTERS
About 4 servings

½ cup dried black mushrooms	2 tablespoons sesame oil
¼ cup dried salt cabbage	1 tablespoon soy sauce
1 cup bamboo shoots	¼ cup stock

1. Separately soak dried mushrooms and salt cabbage.

2. Slice bamboo shoots. Cut mushrooms in half if large. Shred soaked cabbage.

3. Heat sesame oil. Add bamboo shoots and stir-fry 2 to 3 minutes.

4. Add mushrooms and cabbage; stir-fry 2 minutes more. Sprinkle with soy sauce.

5. Add stock and heat quickly. Then simmer, covered, 5 minutes over medium heat, and serve.

Noodle and Rice Dishes

NOODLES

Noodles are the primary staple of northern China and the secondary staple of the South. Many varieties are used: among them a wheat-flour noodle that's firm but delicate, smooth yet chewy. (This noodle, now known as spaghetti, was introduced to the West by Marco Polo when he returned to Italy from the Orient, late in the thirteenth century.) Other types of noodle, ranging from fine and thin to coarse and thick, include the egg, peastarch and rice-flour varieties. Egg noodles are used in soups and many other dishes, as are the delicate peastarch noodles. Rice-flour noodles, favored in the provinces of the South, are often combined with such subtle ingredients as oysters, lily buds and cloud ear mushrooms. The thin and fine rice-flour noodles can also be deep-fried and used as a crisp garnish to set off foods that are soft and creamy in texture.

Chinese noodles are distinguished not only by their constituents but by the way they're prepared. The noodles can be cooked, mixed, blended and combined with just about every variety of meat, seafood and vegetable. They can be added to soup, either alone, or with various toppings. They can be soft-fried in oil, or tossed and cooked through with other ingredients. They can be made into noodle nests or noodle pancakes and topped with various mixtures. They can also be braised, deep-fried or prepared with various sauces. In short, noodles can be served in countless ways: as a side dish, a snack, a garnish or a whole meal.

Noodles in Soup: Most suitable for soup are the egg and peastarch varieties. These are usually added to clear, light soups, although there are exceptions. (Noodles are sometimes served in thick, pungent hot-sour soups.) Noodles should never be cold when added to soup: they will reduce its temperature too much. They should be either freshly cooked or else briefly reheated. Various meat and vegetable toppings can also be added. Some toppings are cooked directly in the soup; others are stir-fried separately and added with the noodles at the very end.

Noodles in Sauce: Noodles, being bland, combine well with various sauces. The noodles and sauce are always cooked separately and then combined either during the last few minutes of cooking or just before serving. Noodles in sauce are usually served as a side dish, but the addition of more substantial ingredients (such as shredded meat and poultry, shrimp, oysters, eggs and vegetables) can convert that dish into a teatime snack or late supper. Noodles in sauce, when made with the gravy of a red-cooked dish, can also be converted to noodles in soup by adding two-thirds water to one-third gravy.

Soft-fried Noodles: Soft-frying calls for parboiled noodles to be reheated in a small amount of oil and tossed—but not very vigorously—by a process that might be described as a cross between stir-frying and pan-frying. The noodles are then combined with various meats and vegetables. (The combination, for example, of noodles, pork, oysters, dried black and cloud ear mushrooms makes for a devastatingly subtle interpenetration of tastes.) When large quantities of noodles are to be soft-fried, they can be managed more easily if divided into smaller portions and rolled up like shredded wheat biscuits.

Crisp-fried Noodles: Crisp or deep-fried egg noodles are southern in origin and served frequently in Chinese-American restaurants as a garnish for soup, or as a topping for various stir-fried mixtures. (The latter is known as Chow Mein to most Westerners. The authentic version of Chow Mein, however, calls for soft-fried, *not* deep-fried crisp noodles.) The deep-fried variety may be prepared at home (see page 827) and will keep about a month, if stored in tightly covered jars. Crisp noodles may also be purchased ready-cooked in vacuum-packed tins.

Quantities of Noodles: The amount of noodles per serving depends on whether the noodles will be a main dish, snack or soup ingredient. For soup,

1 pound of noodles to 6 cups of stock should be enough for 6 to 8 people. For other noodle dishes, about ¼ pound per person should be allowed. NOTE: These quantities are for dried noodles, which produce about 5 cups of cooked noodles per pound. Fresh noodles produce half the amount, or about 2½ cups cooked per pound. (The latter, which are pliable and perishable like homemade noodles, can be purchased in Chinese grocery stores.)

Specific Noodle Dishes: Wo Mein or Wor Mein consists of fine egg noodles and soup, garnished with various bits of meat and vegetables and served in a large tureen. (At banquets it's served as the first course and garnished with shreds of smoked ham.) The restaurant version may include slivers of chicken, pork, ham, shrimp, bamboo shoots, sliced mushrooms, snow peas and mustard cabbage.

Yakko Mein or Yetcamein refers to "an order of noodles" and is actually a one-dish meal. The noodles, served in large individual soup bowls, are topped generously with sliced meats and vegetables, and then a rich, tasty broth is poured over all.

Chow Mein, or "fried noodles," is a casual dish which calls for parboiled noodles (previously drained dry and chilled) to be cooked with other ingredients, somewhat in the manner of fried rice; that is, the noodles and other ingredients are fried separately, then combined and cooked briefly together just before serving. The noodles are soft-fried first in oil, then removed from the pan. Next, the various meats and vegetables are stir-fried separately until nearly done. (These, used in various combinations, include: pork, beef, chicken, duck, ham, shrimp and such vegetables as bamboo shoots, bean sprouts, celery, Chinese cabbage, Chinese lettuce, cucumber, mushrooms, scallions, spinach and water chestnuts.) The soft-fried noodles are then returned at the end only to reheat and blend flavors.

Lo Mein means "tossed or mixed noodles" and calls for parboiled noodles (also previously drained dry and chilled) to be added, not to the hot oil and soft-fried as in Chow Mein, but directly to the meat and vegetable combinations, which have already been stir-fried. These noodles, tossed or mixed and heated through with the cooked combinations, are moister, having more of a sauce than the Chow Mein.

Preparing Noodles in Advance: Since many recipes call for chilled, parboiled noodles, these can be prepared in advance and refrigerated until needed. Parboiled noodles will keep for several days when drained well, tossed in a small quantity of oil—about a tablespoon (to keep them from sticking together)—and stored in a tightly covered container or plastic bag.

RICE

Rice, in addition to being boiled or steamed (see pages 59–61), can be combined with various toppings, prepared as fried rice, or made into a soup called congee.

When fully cooked, rice can be mixed with stir-fried meat and vegetable combinations; (these are added to the rice just before serving). When partially cooked, rice can be topped with ingredients such as raw cut-up chicken, meat and seafood, and cooked with them until all are done. (The steam rising from the rice will actually cook these raw ingredients.)

Fried rice, which originated in Yangchow province, is a versatile dish which combines cooked rice, onions, soy sauce, sometimes eggs, and just about any other ingredient—leftover or fresh—that may be on hand. The ingredient that predominates gives the dish its name: chicken fried rice, roast pork fried rice, shrimp fried rice, etc. When many ingredients are included, the dish is called subgum—or "many varieties"—fried rice.

The starting point for fried rice is cold cooked rice, preferably cooked the day before and refrigerated, so that it becomes firm and grainy and will not stick or become soft when stir-fried. If there is no cold cooked rice on hand, boiled rice can be prepared and broken up while still hot. The rice should then be left to cool for several hours. As long as it's quite cool, it needn't be chilled. It should never, under any circumstances, be rinsed in cold water to speed up the cooling. All of its flavor will be washed way. NOTE: When rice is prepared especially for fried rice, it can be boiled in half-stock and half-water to enrich its flavor.

Since fried rice is essentially a dish of leftovers, many of its ingredients, being already cooked and moist, should be drained well before they are added, to keep the rice from getting soggy. (If the rice becomes too dry, however, small amounts of such drained liquids, stock, leftover gravies or oil can be added at the very end.) Since the finished dish is reasonably dry and aromatic, it goes particularly well with light and simple soups, and the combination makes a good lunch or light supper. The restaurant convention of ordering a dish of fried rice with numerous other "main" courses, or ordering it in place of white rice, is Western and not at all Chinese.

Fried rice, prepared a few hours in advance, can be kept warm in a slow oven. Leftover fried rice will keep several days, if covered tightly and refrigerated. Fried rice can also be frozen and then reheated in the oven without preliminary thawing.

Rice soup or congee is a dish of equal versatility. (It's also known as soft rice or rice gruel. The Chinese call it "jook.") Congee is prepared by simmering a small quantity of rice in a large quantity of water until a smooth creamy broth is formed. Depending on the proportion of rice to water, congee can range from a thin, delicate gruel to a semi-solid porridge. Any type of rice is suitable: long-grain, oval-grain or glutinous. These can be used alone or in combination (glutinous added to long-grain rice makes the congee thicker and stickier). The rice can also be used raw or cooked. Even the seemingly unusable rice crusts, which form at the bottom of boiled rice, can be simmered in water to make this dish.

Congee is eaten for breakfast, lunch, supper and just about any other time of day as a snack. It may be prepared plain or cooked with additional ingredients. The plain congee is never eaten alone but accompanied by various side dishes to contrast with its blandness. For breakfast, it's accompanied by salty and pickled side dishes, designed to wake up the early-morning palate.

These side dishes can include hardboiled eggs, served with soy sauce; salt eggs; preserved eggs; eggs stirred with preserved minced turnips; fried salted fish; salted radishes; salted peanuts; small amounts of red or white bean cheese; savory Chinese sausages; pickled vegetables and pickled ginger. (The contrast between the thin wateriness of the congee and these spicy and stimulating foods provides a refreshing taste of sweetness to the mouth.) Westerners, accustomed to blander breakfasts, may find these combinations too pungent for early-morning tastes and prefer them for lunch or evening snacks instead.

The basic blandness of rice makes it possible to cook congee with just about any meat, poultry and fish, as well as with the bones of pork and chicken, the carcass of roast duck, etc. All these combinations produce dishes which are nutritious and highly digestible. Some of the ingredients used (such as dried shrimp, dried scallops and dried tangerine peel) are added at the start of cooking. Others (such as slices of raw fish or squid) are added at the very end. The latter, when dropped into boiling congee, need a minute or less to cook through. Raw meat or poultry, when cut up fine, also cooks very quickly.

Congee, whatever its ingredients, is always served piping hot, garnished with a bit of green such as minced scallion or Chinese parsley, and seasoned with a few drops of soy sauce. A raw egg is sometimes stirred in at the very end to make it richer. Congee, if refrigerated, will keep for several days (if it becomes thickened and heavy, it can be thinned simply by adding more water when reheating the congee on the top of the stove.)

NOODLE DISHES

PARBOILED NOODLES I
About 4 servings

8 *to* 10 *cups water*　　　　　　　　1 *pound noodles*
1½ *teaspoons salt*　　　　　　　　*peanut or sesame oil*

1. Bring water to a rolling boil. Add salt; then gradually add noodles to keep the water boiling vigorously.

2. Stir noodles from the bottom from time to time and cook until barely done. (Noodles should never be cooked until mushy: the outside should be tender while the inside is still firm and hard. Test for doneness by cutting or biting into a single strand.)

3. Drain noodles in a colander. Rinse at once under cold running water. (Unless this is done, the noodles will continue cooking in their own heat. Rinsing

also keeps the noodles from sticking together because it washes off the excess starch. However, noodles, unlike rice, are never washed before cooking to remove the starch, but *after*.) Drain again.

4. Separate the noodles with a fork. Spread them loosely on a flat plate or tray and mix well with a little peanut or sesame oil. Set aside until needed or keep warm in the top of a double boiler. The noodles can also be reheated by rinsing them in hot water, after they've been rinsed in cold. Use in any noodle recipe.

NOTE: The cooking time depends on the noodles themselves—whether they're egg or wheat-flour, whether they're dried or fresh; whether they're thick or thin. It also depends on how much additional cooking they will get with other ingredients. As a rule, allow 6 to 8 minutes for dried noodles; 4 to 5 minutes for fresh.

PARBOILED NOODLES II
About 4 servings

8 to 10 cups water	1 pound noodles
1½ teaspoons salt	2 cups water

1. Bring water to a rolling boil. Add salt; then drop noodles into water all at once. Bring water to boil again. Add 1 cup cold water.

2. Bring to a boil again. Add a second cup of cold water. Bring to a boil once more. Then pick up steps 3 and 4 above.

STEAMED DRIED NOODLES
About 4 servings

8 to 10 cups water	1½ teaspoons salt
1 pound noodles	

1. Bring water to a rolling boil. Add salt, then noodles; stir once or twice. Remove noodles and drain.

2. Spread noodles out in a large colander. Place colander in a pot containing several inches of boiling water. Cover pot and steam 20 minutes. (See page 831.) Use in any noodle recipe.

NOTE: Use the thinnest variety of dried egg noodles for this recipe.

STEAMED FRESH NOODLES
About 4 servings

2½ cups fresh noodles	1 tablespoon peanut oil

1. Place noodles in a colander. Add oil and toss. Spread noodles out.

2. Place colander in a pot containing several inches of boiling water. Cover pot and steam 10 to 15 minutes (see page 831). Let cool. Use in any noodle recipe.

VARIATIONS: For the peanut oil, substitute 1 teaspoon sesame oil.

For the colander, substitute a flat tray. Place on a rack over boiling water and steam as in step 2.

BASIC NOODLES IN SOUP I
About 4 servings

½ pound egg noodles
6 cups stock
1 scallion

½ teaspoon salt
dash of pepper
2 teaspoons soy sauce

1 tablespoon sherry

1. Parboil noodles as on page 635 or 636.

2. Bring stock to a boil. Stir in noodles, then bring to a boil again. Simmer to heat through (about 2 minutes). Meanwhile mince scallion.

3. Stir salt, pepper, soy sauce and sherry into stock. Sprinkle with scallion and serve at once.

NOTE: Never add noodles to soup until just about ready to serve. If added too far in advance, noodles tend to get mushy.

VARIATIONS: In step 2, *before* adding the noodles, add 1 cup raw chicken, shredded; and/or ½ cup bamboo shoots, cut in strips. Simmer, covered, 10 minutes.

In step 2, *after* adding the noodles, add 1 cup cooked chicken or pork, diced; or 1 cup cooked vegetables, diced. Simmer only to heat through.

For the parboiled egg noodles, substitute ½ pound peastarch noodles (soaked); and 1 cup spinach, shredded. In step 2, simmer both only to heat through.

BASIC NOODLES IN SOUP II
About 6 servings

topping for soup
½ pound egg noodles
2 teaspoons soy sauce

1 teaspoon peanut oil
few drops of sesame oil
⅛ teaspoon pepper

6 cups stock

1. Prepare any of the simple or stir-fried toppings suggested below.

2. Parboil noodles as on page 635 or 636.

3. Place noodles in a bowl. Add soy sauce, peanut oil, sesame oil and pepper, and toss well. Keep noodles warm. Meanwhile bring stock to a boil.

4. Transfer noodles to a large tureen or to individual soup bowls. Arrange topping over noodles; then pour heated stock over and serve at once.

NOTE: When stir-fried toppings are used, the stock is added *first* in step 4, then the topping.

VARIATIONS: Leave the noodles unseasoned. Season the stock instead with ½ teaspoon salt and the pepper.

After step 2, brown the noodles in a little oil before placing them in soup bowls. Season lightly with salt and pepper.

SIMPLE TOPPINGS FOR BASIC NOODLES IN SOUP II

4 scallions, shredded and/or 4 hardboiled eggs, shelled and cut in quarters
½ pound preserved cabbage, rinsed and shredded
¼ cup each of cooked chicken, cooked pork and ham, all shredded
¼ cup each of roast chicken and duck, both shredded
½ cup smoked ham, shredded
1 cup cooked chicken, shredded or cut in strips

NOTE: The cooked meat may be reheated (before it is arranged over the noodles) simply by placing it in a sieve and dipping it briefly in the hot stock.

STIR-FRIED CHICKEN TOPPING I
FOR BASIC NOODLES IN SOUP II

1 cup white meat chicken	½ teaspoon salt
1 cup fresh mushrooms	½ cup stock
½ cup water chestnuts	2 teaspoons cornstarch
2 tablespoons oil	2 tablespoons water

1. Slice chicken, fresh mushrooms and water chestnuts.

2. Heat oil. Add salt, then chicken, and stir-fry until chicken loses its pinkness (about 2 minutes).

3. Add mushrooms and water chestnuts; stir-fry until mushrooms begin to soften (about 1 minute more).

4. Add stock and heat quickly. Then simmer, covered, 3 to 4 minutes over medium heat.

5. Meanwhile blend cornstarch and cold water to a paste; then stir in to thicken chicken mixture. Arrange as a topping over noodles in soup and serve.

VARIATIONS: For the water chestnuts, substitute bamboo shoots.

After step 3, sprinkle the chicken and vegetables with 1 to 2 teaspoons soy sauce.

In step 5, add to the cornstarch paste 1 to 2 teaspoons soy sauce, ¼ teaspoon salt, ¼ teaspoon sugar and a dash of pepper.

STIR-FRIED CHICKEN TOPPING II
FOR BASIC NOODLES IN SOUP II

4 dried black mushrooms	½ cup bamboo shoots
1 cup white meat chicken	½ pound spinach
1 tablespoon soy sauce	2 slices smoked ham
¼ teaspoon sugar	2 tablespoons oil
¼ teaspoon salt	¼ teaspoon salt
dash of pepper	2 teaspoons soy sauce

1. Soak dried mushrooms.

2. Slice chicken. Combine soy sauce, sugar, salt and pepper. Add to chicken and toss to coat.

3. Slice bamboo shoots and soaked mushrooms. Shred spinach and mince ham.

4. Heat oil. Add remaining salt, then chicken and stir-fry until it loses its pinkness (about 2 minutes).

5. Add bamboo shoots, mushrooms and spinach; stir-fry 2 minutes more. Sprinkle with remaining soy sauce.

6. Arrange mixture as a topping over noodles in soup. Garnish with minced ham and serve.

VARIATIONS: For the chicken, substitute shelled and deveined shrimp.

For the spinach, substitute 2 tablespoons cloud ear mushrooms (soaked), sliced; and ¼ cup lily buds (soaked), cut in two.

STIR-FRIED COOKED CHICKEN TOPPING I
FOR BASIC NOODLES IN SOUP II

2 or 3 dried black mushrooms	2 tablespoons oil
1 cup cooked chicken	½ cup stock
¼ cup smoked ham	½ teaspoon salt
2 cups Chinese cabbage	1 tablespoon cornstarch

2 tablespoons water

1. Soak dried mushrooms.

2. Slice cooked chicken and soaked mushrooms. Shred ham and Chinese cabbage.

3. Heat oil. Add cabbage and stir-fry to soften (about 3 minutes).

4. Add chicken, ham and mushrooms; stir-fry ½ minute more. Add stock and salt and heat quickly.

5. Meanwhile blend cornstarch and cold water to a paste; then stir in to thicken mixture. Arrange as a topping over noodles in soup and serve.

STIR-FRIED COOKED CHICKEN TOPPING II
FOR BASIC NOODLES IN SOUP II

1 cup cooked chicken	¼ cup water chestnuts
1 or 2 eggs	¼ cup bamboo shoots
¼ cup smoked ham	2 slices fresh ginger root
1 cup Chinese lettuce	2 to 3 tablespoons oil
1 cup string beans	1 cup stock
1 cup celery	1 tablespoon cornstarch
½ cup canned mushrooms	1 tablespoon soy sauce
½ cup onion	½ teaspoon sugar

2 tablespoons water

1. Slice cooked chicken. Hardboil, shell and slice eggs. Dice ham.

2. Slice Chinese lettuce, string beans, celery, mushrooms, onion, water chestnuts and bamboo shoots. Shred ginger root.

3. Heat oil. Add ginger root and stir-fry a few times. Add all vegetables; stir-fry about 3 minutes.

4. Add stock and heat quickly. Cook, covered, over medium heat until vegetables are done (5 to 7 minutes). Then stir in cooked chicken and ham only to heat through.

5. Meanwhile blend cornstarch, soy sauce, sugar and cold water to a paste; then stir in to thicken mixture. Arrange as a topping over noodles in soup. Garnish with egg slices and serve.

VARIATION: For the chicken, substitute cooked pork, beef, shrimp or lobster.

STIR-FRIED PORK AND SPINACH TOPPING
FOR BASIC NOODLES IN SOUP II

½ pound lean pork
1 leek stalk

½ pound spinach
2 tablespoons oil

1. Shred pork and leek. Stem spinach and cut leaves in half.
2. Heat oil. Add pork and stir-fry until it loses its pinkness (1 to 2 minutes).
3. Add leek and spinach; stir-fry 1 minute more.
4. Arrange mixture as a topping over noodles in soup and serve.

VARIATION: For the spinach, substitute 2 cups Chinese lettuce, cut in 2-inch sections and stir-fry in step 3 until softened. (You may also add, with the Chinese lettuce, ½ cup bamboo shoots, sliced, and ½ cup canned button mushrooms.)

NOODLES IN SOUP WITH CHICKEN
About 6 servings

¼ *pound egg noodles*	½ *cup canned button mushrooms*
½ *pound white meat chicken*	6 *cups stock*
1 *cup bamboo shoots*	½ *teaspoon salt*
¼ *pound peas*	2 *teaspoons cornstarch*

2 tablespoons water

1. Parboil noodles as on page 635 or 636 and keep warm.
2. Dice chicken and bamboo shoots. Shell peas. Drain canned mushrooms.
3. Bring stock to a boil. Add salt, chicken and vegetables; cook, covered, 5 minutes over medium-low heat.
4. Blend cornstarch and cold water to a paste; then stir into soup to thicken.
5. Transfer noodles to a large tureen or to individual soup bowls. Pour thickened soup over and serve.

NOODLES IN SOUP WITH CHICKEN AND HAM
About 6 servings

¼ *pound egg noodles*	6 *cups stock*
¼ *pound white meat chicken*	2 *scallion stalks*
⅛ *pound smoked ham*	2 *slices fresh ginger root*

½ *teaspoon salt*

1. Parboil noodles as on page 635 or 636 and keep warm.
2. Place unsliced chicken and ham in a pan with stock. Bring to a boil; then simmer, covered, 15 minutes. Remove chicken and ham; cut in 2-inch strips and keep warm.
3. Cut scallion stalks in ½-inch sections; mince ginger root. Add both to soup, along with salt, and bring to a boil again.
4. Transfer noodles to individual bowls and pour soup over. Top with chicken and ham strips and serve.

VARIATION: At the end of step 2, reheat the noodles briefly in the soup; then transfer them to individual bowls. Top with chicken and ham strips; garnish with minced ginger root and scallions. Then pour the hot soup over and serve.

NOODLES IN SOUP WITH CHICKEN AND VEGETABLES
About 6 servings

5 *dried black mushrooms*	½ *pound Chinese lettuce*
¼ *pound egg noodles*	6 *cups stock*
1 *cup cooked chicken*	½ *teaspoon salt*

½ *teaspoon soy sauce*

1. Soak dried mushrooms.
2. Parboil noodles as on page 635 or 636.
3. Slice chicken, lettuce and soaked mushrooms.
4. Bring stock to a boil. Add mushrooms and lettuce; then simmer, covered, until softened (3 to 4 minutes).
5. Add chicken, noodles and salt; cook only to heat through. Sprinkle with soy sauce and serve.

NOODLES IN SOUP WITH HAM AND OYSTERS
About 6 servings

¼ pound egg noodles   *1 slice fresh ginger root*
2 slices smoked ham   *2 scallion stalks*
12 medium oysters   *6 cups stock*

½ teaspoon salt

1. Parboil noodles as on page 635 or 636.
2. Cut ham in strips. Shell oysters. Mince ginger root and scallions.
3. Bring stock to a boil. Add ham strips; simmer, covered, 5 minutes.
4. Add oysters, ginger root and salt. Then simmer, covered, about 5 minutes more.
5. Add noodles and scallions; cook only to heat through.

NOODLES IN SOUP WITH PORK
About 6 servings

4 dried black mushrooms   *¼ pound Chinese cabbage*
¼ pound egg noodles   *6 cups stock*
1 cup pork   *1 teaspoon soy sauce*
½ cup bamboo shoots   *½ teaspoon salt*
¼ cup water chestnuts   *dash of pepper*

few drops of sesame oil

1. Soak dried mushrooms.

2. Parboil noodles as on page 635 or 636.

3. Slice pork thin; also bamboo shoots, water chestnuts and soaked mushrooms. Cut Chinese cabbage stems lengthwise in ½- by 1½-inch strips.

4. Bring stock to a boil. Add pork and vegetables and bring to a boil again; then simmer, covered, 5 minutes.

5. Add noodles and cook only to reheat. Then stir in soy sauce, salt, pepper and sesame oil and serve.

NOODLES IN SOUP WITH ROAST PORK I
About 6 servings

¼ pound egg noodles	1 to 2 scallion stalks
¼ pound roast pork	few sprigs of Chinese parsley
2 cups Chinese cabbage	6 cups stock

1. Parboil noodles as on page 635 or 636 and keep warm.

2. Shred roast pork. Slice Chinese cabbage. Mince scallions and Chinese parsley.

3. Bring stock to a boil. Add cabbage and cook, uncovered, over medium heat until tender but still crisp.

4. Transfer noodles to individual bowls and top with pork shreds. Pour soup and cabbage over. Garnish with scallions and parsley and serve.

NOODLES IN SOUP WITH ROAST PORK II
About 6 servings

¼ pound egg noodles	¼ pound preserved cabbage
¼ pound roast pork	½ cup cooked shrimp

6 cups stock

1. Parboil noodles as on page 635 or 636 and keep warm.

2. Shred roast pork. Rinse preserved cabbage; then squeeze dry and shred.

3. Bring stock to a boil. Add pork, cabbage and shrimp; cook only to heat through.

4. Transfer noodles to a large tureen or to individual soup bowls. Pour soup and its ingredients over noodles and serve.

PARBOILED NOODLES WITH SIMMERED CHICKEN BREAST
About 4 servings

3 or 4 *dried black mushrooms*
½ *pound noodles*
1 *chicken breast*
½ *cup bamboo shoots*

1 *cup stock*
1 *or 2 scallions*
¼ *teaspoon salt*
dash of pepper

few drops of sesame oil

1. Soak dried mushrooms.
2. Parboil noodles as on page 635 or 636 and keep warm.
3. Bone and skin chicken breast. Slice chicken thin; also bamboo shoots and soaked mushrooms.
4. Place chicken and vegetables in a pan; add stock and bring to a boil. Then simmer, covered, 3 minutes. Meanwhile cut scallions in 1-inch sections; transfer noodles to a serving dish.
5. Season chicken mixture with salt and pepper; then pour over noodles. Sprinkle with sesame oil, garnish with scallions, and serve.

PARBOILED NOODLES WITH STIR-FRIED COOKED
CHICKEN TOPPING I
4 to 6 servings

½ to 1 *pound noodles*
½ to 1 *cup cooked chicken*
2 *cups bean sprouts*
½ *cup scallion stalks*

1 *garlic clove*
2 to 3 *tablespoons oil*
½ *teaspoon salt*
dash of pepper

1. Parboil noodles as on page 635 or 636 and keep warm.
2. Dice or shred cooked chicken. Blanch bean sprouts. Cut scallion stalks in 1-inch sections. Mince garlic.
3. Heat oil. Add scallions and stir-fry until translucent. Add chicken; stir-fry briefly to heat.
4. Add garlic, bean sprouts, salt and pepper; stir-fry 2 minutes more. Pour mixture over noodles and serve.

VARIATIONS: In step 3, after stir-frying the scallions, add to the pan 1 cup Chinese cabbage and 1 cup celery; cut in 1½-inch sections and stir-fry 1 minute to coat with oil. Then cook, covered, 2 minutes more. Next, add the chicken and stir-fry; then pick up step 4.

In step 4, add with the bean sprouts ½ cup bamboo shoots and 4 dried black mushrooms (soaked), both shredded. After stir-frying, sprinkle with 1 tablespoon soy sauce and blend in. Then pour mixture over noodles.

PARBOILED NOODLES WITH STIR-FRIED COOKED CHICKEN TOPPING II

About 6 servings

½ to 1 pound noodles
½ to 1 cup cooked chicken
½ pound Chinese cabbage
¼ cup celery
2 onions

½ cup bean sprouts
2 to 3 tablespoons oil
1 cup stock
2 teaspoons cornstarch
2 tablespoons water

1. Parboil noodles as on page 635 or 636 and keep warm.

2. Slice or dice cooked chicken, Chinese cabbage, celery and onions. Blanch bean sprouts.

3. Heat oil. Add all vegetables and stir-fry to coat with oil (about 1 minute). Add stock and heat quickly; then cook, covered, 3 minutes over medium heat.

4. Add chicken to vegetables and stir in to heat through. Meanwhile blend cornstarch and cold water to a paste; then stir in to thicken. Pour mixture over noodles and serve.

VARIATIONS: For the onions, substitute ½ cup canned button mushrooms.

In step 4, add with the chicken 1 tomato, peeled and diced.

In step 4, after the sauce thickens, stir in 1 cup canned pineapple, diced, only to heat through.

Before serving, garnish chicken topping with ¼ cup almond meats, blanched and toasted.

PARBOILED NOODLES WITH STIR-FRIED CRABMEAT TOPPING
About 6 servings

½ to 1 pound noodles	3 tablespoons water
1 pound crabmeat	2 to 3 tablespoons oil or lard
4 slices fresh ginger root	½ teaspoon salt
2 scallion stalks	1 to 2 tablespoons sherry
1 tablespoon cornstarch	vinegar

1. Parboil noodles as on page 635 or 636 and keep warm.

2. Pick over and flake crabmeat. Slice ginger root. Cut scallion stalks in ½-inch sections. Blend cornstarch and cold water to a paste.

3. Heat oil. Add scallions and ginger root; stir-fry a few times. Add crabmeat, salt and sherry and stir-fry to heat through (about 2 minutes).

4. Stir in cornstarch paste to thicken; then pour crabmeat mixture over noodles. Serve, either sprinkled with vinegar to taste, or with a dip dish of vinegar on the side.

SOFT-FRIED NOODLES
About 4 servings

4 to 6 cups parboiled noodles	4 tablespoons oil
1 teaspoon peanut oil	salt

1. Parboil noodles as on page 635 or 636; then toss in oil. Refrigerate to chill (2 hours or more).

2. Heat remaining oil very hot. Add noodles and, with chopsticks or a wooden fork, gently separate the strands so they can heat through evenly. Then reduce heat and stir noodles gently. (You may also cover the pan briefly to heat the noodles in their own steam.)

3. After a minute or two, turn noodles over and repeat the process, stirring often. (The noodles are done when heated through, lightly browned and crisp on the outside, but still soft inside.)

4. Sprinkle noodles with salt to taste and mix well. Combine as indicated, with any of the stir-fried mixtures which follow on pages 649–654. Then top with any of the garnishes listed on page 655.

NOTE: Use either wheat-flour or egg noodles. If, during soft-frying, the noodles seem to be sticking, add more oil, pouring it down the sides of the pan, not on the noodles themselves. If the noodles seem to be getting hard and dry, sprinkle with a little water. (Peastarch noodles may also be used. These are not parboiled but soaked first in boiling water to soften, then immersed in cold water for 5 minutes and drained.)

VARIATIONS: In step 1, instead of parboiling the noodles, steam them.

For the peanut oil in step 1, substitute sesame oil or use the two in combination.

In step 2, soft-fry the noodles briefly; then sprinkle lightly with soy sauce, and finish reheating in just enough stock to moisten.

In step 3, sprinkle the noodles with either 1½ tablespoons soy or oyster sauce; then blend in lightly until absorbed.

After step 4, either sprinkle the noodles with vinegar to taste, or serve with a dip dish of catsup mixed with vinegar.

SOFT-FRIED NOODLES (OR CHOW MEIN) I

1. Soft-fry the noodles as above. Place in a large serving dish and keep warm.
2. Prepare any of the stir-fried mixtures on pages 649–654.
3. Pour the stir-fried mixture over the noodles and serve.

SOFT-FRIED NOODLES (OR CHOW MEIN) II

1. Soft-fry the noodles as above. Set them aside.
2. Prepare any of the stir-fried mixtures on pages 649–654. Remove half the stir-fried mixture from the pan and set aside.
3. Return noodles to pan and mix gently with remaining mixture. Then return the other half of the stir-fried mixture; gently blend in with the noodles and serve.

SOFT-FRIED NOODLES (OR CHOW MEIN) III

1. Prepare any of the stir-fried mixtures on pages 649–654. Remove from pan and keep warm.
2. Soft-fry the noodles as above. Then return about ¾ of the stir-fried mixture and stir in gently to blend with the noodles (about 2 minutes).
3. Add 2 tablespoons stock and heat, gently stirring noodles once or twice. Then turn the noodles onto a serving platter and top with the remaining stir-fried mixture. Sprinkle lightly with sherry and serve.

TOSSED NOODLES (OR LO MEIN) I

1. Prepare any of the stir-fried mixtures on pages 649–654.

2. Add the parboiled noodles (see page 635 or 636); toss gently with the stir-fried mixture to blend and heat through; then serve.

TOSSED NOODLES (OR LO MEIN) II

1. Prepare any of the stir-fried mixtures on pages 649–654. Then remove the mixture but leave its liquids in the pan.

2. Add the parboiled noodles (see page 635) and toss gently to heat. (If the noodles seem too dry, add 1 tablespoon oil, pouring it down the sides of the pan.)

3. Return the stir-fried mixture, blend in well with the noodles, then serve.

TOSSED NOODLES (OR LO MEIN) III

1. Prepare any of the stir-fried mixtures on pages 649–654; leave it in the pan. Then add ¼ cup stock and heat.

2. Arrange the parboiled noodles (see page 635) over the top of the stir-fried mixture. Cover pan and cook 2 minutes over medium heat.

3. Sprinkle the noodles with ½ teaspoon sugar and 1½ tablespoons of either soy or oyster sauce; then blend in well and serve.

STIR-FRIED PORK MIXTURE
FOR CHOW MEIN OR LO MEIN

4 to 5 dried black mushrooms	*2 tablespoons oil*
½ pound lean pork	*¼ teaspoon salt*
3 celery stalks	*2 tablespoons soy sauce*
1 onion	*1 teaspoon sugar*
2 or 3 scallion stalks	*½ cup stock*

1. Soak dried mushrooms.

2. Slice pork thin or cut in strips. Slice celery, onion and soaked mushrooms. Cut scallion stalks in 1-inch sections.

3. Heat oil. Add salt, then scallions, and stir-fry until translucent. Add pork; stir-fry until it loses its pinkness (2 to 3 minutes). Then sprinkle with soy sauce and sugar and blend in.

4. Add celery, onion and mushrooms; stir-fry 2 minutes more.

5. Add stock and heat quickly. Cook, covered, another 2 to 3 minutes over medium heat. Then combine with soft-fried or tossed noodles, as indicated above.

VARIATIONS: Shred the pork and vegetables. Omit the stock and additional cooking in step 5.

In step 2, dredge the pork in a mixture of 1 tablespoon cornstarch and 1 tablespoon soy sauce. Omit the soy sauce at the end of step 3.

At the end of step 3, also blend in 1 tablespoon sherry.

In step 4, add with the other vegetables 1 cup Chinese cabbage stems, sliced; and/or 4 water chestnuts, sliced.

After step 4, add 4 snow peas, cut in half.

Omit the soy sauce in step 3. After step 4, add a mixture of 1 tablespoon soy sauce, 2 tablespoons sherry, 2 slices fresh ginger root, minced, and a few drops of sesame oil. Continue stir-frying until pork is cooked through and vegetables are done. Omit step 5.

STIR-FRIED ROAST PORK MIXTURE I
FOR CHOW MEIN OR LO MEIN

1 cup roast pork	2 tablespoons oil
2 cups bean sprouts	1 tablespoon oil
1 cup Chinese cabbage	½ teaspoon salt

2 teaspoons sherry

1. Slice roast pork. Blanch bean sprouts. Cut Chinese cabbage in 1-inch sections.

2. Heat oil. Add vegetables and stir-fry to soften (2 to 3 minutes); then remove from pan.

3. Heat remaining oil. Add roast pork, salt and sherry; stir-fry ½ minute. Return vegetables and stir-fry only to reheat. Then combine with soft-fried or tossed noodles, as indicated on pages 648–649.

STIR-FRIED ROAST PORK MIXTURE II
FOR CHOW MEIN OR LO MEIN

4 or 5 dried black mushrooms	6 snow peas
1 cup roast pork	2 slices fresh ginger root
½ cup celery	1 garlic clove
1 cup Chinese cabbage	2 to 3 tablespoons oil
½ cup bamboo shoots	1 tablespoon sherry
½ cup bean sprouts	½ cup stock

1. Soak dried mushrooms.

2. Slice roast pork, celery, Chinese cabbage and bamboo shoots. Blanch bean

sprouts. Stem snow peas. Shred ginger root and crush garlic.

3. Heat oil. Add ginger root and garlic; stir-fry to brown lightly. Add pork and stir-fry a few times. Then stir in sherry to blend.

4. Add all vegetables except snow peas, and stir-fry 1 minute more.

5. Add stock and heat quickly. Then cook, covered, 3 minutes over medium heat. Stir in snow peas. Combine mixture with soft-fried or tossed noodles, as indicated on pages 648–649.

VARIATIONS: For the roast pork, substitute cooked beef, ham, chicken, duck, crabmeat, lobster or shrimp.

In step 3, add with the garlic and ginger root 2 scallion stalks, cut in ½-inch sections.

When using the mixture as a topping, as in Soft-Fried Noodles I, thicken at the end of step 5 with a paste made of 1 tablespoon cornstarch, 1 tablespoon cold water, 3 tablespoons soy sauce and ½ teaspoon sugar.

STIR-FRIED SHRIMP MIXTURE I
FOR CHOW MEIN OR LO MEIN

4 to 6 dried black mushrooms	*1 tablespoon sherry*
½ pound shrimp	*1 cup Chinese cabbage*
1 or 2 slices fresh ginger root	*1 cup bamboo shoots*
1 tablespoon cornstarch	*2 tablespoons oil*
2 tablespoons soy sauce	*2 tablespoons oil*

½ teaspoon salt

1. Soak dried mushrooms.

2. Shell, devein and dice shrimp. Mince ginger root; then combine with cornstarch, soy sauce and sherry. Add to shrimp and toss to coat.

3. Slice Chinese cabbage, bamboo shoots and soaked mushrooms.

4. Heat oil. Add shrimp and stir-fry until pinkish (about 2 minutes); then remove from pan.

5. Heat remaining oil. Add salt, then sliced vegetables and stir-fry to coat with oil. Cover pan and cook 2 minutes over medium heat. (The vegetables will cook in their own steam.) Then stir-fry vegetables a few times.

6. Return shrimp, stir-frying only to blend in and reheat. Then combine mixture with soft-fried or tossed noodles, as indicated on pages 648–649.

VARIATION: For the Chinese cabbage, substitute 2 celery stalks, blanched and sliced; and 6 snow peas, stemmed.

STIR-FRIED SHRIMP MIXTURE II
FOR CHOW MEIN OR LO MEIN

½ pound shrimp
1 tablespoon cornstarch
½ teaspoon salt
dash of pepper

½ pound zucchini
2 tablespoons oil
1 tablespoon sherry
1 tablespoon oil

1 tablespoon soy sauce

1. Shell, devein and dice shrimp. Sprinkle with cornstarch, salt and pepper, then toss to coat. Cut zucchini in ¼-inch slices.

2. Heat oil. Add shrimp and stir-fry until pinkish. Sprinkle with sherry, then stir-fry until sherry evaporates. Remove shrimp from pan.

3. Heat remaining oil. Add zucchini and stir-fry a few times. Then sprinkle with soy sauce and stir-fry until zucchini softens.

4. Return shrimp, stir-frying only to blend in and reheat. Then combine mixture with soft-fried or tossed noodles, as indicated on pages 648–649.

VARIATION: For the zucchini, substitute broccoli, broken in flowerets and parboiled.

STIR-FRIED PORK AND SHRIMP MIXTURE I
FOR CHOW MEIN OR LO MEIN

½ pound shrimp
1 tablespoon cornstarch
½ pound lean pork
½ pound spinach

2 scallion stalks
2 tablespoons oil
1½ tablespoons soy sauce
1 tablespoon sherry

dash of pepper

1. Shell, devein and dice shrimp; then dredge lightly in cornstarch. Sliver pork, or cut in strips. Wash and stem spinach. Mince scallions.

2. Heat oil. Add scallions and stir-fry a few times until translucent. Add pork; stir-fry until it loses its pinkness (2 to 3 minutes). Then sprinkle with soy sauce.

3. Add shrimp, stir-fry until pinkish, then sprinkle with sherry and pepper.

4. Add spinach leaves and stir-fry until dark green and softened, but not limp. Then combine mixture with soft-fried or tossed noodles, as indicated on pages 648–649.

VARIATION: For the spinach, substitute Chinese cabbage stems, cut in 1½-inch sections and blanched.

STIR-FRIED PORK AND SHRIMP MIXTURE II
FOR CHOW MEIN OR LO MEIN

½ cup cooked pork	2 scallion stalks
½ cup ham	1 garlic clove
½ cup cooked shrimp	1 slice fresh ginger root
2 or 3 eggs	2 tablespoons soy sauce
½ cup Chinese lettuce	1 tablespoon sherry
½ cup bamboo shoots	½ teaspoon salt
½ cup bean sprouts	½ teaspoon sesame oil

3 tablespoons oil

1. Cut cooked pork and ham in strips. Shred cooked shrimp.

2. Beat eggs; then add to meat and shrimp and toss gently to coat.

3. Cut lettuce and bamboo shoots in thin strips. Blanch bean sprouts. Cut scallion stalks in ½-inch sections. Mince garlic and ginger root.

4. Combine soy sauce, sherry, salt and sesame oil.

5. Heat remaining oil. Add scallions, garlic and ginger; stir-fry a few times. Add meat-shrimp mixture and stir-fry 2 minutes more.

6. Add vegetables; stir-fry to soften (1 to 2 minutes). Add soy-sherry mixture and stir-fry 1 minute more. Then combine mixture with soft-fried or tossed noodles, as indicated on pages 648–649.

VARIATION: For the Chinese lettuce and bamboo shoots, substitute celery and fresh mushrooms.

STIR-FRIED VEGETABLE MIXTURE
FOR CHOW MEIN OR LO MEIN

8 to 10 dried black mushrooms	2 to 3 tablespoons oil
1 pound spinach	½ teaspoon salt
1 cup bamboo shoots	1 to 2 tablespoons soy sauce

1. Soak dried mushrooms.
2. Cut spinach leaves in two. Slice bamboo shoots and soaked mushrooms.
3. Heat oil. Add mushrooms and bamboo shoots; stir-fry 3 minutes.
4. Add spinach, salt and soy sauce; stir-fry 1 minute more. Combine mixture with soft-fried or tossed noodles, as indicated on pages 648–649.

VARIATION: Reduce spinach to ½ pound. In step 3, add ½ cup preserved cabbage, rinsed and shredded.

STIR-FRIED CRABMEAT MIXTURE
FOR LO MEIN

½ pound crabmeat
¼ pound bean sprouts
½ cup bamboo shoots
¼ pound fresh mushrooms
1 onion
2 tablespoons soy sauce

1 teaspoon sugar
¼ teaspoon salt
dash of pepper
few drops of sesame oil
3 tablespoons oil
¼ teaspoon salt

1. Pick over and flake crabmeat. Blanch bean sprouts. Slice bamboo shoots, mushrooms and onion.
2. Combine soy sauce, sugar, salt, pepper and sesame oil.
3. Heat remaining oil. Add remaining salt, then onion; stir-fry until translucent. Add mushrooms; stir-fry to soften. Add crabmeat and stir-fry 1 minute more.
4. Add bean sprouts and bamboo shoots; stir-fry to heat through (about 1 minute). Then combine mixture with tossed noodles, as indicated on page 649, gently blending in the soy-sugar mixture during the last minute of cooking.

MISCELLANEOUS STIR-FRIED COMBINATIONS
FOR CHOW MEIN OR LO MEIN

Stir-fry together 1 kind of meat and 1 kind of vegetable (for example, beef and spinach; pork and snow peas).

Stir-fry together 1 kind of meat and 2 kinds of vegetables (for example, pork, Chinese cabbage and bamboo shoots; chicken, mushrooms and bean sprouts).

Stir-fry 2 kinds of meat (such as chicken and ham, chicken and pork, or pork and ham), together with 2 kinds of vegetables; also add shrimp and mushrooms.

GARNISHES FOR CHOW MEIN OR LO MEIN

Almonds, toasted, and left whole or slivered
Chinese parsley, chopped
Egg threads (see page 826)
Hardboiled eggs, shelled and cut in half
Ham, shredded or minced
Roast pork, slivered or minced
Scallions, slivered

NOODLE NEST
About 4 servings

½ pound noodles   *4 to 5 tablespoons oil*

lobster topping

1. Parboil noodles as on page 635 or 636. Then refrigerate to chill (2 hours or more).

2. Heat oil in a deep 8-inch skillet. Add noodles, and with a spatula, press them firmly against the sides and bottom of the pan until they hold a round nest-like shape. Then cook to heat through, but do not brown.

3. Carefully transfer the nest to a heated serving platter and keep warm. Fill the nest with the lobster topping (see below) and serve at once.

NOTE: Thin, medium or broad egg noodles can be used for this dish. If the noodles are not chilled first, shake them out to separate the strands.

LOBSTER TOPPING FOR NOODLE NEST

1 cup cooked lobster meat   *few drops of sesame oil*
¼ pound fresh mushrooms   *1 to 2 tablespoons oil*
¼ cup bamboo shoots   *½ teaspoon salt*
1 onion   *1 tablespoon sherry*
2 teaspoons cornstarch   *½ cup stock*
2 tablespoons water   *dash of pepper*

1. Flake lobster meat. Slice mushrooms thin; also bamboo shoots and onion.
2. Blend cornstarch, cold water and sesame oil to a paste.

3. Heat oil. Add salt, then onion, and stir-fry until translucent. Add mushrooms and bamboo shoots; stir-fry 1 minute more.

4. Add lobster, sherry and stock. Cook, covered, to heat through (about 1 minute). Then sprinkle with pepper.

5. Stir in cornstarch paste to thicken; pour mixture into noodle nest and serve.

VARIATIONS: Omit the sesame oil in step 2 and the pepper in step 4. Instead add to the cornstarch paste 2 teaspoons soy sauce, ½ teaspoon sugar and the pepper.

In step 3, add with the mushrooms and bamboo shoots, 1 cup bean sprouts, blanched.

NOODLE PANCAKE
About 4 servings

½ pound noodles   *1 tablespoon oil*

4 tablespoons oil

1. Parboil noodles as on page 635 or 636; then toss in oil.

2. Heat remaining oil. Add noodles, arranging them like a thick pancake, and brown lightly over medium-low heat.

3. Turn the pancake over and cook the other side. (The pancake is done when it is brown and crispy on both sides but soft in the middle.) Remove from pan and keep warm.

4. Stir-fry any of the toppings below. Then pour over the pancake and serve.

NOTE: When larger quantities of noodles are used, they're easier to handle if divided up and cooked as separate pancakes. If the noodle pancakes are not to be used immediately, they can be kept warm in a slow oven.

VARIATIONS: For the oil in step 1, substitute 1 teaspoon sesame oil.

Instead of making noodle pancakes, divide the noodles in smaller quantities, roll them up like shredded wheat biscuits, and brown on each side as above.

STIR-FRIED CHICKEN LIVER TOPPING
FOR NOODLE PANCAKE

1 pound chicken livers   *½ cup stock*
1 small onion   *1 tablespoon cornstarch*
¼ cup celery   *1 tablespoon soy sauce*
2 tablespoons oil   *2 tablespoons water*

1. Cut each chicken liver in 2 or 3 pieces. Slice onion; sliver celery.

2. Heat oil. Add onion and stir-fry until translucent. Add chicken livers; stir-fry until they begin to change color.

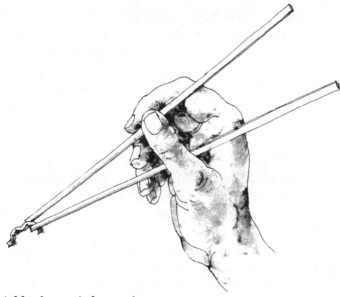

3. Add celery; stir-fry 2 minutes more.

4. Add stock and heat quickly. Then cook, covered, over medium heat until done (2 to 3 minutes).

5. Meanwhile blend cornstarch, soy sauce and cold water to a paste; then stir in to thicken. Pour mixture over noodle pancake and serve.

STIR-FRIED PORK TOPPING FOR NOODLE PANCAKE

1 cup lean pork	½ cup fresh mushrooms
2 teaspoons cornstarch	1 tablespoon cornstarch
2 teaspoons sherry	¼ cup stock
1½ cups Chinese cabbage	2 tablespoons oil
½ cup bamboo shoots	½ teaspoon salt

½ cup stock

1. Shred pork. Combine cornstarch and sherry; then add to pork and toss to coat.

2. Shred Chinese cabbage, bamboo shoots and fresh mushrooms.

3. Blend remaining cornstarch and cold stock to a paste.

4. Heat oil. Add salt, then pork, and stir-fry until pork loses its pinkness.

5. Add shredded vegetables; stir-fry 1 minute. Add remaining stock and heat quickly. Then cook, covered, over medium heat until done (about 2 minutes).

6. Stir in cornstarch paste to thicken. Pour mixture over noodle pancake and serve.

STIR-FRIED PORK AND SHRIMP TOPPING
FOR NOODLE PANCAKE

½ pound pork	2 teaspoons cornstarch
¼ pound shrimp	3 tablespoons water
¼ pound fresh mushrooms	2 tablespoons oil
3 celery stalks	2 tablespoons soy sauce
1 or 2 scallion stalks	½ teaspoon salt

1. Shred pork. Shell and devein shrimp; cut each in two.

2. Slice fresh mushrooms. Cut celery and scallion stalks in 1-inch sections.

3. Blend cornstarch and cold water to a paste.

4. Heat oil. Add pork and stir-fry until it loses its pinkness. Add shrimp; stir-fry until it turns pinkish.

5. Add vegetables; stir-fry 1 minute more. Then sprinkle with soy sauce and salt and stir-fry until done (about another 2 minutes).

6. Stir in cornstarch paste to thicken. Pour mixture over noodle pancake and serve.

STIR-FRIED SUBGUM TOPPING FOR NOODLE PANCAKE

3 dried black mushrooms	¼ cup abalone
¼ cup lean pork	¼ cup smoked ham
1 teaspoon cornstarch	¼ cup bamboo shoots
1 teaspoon soy sauce	2 to 3 tablespoons oil
1 cup shrimp	1 to 2 cups stock
1 teaspoon cornstarch	1 tablespoon soy sauce
1 teaspoon sherry	1 tablespoon sherry
¼ cup chicken	¼ teaspoon salt
½ teaspoon cornstarch	1 tablespoon cornstarch
¼ teaspoon salt	3 tablespoons water

1. Soak dried mushrooms.

2. Sliver pork. Combine cornstarch and soy sauce; then add to pork and toss to coat.

3. Shell and devein shrimp; cut each in two. Combine the second quantity of cornstarch, and sherry; then add to shrimp and toss.

4. Sliver chicken. Dredge in the third quantity of cornstarch, mixed with salt.

5. Sliver abalone, smoked ham, bamboo shoots and soaked mushrooms.

6. Heat oil. Add pork, chicken and shrimp; stir-fry until pork loses its pinkness and shrimp turns pink.

7. Add ham, bamboo shoots and mushrooms; stir-fry 1 to 2 minutes more.

8. Add stock, remaining soy sauce, sherry and salt; bring to a boil. Add abalone and cook, covered, 2 minutes over medium heat.

9. Meanwhile blend the remaining cornstarch and cold water to a paste; then stir in to thicken. Pour mixture over noodle pancake and serve.

VARIATIONS: In step 6, add to the hot oil, before the pork, etc., 1 or 2 slices fresh ginger root, crushed; and 1 scallion stalk, cut in 1-inch sections; stir-fry a few times. Then add other ingredients.

Omit the abalone. In step 7, also add ¼ cup green peas, parboiled.

NOODLES IN MEAT SAUCE
4 to 6 servings

4 dried black mushrooms	¼ cup mushroom-soaking liquid
2 tablespoons cloud ear mushrooms	2 tablespoons oil
10 dried shrimp	2 cups stock
½ pound lean pork	1 pound noodles
2 scallion stalks	2 tablespoons cornstarch
1 tablespoon soy sauce	¼ cup mushroom-soaking liquid
½ tablespoon sherry	2 eggs
2 cups stock	½ teaspoon salt

dash of pepper

1. Soak dried black mushrooms; reserve their liquid. Separately soak cloud ear mushrooms and dried shrimp.

2. Slice pork and both varieties of mushroom. Cut scallions in 1-inch sections.

3. Combine soy sauce, sherry, stock and reserved mushroom liquid.

4. Heat oil. Add pork and stir-fry until it loses its pinkness (2 to 3 minutes).

5. Add sliced mushrooms, then scallions, and stir-fry 2 to 3 minutes more.

6. Add soaked shrimp and soy-sherry mixture; bring to a boil. Gradually stir in and heat remaining stock. Then simmer, covered, 20 minutes.

7. Meanwhile parboil noodles as on page 635 or 636. Keep warm in a double boiler.

8. Blend cornstarch and remaining mushroom liquid to a paste; then stir into meat mixture to thicken.

9. Beat eggs and add gradually, stirring constantly. Then season with salt and pepper.

10. Transfer noodles to a large preheated bowl. Pour meat sauce over and serve.

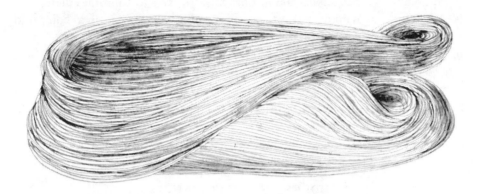

SOY JAM NOODLES

About 6 servings

12 radishes	1 pound noodles
1 small cucumber	½ pound lean pork
4 scallions	1 or 2 slices fresh ginger root
5 stalks celery	4 scallions
½ pound bean sprouts	1 cup soy jam
1 cup Chinese parsley	1 cup water
5 eggs	2 or 3 tablespoons oil

1. Slice radishes. Peel and shred cucumber; then soak briefly in ice water. Shred scallions and celery. Blanch bean sprouts. Trim tough stems from Chinese parsley. Place each vegetable in a separate serving dish.

2. Prepare egg threads (see page 826). Place in another serving dish.

3. Parboil noodles as on page 635 or 636 and keep warm.

4. Mince or grind pork, together with ginger root and remaining scallions.

5. Mix soy jam and water in a bowl.

6. Heat oil. Add pork mixture and stir-fry until pork loses its pinkness (1 to 2 minutes).

7. Stir in diluted soy jam and cook, covered, 10 minutes over medium heat, stirring frequently.

8. Transfer noodles to individual bowls. Place the meat sauce mixture in a serving bowl at the center of the table, with the dishes of vegetables and egg threads nearby. (To eat: the diner spoons 1 or 2 tablespoons of the meat sauce over his noodles, then takes a little of each vegetable and the egg threads and mixes them all together.)

NOTE: This is the family-style way of serving noodles. (Sometimes the noodles are soft-fried first.) Various dishes of diced cooked meat and seafood, diced hardboiled eggs and crushed walnuts or almonds can also be served with the noodles. When they are, a meatless sauce is generally used. (See page 731.)

VARIATIONS: For the soy jam, substitute 8 tablespoons yellow bean paste and 4 tablespoons soy sauce, and mix with the water. Simmer 15 minutes in step 7; then stir in 1 teaspoon sugar.

For the soy jam, substitute 1 cup hoisin sauce. Add in step 7 and stir in to heat. Then gradually add the water and cook 10 minutes as above.

In step 6, before stir-frying pork, add to the hot oil 1 garlic clove, crushed, and/or a few drops of sesame oil.

For the individual vegetables, substitute the following, tossed together and blended: 2 cups celery, shredded and blanched; 1 cucumber, peeled and shredded; 1 tablespoon peanut oil; 1 tablespoon light soy sauce; ½ teaspoon salt; ½ teaspoon sugar; ½ teaspoon sesame oil and a dash of pepper.

NOODLES IN BROWN BEAN SAUCE
About 6 servings

2 or 3 dried black mushrooms	1 garlic clove
shredded vegetables	2 tablespoons oil
egg threads	½ teaspoon salt
¾ pound egg noodles	1 tablespoon hoisin sauce
½ pound lean pork	¼ cup stock
2 tablespoons brown bean sauce	¼ teaspoon sugar

dash of cayenne pepper

1. Soak dried mushrooms.
2. Prepare shredded vegetables and egg threads as in Soy Jam Noodles above.
3. Parboil noodles as on page 635 or 636 and keep warm.
4. Mince or grind pork. Dice soaked mushrooms. Mash brown bean sauce. Crush garlic.
5. Heat oil. Add salt, then garlic, and brown lightly. Add pork and stir-fry until it loses its pinkness (1 to 2 minutes).
6. Add mushrooms; stir-fry ½ minute more. Quickly stir in brown bean sauce, hoisin sauce and stock. Then cook, covered, 5 minutes over medium heat, stirring occasionally. Sprinkle with sugar and cayenne pepper.
7. Transfer noodles to a preheated bowl and pour the sauce over. Garnish with egg threads and shredded vegetables and serve.

VARIATION: For the pork, substitute beef. For the brown bean sauce, substitute yellow bean paste.

NOODLES IN THREE-FLAVORED SAUCE
About 4 servings

1 pound noodles	1 teaspoon hoisin sauce
¼ pound roast pork	½ teaspoon salt
1 Spanish onion	½ teaspoon sugar
1 tomato	dash of pepper
½ cup catsup	2 to 3 tablespoons curry powder

⅓ cup stock

1. Parboil noodles as on page 635 or 636 and keep warm.
2. Shred roast pork. Slice onion. Peel tomato, then cut in wedges.
3. Combine catsup, hoisin sauce, salt, sugar and pepper.
4. In a dry pan, cook curry powder over low heat, stirring constantly for a few seconds. Add onion and continue stirring until curry becomes pungent.
5. Stir in stock, then roast pork, and heat quickly.
6. Stir in catsup-hoisin mixture and mix well to blend.
7. Gently stir in tomato wedges only to heat through.
8. Transfer noodles to a preheated bowl and pour the sauce over. Arrange tomatoes decoratively on top and serve.

VARIATION: In step 8, instead of pouring the sauce over the noodles, add the noodles to the pan and stir in to blend and heat.

STEWED NOODLES
4 to 6 servings

1 pound noodles	1 garlic clove
¼ pound lean pork	2 slices fresh ginger root
¼ pound ham	2 tablespoons oil
½ pound shrimp	2 cups stock
2 scallion stalks	2 tablespoons soy sauce

dash of pepper

1. Parboil noodles as on page 635 or 636 but only very briefly.
2. Cut pork and ham in 1½-inch strips. Shell and devein shrimp; cut each in two. Cut scallions in ½-inch lengths. Mince garlic and ginger root.
3. Heat oil. Add scallion, garlic and ginger root and stir-fry to brown lightly. Add pork and ham; stir-fry until pork loses its pinkness (2 to 3 minutes).
4. Add shrimp and stir-fry until pinkish (2 to 3 minutes).
5. Add parboiled noodles, stock, soy sauce and pepper, and bring to a boil, stirring gently. Then simmer, covered, 8 to 10 minutes and serve.

BRAISED NOODLES
About 4 servings

4 *dried black mushrooms*	1 *tablespoon cornstarch*
2 *tablespoons cloud ear mushrooms*	1 *cup stock*
1 *pound noodles*	2 *tablespoons oil*
¼ *pound lean pork*	½ *teaspoon salt*
1 *small cauliflower*	2 *tablespoons soy sauce*
2 *scallion stalks*	1 *teaspoon sesame oil*

1. Separately soak dried black and cloud ear mushrooms.
2. Parboil noodles as on page 635 or 636 but only very briefly.
3. Cut pork in 1½-inch strips. Break cauliflower in small flowerets. Cut scallions in 1½-inch sections. Slice soaked mushrooms.
4. Combine cornstarch and cold stock.
5. Heat oil. Add salt, then scallion, and stir-fry a few times. Add pork and stir-fry until it loses its pinkness (2 to 3 minutes).
6. Add cauliflower and dried black mushrooms; stir-fry 2 to 3 minutes more. Add cloud ear mushrooms and soy sauce; stir-fry another 2 minutes.
7. Add cornstarch-stock mixture. Cook, covered, 10 minutes over medium heat, stirring occasionally.
8. Meanwhile heat sesame oil in another pan. Add noodles and stir gently until lightly browned.
9. Add pork-cauliflower mixture to noodles; then simmer, covered, another 10 minutes and serve.

COLD MIXED NOODLES
About 4 servings

1 *pound noodles*	½ *pound bean sprouts*
1 *teaspoon peanut oil*	1 *or 2 cucumbers*
½ *pound roast pork*	12 *to 15 radishes*

1. Parboil noodles as on page 635 or 636; then toss in oil. Refrigerate to chill (2 hours or more).
2. Shred roast pork. Blanch bean sprouts. Shred cucumbers and radishes.
3. Place the chilled noodles in individual bowls and the other ingredients in separate serving dishes. To eat: the diner spoons 1 to 2 tablespoons, at a time, of the meat and vegetables over his noodles and mixes them all together. (If he wishes, he may toss the vegetables first in a dip dish of vinegar.)

NOTE: This dish is eaten in summer.

VARIATIONS: For the peanut oil, substitute sesame oil.

For the pork, substitute either spiced beef, shredded; or ½ pound crabmeat stir-fried briefly with 1 or 2 slices fresh ginger root, then sprinkled with 1 tablespoon sherry.

For the vegetables, use the blanched bean sprouts and 2 scallion stalks, minced; then toss with 2 tablespoons peanut oil, 1 tablespoon light soy sauce, 1 teaspoon sesame oil, ½ teaspoon sugar, salt to taste, and a dash of pepper.

Serve the following sauce in a separate bowl to accompany the noodles: Combine 1 tablespoon cornstarch, 1 teaspoon sugar and ½ cup soy sauce and cook, stirring, over medium heat until the mixture thickens and is smooth. (The diner spoons some of the sauce over his noodles, then tops them with about 1 tablespoon of each vegetable, tossed first in vinegar.)

Place the chilled noodles in a large serving bowl. Top with 1 cup cooked pork and ½ cup ham, both shredded; ½ cup shrimp; 1 cucumber, peeled and shredded; and egg threads, made with 2 eggs. In a second bowl, serve the following sauce which has first been heated: 2 cups stock, 2 tablespoons soy sauce, 1 tablespoon peanut butter, 2 teaspoons vinegar, ½ teaspoon salt, and a few drops each of Tabasco Sauce and sesame oil. (The diner transfers some of the noodles and their topping to his own bowl and then spoons some of the sauce over.)

PEASTARCH NOODLES AND EGG SAUCE
About 4 servings

8 cups water	2 tablespoons sherry
½ to 1 pound peastarch noodles	3 eggs
3 cups stock	2 scallion stalks
3 tablespoons soy sauce	1 tablespoon oil

1. Bring water to a boil; add peastarch noodles and cook 15 to 20 minutes. Then drain, rinse with cold water, and drain again. Transfer noodles to individual serving bowls.

2. Heat stock; then stir in soy sauce and sherry.

3. Meanwhile beat eggs and cut scallion stalks in 1-inch sections.

4. Heat oil. Add scallions and stir-fry until translucent; then stir in eggs. While eggs are still liquid, stir in heated stock mixture; and cook, stirring, over moderate heat until the mixture comes to a boil but the eggs have not completely set.

5. Pour the egg sauce over the noodles and serve.

STIR-FRIED PEASTARCH NOODLES WITH SHRIMP AND PORK
About 6 servings

6 dried black mushrooms	1 onion
½ to 1 pound peastarch noodles	2 tablespoons oil
8 cups water	1 tablespoon sherry
½ pound shrimp	1 tablespoon soy sauce
¼ pound lean pork	dash of pepper
½ cup celery	1 cup mushroom-soaking liquid

1. Separately soak dried mushrooms and peastarch noodles. Reserve mushroom-soaking liquid.

2. Bring water to a boil. Add soaked noodles, bring to a boil again; then drain. Rinse with cold water; drain again.

3. Shell, devein and dice shrimp. Slice pork and soaked mushrooms then. Coarsely chop celery and onion.

4. Heat oil. Add onion and stir-fry until translucent. Add pork; stir-fry until it loses its pinkness (2 to 3 minutes).

5. Add shrimp and stir-fry until pinkish. Add sherry; stir-fry until it evaporates. Then sprinkle with soy sauce and pepper.

6. Add chopped celery and mushrooms; stir-fry another 2 minutes.

7. Add reserved mushroom liquid and noodles. Stir in gently to heat through; then serve.

RICE-NOODLE NESTS WITH POACHED EGGS
About 4 servings

½ to 1 pound rice noodles	5 eggs
½ cup baked ham	2 tablespoons oil
1 garlic clove	½ teaspoon sugar
½ can tomato paste	½ teaspoon salt
½ cup water	dash of pepper

soy sauce

1. Parboil rice noodles until cooked through but still firm (about 8 minutes); then drain. Rinse with cold water and drain again. Separate noodles into 5 parts. Arrange each on a warm serving platter, in coils like a nest.

2. Meanwhile, separately mince ham and garlic. In a cup, combine tomato paste and water.

3. Poach eggs (see page 826). Carefully place egg in each noodle nest.

4. Heat oil. Add minced garlic and stir-fry a few times. Add minced ham, diluted tomato paste, sugar, salt and pepper, and cook, stirring, to heat through and blend flavors (about 2 minutes).

5. Pour mixture over eggs; then sprinkle lightly with soy sauce and serve.

VARIATION: For the rice noodles, substitute egg noodles.

RICE NOODLES WITH STIR-FRIED PORK AND VEGETABLES
About 4 servings

½ to 1 pound rice noodles	2 teaspoons cornstarch
½ cup pork	3 tablespoons water
½ cup bamboo shoots	2 tablespoons oil
1 cup Chinese lettuce	2 cups stock

2 to 3 tablespoons oil

1. Parboil rice noodles until cooked through but still firm (about 8 minutes); then drain. Rinse with cold water and drain again.

2. Shred pork, bamboo shoots and lettuce. In a cup, blend cornstarch and cold water to a paste.

3. Heat oil. Add pork and stir-fry until it loses its pinkness (1 to 2 minutes). Add vegetables; stir-fry 1 minute more.

4. Add stock and heat quickly. Cook, covered, 3 to ̣ninutes over medium heat. Then stir in cornstarch paste to thicken. Keep warm.

5. Heat remaining oil in another pan. Add rice noodles and gently stir in to brown lightly. Transfer to a serving platter. Pour the pork mixture over and serve.

RICE NOODLES WITH STIR-FRIED PORK, SHRIMP AND BEAN SPROUTS
6 to 8 servings

6 dried black mushrooms	3 scallion stalks
½ to 1 pound rice noodles	3 tablespoons oil
½ pound shrimp	2 tablespoons soy sauce
½ pound lean pork	2 tablespoons oil
½ pound bean sprouts	1 tablespoon vinegar

dash of pepper

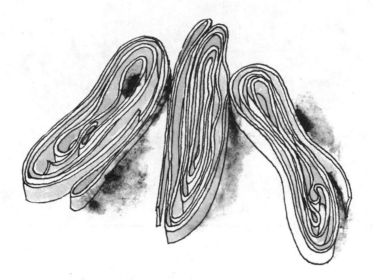

1. Soak dried mushrooms.

2. Soak rice noodles 4 minutes in hot water; then drain, shaking in a colander to remove as much moisture as possible.

3. Shell, devein and dice shrimp. Sliver pork and soaked mushrooms. Blanch bean sprouts. Cut scallion stalks in ½-inch sections.

4. Heat oil. Add scallions and stir-fry until translucent. Add pork; stir-fry until it loses its pinkness (about 2 minutes), then sprinkle with soy sauce.

5. Add soaked mushrooms and stir-fry 2 minutes. Add shrimp; stir-fry until pinkish.

6. Add bean sprouts and stir-fry another 2 minutes. Then remove all ingredients from pan.

7. Heat remaining oil. Add rice noodles and gently stir in to brown lightly.

8. Return pork and shrimp mixture and toss gently with noodles. Cook to blend and heat through (about 2 minutes); then season with vinegar and pepper and serve.

VARIATION: For the vinegar, substitute a few drops of hot sauce.

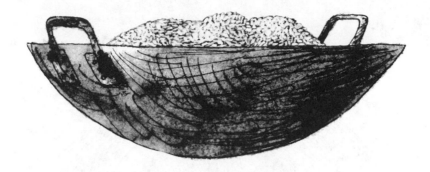

RICE DISHES

POACHED EGG RICE
About 4 servings

2 cups rice
4 to 6 cups water

4 eggs
oyster sauce

1. Boil or steam rice (see pages 59–61).
2. Bring water to a boil in another saucepan. Break eggs one at a time onto a flat dish; then gently ease into boiling water. Reduce heat to medium and poach until the egg whites set, but the yolks are still moist.
3. Arrange cooked rice on a serving platter; top with poached eggs. Sprinkle eggs lightly with oyster sauce and serve.

VARIATION: At the end of step 1, while the rice is still in its cooking pot, make four indentations in its surface with the bottom of a glass. Then break a raw egg into each indentation. Cover the pot and let stand 1 to 2 minutes. (The hot rice will cook the eggs.)

PIMENTO RICE
About 4 servings

2 cups rice
2 tablespoons pimento
1 scallion

3 tablespoons soy sauce
2 tablespoons oil
½ teaspoon sugar

1. Boil or steam rice (see pages 59–61).
2. Dice pimento and mince scallion. Then add to cooked rice, along with soy sauce, oil and sugar. Mix well to blend; then serve.

RICE AND PEAS
About 4 servings

2 cups rice   ½ to 1 pound peas

3 cups water

1. Wash raw rice as for Basic Boiled Rice I (see page 59), and place in a pan.
2. Shell green peas and mix with rice to distribute them. Then add water.
3. Cook as in Basic Boiled Rice I. Let pot stand, covered, 10 minutes before serving.

RICE (PARTIALLY COOKED) WITH TOPPINGS
About 4 servings

topping   2 cups rice

3 cups water

1. Prepare any of the toppings described below.
2. Wash raw rice as for Basic Boiled Rice I (see page 59), and place in a pan with water. Cook as in steps 1 to 3 until most of the water is absorbed.
3. Place topping over rice and cook, covered, over low heat until rice is done (15 to 20 minutes). Let stand, covered, 10 to 15 minutes more; then serve.

NOTE: The topping is cooked as the rice itself steams. Both rice and topping may be stirred together after, but not during, cooking. The rice will stick to the bottom of the pan if stirred too soon.

TOPPINGS FOR PARTIALLY COOKED RICE

BEEF—Mince or grind ¼ pound lean beef; shred 1 slice fresh ginger root. Blend together with ½ teaspoon sugar, ½ teaspoon salt, 1 teaspoon soy sauce, 1 teaspoon sherry, 1 teaspoon oil and a dash of pepper. Arrange over rice and cook as in step 3 above.

CHICKEN AND MUSHROOMS I—Shred ¼ pound white meat chicken. Slice ½ cup fresh mushrooms. Combine 1 teaspoon cornstarch, 1 teaspoon soy sauce, 1 teaspoon sherry and ¼ teaspoon salt; then add to chicken shreds and toss. Arrange chicken and mushrooms over rice and cook as in step 3 above. Then sprinkle with 1 tablespoon oyster sauce and 1 tablespoon chives, chopped.

CHICKEN AND MUSHROOMS II—Slice ¼ pound white meat chicken and ¼ pound fresh mushrooms. Dice 1 celery stalk and ½ cup bamboo shoots. Chop 10 chives. Place in a bowl. Combine 1 tablespoon cornstarch and 1 tablespoon soy sauce; then add to chicken and vegetables and toss. Arrange mixture over rice, sprinkle with 1 tablespoon oil, lard or butter, and cook as in step 3 above.

CHICKEN AND TOMATOES—Shred ¼ pound white meat chicken. Peel and dice 2 tomatoes. Crush 1 garlic clove. Heat 2 tablespoons oil. Add garlic and stir-fry a few times. Add chicken and stir-fry until it loses its pinkness. Add tomatoes, ½ teaspoon salt, ½ teaspoon sugar and a dash of pepper. Simmer, covered, until tomatoes are reduced to a pulp. Chop 1 scallion stalk and sprinkle over rice. Top with stir-fried chicken mixture and cook as in step 3 above.

CHICKEN AND PRESERVED TURNIP—Bone, skin and dice half a spring chicken. Wash and dice ½ bundle preserved turnip. Dice 5 dried black mushrooms (soaked). Mince ½ garlic clove and 2 slices fresh ginger root; then combine in a large bowl with 1 tablespoon oil, 2 tablespoons soy sauce, ½ teaspoon sugar, 2 teaspoons sherry and a dash of pepper. Add diced chicken and toss. Add mushrooms and preserved turnip and toss. Arrange mixture over rice and cook as in step 3 above.

MARINATED CHICKEN—Chop half a spring chicken, bones and all, in 2-inch sections. Mince 1 scallion stalk, shred 2 slices fresh ginger root; then combine in a large bowl with 2 tablespoons soy sauce, 1 tablespoon sherry, ½ teaspoon salt and ½ teaspoon sugar. Add chicken sections and let stand 1 hour, turning occasionally. Drain, reserving marinade. Arrange chicken sections over rice. Strain the marinade and pour over; then cook as in step 3 above.

CHINESE SAUSAGES I—Cut 2 Chinese sausages diagonally in ⅛-inch slices. Arrange over rice and cook as in step 3 above. Then sprinkle with 2 teaspoons soy sauce.

CHINESE SAUSAGES II—Dice 2 Chinese sausages, ¼ cup dried black mushrooms (soaked), and ¼ cup dried shrimp (soaked). Arrange over rice and cook as in step 3 above. Mix well before serving. (For the regular rice, you may substitute glutinous rice.)

CHICKEN AND CHINESE SAUSAGES—Chop 1 chicken breast, bones and all, in 2-inch sections; then dredge lightly with cornstarch. Cut 2 Chinese sausages in ½-inch slices and slice 6 dried black mushrooms (soaked). Arrange all over rice and cook as in step 3 above.

DRIED FISH—Coarsely chop ¼ cup dried salted fish together with 3 to 4 slices fresh ginger root. Add 1 tablespoon oil and toss well to coat. Arrange mixture over rice and cook as in step 3 above. Mix well before serving.

HAM AND CABBAGE—Coarsely chop ¼ pound ham together with ½ pound cabbage (any variety). Arrange mixture over rice; then sprinkle with 1 tablespoon oil or lard, and ½ teaspoon salt. Cook as in step 3 above.

HAM, CHICKEN AND DUCK—Shred ½ cup smoked ham, ½ cup white meat chicken, ¼ cup dried duck, and 1 or 2 slices fresh ginger root. Then mix well with 1 tablespoon sherry and 2 teaspoons soy sauce and arrange over rice. Cook as in step 3 above.

PORK AND DRIED DUCK—Mince or grind 1 cup lean pork, together with ¼ cup dried duck and 3 or 4 water chestnuts. Then blend with ½ teaspoon salt, 2 teaspoons soy sauce and a dash of pepper. Form mixture into a flat meat cake and place over rice. Cook as in step 3 above.

PORK AND MUSHROOMS—Slice thin or sliver ⅛ pound pork. Combine 1 teaspoon cornstarch, 1 teaspoon soy sauce and 2 tablespoons cold water; then add to pork and toss to coat. Slice ½ pound fresh mushrooms and stir-fry in 1 tablespoon oil to soften slightly; then remove from pan and mix well with pork. Sprinkle rice with 1 tablespoon oil and ¼ teaspoon salt. Then top with pork-mushroom mixture and cook as in step 3 above. (You may substitute beef for the pork.)

SEAFOOD—Flake 1 cup lobster or crabmeat; shred 2 slices fresh ginger root. Then mix well with 1 teaspoon cornstarch, 1 teaspoon oil, 2 teaspoons soy sauce, 1 tablespoon sherry, a pinch of salt and a dash of pepper. Arrange mixture over rice and cook as in step 3 above.

SUBGUM—Shred ¼ pound lean pork. Combine 1 teaspoon cornstarch, ¼ teaspoon salt, 1 tablespoon soy sauce and 1 tablespoon sherry; add to pork and toss to coat. Cut 1 or 2 Chinese sausages in small pieces. Shell ¼ pound peas. Arrange all ingredients over rice and cook as in step 3 above. Before serving, sprinkle with 1 tablespoon oyster sauce and garnish with egg threads and minced scallion.

RICE (COOKED) WITH TOPPINGS
About 4 servings

2 cups raw rice   *3 cups water*

topping for rice

1. Cook rice as for any basic boiled or steamed rice (see pages 59–61).
2. While the rice cooks, prepare any of the toppings below.
3. Add to fully cooked rice as indicated below.

BEEF TOPPING I FOR COOKED RICE

½ pound lean beef   *2 tablespoons oil*

1 onion   *1 tablespoon soy sauce*

½ teaspoon salt

1. Shred beef and onion.
2. Heat oil. Add beef and stir-fry until it loses its redness. Then sprinkle with soy sauce.
3. Add onion and salt; stir-fry another 2 minutes.
4. Transfer cooked rice to a serving dish; top with stir-fried beef mixture and serve.

VARIATION: For the onion, substitute any of the following vegetables, shredded: 1 green pepper, ½ pound Chinese lettuce or ½ cup preserved cabbage. (With the preserved cabbage, use less salt.)

BEEF TOPPING II FOR COOKED RICE

½ pound lean beef   *1 teaspoon light soy sauce*

½ bundle preserved turnip   *1 teaspoon peanut oil*

2 slices fresh ginger root   *¼ teaspoon sugar*

dash of pepper

1. Mince or grind beef. Wash and shred preserved turnip; shred ginger root. Then combine and blend with remaining ingredients.
2. Leave the cooked rice still in its pot and spread the beef mixture over. Cook, covered, 2 minutes more over low heat; then serve.

CHICKEN TOPPING FOR COOKED RICE

¾ cup cooked chicken   *½ teaspoon salt*

2 or 3 tomatoes   *dash of pepper*

1. Shred cooked chicken.

2. Peel tomatoes; place in a saucepan. Sprinkle with salt and pepper and let simmer until reduced to a pulp (about 5 minutes).

3. Transfer cooked rice to a serving dish. Pour tomatoes over, top with chicken shreds and serve.

MIXED VEGETABLE TOPPING FOR COOKED RICE

1 *cup carrots*	1 *cup peas*
2 *cups sweet potatoes*	½ *teaspoon salt*
1 *cup tomatoes*	*dash of pepper*
1 *cup string beans*	*stock*

1. Peel and dice carrots, sweet potatoes and tomatoes. Cut string beans in 1-inch lengths. Shell peas.

2. Leave the cooked rice still in its pot and stir in the vegetables, salt and pepper. Then cook, covered, 5 minutes more over medium heat.

3. Reduce heat to low and cook, covered, another 30 minutes. (If necessary, add a small amount of stock to keep the mixture moist.) Then serve.

VARIATION: For the vegetables, substitute asparagus, Chinese cabbage, Chinese white turnips and spinach.

BASIC CONGEE
About 4 servings

½ *cup raw rice*	6 *cups water*

salt

1. Wash rice (see page 58). Place in a saucepan with water. (Since congee boils over easily, always cook it in a deep pot.)

2. Bring to a boil. Then reduce heat to low and simmer, covered, until rice thickens and becomes porridge-like (about 2 hours). Stir occasionally to prevent rice from sticking to the bottom of the pan and burning.

3. Season with salt to taste. Serve either in a large tureen or in individual bowls, with salty or spiced accompaniments (see pages 633–634).

NOTE: Depending on the proportion of water to rice, congee can be made thick or thin. If it becomes too thick during cooking, just add more water. Its texture can also be made creamier by beating the cooked congee with a wire whisk or rotary beater.

VARIATIONS: For the rice, use 3 parts long-grain rice to 1 part glutinous rice.

In step 1, add either 2 slices fresh ginger root or ½ piece dried tangerine peel.

In step 1, add 2 or 3 dried scallops, or 4 or 5 dried shrimp.

In step 3, also add ½ teaspoon sugar.

WITH BEEF: Combine ¼ pound lean beef, minced or ground; 1 scallion stalk or 2 slices fresh ginger root, minced; 1 teaspoon sherry, 1 teaspoon soy sauce, ½ teaspoon oil and ½ teaspoon sugar. Add to congee at the end of step 3 and simmer, covered, 2 to 3 minutes more. (You may also stir in a beaten egg at the very end.)

WITH CHICKEN I: Bone ¼ pound chicken and cut in 1½-inch cubes. Combine 2 slices fresh ginger root, shredded; ½ teaspoon salt, ½ teaspoon sugar, 1 teaspoon sherry, 1 teaspoon light soy sauce, 1 teaspoon oil and a dash of pepper; then add to chicken cubes and toss to coat. Add chicken to congee at the end of step 3 and simmer, covered, until done (8 to 10 minutes more).

WITH CHICKEN II: Bone ¼ pound chicken and cut in slivers. Combine 1 tablespoon soy sauce, 1 teaspoon sherry, 1 teaspoon oil and 1 slice fresh ginger root, minced; then add to chicken and toss. Cook as in the chicken variation above.

WITH WHOLE CHICKEN: Place a small spring chicken, 2 slices fresh ginger root and 2 scallion stalks in a saucepan with 6 or 7 cups of water. Bring to a boil; then simmer, covered, 15 minutes. Add 4 tablespoons sherry and ½ teaspoon salt and simmer, covered, 45 minutes more. Remove the chicken and let cool slightly. Then bone and slice; or chop, bones and all, in 2-inch sections. Meanwhile, in the same pot, cook Basic Congee as above, substituting the chicken broth for water. When the congee is done, add chicken pieces only to reheat. Season to taste with soy sauce, salt and pepper. Garnish with minced scallions; minced smoked ham; or chopped Chinese parsley.

WITH CHICKEN BONES: Place the bones and skin of an uncooked chicken in a saucepan with 6 cups of water (the bird itself is used for other recipes). Bring to a boil; then simmer, covered, 1 hour. In the same pot, cook Basic Congee as above, substituting the chicken broth for the water and leaving the bones and skin to continue cooking (remove these just before serving). Season to taste with salt and pepper. (During the last hour of cooking, you may add ½ pound Chinese white turnips, peeled and diced.)

WITH ROAST DUCK: In step 1 of Basic Congee, add to the water 2 dried scallops and ½ piece dried tangerine peel. Bring to a boil; then add washed rice and bring to a boil again. Reduce heat and simmer, covered, 30 minutes. Then add the bones, lower legs, wings and neck of a roast duck, chopped in small pieces; and 1 or 2 slices fresh ginger root. Cook as in steps 2 and 3 of Basic Congee. Garnish with minced scallion and chopped Chinese parsley.

WITH FISH I: Slice thin ½ pound fish fillets. Combine 2 slices fresh ginger root, shredded; 2 scallions, minced; 1 tablespoon light soy sauce, 2 teaspoons sherry, 1 tablespoon oil, ½ teaspoon salt and ¼ teaspoon sugar; then add to fish and toss gently. Let stand 15 to 30 minutes, then drain. Transfer fish to individual serving bowls and pour the cooked congee over. (The fish needs very little cooking: just pouring the hot congee over is enough.) Top with shredded lettuce; stir and serve.

WITH FISH II: Bone and flake ½ pound haddock. Beat 1 or 2 eggs. At the end of step 3, stir the fish flakes into the congee, followed immediately by the eggs. Stir in for less than a minute. Then stir in 1½ tablespoons soy sauce and serve.

WITH PORK I: Shred ½ pound lean pork; then add 2 tablespoons soy sauce and toss. Let stand 15 minutes. Meanwhile shred ¼ cup onions and chop ½ bundle preserved turnips. Add these to the congee at the end of step 3 and simmer 5 minutes. Next, add the pork and 2 eggs, beaten lightly, and simmer 2 minutes more, stirring constantly. Garnish with chopped Chinese parsley.

WITH PORK II: Mince or grind ½ pound lean pork and ⅛ pound preserved cabbage. Combine 1 tablespoon oil, ½ teaspoon sugar, ½ teaspoon salt and a dash of pepper; then add to pork and cabbage and toss. Add mixture to congee at the end of step 3 and simmer, covered, another 20 minutes. Meanwhile, chop 1 cup Chinese parsley and 4 scallions; add to congee and cook, stirring, 5 minutes more. Just before serving, you may poach several eggs right in the congee. (Allow 1 egg per person, and break 1 at a time onto a flat dish. Then gently ease into congee, whose heat will poach the eggs.)

WITH PORK CHOPS: Rub 2 lean pork chops generously with salt; then sprinkle with 2 teaspoons sherry. Refrigerate, covered, overnight. Add to congee in step 2, during the last 40 minutes of cooking. Then remove chops and cut in bite-size cubes, discarding the bones. Return meat to congee briefly to reheat. Serve congee with a side dish of light soy sauce into which the pork cubes can be dipped before they are eaten.

WITH PORKBALLS: At the end of step 3 of Basic Congee, add ½ pound raw porkballs (see recipe, page 130). Simmer, covered, until cooked through (about 10 minutes). Serve garnished with chopped Chinese parsley. (For the porkballs, you may substitute either shrimpballs or fishballs. These need less cooking—about 5 minutes.)

WITH PORK BONES: In step 1 of Basic Congee add 2 to 3 pounds pork bones. Remove before serving.

WITH SALT EGGS: After congee is brought to a boil in step 2, add 2 salt eggs, still in their shells (rinse them first to wash off the brine). Remove after step 2 and shell; then slice and eat as hardboiled eggs with congee.

WITH SHRIMP: In step 3 of Basic Congee, add 12 shrimp, shelled and deveined, with the salt. Simmer, covered, 10 minutes more. Garnish with shredded lettuce.

WITH TURKEY: Chop a leftover turkey carcass in 6 large pieces. Place in a pan with 4 to 5 quarts of water and bring to a boil; then simmer, covered, 2 hours. Remove bones and skim off excess fat. Cook Basic Congee as above, substituting the turkey broth for the water. Then, at the end of step 3, stir in ½ cup canned ginkgo nuts only to heat through. Serve garnished with ¼ cup cooked turkey and ¼ cup smoked ham, both shredded; and 2 scallions, minced.

BUDDHA CONGEE
4 to 6 servings

3 or 4 *dried scallops*	½ *cup chicken*
4 to 6 *dried shrimp*	1 *tablespoon oil*
½ *cup rice*	½ *teaspoon salt*
6 *cups stock*	2 *tablespoons sherry*

dash of pepper

1. Separately soak dried scallops and dried shrimp.
2. Wash rice. Place in a pan with stock and bring to a boil; then simmer, covered, 30 minutes.
3. Shred soaked scallops; mince soaked shrimp. Add both to rice and simmer, covered, 30 minutes more.
4. Mince raw chicken; then combine with oil. Add to pan and simmer, covered, another 30 minutes.
5. Season with salt, sherry and pepper.

VARIATIONS: For the regular rice, substitute glutinous rice.

For the chicken, substitute smoked ham, or else use half chicken, half smoked ham.

LOTUS SEED CONGEE
4 to 6 servings

½ *cup dried lotus seeds*	1 *cup glutinous rice*
8 *cups water*	4 *tablespoons sugar*

1. Blanch lotus seeds. Place in a saucepan with water and bring to a boil; then simmer, covered, 30 minutes.

2. Meanwhile wash glutinous rice. Then add to pan and simmer until thick and porridge-like (1 to 1½ hours).

3. Stir in sugar and serve.

NOTE: This congee is eaten hot as a snack or dessert.

SIMPLE FRIED RICE
About 4 servings

4 *cups cold cooked rice*
4 *eggs*
2 *tablespoons water*

3 *to 4 tablespoons oil*
½ *teaspoons salt*
dash of pepper

1. Break up and loosen the cold cooked rice so that the individual grains separate and the rice is no longer lumpy. (This is most easily done if you wet your hands first.)

2. Lightly beat eggs with water.

3. Heat oil to smoking in a large deep pan. (The oil and pan must be very hot.) Add rice and stir-fry over high heat, to heat through, turning rice in a folding motion with a spatula so that it heats evenly and doesn't stick to the pan. (Another way to do this is to press part of the rice gently against the pan and let it heat a few seconds; then repeat until all of the rice is well heated.)

4. Add salt and pepper, then beaten eggs. Fold eggs into rice either with the edge of the spatula or a spoon. Then remove from heat and serve, garnished with minced scallion tops or chopped Chinese parsley.

VARIATIONS: In step 2, beat the eggs without the water. Then stir into eggs 2 teaspoons sherry and ½ scallion stalk, minced. (Omit the scallion garnish.)

In step 2, add to the beaten eggs ¼ teaspoon salt and ½ scallion stalk, minced. In step 3, add eggs to the oil *before* the rice and stir-fry ½ minute. Then add the rice and ¼ teaspoon salt, stir-frying to heat through as above. (Omit step 4 and the scallion garnish.)

BASIC FRIED RICE

4 to 6 servings

4 cups cold cooked rice	2 tablespoons oil
1 cup cooked meat or seafood	3 to 4 tablespoons oil
1 cup vegetables	2 tablespoons soy sauce
¼ cup scallions	½ teaspoon salt
1 or 2 eggs	½ teaspoon sugar

1 teaspoon sherry

1. Break up and separate the cold cooked rice, as in step 1 of Simple Fried Rice.

2. Dice or shred meat, seafood and vegetables (see the ingredients and suggested combinations listed on pages 680–682). Keep the fresh vegetables separate from the canned. (The latter should be drained well before using.) Mince scallions; beat eggs.

3. Heat oil in a large deep pan. Add minced scallions and stir-fry a few times. Add fresh vegetables and stir-fry to soften slightly.

4. Add canned vegetables and cooked meat; stir-fry to heat through and blend. Remove all ingredients from pan.

5. Heat remaining oil to smoking. Add rice and heat through completely, as in step 3 of Simple Fried Rice.

6. Return vegetables and meat; fold into rice with a spatula to blend well and reheat.

7. Then quickly blend in soy sauce, salt, sugar and sherry.

8. Fold in beaten eggs with a spatula and turn off heat just as eggs begin to set.

9. Serve hot, garnished with minced scallions or chopped Chinese parsley.

NOTE: When fried rice is eaten as a main dish, accompanied only by soup, allow about 1 cup cooked rice per person plus whatever ingredients are added. When it's eaten with other dishes, allow 3 to 4 cups cooked rice for 6 people.

VARIATIONS: For the oil, substitute lard or bacon fat.

Heat the rice through first (as in step 5) and remove from pan. Then cook the meat and vegetables (as in steps 3 and 4) and add the seasonings (as in step 7). Next, return rice to pan and mix well to blend. Then pick up steps 8 and 9.

Before adding the rice in step 5, combine it first with the beaten eggs, salt and sherry. (This is a way of coating the rice evenly with the eggs.) Cook as in step 5 but over medium-high heat. (The rice will stick at first but then separate later.) Pick up step 6. Omit steps 7 and 8.

In step 7, for the soy sauce substitute either 2 tablespoons oyster sauce (omit the sherry and sugar); or 2 teaspoons shrimp paste (omit the salt, sherry and sugar).

In step 7, if the rice seems too dry, add 2 to 3 tablespoons stock or vegetable liquids with the seasonings.

In step 7, darken the rice as the restaurants do, by adding a few tablespoons of brown gravy or ½ teaspoon of bottled gravy concentrate.

In step 7, add with the seasonings egg threads made with 1 or 2 eggs (see page 826), or scrambled eggs cut in pieces. Omit step 8.

In step 8, instead of adding the beaten eggs, make an indentation in the middle of the cooked rice and break the eggs into it. Let cook a few seconds; then stir the eggs into the rice until they begin to set.

Omit step 8, leaving out the eggs altogether.

For vegetarian fried rice, double the vegetables and omit meat or seafood.

For the cold cooked rice, substitute fresh rice which has been cooked *only* 10 minutes after it reaches the boiling point. Add this in step 4 with the meat and vegetables and stir-fry briefly to reheat. Then cook, covered, 10 minutes more over low heat. (The rice will finish cooking in the liquids of the other ingredients.) Omit steps 5 and 6.

MEATS FOR BASIC FRIED RICE

Roast pork, beef or lamb
Roast duck or turkey
Roast or boiled chicken
Boiled or baked ham
Bacon, pan-fried
Chinese sausage, steamed

SEAFOOD FOR BASIC FRIED RICE

Crabmeat, flaked
Lobster, boiled and diced
Shrimp, cooked

VEGETABLES FOR BASIC FRIED RICE

Bamboo shoots
Bean sprouts, blanched
Celery, blanched
Cucumber (add at the very end, after step 7, so as not to overcook)
Green peas, parboiled
Lettuce

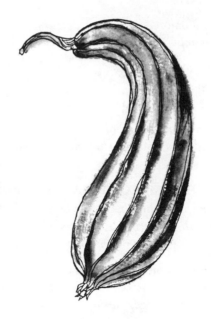

Mushrooms: fresh, canned, or dried (soaked)
Onions
Peppers
Pimentos
Scallions
String beans, parboiled
Tomatoes, peeled (add at the very end, after step 7, so as not to overcook)
Water chestnuts

MISCELLANEOUS INGREDIENTS FOR BASIC FRIED RICE

Almonds, blanched and chopped
Peanuts, chopped
Walnuts, blanched and chopped
Raisins
NOTE: Use these in small quantities (1 to 2 tablespoons).

SUGGESTED COMBINATIONS FOR BASIC FRIED RICE

Beef, onions and green pepper

Bacon, onions, lettuce and tomatoes

Chicken, onions and bean sprouts
Chicken, bamboo shoots, mushrooms and cucumbers

Crabmeat and onions
Crabmeat, bamboo shoots, mushrooms and cucumbers

Ham, onions and green peas
Ham, shrimp and onions
Ham, shrimp and bamboo shoots

Shrimp, bean sprouts and onions
Shrimp, bamboo shoots, mushrooms and cucumbers

SUGGESTED SUBGUM COMBINATIONS FOR BASIC FRIED RICE

Chicken, ham, shrimp, mushrooms, green peas and bamboo shoots
Chicken, ham, shrimp, mushrooms, bamboo shoots, onion and bacon
Chicken, ham, shrimp, lobster, mushrooms, onion and bean sprouts

Ham, shrimp, scallions, almonds, walnuts and raisins
Ham, shrimp, scallions, mushrooms and bamboo shoots
Ham, shrimp, Chinese sausage, mushrooms and green peas

Roast pork, shrimp, ham, lettuce and scallions
Roast pork, bean sprouts, onions, mushrooms, green peppers and tomatoes

BEEF FRIED RICE
4 to 6 servings

½ *pound lean beef*	*4 cups cold cooked rice*
1 *tablespoon cornstarch*	1 *onion*
1 *tablespoon soy sauce*	2 *tablespoons oil*
1 *tablespoon sherry*	3 *tablespoons oil*
½ *teaspoon sugar*	2 *tablespoons stock*

½ teaspoon salt

1. Slice beef thin. Combine cornstarch, soy sauce, sherry and sugar; then add to beef and toss to coat.

2. Break up and separate the cold cooked rice, as in step 1 of Simple Fried Rice. Shred onion.

3. Heat oil. Add onion and stir-fry until translucent. Add beef; stir-fry until it loses its redness. Then remove mixture from pan and keep warm.

4. Heat remaining oil to smoking. Add rice and stir-fry to heat through slightly. Stir in stock and salt; then stir-fry rice to heat through well.

5. Return half the beef and onion mixture to pan and mix thoroughly with rice. Transfer to a serving platter. Top with remaining beef and onions and serve.

CHINESE SAUSAGE FRIED RICE
4 to 6 servings

3 *Chinese sausages*   2 *scallion stalks*

4 *cups cold cooked rice*   2 *to 3 tablespoons oil*

½ *teaspoon salt*

1. Place Chinese sausages on a shallow, but not flat, dish and steam 15 minutes. (See page 831).

2. Let sausages cool slightly; then cut in small pieces. Reserve the drippings.

3. Break up and separate the cold cooked rice, as in step 1 of Simple Fried Rice. Cut scallion stalks in ½-inch sections.

4. Heat oil to smoking. Add rice and stir-fry to heat through partially.

5. Add sausage, drippings, scallions and salt. Stir-fry to heat through completely; then serve.

DUCK FRIED RICE
4 to 6 servings

4 *dried black mushrooms*	2 *tablespoons oil*
1 *cup cooked duck*	2 *tablespoons soy sauce*
½ *pound Chinese cabbage*	1 *tablespoon sherry*
1 *scallion stalk*	2 *to 3 tablespoons oil*
4 *cups cold cooked rice*	2 *tablespoons stock*

½ teaspoon salt

1. Soak dried mushrooms.

2. Cut cooked duck in 1-inch cubes. Dice Chinese cabbage. Mince scallion stalk. Slice soaked mushrooms.

3. Break up and separate the cold cooked rice, as in Step 1 of Simple Fried Rice.

4. Heat oil. Add Chinese cabbage and stir-fry until softened (2 to 3 minutes).

5. Add duck, mushrooms, scallion, soy sauce and sherry. Stir-fry to heat through and blend (about 3 minutes more). Remove all ingredients from pan.

6. Heat remaining oil to smoking. Add rice and stir-fry to heat through completely.

7. Add stock; stir-fry 1 minute more. Return duck and vegetables and add salt; then stir-fry to heat through and blend (about 2 minutes more). Serve hot.

PORK FRIED RICE
4 to 6 servings

1 *cup roast pork*	4 *cups cold cooked rice*
¼ *cup scallions*	2 *to 3 tablespoons oil*
2 *eggs*	½ *teaspoon salt*

1½ *tablespoons soy sauce*

1. Dice roast pork. Cut scallions in ½-inch sections. Beat eggs well.

2. Break up and separate the cold cooked rice, as in step 1 of Simple Fried Rice.

3. Heat oil. Add pork and scallions and stir-fry to coat with oil.

4. Add rice, salt and soy sauce; stir-fry to heat thoroughly. (If necessary, add a few more drops of oil to prevent burning.)

5. Add beaten eggs and fold in until they begin to set. Serve hot.

VARIATIONS: For the pork, substitute ham.

In step 3, before adding the pork, scramble the beaten eggs lightly; then add pork and scallions. (Omit step 5.)

Omit the scallions. In step 3, add with the pork ¼ pound bean sprouts, blanched, and 1 onion, diced; stir-fry together ½ minute. Next, add ¼ cup stock and 2 teaspoons sherry and cook, covered, 1 minute more. Then pick up steps 4 and 5.

SHRIMP FRIED RICE I
4 to 6 servings

½ *pound shrimp*	*4 cups cold cooked rice*
2 *eggs*	2 *tablespoons oil*
1 *cup fresh mushrooms*	2 *or 3 tablespoons oil*
1 *onion*	1½ *tablespoons soy sauce*
1 *or 2 slices fresh ginger root*	½ *teaspoon salt*

1. Shell and devein shrimp. Beat eggs. Slice fresh mushrooms. Chop onion. Mince ginger root.

2. Break up and separate the cold cooked rice, as in step 1 of Simple Fried Rice.

3. Heat oil. Add ginger root and stir-fry a few times. Add shrimp; stir-fry until pinkish, then remove from pan.

4. Heat remaining oil. Add onion and mushrooms; stir-fry to soften slightly (about 2 minutes).

5. Add rice, soy sauce and salt and stir-fry to heat through.

6. Return shrimp; stir in only to reheat. Then fold in beaten eggs until they begin to set. Serve hot.

VARIATIONS: For the soy sauce, substitute oyster sauce.

For the raw shrimp, substitute cooked shrimp. Add in step 3, along with beaten eggs, and stir-fry 1 minute. Then remove from pan. Pick up steps 4 and 5. Return shrimp and eggs in step 6.

SHRIMP FRIED RICE II
4 to 6 servings

1 *cup cooked shrimp*	3 *eggs*
½ *cup smoked ham*	*4 cups cold cooked rice*
½ *cup canned button mushrooms*	3 *tablespoons oil*
1 *large onion*	2 *tablespoons soy sauce*
½ *head lettuce*	½ *teaspoon salt*

dash of pepper

1. Dice cooked shrimp and smoked ham. Drain canned mushrooms. Slice onion. Shred lettuce. Beat eggs.

2. Break up and separate the cold cooked rice, as in step 1 of Simple Fried Rice.

3. Heat oil to smoking. Add ham, onion and rice; stir-fry to heat through.

4. Then add mushrooms and shrimp and stir-fry to heat through.

5. Add beaten eggs and lettuce and fold in until eggs begin to set. Sprinkle with soy sauce, salt and pepper and serve.

YANGCHOW FRIED RICE
4 to 6 servings

½ cup roast pork	4 cups cold cooked rice
½ cup shrimp	3 tablespoons oil
1 cup lettuce	½ teaspoon salt
¼ cup scallions	2 tablespoons soy sauce

1. Dice roast pork. Shell, devein and dice shrimp. Shred lettuce. Mince scallions.

2. Break up and separate the cold cooked rice, as in step 1 of Simple Fried Rice.

3. Heat oil. Add salt, then shrimp, and stir-fry until shrimp turn pinkish.

4. Add roast pork, scallions and lettuce; stir-fry to heat through.

5. Add rice and stir-fry to heat through completely. Then stir in soy sauce and serve.

VARIATIONS: For the meat, use ¼ cup roast pork and ¼ cup cooked chicken; or add to the pork 2 tablespoons smoked ham.

For the raw shrimp, substitute cooked shrimp, tossed in a mixture of ½ teaspoon cornstarch and 2 teaspoons sherry. Add in step 4, with the pork.

In step 4, add with the pork and vegetables ¼ cup green peas, parboiled.

After step 4, add 1 egg, beaten, and scramble until nearly set. Then pick up step 5.

HAM FRIED RICE IN BROTH
4 to 6 servings

2 slices smoked ham	4 cups cold cooked rice
½ cup bamboo shoots	2 tablespoons oil
3 eggs	4 cups stock
½ teaspoon salt	

1. Mince smoked ham. Slice bamboo shoots. Beat eggs.

2. Break up and separate the cold cooked rice as in step 1 of Simple Fried Rice.

3. Heat oil. Add eggs, but do not stir. When eggs begin to set, add rice and stir-fry to heat through.

4. Add stock and half the minced ham. Bring to a boil, stirring; then turn off heat.

5. Transfer rice and broth to a serving bowl. Garnish with sliced bamboo shoots and remaining minced ham. Season with salt and serve.

TEN PRECIOUS RICE
6 to 8 servings

½ cup lean pork	4 cups cold cooked rice
¼ cup smoked ham	2 tablespoons soy sauce
½ cup bamboo shoots	1 tablespoon sherry
½ cup abalone	½ teaspoon salt
1 small chicken breast	dash of pepper
½ cup water chestnuts	3 tablespoons oil
1 scallion stalk	1 cup stock

1. Separately shred pork, ham, bamboo shoots and abalone. Bone and shred chicken breast. Slice water chestnuts; cut scallion in ½-inch sections.

2. Break up and separate the cold cooked rice, as in step 1 of Simple Fried Rice.

3. Combine soy sauce, sherry, salt and pepper.

4. Heat oil. Add scallion and stir-fry until translucent. Add pork; stir-fry until it loses its pinkness (about 2 minutes).

5. Add chicken and ham and stir-fry until chicken loses its pinkness (about 2 minutes). Then quickly stir in soy-sherry mixture.

6. Add rice and mix well to blend. Add stock; bring to a boil, then lower heat.

7. Add bamboo shoots and water chestnuts; simmer, covered, 30 minutes.

8. During the last 3 minutes of cooking, stir in abalone to heat through; then serve.

SIZZLING RICE WITH SHRIMP
About 4 servings

1 pound shrimp	1 cup stock
1 tablespoon cornstarch	1 tablespoon sugar
2 tablespoons sherry	6 tablespoons catsup
½ teaspoon salt	1 tablespoon cornstarch
1 cup rice crusts	3 tablespoons water
2 tablespoons oil	oil for deep-frying

1. Shell and devein shrimp. Combine cornstarch, sherry and salt; then add to shrimp and toss to coat. Break rice crusts in 2-inch pieces.

2. Heat oil. Add shrimp and stir-fry until pinkish; then remove from pan.

3. Heat stock, sugar and catsup; and cook, stirring, 2 minutes.

4. Blend remaining cornstarch and cold water to a paste; then stir in to thicken mixture. Add shrimp to this sauce and cook 1 to 2 minutes to reheat. Keep warm.

5. Meanwhile heat remaining oil. Add rice crusts and deep-fry until they float to the top and are pale gold. Drain quickly; arrange on a heated serving platter.

6. Immediately pour hot shrimp and their sauce over deep-fried crusts and serve. (The initial contact between the two will make the rice sizzle.)

NOTE: Rice crusts are formed from the rice which sticks to the bottom of the pan when Basic Boiled Rice is cooked. Reserve and refrigerate these until you have a cupful for this recipe.

❊ *Eggrolls and Wontons* ❊

EGGROLLS

Eggrolls are thin coverings of unraised dough, wrapped around various meat, seafood and vegetable mixtures, and then usually deep-fried. Originally, these were special snacks served with tea when relatives and friends came to visit after the Chinese New Year. Since the time was early spring, they came to be known as spring rolls. The wrapping of the spring roll was made without eggs, and the rolls themselves were small, thin and delicate. By contrast, the eggroll, said to have originated in Canton and more familiar to Westerners, is larger (it measures 5 to 6 inches) and thicker (its batter is made with eggs). Eggrolls are served either as hors d'oeuvres or with dinner at any time of the year.

PREPARING THE SKINS:

Eggrolls skins are always made first; then the fillings. The skins can either be prepared at home or purchased ready-made in Chinese grocery stores and noodle factories. Ready-made skins come in sheets 8 inches square, average about 20 to the pound, and are always made with eggs. Skins made at home may be prepared with or without eggs.

SPRING ROLL SKINS
About 12 skins

2 cups flour   1½ cups water

1. Place flour in a bowl. Gradually add water, mixing and kneading in one direction until the dough is marshmallow soft.

2. Cover with a damp cloth and let stand 30 minutes.

3. Lightly oil a 6- or 7-inch skillet (by rubbing its surface with a piece of cloth or cotton soaked in peanut oil). Heat pan over a low flame.

4. With a pastry brush, brush on the dough in 5-inch squares. If holes appear, brush on more batter with crosswise strokes. Cook over low heat until set (do not brown). Place skins on a tray and cover with a damp towel.

5. Repeat process until dough is used up, lightly re-oiling the skillet each time.

VARIATIONS: For the flour, use 1⅓ cups wheat flour, ⅔ cup water chestnut flour.

In step 1, add to the dough ½ teaspoon salt and/or ½ teaspoon peanut oil.

In step 4, instead of using a pastry brush, pick up a batch of dough and rub it over the warmed, oiled surface of the skillet until a thin sheet adheres. Or take some dough on the ends of the fingers and spread it over the skillet with a swirling action to form a thin skin.

EGGROLL SKINS
About 12 skins

1½ cups flour	2 eggs
½ teaspoon salt	1½ cups water

1. Combine flour and salt. Beat eggs lightly and blend in.

2. Gradually add water, beating in one direction to make a thin smooth batter.

3. Lightly grease a small skillet, as in step 3 above.

4. Beat the batter again; then pour 2 tablespoonfuls into the skillet, tilting or rotating the pan so that the batter spreads thinly and evenly over the entire surface. (Pour any excess batter back into bowl at once to make the skin as thin as possible.)

5. When the dough shrinks away from the sides of the skillet, quickly pick it up (do not let it brown) and place on a tray. Cover with a damp towel.

6. Repeat process until dough is used up, lightly re-oiling the skillet each time.

VARIATION: In step 1, add 1 tablespoon cornstarch to the flour and salt.

EGGROLL SKINS (UNCOOKED)
About 12 skins

1 egg	½ teaspoon salt
2 cups flour	½ cup ice water

1. Beat egg; then combine with flour, salt and ice water. Knead until smooth and elastic. Cover dough with a damp towel and refrigerate 30 minutes.

2. Place dough on a floured board. Roll out with a rolling pin until paper thin; then cut in six ½-inch squares.

PREPARING THE FILLINGS:

Some eggroll fillings are cooked in advance; others are not. Those containing raw pork are usually stir-fried first, unless the eggroll itself is to be cooked for a longer time. Some fillings are stir-fried in advance, not to be cooked as such, but to blend the flavors of their ingredients.

STIR-FRIED CHICKEN FILLING

4 dried black mushrooms	1½ to 2 cups bean sprouts
¼ pound chicken breast	2 cups spinach
1 teaspoon cornstarch	2 scallion stalks
½ teaspoon salt	2 tablespoons oil
½ teaspoon sugar	1 tablespoon soy sauce
1 teaspoon soy sauce	2 tablespoons oil

1. Soak dried mushrooms.

2. Bone and skin chicken; then shred or cut in thin strips. Combine cornstarch, salt, sugar and soy sauce; then add to chicken and toss gently. Let stand 10 minutes.

3. Meanwhile blanch bean sprouts. Cut spinach in 1-inch sections. Chop scallion stalks. Shred soaked mushrooms.

4. Heat oil. Add scallions and stir-fry a few times. Add bean sprouts, spinach and mushrooms; stir-fry 2 minutes. Sprinkle with remaining soy sauce; then remove all ingredients from pan.

5. Heat remaining oil. Add chicken and stir-fry until it loses its pinkness (about 2 minutes).

6. Return vegetables; stir-fry to heat through and blend (about 1 minute more). Remove; then drain in a colander and let cool.

VARIATIONS: For the scallions, substitute ½ onion, shredded.

For the spinach, substitute ½ cup bamboo shoots, shredded.

In step 2, toss the chicken only in the cornstarch and ¼ teaspoon salt. At the end of step 5, sprinkle the chicken with 1 tablespoon sherry and the soy sauce. (Omit the sugar.)

In step 2, combine with the chicken ¼ pound shrimp, shelled, deveined and chopped; then toss together in the cornstarch mixture.

STIR-FRIED PORK AND SHRIMP FILLING

½ pound lean pork	7 or 8 scallion stalks
¼ pound shrimp	2 or 3 tablespoons oil or lard
½ pound bean sprouts	1 tablespoon soy sauce
½ teaspoon salt	

1. Shred pork. Shell, devein and chop shrimp.
2. Blanch bean sprouts. Slice scallions thin or shred.
3. Heat oil. Add pork and stir-fry until it loses its pinkness (about 2 minutes).
4. Add shrimp and stir-fry 1 minute more.
5. Add bean sprouts and scallions; stir-fry another 2 minutes.
6. Sprinkle with soy sauce and salt; then stir-fry briefly to blend. Transfer mixture to a colander; drain and let cool.

VARIATION: For the shrimp, substitute ½ cup crabmeat, flaked. For the bean sprouts, substitute 8 water chestnuts, minced. (Omit the scallions.) Add crabmeat and water chestnuts in step 4. Omit step 5. In step 6, sprinkle also with 1 tablespoon sherry.

STIR-FRIED ROAST PORK AND SHRIMP FILLING

½ cup roast pork	½ cup celery
¼ cup cooked shrimp	1 cup Chinese cabbage
½ cup bamboo shoots	2 to 3 tablespoons oil
¼ cup water chestnuts	1 tablespoon soy sauce
3 scallions	½ teaspoon salt

dash of pepper

1. Shred or mince roast pork and cooked shrimp.
2. Shred bamboo shoots, water chestnuts and scallions.
3. Blanch celery and Chinese cabbage; drain well. Roll in a clean towel, pressing to remove as much moisture as possible; then shred.
4. Heat oil. Add pork and shrimp; stir-fry only to heat through.
5. Add shredded vegetables, soy sauce, salt and pepper; stir-fry only to heat through.
6. Transfer mixture to a colander; drain and let cool.

VARIATIONS: For the roast pork, substitute roast beef or ham.
For the shrimp, substitute cooked chicken.
For the Chinese cabbage, substitute 1 cup bean sprouts, blanched.
In step 5, add ½ teaspoon sugar with the seasonings.
After step 5, sprinkle mixture with a few drops of sesame oil.

STIR-FRIED SHRIMP FILLING

½ pound shrimp	¼ cup fresh mushrooms
½ teaspoon cornstarch	2 cups celery
¼ teaspoon salt	2 tablespoons oil
1 teaspoon sherry	1 tablespoon oil
½ pound bean sprouts	¼ teaspoon salt

½ teaspoon sugar

1. Shell and devein shrimp; cut in ½-inch pieces. Combine cornstarch, salt and sherry; then add to shrimp and toss to coat.

2. Blanch bean sprouts. Shred mushrooms and celery. Roll celery in a clean towel, pressing to remove as much moisture as possible.

3. Heat oil. Add shrimp and stir-fry until pink; then remove from pan.

4. Heat remaining oil. Add remaining salt, then celery. Stir-fry 2 minutes; sprinkle with sugar.

5. Add mushrooms; stir-fry 1 minute. Add bean sprouts; stir-fry 1 minute more.

6. Return shrimp; stir-fry another minute. Then transfer mixture to a colander; drain and let cool.

VARIATIONS: For the raw shrimp, substitute cooked shrimp; add in step 6, only to reheat; then sprinkle with ½ teaspoon salt and 1 teaspoon sherry. (Omit steps 1 and 3.)

For the bean sprouts, substitute ½ cup bamboo shoots, shredded; or ¼ cup carrots, grated.

UNCOOKED PORK FILLING I

½ pound pork	1 scallion stalk
1 slice fresh ginger root	1 tablespoon soy sauce
1 tablespoon water	

1. Mince or grind together pork, ginger root and scallion stalk.

2. Then blend well with soy sauce and cold water.

NOTE: Eggrolls made with this filling must be steamed for 30 minutes to cook the pork (see Cooking the Eggroll, page 696). They may then be served as is, or deep-fried briefly to make them crisp. (Pork with some fat is best for this filling.)

UNCOOKED PORK FILLING II

6 dried black mushrooms	½ cup bamboo shoots
¼ pound pork	1 cup Chinese parsley
4 slices smoked ham	2 teaspoons cornstarch
6 water chestnuts	½ teaspoon salt
¼ pound shrimp	½ teaspoon sugar
1 pound bean sprouts	¼ teaspoon pepper
2 tablespoons oil	

1. Soak dried mushrooms.

2. Mince or grind together pork, smoked ham and water chestnuts.

3. Shell, devein and mince shrimp. Blanch bean sprouts. Cut bamboo shoots and soaked mushrooms in thin strips. Chop Chinese parsley.

4. Combine meat, shrimp and vegetables with remaining ingredients and mix well to blend.

NOTE: See Note above.

UNCOOKED ROAST PORK FILLING

4 dried black mushrooms	*3 water chestnuts*
1 cup roast pork	*½ cup scallions*
½ cup cooked shrimp	*½ teaspoon salt*

1. Soak dried mushrooms.

2. Shred roast pork. Coarsely chop cooked shrimp, water chestnuts and soaked mushrooms. Mince scallions.

3. Combine ingredients with salt and mix well to blend.

VARIATIONS: For the pork, use half roast pork and half chicken livers. (Parboil and mince the latter.)

For the vegetables, substitute ½ cup Chinese cabbage and ¼ cup each of bamboo shoots and celery, all shredded; also ¼ cup water chestnuts and 2 scallions, both minced. In step 3, add with the salt 1 tablespoon soy sauce, ½ teaspoon sugar and a few drops of sesame oil.

UNCOOKED SHRIMP FILLING

1 pound shrimp	*2 tablespoons Chinese parsley*
⅛ pound pork fat	*1 scallion*
½ cup water chestnuts	*1 tablespoon sherry*
½ teaspoon salt	

1. Shell and devein shrimp.

2. Mince together shrimp, pork fat, water chestnuts, Chinese parsley and scallion.

3. Then add sherry and salt and mix well to blend.

VARIATIONS: For the raw shrimp, substitute cooked shrimp.

For the vegetables, substitute 1 cup celery and ½ cup bamboo shoots, both shredded. (Roll the celery in a towel, pressing gently to remove moisture.) In step 3, omit the sherry, and add instead 2 tablespoons oil, the salt and a dash of pepper.

WRAPPING THE EGGROLL: Before the eggroll is wrapped, three conditions must be met: the filling must be as dry as possible; both the filling and the skin must be cool. Unless these conditions *are* met, the skin could tear during cooking and the filling burst out untidily into the hot oil. It is therefore essential that the filling be drained well in a sieve or colander. (Chinese restaurants have ingeniously adapted regular wine presses to squeeze their eggroll fillings dry.) Stir-fried fillings should be allowed to cool at least 30 minutes after cooking. If time permits, they may be chilled in the refrigerator.

QUANTITIES: Use about 2 tablespoons to ¼ cup of filling per eggroll, or divide the filling into as many parts as there are eggroll skins.

square

triangular

round

ROLLING UP THE EGGROLL SKIN:

Round skins
1. Place the filling slightly below the center of the skin.
2. Fold the skin up from the bottom to cover the filling.
3. Roll the skin fairly tightly around the filling, tucking in the sides as you go, and rolling the skin away from you.
4. Brush the inside of the top edge with a sealing mixture (see below) and press to seal like an envelope flap.

Square skins
1. Place the eggroll skin with one corner of the skin pointing toward you. Place the filling slightly below the center of the skin.

2. Fold the bottom corner up to cover filling. Then fold over the left and right corners.

3. Roll up the skin away from you, pressing tightly to make sure the filling is securely wrapped. Seal as in step 4 above.

Triangular skins
1. Place the filling slightly below the center of the skin.

2. Fold the left corner over the filling; then fold the right corner so that it overlaps the left.

3. Fold up the bottom; then fold over the top to overlap snugly. Seal as in step 4 above.

SEALING THE EGGROLL:

Any of the following may be used:
    1 to 2 tablespoons whole egg, beaten
    1 to 2 tablespoons egg white, unbeaten
    A *thin cornstarch paste made with 1 teaspoon cornstarch and 3 tablespoons water*
    A *flour paste made with 1 tablespoon flour and 2 tablespoons water*
NOTE: When the eggrolls are wrapped, stack them on a damp towel. Then cover with a second damp towel until ready to cook.

COOKING THE EGGROLL:

TO DEEP-FRY:
1. Heat oil for deep-frying to about 375 degrees.

2. Add eggrolls two or three at a time. Reduce heat slightly and deep-fry until each is crisp and golden on both sides.

3. Lift eggrolls out with slotted spoon and drain either on paper toweling or on a rack; or stand eggrolls on end in a colander to drain. (Never stack deep-fried eggrolls one atop the other while still warm; the wrappings will lose their crispness.)

NOTE: When making eggrolls in quantity, you can wrap and deep-fry them at the same time, by wrapping the second batch while the first one cooks in hot oil.

TO STEAM:
1. Place eggrolls on a lightly oiled heatproof platter with enough space between them so they won't stick to one another.

2. Steam 10 to 30 minutes (see page 831).

NOTE: If the eggrolls are to be steamed first and deep-fried afterward, allow 10 minutes for steaming. Then let cool and deep-fry as above. Or dip cooled eggrolls first in beaten egg, dredge lightly in cornstarch and then deep-fry.

If the eggrolls are to be steamed only, and they contain raw pork, allow 30 minutes for steaming. (They may be sprinkled before steaming with a mixture of 1 tablespoon each of lard, soy sauce and water.)

TO PAN-FRY:

1. Heat 2 tablespoons oil. Add eggrolls a few at a time.
2. Brown lightly on both sides.

NOTE: Pan-frying is best when the fillings contain cooked meats or raw vegetables. A Shanghai spring roll filled with bamboo shoots, mushrooms and Chinese parsley, for example, is always pan-fried.

SERVING THE EGGROLL:

1. Cut eggrolls diagonally in 1½-inch sections or in thirds. (This makes them easier to handle with chopsticks.)
2. Serve with hot mustard, plum sauce or slices of lemon or lime.

NOTE: Eggrolls can be kept warm in a slow oven until ready to serve.

STORING THE EGGROLL:

Eggrolls prepared in advance can be pan-fried lightly, cooled and wrapped well in foil or transparent wrap and refrigerated. They can then be deep-fried in a day or two. Or they can be lightly pan-fried and wrapped as above, then frozen, to be unwrapped later and deep-fried without preliminary thawing.

Leftover deep-fried eggrolls may also be frozen. (Bean sprout fillings, however, will lose their crisp texture.) The eggrolls can be reheated without preliminary thawing for about 20 minutes on each side in a slow oven.

Cooked eggrolls will keep 2 to 3 days in the refrigerator. To reheat: Place in a slow oven; cook 10 minutes on each side.

STORING EGGROLL SKINS:

Ready-made eggroll skins are often sold in 5-pound packages. These can be rewrapped in smaller quantities and frozen for future use.

Home-made skins may also be prepared in advance, wrapped and deep-frozen. However, a bit of cornstarch should always be sprinkled between the skins so they will separate and peel off easily.

All frozen eggroll skins should be thawed completely before they are used.

WONTONS

A wonton consists of a skin 2 or 3 inches square, made with flour and eggs, that's filled with a meat or seafood mixture and then cooked. When assembled and folded, the wonton looks like a wisp of cloud. Its Chinese name is "cloud bird" or "cloud swallow."

Wontons can be cooked in various ways: boiled in soup for dinner, or with congee for breakfast; deep-fried and topped with a sweet-and-pungent sauce; or steamed and served as a luncheon dish or teatime snack. In Southern China, a whole meal of wontons, with about 12 to 15 served per person, becomes a Sunday supper or holiday lunch.

PREPARING THE SKINS: As with eggrolls, the wonton skins are made first, then the fillings; and the skins can either be prepared at home or purchased ready-made. (One pound averages 75 to 80 wonton skins.) Instead of buying the special wonton skins, some cooks use the regular 8-inch square eggroll sheets, which, when cut in four 2-inch squares, are just the right size for wontons.

WONTON SKINS
About 40 skins

1½ to 2 cups flour	1 egg
1 teaspoon salt	2 to 3 tablespoons water

1. Sift flour and salt into a bowl. Make an indentation or well in the center.

2. Beat egg lightly; then pour into well and blend in.

3. Sprinkle with cold water and, wetting the hands once or twice, knead mixture to a smooth dough.

4. Place the dough in a bowl and cover with a damp cloth. Refrigerate 30 minutes to an hour.

5. Sprinkle a board with cornstarch or flour. With a rolling pin, roll out the dough in a forward motion, away from you, until it is paper-thin and its edges are even in thickness. (The wonton skins should be semi-transparent.)

6. Cut the dough in 2- to 3-inch strips. Flour them lightly; then stack one atop the other. Cut crosswise through the stack to make 2- to 3-inch square skins.

7. Place skins on a tray. Cover with a damp cloth until ready to use.

NOTE: If the dough is either too moist or insufficiently floured, the skins will stick to one another in step 6.

PREPARING THE FILLINGS:

The following ingredients in various combinations may be used as wonton fillings:

Meats—Beef, chicken, lean pork or roast pork.

Seafood—Crabmeat, fish fillets, lobster or shrimp.

Vegetables—Celery, Chinese lettuce, leeks, onions.

BASIC WONTON FILLING

2 to 2½ cups meat   *1 scallion stalk*
½ to 1 cup vegetables   *1 tablespoon soy sauce*
½ teaspoon salt

1. Mince or shred meat and vegetables. Then combine with soy sauce and salt, blending well.

2. Let stand 30 minutes. Wrap mixture in wonton skins: fold as in the methods described below.

NOTE: The quantities given are for 40 wonton skins or about ½ pound. When raw pork is used, it may be stir-fried first with the scallion until it loses its pinkness, then sprinkled lightly with soy sauce and sherry.

VARIATIONS: For the meat above, use any of the following combinations:

Pork (lean or roast) and shrimp
Pork (lean or roast) and crabmeat
Pork (lean or roast) and fish fillets
Pork (lean or roast) and lobster

For the pork in the variations above, substitute chicken breast.

In step 1, add any of the following, minced or shredded: 1 or 2 dried black mushrooms (soaked); 2 tablespoons bamboo shoots; 2 tablespoons button mushrooms; 4 or 5 water chestnuts.

In step 2, for the soy sauce, substitute 2 tablespoons sherry.

In step 2, also add any of the following: 1 egg, beaten; 1 teaspoon cornstarch; ½ teaspoon sugar; ½ teaspoon ginger juice; 1 tablespoon peanut oil or a few drops of sesame oil.

FOLDING THE WONTONS:

METHOD I:

1. Hold the wonton skin in the palm of your left hand with the lower corner pointing toward you.

2. Place about ½ to 1 teaspoon of filling slightly below the center of the skin.

3. Moisten the two adjacent edges of the skin with beaten egg or other sealing agent (see Eggrolls, page 696, for details). Fold wonton skin diagonally in half to form a triangle.

4. Press the edges to seal, while at the same time gently pressing out any air pockets around the filling.

5. Brush a bit of the sealing agent on the front of the triangle's right corner and on the underside or back of the left corner.

6. With a twisting action, bring the two moistened surfaces together and pinch to seal.

METHOD II:

1. Hold the wonton skin as above.

2. With a knife or chopstick held in your right hand, scoop up about ½ teaspoon of filling and place it slightly below the center of the wonton skin.

3. Fold the lower corner over the knife; then pull the knife out, pressing the skin against it gently so the knife emerges clean.

4. Fold the upper corner of the skin down over the lower corner.

5. Dip the knife or chopstick in sealing agent, and use it to moisten the underside of the skin's left corner and the topside of its right corner.

6. Hold the left corner between thumb and index finger of the left hand, and the right corner in the same way with the right hand. Then, with a twisting motion, bring the two moistened surfaces together and pinch to seal.

COOKING THE WONTONS:

TO BOIL:

1. Drop the wontons into vigorously boiling salted water. (Add them gradually so as not to lower the temperature too abruptly.)

2. Cook until they float (about 10 minutes).

NOTE: For soup, boil the wontons as above, then drain well and add to the soup 1 or 2 minutes before serving. Or parboil the wontons for 2 minutes; then add to hot soup and simmer 5 to 10 minutes to complete the cooking.

TO DEEP-FRY:

1. Heat oil for deep-frying to 375 degrees. Add the wontons a few at a time.

2. Reduce heat to medium and deep-fry until golden on each side. Remove with a slotted spoon; drain on paper toweling.

TO DEEP-FRY BOILED WONTONS:

1. Boil as above. Place in a colander. Rinse with cold water. Drain and dry well (or they will spatter in the hot oil).

2. Deep-fry as above.

TO PAN-FRY:

1. Boil the wontons as above; then rinse and dry.

2. Heat 2 tablespoons oil.

3. Add the boiled wontons several at a time and brown on both sides.

TO STEAM:

1. Place the wontons one layer deep on a lightly oiled heatproof platter. Allow enough space between them so they will not stick together.

2. Steam 10 to 15 minutes (see page 831).

TO BRAISE:

1. Heat 2 tablespoons oil. Add wontons and brown quickly on both sides.

2. Add ½ cup stock or water and bring to a boil. Then reduce heat and cook, covered, until done (3 to 5 minutes).

SERVING THE WONTONS:

Serve deep-fried wontons with hot mustard, plum sauce or a sweet-and-pungent sauce (see pages 735–738).

Serve boiled wontons in individual bowls with clear soup. Garnish with Chinese parsley.

Serve boiled wontons with a vinegar-soy dip; or serve them covered with lobster sauce (see page 735).

STORING THE WONTONS:

Boiled wontons will keep refrigerated for several days. Drain them well and spread on a plate with space between them so they will not stick to one another. Sprinkle with a few drops of cold water and cover with transparent wrap.

Deep-fried wontons may be completely prepared in advance, then cooled, wrapped in foil and frozen. They can be reheated without preliminary thawing either by placing them in a slow oven or by immersing them briefly in hot oil. Leftover deep-fried wontons can be treated in the same way.

STORING WONTON SKINS: Wonton skins will keep about 2 weeks if wrapped well and refrigerated. They may also be wrapped and frozen but must be thawed completely before using.

❊ *Seasonings and Sauces* ❊

COMPARED TO the myriad spices of the West, relatively few condiments are used by the Chinese. Those they do use are designed to bring out the natural flavors of foods, never to mask or overwhelm them. Chinese seasonings are used in various ways: in dips, dressings, marinades and sauces.

Although Chinese food is usually seasoned by the cook, a number of plain-cooked meat, poultry and seafood dishes call for the diner to perform this function. This he does by immersing morsels of food in various dips and mixtures. Some dips, such as soy sauce and hoisin sauce, can be purchased ready-made; others, like hot mustard and pepper-salt mixes, are prepared at home. These at-the-table seasonings make for considerable culinary variety: a plain-cooked dish, served at various times with different dips, becomes in effect a series of different dishes.

The Chinese don't have raw salads as such, but they do toss briefly cooked vegetables in what are essentially salad dressings. (Cold cooked chicken, meat and shrimp are often prepared in a similar manner.) The ingredients of these dressings are few—mainly oil, vinegar, soy sauce, garlic and fresh ginger root—but their variations are many. The salad dressing is always added to the cold dish long enough before serving to flavor the food, but not so long before that it impairs the texture or discolors the brightness.

Marinades play a large and important part in Chinese cooking. These seasoned sauces or mixtures—in which meat, poultry and seafood are allowed to stand or marinate before being cooked—become partially absorbed and act both to flavor and to tenderize the food. Basic Chinese marinades include soy sauce, fresh ginger root, garlic, sugar, salt and pepper.

Chinese sauces are not as a rule superimposed on other ingredients, but created by the natural blending that occurs when vegetables, meat or fish and a few seasonings—such as soy sauce, sherry and salt—are cooked together. There are, however, some separately prepared sauces designed to enhance or enrich plain-cooked foods. These include vegetable sauces for deep-fried Peking chicken, piquant sauces for fish and seafood, meat sauces for noodles and rice, and soy sauce gravies for fried eggs and omelets.

There are also the sweet-and-pungent (or sweet-and-sour) sauces used to flavor cooked, particularly deep-fried foods, such as pork, shrimp, fish and chicken. The basic sweet-and-pungent ingredients are simply sugar and vinegar, to which soy sauce, fruit juices, cooked fruit and raw and pickled vegetables may be added. The sweetness of these sauces is largely a matter of personal taste and can be adjusted by the addition of either sugar or vinegar. In China, such preferences tend to be regional, with certain sections liking their sauces sweeter than others.

Sweet-and-pungent sauces may be prepared in advance, reheated at the last minute and added to the deep-fried food. Should the food have cooled slightly, it may be reheated in the sauce. Should the food have cooled considerably, it is better to reheat it briefly in the original deep-frying oil. (Otherwise, if warmed too long in the sweet-and-pungent sauce, it could lose its crispness.)

Another interesting Chinese sauce is the Master Sauce. This can be started with the gravy of any red-cooked meat or poultry dish. The gravy, however, is not served as a sauce with the dish that produced it. Instead, it is set aside and reserved as a cooking medium to be used again and again in the preparation of other red-cooked meats and poultry. The more this sauce is used in cooking subsequent dishes, the more subtle, rich and complex its flavor becomes. Master Sauces can be kept "alive" indefinitely if refrigerated in a covered container and either used—or brought to a boil—at least once a week. They must also be replenished, from time to time, with such seasonings as soy sauce, sherry and salt.

SEASONINGS

HOT MUSTARD

1 to 2 cups water   *½ cup powdered mustard*

1. Bring water to a boil; then let cool.
2. Gradually add water to dry mustard, stirring in a little at a time, until the mixture becomes smooth, thin and paste-like.
3. Let stand at least 15 minutes to "develop" its flavor (or better still, refrigerate, covered, overnight). Serve as a dip in small condiment dishes.

NOTE: Hot mustard can be prepared in smaller quantities, but the larger the batch, the better the flavor. Between uses, keep refrigerated in a tightly capped jar.

VARIATION: After step 1, add to the water a small amount of salt and vinegar.. (For each ½ cup water, allow ¼ teaspoon salt and 1 teaspoon vinegar.)

HOT PEPPER OIL

4 teaspoons peanut oil   *2 or 3 red chili peppers*

1. Heat oil. Add chili peppers and cook stirring over medium heat until oil becomes dark red.
2. Cool and strain.

NOTE: This seasoning, also known as Red Pepper Oil, Hot Salad Oil, or Szechwan Oil, needs no refrigeration.

VARIATION: For the peanut oil, substitute sesame oil.

For the fresh chili peppers, substitute ½ teaspoon dried, crushed chili peppers.

OYSTER SAUCE

12 oysters   *1 cup oyster liquid*

3 tablespoons soy sauce

1. Shell and mince oysters. Reserve their liquid.
2. Bring oysters and their liquid slowly to a boil; then simmer, covered, 20 minutes.
3. Strain mixture through a sieve, discarding oysters; stir in soy sauce.
4. Pour into a jar, cap tightly, and store in a cool place.

PLUM SAUCE I

½ cup chutney

1 cup plum jelly

1 tablespoon sugar

1 teaspoon vinegar

1. Chop chutney fine; then combine in a saucepan with plum jelly, sugar and vinegar. Blend well and heat thoroughly, stirring. (If mixture is too thick, thin with water.)

2. Pour into a jar, cap tightly, and store in a cool place. Serve as a dip in small condiment dishes.

VARIATIONS: For the plum jelly, substitute peach or apricot preserves.

For the white sugar, substitute brown sugar.

For the vinegar, substitute lemon juice.

PLUM SAUCE II

1 cup plums

1 cup apricots

½ cup pimiento

1 cup sugar

½ cup vinegar

½ cup applesauce

1. Peel and pit fresh plums and apricots; chop pimiento. Combine in a saucepan with sugar, vinegar and applesauce.

2. Bring slowly to a boil, stirring; then simmer, covered, 1 hour.

3. Pour into jars while still warm and cap tightly. Store at least 1 month in a cool, dark place before using.

NOTE: If the mixture is too thick, thin it slightly with water before serving. Sweeten, if desired, with additional sugar.

RED BEAN PASTE I

1 cup Chinese red beans	*½ to ¾ cup sugar*
water to cover	*4 to 6 tablespoons peanut oil*

1. Wash red beans. Place in a saucepan with cold water and bring to a boil. Then simmer, covered, until beans are soft (about 1 hour). Let cool slightly.

2. Strain beans through cheesecloth or force through a ricer. (Discard skins.) Combine beans with sugar and peanut oil.

3. Oil a pan lightly and heat. Add bean mixture and stir over low heat for 5 minutes. (The heat must be very low and the stirring constant to prevent scorching.)

NOTE: This mixture (used in Eight Precious Rice) may be made in advance and frozen.

VARIATIONS: For the white sugar, substitute brown sugar.

Omit step 3. Beat mixture with an electric beater until thick and pudding-like.

RED BEAN PASTE II

1 piece dried tangerine peel	*½ to ¾ cup sugar*
1 cup Chinese red beans	*½ cup water*
water to cover	*4 to 6 tablespoons lard*

1. Soak tangerine peel; then shred fine.

2. Place red beans, tangerine peel and water in a saucepan. Bring to a boil and simmer, covered, until soft (about 1 hour).

3. Transfer beans and their cooking water to a blender and blend at high speed. Then put in a cheesecloth square and squeeze out as much of the liquid as possible. Reserve the mash, discarding the liquid.

4. Bring sugar and remaining water to a boil. Then cook, stirring, over medium heat until the mixture spins a thin thread when a small amount is dropped from the tip of a spoon (3 to 4 minutes).

5. Stir in mash and lard. Cook, stirring constantly, until mixture is thick and pudding-like.

VARIATION: For the red beans, substitute ½ cup red bean powder (also known as red bean flour). Omit steps 2 and 3. Add this powder along with the tangerine peel at the end of step 4 and stir in to dissolve. Then add the lard and cook as in step 5.

SESAME PASTE

¼ cup water	*⅔ teaspoon salt*
¼ cup peanut butter	*few drops of sesame oil*

1. Gradually add water to peanut butter, stirring the mixture to a smooth paste.

2. Then blend in salt and sesame oil.

NOTE: This version approximates the imported variety.

BASIC PEPPER-SALT MIX

2 tablespoons salt   *1 teaspoon Szechwan peppercorns*

1. Heat salt and peppercorns in a dry skillet over medium-low heat. Stir or shake the pan constantly until the salt begins to brown and the odor of pepper is released (about 5 minutes).

2. Remove mixture from pan and let cool slightly. Crush peppercorns with a rolling pin; then strain through a sieve.

3. Store mixture in a tightly capped jar. Use as a table condiment or dip for deep-fried and roasted foods.

NOTE: These mixtures are also known as Fried Salt or Cantonese Salt.

VARIATION: For the peppercorns, substitute either 1 teaspoon ground black or white pepper; or ⅔ teaspoon Chinese red pepper.

CINNAMON-SALT MIX

2 tablespoons salt   *½ teaspoon ground cinnamon*

1. Heat salt in a dry skillet over medium-low heat. Stir or shake the pan constantly until the salt begins to brown; then remove from heat.

2. Let cool slightly; then stir in cinnamon. Store in a tightly covered jar.

VARIATIONS: For the cinnamon, substitute ½ teaspoon ground allspice.

Add with the cinnamon ½ teaspoon sugar and a pinch of Five Spices.

CINNAMON MIX

1 tablespoon ground cinnamon   1½ teaspoons ground ginger
¼ teaspoon ground pepper

1. Heat cinnamon, ginger and pepper in a dry skillet, over medium-low heat. Stir constantly or shake the pan until the mixture is very hot.

2. Serve as a dip with cold red-simmered chicken.

DIPS

SOY-OIL DIP FOR CHICKEN

2 to 3 tablespoons peanut oil   3 to 4 tablespoons soy sauce

1. Heat oil to smoking.

2. Turn off heat; stir in soy sauce. Serve in a dip dish, with white-cooked or roast chicken.

VARIATIONS: In step 1, add to the oil 1 clove garlic, crushed. Brown lightly; then discard.

At the end of step 1, pour the boiling oil over 1 scallion stalk and 2 or 3 slices fresh ginger root, both shredded. Omit the soy sauce.

OIL-SALT DIP FOR CHICKEN

3 tablespoons oil   2 teaspoons salt

1 bunch scallion stalks

1. Heat oil to smoking; then turn off heat.
2. Stir in salt; let cool slightly. Place in a dip dish.
3. Crush scallion stalks with a knife or cleaver blade; then cut in vertical slivers. Arrange in another dish.
4. Dip pieces of white-cooked or roast chicken in oil-salt mixture and eat with slivered scallions.

CHICKEN FAT-SOY DIP FOR CHICKEN

2 to 3 tablespoons chicken fat   1½ teaspoons hot pepper flakes

4 tablespoons soy sauce

1. Heat chicken fat.
2. Stir in and heat pepper flakes and soy sauce. Serve in a dip dish, with white-cooked or roast chicken.

VARIATION: For the hot pepper flakes, substitute ½ teaspoon cayenne pepper and a dash of powdered mustard.

GARLIC-SOY DIP FOR CHICKEN

2 garlic cloves   2 teaspoons Tabasco Sauce

⅛ teaspoon sugar   ½ cup soy sauce

1. Mince garlic; then blend well with remaining ingredients.
2. Serve in a dip dish, with white-cooked or roast chicken.

MUSTARD-SOY DIP FOR CHICKEN

1 tablespoon soy sauce   ½ teaspoon powdered mustard

few drops of sesame oil

1. Combine all ingredients, blending well.
2. Serve in a dip dish, with white-cooked or roast chicken.

HOISIN DIP FOR CHICKEN

1. Serve hoisin sauce in a dip dish. Cut scallion stalks in 1-inch sections and serve in a separate dish.
2. Use both as accompaniments for white-cooked or roast chicken.

SHERRY-SOY DIP FOR DEEP-FRIED CHICKEN

4 tablespoons sherry   *2 tablespoons soy sauce*

½ teaspoon sugar

1. Combine all ingredients, blending well.
2. Serve in a dip dish.

GARLIC-SOY DIP FOR DEEP-FRIED CHICKEN

2 garlic cloves   *1 teaspoon sugar*

2 tablespoons soy sauce   *1 teaspoon hot pepper oil*

1. Mince garlic; then blend well with remaining ingredients.
2. Serve in a dip dish.

VARIATION: For the hot pepper oil, substitute Tabasco Sauce.

DIPS FOR DEEP-FRIED DUCK

Combine Basic Pepper-Salt Mix (see page 708) with 1 to 2 tablespoons of catsup.

Combine plum sauce and a few drops of hot sauce.

CHEKIANG VINEGAR

2 or 3 slices fresh ginger root | ½ cup soy sauce
¼ to ½ cup vinegar | ½ teaspoon salt

1. Mince ginger root; then blend well with remaining ingredients.
2. Serve in a dip dish, to accompany pork.

VARIATIONS: For the ginger root, substitute 2 garlic cloves, minced.
For the salt, substitute ½ teaspoon sugar.
Reduce the soy sauce to 1 tablespoon.
Omit the soy sauce and salt.

SOY-SESAME DIP FOR PORK

¼ cup soy sauce | ½ teaspoon sesame oil

1. Blend soy sauce with sesame oil.
2. Serve in a dip dish.

VARIATIONS: Add any of the following, minced: ½ garlic clove, 2 teaspoons ginger root or ½ scallion stalk.
Add 1 teaspoon light brown sugar and 1 tablespoon vinegar.

SOY-MUSTARD DIP FOR PORK

2 tablespoons soy sauce | 4 tablespoons prepared mustard

1. Blend soy sauce with mustard.
2. Serve in a dip dish.

CHILI-SOY DIP FOR PORK

3 tablespoons Chinese chili sauce | 2 tablespoons soy sauce
pinch of powdered mustard

1. Combine all ingredients, blending well.
2. Serve in a dip dish.

NOTE: This dip is also fine for white-cooked chicken.
VARIATION: For the chili sauce, substitute catsup.

HOISIN DIP FOR PORK

Combine hoisin sauce with a few drops of sesame oil.

ALL-PURPOSE SEAFOOD DIP

2 or 3 slices *fresh ginger root*　　　　　　¼ cup *cider vinegar*

1. Mince ginger root; then blend well with vinegar.
2. Serve in a dip dish.

DIP FOR CLAMS

1 *scallion stalk*　　　　　　　　　　1 tablespoon *sherry*
3 or 4 slices *fresh ginger root*　　　　　1 teaspoon *peanut oil*
2 tablespoons *soy sauce*　　　　　　　few drops of *sesame oil*

1. Mince scallion and ginger root.
2. Blend well with remaining ingredients. Serve in a dip dish.

DIP FOR STEAMED CRAB

2 or 3 slices *fresh ginger root*　　　　3 or 4 tablespoons *soy sauce*

1. Mince ginger root; then blend well with soy sauce.
2. Serve in a dip dish.

NOTE: This dip is also used with deep-fried shrimp.

VARIATION: For the ginger root, substitute any of the following: 1 scallion stalk, minced; 1 garlic clove, crushed; or ½ teaspoon powdered mustard.

DIP FOR POACHED SHRIMP

1 or 2 slices *fresh ginger root*　　　　2 teaspoons *vinegar*
2 teaspoons *sugar*　　　　　　　　　4 tablespoons *soy sauce*

1. Mince ginger root; then blend well with remaining ingredients.
2. Serve in a dip dish.

VARIATION: For the ginger root, substitute ½ teaspoon horseradish.

DIP I FOR DEEP-FRIED SHRIMP

1 *garlic clove*　　　　　　　　　　¼ cup *soy sauce*
2 tablespoons *sherry*　　　　　　　½ teaspoon *salt*
2 tablespoons *honey*　　　　　　　dash of *pepper*

1. Mince garlic clove; then blend well with remaining ingredients.
2. Serve in a dip dish.

DIP II FOR DEEP-FRIED SHRIMP

2 tablespoons catsup   1 tablespoon Chinese chili

1 teaspoon hoisin sauce

1. Combine all ingredients, blending well.
2. Serve in a dip dish.

MISCELLANEOUS DIPS FOR DEEP-FRIED SHRIMP

Light soy sauce and lemon wedges.
Hot sauce and catsup.
Hot mustard and hoisin sauce.

DIP FOR DEEP-FRIED SHRIMP BALLS

1 teaspoon sugar   1 teaspoon water
2 teaspoons hoisin sauce   1 teaspoon sesame oil

1. Combine all ingredients, blending well.
2. Serve in a dip dish.

DIP FOR DEEP-FRIED BEAN CURD

1 tablespoon soy sauce   2 tablespoons peanut oil
1 tablespoon peanut butter   ½ teaspoon hot sauce

1 teaspoon sesame oil

1. Combine all ingredients, blending well.
2. Serve in a dip dish.

DIP FOR DEEP-FRIED WONTON

4 tablespoons soy sauce   2 teaspoons wine vinegar
¼ teaspoon powdered mustard

1. Combine all ingredients, blending well.
2. Serve in a dip dish.

DRESSINGS

SOY-VINEGAR DRESSING

1½ teaspoons sugar   *3 tablespoons vinegar*

3 tablespoons soy sauce   *2 tablespoons peanut oil*

1. Combine sugar, soy sauce and vinegar.
2. Gradually stir in oil to blend. Pour over cold vegetables.

VARIATIONS: For the vinegar, use wine vinegar; or substitute lemon juice to taste.

For the peanut oil, substitute 1 teaspoon sherry and a few drops of sesame oil.

In step 1, add either 1 or 2 slices fresh ginger root, or 1 or 2 garlic cloves, minced. Or add ½ teaspoon powdered mustard and ¼ teaspoon paprika.

SOY-SESAME DRESSING

4 tablespoons soy sauce   *½ to 1 teaspoon sesame oil*

1. Blend together soy sauce and sesame oil.
2. Pour over cold cooked meat or fish.

SOY-OIL DRESSING

2 tablespoons soy sauce	½ teaspoon salt
1 tablespoon peanut oil	½ teaspoon sugar

1. Combine all ingredients, blending well.
2. Pour over cold vegetables, cold cooked meat or fish.

OIL-VINEGAR DRESSING

4 tablespoons oil	¾ teaspoon salt
2 tablespoons vinegar	¼ teaspoon pepper
1 teaspoon sugar	few drops of sesame oil

1. Combine all ingredients, blending well.
2. Pour over cold vegetables, cold cooked meat or fish.

VARIATION: For the salt and pepper, substitute ½ teaspoon powdered mustard and ¼ teaspoon paprika.

CHINESE MAYONNAISE

2 tablespoons vinegar	1 teaspoon peanut oil
1 tablespoon water	½ cup sesame paste
salt and pepper	

1. Combine vinegar, cold water and oil, blending well.
2. Gradually stir in sesame paste (see page 707) to blend. Then season with salt and pepper to taste.

VARIATION: In step 1, add 1 tablespoon soy sauce or a pinch of powdered mustard.

EGG DRESSING

1 egg	1 tablespoon soy sauce
1 slice fresh ginger root	1 tablespoon catsup
1 garlic clove	½ teaspoon sugar
4 tablespoons peanut oil	½ teaspoon salt
dash of pepper	

1. Hardboil egg. Cool under cold running water; then shell. Mince egg and ginger root.
2. Cut garlic clove in two. Rub a bowl with its cut surfaces; then discard garlic.

3. In the bowl combine minced egg and ginger root with remaining ingredients, blending well. Use with cold vegetables.

NOTE: This dressing may be made in quantity, put up in a jar and refrigerated. It will keep for weeks.

MUSTARD DRESSING

1 tablespoon powdered mustard	*2 tablespoons vinegar*
2 tablespoons soy sauce	*1 teaspoon sugar*

few drops of sesame oil

1. Combine all ingredients in a jar. Cap tightly; then shake well to blend.
2. Refrigerate 3 to 4 hours to "develop" the flavor. Use with blanched bean sprouts or cold chicken.

MARINADES

BASIC MARINADE FOR BARBECUED PORK

½ cup soy sauce   *¼ cup sherry*

1 tablespoon sugar

1. Combine all ingredients.
2. Add to pork and marinate. (See pages 190–191.)

VARIATION: Add 2 scallion stalks and 2 or 3 slices fresh ginger root, both minced. Or add ¼ teaspoon ground cinnamon and a dash of pepper.

SUGAR-SOY MARINADE FOR BARBECUED PORK

1 garlic clove	*½ cup soy sauce*
¼ cup sugar	*½ teaspoon salt*

1. Crush garlic; then combine with remaining ingredients.
2. Add to pork and marinate (see pages 190–191).

VARIATION: Add 2 tablespoons catsup in step 1.

SPICED MARINADE FOR BARBECUED PORK

1 *garlic clove*
2 *tablespoons soy sauce*
1 *tablespoon sherry*
1 *teaspoon sugar*

½ *teaspoon salt*
¼ *teaspoon pepper*
¼ *teaspoon cinnamon*
¼ *teaspoon ground cloves*

¼ *teaspoon ground anise*

1. Mince garlic; then combine with remaining ingredients.
2. Rub into pork and let stand 1 hour (see pages 190–191).

PINEAPPLE-SHERRY MARINADE FOR BARBECUED PORK

1 *garlic clove*
1 *cup pineapple juice*

2 *cups soy sauce*
½ *cup sherry*

1½ *tablespoons brown sugar*

1. Crush garlic; then combine with remaining ingredients.
2. Add to pork and marinate (see pages 190–191).

GARLIC-ONION MARINADE FOR BARBECUED PORK

2 *cloves garlic*
⅛ *cup onion*
4 *slices fresh ginger root*

½ *cup soy sauce*
3 *tablespoons sugar*
few drops of sesame oil

1. Mince garlic, onion and ginger root; then combine with remaining ingredients.
2. Add to pork and marinate (see pages 190–191).

HOISIN—FIVE-SPICES MARINADE FOR BARBECUED PORK

1½ *tablespoons soy sauce*
2½ *tablespoons hoisin sauce*
1 *tablespoon sherry*

1 *tablespoon honey*
1½ *teaspoons sugar*
pinch of Five Spices

1. Combine all ingredients.
2. Rub into pork and let stand 1 hour (see pages 190–191).

HOISIN-CHILI MARINADE FOR BARBECUED PORK

2 garlic cloves	4 tablespoons sherry
4 slices fresh ginger root	1 tablespoon hoisin sauce
1 scallion	1 tablespoon chili sauce
2 tablespoons soy sauce	1 tablespoon honey

½ teaspoon salt

1. Crush garlic and ginger root; cut scallion in 2-inch sections. Then combine with remaining ingredients.
2. Rub into pork and let stand 1 hour (see pages 190–191).

SHERRY—BROWN-SUGAR MARINADE FOR BARBECUED PORK

1 scallion stalk	½ cup soy sauce
1 or 2 slices fresh ginger root	1½ tablespoons brown sugar
⅛ cup stock	½ teaspoon salt
¼ cup sherry	2 teaspoons honey

dash of pepper

1. Cut scallion stalk in ½-inch sections; mince ginger root. Then combine with remaining ingredients.
2. Add to pork and marinate (see pages 190–191).

SOY-SHERRY MARINADE FOR BARBECUED PORK

1 teaspoon salt	½ cup soy sauce
2 teaspoons sugar	¼ cup sherry
1 or 2 garlic cloves	1 tablespoon honey
1 scallion stalk	1 tablespoon honey

½ teaspoon sugar

1. Rub pork strips with salt and sugar. Let stand 30 minutes.
2. Meanwhile crush garlic and mince scallion; then combine with soy sauce, sherry and honey. Add to pork strips and let stand 30 minutes more, turning frequently. Drain, discarding marinade.
3. Combine remaining honey with remaining sugar. Brush over the meat and roast (see page 191).
VARIATION: Omit the sugar in step 3. Instead, add a few drops of sesame oil to the honey.

FIVE SPICES MARINADE FOR BARBECUED PORK

1 teaspoon sugar	dash of pepper
½ teaspoon Five Spices	2 tablespoons soy sauce
½ teaspoon salt	1 teaspoon sherry

1. Combine sugar, Five Spices, salt and pepper. Rub mixture over pork strips and let stand 2 hours.

2. Add soy sauce and sherry and toss. Let stand 30 minutes more, turning frequently. Then roast (see page 191).

SHERRY-HONEY MARINADE FOR BARBECUED PORK

2 teaspoons sugar	4 tablespoons soy sauce
1 teaspoon salt	2 tablespoons sherry
2 cloves garlic	2 tablespoons honey

1. Rub pork strips with sugar and salt; let stand 2 hours.

2. Crush garlic; then combine with soy sauce, sherry and honey. Add to pork and let stand 30 minutes more, turning frequently. Then roast (see page 191).

SOY-SUGAR MARINADE FOR BARBECUED PORK

½ cup water	1 teaspoon salt
2 tablespoons sugar	¼ cup soy sauce

1. Heat water. Stir in sugar and salt to dissolve; then add soy sauce.

2. Add to pork strips and let stand 2 hours, turning frequently. Then roast (see page 191).

BROWN BEAN MARINADE FOR BARBECUED PORK

1 teaspoon brown bean sauce	2 tablespoons sugar
1 garlic clove	1 tablespoon soy sauce
½ cup stock	1 tablespoon sherry
1½ teaspoons salt	½ teaspoon Five Spices
½ teaspoon red food coloring	

1. Mash brown beans to a paste; mince garlic. Then combine in a saucepan with stock, salt, sugar and soy sauce. Slowly heat, stirring, but do not boil.

2. Remove pan from heat. Then stir in sherry, Five Spices and food coloring,

mixing well to blend. Add mixture to pork strips and let stand 2 to 3 hours, turning frequently. Then roast (see page 191).

VARIATION: For the food coloring, substitute enough tomato sauce to add color or the liquid from maraschino cherries.

BASIC MARINADE FOR BARBECUED SPARERIBS

1 *garlic clove*   1 *cup soy sauce*
3 *slices fresh ginger root*   1 *tablespoon sugar*
1 *tablespoon sherry*

1. Crush garlic and ginger root; then combine with remaining ingredients.
2. Add to spareribs and marinate (see page 201).

VARIATIONS: Rub the spareribs first with 1 teaspoon salt and 1 teaspoon sugar. Let stand 1 hour; then marinate.

Reduce the soy sauce to ¾ cup; increase the sherry to ¼ cup.

Reduce the sugar to 1 teaspoon and add ½ teaspoon Five Spices. For the sherry, substitute brandy.

Add 2 tablespoons honey and 2 tablespoons of either hoisin sauce or applesauce.

STOCK-SOY MARINADE FOR BARBECUED SPARERIBS

2 *garlic cloves*   ¼ *cup soy sauce*
2 *slices fresh ginger root*   1 *tablespoon sugar*
1 *cup stock*   2 *tablespoons sherry*

1. Mince garlic and ginger root; then combine with remaining ingredients.
2. Add to spareribs and marinate (see page 201).

VARIATIONS: For the white sugar, substitute brown sugar.

Add 3 tablespoons honey and 3 tablespoons vinegar.

Add ½ cup catsup and 1 teaspoon salt.

PINEAPPLE-SOY MARINADE FOR BARBECUED SPARERIBS

1 *garlic clove*	½ *cup pineapple juice*
1 *cup soy sauce*	¼ *cup sherry*

1½ *tablespoons brown sugar*

1. Mince garlic; then combine with remaining ingredients.
2. Add to spareribs and marinate (see page 201).

SOY-SUGAR MARINADE FOR BARBECUED SPARERIBS

1 *garlic clove*	1 *tablespoon sugar*
2 *slices fresh ginger root*	1 *teaspoon salt*
¼ *cup soy sauce*	*dash of pepper*

1. Mince garlic and ginger root; then combine with remaining ingredients.
2. Rub mixture over spareribs. Let stand 1 hour; then roast (see page 201).

VARIATIONS: For the regular soy sauce, substitute 5 tablespoons light soy sauce and 1½ teaspoons heavy soy sauce.

Omit the ginger root. Substitute a second garlic clove. Add 2 tablespoons sherry and ½ teaspoon each of ground cinnamon, anise and cloves. Omit the pepper.

Add 2 teaspoons brown bean sauce, mashed; and ½ teaspoon ground cinnamon.

BROWN SUGAR MARINADE FOR BARBECUED SPARERIBS

2 *slices fresh ginger root*	3 *tablespoons soy sauce*
4 *tablespoons brown sugar*	½ *teaspoon Five Spices*

1 *teaspoon sherry*

1. Mince ginger root; then combine with remaining ingredients.
2. Rub mixture over spareribs. Let stand 1 hour; then roast (see page 201).

FIVE SPICES MARINADE FOR BARBECUED SPARERIBS

1. Cut a garlic clove in two; rub its cut surfaces over the spareribs.
2. Rub Five Spices over the meat. Let stand 1 hour; then roast (see page 201).

NOTE: Allow about ½ teaspoon Five Spices per pound of meat.

RED BEAN CHEESE MARINADE FOR BARBECUED SPARERIBS

2 tablespoons Chinese red bean cheese
½ garlic clove
2 tablespoons soy sauce

1 teaspoon salt
½ teaspoon sugar
½ teaspoon Five Spices

1. Mash red bean cheese and crush garlic; then combine with remaining ingredients.
2. Rub mixture over spareribs. Let stand 1 hour; then roast (see page 201).

CATSUP-HOISIN MARINADE FOR BARBECUED SPARERIBS

1 tablespoon Chinese red bean cheese
½ cup catsup

¼ cup hoisin sauce
2 tablespoons sugar

½ teaspoon salt

1. Mash red bean cheese; then combine with remaining ingredients.
2. Rub mixture over spareribs and refrigerate, covered, overnight. Then roast (see page 201).

HOISIN-SOY MARINADE FOR BARBECUED SPARERIBS

5 tablespoons hoisin sauce
3 tablespoons soy sauce

2 tablespoons sherry
2 tablespoons sugar

¼ teaspoon Five Spices

1. Combine all ingredients.
2. Rub mixture over spareribs. Let stand 1 to 2 hours; then roast (see page 201).

VARIATIONS: For the Five Spices, substitute ground anise or garlic powder.

Omit the sherry, sugar and Five Spices. Substitute 1 tablespoon chili sauce, 2 tablespoons catsup and 2 tablespoons honey.

Add the following, minced: 1 garlic clove, 1 slice fresh ginger root and 2 scallions.

FIVE SPICES MARINADE FOR BASIC ROAST CHICKEN

2 cloves garlic	½ teaspoon Five Spices
4 tablespoons soy sauce	1 teaspoon salt
2 tablespoons oil	1 teaspoon sugar
¼ teaspoon pepper	

1. Mince garlic; then combine with remaining ingredients, blending well.

2. Rub mixture over chicken inside and out and let stand 1 hour. Drain, reserving marinade for basting. Then roast (see page 382).

SCALLION-HONEY MARINADE FOR BASIC ROAST CHICKEN

¼ cup scallion stalks	1 cup soy sauce
2 cloves garlic	2 tablespoons sherry
2 or 3 slices fresh ginger root	1 tablespoon honey
1 teaspoon salt	

1. Cut scallion stalks in ½-inch lengths; mince the garlic and ginger root. Then combine with remaining ingredients, blending well.

2. Rub mixture over chicken inside and out. Let stand 1 hour, turning bird occasionally. Drain, reserving marinade for basting. Then roast (see page 382).

TANGERINE PEEL MARINADE FOR BASIC ROAST CHICKEN

1 piece tangerine peel	1 tablespoon sugar
1 garlic clove	1 teaspoon salt
1½ cups stock	dash of pepper
½ cup soy sauce	few drops of sesame oil

1. Soak tangerine peel; then mince, along with garlic clove. Place in a deep bowl.

2. Heat stock and add with remaining ingredients, blending well.

3. Add chicken; let stand 2 hours, turning occasionally. Drain, reserving marinade for basting. Then roast (see page 382).

HOISIN MARINADE FOR BASIC ROAST CHICKEN

½ cup hoisin sauce	½ cup water

1. Combine hoisin sauce and water; brush over chicken.

2. Let stand 1½ to 2 hours, turning occasionally. Drain, reserving marinade for basting. Then roast (see page 382).

SAUCES

SOY-VINEGAR SAUCE FOR DEEP-FRIED PEKING CHICKEN

½ *leek stalk*
1 *slice fresh ginger root*
½ *garlic clove*

3 *tablespoons soy sauce*
1½ *tablespoons vinegar*
2 *teaspoons sugar*

few drops of sesame oil

1. Mince leek, ginger root and garlic. Then combine in a saucepan with remaining ingredients.

2. Cook 2 minutes over low heat, stirring constantly. Then pour over chicken and serve.

MIXED VEGETABLE SAUCE FOR DEEP-FRIED PEKING CHICKEN

4 *dried black mushrooms*
4 *slices fresh ginger root*
¼ *cup bamboo shoots*
½ *cup Chinese lettuce*
2 *water chestnuts*
2 *tablespoons oil*

½ *teaspoon salt*
½ *cup stock*
½ *teaspoon sugar*
dash of pepper
1 *tablespoon cornstarch*
3 *tablespoons water*

1. Soak dried mushrooms.

2. Shred ginger root. Slice bamboo shoots, Chinese lettuce, water chestnuts and soaked mushrooms.

3. Heat oil. Add salt, then ginger root, and stir-fry a few times.

4. Add all sliced vegetables; stir-fry to heat through (1 to 2 minutes). Add stock and heat quickly. Cook, covered, 2 to 3 minutes; then stir in sugar and pepper.

5. Meanwhile blend cornstarch and cold water to a paste. Then stir in to thicken. Pour sauce over chicken and serve.

GREEN-PEA—CATSUP SAUCE FOR DEEP-FRIED PEKING CHICKEN

1 *cup green peas*
2 *tablespoons oil*
¼ *cup catsup*

2 *tablespoons sherry*
1 *teaspoon sugar*
½ *teaspoon salt*

¾ *cup stock*

1. Shell green peas.

2. Heat oil. Add peas; stir-fry 1 minute. Then stir in catsup, sherry, sugar and salt.

3. Add stock and heat quickly.

4. Add deep-fried chicken pieces. Simmer, covered, to heat through; then serve.

STOCK-SOY SAUCE FOR DEEP-FRIED PEKING CHICKEN

2 *scallion stalks*	1 *teaspoon sherry*
3 *slices fresh ginger root*	¼ *cup water*
2 *tablespoons oil*	1 *tablespoon cornstarch*
2 *tablespoons soy sauce*	3 *tablespoons water*

½ *cup stock*

1. Mince scallion stalks and ginger root.

2. Heat oil. Add scallion and ginger; stir-fry a few times. Then stir in and heat soy sauce, sherry and water.

3. Add deep-fried chicken pieces and cook to heat through, turning once. Remove chicken to a warm platter.

4. Meanwhile blend cornstarch and remaining cold water to a paste.

5. Heat stock in a pan; then stir in cornstarch paste to thicken. Pour sauce over chicken and serve.

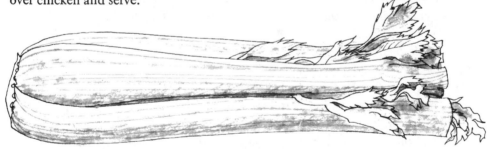

CELERY SAUCE FOR DEEP-FRIED PEKING CHICKEN

2 *celery stalks*	2 *tablespoons oil*
3 *scallion stalks*	1 *cup stock*
1 *tablespoon sherry*	1 *tablespoon cornstarch*
2 *tablespoons soy sauce*	3 *tablespoons cold water*

1. Slice celery stalks thin. Mince scallions. Place both in a saucepan.

2. Add sherry, soy sauce, oil and stock; bring slowly to a boil.

3. Add deep-fried chicken pieces and simmer, covered, to heat through. Remove chicken, leaving liquids in pan.

4. Meanwhile blend cornstarch and cold water to a paste; then stir in to thicken. Pour sauce over chicken and serve.

SIMPLE SAUCE FOR WHITE CUT CHICKEN

1 cup stock	1 teaspoon soy sauce
½ teaspoon salt	1 tablespoon cornstarch

3 tablespoons water

1. Bring stock to a boil; stir in salt and soy sauce.
2. Meanwhile blend cornstarch and cold water to a paste; then stir in to thicken. Pour sauce over chicken and vegetables, and serve.

EGG YOLK SAUCE FOR WHITE CUT CHICKEN

2 egg yolks	2 teaspoons cornstarch
¼ cup water	¾ cup water
2 tablespoons oil	½ teaspoon salt

1. Beat egg yolks and water lightly together.
2. Heat oil. Stir in cornstarch until smooth. Then add remaining water and salt and heat, stirring, until mixture is smooth and bubbling.
3. Gradually pour in beaten eggs, adding them in a thin stream and stirring constantly. Cook, stirring, over low heat until sauce is smooth and creamy. Pour over chicken and vegetables and serve.

MILK SAUCE FOR WHITE CUT CHICKEN

1½ cups milk	1 teaspoon sherry
2 tablespoons butter	½ teaspoon salt
1 teaspoon sugar	1 tablespoon cornstarch

3 tablespoons water

1. Heat, but do not boil, milk. Then, over low heat, stir in butter, sugar, sherry and salt. Cook only to heat through.
2. Meanwhile blend cornstarch and cold water to a paste, then stir in to thicken. Pour sauce over chicken and vegetables and serve.

FRIED EGG SAUCE

1 scallion	½ tablespoon brown sugar
1 tablespoon oil	1 tablespoon soy sauce

2 tablespoons water

1. Mince scallion.
2. Heat oil. Add scallion; stir-fry to brown lightly.
3. Stir in brown sugar, soy sauce and water; cook to heat through. Sprinkle sauce over fried eggs and serve.

EGG FOO YUNG SAUCE I

¾ *cup stock*	1 *teaspoon soy sauce*
½ *teaspoon salt*	2 *teaspoons cornstarch*

2 *tablespoons water*

1. Heat stock; then stir in salt and soy sauce.
2. Meanwhile blend cornstarch and cold water to a paste. Then stir in to thicken.
3. Spoon sauce over each omelet; or serve hot in a side dish as a dip.

VARIATIONS: In step 1, add to the stock ¼ teaspoon sugar, a dash of pepper, and either 1 tablespoon peanut oil or a few drops of sesame oil. Or add 1 tablespoon oyster sauce (omit the salt). Or add 1 tablespoon catsup and/or 2 teaspoons sherry (increase the soy sauce to 1 tablespoon).

Omit the soy sauce in step 1, and add it instead in step 2, increasing it to 1 tablespoon and blending it with the cornstarch. Also blend in 1 teaspoon molasses or dark corn syrup. Omit the water.

EGG FOO YUNG SAUCE II

2 *dried black mushrooms*	1 *tablespoon oil*
2 *tablespoons green peas*	1 *cup stock*
½ *cup bamboo shoots*	2 *tablespoons soy sauce*
½ *leek stalk*	1 *tablespoon cornstarch*

2 *tablespoons water*

1. Soak dried mushrooms. Shell and parboil peas.
2. Shred bamboo shoots, leek and soaked mushrooms.
3. Heat oil. Add shredded vegetables and stir-fry about 2 minutes.
4. Add stock, soy sauce and peas; heat quickly.
5. Meanwhile blend cornstarch and cold water to a paste; then stir in to thicken. Pour sauce over omelets and serve.

NOTE: This sauce is best with simple egg foo yung, not the complex subgum variety.

BEEF SAUCE FOR NOODLES

1 cup beef	½ teaspoon salt
1 garlic clove	¾ cup stock
1 small onion	½ teaspoon sugar
1 tomato	1 tablespoon cornstarch
2 tablespoons oil	3 tablespoons water

Chinese parsley

1. Mince or grind beef. Mince garlic and onion. Peel tomato and cut in wedges.

2. Heat oil. Add salt, then garlic and onion; stir-fry until translucent. Add beef; stir-fry to brown lightly.

3. Add stock, sugar and tomato wedges. Heat quickly, stirring.

4. Meanwhile blend cornstarch and cold water to a paste; then stir in to thicken. Pour sauce over noodles. Garnish with parsley and serve.

VARIATION: Omit the tomato and sugar. Instead, after step 2, add to beef 1 cup fresh mushrooms, 2 celery stalks and 1 green pepper, all diced. Stir-fry 1 to 2 minutes more; then add the stock and simmer, covered, 2 to 3 minutes. Pick up step 4.

HAM SAUCE FOR NOODLES

1 cup ham	1 cup stock
2 celery stalks	1 teaspoon cornstarch
1 small onion	¼ cup water
2 tablespoons oil	1 egg

1. Chop ham coarsely. Dice celery and onion.

2. Heat oil. Add celery, onion and ham; stir-fry 2 minutes.

3. Add stock and heat quickly. Then cook, covered, 3 minutes over medium heat.

4. Meanwhile blend cornstarch and cold water to a paste; then beat egg lightly and blend in.

5. Stir cornstarch paste into stock to thicken. Pour sauce over noodles and serve.

PORK SAUCE I FOR NOODLES

¼ to ½ pound lean pork	½ cup water
1 scallion stalk	2 tablespoons oil
2 tablespoons cornstarch	1 tablespoon soy sauce

1. Mince or grind pork. Mince scallion. Blend cornstarch and water to a paste.

2. Heat oil. Add minced scallion and stir-fry a few times. Add pork; stir-fry

until it loses its pinkness. Then stir-fry 2 to 3 minutes more over medium-low heat.

3. Sprinkle with soy sauce. Then stir in cornstarch paste to thicken mixture. Pour over noodles and serve.

VARIATION: In step 3, add with the soy sauce, 1 tablespoon sherry and a pinch of salt.

PORK SAUCE II FOR NOODLES

½ pound lean pork	1 tablespoon soy sauce
2 to 3 cups vegetables	½ cup tomato sauce
2 scallion stalks	2 cups stock
1 garlic clove	2 tablespoons oil
½ tablespoon brown sugar	1 tablespoon cornstarch
1 tablespoon sherry	2 tablespoons water

1. Mince or grind pork.

2. Dice vegetables. Cut scallions in ½-inch sections. Crush garlic.

3. Combine brown sugar, sherry, soy sauce, tomato sauce and stock.

4. Heat oil. Add scallions and garlic; stir-fry to brown lightly. Add minced pork; stir-fry until it loses its pinkness.

5. Add diced vegetables; stir-fry 2 minutes more.

6. Add brown sugar-sherry mixture and heat quickly. Then cook, covered, 3 to 4 minutes over medium heat.

7. Meanwhile blend cornstarch and cold water to a paste; then stir in to thicken. Pour sauce over noodles and serve.

NOTE: Any of the following vegetables can be used in any combination— bamboo shoots, bean sprouts, celery, Chinese lettuce, green pepper, mushrooms, water chestnuts, and tomatoes. (The tomatoes should be added at the end of step 6, only to heat through.)

VARIATIONS: Omit step 3. After step 4, add the soy sauce and sherry, plus a few drops of sesame oil, and stir-fry the pork 1 minute more. Pick up step 5. In step 6, add only the stock. Then pick up step 7.

In step 7, add to the cornstarch paste 2 teaspoons soy sauce and ½ teaspoon sugar.

PEKING MEAT SAUCE FOR NOODLES

¼ to ½ pound lean pork	2 tablespoons soy sauce
2 teaspoons sherry	1 tablespoon hoisin sauce
½ cup scallions	2 tablespoons oil
½ cup yellow bean paste	1½ cups water

1. Mince or grind pork; then blend in sherry. Mince scallions.

2. Blend together bean paste, soy sauce and hoisin sauce.

3. Heat oil. Add minced pork; stir-fry 1 minute. Add minced scallions and stir-fry 1 minute more.

4. Stir in bean paste mixture. Add water and heat quickly. Then cook, stirring, 2 minutes over low heat.

5. Serve with cooked wheat-flour noodles either mixed together (use about ¼ cup meat sauce for every 1½ cups cooked noodles); or serve the noodles in one dish, the sauce in another so that the diner can mix his own.

NOTE: This dish is always served accompanied by dishes containing such vegetables as shredded radishes and cucumbers, blanched bean sprouts and spinach strips, as well as 4 or 5 minced garlic cloves. The diner tops his noodles and sauce at intervals with a bit of garlic and 1 to 2 tablespoons of vegetables.

CHICKEN STOCK SAUCE FOR NOODLES

1½ tablespoons cornstarch   2 cups stock

1 tablespoon oil

1. Blend together cornstarch and cold stock.

2. Heat oil. Add cornstarch mixture and cook, stirring, over medium heat until thickened and smooth. Pour sauce over noodles and serve.

NOTE: This is best when made with a rich, concentrated chicken stock.

MUSHROOM SAUCE I FOR RICE

1 cup canned button mushrooms   1 tablespoon oil

1 tablespoon cornstarch   1 cup water

2 tablespoons water   2 teaspoons soy sauce

1 teaspoon soy sauce   1 tablespoon sherry

dash of pepper   ½ teaspoon sugar

¼ teaspoon salt

1. Drain canned button mushrooms; then slice.

2. Blend cornstarch, water, soy sauce and pepper to a paste.

3. Heat oil. Add mushrooms, then remaining water and soy sauce; also sherry, sugar and salt. Cook, stirring, only to heat through.

4. Stir in cornstarch paste to thicken; then pour sauce over rice and serve.

NOTE: This sauce is also good as a topping for stir-fried spinach.

VARIATION: At the end of step 4, sprinkle with a few drops of sesame oil.

MUSHROOM SAUCE II FOR RICE

12 *dried black mushrooms*	1 *tablespoon peanut oil*
2 *tablespoons peanut oil*	½ *cup mushroom-soaking liquid*
4 *tablespoons soy sauce*	1 *tablespoon sugar*
1 *tablespoon sherry*	1 *teaspoon cornstarch*
½ *teaspoon salt*	1 *tablespoon water*

1. Soak dried mushrooms; reserve their soaking liquid.

2. Heat oil. Add soaked mushrooms and stir-fry 2 minutes. Stir in soy sauce and sherry, then salt.

3. Add remaining oil, mushroom-soaking liquid and sugar. Heat quickly; then simmer, covered, 30 minutes.

4. Blend cornstarch and cold water to a paste; then stir in to thicken. Pour sauce over rice and serve.

FISH SAUCE I

2 or 3 *slices fresh ginger root*	2 *tablespoons brown sugar*
1 *tablespoon cornstarch*	1 *tablespoon oil*
3 *tablespoons water*	¼ *cup stock*

1. Mince ginger root. Blend cornstarch and cold water to a paste.

2. In a pan, combine sugar, oil, stock and minced ginger. Then bring to a boil, stirring, over medium heat.

3. Stir in cornstarch paste to thicken. Pour sauce over deep-fried fish and serve.

FISH SAUCE II

4 *dried black mushrooms*	1 *tablespoon sherry*
6 *dried lily buds*	½ *teaspoon salt*
½ *cup lean pork*	½ *teaspoon sugar*
½ *cup bamboo shoots*	2 *tablespoons oil*
2 *cups Chinese lettuce*	1½ *cups water*
2 *slices fresh ginger root*	1 *tablespoon cornstarch*
1 *tablespoon soy sauce*	3 *tablespoons water*

1. Separately soak dried mushrooms and lily buds.

2. Cut pork, bamboo shoots, Chinese lettuce and soaked mushrooms in strips. Shred ginger root.

3. Cut soaked lily buds in two; then combine with soy sauce, sherry, salt and sugar.

4. Heat oil. Add shredded ginger and stir-fry a few times. Add pork; stir-fry until it loses its pinkness (2 to 3 minutes).

5. Add julienned vegetables; stir-fry 1 minute more. Add water and heat quickly. Then cook, covered, 2 minutes over medium heat.

6. Meanwhile blend cornstarch and remaining cold water to a paste. First stir in lily bud mixture and heat through; then stir in cornstarch paste to thicken. Pour sauce over deep-fried fish and serve.

FIVE WILLOW SAUCE I

¼ cup green pepper	2 tablespoons sugar
¼ cup carrots	2 tablespoons vinegar
¼ cup tomatoes	1 tablespoon cornstarch
1 cup sweet mixed pickles	1 tablespoon sherry
1 cup water	¼ cup water

1. Shred green pepper, carrots, tomatoes and sweet pickles.

2. Bring water to a boil. Stir in sugar and vinegar to dissolve.

3. Meanwhile blend cornstarch, sherry and remaining cold water to a paste; then stir in to thicken.

4. Add shredded vegetables and simmer 3 minutes, stirring occasionally. Pour over fish and serve.

VARIATION: Omit steps 2 and 3. Instead, combine in a saucepan 1 cup water, 1 tablespoon cornstarch, 2 tablespoons sugar, 2 tablespoons soy sauce and 2 tablespoons vinegar. Bring to a boil and cook, stirring, over medium heat until the sauce thickens. Then add the vegetables and simmer as in step 4.

FIVE WILLOW SAUCE II

1 cucumber	½ cup vinegar
1 carrot	½ cup water
1 Chinese sweet pickle	2 tablespoons sugar
½ cup onions	1 teaspoon salt
2 slices fresh ginger root	1 tablespoon cornstarch
2 garlic cloves	2 tablespoons soy sauce

2 tablespoons oil

1. Peel and seed cucumber; cut in strips. Also cut carrot and sweet pickle in strips. Mince onions and ginger root. Crush garlic.

2. Combine vegetables with vinegar, water, sugar and salt. Let stand 1 hour, turning occasionally.

3. Drain vegetables. Combine their marinade with cornstarch and soy sauce, blending well.

4. Heat oil. Brown garlic lightly. Add marinade mixture and cook, stirring, over medium heat until sauce thickens and is smooth. Discard garlic.

5. Add marinated vegetables, stirring only to heat through. Pour over fish and serve.

NOTE: This sauce can be used also with deep-fried spareribs. Arrange cooked ribs on top of the drained vegetables; then pour the sauce over.

VARIATIONS: For the cucumber and the carrot, substitute green pepper and tomato.

For the soy sauce, substitute 1 tablespoon hoisin sauce.

In step 3, arrange the drained vegetables over the fish. After step 4, pour the thickened sauce over. Next, heat 2 more tablespoons of oil to smoking; then pour over all and serve.

Omit all the vegetables. Combine 2 tablespoons cornstarch, ½ cup sugar, ⅓ cup cider vinegar and ¼ teaspoon ginger juice. Add in step 4 after the garlic has browned and cook, stirring, to thicken. Then pour over the fish and serve.

FIVE WILLOW SAUCE III

1 tablespoon Chinese sweet-and-sour pickles	⅓ cup vinegar
2 slices fresh ginger root	2 tablespoons sugar
1 scallion stalk	½ teaspoon salt
½ garlic clove	2 teaspoons cornstarch
1 tablespoon oil	2 tablespoons water
½ cup fish stock	1 tablespoon oil

1. Shred sweet-and-sour pickles. Slice ginger root. Cut scallion stalk in ½-inch sections. Crush garlic.

2. Heat oil. Add ginger root, scallion and garlic; stir-fry to brown lightly.

3. Stir in fish stock, vinegar, sugar, salt and shredded pickles to heat through.

4. Meanwhile blend cornstarch and cold water to a paste; then stir in to thicken. Blend in remaining oil. Pour sauce over fish and serve.

LOBSTER SAUCE

2 teaspoons fermented black beans	½ teaspoon sugar
1 garlic clove	½ cup water
¼ pound lean pork	1½ tablespoons oil
2 scallion stalks	1 tablespoon cornstarch
1 tablespoon soy sauce	2 tablespoons water
1 tablespoon sherry	2 eggs

1. Soak fermented black beans.

2. Mince garlic; mash together with soaked black beans. Mince or grind pork.

3. Cut scallion stalks in ½-inch sections; then combine with soy sauce, sherry, sugar and water.

4. Heat oil. Add black bean-garlic mixture and stir-fry briefly until pungent. Add pork; stir-fry until it loses its pinkness (about 2 minutes).

5. Add scallion-soy mixture. Heat quickly; then cook, covered, about 3 minutes more over medium heat.

6. Meanwhile blend cornstarch and remaining cold water to a paste; then stir in to thicken.

7. Beat eggs lightly and add to pan, stirring. Remove from heat at once. Pour sauce over lobster and serve.

NOTE: This sauce gets its name not from its ingredients (it contains no lobster) but from its function (it's served *over* lobster). Lobster sauce is also good with stir-fried or deep-fried shrimp.

SWEET-AND-PUNGENT SAUCE I

¾ cup water	1 tablespoon cornstarch
½ cup sugar	1 tablespoon soy sauce
½ cup vinegar	¼ cup water

1. Bring water to a boil. Add sugar, stirring, and cook another minute to dissolve. Add vinegar; cook 1 minute more.

2. Meanwhile blend cornstarch, soy sauce and remaining cold water to a paste. Then stir in to thicken. Pour sauce over deep-fried meat or fish and serve.

NOTE: Sweet-and-pungent sauces, because of their vinegar content, are best prepared in enamel pans. Their color can be enhanced by the addition of 2 tablespoons tomato sauce or ½ teaspoon red food coloring.

VARIATIONS: For the sugar, use brown sugar or honey.

For the vinegar, use cider vinegar.

For the soy sauce, use heavy soy sauce.

For the water in step 1, substitute stock. Or use equal parts of water and tomato juice; or water and pineapple juice; or pineapple juice and tomato juice.

After step 1, add any of the following:

1 to 2 tablespoons sherry
1 to 2 tablespoons catsup or tomato sauce
1 tablespoon molasses
2 garlic cloves, minced
1 scallion stalk, minced
¼ teaspoon salt
¼ teaspoon Tabasco Sauce
few drops of Worcestershire Sauce
few drops of sesame oil
1 teaspoon ginger juice
juice of ½ lemon
½ cup subgum ginger, sliced
½ cup sweet mixed pickles, shredded

Omit the cornstarch paste in step 2. Instead, combine the cornstarch with the water in step 1 before heating it. Then cook, stirring, to thicken as the sugar and vinegar are added.

SWEET-AND-PUNGENT SAUCE II

1 garlic clove   *½ cup water*
½ to 1 cup vegetables   *2 tablespoons soy sauce*
½ cup sugar   *2 tablespoons oil*
½ cup vinegar   *1½ tablespoons cornstarch*
½ cup water

1. Mince garlic. Slice, dice or sliver vegetables.
2. Combine sugar, vinegar, water and soy sauce.
3. Heat oil. Add garlic and stir-fry a few times. Add vegetables; stir-fry until slightly softened (2 to 3 minutes).
4. Add sugar-vinegar mixture. Stir in over medium heat to dissolve and heat through.
5. Meanwhile blend cornstarch and remaining cold water to a paste; then stir in to thicken. Pour over deep-fried meat or fish and serve.

NOTE: For the vegetables, use any of the following in any combination: bamboo shoots, carrots, cucumbers, green peas, green peppers, mushrooms, onions, pickles and snow peas. You may also add, at the end of step 4, fresh tomatoes or canned pineapple chunks, lichees or crab apples. For typical combinations, see page 737.

VARIATIONS: **For the garlic,** substitute 2 slices fresh ginger root and 1 scallion stalk, both minced.

For the oil, substitute chicken fat or lard.

For other substitutions, see variations 1 through 4 of Sweet-and-Pungent Sauce I.

For other ingredients that may be added in step 2, see variation 5 of Sweet-and-Pungent Sauce I.

Omit the cornstarch paste in step 5. Instead, combine the cornstarch directly with the ingredients in step 2, increasing the water to 1 cup. Add, as in step 4, and cook, stirring, to thicken.

TYPICAL COMBINATIONS FOR SWEET-AND-PUNGENT SAUCES

green peppers, onions, carrots, bamboo shoots
sweet red and green peppers, pickles, mushrooms, bamboo shoots
carrots, tomatoes, onions, pickles
carrots, mushrooms, bamboo shoots
carrots and snow peas
green peppers, pineapple chunks, carrots

POSSIBLE COMBINATIONS FOR SWEET-AND-PUNGENT SAUCES

FOR CHICKEN LIVERS: scallions, ginger root, carrots, green peppers, sweet mixed pickles

FOR FISH AND FISHBALLS: ginger root or pickled ginger; carrots, turnips and onions. Or green pepper, pineapple chunks, tomatoes, pickles. (You may also add roast pork, sliced, diced or slivered, when adding the vegetables.)

FOR PORK: green peppers, pineapple chunks, tomatoes, lichee fruit, molasses

FOR SHRIMP: bamboo shoots, crab apples, green peppers, tomatoes, pineapple chunks, catsup

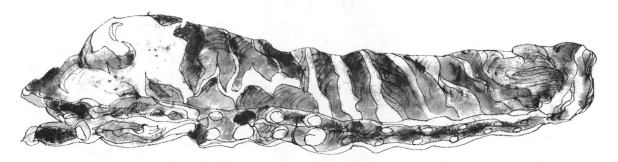

FOR SPARERIBS: carrots, green peppers, honey, pickles, tomatoes, pineapple chunks

FOR WONTONS: onions, pineapple chunks, tomatoes, green peppers, bamboo shoots, pickles, mushrooms, roast pork

SWEET-AND-PUNGENT SAUCE FOR EGGS

1 tablespoon sugar   *1 tablespoon vinegar*

2 tablespoons soy sauce

1. Combine all ingredients in a saucepan. Cook, stirring, over medium heat to blend.
2. Pour sauce over fried eggs and serve.

VARIATION: Omit the soy sauce. Add instead 1 tablespoon oil, ½ teaspoon salt and 1 scallion stalk, minced.

SWEET-AND-PUNGENT SAUCE FOR CARROTS

1 tablespoon cornstarch   *3 tablespoons vinegar*

3 tablespoons sugar   *½ cup water*

¼ teaspoon salt

1. Combine all ingredients in a saucepan. Cook, stirring, over medium heat until sauce thickens and is smooth.
2. Pour over cooked carrots and serve.

NOTE: This sauce also goes well with cooked cabbage.

VARIATIONS: For the water, substitute pineapple juice.

In step 1, also add 1 tablespoon soy sauce.

MASTER SAUCE

TO START: *Cook any basic braised or soy chicken or any red-cooked duck or pork. Strain the sauce through a cheesecloth and reserve. Refrigerate in a covered container. (Remove the fat when it congeals.)*

TO USE: *Bring the sauce to a boil in a large pan. Then add any of the following: pork, beef or lamb (in large pieces or cubed); chicken or duck (whole or in parts); or chicken wings, hearts, livers or gizzards. Simmer covered, until done, turning once or twice for even coloring. Eat hot or cold without the sauce (which is reserved for cooking subsequent dishes).*

NOTE: When using a leg of lamb, sear it first in several tablespoons of hot oil. This may also be done with any of the other meats and poultry. Pork butts, however, are best when parboiled first for 5 minutes.

Master sauce can also be used for pot-stewing eggs. (The eggs must be hardboiled first; then cooled under cold running water and shelled.) Add the eggs to the heated master sauce; then simmer, covered, about 1 hour.

TO REPLENISH: *After each use, strain the master sauce, refrigerate and remove the fat as above. After two or three uses (or more often if desired), add about ¼ cup each of soy sauce and sherry, a sliced scallion stalk, a slice or two of fresh ginger root, a pinch of sugar and about ½ teaspoon salt. At longer intervals, add a pinch of such seasonings as Five Spices, anise pepper or Szechwan peppercorns. To keep the sauce "alive" (if it has not been used for cooking), reheat to the boiling point at least once a week.*

❁ *Sweet Dishes* ❁

WESTERNERS in Chinese restaurants, after being delighted with the variety of "main" courses, often find the desserts limited and disappointing. There's a good reason for this: it's not the Chinese custom to serve any dessert with a meal. Sweet dishes are for snacks or for banquets.

The snacks, served at all hours, usually with cups of tea, include fruits and nuts, cakes and cookies, gelatinous dishes and hot fruit or nut liquids—ranging from thin and delicate to thick and pudding-like—which are known as teas or soups.

The elaborate desserts are reserved for banquets. These include Eight Precious Rice Pudding, Peking Dust and Almond Float. Various fruit and nut teas or soups are often also served. These are sipped from large teacups between courses or at the very end of the banquet.

Cakes prepared at home, such as sponge cake and red date cake, are not baked but steamed. Baked pastries, and particularly the special ones eaten during holidays and festival times, are usually bought at Chinese bakeries. These include the globular rice-flour cakes, that are stuffed with a sweet bean filling, rolled in sesame seeds, and eaten during the Chinese New Year.

There are also small baked cakes (filled with lotus jam—a thick mixture of lotus seeds boiled with sugar—sweet bean fillings, sesame seeds and preserved melon), which are eaten during the moon festival in mid-August.

The fortune cookie, unknown in China, seems to be Western-inspired, although its origins are obscure. Fortune cookies are not baked, but dropped

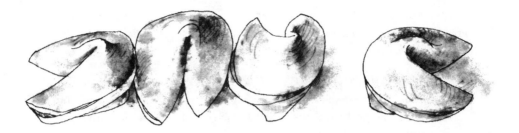

by the spoonful onto a hot grill to form thin, round wafers. While still warm and pliable, each wafer is topped with a strip of paper that has a "fortune" printed on it. The wafer is then folded in half and in half again to enclose its "fortune." When cooled, the cookie hardens and holds its convoluted shape.

HONEYED APPLES
About 4 servings

1 egg
1 cup flour
½ cup water

2 crisp apples
oil for deep-frying
syrup mixture

1. Beat egg; then combine with flour and water to make a smooth batter.
2. Peel and core apples; cut each in ½-inch slices. Dip in batter to coat.
3. Meanwhile heat oil; then deep-fry coated apples until pale golden. Drain on paper toweling.
4. Prepare any of the syrup mixtures below. Then add deep-fried apples and cook, stirring gently, to coat with syrup.
5. Rub a serving platter generously with peanut oil (to keep the fruit from sticking). Transfer apples and syrup to the serving platter and fan a few times to cool slightly.
6. Serve accompanied by a large bowl of water, containing ice cubes. To eat: the diner picks up each apple slice with a fork, tongs or chopsticks; and dips it briefly in the ice water to crystallize the sugar and thus harden the syrup. (The fruit inside will remain warm.)

VARIATIONS: In step 1, prepare the batter by combining 2 egg whites, 2 tablespoons flour and 2 tablespoons cornstarch.

Omit step 1. Instead dip apple slices in beaten egg; then dredge lightly in flour to coat.

In step 4, add with the apples either 1 tablespoon chopped nutmeats or black sesame seeds.

For the apples, substitute sweet potatoes, peeled and cut in ½- by 2-inch strips. Deep-fry these without batter. Add to the syrup as in step 4. Pick up steps 5 and 6.

SYRUP MIXTURES FOR HONEYED APPLES

a. Combine ½ cup sugar with enough peanut oil to moisten, and cook, stirring, over low heat until the sugar dissolves and becomes syrupy. (You may also add ¼ cup light corn syrup.)

b. Bring to a boil, stirring, ½ cup sugar and ¼ cup water. Then stir in 1 tablespoon peanut oil and cook over medium heat until the mixture turns brown and spins a heavy thread when a small amount is dropped from the tip of a spoon. (Add corn syrup as above.)

c. Combine ½ cup honey and ¼ cup peanut oil and cook, stirring, over low heat until the mixture is hot and syrup-like.

HONEYED BANANAS
4 to 6 servings

4 bananas	*2 cups sugar*
4 tablespoons oil	*1½ cups water*

½ tablespoon vinegar

1. Peel bananas; cut either in half lengthwise, or in quarters.
2. Heat oil and, over low heat, pan-fry bananas until lightly browned.
3. Meanwhile, combine sugar, water and vinegar in a saucepan. Bring slowly to a boil, stirring, until mixture spins a thread when a small amount is dropped into cold water.
4. Dip bananas in hot syrup to coat and place on an oiled platter; then dip in ice water to crystallize. (See steps 5 and 6 in recipe above.)

NOTE: These are also called Bananas in Silk Thread.

VARIATIONS: In step 2, add to the oil 1 teaspoon sugar.

In step 3, substitute the following syrup ingredients: ⅔ cup brown sugar, ⅔ cup vinegar, 3 tablespoons cornstarch, ½ teaspoon salt and 1 slice fresh ginger root, minced. Then slowly bring to a boil, stirring, and cook 2 minutes. Pour syrup over the bananas in their pan; cook 2 minutes more over low heat. Then dip coated bananas in ice water.

HONEYED CRAB APPLES
About 6 servings

1 pound crab apples

2 cups sugar

¾ cup water

½ cup light corn syrup

dash of cinnamon

red food coloring

1. Wash and stem crab apples. Place each on a small stick.
2. Combine sugar, water, corn syrup and cinnamon in the top of a double boiler and heat, stirring, until dissolved. Then add enough food coloring to turn the mixture a deep red.
3. Continue to heat mixture gently, stirring until it thickens and forms a ball when dropped from the tip of the spoon into cold water.
4. Remove double boiler from heat. Dip crab apples one at a time into syrup, twirling the sticks to coat evenly. Then let cool and harden either on waxed paper, or on a platter generously coated with peanut oil.

NOTE: The double boiler keeps the syrup fluid while you work.

VARIATIONS: For the crab apples, substitute whole large grapes (with their seeds intact), or large California dates, pitted. Impale several on a stick, or one at a time on toothpicks.

For the syrup, substitute 1 cup sugar, ¾ cup water and ½ teaspoon cream of tartar. Cook as in step 3 until the mixture spins a thread.

STEAMED PEARS
4 servings

4 pears

4 tablespoons honey

1. Cut tops off pears, about 1 inch down, and reserve as lids. Core each pear with a fruit corer to make a deep cavity, but do not cut clear through.
2. Fill cavities with honey and replace the tops.
3. Place pears upright in individual heatproof dishes. Steam until tender (see page 831). (Depending on their size and ripeness, this will take anywhere from 15 to 30 minutes.)
4. Serve pears hot, in their steaming dishes.

NOTE: This not only makes a simple and excellent dessert, but is soothing to the throat as well, and can be taken for coughs and colds.

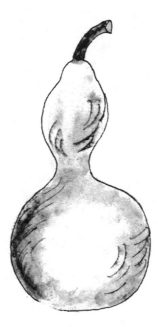

VARIATIONS: For the pears, substitute apples.

In step 2, add with the honey, ¼ teaspoon ground cinnamon for each pear. Or omit the honey entirely and use 1 teaspoon cinnamon instead.

In step 2, stuff the pears with a mixture of chopped California dates and blanched walnut meats. (Allow about ¼ cup of each for 4 pears.) Then spoon honey over each pear and steam as in step 3.

Halve and core the pears. Place each, cut-side down, on a heatproof platter and coat with the honey. Then sprinkle each half with ½ teaspoon preserved ginger candy, minced. Steam as in step 3.

SUGARED WALNUTS
About 4 servings

1½ cups walnut meats	½ cup sugar
1 cup water	½ cup oil

1. Shell walnuts. Bring water to a boil; then pour over walnuts. Let stand 2 minutes; drain well.

2. Add sugar and toss to coat. Let stand overnight to dry.

3. Heat oil and fry walnuts quickly until golden (watch for burning). Drain on paper toweling. Serve hot or cold.

NOTE: A greater quantity of oil can be used and the walnuts deep-fried in a wire basket.

SPICED ROASTED PEANUTS
6 to 8 servings

¼ cup water

1½ teaspoons salt

¼ teaspoon Five Spices

1 pound raw shelled peanuts

1. Preheat the oven to 275 degrees. Meanwhile heat water; stir in salt to dissolve, then Five Spices.

2. Add raw peanuts and mix well together. Then pour mixture onto a roasting pan and spread out flat.

3. Roast until peanuts are a pale golden (about 1 hour), stirring at 10-minute intervals for even coloring and flavor. Serve hot or cold.

NOTE: Use skinless *unroasted* peanuts for this recipe.

GLAZED WHOLE CHESTNUTS
4 to 6 servings

1 pound chestnuts	2 cups sugar
water to cover	¾ cup honey

1. Soak chestnuts overnight in water to cover. Drain, shell and dry.

2. Combine sugar and honey and cook over low heat, stirring frequently, until the mixture dissolves and is syrup-like.

3. Add chestnuts and cook, covered, over very low heat until tender (about 2 hours), stirring frequently.

4. Separate chestnuts. Arrange on a serving platter, which has been either covered with waxed paper or rubbed generously with peanut oil. Let cool; then serve.

SUGARED CHESTNUT BALLS
10 to 12 servings

2 pounds chestnuts	¾ cup powdered sugar
½ cup honey	1 teaspoon cinnamon

1. Score chestnuts. Plunge into boiling water and cook until their shells burst open (20 to 25 minutes). Drain, then let cool and shell.

2. Mince or grind chestnut meats, or force them through a ricer. Blend with honey and shape into small balls.

3. Combine powdered sugar and cinnamon and spread out on a flat plate. Roll chestnut balls in the mixture to coat. Then serve.

GLAZED CHESTNUT BALLS
10 to 12 servings

2 pounds chestnuts	½ cup water
½ cup honey	1 cup sugar
few drops cream of tartar	

1. Prepare chestnut balls with honey as in steps 1 and 2 above.

2. Bring water to a boil; then stir in sugar and cream of tartar. Cook over medium-low heat, without further stirring, until the syrup begins to darken.

3. Remove pan from heat and set at once in a larger pan, containing cold water. Then dip chestnut balls, one at a time, in the syrup to coat lightly. Let dry on waxed paper, and serve.

PEKING DUST I

4 to 6 servings

1 *pound chestnuts*	*pinch of salt*
water to cover	1 *to* 2 *cups heavy cream*
¼ *cup sugar*	2 *tablespoons powdered sugar*

1 *teaspoon vanilla extract*

1. Score chestnuts by making a crisscross cut on the flat side of each one.

2. Bring water to a boil. Add chestnuts and cook until soft (about 40 minutes). Drain, let cool and shell.

3. Mince or grind chestnut meats; then blend in sugar and salt. Shape the mixture as a mound on a serving platter.

4. Whip cream (see page 825). Then fold in powdered sugar and vanilla extract. Arrange as a topping over chestnut mound.

5. Serve garnished with either preserved kumquats or maraschino cherries; or with glazed fruit, which must be prepared in advance (see recipe below).

VARIATION: In step 4, fold half the sweetened whipped cream into the chestnut mixture. Pack the mixture into an oiled mold or bowl; then carefully invert onto a serving platter. Top with remaining whipped cream, and garnish as in step 5.

GLAZED FRUIT FOR PEKING DUST

12 *almonds*	½ *cup sugar*
1 *or* 2 *oranges*	¼ *cup water*

⅓ *cup light corn syrup*

1. Shell and blanch almonds. Peel oranges and separate into segments. Rub a serving platter generously with peanut oil.

2. Combine sugar, water and light corn syrup in a saucepan and bring to a boil, stirring, over medium heat.

3. Dip nuts and fruit, one piece at a time, into the syrup to coat. Place on the oiled serving platter to cool and harden.

PEKING DUST II

10 to 12 servings

2 pounds chestnuts	1 egg white
water to cover	⅛ teaspoon cream of tartar
milk to cover	pinch of salt
1 teaspoon vanilla extract	¼ cup sugar
⅛ pound butter	½ teaspoon vanilla extract
¼ cup sugar	1 cup heavy cream
2 tablespoons brandy	1 cup powdered sugar

¼ cup maraschino cherries

1. Shell chestnuts. Place in cold water and bring to a boil. Boil 3 minutes; then drain.

2. Add milk and vanilla extract to chestnuts and heat (but do not boil). Simmer, covered, until chestnuts are tender (20 to 30 minutes). Drain, discarding milk.

3. Mash chestnuts together with butter, sugar and brandy. (The mixture should have the consistency of mashed potatoes. If it doesn't, add some heavy cream.)

4. Meanwhile heat the oven to 275 degrees. Beat egg white with cream of tartar until stiff, but not dry.

5. Fold in salt, then sugar, then remaining vanilla extract. Transfer egg mixture to a pastry tube.

6. Line a baking sheet with foil. Squeeze egg mixture out of tube in the shape of a nest. Bake until golden (40 to 50 minutes). Remove from oven and let cool slightly. Then transfer to a serving platter.

7. Meanwhile transfer the chestnut mixture to the pastry tube. Then squeeze it out in thin threads over the baked egg nest to form a mound on top.

8. Whip heavy cream (see page 825). Then sweeten it with powdered sugar. Arrange as a topping over chestnut mound. Garnish with maraschino cherries and serve.

VARIATION: For the brandy, substitute rum.

SWEET ORANGE TEA I

About 4 servings

3 oranges	½ cup sugar
2 tablespoons cornstarch	3 cups water

1. Peel oranges. Remove seeds and membranes over a bowl, to catch the juice; then break pulp into small pieces. (Or cut oranges in half and, with a small sharp spoon, scoop the pulp and juice into a bowl.)

2. Combine cornstarch, sugar and water; then bring to a boil, stirring constantly.

3. Add orange pulp and juice and cook, stirring, only to heat through. Serve hot, in small bowls.

VARIATIONS: For the cornstarch, substitute 3 tablespoons glutinous rice flour. In step 3, simmer the pulp and juice, covered, for 2 minutes.

In step 3, add with the orange 1 slice canned pineapple, shredded; or ½ pound muscatel grapes, peeled, pitted and mashed.

For a thinner drink, use 4 to 5 cups of water.

SWEET ORANGE TEA II
About 4 servings

3 oranges	*water*
4 tablespoons glutinous rice flour	*3 cups water*
½ cup sugar	

1. Peel and seed oranges as in step 1 above.

2. Place glutinous rice flour in a bowl. Mix with a small amount of water to form a stiff paste (add water gradually, one teaspoonful at a time). Roll the paste into small (⅜-inch) balls.

3. Bring remaining water to a boil; then stir in sugar to dissolve. Drop flour balls in and continue boiling until they float and are soft.

4. Stir in orange pulp and juice; cook only to heat through. Serve hot, in small bowls.

VARIATION: For the oranges, substitute 5 tangerines.

SWEET GRAPEFRUIT TEA
About 4 servings

2 cups water
1 16-ounce can grapefruit sections
½ cup sugar

2 cups water
2 tablespoons cornstarch
2 tablespoons water

1. Bring water to a boil. Add grapefruit sections, their syrup and sugar; and heat, stirring. Then add the second quantity of water and heat.

2. Meanwhile blend cornstarch and remaining water to a paste. Then add and bring to the boiling point, stirring until the mixture thickens. Serve hot, in small bowls.

VARIATIONS: For the grapefruit sections, substitute either 2 small cans of mandarin oranges or 1 large can of fruit cocktail. Or substitute 2 cups of fresh fruit, diced. (For the latter, use orange or pineapple juice for the first 2 cups of water and add another ½ cup sugar in step 1.)

SWEET PINEAPPLE TEA
About 4 servings

½ cup sugar
¼ cup honey

3 cups water
1 16-ounce can crushed pineapple

1. In a saucepan, combine sugar, honey and water with crushed canned pineapple and its syrup.

2. Bring to a boil; then simmer gently for 15 minutes, stirring frequently. Serve hot, in small bowls.

VARIATION: For the crushed pineapple, substitute 1 pound fresh cherries, pitted and shredded; or the pulp and juice of 3 oranges.

SWEET ALMOND TEA I
About 6 servings

½ cup raw rice
water to cover
1½ cups almond meats
6 cups water

water
½ cup sugar
pinch of salt
1 teaspoon vanilla

1. Wash raw rice. Soak overnight in water to cover. Then drain well.

2. Blanch almonds. Grind almonds and rice to a fine powder, either by hand (with a mortar and pestle), or in a food mill.

3. Place mixture in a bowl. Add the second quantity of water and let stand 1 hour; then stir thoroughly.

4. Strain mixture through a double thickness of cheesecloth into the top of a double boiler. Gather together corners of the cheesecloth, and squeeze the remaining liquid into the pan.

5. Boil remaining water in the lower half of the double boiler; then reduce heat to medium. Cook almond-rice mixture over it, stirring until it thickens. (During this period, "milk" the cheesecloth into the pan several times.)

6. Next stir in sugar, salt and vanilla extract to dissolve; then turn up heat to bring mixture quickly to a boil. Serve hot, in small bowls.

Note: This tea, which has the consistency of custard, is a wonderful snack on cold days.

variations: Omit the rice, salt and vanilla extract. In the top of the double boiler, blend to a smooth, thick paste the ground almonds, 4 tablespoons cornstarch, ½ cup sugar and 1 cup cold water. Then stir in 1 large can of evaporated milk and 6 more cups water. Cook until the mixture thickens, stirring occasionally.

Omit step 3. Combine ground almonds and rice in a saucepan with the sugar and 4 cups water. Bring to a boil; then simmer, covered, 30 minutes, stirring occasionally. Pick up step 6, adding the salt and vanilla extract.

In step 5 add to the almond-rice mixture, 12 Chinese red dates which have been cooked in 1 to 2 cups boiling water until soft (about 20 minutes), then pureed through a fine sieve or ricer to remove the skins and pits.

SWEET ALMOND TEA II
About 4 servings

5 tablespoons almond paste	3½ cups water
⅓ cup rice flour	⅓ cup sugar
½ cup water	1 teaspoon almond extract

brown sugar

1. In a saucepan, blend almond paste, rice flour and water until smooth. Gradually stir in remaining water.

  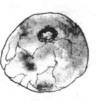   

2. Then bring to a boil over medium heat, stirring constantly.

3. Add sugar and almond extract and cook, stirring, to dissolve. Then sprinkle lightly with brown sugar and serve hot, in small bowls.

VARIATION: Omit the rice flour and almond extract. Combine the almond paste with 4 cups water and beat until smooth, using an eggbeater or a blender. Strain into a pan through cheesecloth. Then heat until hot, but not boiling. Stir in the white sugar to dissolve, and serve.

SWEET ALMOND TEA III
About 8 servings

7½ cups water
½ cup sugar
¾ cup evaporated milk

¼ cup cornstarch
½ cup water
1 tablespoon almond extract

1. Bring water to a boil; then stir in sugar to dissolve. Add evaporated milk and heat, but do not boil.

2. Meanwhile blend cornstarch and remaining cold water to a paste. Then stir in to thicken mixture.

3. Stir in almond extract and cook 1 minute more. Then serve hot, in small bowls.

VARIATIONS: For the evaporated milk and water in step 1, substitute 4 to 5 cups whole milk.

In step 3 add, with the almond extract, ½ teaspoon vanilla extract.

SWEET WALNUT TEA
About 6 servings

½ cup raw rice
water to cover
2 cups walnut meats
1 cup water

2 cups water
1 cup sugar
3 cups water
water

1. Wash raw rice. Soak overnight in water to cover. Then drain well.

2. Blanch walnuts. Grind walnuts and rice to a fine powder, either by hand (with a mortar and pestle) or in a food mill.

3. Gradually stir the powder to a smooth paste with the second quantity of water; then stir in the third quantity.

4. Strain mixture through a double thickness of cheesecloth into the top of a double boiler. Gather together corners of the cheesecloth and squeeze every possible drop of liquid into the pan. Add sugar and the fourth quantity of water.

5. Bring remaining water to a boil in the lower half of the double boiler; then reduce heat to medium. Cook walnut-rice mixture over it, stirring constantly until it thickens (7 to 10 minutes). Serve hot, in small bowls.

NOTE: This mixture, also known as Flowing Walnut Pudding, may be reheated, but only over extremely low heat to prevent burning.

VARIATIONS: For the rice, substitute ½ cup glutinous rice. Wash thoroughly; then soak 10 minutes in water to cover. In step 3, use 1 cup of the rice-soaking water to make the smooth paste.

Omit the rice. After grinding the walnuts, simmer them 30 minutes in water to cover. (Omit step 3.) Strain the walnuts as in step 4; then add the sugar and water. Pick up step 5, adding to the mixture ¼ cup rice flour.

In step 5, add to the walnut-rice mixture 12 Chinese red dates which have been cooked in 1 to 2 cups boiling water until soft (about 20 minutes), then pureed through a fine sieve or ricer to remove the skins and pits.

HOT LOTUS TEA
About 6 servings

4 cups water	*5 cups water*
½ teaspoon baking soda	*1 cup sugar*
1 pound lotus seeds	*2 eggs*

1. Bring water to a boil; stir in baking soda. Then pour over lotus seeds and let stand 5 to 10 minutes.

2. Rub lotus seeds with fingers to husk; rinse and drain.

3. Bring remaining water to a boil; then stir in sugar to dissolve. Add lotus seeds and simmer, covered, 1 hour.

4. Beat eggs lightly. Gradually stir into mixture and remove from heat at once. Serve hot, in small bowls.

SWEET PEANUT SOUP
About 6 servings

6 cups water

2 teaspoons baking soda

2 cups raw peanuts

½ to 1 cup brown sugar

1. Heat water to lukewarm; then stir in baking soda.

2. Add raw peanuts and bring to a boil. Then simmer, covered, until completely softened (about 1½ hours).

3. Add brown sugar and cook, stirring, until dissolved. Serve hot, in small bowls.

GINGER SOUP
About 6 servings

½ cup fresh ginger root

2 cups brown sugar

7 cups water

1. Slice ginger root thin. Place in a saucepan with water and sugar.

2. Bring to a boil, stirring; then simmer, covered, 15 to 20 minutes. Discard ginger. Serve the hot liquid in small bowls.

NOTE: Ginger soup is eaten with steamed crabs. It's also eaten as a midnight snack, and served to visitors any time of the day. During the Chinese New Year it's served with dumplings (see below).

DUMPLINGS FOR GINGER SOUP

1. Gradually add enough cold water to 2 cups glutinous rice flour (kneading the mixture) to make a dough that has the consistency and pliability of wet clay.

2. Pinch off about 1 tablespoon of the dough at a time and roll it between the palms of the hands to make a ball. Place on waxed paper.

3. Bring the ginger soup to a boil. Drop the dough balls in and cook 5 minutes over medium heat. To serve: place several dumplings in each bowl. Ladle the hot soup over.

ALMOND FLOAT I

4 to 6 servings

2 to 3 cups sweetened water	2 cups water
½ pound almond meats	½ cup agar-agar
2 cups water	3 cups water

1. Prepare the sweetened water (see recipe below).

2. Blanch almonds. Place half of them in a blender with water and blend to a smooth paste.

3. Strain mixture into a bowl through a double thickness of cheesecloth. Gather up corners of the cheesecloth and squeeze out every last drop of liquid; then discard residue.

4. Repeat this process with remaining almonds and the second quantity of water.

5. Break agar-agar in 1-inch sections and place in a saucepan with remaining water. Bring to a boil, stirring, and cook until agar-agar dissolves and begins to thicken. Then stir in almond liquid and cook 1 minute more.

6. Pour the mixture into a shallow rectangular pan. Let cool; then refrigerate until set. Cut in ½-inch cubes or diamond shapes.

7. Transfer to a deep serving dish. Serve with enough sweetened water poured over so almond cubes float. Garnish with slivered almonds, fresh strawberries or canned fruit such as mandarin orange sections, pineapple chunks, lichees or fruit cocktail.

NOTE: This dish has many names—Almond Curd (because it's similar in consistency to bean curd), Almond Junket, and Almond Lake. It can be converted to a party punch by cutting the almond curd into finer pieces and using more of the sweetened water.

VARIATIONS: For the sweetened water, substitute the heavy syrup of any canned fruit.

In step 2, grind the almonds instead; then bring to a boil with 3 cups water and simmer, covered, 5 minutes. Strain through the cheesecloth as in step 3.

SWEETENED WATER

2 cups water	½ cup sugar

1. Bring water to a boil. Stir in sugar and cook, stirring, until dissolved.

2. Let cool; then refrigerate to chill. (Allow about ¼ cup sweetened water per serving.)

VARIATIONS: For the sugar, use either brown sugar; or about ¼ pound rock candy.

In step 1, also add ½ cup light syrup from canned mandarin oranges.

After step 1, stir in 1 teaspoon almond extract.

ALMOND FLOAT II
4 to 6 servings

1½ envelopes gelatin	3 cups water
½ cup water	4 tablespoons sugar
1 cup evaporated milk	1 tablespoon almond extract

1. Add unflavored gelatin to cold water to soften.

2. Heat, but do not boil, evaporated milk and remaining water. Stir in sugar to dissolve.

3. Slowly add the softened gelatin and cook, stirring, over low heat to dissolve completely.

4. Let cool slightly; then stir in almond extract. Pour into a shallow pan and refrigerate. Cut up and serve with the sweetened water and fruit garnish as in Almond Float I.

VARIATION: For the evaporated milk and water, substitute 4 cups whole milk. Or else, substitute ½ cup condensed milk; increase the water in step 2 to 4 cups and omit the sugar.

BANANA GELATIN
4 to 6 servings

4 cups water	1 cup evaporated milk
½ cup sugar	1 teaspoon banana extract
½ cup agar-agar	few drops of yellow food coloring

1. Bring water to a boil in a saucepan. Add sugar and agar-agar and cook, stirring, until the mixture begins to thicken.

2. Stir in evaporated milk, banana extract and food coloring. Remove pan from heat.

3. Pour mixture into a shallow rectangular pan. Let cool; then refrigerate until set. Cut in 1-inch squares.

4. Serve in individual dessert dishes, either plain or with Chinese preserved fruits in syrup.

PINEAPPLE GELATIN
About 6 servings

½ *cup sugar*	½ *cup agar-agar*
3 *cups water*	*few drops of yellow food coloring*
1 *cup pineapple juice*	½ *cup pineapple chunks*

1. Combine all ingredients except pineapple chunks in a saucepan. Bring to a boil over medium-high heat and cook, stirring, until the mixture begins to thicken. Let cool slightly.

2. Meanwhile place a pineapple chunk in the center of individual gelatin molds. Then pour the warm liquid over and refrigerate until set.

VARIATION: For the pineapple chunks, substitute either canned kumquats or canned lichee fruit.

GREEN PEA PUDDING
4 to 6 servings

1½ *pounds dried split peas*	½ *cup sugar*
2¼ *cups water*	2 *tablespoons cornstarch*

4 tablespoons water

1. Soak dried split peas overnight in water.

2. Bring to a boil, using the same water. Then simmer, covered, until peas are soft (1½ to 2 hours).

3. Strain into a bowl through a fine sieve. Then stir in sugar. Return to saucepan and reheat over very low flame, stirring frequently to prevent burning.

4. Meanwhile blend cornstarch and remaining cold water to a paste. Then stir in over medium-low heat to thicken.

5. Pour into a shallow rectangular pan, to a depth of 1 inch. Let cool; then refrigerate until set.

6. Cut the pudding in 1-inch cubes and pile these, pyramid fashion, on a serving platter. Garnish with maraschino cherries and serve.

NOTE: This dish, also known as Pea Cubes, Pea Jelly Squares and Green Pea Cake, is eaten like a candy with toothpicks or small dessert forks. In China, it is served in the summertime with afternoon tea.

VARIATION: In step 3, before returning the mixture to the saucepan, heat 2 tablespoons oil or lard; then pour in the strained pea puree and stir constantly over very low heat to thicken. (Watch out for burning.) Omit the cornstarch paste. Pick up steps 5 and 6.

WATER CHESTNUT PUDDING
About 4 servings

1 cup water-chestnut flour
½ cup water

½ cup sugar
2½ cups water

1. Place water-chestnut flour in a heatproof bowl. Gradually stir in cold water to make a smooth paste. Then blend in sugar and remaining water.
2. Steam 1 hour (see page 831). Serve hot or cold.

TURKISH BARLEY PUDDING
About 6 servings

1 cup pearl barley
2 cups water
pinch of salt
1 cup sugar

2 cups milk
1 cup walnut meats
⅓ cup raisins
dash of cinnamon

1. Wash barley. Place in a saucepan with cold water and salt. Bring to a boil; then simmer, covered, 1 hour.
2. Transfer cooked barley to the top of a double boiler. Add sugar and milk; cook 3 hours more over low heat.
3. Blanch walnuts and chop coarsely. Add with raisins to barley mixture; cook 10 minutes more. Sprinkle with cinnamon and serve hot.

NOTE: This is customarily eaten as a dessert with Mongolian Grill-cooked meats.

EIGHT PRECIOUS PUDDING
About 8 servings

1 cup red bean paste
1½ to 2 cups fruit and nuts
2 cups glutinous rice

4 cups water
½ to 1 cup sugar
2 tablespoons oil

1. Prepare the red bean paste (see page 707).
2. Generously oil a heatproof bowl, about 8 to 9 inches in diameter. Arrange

the fruit and nuts (see below) at the bottom in a decorative circular design. (This design may also extend up the sides of the bowl.)

3. Meanwhile wash glutinous rice to remove excess starch. Transfer to a heavy pan and add water. Bring to a boil over high heat; then cook, covered, 5 minutes. Reduce heat to low; cook, covered, 20 minutes more.

4. Add sugar and oil to rice, mixing well to blend. Spoon half the rice into the heatproof bowl, being careful not to disturb the fruit and nut pattern.

5. Spread red bean paste over rice. Then cover with remaining rice, leaving about 1-inch headroom at the top of the bowl. (Make sure the bean paste is completely covered with rice; otherwise it will run into the rest of the pudding and spoil its appearance.)

6. Cover the bowl with foil. Steam 45 minutes to 1 hour (see page 831).

7. Remove the bowl and place a large flat serving plate over the top. In one quick, decisive motion, invert the contents of bowl onto the plate so the pudding, with its fruit and nut pattern on top, is intact. (The edges of the pudding may be loosened with a spatula before the bowl is inverted.)

8. Serve hot or cold with or without a sweetened water syrup (see page 761).

Note: This dish, also called Eight Jewel or Eight Treasure Pudding, is primarily a banquet dessert. It may be cooked in advance, refrigerated in its bowl, then reheated by steaming another 45 minutes or so. It may also be frozen, *before* steaming, and later cooked without preliminary thawing; or else frozen *after* steaming and reheated in the same manner.

VARIATIONS: For the oil, substitute lard.

For the red bean paste, substitute pureed Chinese red dates, canned chestnut paste or canned coconut filling.

Before arranging the fruit and nuts in step 2, put down a thin layer of cooked rice at the bottom of the bowl; then press fruit and nuts well into the rice so that they'll show through when the pudding is inverted.

Arrange ¾ of the fruit and nuts at the bottom of the bowl, the remainder on top.

In step 3, simmer the rice, covered, 15 minutes, in 3½ cups water. Add ¼ cup sugar and ½ cup water and simmer, covered, 15 minutes more. In step 4, add with the oil only ¼ cup sugar.

In step 3, after cooking the rice 5 minutes, add ¼ cup sugar and ½ cup ground suet; then continue the cooking. In step 4, add ¼ cup sugar, but omit the oil.

For the rice, substitute half-rice and half-barley, both cooked. Arrange in alternating layers.

Instead of cooking the pudding in one large bowl, steam in individual custard cups or molds.

FRUIT AND NUT COMBINATIONS FOR EIGHT PRECIOUS PUDDING

The original recipe calls for 2 ounces each of dried red plums, dried green plums, honey dates, candied lotus seeds and cooked chestnuts. Since these are available in Chinese food stores only during the Chinese New Year, any of the following, in any combination, may be substituted:

FRUIT: Dates, raisins, prunes, maraschino cherries, preserved or candied kumquats; candied ginger, citron, orange peel, red or green cherries; or mixed glacéed fruit.

NUTS: Almonds, chestnuts, walnuts, lichee nuts, dried dragon's eyes, watermelon seeds, canned ginkgo nuts.

NOTE: The preserved fruit should be pitted, then cut in quarters if large, in half if small, or chopped coarsely. The candied fruit should be cut in narrow strips; the nuts, shelled and blanched.

SWEETENED WATER SYRUP FOR EIGHT PRECIOUS PUDDING

½ *cup sugar*
1 *cup water*

1 *tablespoon cornstarch*
3 *tablespoons water*

1. Heat sugar and water, stirring to dissolve.

2. Blend cornstarch and remaining cold water to a paste; then stir in to thicken.

3. Spoon the syrup, boiling hot, over individual servings of the pudding.

VARIATIONS: In step 1, add ¼ cup light corn syrup.

After step 1, add ½ teaspoon almond extract.

ALMOND COOKIES
About 35 cookies

35 *almonds*
10 *almonds*
1 *cup lard*
1 *cup sugar*

1 *egg*
1 *teaspoon almond extract*
2½ *cups flour*
1½ *teaspoons baking powder*

⅛ *teaspoon salt*

1. Blanch almonds. Leave the first quantity whole; grind the remainder to a fine powder. Preheat the oven to 350 degrees.

2. Cream together lard and sugar in a mixing bowl. Beat egg and add, along with ground almonds and almond extract. Blend in well.

3. Sift flour together with baking powder and salt. Gradually add to bowl,

mixing with the hands to blend. Then knead into a dough. (If the dough is too stiff, add water a drop at a time to make it more pliable, but do not soften too much.)

4. With a rolling pin, roll the dough out to a thickness of ½-inch. Then, with a cookie cutter, cut in 1½-inch circles. (Or pinch off the dough and form into small balls which, when flattened, will make cookies of the same size.)

5. Grease a baking sheet with peanut oil; arrange cookies on top. With chopsticks or finger, make an indentation in the center of each cookie; then press in a whole almond. Bake until pale golden (about 15 minutes).

NOTE: Almond cookies may be baked in advance, wrapped in foil and frozen.

VARIATIONS: For the lard, substitute either butter or ½ cup peanut oil. (One teaspoon sesame oil may be added to the latter.)

For the flour, substitute rice flour; for the white sugar, light brown sugar.

For the almond extract, use half-almond, half-vanilla extract.

In step 5, before topping with almonds, glaze the cookies by brushing them with a mixture of 1 egg yolk and 1 tablespoon water, beaten together.

In step 5, omit the almonds. Instead, dip the end of a chopstick into red food coloring and lightly touch the indented center of each cookie to decorate.

SESAME SEED COOKIES
About 35 cookies

1 teaspoon oil	1 egg
2½ tablespoons white sesame seeds	2 cups flour
½ cup lard	1 teaspoon baking powder
1 cup sugar	pinch of salt

½ teaspoon nutmeg

1. Heat oil. Add sesame seeds and toast lightly (stir constantly to prevent burning). Meanwhile preheat the oven to 350 degrees.

2. Cream together lard and sugar in a bowl. Beat egg; then blend in. Stir in 1½ tablespoons of the toasted sesame seeds.

3. Sift flour, together with baking powder, salt and nutmeg. Gradually add to bowl and blend in. Then knead the dough well: push it away with the palms of the hands, pull it up with the fingers, and fold the dough back over, repeating the process a number of times. (If the dough is too stiff, add water a drop at a time to make it more pliable.)

4. Refrigerate the dough several hours to chill.

5. Lightly flour a pastry board. With a rolling pin, roll the dough to a

thickness of ⅛-inch; then cut with a cookie cutter.

6. Grease a baking tin with peanut oil; arrange cookies on top. Sprinkle with remaining sesame seeds; press these in gently. Bake until cookies are browned (about 15 minutes).

VARIATIONS: For the lard, substitute either butter or ½ cup peanut oil.

In step 5, instead of rolling the dough, shape it into a long cylinder, ½ inch in diameter. Then cut into ⅛-inch rounds. Or pinch off the dough in small pieces and roll these into balls between the palms of the hands. Then, using the bottom of a glass that's been covered with a damp cloth, press these balls into flat wafers, about ⅛-inch thick.

Separate a second egg. Beat the yolk and brush lightly over the cookies at the beginning of step 6. Then turn the cookies over and top with the sesame seeds. Brush lightly with egg white; then bake.

STEAMED RED DATE CAKE
About 20 small cakes

2 cups Chinese red dates   water to cover
1 cup glutinous rice flour

1. Wash red dates and place in a saucepan with water. Bring to a boil; then cook, uncovered, over medium heat until softened (about 20 minutes).

2. Skin and pit dates. Puree the pulp by forcing it through a ricer or fine sieve.

3. Gradually add glutinous rice flour to the puree and knead the mixture to a stiff paste-like dough.

4. Form the dough into a long cylinder about 1 inch in diameter. Then cut in ½-inch rounds and flatten each slightly.

5. Line a small baking tin with foil or waxed paper, arrange the rounds on top. Steam until the cakes are done (about 10 minutes). (See page 831.) Serve hot.

NOTE: In China, the dough was shaped in wooden molds. The cakes themselves were steamed on bamboo leaves to keep them from sticking, then served right on the leaf.

VARIATIONS: In step 3, add 1 tablespoon lard to the dough.

After step 4, prepare the following mixture to use as a cake filling: Heat 2 tablespoons peanut oil. Add 1 tablespoon sesame seeds and stir once or twice. Then add ½ cup walnut meats, blanched and chopped fine, and ⅓ cup sugar. Toss quickly to coat seeds and nuts with the sugar. Add 1 teaspoonful of this mixture to each disk of dough; pinch the disk into a ball to enclose the filling. Arrange, pinched-side down, on a baking tin and steam as in step 5.

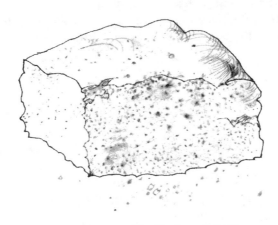

STEAMED SPONGE CAKE

6 eggs
1 to 1½ cups sugar
2½ tablespoons water

1½ cups flour
½ teaspoon baking powder
1 teaspoon vanilla extract

1. Separate eggs. Beat yolks in a large bowl. Add sugar and water; beat until fluffy.

2. Sift together flour and baking powder. Gradually add to eggs, mixing well. Then blend in vanilla extract.

3. Beat egg whites until they form peaks and are stiff but not dry. Fold into batter.

4. Line a cake pan (about 8 or 9 inches square and about 3 inches deep) with waxed paper or foil. Pour batter into pan. Rap the pan sharply on the table several times to remove large air bubbles.

5. Steam until done (20 to 25 minutes). See page 831. Test for doneness by inserting a toothpick: If no batter adheres, the cake is done.

6. Let cake cool slightly. Place a large flat platter over the pan and invert cake onto it. Remove waxed paper or foil. Turn the cake right-side up and cut in 2-inch squares. Serve hot or cold. (Hot is better.)

NOTE: This cake is fine for summer since it needs no oven-baking. It's also excellent for low-fat diets. To keep it dry, place a cloth under the steamer lid to catch and absorb the steam drippings.

VARIATIONS: For the sugar, substitute powdered sugar.

For the vanilla extract, use either half-vanilla and half-almond extract; or half-vanilla and half-lemon extract.

Use an electric mixer: Beat the egg whites until stiff. Gradually add the sugar and beat 2 minutes. (Omit the water.) Add the egg yolks and vanilla extract; beat 2 minutes more. Sift in the flour and baking powder, and mix well with egg mixture to make a smooth batter. Pick up steps 4, 5 and 6.

In step 4, line a Chinese bamboo steamer with a damp cloth; pour in the batter and steam. Or pour the batter into paper cupcake cups or greased custard cups.

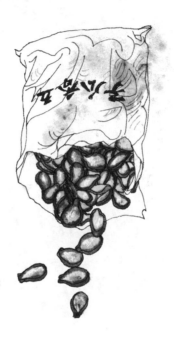

* Firepot and Other Do-It-Yourself Cooking *

THE CHINESE FIREPOT, a festive type of chafing-dish cookery, is used not for single dishes but for preparing whole meals. Although the cook does all the advance preparation, the *actual* cooking is done by the diners right at the table.

The basic technique is a simple one. It calls for a large pot of simmering stock; a wide variety of meat, fish and vegetables, all raw, all cut wafer-thin; and a selection of condiments. The diner, with chopsticks (or other utensils), picks up one piece of food at a time and immerses it in the stock just long enough to cook it. (Cooking time is extremely brief, ranging from a few seconds for leafy vegetables to a minute or two for pork.) The diner then dips the food in a blend of condiments he has mixed in his own bowl and eats it. The meal proceeds at a leisurely pace, in a relaxed, party-like atmosphere, and usually takes anywhere from two to three hours.

Firepot cookery is essentially a winter activity, most appropriate when the weather is cold, brisk and nippy. It's known by many names: Boiling Firepot, Stove Party, Winter Chafing Dish or Chrysanthemum Pot (the latter, because white chrysanthemum petals are sometimes used as a garnish.) The Chinese name is Ho Go or Huo Kuo.

EQUIPMENT: The firepot is literally a pot with a fire in it, fueled with either charcoal or alcohol. It is large, round, and made of shiny brass, with a funnel, like a small chimney, in the center. Surrounding the funnel is a container for the stock. Brass firepots, imported from the Orient and available in Chinese hardware stores, are luxury items. Other utensils, such as electric deep-fat fryers and large electric saucepans, can substitute nicely. (They should be set at high heat to bring the stock to a boil, then set at medium to maintain the simmering.) Large chafing dishes, earthenware casseroles, or simply large soup pots set on electric hotplates or hibachi stoves can also substitute. (With hot plates and hibachis, which do not generate very strong heat, the stock can be brought to a boil first over the kitchen stove.)

THE STOCK: Firepot soup can be made with chicken stock, meat stock, or just plain water. As a rule the stock is served clear, although sometimes ingredients such as porkballs, smoked ham, sliced Chinese cabbage, mushrooms, bean curd and bamboo shoots may be added in advance to further enhance the flavor. During the party cooking time, the pot should be kept half full of stock, with more being added as it evaporates. It must also be kept constantly bubbling and simmering.

SAMPLE FIREPOT STOCK
8 to 10 servings

5 *quarts water*	1 *pint oysters*
1 *chicken*	1 *pint clams*
1 *ham bone*	1 *can abalone*
6 *dried scallops*	*salt*
1 *pound roast pig*	2 *cakes bean curd*

1. Bring water to a boil in a 10-quart pot. Meanwhile bone chicken, reserving and refrigerating meat for use later. Add carcass to the pot along with ham bone, dried scallops and roast pig (not roast pork; see Glossary).

2. Shell oysters and clams; drain canned abalone. Add liquids to the pot, reserving and refrigerating meat. Bring to a boil; then simmer, covered, 1½ hours.

3. Strain stock, discarding bones and other particles. Return stock to pot and season with salt to taste. Cut each bean curd cake in 9 cubes and add.

NOTE: Although any stock can be used for the Firepot, this recipe has the advantage of using the chicken and seafood for the broth and also for the ingredients added later.

THE INGREDIENTS: While the stock cooks, the raw ingredients can be sliced wafer-thin, then arranged attractively one layer deep on separate plates. To suit all tastes, about a dozen varieties should be provided. These can include:

MEAT AND POULTRY—beefsteak, lean pork, roast pork, chicken, duck, ham, lamb, chicken livers and gizzards, calves' liver and pork kidneys. All raw meat should be cut as thin as possible, then in 1- by 1½-inch strips. (The meat may be frozen first, thawed slightly, then sliced paper-thin and arranged on plates to complete the thawing.) Pork kidneys should be cleaned and parboiled before they are sliced.

SEAFOOD—clams, oysters, prawns, shrimp, lobster, fresh and dried squid, fishballs, mussels; and fish such as black bass, striped bass, halibut, pike, rock cod and sole. Clams and oysters are left whole, or cut in half, if large. Prawns, shrimp, lobster, mussels and fresh squid are sliced. (Dried squid must be soaked first.) Fish is boned, sliced as thin as possible, then cut in 2-inch squares.

VEGETABLES—spinach, Boston lettuce, mustard cabbage, water cress, Chinese lettuce, bamboo shoots, snow peas, water chestnuts, bean curd, cucumbers, mushrooms, dandelion greens and vegetable steak (see page 871). Spinach and lettuce leaves are left whole, Chinese lettuce and mustard cabbage cut in 2-inch sections; all other vegetables sliced thin. The tough stem ends of water cress should be trimmed off.

CONDIMENTS AND SEASONINGS: Condiments are never added directly to the stock, but each is served separately in a small sauce dish. They can include several of the following: soy sauce, sherry, hoisin sauce, oyster sauce, sesame oil, sesame paste, sugar, vinegar, red bean cheese, shrimp paste, soybean paste, plum sauce or hot mustard. Other dishes can include a selection of such seasonings as ginger root, fresh or pickled; leeks, scallions, garlic, Chinese parsley or tea melon, each served separately. The soy sauce and the hot mustard should always be available and in the largest quantities—about three sauce dishes each. For the others, allow ¼ to ½ cup each. Ginger root should be finely shredded or chopped, scallions and leeks cut in 1-inch sections; the tough ends of parsley should always be trimmed off.

NOTE: Other ingredients which can be set out include cornstarch (to be mixed with soy sauce and sherry as a coating for the meat *before* cooking) and raw eggs (to be combined with various condiments or poached directly in the soup at the end of the meal).

THE TABLE SETTING: The table should be round, insulated against the heat of the firepot and protected against staining. (A formica-topped table with an asbestos pad is best.) At its center, within easy reach of all, is the firepot, and around it the plates of raw ingredients and the condiment dishes.

The individual place settings should include the following:

   one dinner plate
   one soup bowl
   one soup spoon
   one pair of chopsticks (for cooking); or an individual wire mesh
   strainer, like a tea strainer (for dipping the ingredients); or a small
   skewer; or a fork and spoon. Separate sets of chopsticks or silverware
   may be served for eating purposes.

THE COOKING TECHNIQUE: The diner picks up whatever ingredients he wishes (meat, poultry and seafood at the beginning of the meal; vegetables toward the end) and dips that ingredient into the section of the firepot directly in front of him. He may plunge the raw ingredient, as is, into the broth, or dip it first in a mixture of cornstarch, soy sauce and sherry. As soon as the meat changes color—or any other ingredient is cooked to his taste—he removes it and either eats it directly or dips it in a sauce mixture he has prepared in his own bowl. (He makes this mixture by taking small quantities from the various condiment dishes and blending them to suit himself. He may, for example, make an elaborate mixture with 1 tablespoon each of sugar, vinegar and sherry; 2 tablespoons soy sauce, 1 teaspoon minced scallion, 1 teaspoon red bean cheese and ½ teaspoon sesame oil. He may also have a second bowl in which to beat a raw egg; and may, for example, make a simple mixture by combining a small quantity of egg with 1 tablespoon of soy sauce and a few drops of sesame oil.) He then eats the seasoned morsel along with a bit of parsley, garlic or scallion.

The diner usually puts only one or two pieces of food into the stock at once and hangs on to them until they're done. He can, however, if he wishes, leave a few pieces in the pot to flavor the soup. About halfway through the meal, a small quantity of peastarch noodles (separately soaked in boiling water about 20 minutes to soften) is added to the stock. At the very end of the meal, the diner helps himself to the soup, which by then has become subtly and marvelously flavored by all the ingredients cooked in it. He adds this soup, spoonful by spoonful, to his bowl (which still contains some of his previously mixed condiments) until he gets the balance he likes between soup and seasonings. He then transfers to his bowl some of the peastarch noodles, which have now absorbed the good soup flavor. He may also add a raw egg to thicken his soup; or poach an egg directly in the stock pot and eat it at the very end.

The finale of the meal comes when the majority of diners feel they've had enough to eat. There is no dessert as such. Sometimes a hardboiled egg floating in warm sugar-water is served at the end of the meal.

SAMPLE INGREDIENTS FOR 8 TO 10 PEOPLE

10 to 12 cups stock
2 pounds chicken meat
1 pound pork, beef or lamb
1 chicken gizzard and liver
1 pound calf liver

1 large fish
1 pound spinach
1 pound Chinese cabbage
6 scallions
¼ to ½ pound peastarch noodles

8 to 10 eggs

MOHAMMEDAN FIREPOT

A variant of the Firepot, from Northern China, where lamb predominates, is known as the Mohammedan Firepot. Although rice may be served with it, the usual accompaniments are steamed breads, steamed dumplings, sesame seed buns or onion biscuits. (Hot rolls or toasted buns can substitute for these.)

SAMPLE INGREDIENTS FOR 8 TO 10 PEOPLE

10 to 12 cups beef or mutton stock
3 to 4 pounds lamb fillet
2 pounds lamb or beef liver

2 pounds lamb kidneys
2 pounds Chinese cabbage
1 pound spinach

¼ pound rice noodles

NOTE: The liver is cooked lightly, the kidneys longer.

THE MONGOLIAN GRILL

Another type of do-it-yourself cooking, which comes out of Northern China and features lamb, is known as the Mongolian Grill. Unlike the firepot, this is a barbecue technique requiring a large open charcoal stove with a fine iron grating on top. (A good-sized hibachi with wire mesh covering can substitute.) For the fuel, pinewood—with the bark left on—is favored, with charcoal the second choice.

The Mongolian Grill technique is suitable indoors or out. It calls for each diner to be given a bowl of mixed seasonings (see below) in which he marinates a paper-thin slice or two of lamb for a minute or so. Then he tosses the lamb onto the grate (the fuel has now been fanned to blazing) and quickly flips the slice back and forth with long chopsticks until it's grilled to his taste. (Some like their lamb crisp, others less well done; in either case, the meat, being paper-thin, cooks in a matter of seconds.) The lamb is then eaten with plain buns or biscuits; the next slice is prepared in the same manner.

SEASONING MIXTURE FOR THE MONGOLIAN GRILL

½ cup scallions, cut in slivers

2 garlic cloves, crushed

¼ cup parsley, chopped

1 cup water

½ cup soy sauce

1 tablespoon sugar

NOTE: These ingredients are sufficient for 4 people. They should be mixed well in a bowl, then divided into 4 smaller bowls. Allow about ¼ pound tender fillet of lamb per person. Beef (also sliced paper-thin) can substitute.

BRAZIER-GRILLED LAMB

A variant of the Mongolian Grill, known as Brazier-Grilled Lamb (and a favorite winter pastime in Peking), calls for the meat to be grilled as above, but *not* seasoned first. Instead, after each slice is cooked, it is dipped briefly in beaten egg to cool and coat, *then* in a bowl of mixed seasonings. (This lamb is also eaten with plain buns or biscuits.)

SEASONING MIXTURE FOR BRAZIER-GRILLED LAMB

1 garlic clove, crushed

1 scallion, minced

1 tablespoon soy sauce

1 tablespoon soy paste

1 tablespoon sweet soy jam

½ teaspoon Chinese chili sauce

½ teaspoon sesame oil

NOTE: Since each person prepares his own seasoning mixture here, the quantities given are for the individual seasoning bowls. Also allow 1 egg per diner, served in a separate bowl. If soy paste and sweet soy jam are not available, substitute peanut butter and black currant jam.

❊ *Banquet Dishes* ❊

ALTHOUGH many Chinese banquet dishes are within the range of the home cook, several are not often prepared at home because they demand special skills and facilities. These include shark's fin and bird's nest soups, Winter Melon Pond and Peking Duck.

Shark's fin soup, for example, requires particular culinary skills to produce a dish which is creamy, yet not heavy; rich in fragrance, yet still mild; with the shark's fin soft and gelatinous, but not completely dissolved. Bird's nest soup, made with one of the rarest and most expensive of Chinese ingredients, must also be delicately prepared and served in a festive setting to match its rarity. Winter Melon Pond (a soup cooked right in the melon itself) poses physical rather than culinary problems. The melon's cumbersome size requires expansive stove facilities, and a strong back is needed to transfer the melon's great weight to the table when the soup is done.

The most demanding of all is Peking Duck. Considered one of the greatest Chinese dishes and the high point of every Peking banquet, it calls for special cooking facilities and training on the part of the cook. It also calls for a specific breed of duck, known as Imperial Peking.

In China, students of the Peking cuisine were required to take a one-year course devoted exclusively to the art of preparing Peking Duck. In addition to mastering the actual cooking techniques, they learned to raise and fatten the birds: the ducks were force-fed and housed in small cages to keep them inactive so that they would be plump and tender. The apprentice cooks also learned to slaughter and dress the ducks: the heads and necks had to be intact and the birds wet-dressed (plucked, singed and drawn while freshly killed), with the innards carefully removed so that the skin remained smooth and unbroken.

Peking Duck has no peer among barbecued ducks. Its skin is uniquely crisp, fragrant, glistening and golden. The secret of the skin's special quality is air—air which is forced or pumped between the skin and meat of the breast before roasting. This air, introduced through a shallow cut made in the side of the neck, is blown under the skin until the entire duck is inflated. Originally this was done directly or through a paper straw; now mechanical blowers are used. (The bird's neck is tightly tied with string and the bottom opening sewn or sealed to prevent the air's escape.)

The inflated duck is next scalded with boiling water, brushed with a malt-sugar or honey syrup and hung up to dry in a cool, airy place until its skin is quite hard. (Under ideal conditions and at controlled room temperatures, this drying process takes about 24 hours.) The duck is then suspended vertically in a special cylindrical pit made of brick or concrete, or in a heavy, insulated restaurant-type barbecue box. It is roasted over moderate heat until glistening and golden.

The skin, which is the primary delicacy, is cut from the duck in small squares or rectangles and either arranged on a serving platter or placed back on the duck in its original form. It is eaten immediately after roasting, while still hot and crisp (accompanied by steamed buns and small, thin, flat wheatcakes called Peking doilies; and by scallions and a dip, usually hoisin sauce). The tender meat, which is of secondary interest, is cut up and served later in the banquet as a separate dish, or else eaten at another meal entirely.

BIRD'S NEST SOUP I
About 6 servings

¼ *pound dried bird's nest*	2 *egg whites*
6 *cups stock*	½ *scallion stalk*
½ *cup white meat chicken*	1 *tablespoon cornstarch*
1 *tablespoon sherry*	3 *tablespoons stock*
⅓ *cup stock*	½ *teaspoon salt*

1. Soak bird's nest.

2. Bring stock to a boil. Add soaked bird's nest and simmer, covered, 30 minutes.

3. Meanwhile mince chicken. Mix with sherry and the second quantity of cold stock until smooth; then blend in egg whites.

4. Mince scallion. Blend cornstarch and remaining cold stock to a paste.

5. Add salt to heated stock, then chicken mixture, stirring constantly to blend well.

6. Stir in cornstarch paste to thicken stock. Sprinkle with scallion and serve.

NOTE: Bird's nest soup may be made in advance, refrigerated and reheated. The stock should be clear and rich with no trace of fat. A concentrated stock can be prepared by cooking a 3-pound chicken in 8 cups of water. (The bird may be served as white cut chicken at the same meal.)

VARIATIONS: In step 3, mince the chicken as in Chicken Velvet, adding water instead of stock one drop at a time (see page 387). Then add to the cornstarch paste 1 tablespoon sherry. Add the paste after the salt in step 5, and when the soup thickens, remove pan from heat and pour in chicken mixture in a thin stream, stirring gently to blend. Garnish with scallion.

Omit the cornstarch paste. After adding the salt in step 5, remove pan from heat and stir in chicken mixture. Return to stove for a moment to reheat. Garnish with scallion.

Instead of adding the egg whites in step 3, stir them in after step 5 to thicken the soup. Omit the cornstarch paste.

For the minced scallion garnish, substitute ¼ cup smoked ham, shredded or minced; or 4 snow peas, blanched and shredded.

BIRD'S NEST SOUP II
About 6 servings

¼ *pound dried bird's nest*	6 *cups stock*
½ *cup white meat chicken*	½ *teaspoon salt*
¼ *cup smoked ham*	2 *egg whites*

1. Soak bird's nest.

2. Separately shred chicken and smoked ham.

3. Place stock, salt, soaked bird's nest and chicken in a pan. Bring to a boil; then simmer, covered, 30 minutes.

4. Beat egg whites lightly and stir in until they set. Garnish with shredded ham and serve.

VARIATIONS: Use cooked instead of raw chicken. In step 3, bring the stock to a boil. Add the soaked bird's nest and simmer, covered, 20 minutes. Add the chicken and ham only to heat through. Then add the salt and egg whites.

In the above variation, for the ham, substitute ½ cup fresh mushrooms, coarsely chopped.

Omit the chicken and increase the number of egg whites to 6.

At the end of step 4, stir in a cornstarch paste made of 1 tablespoon cornstarch and 3 tablespoons cold water to thicken soup. Omit the egg whites.

STEAMED CHICKEN STUFFED WITH BIRD'S NEST
6 to 8 servings

¼ *pound dried bird's nest*	1 *tablespoon sherry*
½ *cup smoked ham*	½ *teaspoon salt*
¼ *cup water chestnuts*	1 *chicken (3 to 4 pounds)*

5 cups stock

1. Soak bird's nest.

2. Mince smoked ham and water chestnuts. Blend well with sherry, salt and soaked bird's nest.

3. Wipe chicken with a damp cloth. Make an incision along its backbone, but do not cut through bone. Stuff chicken with bird's nest mixture and sew up securely or skewer.

4. Place bird in a large heatproof bowl and pour stock over. Steam over low heat until tender (2 to 3 hours). See page 831.

NOTE: A rich clear stock should be used for this dish. See the Note for Bird's Nest Soup I.

SHARK'S FIN SOUP I
About 6 servings

½ *pound dried shark's fin*	¼ *cup smoked ham*
1 *cup white meat chicken*	1 *to 2 scallion stalks*
cornstarch	6 *cups stock*

½ teaspoon salt

1. Soak and process shark's fin.

2. Shred chicken; then dredge lightly in cornstarch. Mince smoked ham and scallion stalks.

3. Bring stock to a boil. Add shark's fin and simmer, covered, 20 minutes. Add chicken; simmer, covered, 10 minutes more.

4. Season with salt. Garnish with ham and scallion and serve.

NOTE: A rich clear stock should be used and the fins cooked until their gelatinous content dissolves partially, thickening the stock. The fins should be eaten when soft but still firm.

VARIATIONS: For the chicken, substitute any of the following: 1 cup crabmeat, picked over and flaked; or ½ cup chicken and ½ cup crabmeat; or 1 cup lobster meat.

In the variation above, also add ½ cup bamboo shoots, shredded; and 4 dried black mushrooms (soaked), shredded.

In step 3, before adding the shark's fin, add to the stock 1 tablespoon sherry, 1 teaspoon sugar and 1 slice fresh ginger root, minced.

In step 3, add with the shark's fin ½ cup bamboo shoots and ¼ cup water chestnuts, both minced.

In step 4, after adding the salt, either stir in 1 to 2 egg whites, lightly beaten, until set; or thicken the soup with a cornstarch paste made of 2 teaspoons cornstarch, 2 teaspoons sherry, ½ teaspoon soy sauce and 2 tablespoons cold water.

SHARK'S FIN SOUP II
8 to 10 servings

4 *dried black mushrooms*	2 *scallion stalks*
2 *scallion stalks*	3 *tablespoons oil*
3 *slices fresh ginger root*	5 *cups stock*
1 16-*ounce can shark's fin*	1 *teaspoon salt*
2 *tablespoons sherry*	2 *tablespoons sherry*
4 *cups water*	2 *tablespoons cornstarch*
1 *chicken breast*	1 *cup stock*

1. Soak dried mushrooms.

2. Trim scallion stalks; slice ginger root and combine in a pan with canned shark's fin, sherry and water.

3. Bring to a boil, then simmer, covered, 15 minutes. Drain shark's fin, discarding liquid, scallions and ginger root.

4. Meanwhile skin, bone and shred chicken breast. Shred soaked mushrooms; cut remaining scallions in 2-inch sections.

5. Heat oil. Brown scallion sections lightly and discard. Add chicken shreds and stir-fry until they lose their pinkness (about 1 minute).

6. Add stock, salt, shark's fin, mushrooms, and remaining sherry. Bring to a boil; then simmer, covered, 30 minutes.

7. Blend cornstarch and remaining cold stock; then stir in to thicken soup, and serve.

SHARK'S FIN IN HAM SAUCE
About 8 servings

1 *pound shark's fin*	2 *tablespoons soy sauce*
½ *cup smoked ham*	1 *tablespoon sherry*
2 *cups stock*	½ *teaspoon sugar*
½ *cup water*	1 *tablespoon soy sauce*

1. Soak and process shark's fin.

2. Chop smoked ham coarsely; then combine with stock, water, soy sauce and sherry. Bring to a boil; then simmer, covered, 50 minutes.

3. Add sugar and simmer, covered, 10 minutes more.

4. Strain broth into another pan, discarding ham. Add shark's fin and simmer, covered, 10 minutes. Stir in remaining soy sauce and serve at once.

NOTE: A rich clear stock should be used for this dish.

WINTER MELON POND
Allow about ½ pound melon for each serving

1. This dish requires a whole winter melon. Clean it first by scrubbing its skin thoroughly with a brush. Then set the melon upright and cut a slice off the top, anywhere from 3 inches down to ¼ of the whole melon. This will serve as a lid. (For a more attractive effect, notch the lid as you cut it.)

2. Scoop out the seeds and spongy pulp, scraping the inside surface clean. Stand the melon upright in a large heatproof bowl.

3. Prepare any combination of soup ingredients described below. Place in the melon, as directed, adding enough stock so that the melon is about ¾ full. Cover melon with its lid.

4. Place the bowl on a rack and steam the winter melon; or steam by the bowl-in-a-pot method (with enough boiling water added to the pot to cover about ⅞ of bowl). See page 831. In either case, the pot should be large enough so the bowl can be lifted out easily when the melon is done. If necessary, use a large roasting pan, placed over *two* burners on the stove.

5. Steam the melon until translucent and tender, but still firm enough to hold its shape. (Allow 3 to 4 hours for a 4- to 5-pound melon; about 5 hours for a 6- to 10-pound melon.) During the last half hour, add more stock if necessary to keep the melon ¾ full.

6. When the melon is done, bring it to the table right in its steaming bowl. (Should you wish to serve it in another bowl, tie the melon at the end of step 2 with heavy string in a sling-like or basket-like arrangement with a handle—make it strong and secure so it can support the whole melon and its contents. Then, after steaming, lift out and transfer the melon.)

7. To serve: Cut a horizontal slice of melon near the top. Place in an individual soup bowl and ladle some soup over. Or scoop out some melon meat and mix with the soup. Serve in individual bowls, garnished with shredded smoked ham.

NOTE: This dish is also called Eight Precious Melon Bowl.

VARIATIONS: In step 1, lay the melon on its side. Cut a hole about 6 inches in diameter on its top surface. Reserve this as the lid. Clean the melon as in step 2, and stand it not upright, but on its side. Pick up step 3, etc.

Steam the melon by itself until done. Prepare the soup separately, either simmering it for about 40 minutes until done, or dicing the ingredients so fine that they need only be brought to a boil. Pour the cooked soup into the steamed melon and serve.

SOUP INGREDIENTS FOR WINTER MELON POND
CHICKEN I
1 chicken (3½ pounds), boned and diced
¼ cup dried lotus seeds, blanched and husked
1 teaspoon salt (added just before serving)

CHICKEN II
½ pound white meat chicken, diced
¼ cup dried lotus seeds, blanched and husked
¼ cup bamboo shoots, diced
¼ cup button mushrooms
½ cup green peas, parboiled (added just before serving)
1 teaspoon salt (added just before serving)

CHICKEN III
2 cups chicken, diced
2 cups lean pork, diced
½ cup smoked ham, diced
½ cup ginkgo nuts, shelled and blanched
¼ cup dried black mushrooms (soaked), diced
¼ cup button mushrooms

Duck I

1 duckling, boned and diced
1 cup smoked ham, diced
6 dried black mushrooms (soaked), diced
¼ pound fresh mushrooms, diced
¾ cup sherry
½ teaspoon ground anise
2 teaspoons soy sauce

Duck II

1 pound duck, boned and diced
½ cup lean pork, diced
¼ pound dried lotus seeds, blanched and husked
6 dried black mushrooms (soaked), diced
½ cup bamboo shoots, diced
½ cup water chestnuts, diced

Subgum I

1 cup white meat chicken, diced
1 cup roast duck, diced
½ cup smoked ham, diced
½ cup dried lotus seeds, blanched and husked
4 dried black mushrooms (soaked), diced
½ cup fresh mushrooms, diced
½ cup bamboo shoots, diced
6 Chinese red dates, cut in half and pitted
1 scallion stalk, minced (added just before serving)
1 teaspoon Chinese parsley, minced (added just before serving)
1 teaspoon salt (added just before serving)

Subgum II

¼ cup white meat chicken, diced
¼ cup dried lotus seeds, blanched and husked
¼ cup fresh mushrooms, diced
1 tablespoon sherry
1 teaspoon sugar
¼ pound shrimp, shelled and deveined (added during last 5 minutes of cooking)
¼ cup abalone, diced (added during last 5 minutes of cooking)
¼ cup smoked ham, diced (added during last 5 minutes of cooking)
¼ cup roast duck, diced (added during last 5 minutes of cooking)
1 teaspoon salt (added just before serving)

PEKING DUCK (MODIFIED VERSION)
6 to 8 servings

1 duck (4 to 5 pounds)   1 cup water
8 cups water   ½ cup honey

½ cup sesame oil

1. Have a whole duck wet-picked and dressed, with the head and neck retained and the skin kept completely intact.

2. Tie the neck tightly with string. Sew up or skewer the bottom opening. In the side of the neck below the string, cut a small slit (about ½-inch long and ⅛-inch deep); insert a straw and blow air under the skin, until entire duck is inflated.

3. Suspend duck over a basin, with an electric fan set nearby and let dry 1 hour.

4. Bring water to a boil. Scald duck until its skin is almost white: either by pouring boiling water over the suspended bird, or immersing the duck in water about 1 minute. Drain well; dry with paper toweling.

5. Bring remaining water to a boil. Then stir in honey to dissolve. Rub diluted honey over duck skin, saturating it completely.

6. Suspend duck in a cool, airy place to dry until its skin is hard. (This will take 2 to 3 hours with an electric fan; 8 to 10 hours without one.) To suspend duck: bend a heavy piece of wire (about 10 inches long) at each end to form a hook. Hook duck through the tail and hang it up. Spread the wings apart by wedging a bamboo chopstick between them. Place a pan underneath to catch the drippings.

7. Preheat the oven to 350 degrees. Remove all but the topmost rack and suspend the duck vertically from it, using the wire hook again. Place a foil-lined drip pan underneath. Roast duck until done (about 1½ hours), basting with sesame oil

at 15-minute intervals. (To prevent shrinkage during roasting, place a bamboo chopstick horizontally *inside* the duck cavity. If the skin browns unevenly, cover overdone sections with pieces of foil.)

8. Remove duck from oven. While the skin is still sizzling and crisp, carefully cut it off with a sharp knife in 2-inch squares or in 1- by 2-inch rectangles. (Leave as little meat attached to the skin as possible.) Serve the skin at once on a warm platter, accompanied by scallions or cucumbers, a hoisin or soybean paste dip and Peking Doilies (see below).

9. To eat, place one or two pieces of crisp skin in the middle of a Peking doily; dab with about ¼ teaspoon of the dip and top with a piece of scallion. Then roll up the doily or fold over twice. (With steamed buns, place the skin, scallion and dip between the layers of the bun.)

10. After the skin is eaten, cut the meat in 1½-inch cubes and serve as a side dish at the same meal, or at another meal as leftovers. (Reserve the duck carcass for stock.)

NOTE: Peking duck must be roasted at moderate heat. If the heat is too high, the skin will shrink and stretch thin. If it's too low, the skin will not be crisp and succulent.

VARIATIONS: After step 4, rub the duck cavity with ½ teaspoon salt and ½ teaspoon Five Spices.

After step 6, rub the duck cavity with a mixture of 3 tablespoons hoisin sauce, 2 tablespoons sherry, 1 teaspoon sugar and 1 teaspoon vinegar.

ACCOMPANIMENTS FOR PEKING DUCK

Scallions, cut lengthwise in half or in quarters, then crosswise in 3-inch sections; or made into onion brushes (see page 828).
Cucumbers, peeled, seeded, and cut in thin strips, about 3 inches long.

DIPS FOR PEKING DUCK

Combine any of the following:
4 tablespoons hoisin sauce and 2 tablespoons sugar
¼ cup hoisin sauce, 2 tablespoons soy sauce and ½ teaspoon sesame oil
2 tablespoons soybean paste, 2½ tablespoons water, 1 teaspoon sugar, and a few drops sesame oil. (Cook 5 minutes over low heat, stirring frequently.)

PEKING DOILIES

4 to 5 servings (allowing about 3 doilies for each person)

1 cup water	*flour*
2 cups flour	*peanut oil*

1. Boil water; then gradually add to flour, blending with a wooden spoon. Transfer the dough to a board and knead until soft (do not work it too much). Cover with a damp towel and let stand 15 to 20 minutes.

2. Flour the board lightly. Roll and pull out the dough to form a long thin cylinder, about 2 inches in diameter.

3. Cut the cylinder crosswise in ½- to 1-inch slices (or pinch off walnut-size pieces and roll into balls; then press into ½- to 1-inch disks).

4. Flatten slices or disks with the palm of the hand until they're about ¼-inch thick. Then lightly brush their tops with oil.

5. Stack the slices in pairs, with their oiled surfaces touching. (This makes it possible to separate them easily after they're cooked.) Dust the outside surfaces lightly with flour.

6. With a rolling pin, roll each pair into a thin round cake, about 4½ inches in diameter. (Work lightly and evenly from the center, rolling each as paper-thin as possible. Turn each pancake pair over to check the edges for uniform thickness.)

7. Heat an ungreased (6-inch) skillet over medium-low heat. Add one pancake pair at a time and cook about 1 minute on each side to brown lightly. (Some cooks like to work with rolling pin and board near the stove so they can roll out the second pancake while the first one cooks.)

8. As soon as each pair is done, tear it apart to separate the doilies. Then stack the doilies and cover with a damp cloth until ready to serve.

NOTE: Peking doilies are also called Moo Shoo Pancakes, Mandarin Pancakes or Spring Cakes. These delicate pancakes are always cooked in pairs, because when rolled out, they are too fragile to be cooked alone. If they are not to be used immediately, wrap and refrigerate them; then steam about 10 minutes to soften before using. (They can even be steamed with basic boiled rice if a piece of foil is placed between the rice and the doilies to keep them from sticking.) Peking doilies may also be cooked in advance, frozen, then steamed—without preliminary thawing—to soften.

VARIATION: For the peanut oil, substitute either sesame oil or melted lard.

PART III

Supplementary Information

Preparing a Complete Meal

SINCE THE CONCEPT of a "main" dish as such does not exist in Chinese cooking, a meal will consist of several dishes, each as important as the next. A typical dinner, even in the most modest home, usually includes separate meat, seafood and vegetable dishes, as well as soup, rice and tea. (This does not mean, however, that twice as much fish and meat is consumed. These ingredients, always combined with vegetables, are actually used in smaller quantities than in Western meals.)

To attempt a complete Chinese meal from the start, therefore, is not recommended for the beginner. She would do far better learning to cook one dish at a time, until she knows what she's about. That dish (which could then be incorporated into an otherwise Western meal) might be a soup, Chinese-style vegetable, meat, seafood or sweet dish. Thus, with each meal, the beginner can learn the techniques, sharpen her skills, build her repertory and, most important of all, develop a feeling for Chinese cooking.

Since there is no single main dish, the question inevitably arises: How many dishes should there be? The answer: Plan on as many as there are people to be served. This is the general pattern:

For 2 — soup, a meat or seafood dish, rice
For 4 — soup, a meat dish, a seafood dish, vegetable dish, rice
For 6 — soup, 2 meat dishes, 2 seafood dishes, a vegetable dish, rice
For 8 — soup, 3 meat dishes, 2 seafood dishes, 2 vegetable dishes, rice

NOTE: This is a guidepost, not a hard-and-fast rule. If these menus seem too involved, adapt them to your own needs. Plan on fewer dishes, prepared in larger quantities. (And should unexpected guests drop in, a dish can be stretched with more vegetables and rice.) Also, desserts are not indicated since the Chinese do not generally serve them with their meals. If you include dessert, count it as a "main" dish.

Planning the meal: Planning a Chinese meal is an art in itself. It calls for the selecting of individual dishes, relating them to one another and working out the harmonies and contrasts between them. When planning a Chinese menu, remember that pork is the favorite, followed by duck and chicken; that characteristic seafoods are fish, shrimp or crab and that the vegetable can be whatever is in season. Egg dishes are also popular, with custard-like steamed eggs often served in place of soup, meat or seafood.

Whatever the ingredients, whether simple or costly, each dish should stimulate the eye, the imagination and the palate. It should be colorful— never dull, dreary or drab. (If it has no color of its own, garnish it with yellow egg threads, pink slivers of ham or green scallion tops.) Its taste and aroma should always be delightful too.

Within the meal itself, there should be proportion, balance and variety. Variety, for example, can be achieved in many ways: by the ingredients themselves, the way in which they're cut, and the methods by which they're cooked. As for proportion, the same ingredients should not be repeated too often. (Too many meat dishes are as bad as too many vegetable dishes.) For balance, a heavy meal is best preceded by a clear, light broth; a light meal, by a soup that's rich and hearty. A smooth dish should be offset by a crunchy one; a pungent dish by one that's bland.

No meal is enjoyable for the hostess if she has worn herself out preparing it. Confusion and its counterpart—fatigue—can be kept to a minimum by following a few simple rules: Allow plenty of time for preparation. Choose a few dishes that can be prepared well in advance or that can be conveniently managed the same day. Choose only one that calls for last-minute cooking. And never plan on two dishes which need the same cooking pan at the same time.

It's essential always to be realistic about what can be comfortably managed in the kitchen. If a stove has four burners, the first can be used for soup; the second for a slow-cooked dish; the third for rice; and the fourth, first for tea, and then at the last moment for a stir-fried or deep-fried dish. (If you're a beginner, don't attempt both stir-frying and deep-frying at the same meal since these call for too much last-minute attention.) If there's to be a fifth dish, it can be barbecued meat or poultry roasted in the oven. Some dishes can be prepared in advance: cooked earlier in the day and reheated at the last minute; or partially cooked a day or two ahead and refrigerated. In the case of long-simmering dishes, some cooks divide the simmering over a period of several days. The final cooking is then synchronized with the last-minute dishes.

It's always advisable to cook ahead as much as possible. The Chinese do. They get such variety in their meals because they rarely start from scratch. They prepare all sorts of dishes in advance—slow-cooked, cold, and deep-fried dishes, soups and rice. Even spareribs can be barbecued a day or two ahead, then reheated and browned before serving. Still another way to get more mileage out of four burners is to cook the rice and soup, then remove them from the stove and keep them covered so they'll stay hot. This will give you two more burners for last-minute cooking or reheating.

Getting Organized: Menu planning should be done, not at the last minute, but a day or two ahead. Begin by listing the dishes you want to include; then check the ingredients they call for against the supplies on hand. Draw up a shopping list to cover the missing items. Also indicate second-choice dishes just in case you can't get ingredients for the first.

Work out the cooking time for each dish, including preparation time. Then draw up a timetable to indicate when each should be started. (Work backward from the time dinner is to be served.) Post your menu where you can see it so nothing is forgotten.

If, for example, your dinner is to be at 7:30, and you're serving a cold vegetable dish, sesame ham sticks, red-cooked duck, mushroom soup, stir-fried pork and vegetables, rice and tea, your timetable for relaxed and leisurely preparation might read something like this:

5:00 P.M.—*Get ingredients ready for slow-cooked duck. Put these in pot.*

5:30 P.M.—*Put slow-cooked dish on stove. (Once this is on the fire, it may virtually be ignored. It can cook an extra half hour without harm and will remain warm for some time after the heat is turned off.)*
Start organizing stir-fry ingredients. (The more advance preparation you do here, the better. For details, see the "Guide to Stir-Frying.") Cut meat. (If frozen, let thaw.) Soak dried ingredients.
Start soup. Get out stock, other ingredients. Wash, peel, and cut vegetables for soup.

6:00 P.M.—*Wash rice. Put in pot with water, let sit quietly. Continue preparations for stir-fried dish (washing, cutting, parboiling, mixing sauces, etc.).*

6:30 P.M.—*Put rice on fire.*

6:45 P.M.—*Put soup on fire.*
Prepare the cold vegetable.

7:00 P.M.—*Turn heat off under rice. (Rice tastes better when it sits quietly both before and after cooking. When the heat is turned off, do not lift the lid but let the rice continue to cook in its own steam.)*
Add dressing to cold vegetable and refrigerate.

7:15 P.M.—*Set the table. Boil water and scald the teapot. Keep the pot warm.*
Slice the cold ham. Add dressing.
Set out all ingredients for stir-frying, all utensils, all serving dishes.
Boil fresh water for tea. (This is assuming you plan to serve tea with the meal, Cantonese-style. It may, of course, also be served as an after-dinner beverage.)

7:25 P.M.—*Brew tea.*

7:30 P.M.—*Serve soup, ham, cold vegetable. Stir-fry the pork dish.*

7:38 P.M.—*Serve the stir-fried pork, duck, rice and tea.*

LEFTOVERS

Leftovers are no problem to the Chinese, who come from a long tradition of wasting nothing. Sometimes leftovers are reheated * and eaten for lunch the next day. More often they're completely transformed: bits of meat and vegetables become key ingredients in fried rice, noodle dishes, soups and egg foo yung. Plain rice turns up in soups, casseroles and congees. Leftover meat shreds garnish freshly cooked or cold vegetables. Leftover fried fish becomes a delicacy when reheated two or three minutes in a sweet-and-pungent sauce.

If any ingredient is remotely edible, the Chinese have found a use for it. Bones from chicken, duck and pork go into stock, as do the liquids from

* When reheating leftovers, add a few tablespoons of water to replace the liquid which has evaporated. (When leftovers are reheated by steaming, this is not necessary.) When reheating deep-fried foods in the oven, put them on a rack over a drip pan so the excess oil can drain away. When reheating dishes made with cornstarch paste, add fresh paste because cornstarch tends to turn watery in leftovers. Finally, *never* reheat steamed fish and seafood leftovers. Resteaming makes them tough and flavorless. They are better eaten cold.

parboiled vegetables and certain soaked ingredients. Vegetable tops and the outer leaves of cabbage are never discarded but added to soup. Chicken and pork fats are saved for stir-frying. (These should never be mixed; they should be stored in separate containers.) Even ham skins, melon rinds and leftover tea leaves have their uses: ham skins, boiled until soft, are diced and used in soups and stews; melon rinds stir-fried as a vegetable; and tea leaves used in smoking fish and flavoring hardboiled eggs.

In a sense, the Chinese also plan for leftovers through their sparing use of ingredients. It's not unusual for a housewife to buy a single chicken that will eventually appear as three separate dishes, served at three separate meals. (The chicken breast may be stir-fried, then the giblets deep-fried and the dark meat braised. Or perhaps the legs and wings will be steamed, the bones used in congee, the neck and giblets for stock, the legs and back deep-fried.)

Fresh vegetables, too, are rarely used up all at once. Over a period of days, a given vegetable will be added a little bit at a time to soups and stir-fried dishes. Canned Chinese vegetables also go a long way. Water chestnuts, mushrooms and bamboo shoots, sparingly used, add a touch of crispness or taste to a variety of dishes.

In addition to utilizing leftovers, the Chinese also cook ahead to maintain a constant supply of ingredients. They frequently have on hand cooked rice and noodles, meats which have been slow-cooked and roasted, fishballs and meatballs. These ingredients make many shortcuts possible. With them as the starting point, a vast range of dishes can be prepared. For example, cooked meats and fresh vegetables can readily be stir-fried together: the raw ingredients are added to the pan first, and the cooked ones put in at the end only to be reheated. Countless other variations are also possible by the addition of canned or dried ingredients.

Since much Chinese cooking is improvisational, having a bit of this and a bit of that on hand is not a burden but a delight. Inevitably these ingredients stimulate the imagination and suggest all kinds of combinations: a few peas can be tossed in for color, a few shrimp for flavor, a bit of bean curd for contrast. All this makes possible greater variety and complexity within a given dish, greater interest and richness within a given meal.

❈ *Serving a Chinese Meal* ❈

A CHINESE MEAL can be served Western-style (starting with soup and ending with dessert), or buffet-style (including hot, cold, and stir-fried dishes, provided the hostess has prepared everything in advance for the latter. She can then disappear briefly into the kitchen and stir-fry the dish without being missed). Or the meal can be served as the Chinese themselves serve it, either formally or informally. The informal style is the family meal; the formal, the feast or banquet. The difference between the two is not so much the menu (although there are special banquet dishes), but the number of dishes, and the sequence in which these are served.

THE FAMILY MEAL

There are no separate courses: the entire meal is set out all at once in serving dishes at the center of the table. Each diner can see exactly how much food there is and pace himself accordingly. Once the food is served, the cook can remain seated like everyone else throughout the entire meal.

The beginning of the meal is signaled when the head of the family or host raises his chopsticks. Then host or hostess ladles out the soup (served in a large tureen), and the diners at the same time may help themselves from the central serving dishes. All these dishes are shared. Rice, however, is not shared: each diner receives his own rice bowl, which he can have refilled whenever he wishes. (Rice in a bowl not only keeps hot, but is easier to manage with chopsticks.) Using his chopsticks, the diner takes a small quantity of food from a central serving dish and either eats it directly or transfers it to his rice bowl. En route, he may dip it in hot mustard or plum sauce. He continues serving himself in this manner from each central dish until he's had enough to eat.

NOTE: Sometimes informal family dining is described as village-style or dinner-style. This distinction is based on the dishes served. Village-style is peasant-style and characterized by such simple and hearty fare as mustard cabbage soup, minced pork steamed with salt fish and various bean curd dishes. Dinner-style is characterized by the dishes served in most Chinese restaurants.

THE FORMAL MEAL

Feasts and banquets are held on very special occasions: to observe holidays, honor guests or celebrate weddings and birthdays. On such occasions, anywhere from ten to thirty-two dishes, served as separate courses, follow each other one at a time, in opulent progression. (Such banquets, obviously too big and elaborate for the home cook, are usually given in restaurants.)

The sequence of the banquet reverses the classic Western pattern of soup to nuts. The Chinese feast literally runs from nuts to soup. The nuts (almonds, salted peanuts, etc.), along with dishes of fresh fruit, appear on the table before the guests are seated. The soup, a sweet, hot liquid made with oranges, almonds or walnuts, is served in a large bowl, and takes the place of dessert at the end of the meal.

The guests begin by nibbling at the nuts and fruit until the appetizers appear. (Sometimes these too are set out on the table before the guests are seated.) There are usually four or five of these appetizers, including cold

meats, preserved eggs, shrimp toast, smoked fish and vegetable relishes, all beautifully arranged either on separate dishes or on one large platter. The appetizers are accompanied by yellow rice wine, similar to a medium-dry sherry but rougher in taste and served warm. The host then proposes a toast which in effect says: Drink up. The guests in turn express appreciation for his generous hospitality.

At some banquets, the appetizers are followed by a series of stir-fried dishes, or by several hot and delicate dishes such as shrimp, fish and chicken. At other meals, the principal or prestige dish, such as Bird's Nest Soup, takes precedence. Other prestige dishes include Peking Duck and Shark's Fin Soup (which, like the Bird's Nest, is more of a stew than a soup). These represent the high point of the feast. A number of braised and slow-cooked foods are also served. These include whole ham, roast suckling pig, and duck or chicken in soup.

Because of the abundance of food, rice is eaten in relatively small quantities. (In family-style meals, the dishes are considered an accompaniment to rice. In banquet-style, it's the other way around.) When rice appears midway through the meal (served either plain or as congee) it comes as a welcome change after a series of heavy or highly seasoned dishes. Other changes of pace, served throughout the meal to stimulate flagging appetites, include dainty sweet dishes and salty pastries, clear and delicate soups and hot tea. All of these act to clear the palate and prepare the diner for the more filling foods to follow.

Here are samples of two actual banquet menus:

FORMAL MENU I

PLATES OF NUTS AND FRESH FRUIT

APPETIZERS: Sliced chicken breast
Preserved eggs
Chinese cabbage relish
Slivered cucumber and chicken

MAIN DISHES: Bird's nest soup
Red-cooked abalone
Pineapple duck
Sweet-and-pungent fish
Shrimp and bamboo shoots
Stir-fried Chinese cabbage
Eight Precious pudding
Scallops and radishes
Chicken and peppers
Beef and cauliflower
Steamed bread
Rice

FORMAL MENU II

PLATES OF NUTS: Almonds
Watermelon seeds
Apricot kernels
Pine nuts
Candied walnuts

PLATES OF FRUIT: Bananas
Oranges
Apples
Pears

APPETIZERS:	Cold chicken vinaigrette
	Ducks' tongues
	Preserved eggs
	Sliced ham
	Smoked fish
STIR-FRIED DISHES:	Chicken
	Fish fillets
	Shrimp
	Bêche-de-mer
STEAMED FOODS:	Rolls
	Dumplings
	Cakes
	Honey cakes
MAIN DISHES:	Bird's nest soup
	Shark's fin soup
	Pigeon eggs
	Fish's maw
	Abalone
	Cloud ear mushrooms
ROASTS:	Roast duck
	Roast suckling pig
RICE DISHES:	Rice
	Congee
	Eight Precious pudding

Seating arrangements: The Chinese prefer round tables to rectangular ones for both social and practical reasons: Everyone is literally gathered around and conversation is much easier. The food at family meals does not have to be passed since each person is the same distance from the central serving dishes and all can reach them with equal ease. (In Imperial China, however, square tables seating eight were traditional at banquets. The custom now at banquets is to seat ten people at a round table.) Seating arrangements follow this pattern: The host and hostess sit side by side, with their backs to the door. (These seats are considered the lowliest.) Directly opposite, across the table from them, sits the guest of honor. (His is the highest, being the exact reverse of the lowliest.) On his left is the second-highest seat; on his right, the third; and so on, alternating around the entire table. Thus, those seated closest to the guest of honor occupy the highest seats; those nearest the host and hostess occupy the lowliest.

Etiquette: Chinese etiquette requires that each person finish the food in his bowl before reaching for any more of the same dish. (It's considered greedy to put a quantity of food on your plate at once.) Also, you never should take the most tender or delicate morsels for yourself. Someone else at the table, however, may pick up a dainty morsel and put it on your plate for you. Sometimes the host and hostess will have an extra-long pair of chopsticks with which to pass such delicacies to their guests. Sometimes they will simply turn their own chopsticks around, using the square ends to serve food to others. Good manners also require that the diner eat every last grain of rice in his bowl. When he finishes eating, he indicates this by placing his chopsticks across the top of his rice bowl.

NOTE: Often at the end of the meal, each diner is handed a small, white, steaming hot towel, similar to a terry washcloth. This has been dipped in boiling water (to which a slight fragrance has been added), then wrung out. The towel, used for wiping hands as well as face, is particularly refreshing when anything sticky has been eaten.

❀ *Setting a Chinese Table* ❀

CHINESE FOOD can be served on any kind of dinnerware. However, when authentic Chinese dishes are used, they add interest, atmosphere and beauty to the meal. (These dishes, which are available in a variety of sizes, shapes, designs and colors, are relatively inexpensive and can be purchased in any city with a sizable Chinese community.) The dining table itself is covered with a simple white cloth. Flowers or other decorations are never used. The beauty of the food itself is sufficient.

SERVING DISHES

The serving dishes are placed in the center of the table, forming a central square, with a platter at each corner. The soup bowl is set in the middle. (Since most Chinese tables are round, this square shape in the center provides an interesting contrast.) These are the kinds of serving dishes used:

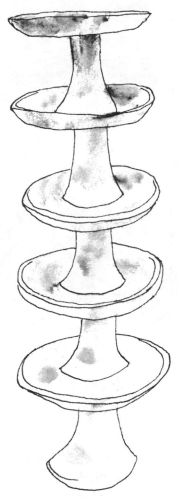

Soup bowl: Big and deep with straight sides, like a soufflé dish. Large enough to hold a quart or two of soup.

Other serving dishes: For stir-fried and deep-fried foods, both deep bowls and shallow dishes on short pedestals. For whole fish, long platters. For cold foods, round platters. For slow-cooked meats, large shallow bowls.

Serving spoons: Either porcelain or metal, in various sizes, for ladling soup and serving other dishes.

Dip dishes: Small saucers, about 3 inches in diameter. (These are used for table condiments such as fresh mustard, pepper-salt mix, plum sauce, etc. For soy sauce, hot sauce and vinegar, small cruets are used.

Teapot: Porcelain or ceramic—large enough to hold 4 to 6 cups of tea— preferably with its own cozy. (The more expensive Chinese teapots come with their own basket-like cozies, whose padded interiors are lined with brightly colored fabrics.)

THE PLACE SETTING

Each setting includes a soup bowl set on a plate. The soup spoon is either in the empty bowl, or to the right, on the plate. A pair of chopsticks is to the right of the plate; above them, the teacup.

If a second bowl is used, it's placed upper left. (When soup and rice are to be eaten simultaneously, separate bowls are used. Otherwise, the same bowl is filled first with soup, later with rice.) If an individual dip dish is used, it's upper center (directly in front of the place setting). If a wine cup is used, it's upper right, alongside the teacup. The dishes used in place settings are:

Bowl: China or porcelain, about 4½ inches in diameter, cup-like without handles; used for soup and rice.

Plate: Medium-size and all-purpose. The bowl sits on it. The plate is also used for various discards, such as lobster shells, bits of bone, etc. (Sometimes small tissue-like squares of paper, to wipe the chopsticks and soup spoons, are placed on it before the meal begins.)

Soup spoon: Porcelain. (This doesn't conduct heat as metal does and therefore cannot burn the lips.) Brightly decorated or unadorned white.

Wine cup: Tiny, handleless porcelain cup. Not much taller than a thimble, about 1½ inches in diameter. (Wine cups and pots are used only at formal meals. The pots, made of pewter, brass or porcelain, are set in containers of boiling water to keep the wine warm.)

Teacup: Small, handleless porcelain cup, about 3 inches in diameter. Often matches the teapot. (A more formal teacup is slightly larger, has its own saucer and lid.)

Chopsticks: Made of a variety of materials; bamboo is most popular. Used in eating everything but soup. (See next section for details.)

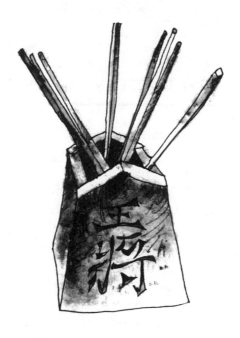

❀ *Chopsticks and How to Use Them* ❀

CHINESE FOOD seems to taste better when eaten with chopsticks. Since only a few morsels can be picked up at a time, the tempo of the meal is generally more relaxed and enjoyable. In addition, each individual morsel can be more fully savored, as can the interchange of flavors between one ingredient and the next, between the sauce and the ingredients. When chopsticks are used, the sauce can never drown the food: only the amount of sauce which clings to each morsel can be carried to the mouth. Chopsticks have other advantages: There is no metallic taste to impair food flavors and, being nonmetallic, chopsticks cannot burn the tongue.

Types of chopsticks: Most chopsticks are 10 to 12 inches long, and about the thickness of a pencil. (Those for children can be as short as 5 inches; those for the host and hostess—to pass special delicacies to their guests—as long as 20 inches.) The top half is square (to be held in the hand); the bottom half round (to pick up the food). Chopsticks are made of various materials: bamboo, wood, plastic, coral, jade, silver or ivory. Those made of ivory are to the Chinese what sterling silver flatware is to Westerners. (Expensive chopsticks are often linked together at the top by a silver chain to keep them from being separated or lost.)

NOTE: Ivory chopsticks, which develop a slight yellowish cast as they age, must be treated with particular care. They're sensitive to temperature changes: exposure to extreme heat will cause them to warp, or to brown and crack. After each use, they should be dipped briefly in lukewarm suds, then rinsed and dried thoroughly.

How to use chopsticks: Chopsticks are always used in pairs for eating. (For cooking, they're often used singly.) Although the two are alike, each differs in function. One is stationary; the other moves. Together they act like a pair of tongs.

To understand how chopsticks function, begin with the stationary stick. Hold your right hand in a relaxed, half-open position. Place the first chopstick between the tip of your ring finger and the base of your thumb. (The thumb on the square section, the ring finger at the halfway point of the chopstick.) Hold the stick lightly but firmly, bracing it against the ring finger with the middle of your thumb. Keep the stick in this fixed position. (The tips of your thumb, index and middle fingers should be free to hold the second stick.)

The second stick is the one which moves. Place it between the tip of your thumb and the tips of your index and middle fingers. Hold it lightly. Move it up and down against the stationary stick.

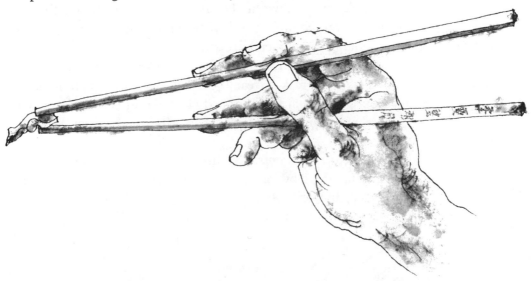

To pick up a piece of food, push upward with the middle finger. (This opens the tips of the chopsticks.) To grasp the food, push down with the same middle finger. (This brings the tips of the chopsticks together, pinches the food against the lower chopstick so it is grasped tightly and held.) Then it's just a matter of raising the food to the mouth with a wrist-and-arm action. It's important to keep the tips of the chopsticks level with each other at *all* times. (You can do this by tapping them lightly together on the plate or on the palm of your hand.) If the tips are not even, the chopsticks will not work.

It's considered poor etiquette to point your elbows outward when using chopsticks. Elbows should always be held close to the body, so as not to crowd or annoy fellow diners either to the left or right. By the same token, some consider it ill-mannered to eat with the left hand. The reason again is a practical one: One left-handed person seated at a round table with a group of right-handers can cause quite a tangle. (Left-handed people, therefore, have to eat with particular care so their chopsticks won't collide with their neighbor's.

NOTE: A few rare people can pick up chopsticks for the first time and use them in a relaxed, natural way. For most, chopsticks seem awkward at first. Beginners tend to hold chopsticks too tightly. This makes for muscle tension and the manual equivalent of "tennis elbow." When chopsticks are held firmly but lightly, there's no strain at all. With practice, their use becomes automatic. As a matter of fact, chopsticks can move with such speed and nimbleness that the Chinese name for them is "quick little boys."

Chopsticks and cut-up ingredients: Chopsticks can pick up any solid foods when they're cut in bite-size pieces. Rough-textured meats, for example, are gripped squarely between the tips of the sticks. Food that is larger in size but tender can be broken in half by chopsticks: Hold the sticks parallel to each other and perpendicular to the food. Pierce the food in the middle with the sticks, then open the tips and spread them so they pull away from each other. (This will break or tear the food.) Smooth, finely minced foods are often scooped up rather than gripped. The chopsticks, held parallel to each other, are slipped under the food, then lifted with a gentle wrist action.

Chopsticks and uncut ingredients: Certain naturally tender foods (fish), or those reduced to tenderness by long-simmering (duck), are often *not* cut up before being served, but left whole. This is because chopsticks make it possible to pick the meat off the bones with ease and grace. Fish, particularly, can be eaten with great delicacy. Chopsticks won't bruise its flesh or disturb its fine bones. Other uncut ingredients call for a different approach. Large whole shrimp, for example, are grasped firmly with chopsticks, then consumed neatly in several bites. In the case of noodles, a dozen or so are picked up at once and bitten off a mouthful at a time; the rest eased back into the diner's bowl so the chopsticks can be used for sampling other foods, which are eaten alternately with the noodles.

Chopsticks and rice: The Chinese eat rice from a bowl held in the left hand, with the thumb resting on the rim, the index and middle fingers grasping the bottom. Chopsticks used with the right hand then transfer rice from bowl to mouth with the same gentle scooping action used for finely minced ingredients. To get the last few grains at the bottom, the bowl is brought to the lips in a drinking position, and the rice scooped into the mouth, quickly and directly. (Beginners should never try to eat rice from a flat plate with chopsticks. Even an experienced chopstick wielder might drop half the grains en route.)

❀ *Suggested Menus* ❀

MENUS FOR 2

Mushroom soup
Basic stir-fried chicken with walnuts
Stir-fried spinach with white cheese

———

Lobster Cantonese
Deep-fried sweet-and-pungent
    spareribs
Fresh fruit

———

Pork and cucumber soup
Deep-fried cubed and marinated
    chicken
Braised eggplant with bacon and
    tomatoes

———

Stir-fried chicken with almonds and
    vegetables
Basic steamed fish with mushrooms
Sesame seed cookies

———

Egg pouch omelets
Basic braised chicken with mushrooms
    and red dates
Almond float

———

Basic pan-fried egg foo yung with
    chicken
Stir-fried Chinese cabbage and dried
    shrimp
Canned lichee fruit

———

Eggrolls
Basic noodles in soup with stir-fried
    pork and spinach topping
Fresh fruit

———

Marinated and deep-fried chicken
    livers

Basic stirred eggs with crabmeat
Almond cookies

Basic stir-fried shrimp with peas
Basic stir-fried cooked chicken and
    peppers
Steamed pears

Stir-fried pork and bean sprouts
Deep-fried cubed chicken
Sweet orange tea

Barbecued spareribs
Basic steamed fish with lily buds
Almond cookies

Basic braised soy fish
Stir-fried string beans and white
    cheese
Honeyed bananas

Stir-fried pork and cucumber
Braised chicken with fresh mushrooms
Sweet almond tea

Deep-fried shrimp with bacon
Stir-fried mixed vegetables
Preserved kumquats

Stir-fried beef and celery
Steamed lobster
Honeyed apples

Stir-fried chicken and peppers
Deep-fried coated butterfly shrimp
Banana gelatin

Fish fillet soup
Deep-fried pork with sweet-and-
    pungent sauce

Stir-fried broccoli

Egg drop soup
Deep-fried sweet-and-pungent shrimp
Fresh fruit

Basic bean curd and spinach soup
Basic red-simmered pork with Chinese
    turnip
Stir-fried shrimp and lettuce
Braised anise beef
Stir-fried spinach and mushrooms
Steamed sponge cake

Pork and Chinese cabbage soup
Steamed chicken stuffed with lobster
Sweet almond tea

Stir-fried ham and spinach
Deep-fried sweet-and-pungent fish
Sweet orange tea

Wonton soup
Spinach salad with shrimp
Eggrolls
Tossed noodles with stir-fried pork

Pork and water cress soup
Deep-fried shrimp with croutons
Stir-fried chicken and bamboo shoots

Stir-fried pork and clams
Creamed Chinese cabbage
Preserved kumquats

Pork and seaweed soup
Barbecued spareribs
Soft-fried noodles with shrimp
    topping

Deep-fried coated butterfly shrimp

Stir-fried beef and bamboo shoots
Almond cookies

———

Red-simmered chicken wings
Deep-fried shrimp and peas
Steamed Chinese lettuce

———

Simmered crabs with pork

Stir-fried Chinese cabbage and white
    cheese
Sweet pineapple tea

———

Basic braised chicken with eggs
Stir-fried beef and tomatoes
Fresh fruit

MENUS FOR 3

Basic bean curd and Chinese cabbage
    soup
Stir-fried beef and peppers
Deep-fried fish with vegetables
Steamed red date cake

———

Basic steamed fish with mushrooms
Stir-fried pork with Five Spices
Basic stir-fried beef with cucumber
Sweet grapefruit tea

———

Wonton soup
Deep-fried oysters
Braised honey chicken
Fresh fruit

———

Bird's nest soup
Stir-fried cauliflower with mushrooms
    and water chestnuts

Stir-fried beef with oyster sauce
Red-cooked chicken

———

Marinated mushrooms
Spring rolls
Steamed whitefish steak
Stir-fried Chinese cabbage
Sugared walnuts

———

Pork and winter melon soup
Deep-fried paper-wrapped chicken
Steamed stuffed eggplant
Almond cookies

———

Fish fillet soup
Roast pork
White cut chicken
Almond float

MENUS FOR 4

Abalone soup
Basic pan-fried egg foo yung
Gold coin chicken
Stir-fried broccoli

Fresh fruit

———

Jellied chicken
Basic deep-fried shrimp

Basic steamed eggs with Chinese
    sausage
Stir-fried Chinese cabbage
Canned lichee fruit

————

Mushroom soup
Steamed eggplant
Red-cooked deep-fried squab
White-cooked pork with lotus root
Stir-fried shrimp in shells

————

Pork and water cress soup
Braised anise beef
Stir-fried shrimp with peppers and
    tomatoes
Stir-fried spinach
Fresh fruit

————

Egg drop soup
Pork and shrimp egg foo yung
Stir-fried beef and preserved mustard
    cabbage
Basic deep-fried shrimp
Almond cookies

————

Three delicious soup
Stir-fried beef and oyster sauce
Braised pork and bean curd
Sweet-and-pungent mustard cabbage
Basic pan-fried egg foo yung with
    shrimp

————

White cut chicken
Slivered bean curd and shrimp
Deep-fried pork strips and walnuts
Stuffed mushrooms with fish
Stir-fried mustard cabbage

————

Wonton soup
Soy eggs

Basic deep-fried sweet-and-pungent fish
Stir-fried pork and ginger root
Hot lotus tea

————

Pork and Chinese cabbage soup
Stir-fried chicken and peppers
Stir-fried beef and onions
Soft-fried noodles with stir-fried pork
    and shrimp
Almond float

————

Spinach soup
Smashed radishes; smashed
    cucumbers
Chicken velvet and corn
Soft-fried noodles with roast pork
Basic stirred eggs with crabmeat

————

Basic bean curd soup with bean sprouts
Stir-fried beef and peppers
Basic stir-fried roast pork with Chinese
    cabbage
Steamed chicken with anise
Sweet orange tea

————

Crabmeat soup
Roast orange duck
Stir-fried beef and Chinese cabbage
Ham foo yung
Fresh fruit

————

Pork and water cress soup
Basic steamed eggs with clams
Gold coin pork
Stir-fried chicken and leeks
Sesame seed cookies

————

Chicken velvet and lettuce soup
Lobster Cantonese
Stir-fried pork and bean sprouts

Braised marinated beef
Fresh fruit

———

Chicken and fuzzy melon soup
Stir-fried beef and mushrooms
Basic deep-fried shrimp
Steamed minced pork with tea melon
Banana gelatin

———

Pork and winter melon soup
Stir-fried shrimp and vegetables
Deep-fried chicken cubes wrapped in
    bacon
Basic braised beef with bamboo shoots
Fresh fruit

———

Vegetarian soup
Stir-fried chicken and Chinese
    cabbage hearts
Braised spareribs with black bean
    sauce
Oyster omelet
Almond float

———

Basic noodles in soup
Basic omelet with shrimp
Deep-fried fish fillets with vinegar
    sauce
Basic braised chicken with Chinese
    lettuce
Sweet almond tea

———

Pork and Chinese cabbage soup
Basic steamed fish with bean curd
Basic deep-fried porkballs
Braised beef with string beans
Stir-fried chicken with almonds and
    vegetables

———

Pork and cucumber soup

Braised fragrant pork
Basic steamed fish with ham
Stir-fried asparagus with egg sauce
Almond float

———

Basic bean curd soup with mustard
    cabbage
Basic deep-fried fish in pieces
Stir-fried pork and lily buds
Smashed cucumbers
Fresh fruit

———

Abalone soup
Deep-fried sweet-and-pungent fish
Steamed stuffed bitter melon
Stir-fried Chinese cabbage
Steamed sponge cake

———

Hot-sour soup
Lobster Cantonese
Stir-fried string beans and white bean
    cheese
Stir-fried pork with vermicelli
Steamed red date cake

———

Deep-fried paper-wrapped chicken
Braised spareribs with pineapple
Basic steamed fish with shrimp sauce
Stir-fried pork and bean sprouts
Creamed Chinese cabbage

———

Beef and Chinese lettuce soup
Stir-fried chicken and button
    mushrooms
Braised pork with shrimp sauce
Stir-fried asparagus
Glazed chestnut balls

———

Chicken and bitter melon soup

Basic braised beef with hard-boiled
    eggs
Basic stir-fried pork with Chinese
    lettuce and peppers
Smashed radishes
Peking dust

———

Fish's maw soup
Braised duck with bamboo shoots
Steamed cubed pork with Five Spices
Stir-fried Chinese cabbage
Steamed pears

———

Chicken and fuzzy melon soup
Braised duck with sweet potatoes
Steamed sliced pork with shrimp sauce
Stir-fried mixed vegetables
Smashed cucumbers

———

Pork and mustard cabbage soup
Shrimp toast
Stir-fried beef and onions
Basic steamed fish with tea melon
Braised bamboo shoots

———

Beef and lotus root soup
Simmered stuffed green peppers
Basic stir-fried shrimp with peas

Stir-fried Chinese cabbage
Spinach and peanuts

———

Pork and fuzzy melon soup
Braised pork and spinach
White cut chicken
Deep-fried shrimp in shells
Basic stir-fried beef with asparagus

———

Basic soup with pork
Marinated abalone
Red-cooked chicken
Roast pork
Stir-fried beef and cauliflower

———

Braised anise beef
Basic steamed eggs with crabmeat
Stir-fried pork and bitter melon
Deep-fried shrimp in shells
Canned lichee fruit

———

Pork and mustard cabbage soup
Stir-fried sweet-and-pungent chicken
    livers
Stir-fried pork and bean sprouts
Smoked beef
Steamed eggs and fish fillets

MENUS FOR 6

White-simmered duck in soup
Basic stir-fried cooked chicken and
    pineapple
Stir-fried shrimp and asparagus
Shark's fin omelet
Steamed spareribs with black bean
    sauce

Almond float

———

Mushroom soup
Smoked chicken
Basic stir-fried pork with bamboo
    shoots
Drunken shrimp

Braised Tung-Po pork
Basic steamed clams
Stir-fried bean curd with fresh
    mushrooms

———

Whole fish soup
Stir-fried chicken and walnuts
Lobster Cantonese
Stir-fried beef and string beans
Bean sprout salad
Deep-fried sweet-and-pungent
    crabmeat balls
Sweet orange tea

———

Pork and water cress soup
White cut chicken and vegetables
Stir-fried fish with vegetables
Basic steamed minced pork with salt
    egg
Stir-fried Chinese cabbage
Preserved kumquats

———

Chicken and lotus seed soup
Smashed radishes
Braised pork balls and lily buds
Drunken duck
Stir-fried squid with mushrooms
Stir-fried beef and peas
Steamed sponge cake

———

Pork and winter melon soup
Chicken velvet sautéed
Braised duck with pineapple
Stir-fried sweet-and-pungent spareribs
Steamed shrimp
Sweet orange tea

———

Fish fillet soup

Braised bamboo shoots
Shrimp toast
Braised chestnut chicken
Steamed duck with ham and leeks
Soy eggs
Stuffed mushrooms with pork
Sweet walnut tea

———

Wonton soup
Deep-fried marinated duck stuffed
    with glutinous rice
Stir-fried beef and tomatoes
Spinach salad with shrimp
Braised five-flower pork and red bean
    cheese
Basic stirred eggs with crabmeat
Stir-fried lettuce

———

Pork and water cress soup
Roast pork
Stir-fried fish and bean sprouts
Steamed three-kinds-of-eggs
Red-cooked spiced chicken
Stir-fried beef and mushrooms
Fresh fruit

———

Chicken velvet and corn soup
Eggrolls
Aromatic roast duck
Braised pork and spinach
Stir-fried beef and celery
Almond float

———

Pork and Chinese cabbage soup
Braised curried chicken
Barbecued spareribs
Crabmeat soufflé
Stir-fried pork with lettuce

Deep-fried shrimp without batter
Sweet orange tea

———

Abalone soup
Preserved eggs
Eggplant salad
Red-simmered pork with mushrooms
Steamed eggs and fish fillets
Stir-fried beef and Chinese cabbage
Braised lily bud chicken

———

Fish fillet soup
Steamed dried mushrooms
Stir-fried sweet-and-pungent chicken
    livers
Deep-fried shrimp with sherry sauce
Basic braised pork with eggs
Honeyed bananas

———

Vegetarian soup
Shrimp toast
Deep-fried marinated sweet-and-
    pungent fish
Lion's head
Stir-fried chicken with oyster sauce
Drunken duck
Sweet almond tea

———

Ten precious soup
Deep-fried paper-wrapped pork
Stir-fried chicken and tomatoes
Stir-fried beef and peppers
Crabmeat and cucumbers
Canned loquats

———

Basic bean curd soup with mushrooms
Basic steamed eggs with crabmeat
Red-cooked duck with Five Spices
Smashed radishes
Stir-fried pork and peppers

Fresh fruit

———

Pork and winter melon soup
Steamed shrimp
Red-simmered duck and pineapple
Stir-fried beef and cauliflower
Smashed cucumbers; smashed radishes
Sweet orange tea

———

Pork and Chinese cabbage soup
Stir-fried beef and tea melon
Liquid-filled roast duck
Red-simmered pork with mushrooms
Deep-fried shrimp stuffed with bacon
    and almonds
Stir-fried mustard cabbage

———

Chicken velvet and corn soup
Soft-fried noodles with stir-fried
    shrimp
Boneless roast chicken stuffed with
    pork
Basic omelet with ham
Basic braised soy fish
Stir-fried spinach and mushrooms

———

Pork and winter melon soup
Nanking salt duck
Simmered stuffed green peppers
Pan-fried fish cakes
Steamed pork strips with glutinous
    rice flour
Braised Chinese lettuce and chestnuts
Fresh fruit

———

Basic braised shrimp balls with
    Chinese cabbage
Deep-fried Chinese steak
Drunken duck

Basic steamed eggs with clams in their
    shells
Stir-fried pork kidney and snow peas
Stir-fried water cress
Almond cookies

Fish fillet soup
White cut chicken
Steamed pork balls with glutinous rice
Basic stir-fried beef with asparagus
Lobster Cantonese
Stir-fried spinach

Chicken velvet and corn soup
Stuffed mushrooms with crabmeat
Pan-fried marinated fish steaks
Stir-fried beef and tomatoes
Basic steamed eggs with roast pork
Red-cooked chicken
Deep-fried pork strips and walnuts

Oyster soup
Eggrolls
Deep-fried sweet-and-pungent pork
Stir-fried chicken and peppers
Smoked fish
Braised porkballs and cauliflower
Fresh fruit

Chicken and fuzzy melon soup
Deep-fried wonton
Cold roast duck with pineapple sauce
Deep-fried fish fillets with sesame
    seeds
Basic braised beef with lily buds
Chicken velvet sautéed
Stir-fried mixed vegetables

Wonton soup
Cold shrimp and cauliflower

Simmered and deep-fried chicken
    livers
Steamed duck with pineapple and
    preserved ginger
Deep-fried sweet-and-pungent fish
Roast pork
Sweet almond tea

Pork and water cress soup
Smoked fish
Marinated and deep-fried chicken
    livers
Stir-fried chicken with almonds and
    vegetables
Deep-fried coated butterfly shrimp
Stir-fried bamboo shoots and
    mushrooms
Sugared walnuts

Beef and lotus root soup
Barbecued spareribs
Basic deep-fried shrimp
Braised chicken with fresh mushrooms
Stir-fried beef and peppers
Basic steamed fish with black bean
    sauce
Honeyed bananas

Oyster pancakes
Braised duck with Chinese lettuce
Steamed sliced pork with white cheese
Red-simmered beef
Stir-fried spinach
Fresh fruit

Pork and mustard cabbage soup
Tea eggs
Red-cooked duck with tangerine peel
Stir-fried beef and string beans
Deep-fried shrimp balls in batter

Stir-fried cauliflower with mushrooms
    and water chestnuts
Sweet almond tea

———

Basic bean curd soup with mushrooms
Marinated and deep-fried chicken
    livers
Basic braised soy fish
Stir-fried beef and Chinese turnips
Basic steamed eggs with pork
Stir-fried broccoli
Green pea pudding

———

Pork and mustard cabbage soup
Chinese sausages
Chicken velvet and corn
Deep-fried steamed duck with
    mushrooms and bamboo shoots
Stir-fried beef and cauliflower
Basic steamed eggs with shrimp
Canned lichee fruit

———

Basic soup with pork
Stuffed mushrooms with ham
Basic steamed fish with lily buds
Braised duck with bamboo shoots
Stir-fried chicken and peppers
Smashed cucumbers
Steamed fruit

———

Basic noodles in soup
Red-simmered duck with glutinous
    rice
Clear-simmered fish
Stir-fried chicken livers with snow peas
Roast pork
Stuffed mushrooms with shrimp
Stir-fried mixed vegetables

———

Mushroom soup

Basic braised shrimp balls with spinach
Stir-fried bean sprouts
Red-simmered duck with pineapple
Twice-cooked pork
Sweet almond tea

———

Porkballs and vermicelli soup
Deep-fried fish fillets with egg whites
Jellied chicken
Stir-fried pork and string beans
Red-simmered beef
Stir-fried sweet-and-pungent preserved
    cabbage
Fresh fruit

———

Pork and water cress soup
Braised chestnut chicken
Basic stir-fried crabmeat with
    mushrooms
Red-simmered pork strips
Stir-fried spinach
Sweet walnut tea

———

Basic bean curd soup with bamboo
    shoots
Liquid-filled roast chicken
Gold coin pork
Braised soy fish with red dates
Red-simmered beef
Stir-fried bamboo shoots

———

Chicken and bitter melon soup
Preserved eggs
Mushrooms stuffed with pork and
    shrimp
Braised curried chicken
Deep-fried fish
Stir-fried beef and Chinese cabbage
Steamed sponge cake

MENUS FOR 8

Basic fishball soup
Stir-fried beef and oyster sauce
Basic steamed minced pork with salt
    fish
Deep-fried paper-wrapped chicken
Chinese sausages
Basic braised soy fish
Stir-fried spinach
Smashed radishes
Almond float

———

Basic soup with pork
Egg pouch omelets
Stir-fried chicken and peppers
Steamed sliced pork with ham and
    bean curd
Stir-fried beef and preserved mustard
    cabbage
Deep-fried sweet-and-pungent
    spareribs
Stir-fried shrimp and bean sprouts
Stir-fried pumpkin
Fresh fruit

———

Clam soup
Deep-fried fishballs and Chinese
    cabbage
Pickled turnips
Preserved eggs
Chinese sausages
Steamed duck with two kinds of
    mushrooms
Braised pork and bean curd
Basic stir-fried beef with black bean
    sauce
Fresh fruit

———

Pork and winter melon soup
Smashed cucumbers
Eggplant salad
Braised anise beef
Braised lily bud chicken
Stuffed mushrooms with crabmeat
Basic stir-fried pork with
    water chestnuts
Deep-fried sweet-and-pungent
    spareribs
Sweet almond tea

———

Porkballs and vermicelli soup
Peking duck
Stir-fried beef and onions
Deep-fried shrimp in shells
Stir-fried creamed Chinese cabbage
Crabmeat soufflé
Deep-fried eight piece chicken

———

Wonton soup
White-cooked pressed pork
Marinated abalone
Shrimp toast
Basic stir-fried chicken with lily buds
Stir-fried pork with lettuce
Red-simmered duck with pineapple
Basic braised beef
Sweet orange tea

———

Pork and water cress soup
Sweet-and-pungent lotus root
Oyster sauce mushrooms
Spring rolls
Chicken velvet sautéed
Stir-fried ham and spinach

Pan-fried fish fillets with pineapple
Stir-fried beef and celery
Sweet walnut tea

———

Abalone soup
Smoked fish
Soy eggs
White cut chicken
Smashed cucumbers
Stir-fried chicken and peanuts
Basic deep-fried shrimp balls
Basic braised pork with eggs
Shark's fin in ham sauce
Stir-fried mixed vegetables
Almond float

———

Wonton soup
Sesame ham sticks
Bean sprout salad
Bird's nest soup
Stir-fried chicken and oyster sauce
Basic steamed fish with lily buds
Stir-fried bamboo shoots
Braised beef
Spring rolls
Steamed red date cake

———

Egg drop soup
Chinese pickles
Shrimp toast
Stir-fried chicken and bamboo shoots
Steamed duck with sherry
Deep-fried sweet-and-pungent fish
Steamed deep-fried squab
Stir-fried pork and ginger root
Sweet almond tea

———

Pork and water cress soup
Pickled Chinese cabbage
Dried jellyfish and turnips
Pan-fried fish fillets with pineapple
Stir-fried chicken and snow peas
Steamed duck with ham and leeks
Tea eggs
Stir-fried beef and rice-flour noodles
Sweet walnut tea

———

Pork and water cress soup
Deep-fried steamed duck stuffed with
    lotus seeds
Red-simmered beef
Braised fragrant pork
Deep-fried sweet-and-pungent fish
Stir-fried mixed vegetables
Sweet almond tea

———

Hot-sour soup
Spinach salad with shrimp
Nanking salt duck
Stir-fried shrimp in shells
Basic red-simmered pork with Chinese
    turnip
Stir-fried beef and peppers
Sweet-and-pungent mustard cabbage
Peking dust

———

Steamed lobster tails stuffed with pork
Barbecued spareribs
Stir-fried fish with vegetables
Braised curried chicken
Roast turkey
Eggplant salad
Smashed cucumbers
Almond float

MENUS FOR 10–12 (BANQUETS)

Hors d'oeuvres:
Marinated abalone
Pickled Chinese lettuce
Sesame ham sticks
Smashed cucumbers
White cut chicken
Smashed radishes
Stir-fried shrimp in shells

Soup:
Pork and winter melon soup

Small dishes:
Chicken soufflé
Basic stir-fried pork with mushrooms
Stir-fried fish with lily buds
Stir-fried miniature shrimp and peas

Big dishes:
Clear-simmered fish
Eight precious duck
Lion's head

———

Hors d'oeuvres:
Marinated abalone
Marinated mushrooms
Preserved eggs
White-cooked pressed pork

Soup:
Hot-sour soup

Small dishes:
Stir-fried chicken and walnuts
Deep-fried coated butterfly shrimp
Stir-fried beef and oyster sauce
Stir-fried snow peas with mushrooms

Big Dishes:
Shark's fin in ham sauce
Deep-fried marinated sweet-and-pungent fish
Basic red-simmered pork with eggs
Peking duck

Dessert:
Sweet almond tea

———

Hors d'oeuvres:
Sesame ham sticks
Deep-fried chicken gizzards
Tea eggs
Roast pork

Soup:
Pork and winter melon soup

Small Dishes:
Stir-fried miniature shrimp and peas
Stir-fried pork and string beans
Stir-fried beef and snow peas
Deep-fried squab

Big Dishes:
Steamed pork strips with glutinous rice flour
Braised chestnut chicken
Peking duck
Deep-fried marinated sweet-and-pungent fish

Desserts:
Eight precious pudding
Sweet orange tea

———

Hors d'oeuvres:
Marinated and deep-fried chicken
 livers
Cantonese sausage
Preserved eggs
Pickled Chinese lettuce

Soup:
Pork and mustard cabbage soup

Small dishes:
Stir-fried shrimp balls and
 tomatoes
Deep-fried squab
Stir-fried beef and peppers
Deep-fried paper-wrapped chicken

Big dishes:
Steamed chicken stuffed with bird's
 nest
Red-simmered pork shoulder
Deep-fried steamed eight precious
 duck
Basic steamed fish and bean curd

Desserts:
Peking dust
Sweet almond tea

Hors d'oeuvres:
Red-simmered chicken
 wings
Preserved eggs
Steamed dried mushrooms

Soup:
Squab and ginseng root soup

Small Dishes:
Deep-fried coated butterfly
 shrimp
Basic stir-fried pork with walnuts
Stir-fried bean curd with mushrooms
Deep-fried squab

Big dishes:
Shark's fin in ham sauce
Deep-fried marinated duck stuffed
 with glutinous rice
Red-simmered fresh ham and
 chestnuts
Steamed chicken stuffed with bird's
 nest
Deep-fried marinated sweet-and-pun-
 gent fish

Desserts:
Eight precious pudding
Almond float

❀ *Other Useful Information* ❀

HOW-TO SECTION

ALMONDS—*To blanch:* Shell the almonds. Soak 5 minutes in hot water. Rinse in cold water. Drain. Slip off skins.

ALMONDS—*To toast:* Heat 2 tablespoons peanut oil in a skillet. Sauté blanched almonds in hot oil until golden. (Keep them moving or they'll burn.) Chop or sliver.

Or: Bring several cups of peanut oil to a boil. Place the blanched almonds in a sieve. Dip sieve in oil until nuts turn golden. Remove and drain.

Or: Place the blanched almonds in a dry pan with several tablespoons of salt. Stir constantly over very low heat until almonds turn golden.

BARBECUE RACK—*To make your own:* Buy 8 or 10 curtain end hooks (the single, not double, variety) at the dime store. Bend them so they hook at each end. Hook one end of each onto the crossbar of the oven shelf; the other into the meat to be barbecued (such as a rack of spareribs). Set the shelf as high in the oven as possible. Place a large pan containing water on the floor of the oven to catch the drippings and prevent their burning. Replenish the water from time to time.

NOTE: This is the best method for barbecuing spareribs. Second best is laying them flat on a rack over a drip pan.

BEAN CURD—*To press:* Place a sheet of wax paper on a cutting or other flat board. Set the cakes of bean curd side by side on the paper. Cover with a second sheet of wax paper, another flat board. Weight the top board with heavy objects: thick books, a kettle filled with water, etc. Let stand until bean curd cakes become compressed and solid (about 5 hours or overnight).

Or: Wrap each bean cake individually in cheesecloth. Place between two flat boards. Weight as above, gradually increasing the weight at 20-minute intervals. Unwrap after 1 hour.

NOTE: Pressing fresh bean curd makes it more compact, less fragile, and easier to handle. Some cooks parboil the bean curd first in salted water to make it keep longer. When the cakes float, they are removed, drained and pressed as above.

BEAN SPROUTS—*To grow your own:* Bean sprouts can be grown from tiny dried mung green peas if kept warm, moist, and away from light. (They need a room temperature of about 68 to 75 degrees.)

The simple equipment required is a rack or perforated pan. (A non-rusting window screen, an ordinary colander or an old pan with holes punched in the bottom, can be used. Also suitable is a scrubbed-out clay flower pot lined with a layer of clean pebbles.) Other necessary items are cheesecloth and a basin for draining.

Wash the peas, then soak overnight in warm water (they will nearly double in size). Then rinse until the water runs clear. Next, place a double layer of cheesecloth on the rack. Using warm water, sprinkle the cloth to moisten thoroughly; then spread the peas over the cloth in a single even layer. Cover with another double thickness of cheesecloth. Again sprinkle with warm water to moisten well. Place the rack over the draining basin and put in a dark place such as a basement, oven, cupboard or closet. The darkness will keep the sprouts white and tender. (If no such place is convenient, cover the rack with a black or dark-colored cloth to keep the light out. Dampen this too.)

Keep the cheesecloth moist by sprinkling it with half a cup of warm water at 4-hour intervals during the day. See that the excess water drains off properly into the basin. When the basin is full, pour off the water. Don't let it stand: it will become stagnant and give the sprouts an unpleasant muskiness. Should mold begin to form on the growing sprouts, add to the last sprinkling water of the day a pinch of chlorinated lime (which can be purchased at the drugstore). Do not stir or disturb the sprouts. If they turn pinkish, moisten the cheesecloth with cool, but not ice, water.

In 4 to 5 days, the bean sprouts will mature (sooner if the room is warm, later if it's cool). They will have expanded to about four times their original size, with the sprouts plump, and measuring about an inch or so in length. Remove only those sprouts you plan to use. Keep the remainder covered and moist. They'll keep fresh and tender for several days. (One-fourth pound of mung peas will yield more than a pound of bean sprouts. On your first try, however, limit yourself to 3 to 4 tablespoons of peas.)

NOTE: Soybean sprouts may be grown from black soybeans in exactly the same way. These take longer to mature (6 to 8 days) and have 3-inch sprouts.

BEAN SPROUTS—*To husk:* Immerse the sprouts in cold water. Plunge up and down several times. The husks or hoods will rise to the surface. Skim off

husks and discard. Change the water. Repeat process until most husks are removed, then drain. (This is for the soy rather than the mung sprouts. The hoods of the latter are delicate and don't really need husking.)

BEAN SPROUTS, CANNED—*To restore crispness:* Several hours before using, open the can and drain the sprouts. Rinse thoroughly with cold running water. Immerse in fresh cold water or ice water and refrigerate. Drain when ready to use.

BEEF—*To tenderize:* Dissolve 1 teaspoon baking soda in 2 tablespoons water. Spread over beef. Let stand 1 hour.

Or: Combine ½ teaspoon baking soda, ½ teaspoon salt, ½ teaspoon peanut oil, a pinch of sugar and a dash of pepper. Add mixture to beef shreds or slivers and toss. Let stand 1 hour.

Or: Pound stewing beef lightly with the side of a cleaver blade or bottom of a glass, and pierce all over with a fork. Combine 3 tablespoons soy sauce, 2 tablespoons sherry and 1 teaspoon salt. Rub into meat. Let stand 1 hour, then braise.

Or: Add 1 tablespoon brandy for every 2 cups of liquid in which red-simmered beef will cook.

CHESTNUTS—*To shell:* With the point of a sharp knife, cut 2 cross-wise gashes on the flat side of each chestnut. Place chestnuts and 1 teaspoon peanut oil in pan over high heat. Shake pan until nuts are coated with oil.

Then place for a few minutes in a moderate oven until shells loosen. Remove shells and inner membranes.

Or: Cover chestnuts with boiling water. Boil 20 to 25 minutes. Drain. Remove shells and membranes.

Or: Cut a gash on the flat side of each chestnut. Drop in boiling water. Boil 5 minutes. Let stand in the water 10 minutes. Shell while warm. Remove inner membrane.

CHICKEN—*To bone:* Make a lengthwise slit in the skin at the back of the neck, cutting downward to base of the neck. Loosen skin. Remove crop. Cut through neckbone. Roll back skin at shoulders. At wing joints, cut through sinews. Make a cut along the wing bone, following the bone closely with the knife. Push up the bone and cut it off at the second joint. (Don't remove bone from lower wings.)

Slip knife along breastbone, one side at a time: separate meat from bone, pushing meat toward the back and cutting it loose crosswise at the back; loosen the meat with the back of the knife, slipping it further off the body.

Where legs join body, break the joints, cut through the sinews. The meat should now be inverted with the legs attached. Separate meat from carcass by cutting it wherever it's still attached. Loosen meat from thighs. Push bone up and cut off at first joint. Loosen meat of next leg section, by cutting along bone. Turn meat inside out to remove leg bone. The entire chicken should now be inside out. Turn it back to its original shape. (If boning a chicken seems too difficult, have the butcher do it, or leave the bones in. In the latter case, carve the chicken Western-style.

CHICKEN, COOKED—*To cut up:* With a sharp cleaver, remove the legs and wings at their joints. Chop each thigh, bones and all, in 2 pieces; each drumstick in 2 pieces. Cut off the lower or bony part of each drumstick. Chop each wing in 2 or 3 pieces. Chop the neck in 3 pieces. Split the bird lengthwise down the spine and through the breast. Remove each half of the breast, cutting it first into quarters, then into slices about 1 inch thick (bones and all). Chop the upper and lower back in 3 pieces each. Lay these down on the serving dish. Then place the neck, wing and leg sections, skin-side up, approximately back in their original positions. Finally, place the slices of breast meat down the middle in 2 neat rows to reconstruct the natural shape of the chicken. (An easy way to do this: as the chicken is chopped, section by section, scoop up the pieces with the broad cleaver-knife blade and slide them directly onto the serving platter.)

CORNSTARCH PASTE—*To thicken with:* Blend the specified amount of cornstarch, cold water (and whatever seasonings may be called for in the recipe) to a smooth paste. Add gradually to the pan when directed and cook, stirring, over medium-high heat until the sauce thickens and is smooth. When the dish contains a fragile ingredient such as fresh bean curd, it's advisable to thicken the sauce first and *then* add that ingredient.

NOTE: If the cornstarch paste is prepared in advance, always re-stir before using. Otherwise it will separate, with the solids sinking to the bottom.

CREAM—*To whip:* Place fresh cream in a bowl. Set the bowl in a large container filled with ice cubes. Whip with an egg beater to the desired consistency. Note: This is used with Peking Dust.

DUCK—*To bone:* Chop off the lower wings. Cut carefully downward along the spine, working close to the bone. Separate meat from bone without tearing either meat or skin. Lift one leg of duck and move it in all directions to loosen the thigh joint. Insert the knife point, hitting thigh joint lightly but firmly until joint and pelvis separate. Repeat with the other leg and with both shoulder joints to loosen. In the fleshier portions, such as breast and thighs, alternately cut and pull the meat away from the bones, to separate the flesh from the carcass. When meat and bones are completely separated, draw the bony neck out as far as possible through the skin. Chop neck off. Draw out the windpipe and esophagus. Remove as much tail bone as possible, but do not chop off tail. Carefully remove oil sacs near the tail. Wash duck in cold water. Hang by tail to drain thoroughly.

DUCK, COOKED—*To cut up:* Cut off the legs at the thigh joints, the wings at the shoulder joints. Split duck in half along the backbone. Carefully separate breast meat from bone, using a cutting and tearing action. Cut breast meat in 2-inch strips. With a cleaver, chop legs and upper wings in 2-inch sections. To serve: Place neck on platter. Arrange wing, leg and breast sections to approximate original shape of duck.

DUCK, COOKED—*To bone and carve:* Cut off legs at the thigh joints. Slip out leg bones and cut meat in 1- or 1½-inch strips. Cut off wings at shoulder joints. With a sharp knife, make a vertical incision along the center line of the breast. Slip the knife in to separate meat and bone. Cut meat in 1- or 1½-inch strips.

EGG CUBES—*To prepare:* Beat 2 eggs lightly. Add ½ teaspoon salt, ½ teaspoon sugar, and a dash of pepper. Heat 1 tablespoon oil in a skillet. Add the eggs and scramble until set. Cool slightly. Cut into cubes.

NOTE: These, used as a soup garnish, are added at the end, only to be heated through.

EGG THREADS—*To prepare:* Beat an egg lightly. (You may, if you wish, add a pinch of salt and ½ teaspoon sherry.) Grease a skillet and heat. Add the egg and tip the pan so it spreads thinly and evenly. Cook over low heat until egg sets but is not dry. (Its edge should be slightly browned.) Invert onto a platter. Let cool. Cut into short narrow strips about ⅛-inch wide, 2 inches long.

EGGS—*To poach:* Bring water to a boil in a skillet or shallow pan. Add ½ teaspoon salt and ½ teaspoon vinegar. Reduce heat to a simmer. Break the eggs one at a time into a saucer, then slide each gently into the simmering water. Cook until the white sets. Remove carefully with a slotted spoon.

EGGS, PRESERVED—*To shell:* Soak the egg in cold water until its black outer coating is soft enough to scrape off with a knife (about an hour). Then crack and remove shell, taking care not to bruise the egg itself. Slice egg with a sharp knife.

Or: Crack the black outer coating by tapping the egg gently on a flat surface, or with the side of a knife. Remove coating and rinse. Then crack and remove shell; slice egg.

NOTE: Either procedure is best done at the sink right from the start.

FLAVOR—*To improve:* If the food is too salty, add a little sugar and vinegar during cooking. The next time you cook the dish, reduce the amount of salt first. If it's still too salty, reduce the amount of soy sauce to taste. If the food is too sour or vinegary, add salt. If it's too sweet or cloying, also add salt.

GINKGO NUTS—*To blanch:* Shell with a nutcracker. Pour boiling water over nutmeats. Let stand 5 to 10 minutes. Drain. Remove and discard pinkish inner skin.

GLUTINOUS RICE—*To cook:* Wash rice under cold water until the water runs clear. Place the rice in a saucepan with fresh water (use 2 cups of water for each cup of rice). Bring to a boil, then reduce heat to low and cook, covered, until the water is absorbed (about 30 minutes). NOTE: Do not remove the lid during cooking.

LARD, LEAF—*To render:* Cut the lard in 2-inch pieces. Heat in a pan, while at the same time pressing leaves gently with either fork or chopstick to extract liquid. Continue until the leaves become crisp and brown. Pour liquid lard into a container. Let cool.

LOTUS SEEDS—*To blanch:* Soak the seeds 5 minutes in hot water. Rub off the husks. Insert a toothpick in one end of each seed. Push out and discard the bitter-tasting green heart. Rinse. Boil 10 to 15 minutes. Drain.

MUNG PEAS—See BEAN SPROUTS.

MUSHROOMS—*To dry*: With a needle and strong white sewing thread, string fresh mushrooms through their stems and caps, spacing them about an inch apart. Hang up to dry in the sun for a few days.

NOODLES, EGG—*To deep-fry*: Parboil the noodles, then drain dry. Heat deep-frying oil to about 325 degrees. Place the noodles in a sieve or strainer and immerse in the oil for a minute or two. (This preliminary deep-frying keeps the noodles from absorbing too much oil later and puffing up like popcorn.) Drain and let cool about 5 minutes. Reheat the deep-frying oil; then return noodles and stir constantly until they're crisp and golden. Drain on paper toweling.

NOODLES, RICE-FLOUR—*To prepare as a garnish*: Break off the required amount of noodles and separate the strands. Heat deep-frying oil to 350 degrees. Add noodles and deep-fry quickly until crisp, puffed up and snow white (about 20 seconds on each side). Do not brown. Drain on paper toweling and let cool.

OIL, PEANUT—*To enhance*: Pour the oil into a pan. Add a slice or two of fresh ginger root and a leek or scallion stalk, cut in 1-inch sections. Heat oil until ginger and leek begin to brown, then remove these and discard. Let oil cool. Strain and store in a covered container.

NOTE: Peanut oil, unlike other oils, does not absorb cooking odors or need clarification. Many cooks, however, like to enhance its flavor, as described above, after using the oil for deep-frying.

ONION BRUSHES—*To make:* Discard both the leafy green tops and root ends of thick scallions, leaving only the white stalks. Make a number of vertical, parallel cuts about ½-inch deep at one end. Then make a number of other parallel cuts at right angles to the first set to form a grid pattern. (You may do this at one or both ends of each stalk.) Soak 1 hour in ice water. (The shredded ends will open and become frilly.) Drain. Place in a serving dish.

NOTE: Onion brushes are served with Peking Duck or as a relish with hoisin sauce.

PAPER-WRAPPING—*How to:* Use a heavy tissue, rice paper, parchment-type, or wax paper. Do not use aluminum foil. (The wrapping must be porous.)

Cut the paper in 4-inch squares. Place each square with the lower corner pointing toward you. Grease paper with a drop of oil (peanut or sesame, lard or chicken fat). Place the meat or chicken well below the center line of the square.

Fold up the lower corner to cover the meat. Then fold the lower section once more (to the center line). Next, fold the left corner over and the right, envelope-style. Finally, fold the remaining top corner down, like an envelope flap, and tuck its end in securely. Repeat until all meat or chicken is paper-wrapped.

NOTE: Paper-wrapping, used with deep-fried foods, acts much like a batter coating in insulating ingredients against the hot oil. (If the meat is cut in narrow strips, 2 pieces may be enclosed in each wrapping. The paper may also be cut in smaller, or 2½-inch, squares.)

PEANUTS—*To toast:* See ALMONDS.

POULTRY—*To suspend and dry:* If the bird is intact, suspend it by its neck, using clean white string. Otherwise, suspend the bird by its tail section, using a curtain hook or similar wire device to support it. Hang in a cool, airy place to dry, with a drip pan underneath.

POULTRY—*To truss:* Place the bird breast-side up. Take a length of clean white string; slip it around the back, then under and around the wings. Cross the ends of the string at the tip of the breastbone and pull them taut to hold the wings down. Then loop one end around each leg and tie securely.

SMOKING—*How to:* Line a thick pan, preferably cast-iron, with enough heavy-duty foil so it can be folded over and sealed completely at the top. (If necessary, use two sheets of foil, folding them together several times at the bottom to make a strong airtight seam.) Sprinkle the brown sugar—and other specified ingredients—over the foil. Place the food on a flat dish. Set the dish over the sugar, using a small rack device. (Either use an old dish or cover it completely first with additional foil since it will char.) Then fold the top edges of the foil several times to make an airtight seam so the ingredients are completely sealed in. Heat the pan over medium-low heat until the sugar burns and smokes. (Make a pinhole in the foil to check this, then pinch it closed.) Cover the pan and let smoke as directed in the recipe. Then turn off the heat and slowly open the foil wrapping to let the smoke escape gradually.

SQUAB—*To cut up:* Use the same method as for chicken but cut the squab in quarters or eighths. Leave the leg and wings whole.

STEAMERS—*To make your own:* Get a large wide pot (such as a Dutch oven or roaster) with a close-fitting lid. Add about 2 to 3 inches of boiling water. In the pot, set a rack device—standing 3½ to 4 inches high—which will support the dish of ingredients to be steamed and at the same time keep it elevated *above* the boiling water. The rack device can be any of the following: (1) an upright coffee cup, on which is set an inverted metal pie pan with a few dozen holes punched in it; (2) a 1-pound coffee can (the type that's 3½ inches tall) with a few dozen holes punched in the bottom, placed upside down—without its lid—at the bottom of the pot; (3) any 1 or 2 can with both the top and bottom removed, set upright in the pot. (If the dish of ingredients to be steamed is large, two cans of the same size can be used for steadier support.); (4) a rack-like cake cooler that stands about 3½ inches

high; (5) a vegetable steamer set out flat rather than in its characteristic basket-like shape; or (6) a roaster rack set on 2 upright coffee cups.

NOTE: The devices above are used for steaming fish, eggs, meatballs, pastries and any small or finely cut ingredients which will fit in a shallow dish that is to be set on the rack. However, when a large cut of meat or whole poultry is involved, this is usually placed in a deep heatproof bowl. The bowl can then be set on a rack (if the pot is deep enough) or else it can be set directly on the bottom of the pot in a few inches of boiling water. The latter is known as the bowl-in-a-pot or pot-within-a-pot method. Whichever method of steaming is used, whether it be rack or bowl, the outer pot is *always* covered to contain the live steam which will cook the food.

Still another way to handle particularly large cuts of meat or poultry is to use a big enamel basin with a rack in it, covered with a second enamel basin of the same size. Or to suspend a colander in a pot large enough to hold it and place a whole chicken or duck in that colander. Boiling water is then added to within one inch of the bottom of the colander and the pot is covered with its own lid, or else the colander itself is covered tightly with aluminum foil to contain the steam.

STEAMING—*How to:* For the rack method, place the small or finely cut ingredients in a heatproof dish—as a rule, the shallower the dish, the better. Meanwhile bring several inches of water to a boil in a large pot, wok or roaster. Place in the pot a rack device that will clear the water level by 1 or 2 inches (see STEAMERS above). Then place the heatproof dish on that rack. Cover the pot and steam for the time specified in the recipe. As the boiling water evaporates, add more of the same from time to time to maintain its general level.

For the bowl-in-a-pot method: Place the large cut of meat or whole poultry in a heatproof bowl. Set the bowl in a large pot, wok or roaster and surround the bowl with boiling water to about two-thirds of its height. Cover the pot, steam as specified and replenish the boiling water with more of the same, as necessary. (At no point should the water be permitted to evaporate *below* the bowl's halfway mark.)

NOTE: To guard against burned fingers when removing the steamed foods, turn the heat off first, set the pot lid aside and let the steam disperse for a few seconds. Then lift out the dish or bowl with potholders or rubber gloves. Also don't bend your head too close for the first few seconds after removing the lid, since the concentrated steam tends to be scalding.

TOMATOES—*To peel:* Insert a 2-pronged fork in the tomato's stem end. Dip the tomato into rapidly boiling water for about 20 seconds. Remove. Slip off the skin at once with a paring knife.

VEGETABLES—*To blanch:* Wash, peel and cut up vegetable. Then pour boiling water over, stir once or twice, and drain at once in a colander or sieve. Rinse the vegetable immediately with cold running water. (This will stop the cooking action.) Drain again.

Or: Bring the water to a boil in a large pot and add the cut-up vegetable. Turn off the heat at once and let the vegetable stand a minute or two. Then drain; rinse immediately with cold running water and drain again.

VEGETABLES—*To parboil:* Wash, peel and cut up the vegetable. Bring the water to a rolling boil in a pot large enough to allow plenty of space for the vegetable. Add salt; then add the vegetable gradually so that the water is kept at a rolling boil. Stir gently for even cooking. (Depending on the tenderness or toughness of the vegetable and the way it's cut, parboiling will take from 1 to 4 minutes.) Remove green vegetables from the heat as soon as they begin to turn a very bright green. Remove the non-green vegetables when slightly softened but still crisp. Drain at once in a colander or sieve. (Reserve the vegetable liquid for soups and sauces; it's not only tasty but full of nutrients.) Cool the vegetable immediately under cold running water; then drain again.

NOTE: These techniques of blanching and parboiling are sometimes also used with meat, poultry and seafood as specified in certain recipes.

WALNUTS—*To blanch:* Shell the walnuts with nutcracker. Cover nutmeats with cold water. Bring to a boil and cook 3 minutes. Drain at once. Dry on paper toweling.

Or: Cover the nutmeats with boiling water. Let stand 15 minutes. Drain and dry.

WALNUTS—*To toast:* Heat oil for deep-frying to 300 degrees. Place blanched walnuts in a sieve. Dip sieve in the oil, then quickly lift out. With a ladle, pour hot oil over walnuts until light brown and crisp. Drain on paper toweling.

Or: Coarsely chop blanched walnuts. Place under an oven broiler for a few minutes.

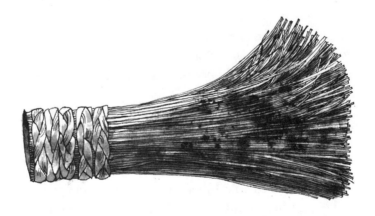

WOK—*To treat a new one:* Wash the wok thoroughly with hot water and detergent. Rinse and dry. Heat 2 tablespoons peanut oil in the wok until the oil seems to move around at the bottom. Tilt pan so oil coats entire inside surface. Turn off heat. Let cool. Pour off the oil. Wipe wok with paper towel until its surface is smooth and lightly oiled.

Or: Clean, rinse and dry as above. Rub the entire inside surface of the wok with oil. Heat 1 minute over high flame. Rinse with hot water. Rub on more oil. Repeat the process. Wash carefully with hot water. Dry with paper towel.

NOTE: Iron woks are seasoned in this way to seal up the "pores" of the metal. This keeps the food from sticking.

WOK—*To clean:* Once seasoned, the wok should never be scoured with strong detergents or metal cleaners. Remove food scraps and excess oil with paper toweling. If food sticks, scour the wok with salt to build up a seasoned finish like that of an omelet pan.

NOTE: The Chinese scrape the wok clean with a stiff brush, rinse it in very hot water, then dry it immediately to prevent rusting by placing it over a gas jet for a few seconds.

GUIDE TO STIR-FRYING

At first stir-frying may seem complex and baffling, but when broken down into its component parts, it's extremely logical and not at all difficult. Success in stir-frying depends on two things: understanding the underlying principles of this cooking method, and getting organized before you begin.

Principles of stir-frying: Stir-frying consists of the following steps: heating the pan and oil; adding the first seasonings (garlic, ginger root, etc.); then the meat; liquid seasonings; vegetables; stock; and a cornstarch paste. This sequence can vary slightly from one recipe to the next: sometimes the vegetable is added *before* the meat.*

Heating the pan and oil: Always start with the pan dry. Heat it over high heat until the metal becomes hot enough to make a drop of water sizzle. Then add the oil and heat until bubbling, but not smoking. It should be thin and easy flowing. (If oil and pan are not sufficiently hot, the ingredients will stick and become limp.)

Adding the first seasonings: When the oil is heated, add the salt. Stir once or twice. (It will dissolve quickly.) Add the garlic,† and stir-fry constantly. Watch for burning. You may also at this point add and stir-fry sliced scallion stalks and/or ginger root. Other seasonings that can also be added at this point are the fermented black beans or brown bean sauce. As soon as any of these begin to brown and become aromatic, add the meat. (This will immediately lower the pan temperature and prevent burning.)

NOTE: As a short cut, some restaurants keep on hand a mixture of peanut oil, salt and minced garlic. The home cook can do the same, if she wishes, putting the mixture up in a jar. It should be tightly covered and refrigerated when not in use.

Adding the meat: Meat is always stir-fried by itself first in very hot oil. It is vigorously tossed and flipped about (to assure even heating and prevent burning) until partly cooked: Beef is partly cooked when it loses its redness and turns brown; pork and chicken when they lose their pinkness and turn white; shrimp when it starts to turn pink. No other liquid is added at this point. If the pan becomes too dry more oil is added, but never poured directly on the meat. (The oil is added with a wide circular motion inside the rim so

---

* The vegetable is removed, however, when partly cooked, along with its liquids to permit the meat to cook directly in fresh oil. When the meat is partly cooked, the vegetable is returned and they complete their cooking togther.

† The hot oil brings out the garlic's flavor and aroma. The way garlic is added to the pan determines its strength in the final dish. When the clove is cut in half, impaled on a fork and rubbed on the pan's surfaces as the oil heats, garlic is mild and best for such delicate dishes as asparagus. When crushed and browned in the hot oil but removed before the other ingredients are added, the garlic is stronger. When minced fine, browned lightly in the oil and left in the pot to cook with the other ingredients, it's the most aromatic of all.

that it runs down the sides and is heated by the metal before actually touching the meat. Another way to add oil is to make a well or small clearing at the bottom of the pan—by pushing the ingredients aside—then pouring the oil directly into this so it hits the hot metal before touching the meat.)

NOTE: More than 1 pound of meat should never be added to the pan at once. (A greater quantity would make the temperature of the pan drop too quickly.) When cooking meat in larger quantities, stir-fry it a pound at a time.

The meat should be dry when added. If moist, a layer of steam will form between meat and oil, interfering with the searing process which seals the meat and keeps it juicy. To prevent this, the meat is often tossed first in a cornstarch paste, to give it a tight dry outer coating.

Adding the liquid seasonings: Liquid seasonings such as soy sauce and sherry are added in small quantities but not until the meat is partly cooked. (If the meat is too raw, the liquid will toughen it.) When added at the right time, liquid seasonings enable the meat to keep cooking at high temperatures without burning. They also blend with the juices of the meat and bring out its natural flavors. To do this, the liquid seasonings should be slightly heated before contact with the meat. This is done by adding them to the pan like the oil—in a circular motion inside the rim, or else by pouring them directly into a well at the bottom. (This prevents their being absorbed and concentrated in only one part of the pan.)

Adding the vegetables: Like the liquid seasonings, the vegetables usually are added *after* the meat is partly cooked. The reason is the same: if the meat were still raw, the vegetable juices would toughen it. As a rule, vegetables require less heat than meat and more cooking time. (The coarse vegetables need the longest time and go into the pan before the tender ones.) Pork is usually left in the pan to cook with the vegetables, but beef generally is temporarily removed and returned at the end. Vegetables are stir-fried quickly but gently so they won't break or become mushy. Fragile ingredients such as bean curd are not stirred at all. (They'd be demolished.) The pan is either tilted or shaken to coat them with hot oil and seasonings, or else the pan is rotated quickly and sharply while at the same time, the delicate bean curd is gently pushed about with the back of a spoon to expose all its surfaces to the hot oil.

Note: Add the vegetables to the pan a fistful at a time, instead of all at once, so that their initial contact with the oil is at the high pan temperature. This temperature is then maintained until the vegetables are coated with the oil and partially cooked.

Adding the stock: A little stock or water is added to the vegetables to soften them and blend their flavors. This stock—like the other liquid

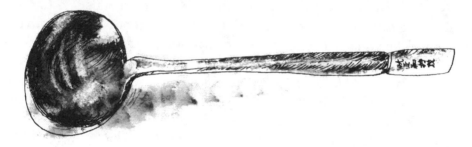

seasonings—is never poured directly onto the ingredients but heated slightly first in the same way the liquid seasonings are. The precise amount of stock needed for a given dish is best determined by experience: Some ingredients, being more tender, need less liquid; others, being tougher, need more. Some which are juicier give off more liquids; others which are drier give off less. In the case of certain vegetables, stock is omitted altogether. (Spinach, water cress and lettuce produce enough liquid of their own.) With others, the heat can be lowered and the pan covered a few seconds. (This will generate just enough steam to cook the vegetable without additional stock.)

Stir-fried dishes are better dry than wet: stock should moisten the dish, not drown it. If the dish has too much sauce, the excess should be poured off before it is served.

Adding the cornstarch paste: Although restaurants invariably thicken their sauces, many home cooks do not. This is a matter of personal preference. The thickening agent (a cornstarch paste, made by blending cornstarch, cold water, and occasionally other seasonings) performs a number of useful functions: It enables the sauce to adhere to, coat and flavor the cut-up ingredients. It also gives the dish a glistening, finished appearance. Cornstarch paste goes into the pan at the very end of stir-frying. It is added gradually to the hot liquid and continuously stirred until the sauce is thick, smooth and velvety.

Serving the stir-fried dish: As has been indicated earlier, stir-fried food, to be at its best, should be served the moment it's done. It is possible, however, to stir-fry certain hard and semi-hard vegetables partially in advance (although not more than about an hour ahead) and then to combine these with the meat, poultry or seafood for the last minutes of cooking.

NOTE: Just before taking the food from the pan, some cooks like to hold the serving dish over the pan for a few seconds to give that dish an additional "taste" or aroma of the stir-fried mixture.

Preparation—Getting Organized: The beginner in stir-frying does her best when she's relaxed and not under any undue pressure. The following suggestions on getting organized should help prevent frayed nerves and frazzled tempers:

1. Read the recipe well in advance to see what ingredients are needed and what preparation they require.

2. If dried ingredients are called for, allow time enough for soaking.

3. Slice and neatly stack the meat, poultry or seafood. (These may be sliced several hours in advance, wrapped in foil or transparent wrap and refrigerated until needed.) If they are to be dredged or marinated, allow time for this.

4. Wash, drain and cut the vegetables. (Always have ingredients as dry as possible to prevent spattering.) If parboiling is called for, allow time for this.

5. If more than one vegetable is used, check to see which will be added to the pan first. Separate the longer-cooking from the shorter-cooking vegetables. Stack them separately and neatly. (Stacking them on separate dishes means more dishes to wash. An easier way is to stack them on a stainless steel tray, or rectangular cookie tin. The 14- × 17-inch size is a good one for the latter.)

6. Mix the liquid seasonings (the soy sauce, sherry, etc.).

7. If a cornstarch paste is called for, mix and set this aside.

8. Get out all the other ingredients such as peanut oil, salt, garlic, ginger, scallions, stock, garnish, etc. Arrange these, along with the above ingredients, from left to right, on a table or counter near the stove, setting them out in the same order in which they are to be added to the pan.

9. After measuring and mixing, put away all bottles and jars, etc. Dispose of the disposable as soon as possible. Wash the dirty dishes a few at a time. Don't let them accumulate.

10. Set out the cooking pans, utensils and serving dishes. Set the table.

11. Read the recipe once more to review the cooking pattern (the exact sequence of what should be happening when).

12. Double-check to see that everything is in place. Then light the stove and you're off.

Preparation—Cutting: Cutting the ingredients properly is essential for successful stir-frying. The following tips will prove helpful:

Trim all fat and gristle from the meat.

Always cut meat for stir-frying against the grain. (First determine the general direction of the fibers, then hold the knife perpendicular to them. For diagonal slicing, shift the angle of the knife slightly.)

Meat for stir-frying should always be sliced thin. This is particularly true for pork: Slice it about $\frac{1}{16}$-inch thick. Poultry and beef may be sliced in $\frac{1}{8}$-inch, or slightly thicker slices.

Paper-thin slicing is easiest when meat and poultry are partially frozen. (Freeze them completely first, then let thaw slightly before slicing.) Before cooking, defrost completely, or the meat's flavor and tenderness will be impaired.

If the meat seems to be tough, slice it as thin as possible; then lay the slices out flat. Pound each slice once with the side of a cleaver-knife blade. (This will tenderize it.)

Slippery ingredients such as garlic, scallions, ginger root and nuts behave better if crushed slightly with the side of a knife blade. They will then lie flat for easier mincing or shredding.

To peel garlic, first tap it lightly with the side of a knife blade. This will loosen the skin for easy peeling.

When shredding ginger, follow the pattern of the fibers, which run vertically down the root.

Keep cutting boards clean. After chopping onions or other strong-flavored foods, always turn the cutting board over before slicing other ingredients.

CHINESE TEAS

GREEN TEAS—*Dragon Well* (Lung Ching, Loong Chin, Lown Jeng or Long Jang): From Hangchow. Considered the finest tea. (The name is often used generically to mean any high-grade green tea.) Has a light, fresh color and flavor; a smooth, soothing quality. Delicious and fragrant. May be served either night or day.

Dragon's Beard or Dragon's Whiskers (Lung So or Loong Soo): From Kwangtung. Light-colored and delicately flavored. Served in the afternoon as a social pastime drink.

Water Nymph (Sui-Sing, Shui-Sen, Shuy Seen or Suy Sien): From Kwangtung. Refreshing, light and pleasant. Drunk in mid-morning.

Eyebrows of Longevity (Sow Mee, Sho May or Soo May): From Kwangtung. Served out-of-doors in the spring.

Silver Needle (Gon Jim or Ngun Jum): From Kwangtung. Delicate but also somewhat astringent. Served with meals. Considered ideal for refreshing the palate during banquets.

Cloud Mist (Wun Mo): From Kiangsi. Exquisitely flavored and delectable. Drunk like a liqueur.

NOTE: This tea grows on the highest mountain peaks at altitudes where men seldom climb. Monkeys have been trained to scale these peaks, pluck the delicate leaves, fill baskets with them, and bring them down the mountain. This is why the tea is also called "Monkey Pluck."

BLACK TEAS—*Keemun:* From Kiangsu and northern China. One of the best of the blacks. Full-bodied, fragrant, spicy and smooth. Has a rich aroma, a superb bouquet. Excellent with meals.

Lapsang Souchang (Su Tang): From Hunan and Fukien. Hearty and rich with distinctive smoky taste.

Clear Distance (Lu An): From Kwangtung. Strong. Served with meals and late at night.

Iron Goddess of Mercy (Iron Kwan Yin, Tee Goon Yum, Tit Koon Yum or Tweet Gwoon Yum): From Fukien and Amoy. Thick and rich, with an exquisite fragrance. Drunk in small quantities like fine brandy.

SEMI-FERMENTED TEAS—*Black Dragon* (Oolong or Woo Long): From Formosa, Foochow, Amoy and Canton. Most common for family use. Well flavored and naturally sweet. Pungent and piquant. Served with heavy food, with the evening meal.

NOTE: The best grades of oolong make a pure straw-colored brew; the lower grades, a brown or red brew.

SCENTED TEAS—*Jasmine* (Mook Lay Far): From Formosa. Oolong or black tea and dried or fresh jasmine buds. Pale yellow, delicate, aromatic, fragrant and romantic. Taken at afternoon teas, between meals. Served at banquets and with rich, oily foods.

Lichee (Lay Jee): From Taiwan. Oolong or black tea and yellow lichee

blossoms. Faintly sweet. Popular with the Cantonese. Considered good for renewing friendships.

Chrysanthemum (Hung Pien or Herng Peen): From Chekiang. Dragon Well tea and dried chrysanthemum petals. Fragrant. Taken with Chinese pastry. Often sweetened with rock sugar.

CHINESE WINES

Chinese wines are drunk at formal banquets, or with snacks, or for medicinal purposes. (At banquets the wine is heated in special porcelain wine pots, poured into tiny, delicate thimble-like cups, and sipped before each dish.) Wine is also used widely in cooking.

Chinese wines are not wines in the Western sense; they aren't pressed from grapes. They're more like liqueurs and whiskeys; they're distilled from rice and other grains. Some are mild, others strong as brandy. There are 2 basic types: yellow and white.

YELLOW WINES—*Shaoshing* (Shoo Ching): From central China. Made from rice. Amber-colored and mild. Similar to sherry. The high grade is used for drinking, the low for cooking.

Shantung (Noo Mei Dew or Noh Mei Jow): From Peking. Used in cooking.

Five Companies (Eng Ga Pay or Ng Ga Pai): From Canton. Flavored with herbs. Dark yellow with strong, slightly bitter flavor. Reminiscent of bourbon.

WHITE WINES—*Kaoling*: Made from a rice-like grain that grows in northeast China. Similar to gin and vodka in its water-like clarity, but stronger and very intoxicating. Drunk as a liqueur after meals.

Pai Gar (Pai-ka-erh): From western China. A clear distillation made from corn. Very potent.

Rose Petal (Mur Guri Low, Mooey Gway Low, or Mui Kwe Lu): Fragrant and rose-petal flavored, but not sweet. Very strong. (Its alcoholic content is about 96 proof.) Often sold in decorative bottles.

Pear Wine (Shot Lee Low or Sewt Lay Low): Mild and pleasant.

Orange Wine (Chang Far Low or Charng Fa Low): Mild, but decidedly orange-flavored.

NOTE: Most Chinese wines do not travel well. Although sometimes available outside the Orient, the selection is limited. For alternatives, see the section on Substitutions.

❀ *Glossary of Chinese Ingredients* ❀

abalone: A distinctively flavored mollusk with iridescent shell, smooth-textured meat. Used in soups, stir-fried dishes and salads. Available fresh (in California), dried and in cans. The dried variety—silver-gray, flat elliptically shaped—requires extensive soaking and cooking. The canned variety, already cooked, is easiest to use: Its meat is suitable for stir-frying; its liquid excellent for soups. Cooking time must be kept extremely brief; heat toughens abalone, makes it rubbery. The canned variety comes from Japan, South Africa and Mexico. (See Storing Information, page 876; Soaking Information, page 881.)

agar-agar (*kanten*): A dried seaweed. Comes in long, thin, white strips. Looks like transparent noodles. Acts like unflavored gelatin. Must be soaked. Used in aspics, sweet dishes and salads. Sold packaged by weight. (See Soaking Information, page 881; Substitutions, page 873.)

almond paste: Sweetened ground almonds, used in sweet dishes. Available in cans. Sold in fancy food stores.

almonds: Nuts used blanched and toasted, primarily as garnishes for meat, poultry and seafood. (See How-To Section, page 820.) Available already toasted in cans.

ancient eggs: See *eggs, preserved.*

anise, star: Small, dry, brown seed cluster, or clove, shaped like an eight-pointed star. Licorice-like, it's used to flavor red-cooked meat and poultry dishes. (The cloves can be tied loosely in cheesecloth for easy removal after cooking.) Sold by weight. (See Substitutions, page 873.)

anise, star, powdered (weihsion powder): Ground cloves of star anise. Should be used sparingly. Sold by weight. Note: 3 or 4 cloves ground (in an electric blender) equal 1 teaspoon powdered star anise. (See Substitutions, page 873.)

anise pepper: See *pepper, anise.*

baby shrimp: See *shrimp, miniature.*

balsam pear: See *bitter melon.*

bamboo shoots: Young, tender, ivory-colored shoots of an Oriental plant. Used as a vegetable. Adds sweetness, delicacy and crispness to soups, seafood and poultry. There are two varieties: winter and spring. The former—smaller and more tender—is preferred. Occasionally available fresh (submerged in pails of water), more commonly available canned. The fresh variety must be parboiled 15 minutes. The canned variety comes either whole or in chunks. The whole shoots packed in water, not brine, are best. Bamboo shoots should always be rinsed before they are used. (See Storing Information, page 876; Substitutions, page 873.)

bamboo shoots, pickled: Thin, crisp membranes of bamboo shoots with a stimulating salty-sour taste. Can be steamed with pork or beef. Available in cans, sometimes in bulk.

bean curd (bean cakes): Bland, smooth, creamy, custard-like product, made by pureeing soybeans, then pressing the mixture into cakes about 3 inches square, 1 inch thick. Used as a vegetable. Is easily digested, highly nutritious (strong in protein) and very inexpensive. Also delicate, perishable, and fragile. Requires brief cooking time; since it's already cooked, only reheating is necessary. Extremely versatile: can be boiled, steamed, stir-fried, baked, marinated, pressed, deep-fried, or eaten fresh. (When eaten fresh with various dips or condiments, the Chinese call it "meat without bones.") Has a slight, subtle taste which readily absorbs and complements stronger food flavors. Combines well with just about any meat, fish, soup, egg, vegetable or poultry dish. Sold singly by the cake, by the pint, and in cans. (See Storing Information, page 877.) Note: Bean curd is available in a number of other forms. Among them are deep-fried bean curd (eaten stuffed as snacks or used in stir-fried and vegetarian dishes); spiced bean curd pressed into thin, flat cakes, then cooked and mildly flavored with anise (served cold or stir-fried with vegetables); and watery bean curd served sweetened as a snack.

bean curd sauce: See *cheese, Chinese white.*

bean curd sticks (*dried bean curd*): Long, dried, cream-colored sticks, about ½ inch wide and 20 inches long, but bent in two. Are stiff and striated with a shiny, enamel-like surface. (Sometimes called "Second Bamboo" because they come from the residue or second layer of creamy bean curd.) Must be soaked; then become chewy in texture, nutlike in flavor. Used as a vegetable with soup, steamed fish, stir-fried and braised pork. Sold packaged by weight. (See Storing Information, page 876; Soaking Information, page 881.) Note: Other dried varieties include sweet bean curd sticks, which are similar, but thicker, and are used in fish and vegetarian dishes; and glazed bean curd skin in the form of stiff thin sheets. The latter is used in vegetarian dishes, and for pastries and egg rolls.

bean paste, red: A sweetened puree of Chinese red beans used in steamed pastries and sweet dishes. Available in cans; may also be prepared at home. (See Seasonings and Sauces, page 707; Substitutions, page 873.)

bean paste, yellow (*yellow sauce*): Salty, pungent ground soybean product, used to flavor and preserve food. (In North China, it's used as a dip for raw scallions.) Sold in cans. (See Storing Information, page 877; Substitutions, page 873.)

bean sauce, brown: See *brown bean sauce.*

bean sprouts: Tiny white shoots with pale green hoods; not actually the sprouts of beans but of tiny mung peas. Called nature's most convenient vegetable since they can be grown in a few days at any time of the year. Add texture and delicate taste to meat, omelets, shellfish, salads, soups, other vegetables. Should be cooked only briefly, so that their crunchiness is retained. (Because of this crunchiness, the Chinese call them "teeth vegetable.") Available fresh by weight and in cans, which must be drained before being used. (See Storing Information, page 877; Substitutions, page 873; How-to Section, page 822.) Note: Chinese food shops also carry another variety called yellow soybean sprouts. These are larger and coarser than the mung sprouts, and must be husked. They also have a stronger, more woodsy flavor.

bean threads: See *noodles, peastarch.*

beans, black: Dried, oval black beans, the size of peas. Used in slow-simmered soups. Must be soaked. Sold by weight. (See Soaking Information, page 881.) Note: Sweetened black beans used as pastry filling are sold in Chinese bakeries.

beans, black fermented (*black bean sauce* or *salted black beans*): Small, black preserved soybeans. Extremely strong, pungent and salty. Used in conjunction with garlic as a seasoning. Subdues the fishiness of fish; heightens the flavor of pork, lobster, beef and chicken. Must be soaked. Available in cans and plastic bags. (See Storing Information, page 877; Soaking Information, page 881; Substitutions, page 873.)

beans, red: Tiny, smooth red beans used in soups, and as red bean paste in sweet dishes. Sold by weight. Also available in powdered form.

bêche-de-mer (*sea cucumber, sea slug,* or *trepang*): Dried, black spiny mollusk, measuring 4 to 12 inches in length. Considered a great delicacy and served frequently at banquets. Must be soaked; then expands considerably, becomes soft, delicate, gelatinous. Used in soups, and with pork and poultry. Can also be cooked sweet-and-sour. Sold packaged, either whole or in segments. (See Soaking Information, page 881.)

bird's nest (*swallow's nest*): Rare, expensive dried delicacy whose origins go back ten centuries. Not ordinary bird's nest, but an edible gelatinous coating produced by tiny swallows or swiftlets indigenous to the South China Sea. The nests, beige in color, look like finely shredded and glazed coconut. Must be soaked and cleaned before use. When cooked, they separate into shreds and have a subtle, distinctive taste. (They're also high in proteins and vitamins because of the bird's diet of seaweed and marine plants.) Bird's nest soup is considered a mark of great hospitality and the high point in formal dinners. It's also used as a poultry stuffing and prepared with rock sugar as a sweet dish for wedding feasts. Bird's nest is available in three grades: The rarest and most expensive grades are the whole nests which look like small, shallow, transparent cups. (The best of these are nearly white, with few twigs and feathers.) Next are the curved chips of broken nests or "Dragon's Teeth." Last are ground-up bird's nest fragments, made into porous, brittle cakes. (Most restaurants serve these.) All grades are sold in boxes by weight. (See Storing Information, page 877; Soaking Information, page 881.)

bitter melon (*balsam pear*): Cucumber-like vegetable with clear, green, shiny and very wrinkled skin. Can be stir-fried with pork, beef, chicken and seafood, simmered in soup, steamed or braised. Seems to taste acrid at first, because of its quinine content, but is actually cool, mintlike and refreshing. Popular during the summer months. Sold fresh by weight. To use: Slice off stem end. Cut lengthwise in half. Scoop out spongy pulp, pinkish seeds: then slice and parboil 3 minutes (it will be too bitter otherwise). Also available in cans. (See Storing Information, page 877; Substitutions, page 874.)

black bean sauce: See *beans, black fermented.*

black pepper: See *pepper, black.*

bok choy: See *cabbage, Chinese.*

bottle gourd: See *squash, bottle.*

broccoli, Chinese: Similar in color to the familiar broccoli, but much more leafy and somewhat longer (about 12 to 14 inches). Has irregularly shaped stalks, large flowerets with yellow and white blossoms. Its taste is fresh and delicate. Can be stir-fried alone as a vegetable or with meat. Sold fresh by weight. (See Storing Information, page 877.)

brown bean sauce: Thick, spicy, aromatic paste made with yellow beans, flour and salt, fermented in a semi-mash. Adds salty, full-bodied flavor to foods. Used to season fish, beef and duck; also bean curd and bland vegetables. (Cannot be used as a table condiment; must always be cooked.) Often used interchangeably with fermented black beans. Available in cans and jars. (See Storing Information, page 877; Substitutions, page 874.)

brown fungus: See *mushrooms, cloud ear.*

cabbage, celery: See *lettuce, Chinese.*

cabbage, Chinese (bok choy, Chinese chard, Chinese greens, or Shanghai cabbage): Tender, delicate vegetable with long smooth milk-white stems and large crinkly dark-green leaves. The Chinese call it "White Vegetable." Extremely versatile and popular. Has a clear, light taste, requires little cooking. Can be stir-fried with any meat, poultry or seafood; can be quick-cooked in soups. Sold fresh by weight. Available year-round, with the winter crop considered choicest. Note: The center section or heart, topped with yellow flowerets, is particularly delicate and tender and is usually sold separately. (See Storing Information, page 877; Substitutions, page 874.)

cabbage, Chinese dried: The same vegetable as above, available dried for use in slow-simmered soups. Sold by weight.

cabbage, mustard (mustard greens): Dark jade-green vegetable, similar in size and texture to small round cabbage. Has tightly packed leaves that are curved, fluted and fanlike. Is slightly cool and bitter in taste. Combines well with stir-fried beef, pork and bamboo shoots. Is good in soups; can also be cooked sweet-and-sour. Sold fresh by weight. Note: A smaller variety, called Baby Mustard Greens, is used primarily in soups. (See Storing Information, page 877.)

cabbage, pickled (Chinese sauerkraut, pickled mustard greens, preserved cabbage or winter vegetable): Whole mustard cabbage, packed in brine and fermented. Yellow-green in color, with crisp stalks, limp leaves. Can be stir-fried or steamed with meat and fish. Adds tang to soup, beef, pork and noodles. Sold in jars, cans and in bulk right from the pickling barrel. To use: Rinse well with cold water. Wring dry. Slice diagonally. (Before using it in stir-fried dishes, restore its crunchiness by stir-frying it alone first for 2 minutes in a dry pan over high heat.) Note: There are a number of varieties, pickled in different ways, with names such as Hom Choy, Choan Choy, Mooey Choy and Doan Choy.

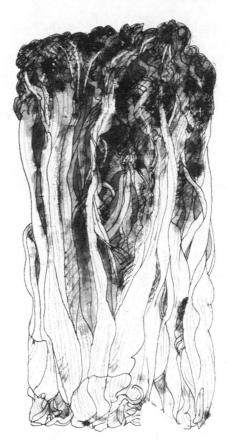

cabbage, salt-cured: Tightly wrapped small bundles of cured and pungent brownish-green cabbage. About 2 inches in diameter, salty and moist. Used to flavor steamed pork and fish. Must be washed and chopped. Sold individually and in packages.

cabbage, salted (cured mustard greens, dried cabbage, or *Chungking cabbage):* Pressed, salted and dried mustard cabbage. Used in flavoring soups, stews and steamed pork. Must be soaked. Sold by weight. (See Soaking Information, page 882.)

California rice: See *rice, oval-grain.*

Cantonese sausage: See *sausage, Chinese.*

celery cabbage: See *lettuce, Chinese.*

cellophane noodles: See *noodles, peastarch; noodles, seaweed.*

century eggs: See *eggs, preserved.*

chard, Chinese: See *cabbage, Chinese.*

cheese, Chinese red (red bean curd cheese, spiced red bean curd, or *southern cheese):* Pressed bean curd cubes, fermented in rice wine, spices and salt until brick-red and very pungent. Used as a seasoning to give an "aging" taste to braised pork, chicken and duck; also as a side dish to accompany rice. Available in cans. To use: Mash cubes until smooth. (See Storing Information, page 877.)

cheese, Chinese white (*bean curd sauce, white bean curd cheese,* or *white bean sauce*): Pressed, buff-colored bean curd cubes, 1½ inches square, fermented in rice wine and salt. Similar in taste and texture to Camembert cheese. Used as a pungent, tangy seasoning with fish, pork, chicken, noodles and vegetables. Can also be used uncooked as a table condiment (mixed with peanut oil, sprinkled with sugar) for rice or congee. Available in jars. (See Storing Information, page 877.)

chestnuts, dried: Shelled, dried chestnuts used as a flavoring. Add a rich, sweet, smoky taste to braised chicken and pork dishes. Sold by weight. (Also sold in Italian food stores.) To use: Parboil 10 minutes. Strip off skin covering. Note: These can also take the place of fresh chestnuts in sweet dishes. To use: Simmer 2 hours in 5 cups of water per pound.

chili peppers: See *peppers, chili.*

chili sauce, Chinese: Hot sauce made with small red chili peppers, apricots, lemon and garlic. Used to season fish, pickled vegetables, salted cabbage. Very hot. Should be used sparingly. Sold in bottles. (See Substitutions, page 874.)

Chinese broccoli: See *broccoli, Chinese.*

Chinese cabbage: See *cabbage, Chinese.*

Chinese chard or *Chinese greens:* See *cabbage, Chinese.*

Chinese chives: See *chives, Chinese.*

Chinese lettuce: See *lettuce, Chinese.*

Chinese okra: See *okra, Chinese*

Chinese onions: See *onions.*

Chinese parsley: See *parsley, Chinese.*

Chinese peas: See *snow peas.*

Chinese pepper: See *pepper, Chinese.*

Chinese pickle: See *tea melon.*

Chinese pickles: See *pickles, Chinese.*

Chinese sauerkraut: See *cabbage, pickled.*

Chinese sausage: See *sausage, Chinese.*

Chinese squash: See *squash, Chinese.*

Chinese turnips: See *turnips, Chinese.*

chives, Chinese: Members of onion family, with narrow, flat green leaves about 6 inches long. Look like a cross between scallions and chives. Add sharp, pungent flavor to noodle dishes, eggs, stir-fried beef. Sold fresh by the bunch. (See Storing Information, page 877.)

Chungking cabbage: See *cabbage, salted.*

cilantro: See *parsley, Chinese.*

cinnamon bark: Highly aromatic tree bark used as a spice with slow-cooked meats. (A 2-inch stick is sufficient for 5 pounds of meat.)

clams, dried: Dehydrated razor clams. Used primarily to flavor soups, noodles, vegetables. Must be soaked. Sold by weight. (See Soaking Information, page 882.)

cloud ears: See *mushrooms, cloud ear.*

cornstarch (corn flour): Powdered corn product used to dredge fish and meat. Performs a number of functions: Seals in the juices during cooking. Produces a golden-brown surface in deep-frying. Acts as a binder with minced meat. Gives coarse meats a smoother texture. Thickens soups and sauces. (When used as a thickener, it must first be blended with cold water to a smooth paste.) Sold packaged by weight.

cucumber pickle: See *tea melon.*

cured mustard greens: See *cabbage, salted.*

curry: A seasoning powder from India introduced to China centuries ago. Used in many seafood and meat dishes. Particularly favored in winter. (Often cooked in a dry pan over low heat before other ingredients are added. Must be stirred constantly to prevent burning.) Sold packaged by weight.

cuttlefish, dried: A dehydrated mollusk, thicker and larger than squid. Used primarily in slow-cooked soups. Must be soaked. Sold packaged by weight. (See Soaking Information, page 882.)

dragon's eyes (longans): Cherry-sized fruit with cinnamon-colored shell; transparent, pulpy flesh; and large pit. Subtly delicate. Related to the lichee but not as fragrant. Fresh variety is rare. The canned variety, already pitted, is used in sweet dishes. The dried variety, nut-like, shelled and about ¾ inches in diameter, is used to flavor slow-cooked soups. The latter is sold by weight in boxes. (See Substitutions, page 874.)

dried cabbage: See *cabbage, salted.*

duck feet: Dried, cured, used primarily as a stock ingredient. Can also be braised

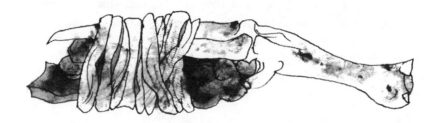

with mushrooms, bamboo shoots and water chestnuts. Considered a delicacy. Must be soaked and boned. (See Soaking Information, page 882.)

duck liver, cured: Hard, dark-brown duck liver wrapped in cured duck feet. Usually steamed with minced pork. Considered a delicacy. Its flavor is intense, concentrated and meaty. It must be soaked, then chopped. (See Soaking Information, page 882; Substitutions, page 874.)

duck, preserved: Boned, pressed precooked duck immersed in peanut oil. Needs additional cooking. Is usually rinsed in cold water, diced, then steamed until tender (about 30 minutes), either alone, or with rice or fresh duck. Can also be minced with beef or pork and steamed. Sold by weight.

duck, roast: Whole duck sold already roasted. Can be eaten cold, reheated in the oven or stir-fried with snow peas, other vegetables, lichees and pineapple. Sold by weight, whole or in pieces.

duck, salted: Another preserved variety is salted duck, dried in the sun. This is used in small quantities to flavor soup and rice.

duck sauce: See *plum sauce.*

eggplant, Chinese: White eggplant, similar in shape and texture to the more common purple variety, but smaller (about the size of a cucumber), less pulpy and more delicate. Can be steamed with fish or white bean cheese, braised or stir-fried. Sold fresh by weight.

eggroll skins: Egg-dough wrappings which, when stuffed with minced meat and vegetables and deep-fried, make eggrolls. Sold in 5- by 8-inch sheets by weight. Note: Sometimes available only in 5-pound packages. Can be rewrapped in smaller quantities and frozen for future use, but must be completely defrosted before use. (See Storing Information, pages 697, 878.) Can also be made at home. (See page 689.)

eggs, preserved (*ancient eggs, century eggs, hundred-year eggs, Ming Dynasty eggs,* or *thousand-year eggs*): Eggs coated with a claylike mixture of lime, ashes and salt, then buried in shallow earth for about 100 days. The lime "petrifies" the eggs: makes the whites firm, gelatinous and amber-colored; the yolks, spinach-green and cheeselike. (The Chinese call these "eggs with skin" because of their black outer coating. The English names, although romantic and exaggerated, describe their antique appearance—they do look as though they've been buried for centuries.) Preserved eggs usually are eaten uncooked for breakfast or as hors d'oeuvres, and served frequently at banquets. (Good accompaniments are soy sauce, minced ginger root and vinegar.) They can also be diced and cooked in omelets or steamed with fresh eggs. The black outer coating must always be removed first. They're sold individually. (See Storing

Information, page 878; How-To Section, page 826.) Note: These are usually chicken eggs. Sometimes duck or goose eggs are also preserved in this way.

eggs, salted: Duck eggs soaked in brine for 30 to 40 days. The saline makes the whites salty, causes the yolks to become firm and turn bright orange. Must be cooked. Add taste and tang to bland dishes. Can be hardboiled and eaten with rice, steamed with minced pork, pot-stewed or used in omelets. (When hardboiled and eaten with rice or congee, are called "the lazy man's dinner.") Sold individually. Note: Although chicken eggs can also be salted, the stronger, tougher duck eggs are better for this kind of preservative handling.

fish, dried (*salted fish*): Fish preserved by salting and drying. Some are immersed in oil; others are not. Includes many varieties: flounder, haddock, blowfish, and the sardine-like pilot fish and silverfish. Domestic dried flounder is relatively bland, the imported varieties stronger and saltier. Can be steamed with ginger or minced pork, combined with red-cooked meats or cut in small pieces and deep-fried (smells like ripe cheese during frying). Is often soaked first. Should be used sparingly. Sold by weight. (See Storing Information, page 878; Soaking Information, page 882.)

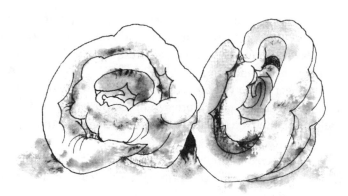

fish's maw: The dried and deep-fried stomach lining of fish. Comes in large, curved, crisp-looking pieces, the color of parchment, the texture of pork rind. Must be soaked; then increases about four times in volume, becomes light, honeycombed, delicate. Has no fishy taste. Used in soup, pork and ham dishes. Sold by weight. (See Storing Information, page 878; Soaking Information, page 882.)

Five Spices (*five-flavored powder* or *five-fragrance spice powder*): A cocoa-colored, ready-mixed combination of five ground spices (star anise, anise pepper, fennel, cloves and cinnamon). Fragrant, slightly sweet, very pungent. Used in seasoning red-cooked and roasted meat or poultry. Must be used sparingly. Sold by weight. Note: The component spices may be purchased by weight individually. (See Substitutions, page 874.)

flavoring powder: See *monosodium glutamate.*

flour, glutinous rice (*glutinous rice powder*): Flour ground from glutinous rice. Used in pastries, savories, sweet dishes and steamed pork. Sold by weight.

flour, rice: Flour ground from rice. Used in sweet dishes such as walnut and almond teas. Sold by weight.

flour, water-chestnut: Dried water chestnuts ground to a fine powder. Used as a thickener, binder, and batter ingredient. Makes for a light, crisp coating in deep-fried foods. Sold packaged by weight. Expensive. (See Substitutions, page 874.)

fuzzy melon (*fuzzy squash, hairy melon* or *summer melon*): Cylindrical, green vegetable, about 6 inches long, and covered with a fine, hairlike fuzz. Used primarily as soup ingredient, but may also be stir-fried or braised. Popular in summer. Must be peeled before use. Sold fresh by weight. (See Storing Information, page 878; Substitutions, page 874.)

garlic: Member of the onion family, used in seasoning meat, seafood, poultry and vegetables. Often used crushed or minced and cooked directly in hot oil to bring out its flavor. Should be purchased fresh by the bulb: the individual cloves should be pinkish and firm.

ginger, preserved: Ginger preserved in red syrup. Used to color and flavor fruit dishes and salads. Sold in jars. Note: Another preserved variety is candied ginger, available either crystallized or in jars with syrup. (See Storing Information, page 878.)

ginger, red: Pinkish-red cooked ginger prepared with salt and sugar. Used as a garnish, color accent or flavor contrast with fish, congee and other dishes. Available in jars and cans.

ginger, subgum (*mixed Chinese pickles* or *pickled ginger*): Sweet-and-sour combination of preserved ginger, fruit, vegetables and spices. Can be eaten cold as a garnish or relish; or cooked with spareribs and sweet-and-sour sauces. Sold in jars and cans. (See Storing Information, page 878.)

ginger root: Gnarled, potato-like root, about 3 inches long. Brown and flaky outside: rich ivory when peeled. Has pungent, fresh, spicy taste. Used as basic seasoning. Adds subtle flavor to soups, meats, vegetables and sweet dishes. Always used with seafood: it neutralizes fishy odors. (The younger the roots, the more delicate the flavor. Young roots, available in spring, have skins like those of new potatoes.) Sold by weight. To use: Lightly scrape skin and slice.

Then crush, shred or mince according to recipe directions. When a slice is specified, it should be about 1 inch in diameter, from ⅛ to 1/16 of an inch in thickness. Note: To extract ginger juice (called for in quick-cooked soups, shrimp balls and other delicate dishes), slice the root, squeeze it in a garlic press. (See Storing Information, page 878; Substitutions, page 874.) Has recently become available canned; also available dried.

ginkgo nuts (white nuts): Small fruit of the ginkgo tree, with tough beige-colored shells, ivory-colored meat. Used in soups, with slow-cooked poultry and in vegetarian dishes. Dried variety, sold by weight, must be shelled and blanched. (See How-To Section, page 826.) Canned variety is shelled and ready for use.

ginseng root: Aromatic root plant with sweet licorice-like taste, originating in Korea. Prized by ancient Chinese aristocracy as "the root of life." Its name derives from two Chinese characters meaning "human-shaped root." Tradition ascribes to it the power to cure everything from loss of appetite to heart ailments; from barrenness in women to a decline in masculine virility. (Modern laboratory tests have found it contains an ingredient effective in treating high blood pressure.) When taken freshly from the field, washed, peeled and dried in the sun, it's known as white ginseng. When steamed and fired (as it is for better preservation and for export) it takes on a reddish tint and is known as red ginseng. Used in one form as a soup ingredient, in another as a medicinal tonic. Also exported in the form of spirits and tea. Very expensive.

glutinous rice: See *rice, glutinous*.

glutinous rice flour: See *flour, glutinous rice*.

golden needles: See *lily buds*.

greens, Chinese: See *cabbage, Chinese*.

hair vegetable: See *seaweed, hair*.

ham: Cured, smoked pork used in small amounts to improve the flavor and aroma of soups and many other dishes. Also used as a decorative garnish. (See Storing Information, page 878; Substitutions, page 874.) Note: The Smithfield variety is most similar to Chinese ham; the redder the color, the better.

hoisin sauce (haisein sauce, Peking sauce, red seasoning sauce, red vegetable sauce, sweet vegetable paste, or sweet vegetable sauce): Thick, dark brownish-red sauce, made from soy beans, spices, garlic and chili. Sweet and spicy. Used in cooking shellfish, spareribs and duck; also as a table condiment for shrimp, plain-cooked pork and poultry. Sold in cans and bottles. (See Storing Information, page 878.) Note: Another variety, called Ten-Flavored Sauce, is somewhat smoother and spicier.

hundred-year eggs: See *eggs, preserved*.

jellyfish, dried: Dehydrated marine animal used as an ingredient in cold dishes. Adds bland flavor, crisp texture. Must be soaked and shredded. Sold by weight. (See Soaking Information, page 883.)

jujubes: See *red dates.*

kanten: See *agar-agar.*

kumquats: Tiny, oval-shaped citrus fruit, orange-yellow in color, with strong orange flavor. Sometimes available fresh; more often preserved in thick syrup. Are served alone, with other fruits or in sweet dishes. Available in cans and jars. (See Storing Information, page 878.)

lard: Soft white fat of pork. Commonly used as a cooking medium. Gives clear color and rich flavor to stir-fried dishes, particularly vegetables. Also used for pastries. Is never used with cold dishes (it congeals); or for deep-fried foods (it makes them soft, not crisp). Pure leaf lard is favored. Sold by weight. (See How-To Section, page 826.) Note: Ingredients cooked in lard don't lend themselves to reheating. They taste best when freshly cooked.

lettuce, Chinese (celery, Napa or *Tientsin cabbage):* Crisp, tightly packed vegetable, about 10 to 12 inches long. Has firm, vertical, yellow-white leaves, tinged at the top with pale green. Can be eaten raw in salads Western-style, but is delicious stir-fried with beef or pork; or quick-cooked in soups. Has a distinctive but not strong taste, somewhere between lettuce and cabbage. Sold fresh by weight. Sometimes available in neighborhood fruit stores and supermarkets. (See Storing Information, page 878; Substitutions, page 874.)

lichee fruit: Small, delicate and juicy, oval-shaped fruit. Its skin is rough-textured, shell-like and strawberry red; its pulp milky-white and translucent. The seed is smooth, hard and brown. The canned variety (peeled, pitted and preserved in light syrup) is used as a sweet dish, also with chicken, duck, and sweet-and-pungent pork. The fresh variety, available only in July, is very expensive. (See Storing Information, page 878.)

lichee nuts: Dried lichees with paper-thin brownish-red shells, firm dark prune-like flesh. Have smoky, sweetish taste. Are eaten like nuts or candy. Sold by weight and in boxes.

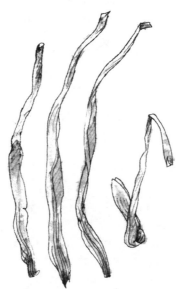

lily buds (*golden needles*, *lily flowers*, or *tiger lilies*): Dried, elongated lily buds about 2 to 3 inches long. Pale gold in color (the paler the better), fragile and lightweight. Have delicate, musky taste, high nutritive value. Used as a vegetable or flavoring with fish, pork, poultry (often in combination with cloud ears and other dried ingredients). Can be either stir-fried or slow-cooked. Must be soaked. Sold by weight. (See Soaking Information, page 883.) Note: Some have hard stems which should be removed after soaking. If very long, lily buds should be cut crosswise in two.

long beans: Light, green summer vegetable, resembling attenuated string beans. Used in stir-fried dishes, either diced or cut in 2-inch lengths. Lose their fresh

taste and become mushy if overcooked. Sold fresh in bunches by weight. (See Substitutions, page 874.)

long rice: See *noodles, rice-flour.*

longans: See *dragon's eyes.*

loquats: Small yellow fruit, similar in size and texture to the apricot. Subtle, delicate, juicy. Used as a sweet dish. Can also be cooked with chicken. Available in cans. (See Storing Information, page 878.)

lotus leaves: Leaves of the water-lily plant, used both fresh and dried. The fresh impart flavor and fragrance to foods. The dried serve as wrappings for rice, meat and sweet mixtures which are then steamed.

lotus root (*water-lily root*): Reddish-brown tuberous stem of the water lily. Measures roughly 2 inches in diameter, about 8 inches in length per section. (Looks like several sweet potatoes linked together.) Similar in texture to the potato but better-tasting and less woody. Used as a vegetable. Can be stir-fried to retain its crunchiness, or slow-simmered in soups and stews. It can also be prepared as a sweet dish: stuffed with glutinous rice and steamed. Must be peeled. (To prevent discoloration, soak in water with a small amount of vinegar added.) Sold fresh by weight from July through February. Also available canned and dried. (See Storing Information, page 879; Soaking Information, page 883.)

lotus seeds: Small, delicately flavored water-lily seeds, ½ inch long and oval in shape. When young and juicy, are eaten raw as fruit, or boiled with sugar. When ripe, have dark brown husks resembling those of filberts; are then dry and nut-like and are used in duck and winter melon soups. Are also candied and sweetened as pastry fillings. Must be blanched. Sold by weight; or already blanched, in cans. (See Substitutions, page 874, and How-To Section, page 826.)

mandarin orange peel: See *tangerine peel.*

matrimony vine: A thorny vine with dark green leaves about 1 inch long. Used as a flavoring to add a cool, slightly bitter taste to soup. Sold fresh by weight.

melon seeds: Dried watermelon seeds, eaten like nuts or used in sweet dishes and pastries. Come in 2 varieties: black and red. (Red is more expensive.) Sold by weight.

Ming Dynasty eggs: See *eggs, preserved.*

mixed Chinese pickles: See *ginger, subgum.*

monosodium glutamate (*flavoring powder,* or *seasoning powder*): White crystalline extract of grains and vegetables, said to enhance the natural flavor of certain foods. Considered a seasoning, not a chemical additive. (Does not replace salt or other seasonings.) Has no significant flavor of its own. Used in fairly large amounts by restaurants, food processors and food service institutions. There are two schools of thought on its value for home cooking: one that it heightens flavor, the other that it's not necessary when food is of good quality and well-prepared. Can be added to any dish except sweet dishes and eggs. Must be used sparingly so as not to mask food flavors (excessive use tends to give all dishes a mechanical sameness, a pseudo-taste). Sold in cans and jars under a variety of brand names. Note: If a recipe is doubled or tripled, the monosodium glutamate should *not* be increased correspondingly.

mung peas: Tiny, hard, dried, smooth-textured green peas. Used in making peastarch noodles and in growing bean sprouts. Sold by weight. (See Storing Information, page 879; How-To Section, page 822.)

mushrooms: Basic, versatile ingredient used as vegetable and flavoring in soups and many dishes. All types—fresh, dried and canned—are used. (Fresh mushrooms can also be dried at home: See How-To Section, page 827.)

mushrooms, black dried (*winter mushrooms*): Brownish-black mushrooms from the Orient, with caps about ½ to 2 inches in diameter. Meaty, succulent and savory. (The large thick ones with light skins, curled edges and highly cracked surfaces are best.) Can be stir-fried, stuffed, braised, steamed or simmered. Must be soaked. Should be used sparingly: 6 are the equivalent of a 6-ounce can of mushrooms. Sold by weight. Note: A second variety is flower-shaped.

thicker, rarer and more expensive. It's used in banquet dishes. (See Storing Information, page 879; Soaking Information, page 883; Substitutions, page 874.)

mushrooms, button: Small, white, tender young mushrooms used in soups and delicate stir-fried dishes. Sometimes used fresh, more commonly canned, particularly the canned variety from France. (See Storing Information, page 879.)

mushrooms, cloud ear (brown fungus, tree fungus, or *wood ears):* Small, dried, charred-looking fungus, about 1 inch long and irregularly shaped. Must be soaked. Expands to 5 or 6 times its original size, becomes brown and gelatinous. Resembles a convoluted flower or well-shaped ear. Can be stir-fried, braised or steamed. Used in pork, chicken, noodle, egg and vegetable dishes (often in combination with lily buds). Has a tender, delicate taste, somewhat crunchy texture. Sold by weight. Note: A second larger, thicker and tougher variety is used in quasi-medicinal soups. (See Storing Information, page 879; Soaking Information, page 883.)

mushrooms, grass (straw mushrooms): Tall, thin leafy mushrooms, crisp in texture, fragrant and very tasty. Must be soaked. Used with steamed chicken. (See Soaking Information, page 883.)

mushrooms, snow (white fungus): Dried cultivated fungus used in soups, in braised and vegetarian dishes. Considered high in tonic qualities. Must be soaked. Sold by weight. (See Soaking Information, page 883.)

mustard: Frequently used table condiment made by blending powdered English mustard and water to a paste. (See Seasonings and Sauces, page 705.) Very strong and hot. Should be used sparingly. Powdered mustard is available in cans by weight.

mustard greens: See *cabbage, mustard*.

mustard greens, pickled: See *cabbage, pickled*.

Napa cabbage: See *lettuce, Chinese*.

noodles, egg: An alimentary paste made of flour and eggs. Can be boiled, braised or fried. Combines with pork, beef, poultry, soup and vegetables. Sold by weight both fresh and dried. (See Storing Information, page 879.)

noodles, peastarch (bean threads, cellophane noodles, powdered silk noodles, shining noodles, transparent noodles, or vermicelli): Hard, opaque, fine white noodles made from ground mung peas. Must be soaked, then cooked briefly. (They absorb some of the liquid in which they're cooked and become translucent, gelatinous, slippery.) Have more texture than flavor, but readily absorb the flavor of other ingredients. Can be simmered in soups, stir-fried with beef, lobster, shrimp, pork and vegetables. Should be served at once when cooked; otherwise they become shapeless and mushy. Sold in long bundles, packaged by weight. (See Soaking Information, page 883; Substitutions, page 874.)

noodles, rice-flour (long rice or rice sticks): Noodles made from rice pounded into flour. Look like long white hairs. Are thin, brittle and opaque, about 5 inches long, and have a distinctive flavor. Combine well with fresh oysters, dried mussels, scallions, pork, cloud ears and lily buds. Can be parboiled, steamed, simmered and deep-fried. (When deep-fried briefly, they become puffy and crisp, and are used as a garnish.) Can also be stir-fried but must be soaked first. Sold by weight in bundles. Another variety, known as Rice Sticks, is about ¼-inch wide. (See Soaking Information, page 883; How-To Section, page 827.)

noodles, seaweed (cellophane noodles or vermicelli): Transparent, threadlike noodles made from seaweed. Are thinner, finer, more gelatinous than peastarch noodles. Must be soaked. Used mainly in cold dishes. Sold in boxes. (See Soaking Information, page 883; Substitutions, page 874.)

noodles, wheat-flour: An alimentary paste, whiter and smoother than egg noodles. Prepared in the same way, but cooked longer. Usually boiled first until nearly done, then added to stir-fried dishes and soups. Sold packaged by weight. (See Substitutions, page 874.)

oil, peanut: Clear, golden liquid shortening made from peanuts. A commonly used cooking medium for both deep- and stir-frying. Imparts a distinctive, subtle flavor to foods, keeps them from sticking. Can be heated to high temperatures without burning. Can also be used again and again without clarification. Sold in bottles and cans. (See Storing Information, page 879; Substitutions, page 874; How-To Section, page 827.)

oil, sesame: Amber-colored oil made from toasted white sesame seeds. Strong, nutlike, aromatic and fragrant. Generally used as a flavoring. Adds subtle taste to soup, poultry, shrimp, turnips, stuffings and cold dishes. (A few drops will improve any dish.) Should be used sparingly. Available in bottles. Expensive. Note: The paler sesame oil sold in many supermarkets is not this concentrated variety. The latter must be purchased in Oriental food stores.

okra, Chinese (pleated squash): Long, narrow, light-green summer vegetable, the size of a cucumber. Segmented lengthwise, with sharp, tough edges. Has a refreshing, slightly sweet taste. Used in stir-fried dishes, in quick-cooked soups. Sold fresh by weight. To use: Cut away hard stringy edges. Scrape skin. Cut in thin slices for stir-frying, in triangular chunks for soup.

olives, dried: Purplish-black cured and dried olives, cut in half and pitted. Add pungency to steamed fish, meat and vegetarian dishes. Can be steamed, with oil, sugar and ginger and used as a snack. Must be soaked. Sold by weight. (See Soaking Information, page 883.)

onions: Most frequently-used is the scallion or green onion. The white root end is preferred (the green top tends to be peppery); and cooked directly in hot oil to extract its flavor. Both tops and root ends, minced or shredded, are popular as garnishes. Note: Other onions used are leeks, shallots and Spanish onions.

orange peel: See *tangerine peel.*

Oriental rice: See *rice, long-grain.*

oyster sauce: A concentrate of oysters cooked in soy sauce and brine: a thick, grayish-brown liquid with fine bouquet. Used as a seasoning. Intensifies food flavors, without imparting its own. Makes food smooth, rich, subtle and velvety. Used with stir-fried meat, poultry, seafood, with congee and fried rice. Also used as a table condiment with roast pork, fried eggs, cold chicken and beef. Sold in cans and bottles. (See Storing Information, page 879.)

oysters, dried: Reddish-brown dried oysters with strong, tasty flavor. Can be stir-fried with vegetables, steamed with minced pork, simmered in soups and stews. Must be soaked, then cleaned. Sold by weight. (See Soaking Information, page 883.)

parsley, Chinese (cilantro or fresh coriander): Medium-green herb with willowy stem, broad flat serrated leaves. Stronger and more distinctively flavored than the common frilly variety. Highly aromatic (it's called "Fragrant Green" in Chinese). Used as a garnish for soups and cold dishes, as a herb bouquet for poultry, as a flavoring for chopped meats. Should be used sparingly. Sold fresh by weight. To use: Wash. Discard tough stems. Chop leaves, or leave them whole. (See Storing Information, page 879.)

parsnips, preserved: See *turnips, preserved.*

patna rice: See *rice, long-grain.*

pea pods: See *snow peas.*

pea sprouts: See *bean sprouts.*

peanuts: Raw, shelled peanuts (not salted or roasted). Used in slow-cooked soups, also with chicken. Or spiced, as an hors d'oeuvre or eaten plain as snacks. Can also be toasted and used as a garnish, or combined with sesame seeds as a candy. Sold by weight. Note: There are two varieties: those with thin, reddish skin coverings and those without. The latter, already blanched, are easier to use. (See Storing Information, page 879; How-To Section, page 828.)

peas, Chinese: See *snow peas.*

Peking sauce: See *hoisin sauce.*

pepper, anise: Tiny, whole, reddish peppercorns with dark brown seeds. Used as pungent seasoning in slow-cooked dishes. Sold by weight.

pepper, black: Ground black peppercorns used chiefly in seasoning noodle dishes and soups. Can also be heated with salt and used as a table condiment for deep-fried poultry. (See Seasonings and Sauces, page 708.)

pepper, Chinese red: Aromatic red pepper flakes, used in seasoning stir-fried dishes. Sold by weight. (See Substitutions, page 875.)

pepper, Szechwan (wild pepper): Mildly hot spice with pleasant aroma. Resembles the black peppercorn but contains a small seed. Used with red-cooked meat and poultry, Chinese pickles, and pepper-salt mixes. Sold by weight.

peppers, chili: Green chili peppers used as a hot seasoning, primarily in Szechwanese cooking.

pickle, Chinese: See *tea melon.*

pickled ginger: See *ginger, subgum.*

pickled mustard greens: See *cabbage, pickled.*

pickled vegetables: See *pickles, Chinese.*

pickles, Chinese (pickled vegetables): Various vegetables such as cucumbers, turnips, ginger, etc., shredded and pickled in soy sauce. Used with noodles, soups, and as a relish for congee. Sold in cans and jars. (See Storing Information, page 879.)

pickles, mixed Chinese: See *ginger, subgum.*

pig, roast: Glazed whole roast pig with crackling golden skin and sweet, rich fatty meat. Can be eaten as is, hot or cold, or steamed with shrimp sauce. Sold in pieces by weight.

plum sauce (*duck sauce*): Amber-red chutney-like sauce made from plums, apricots, chili, vinegar and sugar. Piquant and thick. Used as a table condiment with roast duck, roast pork, spareribs and egg rolls. Also used occasionally in cooking. Sold in cans and bottles. (See Storing Information, page 879.) Note: If taste is too tart, add a pinch of sugar.

pomelo: Large yellow citrus fruit resembling a grapefruit but pointed rather than flat on top. Of delicate texture and sweet, delicate taste.

pork, roast: Thick strips of barbecued pork prepared with spices and honey. Sold already roasted. Can be reheated in the oven or eaten cold with various dips (oyster sauce is excellent). Can also be cooked in soup or stir-fried with vegetables. (Should be added at the end of cooking since it needs only brief reheating.) Sold by weight. (See Storing Information, page 879.)

powdered silk noodles: See *noodles, peastarch.*

preserved cabbage: See *cabbage, pickled.*

preserved cucumber or preserved sweet melon: See *tea melon.*

preserved parsnips: See *turnips, preserved.*

purple laver: See *seaweed, dried.*

red bean curd cheese: See *cheese, Chinese red.*

red bean sauce: Sauce made from mashed red soy beans. Highly odoriferous. Used in poultry and meat dishes, with braised beef and eggplant. Available in cans.

red berries: An herb considered a nutrient tonic. Used in soups. Must be soaked. Sold by weight. (See Soaking Information, page 884.)

red dates (*jujubes*): Small dried reddish fruit with shiny withered skin. Used to impart subtle sweetness to soups, stews, slow-cooked and steamed dishes, particularly fish and chicken. Also used in sweet dishes. (Is usually soaked for the latter.) Sold by weight. (See Soaking Information, page 884; Substitutions, page 875.)

red seasoning sauce or red vegetable sauce: See *hoisin sauce.*

rice, glutinous (starchy rice, sticky rice, or *sweet rice):* Short-grained, opaque, pearly-white rice. Becomes sticky when cooked. Used with meat balls, as a stuffing for chicken and duck. Also in sweet congees, pastries, puddings, dumplings and banquet dishes. Must be washed and sometimes soaked before being used. (See Soaking Information, page 884; How-To Section, page 826.)

rice, long-grain (Oriental rice, patna rice): Long, narrow-grained rice, most commonly used in South Chinese cooking. Absorbs more water than the oval-grained variety. Yields a larger quantity, a fluffier rice. Can be boiled, steamed or used in fried rice. Sold by weight.

rice, oval-grain (California rice, or *short-grain rice):* Rice with short, wide, oval grain. Requires less water, longer cooking to produce same consistency as long-grain variety. Tends to be softer and starchier. Can be boiled, steamed or used in congee. Sold by weight.

rice flour or *rice powder:* See *flour, rice.*

rice flour, glutinous: See *flour, glutinous rice.*

rice sticks: See *noodles, rice-flour.*

rice vinegar: See *vinegar.*

roast duck: See *duck, roast.*

roast pig: See *pig, roast.*

roast pork: See *pork, roast.*

rock sugar: See *sugar, rock.*

salted black beans: See *beans, black fermented.*

salted fish: See *fish, dried.*

sauerkraut, Chinese: See *cabbage, pickled.*

sausage, Chinese (Cantonese sausage): Cured waxy pork sausage. Comes in narrow red and white links, each about 6 inches long, tied together as pairs. Sweet and savory. Can be steamed with rice, chicken or pork, combined with omelets and bean curd, or stir-fried with other meats and vegetables. Can also serve as an hors d'oeuvre. Sold by weight (4 pairs are about 1 pound). To use: Remove string. Wash with warm water. Steam or simmer until translucent, about 20 minutes. (See Storing Information, page 879.)

sausage, liver: Duck-liver sausage, similar in size and shape to the pork sausage but darker and not as sweet. Also sold in pairs by weight. Can be cooked with Chinese cabbage and other vegetables. (See Storing Information, page 879.)

scallions: See *onions.*

scallions, pickled: The bulb-like white tips of scallions pickled in vinegar, sugar and salt. Add crispness and flavor to sweet-and-sour fish sauces. Serve as a garnish for preserved eggs. Available in jars.

scallops, dried: Coarse, strong, salty and highly nutritious sea scallops. Look like dried amber-colored disks. Measure about 1 inch in diameter, ½ inch in thickness. Used to add rich flavor to soups, congees and slow-cooked dishes. Can also be steamed with ham, stir-fried with Chinese cabbage, combined with eggs, turnips and radishes. Must be soaked. Sold by weight. (See Soaking Information, page 884.)

sea cucumber or *sea slug:* See *bêche-de-mer.*

seasoning powder: See *monosodium glutamate.*

seaweed, dried (purple laver): Dark purple marine plant. Comes in tissue-thin sheets, 7 by 8 inches, folded in half. Called "paper vegetable" in Chinese. Must be soaked; then doubles in size. Used in soup. Has a fresh, tangy sea-sweet taste. Is highly nutritious. Sold in packages by weight. (See Soaking Information, page 884.)

seaweed, hair: Fine hairlike black seaweed. Used mainly in savories and Buddhist vegetarian dishes. Must be soaked. Sold by weight. (See Soaking Information, page 884.)

sesame oil: See *oil, sesame.*

sesame paste: Ground sesame seeds, similar in taste and texture to peanut butter. Used in sauces and cold chicken dishes. Available in cans; also sold under the name of "taheeni" in grocery stores specializing in Middle Eastern products, and sometimes in health food stores. (See Substitutions, page 875.)

sesame seeds: Small, flattish seeds used in flavoring cakes, candies, cookies. Available in two varieties: black and white. Sold by weight.

Shanghai cabbage: See *cabbage, Chinese.*

shark's fins: Rare, dried delicacy from the South Seas. Used mainly in thick, rich soups (served at formal Chinese dinners and banquets). Actually the cartilage of the fin, which is tasteless when fresh, but translucent, tasty and threadlike when dried. Is rich in vitamins, high in calcium and protein. Must be soaked. Available both with and without rough outer skin. The latter (which comes as

hard, dry, grayish-white shreds) is preferable: it requires less preparation. Available in a number of grades: top grade is 5 inches long; medium grade 2 to 3 inches; the remnants about 1 inch. Can also be used as a poultry stuffing, or with omelets, crabmeat, and pork. Sold by weight and in boxes. Very expensive. Also available canned. (See Storing Information, page 879; Soaking Information, page 884.)

shining noodles: See *noodles, peastarch.*

short-grain rice: See *rice, oval-grain.*

shrimp, dried: Tiny, hard pink-and-white shelled shrimp, about ½ inch in length. Enrich the flavor of bean curd, cucumbers, Chinese cabbage, spinach and eggplant. Can also substitute for pork or ham in soup. Must be soaked, or softened by steaming. Sold by weight. Note: There's also a larger variety of dried shrimp used in stews and slow-cooked soups. (See Soaking Information, page 884; Substitutions, page 875.)

shrimp, miniature (baby shrimp): Tiny, shelled, deveined shrimp from South America. Sweet and tender, used frequently by Chinese restaurants in stir-fried dishes and egg-roll stuffings. Available frozen only in 5-pound blocks, from which 1 or 2 pounds can sometimes be purchased.

shrimp chips: Dried shrimp slices colored white, pink and yellow. Must be deep-fried. Are eaten like potato chips with fried chicken or as a snack. Sold packaged by weight.

shrimp sauce (shrimp paste): Grayish-pink concentrate of dried ground shrimp preserved in brine. Very pungent. Similar to anchovies in saltiness. Used as a zesty flavoring for fish, pork, chicken, fried rice, bean curd and vegetables. Should be used sparingly. Sold in jars. (See Storing Information, page 879; Substitutions, page 875.)

snow fungus: See *mushrooms, snow.*

snow peas (Chinese peas, pea pods or sugar peas): Special variety of pale-green pea pods, picked before maturity. Add crispness, subtle taste and color to meat, poultry, seafood and vegetables. Very tender. Require little cooking. Are always stir-fried to retain delicate color, flavor and vitamin content. Sold fresh by weight. Available year-round, but most inexpensive May through September. To use: Break off tips, remove strings. (See Storing Information, page 879; Substitutions, page 875.) Note: Frozen snow peas are now available in a number of markets.

southern cheese: See *cheese, Chinese red.*

soy jam (*soybean paste*): A thick, dark paste, the sediment of soy sauce. Similar to molasses in color and texture. Very subtle. Used to color, flavor and thicken sauces of slow-cooked pork, beef, poultry. Also used to season string beans, fish and lobster. Sold in cans. (See Storing Information, page 879.)

soy sauce: Salty, savory brown sauce made from soybeans, wheat, yeast and salt. Essential in Chinese cooking. Enhances the flavor of meat, poultry, fish, vegetables. Colors and flavors gravies, sauces, marinades and dips. Comes in many grades and types, ranging in color from light to dark, in density from thin to thick. Specific types are: light, dark and heavy. Light soy (made with soybean extracts, flour, salt and sugar) is light-colored and delicate. It's used as a table condiment and in dishes such as clear soups where soy flavor but not color is desired. Dark soy (made from the same ingredients, plus caramel) is blacker, richer and thicker. It's used as a table condiment; and also in cooking, when both full-bodied flavor *and* color are wanted. Heavy soy, made with molasses, is thick and viscous. It's used more for color than taste, in the rich, dark-brown sauces of sweet-and-pungent spareribs and stir-fried beef and peppers. Good quality soy is essential for good sauces and marinades. Many grades are available; best are the Oriental imports. These are made slowly by a natural fermentation and aging process. (Domestic soys, made quickly by a chemical process, tend to be highly concentrated, salty and bitter. These must be used in reduced quantities.) Chinese soy is available in the light, black and heavy varieties. Japanese soy, made with malt, is somewhere between the light and the black. Both types are sold in bottles and cans. (See Substitutions, page 875.)

spiced red bean curd: See *cheese, Chinese red.*

spring roll skins: See *eggroll skins.*

squash, bottle (*bottle gourd*): Green marrow, shaped like a squat bowling pin. A spring and summer vegetable. Used in soup and stir-fried dishes. Sold fresh by weight. To use: Peel and slice.

squash, Chinese: Green marrow, either cylindrical or round and flat, with thin yellow stripes. Can be stir-fried by itself as a vegetable, or combined with beef, ham or fish. Sold fresh by weight. To use: peel and slice. (See Substitutions, page 875.)

squash, pleated: See *okra, Chinese.*

squid, dried: Dehydrated and tentacled mollusk. Brown in color with a coating of whitish powder. Can be stir-fried with vegetables, prepared sweet-and-sour, simmered in soup or steamed. Must be soaked. Sold by weight. (See Soaking Information, page 885.) Note: The fresh variety is usually stir-fried.

star anise: See *anise, star.*

starchy rice or *sticky rice*: See *rice, glutinous.*

straw mushrooms: See *mushrooms, grass.*

sugar, rock: Amber-colored sugar used to sweeten certain teas, to glaze chicken. Sold by weight.

sugar peas: See *snow peas.*

summer melon: See *fuzzy melon.*

swallow's nest: See *bird's nest.*

sweet cucumber or *sweet melon*: See *tea melon.*

sweet rice: See *rice, glutinous.*

sweet root: A Chinese herb, a nutrient tonic used in soups and other dishes. Must be soaked. Sold by weight. (See Soaking Information, page 885.)

sweet tea pickle: See *tea melon.*

sweet vegetable paste or *sweet vegetable sauce*: See *hoisin sauce.*

tangerine peel (*mandarin orange peel* or *orange peel*): Dried, preserved tan-colored tangerine skin. Used as a flavoring. Imparts fresh, subtle taste to meat, poultry (particularly duck), soups and congees. Must be soaked. Should be used sparingly. (The older the skin, the more prized and expensive; some rare ones are said to be one hundred years old.) Sold by weight. (See Soaking Information, page 885.)

taro: Starchy, tuberous, rough-textured brown root, about the size of a large potato.

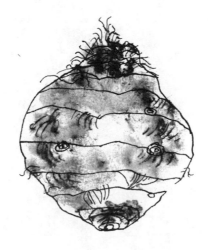

Can be stir-fried, braised with duck or steamed with Chinese sausages. Can also be shredded and deep-fried as a savory. Sold fresh by weight.

tea melon (*Chinese pickle, cucumber pickle, preserved cucumber, preserved sweet melon,* or *sweet tea pickle*): Tiny, 2-inch miniature cucumber-like melon, preserved in honey and spices. Amber-colored, sweet and crunchy. Used as a flavoring. Can be steamed with pork, beef or fish, added to noodle dishes, or eaten cold as a relish. Available in cans and jars. (See Storing Information, page 880.)

thousand-year eggs: See *eggs, preserved.*

Tientsin cabbage: See *lettuce, Chinese.*

tiger lilies: See *lily buds.*

transparent noodles: See *noodles, peastarch.*

tree fungus: See *mushrooms, cloud ear.*

trepang: See *bêche-de-mer.*

turnips, Chinese: Vegetable resembling large, white horseradish. Very subtle in taste. Combines with beef, pork, bacon, fish and shrimp. Can be stir-fried or braised. Also slow-cooked in soup and marinated for cold dishes. Plentiful and best in winter months. Sold fresh by weight. To use: Peel and slice. (See Substitutions, page 875.)

turnips, dried: Dehydrated turnips. Can be stir-fried or slow-cooked. Combine with pork and snow peas. Must be soaked. Sold by weight in flat sheets. (See Soaking Information, page 885.)

turnips, preserved (*preserved parsnips*): Small, brown, pungent bundles of cut-up

turnips, tops and all, steamed, preserved with salt and dried. Have salty, aromatic flavor, chewy texture. Used as seasoning in soups, congees, steamed fish and pork. Sold by weight. To use: Rinse. Drain. Unroll. Shred or chop fine. In most cases, half a bundle is sufficient. (See Storing Information, page 880.)

vegetable steak (*choplets*): A high-protein soy-bean product used as a meat substitute. Needs little cooking. Available in cans in health food stores.

vermicelli: See *noodles, peastarch; noodles, seaweed.*

vinegar: Rice vinegar used in flavoring soups and sauces; as a table condiment for seafood, meat and noodles. Comes in three types: white, red and black. White rice vinegar is used with sweet-and-pungent dishes; red rice vinegar, as a dip for boiled crab; and black rice vinegar, with braised dishes and as a general table condiment. All are available in bottles. (See Substitutions, page 875.)

walnuts: Nutmeats used as a garnish and in sweet dishes. (See How-To Section, page 832.)

water-chestnut flour: See *flour, water-chestnut.*

water chestnuts: Aquatic bulbs of an Asian marsh plant; about the size of large walnuts. Have tough, purplish-brown skins; usually covered with mud to prevent their drying out. (Are called "Horse's Hooves" in Chinese because of their color, texture and shape.) Used as a vegetable. Must be washed and peeled. Their meat is crisp, white, sweet and delicate. Can be stir-fried with pork, beef, poultry, seafood or with other vegetables. Are also used in soups and cold dishes. Sold fresh by weight. Also available canned. (See Storing Information, page 880; Substitutions, page 875.)

water-lily root: See *lotus root.*

weihsion powder: See *anise, star* (*powdered*).

white bean curd cheese or *white sauce:* See *cheese, Chinese white.*

white fungus: See *mushrooms, snow.*

white nuts: See *ginkgo nuts.*

wild pepper: See *pepper, Szechwan.*

wine: Used as a marinade and liquid seasoning. Flavors meat, neutralizes the strong taste of fish and duck. The Chinese use a yellow rice wine which doesn't travel well. A good quality, medium-dry or pale-dry sherry, *not* cooking or cream sherry, can substitute. (See Substitutions, page 875.)

winter melon: Very large round melon; frosty, green and tough on the outside, delicate and pulpy-white on the inside. Needs little cooking. Can be stir-fried as a vegetable, or combined with pork in soup. (For banquets and special occasions, this soup is often cooked right inside the melon itself.) Can also be glazed with sugar as a candy or sweet-dish ingredient. Sold fresh by weight, either whole or in wedges. To use: Remove rind with a sharp knife and discard. Scrape out yellow seeds. Slice or dice meat. (See Storing Information, page 880.)

winter mushrooms: See *mushrooms, black dried*.

winter vegetable: See *cabbage, pickled*.

wonton skins: Thin egg-flour skins or wrappings, about 3½ inches square, which are stuffed with minced pork, seafood or vegetables. Can be deep-fried, pan-fried, steamed or boiled. Boiled wontons are usually eaten in soup; the others, served with soy sauce and vinegar dips. Wonton skins can be purchased fresh by weight, or made at home. (See Storing Information, page 880; Eggrolls and Wontons, page 701.)

wood ears: See *mushrooms, cloud ear*.

yellow sauce: See *bean paste, yellow*.

❊ *Substitutions* ❊

SUBSTITUTES can be used for Chinese ingredients if they approximate either their texture or taste. When cooked the Chinese way, these substitutes are no less the real thing. This is the true versatility of Chinese cooking. Almost any ingredient can be used to create authentic-tasting Chinese dishes, provided the nature of that ingredient and its cooking requirements are understood. Some suggested substitutes follow:

agar-agar: Unflavored gelatin.

anise (either powdered or star anise): Cinnamon in powdered or stick form; or anise extract, which is sold in some markets and drugstores. Use only a few drops of the latter.

bamboo shoots: Coarse-textured vegetables such as celery, green pepper, carrots, young cabbage, rutabagas and string beans. Chop or shred these for stir-frying.

bean paste, red (for desserts): Coconut or chopped California dates.

bean paste, yellow: Japanese Miso, half-white, half-dark.

bean sprouts: Shredded onions or parboiled and shredded string beans.

beans, black fermented: Salt.

bitter melon: Cucumber.
brown bean sauce: Bovril.

cabbage, Chinese: Spinach, lettuce, young celery, young cabbage.
chili peppers (*fresh*): Dried crushed chili peppers (allow about ½ teaspoon for each pepper).
chili sauce, Chinese: Tabasco Sauce or Louisiana-type hot sauce.
cornstarch: (Never substitute flour in cornstarch pastes. It will make sauces cloudy and heavy rather than smooth and clear.)

doilies (*for Peking Duck or Moo Shoo Pork*): Wheat tortillas.
dragon's eyes (*dried*): White seedless raisins.
duck liver: Smoked ham.

Five Spices: Allspice or a combination of powdered cinnamon, cloves, ginger and nutmeg.
flour, glutinous rice: (Never substitute ordinary rice flour. It turns hard when steamed.)
flour, water-chestnut: Cornstarch.
fuzzy melon: Cucumber or zucchini.

ginger root: Preserved ginger with the syrup washed off. Dried ginger in smaller quantities. (Never substitute powdered ginger. It's too strong and is better omitted entirely.)
ginkgo nuts: Blanched almonds.

ham, Smithfield: Any good-quality smoked ham or Italian prosciutto.

lettuce, Chinese: Celery, Swiss Chard, young white turnips, young carrots.
long beans: String beans.
lotus seeds: Blanched almonds.

mushrooms, black dried: Dried mushrooms from central Europe and Italy. Use in smaller quantities since their flavor is stronger.

noodles, peastarch: Vermicelli.
noodles, seaweed: Vermicelli.
noodles, wheat-flour: Number 8 or 9 spaghetti or Japanese somen.

oil, hot pepper: Chinese chili sauce.
oil, peanut: Corn oil or any clear, tasteless and odorless vegetable oil. For stir-frying

lard can be used, particularly with vegetables. (Never substitute butter, which will burn; olive oil, which is too strong; or shortenings, which congeal and spoil the texture of food.)

pepper, Chinese red: Tabasco Sauce.

red dates: Prunes. (Never substitute California dates.)

scallions: Chopped onions in smaller quantities.
sesame paste: Peanut butter with a few drops of sesame oil added. (See page 707.)
shrimp, dried: Shelled and cooked shrimp. Use ½ cup for every 6 dried shrimp.
shrimp sauce: Anchovy paste.
snow peas: Fresh green peas. (Don't use the pods, which are invariably too tough.)
soy sauce: Salt or a bouillon cube. For every 2 tablespoons of soy sauce, use either 1 teaspoon salt or 1 beef bouillon cube dissolved in 3 tablespoons hot water. (Never substitute bouillon when *large* quantities of soy are called for: its taste is too different.)
squash, Chinese: Cucumber or zucchini.

taro: Sweet potato or white potato.
turnips, Chinese (for cold dishes): White radish.

vinegar, rice (white): Cider or wine vinegar.

water chestnuts: Crisp vegetables such as green pepper, celery, cabbage hearts, rutabagas or small young potatoes (all diced). In pork dishes, apples sometimes can be substituted. (Use ½ cup apples, peeled and diced, for 10 water chestnuts.)
wine (for cooking): Medium-dry or pale-dry sherry (never cream or cooking sherry). Also white wines such as sauterne or the German Liebfraumilch; and brandy, cognac, gin, or Japanese sake.
(*for drinking with Chinese food*): Premium white wines from California; dry French Graves or Chablis; the Italian Soave Bolla; the Rhine wine, Spätlese; or the German Liebfraumilch. (Medium-dry sherry is too heavy. Red wines are not recommended but can be served with specific dishes such as slow-cooked duck in rich gravy.) Japanese sake, slightly heated, can be served for formal dining.
NOTE: Beer is also fine with Chinese food.

❀ *Storing Information* ❀

CHINESE ingredients are stored like other foods: Fresh vegetables and other perishables are refrigerated. Tea, spices and ground ingredients are kept in tightly covered containers. Dried ingredients are stored in jars or plastic bags and kept in a cool, dry place. (Should these become moist under humid conditions, they can be dried again in the sun or in a very slow oven.) Canned items, when not used up at a single meal (which is usually the case), are transferred to jars or other covered containers and refrigerated.

Here are the details:

abalone (*canned*): Drain. (Reserve liquid for soups.) Rinse with cold water. Place in jar with water to cover. Cap tightly. Refrigerate. Change water every other day. (Will keep about a week.)

bamboo shoots (*canned*): Store as for *abalone*. (Will keep more than a week.)

bean curd (*dried*): Keep well wrapped. Needs no refrigeration, but should be used within a few months. It may be soaked a day or two before use and refrigerated in water in a tightly covered container.

bean curd (fresh): Place in container with water to cover. Close tightly and refrigerate. Change water daily. (Will keep about a week.) For longer storage, keep in salted water. Change water every other day. (Will keep about 2 weeks.)

bean curd (fried): Wrap in foil or transparent wrap. Refrigerate. Use within 3 or 4 days.

bean paste, yellow: Place in a tightly covered jar. Refrigerate. (Will keep for months.)

bean sprouts (fresh): Wash well. Place in jar with water to cover and refrigerate. Change water every day. (Will keep 4 to 5 days.) They may also be blanched first, then stored as above. (They will keep longer but lose their crunchiness and some of their nutritional value.) Note: Bean sprouts can also be quick-frozen. Wash. Parboil 1 to 2 minutes. Drain well. Place in plastic bag. Freeze. (Thaw fully before using.)

beans, black fermented: Place in a tightly covered jar or plastic bag. If they seem to be drying out, add a few drops of peanut oil.

bird's nest: Keep well wrapped. Needs no refrigeration.

bitter melon: Refrigerate in vegetable bin or perforated plastic bag. (Will keep about a week.)

broccoli, Chinese: Store as for *bitter melon*. (Will keep several days.)

brown bean sauce: Refrigerate in covered jar. (Will keep for months.)

cabbage, Chinese: Store as for *bitter melon*. (Will keep several days.)

cabbage, mustard: Store as for *bitter melon*. (Will keep more than a week.)

cabbage, pickled: Refrigerate in covered jar. (Will keep more than a week.)

cheese, Chinese red: Refrigerate in covered jar. (Will keep several weeks.)

cheese, Chinese white: Needs no refrigeration. Will keep indefinitely.

chili sauce, Chinese: Needs no refrigeration.

chives, Chinese: Store as for *bitter melon*. Use as quickly as possible. (These will keep a week, but become progressively stronger.)

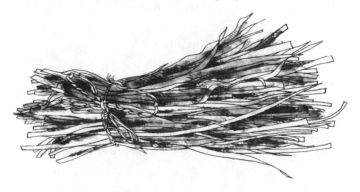

duck, preserved: Needs no refrigeration.

eggroll skins: Wrap in foil, transparent wrap or wet towel. Refrigerate. (Will keep 4 to 5 days.) May also be frozen.

eggs, preserved: Need no refrigeration for short periods; will keep for a couple of weeks. Refrigerate to keep for a month or so.

eggs, salted: Refrigerate. (Will keep about a month.)

fish, dried: Needs no refrigeration but should be wrapped well in plastic because of its penetrating odor.

fish's maw: Needs no refrigeration. (Will keep for several weeks.)

fuzzy melon: Store as for *bitter melon.* (Will keep about 2 weeks.)

ginger, preserved: Needs no refrigeration.

ginger root, fresh: May be stored in any one of the following ways:
1. Store like potatoes in a cool, dry place.
2. Keep in moist earth or sand, and water frequently. Dig up whenever needed.
3. Place in plastic bag. (Do not wash or peel.) Freeze. Slice or shred while still frozen.
4. Peel. Grate finely. Place in covered jar. Refrigerate. Drain before using.
5. Peel. Wash. Dry thoroughly. Place in jar with sherry to cover. Cap tightly. Refrigerate in warm weather; keep on shelf in cool weather.
6. Scrub with brush. Chop. Cook a few minutes in peanut oil. Drain. Refrigerate in covered jar. (Will keep several months.)
7. Refrigerate in vegetable crisper. (Will keep about 3 weeks.)

ginger, subgum (*canned*): Place leftovers in covered jar. Refrigerate.

ham, Smithfield: Remove dark outer coating and fat. Wash and dry. Steam or boil 20 minutes. Cool. Wrap in foil. Refrigerate. (Will keep several weeks.)

hoisin sauce: Place in tightly covered jar. Refrigerate. (Will keep for months.)

kumquats (*preserved*): Need no refrigeration.

lettuce, Chinese: See *broccoli, Chinese.* (Will keep more than a week.)

lichee fruit (*canned*): Place leftovers in covered jar. Refrigerate.

lichee fruit (*fresh*): Refrigerate. Use as soon as possible. (They lose color and taste very quickly.)

loquats (*canned*): Place leftovers in covered jar. Refrigerate.

lotus root: Store like potatoes in cool, dry place; or refrigerate in vegetable crisper. (Will keep about 3 weeks.)

mung peas: Store in covered jar. (Will keep several months.)
mushrooms (canned): Store as for *abalone.*
  (dried): Store in covered jar. Leftover soaked mushrooms should be drained, wrapped well in foil or transparent wrap and refrigerated. (Will keep several days.)
mushrooms, cloud ear: Store in covered jar. After soaking, may be kept in water in covered container and refrigerated. Change water every other day. (Will keep about 6 days.)

noodles, egg (dried): Keep in original wrappings or plastic bags.
  (fresh): Refrigerate in tightly sealed plastic bags. (Will keep 3 weeks.)

oil peanut: Needs no refrigeration. (Will keep indefinitely.)
oil, sesame: Needs no refrigeration. (Will keep indefinitely.)
oyster sauce: Needs no refrigeration. (Will keep indefinitely.)

parsley, Chinese: Place in uncovered jar with stems only in water. Refrigerate. Change water every other day. (Will keep about a week.)
peanuts (raw or roasted): Store in covered jar. (Will keep for weeks. If stored too long, will darken and become rancid.)
pickles, Chinese: Need no refrigeration.
plum sauce: Refrigerate in covered jar. (Will keep for months.)
pork, roast: Refrigerate in covered container. (Will keep a week or more.) Can also be frozen.

sausage, Chinese: Wrap and refrigerate. (Will keep several months.)
sausage, liver: Store as for *sausage, Chinese.*
sesame paste: Refrigerate in covered jar. (Will keep for months.)
shark's fins (soaked): Place in bowl with cold water to cover. Refrigerate. (Will keep several days.)
shrimp sauce: Needs no refrigeration. (Will keep indefinitely.)
snow peas: Refrigerate in perforated plastic bag. (Will keep about a week, but are better used within a day or two.)
soy jam: Needs no refrigeration.
soy sauce: Needs no refrigeration. (Will keep indefinitely.)

tea: If bought in a cardboard box, transfer immediately to airtight metal or plastic container. Do not keep longer than 6 months.

Note: Tea, unlike wine, does not improve with age. The sooner it's used, the better. Tea is at its best when freshly opened, then properly stored: It cannot take much exposure to air; its leaves absorb moisture, other flavors and odors. Its volatile oils evaporate quickly, causing loss of fragrance and flavor. Tea also reacts unfavorably to light, and so should never be stored in *clear* glass containers.

tea melon: Refrigerate in covered jar. (Will keep for months.)

turnips, preserved: Store in covered jar. Need no refrigeration.

water chestnuts (fresh): Refrigerate. Will keep several days.

    (canned): Store as for *abalone.* (Will keep about a month.)

winter melon: Cover cut surfaces with transparent wrap. Refrigerate (Will keep about 3 to 5 days.)

wonton skins: Store as for *eggroll skins.*

SOAKING INFORMATION

Dried ingredients must be soaked before use to "develop" their flavor and texture and restore them to their original size and shape. The soaking time is based on the nature of the ingredient itself and how it's to be cooked. The same dried ingredient needs less soaking time for a slow-cooked dish than for a stir-fried one. Some ingredients are not only soaked, but simmered as well. Generally speaking, it's better to oversoak than undersoak. In many cases, the longer the soaking, the better the ingredient's texture and taste.

Soaking is done in two ways: The ingredient is rinsed and cleaned first, then soaked; or soaked first until it expands, rinsed clean, then soaked again until soft. In either case, the dried ingredient should always be immersed in water, always rinsed in cold water and always drained thoroughly, before use. Here are the details:

abalone (*for braising*): Clean in warm water. Scrub thoroughly. Soak 4 days in cold water. Change water every day.

(*For stir-frying*): Soak overnight in cold water. Drain. Pour boiling water over. Simmer covered 6 hours. Let cool in the liquid. Clean each abalone and drain.

agar-agar (*for gelatins*): Soak in hot water until dissolved. Strain if lumpy.

(*For salads*): Soak 2 hours in cold water. Change water 2 or 3 times. Drain well. Cut in 2-inch sections.

bean curd sticks: Break in 2-inch lengths. Boil until soft (about 20 minutes).

Or: Soak 2 hours in warm water. Drain. Cut in 2- or 3-inch sections.

bean curd sticks, sweet: Soak 1 hour in warm water.

beans, black: Soak 2 to 3 hours in cold water. Drain.

beans, black fermented. Soak 10 minutes in cold water. Rinse to remove salt. Drain.

bêche-de-mer: Soak a few hours in cold water. Brush and clean thoroughly. Cover with fresh water. Boil 5 minutes. Remove. Drain. Let cool. Brush and clean again thoroughly. Cut underside; remove internal organs. Repeat process at least 10 times (Unless absolutely clean, bêche-de-mer will not expand and soften.)

Or: Soak 24 hours in warm water. Change water several times. Cut underside, remove internal organs. Rinse. Cover with fresh water. Simmer 4 hours. Rinse thoroughly.

bird's nest: Soak overnight in cold water. Clean, removing loose feathers with tweezers. Parboil 10 minutes. Rinse.

Or: Place in cold water in a saucepan. Bring to a boil. Simmer covered 1 hour. Let cool; clean and rinse.

Or: Soak 4 hours in cold water. Drain. Rinse. Boil 5 minutes at high heat in water to cover (with ½ teaspoon baking soda added). Drain. Discard liquid. Place in pot with 7 cups stock. Boil 15 minutes over high heat. Discard stock.

(*For chips*): Pour 3 cups boiling water over 1 cup dried bird's-nest chips. Let stand overnight. Drain. Transfer to saucepan. Add 4 cups hot water. Simmer 30 minutes. Drain and cool. Squeeze out excess water. Remove feathers and impurities.

(*For stuffing*): Place in hot water to cover and boil 10 minutes. Transfer to a colander. Rinse with cold running water. Remove foreign materials. Drain. (Stuff into poultry and steam according to recipe directions.)

cabbage, salted: Soak in warm water 15 minutes or until soft. Rinse 2 to 3 times with cold water to remove impurities.

chestnuts, dried: Parboil 10 minutes. Strip off outer covering.

clams, dried: Soak as in *oysters, dried.*

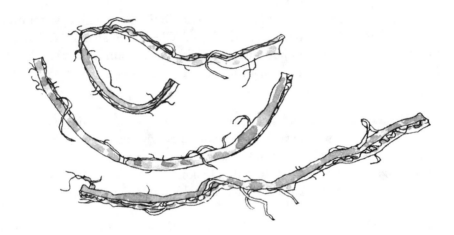

cuttlefish, dried: Soak overnight in cold water to cover. Rinse several times under cold running water. Peel off membranes. Remove cuttle bone. Cut body and tentacles in 1-inch squares or large strips.

duck feet, dried: Wash. Pour boiling water over to cover. Soak 5 minutes. Drain. Remove skin and discard. Clip claws. Remove bones. Cut each foot in two.

duck liver, cured: Soak 2 hours in cold water. Rinse and drain.

(*For steaming*): Soak 30 minutes.

fish, dried: Soak 4 hours in cold water. Rinse.

(*For steaming*): Soak 10 minutes in cold water. Rinse and drain.

fish's maw: Soak 3 hours in cold water. (It will expand to four times its volume.) Drain. Place in boiling water with ½ teaspoon vinegar, 1 teaspoon ginger juice and 1 tablespoon sherry added. Simmer 5 minutes. Drain. Rinse in cold water to remove all traces of oil. Squeeze dry.

Or: Soak overnight in cold water. Squeeze dry. Parboil 5 to 10 minutes. Rinse. Squeeze dry.

Or: Soak 1 hour in hot water. Wash several times in warm water to remove excess fat. Rinse. Wring out 4 to 5 times. Pour 2 tablespoons sherry over and let stand 15 minutes. Wring dry again.

jellyfish, dried: Soak overnight in warm, not hot, water. Drain. Remove red matter. Cut in narrow strips, about 1½ inches long. Quickly rinse in boiling water. Drain. (Strips may then be soaked for weeks in water, and used as needed. The water, however, should be changed every day.)

lily buds: Rinse with cold water to clean. Soak 30 to 60 minutes in warm water. Rinse. Cut off tough stem ends.

lotus root: Soak 20 minutes in hot water. Rinse.

mushrooms, black dried: Rinse with cold water to clean. Soak 30 to 60 minutes in warm water. Rinse. Drain. Squeeze dry. Cut off tough stems. (Reserve stems and soaking liquid for stock.)

Or: Cover with hot, but not boiling, water. Let stand 15 to 20 minutes.

mushrooms, cloud ear: Rinse with cold water. Soak 30 minutes in warm water. Wash. Rinse with cold water several times to clean. Snap off hard stems. (When using the tougher variety: Rinse. Simmer 1 hour. Wash and rinse.)

mushrooms, grass (For steamed dishes): Soak 15 minutes in warm water.

mushrooms, snow: Soak 5 or 6 hours. Transfer to fresh water, boil 5 minutes. Then drain.

(*For soup*): Soak 30 minutes in warm water. Clean. Rinse. Squeeze dry.

noodles, peastarch: Soak 20 minutes in boiling water to soften. Drain. Rinse with cold water. Drain again.

(*For stir-fried dishes*): Soak 10 minutes in hot water; 30 minutes in cold. Drain.

(*For soup*): Soak 30 minutes to 1 hour in cold water. Drain.

noodles, rice-flour: Soak 30 to 60 minutes in hot water. Drain.

Or: Soak 10 minutes in warm water. Drain. Simmer 10 minutes in stock.

noodles, rice-flour (sticks): Parboil 5 to 10 minutes. Drain. Rinse in cold water. Drain again.

noodles, seaweed: Soak as for *noodles, peastarch.*

olives, dried: Soak 30 minutes in cold water. Drain. Chop fine.

oysters, dried: Soak 1 hour in cold water. Wash thoroughly. Soak 8 hours in warm water. Slit hard portion. Clean out sand. Rinse.

(*For stewing*): Soak 2 hours in warm water. Clean as above.

(*For stir-frying or braising*): Soak overnight in cold water. Rinse several times to remove grit. Then pour boiling water over and simmer, covered, 30 minutes. Rinse in cold water. Drain.

red berries: Soak 30 minutes in cold water. Wash and drain.

red dates (*For braising*): Need no soaking.

(*For sweet dishes*): Soak 25 minutes in cold water.

rice, glutinous (*For cooking*): Soak 30 minutes in cold water. Rinse until liquid runs clear. Drain. Add required cold water. Let stand 10 minutes. Cook according to recipe directions.

(*For coating and stuffing*): Soak 3 hours or overnight in cold water. Rinse.

scallops, dried (*for braising*): Soak overnight in warm water or a few tablespoons of sherry.

(*For soup*): Soak as above.

(*For stir-frying*): Soak 2 hours in cold water or sherry. Boil or steam 10 minutes; then shred.

seaweed, dried: Tear into squares. Soak 1 hour in cold water. Rinse by lifting out of water repeatedly. Squeeze dry.

Or: Soak 10 minutes in warm water. Rinse several times. Squeeze dry.

seaweed, hair: Soak 1 hour in warm water. Rinse until water runs clear. Drain in colander. Pour 2 tablespoons oil over. Squeeze to let oil penetrate. Rinse in cold water. Drain again. Add 1 to 2 tablespoons sherry. Squeeze to let sherry penetrate. Rinse and drain again.

Or: Parboil 2 to 3 minutes. Drain. Rinse in cold water. Drain again.

shark's fins (*skinless*): Rinse in cold water. Soak overnight in warm water. Wash. Drain. Simmer 1 hour (with a garlic clove, small piece of ginger root or leek). Rinse.

Or: Soak 30 minutes in warm water. Wash. Drain. Simmer as above for 2 hours.

Or: Soak overnight in warm water. Cook 2 hours in chicken broth, using the bowl-within-a-pot method of steaming.

Note: Already processed shark's fins are available in some Chinese food stores, but must be ordered several days beforehand. They are quite expensive.

shrimp, dried: Rinse. Soak 30 to 60 minutes in warm water or sherry.

squid, dried: Rinse. Soak 24 hours in warm water. Remove black outer skin. Split open. Clean out internal organs. Remove center bones. Cut off tentacles and

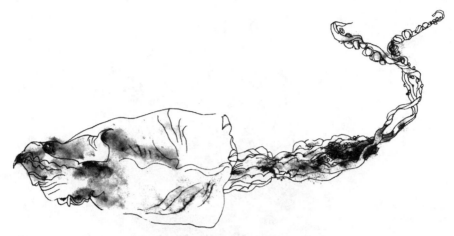

slice in 1-inch pieces. Score inside of body diagonally in a grid pattern. Cut in small squares. (When cooked, these roll up like balls.)

sweet root: Soak 30 minutes in cold water. Wash and drain.

tangerine peel: Soak 30 minutes in warm water. Scrape inside of peel. Rinse.

turnips, dried: Soak 15 minutes in cold water. Wash. Separate, divide in small pieces. Rinse. Soak in fresh cold water 45 minutes more.

vermicelli: See *noodles, peastarch.*

❋ *Chinese Terminology* ❋

MANY Chinese ingredients either have no comparable English names or have several. The confusion is further compounded by the fact that their Chinese names sound quite different from one dialect to the next (although they are always the same in the written language). Some rudimentary Chinese vocabulary, however, can prove helpful in purchasing special ingredients or ordering a meal in a Chinese restaurant. For this reason a listing of Chinese food terminology is given here. (It is given in the Cantonese dialect—the one most frequently spoken in the United States.) It must be clearly understood, however, that since Chinese bears no resemblance at all to English, simple phonetic equivalents are virtually impossible. The spellings below are therefore very rough approximations.

abalone: Bow Yee or Bau Yew
abalone, dried: Bow Yee Gawn
agar-agar: Tai Choy Go
anise, star: Bot Gok

bacon, Chinese: Lop Yuk or Lop May

bamboo shoots: Jook Sun (or Soon)
bamboo shoots, pickled: Sun (or Soon) Yee
bean curd: Dow (or Dau) Foo
bean curd, deep-fried: Dow Foo Pok
bean curd, spiced: Dow Foo Kon

bean curd, watery: Dow Foo Fa
bean curd sticks: Foo Jook (or Joke)
bean curd sticks, sweet: Tim Jook or Tiem Joke
bean paste, red: Dow Sha (or Cha)
bean paste, yellow: Wong Dow Sa
beans, black: Woo Dow
beans, black fermented: Dow See or Doe Shee
beans, sweet black: Dow Sa
beans, red: Hoong Dow
bean sprouts, Mung: Gna (or Ngah) Choy
bean sprouts, soy: Dow Gna (or Ngah)
bêche-de-mer: Hoy Sum (or Sharm)
beef: Ngow Yuk
beef, white abdomen: Ngow Bark Nahm
bird's nest: Yin Wor or Yeen Woh
bird's nest, whole: Yin Wor Jon
bitter melon: Foo Gaw (or Quar)
broccoli, Chinese: Gai Lan or Guy Lon
brown bean sauce: Min (or Mien) See Jeung

cabbage, Chinese: Bok Choy
cabbage, dried: Bok Choy Gawn (or Gon)
cabbage, mustard: Gai (or Guy) Choy
cabbage, pickled: Hom Choy
carp: Li Yee (or Yew)
catsup: Fon Ker Jeung
cheese, Chinese red: Nom Yee or Narm Yoo
cheese, Chinese white: Foo Yee (or Yoo)
chestnuts, dried: Loot Jee
chicken: Guy or Gai
chicken giblets: Guy Foo Chee
chicken wing: Guy Yick

chili sauce, Chinese: Lar Dew Din
chives, Chinese: Gow Choy
clams: Gup Guy
clams, dried: Hing Yoke
crab: Hwa or Hy
crabmeat: Hwa Yuk or Hy Yoke
curry: Gar Lay
cuttlefish, dried: Muck Yee

dragon's eyes: Loong Nan or Loan Ngon
dragon's eyes, dried: Loong Nan Gawn
duck: Opp
duck liver, cured: Opp Geoke Bow
duck, preserved: Yu Dim (or Yo Jum) Lop Opp
duck, roast: Shew Opp
duck, salted: Lop Opp

eel: Shan Yee
eggplant, Chinese: Bok Ker (or Quar)
eggroll skins: Chuen Guen Pay
eggs, preserved: Pay Don
eggs, salted: Hom Don

fish, dried: Hom Yee (or Yew)
fish's maw: Yee (or Yew) Toe
Five Spices: Ng Heung (or Heung New) Fun
flounder, salted: Yow Dai Day
flour, glutinous Rice: Naw May Fan (or Fun)
flour, rice: Doug Mein Fan (or Fun)
flour, water-chestnut: Mar Tie Fan (or Fun)
fuzzy melon: Jeet Quar or Mo Gwa

ginger root: Sang Geung (or Geong)
ginger, preserved: Tong Geung
ginger, red: Hoong Geung

ginger, subgum: Subgum Geung
ginkgo nuts: Bok Gwar (or Gwa)
ginseng root: Yun Sharm

ham, Smithfield: Gum Wah Tuey
hoisin sauce: Hoy Sin (or Sein) Jeung

kumquats: Kum Quat

lamb: Yeung Yuk
lettuce, Chinese: Wong Nga (or Lung Gna) Bok
lichee nuts: Ly Chee or Lay Chee
lily buds: Gum Jum
lily petals, dried: Bok Hop
lobster: Lung (or Loong) Har
long beans: Dow Gok
loquats: Pay Pa Gwor
lotus root: Lin Gow or Leen Ngow
lotus root, dried: Lin Gow Gawn
lotus seeds: Lin (or Leen) Gee

matrimony vine: Gow Gay
melon seeds: Quar (or Gwa) Gee
mung peas: Look Dow
mushrooms, black dried: Dong Koo or Doong Goo or Tung Kuo
mushrooms, button: Moo Goo
mushrooms, cloud ear: Wun (or Won) Yee
mushrooms, cloud ear, tough: Mook (or Mok) Yee
mushrooms, grass: Cho Gook (or Koo)
mushrooms, snow fungus: Sewt Yee

noodles: Mein
noodles, dried egg: Gawn Don Mein
noodles, fresh egg: Don Mein (or Meen)
noodles, peastarch: Fun See (or Shee)

noodles, rice-flour: May (or Mai) Fun
noodles, rice (sticks): Sha Ho Fun
noodles, seaweed: Yang Fun
noodles, wheat-flour: Mein Fun

oil, peanut: Far Sung Yow
oil, sesame: Jee Ma Yo (or Yow)
okra, Chinese: Sing Quar (or Gwa)
olives, dried: Lom (or Larm) Gok
onion sprouts, dried: Chung Choy
oyster sauce: Ho Yo (or Yau) Jeung
oysters, dried: Ho See (or She) Gawn

parsley, Chinese: Een Sigh
peanuts: Far Sang (or Sung)
pepper, anise: Far Jui (or Jeel)
pepper, black: Woo Joo Fun
pepper, Chinese red: Far Joo
pepper, Szechwan: Hwa Jo
pickles, Chinese: Char Quar Kan
pig, roast: Siew Gee Yuk
plum sauce: So Moy (or Shuen Mooey) Jeung
pomelo: Pom Elow
pork, roast: Char Shew or Ta Siew

red bean sauce: Saang See (or Sharng She) Jeung
red berries: Gay (or Go) Jee
red dates: Hoong Jo
rice, cooked: Fan
rice, glutinous: Naw May

sausage, Chinese: Lop Chong
sausage, liver: Gum Gnun Yuen
scallions, pickled: Kew Tow
scallops, dried: Gong Yu Chee
seaweed, dried: Gee Choy
seaweed, hair: Faht Choy

sesame paste: Jee Ma Jeung
sesame seeds: Jee Ma
shark's fins: Yu Chee
shrimp: Har
shrimp chips: Har Peen
shrimp, dried large: Har Gawn
shrimp, dried small: Har Mi (or May)
shrimp sauce: Hom Har Jeung
snow peas: Ho Lon Dow
soy jam: Yewn She Jeung
soy sauce: See Yu or Shee Yau or Sho Yu
soy sauce, light: Sang Chau
soy sauce, dark: Chow Yau or Cho Yo
soy sauce, heavy: See (or Jeow) Yau
squab: Bok Opp
squash, bottle: Foo Loo Quar (or Gwa)
squash, Chinese: Fon Quar (or Gwa)
squid, dried: Dew Peen
squid, fresh: Yo Yee (or Yew)
sugar, rock: Bing (or Bung) Tong
sweet root: Why Shon

tangerine peel, dried: Gor (or Gwaw) Pay
taro: Woo Tow
tea: Cha
tea (black): Hung Cha
tea (green): Ching Cha
tea melon: Cha Quar (or Gwa)
ten-flavored sauce: Subgum Jeung
turnips, Chinese: Lo (or Lor) Bok
turnips, dried: Choy Pin

vinegar, rice (black): Hak Mi Cho
vinegar, rice (red): Jit Cho
vinegar, rice (white): Bok Cho

water chestnuts: Mar (or Mah) Tie
water cress: Gwa Jee Choy

winter melon: Doong Quar (or Gwa)
wonton skins: Won Ton Pay

CHINESE COOKING TERMS

boil: Po or Bo
braise: Min or Mun
deep-fry: Jow
roast: Shu or Siew
sauté: Lok
slow-cook (red): Hoong Shu (or Shew)
steam (wet): Jing
steam (dry): Dunn
stir-fry: Chow or Chau

CUTTING TERMS

dice (chunks): Kar
dice (cubes): Ding
mince: Soong
mince (to a pulp): Yoong
shred: See
slice: Pan or Peen

KITCHEN EQUIPMENT

chopsticks (bamboo): Fi Gee
cleaver-knife (big): Die Doh
cleaver-knife (small): Choy Doh
cutting board: Jum (or Jahm) Bahn
ladle: Siou Hok (or Huak)
skillet: Wok
spatula: Wok Chan or Wok Lay
steamer, bamboo: Jing Loong

MISCELLANEOUS

assorted vegetables: Quar Choy
boneless: Wor
buns, steamed: Bau

congee: Jook

custard (steamed eggs): Jing Don

dried: Lop

many precious mixture: Subgum*

morsels: Kew

pastry savories (tea lunch): Deem Sum

patties, pork: Shu My or Shew My

soup: Tang or Tong

spareribs: Pai Goot (or Guk)

spareribs, barbecued: Su Pai Goot

stuffed: Young

sweet-and-pungent: Tiem Shuen

* Means "miscellaneous ornament," and is usually applied to dishes which include many vegetables in small amounts.

❋ *Mail Order Sources* ❋

Sun Sun Company
340 Oxford Street
Boston, Massachusetts

*Cathay Food Products, Inc.
115 Broadway
New York, New York

Mee Wah Lung Company
608 H Street N.W.
Washington, D.C.

Sam Wah Yick Kee Company
2146 Rockwell Avenue
Cleveland, Ohio

Kam Shing Company
2246 South Wentworth Street
Chicago, Illinois

Chung Hing
202 Milam Street
Houston 2, Texas

Adler's Fine Foods
2012–14 Broadway
San Antonio, Texas

Wah Young Company
717 South King
Seattle, Washington

Gim Fat Company
953 Grant Avenue
San Francisco, California

Kwong On Lung Importers
686 North Spring Street
Los Angeles, California

❀ INDEX ❀

GLORIA BLEY MILLER

Gloria Bley Miller is a professional writer with a varied background in education and in the fine arts. A native New Yorker, Mrs. Miller attended schools in New Mexico, Philadelphia and New York and holds degrees from both Hunter College and the Bank Street College of Education.

When first introduced to authentic Chinese food more than a decade ago in San Francisco, Mrs. Miller became fascinated with its subtle taste and beauty and was determined to learn how to cook that way for herself. However, when she sought a basic cookbook on the subject she discovered there weren't any that provided in detail the essential information she needed. She then began to pursue the knowledge of Chinese food on her own: tracking down every available scrap of information, haunting Chinese grocery stores, eating in all kinds of Chinese restaurants both here and abroad, comparing notes with Chinese friends, and, most important, constantly cooking and experimenting in her own kitchen. She soon came to feel that the information she was gathering should be shared with others. This cookbook is the result.

Mrs. Miller lives in Greenwich Village with her husband, Richard McDermott Miller, the Figure Sculptor of Soho, whose studio is near Chinatown and who shares her enthusiasm for Chinese food. Both, on recent visits to China, had the opportunity to sample little-known restaurants in Peking and elsewhere as well as the more popular ones. At home, Mrs. Miller frequently serves up Chinese feasts to the delight of family and friends.